Job Training for Women

The Promise and Limits of Public Policies

EDITED BY

Sharon L. Harlan and Ronnie J. Steinberg

Temple University Press

Philadelphia

Temple University Press, Philadelphia 19122
Copyright © 1989 by Temple University. All rights reserved
Published 1989
Printed in the United States of America

Library of Congress Cataloging-in-Publication Data
Job training for women.
(Women in the political economy)
Bibliography: p.
Includes index.
1. Occupational training for women—United States.
2. Vocational guidance for women—United States.
I. Harlan, Sharon.   II. Steinberg, Ronnie J., 1947–
III. Series.
HD6059.6.U6J63   1989   331.4'2592'0973   88-28492
ISBN 0-87722-614-8 (alk. paper)

Job Training for Women

The Promise and Limits of Public Policies

In the series
Women in the Political Economy,
edited by Ronnie J. Steinberg

TO OUR CHILDREN
Jocelyn
Brian and Elizabeth

Preface and Acknowledgments

The origins of this book take us back to the spring of 1979 as Sharon Harlan was preparing to take a job at the Wellesley College Center for Research on Women and Ronnie Steinberg was preparing to leave the Center. That is when we met for the first time. Over the next few years we crossed paths only occasionally, yet often enough to know that the other was also studying the impact of federal job training policy on women. Harlan had a grant from the National Science Foundation to study the effects of the Comprehensive Employment and Training Act (CETA) on gender differences in employment outcomes. Steinberg, then located at the Center for Women in Government, State University of New York at Albany, was funded by the U.S. Department of Labor to survey the effectiveness of CETA training programs for women in nontraditional occupations.

From these quite different studies emerged a shared perception that something was wrong with the way job training policy was being formulated, implemented, and evaluated at the national level. Each of us arrived independently at the conclusion that most research in this area was stressing technique while downplaying substance. As sociologists treading on territory where economists were regarded as the legitimate experts, we felt that too much attention to narrowly-defined economic outcomes had resulted in a lack of awareness about grass-roots innovation in training strategies and a lack of critical perspectives on national policy. As feminists analyzing historically male-centered programs and policies, we were incensed by the widely disseminated finding that women "gained more" than men from participation in these programs, even as men continued to have higher employment rates and substantially higher wages during and after CETA.

By 1984, when we found ourselves both living in the Albany, New York, area, we were faced with yet another concern about training policy that impelled us to begin our work on this edited volume. The Job Training Partnership Act (JTPA) of 1982 threatened women's enrollment opportunities and their expectations, which had grown in the wake of progressive federal regulations promulgated after the 1978 CETA reauthorization. JTPA more perfectly embodied the conservative Reagan economic and political agenda that encouraged the private sector to set directions and priorities for public training funds.

We decided it was time to take stock of the many accomplishments of the CETA era, to broaden thinking about job training for women, and to articulate promising new directions for future policies, in the hope that a more favorable political climate would emerge. We felt it was necessary to move beyond CETA/JTPA programs to examine the range of publicly funded training programs, including the workfare and job search programs associated with efforts at "welfare reform." Most important, we wanted to show how training policies for poor women reflect a broader pattern of segregation and discrimination against all women that permeates the entire establishment of occupational education. Therefore, the chapters that follow explore the complex reciprocal relationship between the structure of many different kinds of training programs and gender inequalities in the labor market. By articulating the direct linkages between public training programs and labor market outcomes, we hope to stimulate more research and to lend intellectual support to the advocates who have lobbied successfully for expanding women's opportunities.

In the four years during which we worked on this book, it was discussed, written, and revised in our kitchens and backyards, in restaurants, and once in a beauty parlor and an airport. And while we met often in Albany, on several occasions, parts of the manuscript made their way to meetings in New York, Chicago, Washington, and Philadelphia. Once in a while, we even worked on it in our offices.

The first and most important persons to thank for bringing this book into being are the contributors, who prepared original chapters based on vast experience and knowledge in their own fields. Their commitment to achieving greater economic opportunities for women is self-evident in their writings. We owe a special thanks to Lois Haignere, one of the contributors and an early collaborator on the book, for helping us to formulate an outline of its contents. We are also indebted to the reviewers who read and commented on drafts of chapters. Alice Cook and Roslyn Feldberg were particularly helpful in pointing out errors of omission in an early version of the manuscript, and they were influential in suggesting the final format as well as revisions in several chapters. Prudence Brown, Sumru Erkut, Mary Ann Etu, Lucy Gorham, Edward Hackett, Lois Haignere, Ruth Jacobs, Erika Kates, Ruth Milkman, Sue Mitchell, Brigid O'Farrell, Julie Wilson, and Rick Worthington read individual chapters and provided valuable suggestions and guidance to the contributors. Michael Ames, David Bartlett, and Jennifer French of Temple University Press provided enthusiasm, encouragement, and many good ideas.

Edward Hackett provided support at home that made it possible for

Sharon to devote a great deal of time to this book. Michael Ames appreciated the significance of our efforts and offered Ronnie loving support throughout the completion of this project, including doing more than his share of household work. Kathy Trent was a loyal friend and supportive colleague.

We have dedicated this book to Sharon's daughter, Jocelyn Hackett, and to Ronnie's stepchildren, Brian and Elizabeth Ames—the next generation—whom we hope will inherit and expand on our efforts to create a more egalitarian society.

Contents

xi

Part V. Public Training for the Private Sector
SHARON L. HARLAN

Job Training for Women

The Promise and Limits of Public Policies

1/Job Training for Women: The Problem in a Policy Context

Sharon L. Harlan and Ronnie J. Steinberg

In a classic study of women's jobs, Louise Kapp Howe (1977) recounts the scene of an awards ceremony that took place in the banquet room of a Chicago hotel. Most of the 1,000 people in attendance were young women about to graduate from high school. The hushed anticipation of the audience was broken periodically by loud applause and cheers each time the master of ceremonies announced another award. The occasion was the annual competition of the office education program of the city's public schools.

Seventeen- and 18-year-old winners, proud and smiling, carried away awards recognizing their superior achievements in . . . filing . . . typing . . . bookkeeping . . . data entry . . . and the highest honor of all, overall excellence in clerical skills. After the ceremony, one of the school officials explained to Howe that the participants were mainly "Terminal Students." Instead of continuing on to college, within a few weeks the young women would be looking for full-time jobs where they could use their newly acquired skills. Many of them, as Howe discovered, would find those jobs in the back offices of the insurance companies and banks that make up Chicago's great financial industry. The training and job prospects of these young women were typical, both then and now, for female high school graduates who do not attend college.

The winners of the awards competition were justifiably proud of their accomplishments in mastering office skills. But they were probably unaware of the social context in which they chose clerical training as preparation for paid employment. Most of them probably did not realize that their skills would not be well remunerated compared to other kinds of skills they might have received in the same institution and in the same amount of time. They probably had not considered that clerical work offers few promotional paths. However, despite the low wages and limited advancement opportunities that are characteristic

3

of clerical work, the women Howe studied were still better off than many others in important respects. They were completing high school, they had learned some job skills, and they had done these things while they were young. They also might find one of the few female-dominated jobs for women with their educational level that would enable them to earn more than poverty-level wages.

In the decade since Howe wrote *Pink Collar Workers*, a confluence of social and economic trends has produced greatly increased interest and activity regarding publicly supported training for women. The services and opportunities that job training has to offer are in greater demand by women because their labor force participation rate has risen dramatically and is expected to continue rising. Between 1986 and 2000, the number of women in the labor force will increase from 52 million to 66 million. These figures signify a participation rate that is rising twice as fast as men's (U.S. Department of Labor [USDOL] 1987). By the year 2000, women will constitute 47 percent of the labor force.

The advances women have made in federally supported training programs are remarkable considering that historically women have been discouraged and even prohibited from participating. Public vocational education, available to everyone and with origins in federal sponsorship dating to early in the century, has traditionally offered wage-earning occupational training in agriculture, trade, and industry to men. Until relatively recently, women's participation was confined to consumer home economics and homemaking courses. Training programs targeted to the poor and unemployed, which first appeared during the 1920s and 1930s and then re-emerged as a major federal initiative in the 1960s, have focused primarily on young men and male family breadwinners. Prior to the 1970s there were almost no women apprentices in the oldest form of occupational training in recorded history. In the U.S. armed forces, a major source of occupational training for young men, women were not even permitted to be permanent members until the end of World War II, and as late as 1973, they were less than 2 percent of military personnel.

This historical neglect of women is changing. Federal involvement in occupational education has always been motivated by industry's desire for a skilled, productive labor force. So, some of the gains women have made are attributable to demand for women to fill clerical, sales, and service positions in the labor market. But in large part, we also owe the existence of the vocational education and job training system to the value Americans place on equal educational opportunity. This society has always believed that the educational system is the basis for providing equal access to the attainment of economic rewards in the marketplace, and the system has been called upon to create mobility opportunities for the lower classes, immigrants, and racial minorities. As the twentieth century has progressed, concern for equitable treatment of disadvantaged groups has become more explicit in federal legislation. In the past decade or so women have finally begun to benefit from the implementation of equal opportunity legislation.

Women's right to participate in training on an equal basis with men is formally guaranteed by federal laws, beginning with Title VII of the Civil Rights Act of 1964, which prohibits sex discrimination by employers in training, including on-the-job training and apprenticeship. However, it was not until the 1970s that additional legislation and administrative regulations really began to spur action. Title IX of the Education Amendments of 1972 protects women from discriminatory practices in any educational program or activity that receives federal funds. Later, Title II of the 1976 Education Amendments to the Vocational Education Act of 1963 required states to eliminate sex discrimination in vocational education programs. In 1978, the U.S. Department of Labor established goals and timetables for hiring women in apprenticeships in the skilled trades. The legislation which authorized the Carl D. Perkins Vocational Education Act of 1984 and the Job Training Partnership Act (JTPA) of 1982 enjoins states, localities, and program operators to provide equal opportunities for women and to increase their participation in nontraditional jobs. Even the armed forces, which still restrict the assignment of women to noncombat jobs, have somewhat improved women's access. In 1967 Public Law 90-130 lifted the restriction on the number of women in the military and the limits on the military rank women could obtain. In 1984 the secretary of defense established the Task Force on Equity for Women to evaluate women's opportunities (USDOL 1985).

Job search, training, and employment programs for women are also at the heart of major changes taking place in the welfare system. There is continuing experimentation with programs that attach work requirements to the receipt of Aid to Families with Dependent Children (AFDC), a cash public assistance program in which all but a very small percentage of recipients are in families headed by women.

At the same time that women have become a more important constituency of training programs, the federal government's responsibility for occupational education and job training has expanded. Although training programs for the economically disadvantaged have endured reductions in funding levels since 1980, the government still spends far more than it did on training programs for disadvantaged workers in the 1960s. For example, federal expenditures on training programs under the Manpower Development and Training Act and the Economic Opportunity Act totaled $1 billion in 1966 (USDOL 1974, 358), whereas 1986 federal appropriations under JTPA were $3.5 billion (see Table 1-4 below). More important, with few exceptions, the legitimacy of the federal government's role in sponsoring these programs is no longer questioned as it once was. They appear to be a permanent part of the training system, having survived even the conservative Reagan economic agenda to drastically reduce federal spending. Looking to the future, some observers, such as Osterman (Chapter 20), are even calling for an expanded training system to function as part of a broader national industrial policy.

Finally, technological change in work, which has always been an important rationale for government involvement in training, is occurring at a very fast pace. Labor Department projections indicate that most entry-level jobs will require more training in the future and most workers can expect to be retrained periodically to adapt to changes in their jobs. The effects of technological change include, but are not limited to, jobs in "high tech" industries. Clerical occupations, in which 80 percent of the work force is women, are among those experiencing dramatic change as computers and word processors become standard equipment in many firms. Employers expect women to already have acquired these skills when they are hired (see Greenbaum and Watson, Chapter 8), and much of this training takes place in the vocational education system. Some traditionally male jobs (in manufacturing or printing, for example) are also more accessible to women as they are transformed by technology to require less physical exertion. Thus, skill training that will enable women to qualify for newly emerging jobs is a high priority for training policy (see Giese, Chapter 13).

This book is about the public system of occupational education and job training for women in the United States. It is the first book of its kind: a comprehensive review of the system that places the treatment of women in a historical and political context. Its focus is on education and training for occupations that require less than a four-year college degree, including clerical, service, and blue-collar occupations, where the overwhelming majority of today's working women earn their living.[1] We examine the major public training programs that are aimed at individuals who are entering the labor market for the first time and at workers of all ages who need employment assistance: federal programs for the economically disadvantaged, public vocational education, occupational training in the armed forces, apprenticeship, and employment and training in the welfare system.

It has been difficult to focus scholarly and public attention on equal opportunity efforts directed explicitly at women without a college education. Instead, most of the notice has gone to the minority of women who have, or who will obtain, a college degree. Much more has been published on how women prepare for and get professional and managerial jobs.[2] Colleges, universities, and professional schools have been the targets of public controversy over sex discrimination much more often than have vocational or technical schools. And many of the celebrated media accounts of breaking down barriers in traditionally male jobs have been about women in professional careers. Fewer corporate resources have been spent on integrating nonprofessional jobs (Shaeffer and Lynton 1979).

This biased focus tends to obscure many of the ways by which the labor market confines and channels the majority of women into low-status and low-paying clerical, service, and blue-collar occupations. It reflects as well the undervaluation of these jobs as women's work and even more so, the widely held belief that these women are secondary earners and, therefore, unimportant. This, in turn, hinders efforts to improve their status because neither social scientists nor policy makers adequately understand the institutional structures within which the average woman is trained and subsequently employed.

Nevertheless, as the federal job training system has expanded and women have begun to claim a larger share of its resources, the business of designing programs for women and evaluating the effects has proliferated. A considerable amount of knowledge has accumulated from both research and practice about the strengths and weaknesses of the system. However, the literature is limited in important ways. There are many descriptive studies of individual vocational education and job training programs as well as several overviews of women and federal policy initiatives. Yet these are largely unpublished reports and papers and therefore not readily available to the general community of social scientists who could incorporate this knowledge into more general theory and research on labor market behavior and gender inequality. Neither have they persuaded policy makers and educators of the importance of training for women and of the role that training must play in a more comprehensive economic equality policy.

In the published literature, by contrast, we find a large number of econometric evaluations which are increasingly casting research and policy issues in narrow intellectual and methodological frameworks. Their sole intent is to measure the net program impact on participants' earnings by comparing earnings before and after participation while taking into account other factors that might cause change. This is a highly oversimplified definition of program impact because, among other things, it ignores any meaningful context of family or individual economic well-being. It also often suggests the misleading conclusion that women do "better" than men as a result of training (see Harlan, Chapter 2). The econometric studies, which have captured the attention of policy makers as well as the lion's share of research funding, hardly begin to answer the complex question of whether education and training is effective for women. Almost none of the literature—published or unpublished—attempts to discern the lessons learned during the past decade of program growth and experimentation. Nor does it address broader employment goals for diverse groups of women with differing training needs.

This book examines women's occupational options within the public training system and assesses the impact of training on women. We, and our contributing authors, consider training in traditionally female clerical fields but also look at training opportunities for women in traditionally male jobs, such as firefighters, coal miners, electronic technicians, the skilled trades, and entrepreneurs. We take into account the diversity among women in circumstances and need, and we try, where possible, to evaluate training outcomes by the yardstick of improvement in living standards and well-being. Some chapters measure earnings gains, whereas others adopt broader standards of effectiveness: self-sufficiency and economic opportunity. The quality and long-run earning potential of jobs for which women are trained are important to us. Where the availability of data permits, the chapters look at the options and impact of training from multiple perspectives: policy makers, evaluation researchers, educators, employers, society, and the women themselves.

Perspectives on Women's Needs for Training

The rising educational attainment of the labor force in the United States and, in particular, women's increasing share of bachelor's, graduate, and professional degrees sometimes obscures the fact that the job training needs of ordinary women will place the greatest future claim on public educational and training resources. Most of the women in the labor force today, as well as most of those who will enter it in the future, are not and will not be college graduates. Four-year colleges and universities train only a small fraction of all workers.

To be sure, the percentage of college graduates and the median years of school completed have been increasing steadily in the United States (see Table 1-1). Yet, looking at the 1984 figures for women most likely to have completed their education and to be in the labor force (that is, the civilian noninstitutional female population between ages 25 and 64), 82 percent had less than four years of college. Of those women, 12 million or 20.6 percent had not finished high school; 26.3 million or 44.7 percent had only a high school diploma; and 10 million or 17.1 percent had attended one to three years of college. Only 10 million women, or fewer than one in five, had at least a four-year college degree. Moreover, current trends do not portend any dramatic increase in aggregate levels of educational attainment for young women.[3]

Women who have not graduated from a four-year college (and even some who have) are potential candidates for participation in one or more of the public vocational education or job training programs examined in this book. Among those women there is a great deal of diversity in education, race, class background, and other factors which influence specific training needs. High school dropouts, for example, require different treatment from the job training system than do women who have completed a high school vocational education curriculum. And high school graduates who pursue postsecondary training in, for example, electronics, the building trades, or health sciences, have different needs than does either group of women with less education.

Table 1-1/Years of School Completed by Female Population 25 Years Old and Over, 1960 to 1984

YEAR, RACE, AND SPANISH ORIGIN	POPU-LATION (N × 1,000)	YEARS OF SCHOOL COMPLETED (% OF FEMALE POPULATION)					MEDIAN SCHOOL YEARS COM-PLETED
		Elementary School	High School		College		
		8 YEARS OR LESS	1–3 YEARS	4 YEARS	1–3 YEARS	4 YEARS OR MORE	
1960							
White	46,322	35.7	19.6	29.2	9.5	6.0	11.2
Black	4,814	57.7	20.5	14.3	4.1	3.3	8.6
1970							
White	51,718	25.5	19.4	35.5	11.1	8.4	12.1
Black	5,661	41.1	26.4	22.2	5.8	4.6	10.1
Spanish origin	2,014	47.9	18.0	23.1	6.7	4.3	9.3
1980							
White	60,349	16.5	15.5	39.1	15.6	13.3	12.6
Black	7,300	25.6	22.9	30.0	13.2	8.3	12.0
Spanish origin	3,493	41.3	16.1	26.0	10.6	6.0	10.6
1984							
White	64,627	13.1	12.2	42.8	15.8	16.0	12.6
Black	8,035	21.1	19.3	35.4	13.9	10.4	12.3
Spanish origin	3,880	39.2	15.0	28.2	10.5	7.0	11.0
All women, civilian non-institutional population, 25–64 years old [a]	58,901	8.6	12.0	44.7	17.1	17.6	

Source: U.S. Bureau of the Census 1986.
Note: Percentages may not add to exactly 100 because of rounding.
[a] Young 1985 (Current Population Survey, March 1984).

Thus, the women who are eligible for occupational education and job training programs are a large and heterogeneous population which presents a variety of challenges to the training system and demands a diversity of resources if such programs are to be effective. Let us look in greater detail at each group of women and outline some of these training needs.

High School Dropouts
Contrary to public perceptions, girls are as likely as boys to quit school. Almost a half million girls drop out annually before completing high school

(USDOL 1983, 120). The national high school dropout rate is 10 percent for white youths between the ages of 14 and 21, 15 percent for blacks, and 23 percent for Hispanics (Rumberger 1983, 200).[4] Moreover, only about 38 percent of dropouts finish a General Educational Development (GED) program within two years of their expected high school graduation date (Earle, Roach, and Fraser 1987, 12).

Reasons related to pregnancy or marriage account for between 33 percent and 40 percent of the girls who drop out of school (Rumberger 1983, 201; Earle, Roach, and Fraser 1987, 9). As Polit discusses in Chapter 6, educational programs to help teenage mothers finish school are a key strategy in improving their future employability. Among other causes of dropping out for girls, the most important self-reported reasons are school-related, such as disliking school or poor grades, and economic pressures at home. (These are also some of the same factors that lead to early childbearing.)

Family background characteristics are strongly correlated with quitting high school. The most important of these are low family socioeconomic status (SES), being black, and living in an urban area. A student from a low SES family, measured by parents' income, occupation, and education, is more than three times as likely to drop out than is a student from the highest SES background (U.S. General Accounting Office [USGAO] 1986). Girls' dropout rates are more conditioned by SES than are boys'.

According to the National Association of State Boards of Education (Earle, Roach, and Fraser 1987; see also references cited therein), the factors which put young women at risk of dropping out are becoming more prevalent. Most states have toughened their high school graduation standards since 1980 as a result of federal pressure for educational "reform." As this was done, however, no special efforts were made to address factors, such as alternative teaching styles, scheduling, or child care assistance, which might encourage students to stay in school. Moreover, because of federal budget reductions, many sex equity coordinators have been eliminated from schools. Among other duties, the coordinators had worked with high-risk girls to prevent them from dropping out.

Dropouts have limited options in the public training system, yet they are among those who need it most. The most fundamental need of school dropouts is for a training system that can provide basic language, reading, and mathematical skills, which are prerequisites for higher-level occupational training. Without this kind of remedial help, the problems associated with low educational attainment in adolescence—unemployment; low-wage, low-status jobs; poverty; and welfare dependence—extend into adulthood for many women.

Without a high school diploma, postsecondary education opportunities are largely closed to women. Even the U.S. Army requires enlisted women

Table 1-2/Plans of U.S. High School Seniors, High School and Beyond Survey, Spring 1980

MAIN ACTIVITY PLANNED FOR FIRST YEAR AFTER HIGH SCHOOL	GIRLS (%)	BOYS (%)
Attend four-year college	38.6	36.4
Attend junior college (academic program)	10.0	6.9
Attend junior college (technical or vocational program)	6.3	5.0
Attend trade or business school	6.6	5.2
Apprenticeship or on-the-job training	1.5	3.3
Military service	1.6	5.3
Full-time work	26.4	30.8
Part-time work without school or college attendance	2.1	1.5
Full-time homemaking	2.1	0.2
Other	3.2	3.1
Not reported	1.5	2.2

Source: USED 1983, 74–75.

(but not men) to be high school graduates. Similarly, many company training programs and all postsecondary vocational education programs are unavailable to female dropouts. As a result, the occupational options and earnings capacity of these women are extremely limited. The majority are either not in the labor force or unemployed. Of female dropouts who are employed, two-thirds work in service and blue-collar factory operator occupations. Textile sewing machine operators (average annual full-time 1986 earnings of $9,204) and nursing aides (earnings of $10,504) are typical job titles.[5] For such women to improve their labor market position, the public job training and educational system must provide, at a minimum, a means for them to acquire basic educational competencies and a high school credential.

High School Graduates
The high school graduate population encompasses women with a wide array of educational credentials and needs. A national longitudinal survey of high school seniors in spring 1980 found that 61.5 percent of the girls planned on enrolling in postsecondary education (four-year colleges, two-year colleges, and trade or business schools) (see Table 1-2). Boys were somewhat less likely than girls to plan on attending postsecondary schools but slightly more likely to plan on apprenticeship or military service where they would receive job training. A later segment of the same survey in fall 1980 found that 56 percent of female high school graduates, compared to 49 percent of males, actually participated in postsecondary education immediately after high school graduation (U.S. Department of Education [USED] 1985, 224). Another 15

percent of graduates enrolled in postsecondary education during the 3.5 years after graduation (USED 1987b, 33). Thus, in the short run, *29 percent of female graduates did not pursue any form of additional training.*

As with high school dropouts, the chances of young people's ending their education after high school are strongly associated with family SES, school performance, and race and ethnicity. Among 1980 female high school graduates from high SES families, only 18 percent did not attend postsecondary education immediately, whereas 42 percent of middle SES girls and 63 percent of lower SES girls did not attend. Lower SES girls were far less likely than others to be in four-year institutions. Low performers in school were two to three times less likely to attend postsecondary school compared to high performers of the same SES background. Overall, blacks were less likely than whites to participate in postsecondary education and Hispanics were less likely to than either of the other groups (USED 1985, 224).

Only some of the sizeable minority of women who end their education after high school are prepared to enter an occupation, and even when they are prepared, there is no guarantee that they will earn a decent living. Vetter (Chapter 3) reports that only about half the high school students enrolled in vocational courses have developed salable job skills. Most of the girls in this category, like the Chicago high school students of *Pink Collar Workers*, are trained in office occupations. In fact, nearly 40 percent of employed women with only a high school education worked in administrative support, including clerical occupations (see Table 1-6 below). Among all women who worked year-round and full-time, the largest single occupational title was secretary (average annual full-time 1986 earnings of $14,924; see n. 5).

As both Vetter and Giese (Chapters 3 and 13) point out, the most important service that high school vocational education could perform for young women is to expand their occupational options. To do this, women need to participate in a broader array of traditionally male curriculums, such as the numerous specialties in agriculture or trade and industry, which lead to higher-wage jobs. Moreover, within the office occupations curriculum, there is a need to train women for computerized information processing (Greenbaum and Watson, Chapter 8), to teach them entrepreneurial and business skills (Giese), and to prepare them for higher-level administrative and supervisory positions (Vetter).

A far larger number of female "terminal" high school graduates leave school without any occupational preparation. This includes students in the vocational curriculum who have not taken enough courses to acquire marketable skills as well as students in the general high school curriculum. According to a national survey, about half of all high school students were in a general high school curriculum in 1979 (Crowley, Pollard, and Rumberger 1983), and only 35 percent of general curriculum students attend postsecondary education

(Vetter, Chapter 3). Not surprisingly, general curriculum students have worse labor market outcomes, on average, than do vocational students (Grasso and Shea 1979).

Many of those young women who enter sales, service, or factory occupations directly from high school will be forced to return to the training system at some point for skill training because they will find that the female-dominated occupations for which they qualify are marginal, seasonal, or part-time employment with low pay. For example, a sales-counter clerk working full-time, year-round in 1986 had average earnings of $8,840, while a maid in a commercial establishment earned an average of $9,256 (see n. 5). Many women who return to the training system after working or raising families for a while have dependent children whom they are supporting, perhaps by themselves. They may also be enmeshed in the welfare system with its tangled and restrictive rules about what kinds of education are "acceptable" for them (see Gittell and Moore, Chapter 18). Thus, the public training system must be prepared to provide not only skill training but also an array of support services and financial assistance that will enable them to participate.

Young women who attend postsecondary education immediately after high school graduation, and especially those who acquire a credential beyond high school in community colleges, trade, technical, or business schools, will be better off than other high school graduates. Because they have basic educational competencies *and* marketable job skills, a somewhat larger percentage of them are able to work in better-paying managerial, professional, and technical jobs (see Table 1-6 below). For example, over 90 percent of vocational education in technical occupations and 80 percent in health occupations occurs at the postsecondary level.

Yet, the training system as it is currently structured funnels these women disproportionately into a narrow range of female-dominated occupations, such as nurses, secretaries, and therapists. While these occupations are vital to society and personally rewarding to many individuals, we argue throughout this book that (along with pay equity to raise the wages for historically female work) the range of options for women in postsecondary occupational training should be expanded in order to increase their wage-earning capacity. The equitable treatment of women in postsecondary occupational training includes increased access to school-based training in male-dominated occupational fields and, equally important, greater in-roads into male-dominated training institutions, such as apprenticeship and the military, which provide many benefits and higher-paying jobs that have been denied to women.

Race and Ethnicity
For a variety of reasons centering on lower rates of high school completion and college attendance, women of color are more likely than white women to

depend upon nonacademic training programs. They are more likely to need basic education, high school equivalency credentials, and occupational skills training. Moreover, the large influx of Spanish-speaking minorities into the labor market (USDOL 1987a, 10) suggests a need for training programs that include instruction in the English language.

Average educational attainment has increased for white, black, and Hispanic (Spanish origin) women and the educational gap between white and minority women has decreased since 1960 (see Table 1-1). Yet, even though a greater percentage of young minority females are graduating from high school than in the past, we have seen that they still quit high school at higher rates than do white females. Unmarried black teenagers have higher birth rates than do whites, a leading cause of dropping out of school. In contrast to white youth, among whom the propensity for males and females to return and complete high school is about equal, black and Hispanic males are more likely to go back than are black and Hispanic females (Kolstad and Owings 1986). Earle and her colleagues (1987, 12) report, "When these factors [low return rates] are added to the fact that minority status and the urban setting are highly associated with dropping out, the academic consequences for urban, minority young women are particularly severe."

Despite the higher dropout rates for most groups of minority women, the rise in the proportion of them completing high school is responsible for closing the educational gap between them and whites. In contrast, the rate of college attendance for blacks has fallen since 1975 and the disparity between the percentages of white and black women college graduates has increased. The national percentage of black female high school graduates between the ages of 18 and 24 enrolled in college decreased from 31.5 percent in 1975 to 26 percent in 1984.[6] During the same period, the percentage of comparable white females rose from 28.6 percent to 31.1 percent (U.S. Bureau of the Census 1986, 149). Moreover, black women are only 5 percent of the students in higher education nationally and they are far more likely than whites to be in two-year colleges where costs are lower (Wilkerson 1987, 88).

Although these educational inequalities between whites and people of color are clearly in need of redress, they suggest that in the current educational and economic environment, vocational education and other forms of nonacademic training are especially important for black women and Hispanic women. The high rates of nonmarital teenage childbearing and single-female family headship among black women also indicate that they are an important target group.

Yet, these forms of education, too, may be failing women of color. Occupational data indicate that among women without college degrees, women of color work in jobs that require less training (and therefore, pay less and have less status). For example, Hispanic women are more likely than blacks or whites to work as factory operatives, whereas blacks work disproportionately in service occupations and are underrepresented in clerical jobs (USED 1986, 208). While there is some evidence that these patterns are changing among younger cohorts of women (Taeuber and Valdisera 1986, 22–23), much progress remains to be made in integrating and expanding options for women of color in all kinds of job training programs.

This section has illustrated a variety of training needs among women of different educational backgrounds. The ideas expressed here—basic educational competencies, expanded occupational options, support services, and financial assistance—are repeated again and again in the chapters of this book. Another point that is implicit when we discuss training for women is the need for a training system structured in such a way that it provides opportunities for women who have already been failed by it at least once. Too many women do not make good initial choices about education and employment, either because they have poor information or because they lack the freedom to do what is best for their long-term security. Therefore, the single most important common need women have is for a training system that is flexible; that is, one that can accommodate individual timetables, family and financial situations, geographic location, and occupational aspirations. With this thought in mind, we now turn to examine the structure of occupational education and training in the United States.

Training: Institutional Perspectives

Occupational education and training in the United States takes place in a vast array of institutional settings involving large numbers of diverse individuals who participate in publicly and privately financed programs. People train and retrain for occupations in high school and throughout their adult lives, so that participants are of all ages and have a wide range of previous educational and labor market experiences. A substantial amount of noncollege training is based in public secondary and postsecondary schools, but other institutions, such as proprietary schools, the military, and private sector firms, also perform important training functions. The credentials awarded to students range from none to high school diplomas, certificates, licenses, and associate degrees.

A recent sample survey by the Bureau of the Census found that 55 percent of the U.S. work force said they needed at least one kind of training to qualify for their current job (see Table 1-3 derived from original survey results).[7] Not surprisingly, a higher percentage of workers in more skilled occupational categories required training. Schooling of any kind (vocational, trade, technical, college, or professional) is an important source of training to qualify for jobs: 29 percent of workers in the survey mentioned schooling as a necessary job

Table 1-3/Sources of Training Needed by Workers 16 Years Old and Over to Qualify for Their Current Jobs, by Major Occupational Group

| OCCUPATIONAL GROUP | Any Source of Training | School | | | | | | Formal Company[a] | Informal OJT | Armed Forces | Correspondence Courses | Friends and Other[b] |
| | | Any School | High School Vocational Education | POST–HIGH SCHOOL VOCATIONAL EDUCATION | | Junior College or Technical Institute | College, 4 years or More | | | | | |
				Private	Public							
Executive, administrative, and managerial occupations												
N × 1,000	7,738	4,674	333	169	134	581	3,638	1,346	4,242	314	140	341
(% of total employment)	(71)	(43)	(3)	(2)	(1)	(5)	(34)	(12)	(39)	(3)	(1)	(3)
Professional specialty occupations												
N × 1,000	11,797	10,397	208	367	213	906	8,961	1,184	2,767	281	118	331
(% of total employment)	(93)	(82)	(2)	(3)	(2)	(7)	(70)	(9)	(22)	(2)	(1)	(3)
Technicians and related support occupations												
N × 1,000	2,579	1,759	149	168	185	600	774	442	962	152	54	47
(% of total employment)	(85)	(58)	(5)	(5)	(6)	(20)	(24)	(14)	(32)	(5)	(2)	(2)
Sales occupations												
N × 1,000	4,867	1,643	185	163	90	356	941	1,315	3,148	90	113	330
(% of total employment)	(43)	(15)	(2)	(1)	(1)	(3)	(8)	(12)	(28)	(1)	(1)	(3)
Administrative support occupations, including clerical												
N × 1,000	9,157	5,262	2,659	506	367	1,282	976	1,198	4,945	136	101	198
(% of total employment)	(57)	(33)	(16)	(3)	(2)	(8)	(6)	(7)	(31)	(1)	(1)	(1)

qualification (see Table 1-3). Even more important than all kinds of schooling in qualifying for jobs is training while working for a company, including both informal and formal training. In fact, 28 percent of workers in the survey reported using informal on-the-job training (OJT). Whereas school-based training is more commonly required for executive, professional, lower white-collar, and some service occupations, OJT is relatively more important in blue-collar occupations. Manual jobs, such as the construction trades, assembly, or machine operation, are frequently learned through OJT. An advantage of OJT is the opportunity to earn while learning. Under JTPA, for example, employers can provide economically disadvantaged participants with training in a specific occupation in exchange for a federal wage subsidy (see Harlan, Chapter 2).

Training can be characterized not only according to its form but also according to its function. A primary function of training is to provide participants with specific job skills. However, it is often erroneously assumed that the acquisition of a specific job-related skill is all that is needed for participants to capitalize on their educational "investment." As we suggested above, a second important function of training for many individuals is the provision of basic educational competencies (reading, math, English language communication) which they did not acquire in school and which they must have before skill training can even begin. Third, and especially important to women, is the function of occupational and personal counseling that helps to shape occupational aspirations by broadening awareness of the available options and the consequences of choices. A fourth function of training, which is sometimes overlooked, is assistance in job placement.

Training, as it is currently operated, does not always serve all of these functions where they are needed, as we will see. For example, while apprenticeship has traditionally combined extensive skill training with placement of its participants as well-paid journey-level craftworkers, it has only minimally expanded women's opportunities in the system through specific outreach and recruitment procedures targeted to them (see Glover, Chapter 11). At the other end of the spectrum, current welfare regulations permit job search programs which do not provide any skill training and can lead to direct placement in minimum-wage jobs for a predominately female clientele (see Goldman, Chapter 16).

The length of training is another aspect which varies substantially across programs. Apprenticeships, which typically last between four and six years, can be contrasted with the one or two years required for most postsecondary vocational credentials. Both of these are substantially longer than the average 14-week training program in JTPA which prepares many female participants for entry-level jobs as typists or nursing aides.

Sources of Training

The most important source of occupational training for youth who have not yet entered the labor market is vocational education (Doeringer 1981, 3). Vetter (Chapter 3) reports that 5.8 million individuals were enrolled in occupationally specific instruction programs in the public vocational education system, including secondary and postsecondary. Girls and women were 47 percent of the participants. These programs take place in a variety of institutions, such as high schools, vocational high schools, community colleges, hospital schools, and technical institutes.

Both the number of community colleges and their enrollments (4.7 million in 1983) have been increasing substantially, and those trends are expected to continue (USED 1986, 112). A growing proportion of enrollments are now in vocational rather than academic programs. Moreover, many two-year colleges, "sometimes dismissed as the poor relations of higher education, are carving a new role for themselves delivering customized job training and technical education to manufacturers and businesses in their towns" (*New York Times*, 20 June 1988, Sec. A). (See also Goldstein, Chapter 19).

Although public institutions are the principal providers of vocational training in the educational system, proprietary schools are also important. Wilms (1981, 31, 33) estimates that there are more than 10,000 such schools enrolling between 1.3 and 3 million students annually. Large proportions of their courses are in business and office occupations (25 percent), cosmetology and barber (10 percent), and trades (9 percent).

Federal and state governments jointly operate programs for economically disadvantaged individuals under JTPA and the Omnibus Budget Reconciliation Act (OBRA) of 1981. Approximately 1.8 million new participants were enrolled in JTPA during program year 1986 and women were slightly more than half of all participants in the largest JTPA titles.[8] JTPA is the successor to the Comprehensive Employment and Training Act (CETA) of 1973 and other employment and training programs initiated during the Great Society era of the 1960s (see Harlan, Chapter 2). Although these programs typically enroll poor people with a variety of employment difficulties, historically men, and not women, have been the primary target group. To some degree under CETA, and now especially under JTPA, one group of poor women is receiving more attention: nearly one-quarter of JTPA Title IIA participants are recipients of AFDC. Not coincidentally, this targeting strategy of JTPA occurred at the same time that federal efforts were under way to link the receipt of public assistance payments to employment and training requirements for recipients.

Under OBRA, the states gained much more flexibility in their ability to restructure welfare-related work programs (see Gueron, Chapter 15). Many of them are using this authority to experiment with a variety of voluntary and mandatory programs for AFDC recipients, such as community work experience, job search, and employment and training programs like ET Choices in Massachusetts (Werner, Chapter 17). The WIN (Work Incentive) Demonstration Projects authorized by OBRA and operated by the states enrolled approximately 680,000 AFDC recipients in fiscal 1985.[9] These welfare-related work programs authorized by OBRA are separate and distinct from employment and training policy under JTPA, but a convergence of purpose is strengthening the ties between them. The use of employment and training programs *for women* (on such a massive scale) to reduce the number of families on public assistance is a precedent both for training policy and welfare policy.

JTPA trainees may be enrolled in schools, but they may also be working in private-sector on-the-job training programs or be students in other programs, such as community-based organizations, Job Corps centers, or other educational programs. Most JTPA participants are engaged in job-related training, but other JTPA activities include job search, work experience, direct job placements, and remedial education for summer youth participants (USDOL 1987b; USGAO 1987a). The WIN Demonstrations, on the other hand, are not primarily concerned with education and training activities. The majority of participants in welfare-related work programs are engaged in job search activities (see Gurin, Chapter 15, and Goldman, Chapter 16), while only 10 percent of WIN Demonstration participants received education and training services (USGAO 1987b, 70). These programs vary widely by state.

Two other public training sources, which enroll few women but which are very important parts of the training establishment are apprenticeship, jointly regulated by the U.S. Department of Education and the U.S. Department of Labor, and the armed forces. Glover (Chapter 11) reports that there were approximately 250,000 active apprenticeships in 1986 and most of them were in the building trades, metalworking, and repair occupations. About 6 percent of all apprentices were women. In fiscal 1986, the armed forces numbered approximately 1.9 million enlisted personnel, 10 percent of whom were women (Devilbiss, Chapter 4). Skill training in over 2,000 military job specialties accounts for at least half of all military training (Wilms 1981, 39).

The federal budget for occupational education and training is quite large and dispersed across many agencies, as shown in Table 1-4. One must add to this, expenditures from state and local governments' budgets, which provide 90 percent of the funding for public vocational education and between 10 percent and 50 percent matching funds for welfare-related work programs. Some states also use their own funds for special training interests. For example, the first legislation authorizing programs for displaced homemakers was passed by California in 1975, followed by several other states (Miller, Chapter 5). Although the appropriations for state programs are relatively small, this movement strengthened the case for federal targeting of displaced homemakers under CETA. States also contribute to comprehensive education and employ-

Table 1-4/Federal Appropriations for Vocational Education and Employment and Training Programs, Fiscal 1986

PROGRAMS BY ACTIVITIES	1986 APPROPRIATIONS (× $1,000)
VOCATIONAL EDUCATION [a]	
Basic state grants and set asides	845,962
Community-based organizations	6,460
Consumer and homemaking education	30,311
State councils	6,761
National programs	10,165
Other	6,852
Total (vocational education)	906,511
ADULT EDUCATION [b]	
Grants to states	109,791
EMPLOYMENT AND TRAINING [c]	
Grants to states:	
Block grant	1,781,562
Summer youth employment and training	724,549
Dislocated worker assistance	126,252
Federally-administered programs	891,217
Other	2,459
Total (employment and training)	3,526,039
APPRENTICESHIP SERVICES [d]	12,185
WORK INCENTIVE (WIN) PROGRAM [e]	
Grants to states	202,884
TOTAL APPROPRIATIONS	4,757,410

Source: Executive Office of the President 1987a.

[a] Funds appropriated under the Carl D. Perkins Vocational Education Act. Basic grants to states for expansion, innovation, and improvement in vocational education.

[b] Funds appropriated under the Adult Education Act. Grants to states to eliminate illiteracy among adults and help them to obtain a high school diploma or equivalent.

[c] Funds appropriated under the Job Training Partnership Act. Block grants to states for designing and operating training programs, including remedial education, basic institutional programs, and on-the-job training. Federally administered programs for special segments of the population, including native Americans, migrant farm workers, and veterans—also includes Job Corps.

[d] Funds appropriated under the Department of Labor Appropriations Act, 1986, to promote apprenticeship as a method of skill acquisition through a federal-state administrative structure.

[e] Funds appropriated under the Department of Health and Human Services Appropriations Act, 1986, as authorized by Title IV of the Social Security Act. Grants to states for registration, appraisal, and employability planning; job search; training and child care services for AFDC recipients; and WIN Demonstrations. Scheduled to be replaced by new initiatives.

ment programs for teenage parents sponsored jointly with the federal government (Polit, Chapter 6).

Private sector employers also provide training opportunities to some workers. The Conference Board found in a 1975 study that education and training opportunities were concentrated in the largest firms (of more than 10,000 employees), which accounted for 8 percent of all firms in the U.S. and for 75 percent of training expenditures (Lusterman 1977). It is unlikely, they said, that formal in-house training and education programs exist for employees in firms that employ fewer than 500 workers. Based on the survey, Lusterman projected that private firms spent about $2 billion in *direct* costs on training in 1974–75, most of it for in-house programs.[10]

Financial and insurance companies led all other industries in the prevalence, employee participation, and median expenditures per employee for training in the study. Transportation, communications, and utilities ranked next, and trade and manufacturing industries were last. Across all industries, however, the employees most likely to participate in training were in managerial, professional, and sales occupations. These are predominately male jobs. Only 19 percent of nonexempt salary and 11 percent of nonexempt hourly workers (far less than any other category) participated in courses. In a follow-up study 10 years later, larger proportions of employees in all major categories were involved in formal training (Lusterman 1985). *But at the time of the follow-up, secretarial/clerical and operatives/craftworkers were least likely to have increased their participation levels.* When they did make gains, it was because of the need to learn new technology associated with computers used in information processing and production. The greatest gains in training participation were for supervisors and mid-level managers as firms tried to tie training programs more closely to strategic corporate goals. Later in this book, Goldstein (Chapter 19) presents an excellent case study of how business goals in high tech industries shape training decisions that turn out to be detrimental to female production workers and most beneficial to male technicians.

The Promise and the Limits of Public Training

A substantial amount of training takes place in the private sector as well as in the public sector, but we have focused this book almost exclusively on publicly supported training because of its scope, accessibility, and legal obligation to provide equal opportunity for women.[11] Public training has the capacity to reach a large and diverse population of women who would probably not get training from any other source.

The functions of public training programs are particularly significant for women. Training can help participants to gain access to entry-level jobs by providing basic educational requirements, occupational counseling, job skills training, and job search assistance. These are important to first-time labor market entrants and re-entrants with limited work experience, many of whom are women. Skill training is also imperative in enabling women to enter non-traditional jobs (that is, jobs that are predominately held by men). Typically, women do not have the educational background or occupational socialization necessary to enter those occupations without training assistance. Public training policy also has a mandate to serve special populations, such as welfare recipients, teenage mothers, and displaced homemakers. Not only do these women encounter the educational and labor market barriers experienced by other women, but they are disadvantaged as well by particular social situations in which they must simultaneously assume the demanding roles of sole family caretaker and breadwinner. These situations are unique to women because of their gender and require a special kind of training and public support that is unnecessary for men.

Public programs reach a much broader cross section of the population, and more women, than does either private vocational education or employer-sponsored training programs. Access to training in private schools is limited to those who can pass entrance requirements and pay the tuition costs. Such programs are inaccessible to the economically disadvantaged population, most of whom are women, because they cannot afford it. Access to employer-sponsored training is, for the most part, limited to employees who work in the largest corporations. Female-dominated and working-class jobs are not targets of corporate training policies. Thus, many women who are the subjects of this book would never have the opportunity to participate in private sector training programs, as they are currently structured, either on or off the job. Public-sector job training is their only option.

This is not to say that the public system is a perfect vehicle for delivering training. One of its major limitations is that these programs operate outside the labor market. Public programs teach occupational skills that are an asset in finding entry jobs in some occupations, but they do not help participants gain access to the internal labor markets of many large firms that do not require specific occupational skills of new hires. Yet these firms often pay the highest wages and provide the most stable employment opportunities. (See section below, "Job Training and Equal Employment.")

The public training system also suffers from inadequate resources. Despite the fact that millions of individuals channel through the public system, the opportunities specifically targeted to the economically disadvantaged are not nearly adequate to meet the need for education and training assistance. For example, Title IIA of JTPA, the largest training title, is estimated to enroll only 4 percent of the population that is eligible to participate. In states with full-year WIN Demonstrations in 1985, only about 22 percent of all adult AFDC recipients participated in any welfare-related work programs.[12] Even for those who are fortunate enough to participate in training programs, scarce resources often lead to short, inexpensive, and inadequate training strategies.

It is harder to gauge whether enrollment opportunities in other parts of the system adequately meet the needs of eligible, interested individuals. However, we do know that the U.S. government subsidy for skill training is lower than in almost any other industrialized country (Woodcock 1977). Moreover, the federal budget for many civilian training programs has decreased since 1980.

Regardless of its faults, the public occupational education system is unique and important because it serves a *compensatory* function for those who were passed over in the initial stages of education, a *redistributive* function for those who have been denied training opportunity elsewhere, and an *entitlement* function for those who cannot afford other educational options. It is compensatory because it can give a second chance for educational opportunities to individuals who would otherwise be at a life-long disadvantage. It is redistributive because it is more accessible than any other source of training to women, people of color, and all individuals who face systemic barriers to educational opportunity. Finally, it is an entitlement because it extends to the lower and working classes a right to an education, which is highly valued in American society.

Achieving sex equity in federal training programs is a pressing policy issue. It is essential that federal training policy set an exemplary standard for, and maintain a consistent posture toward, equal opportunity for women. After all, the private sector takes its cues from the government in complying with equal opportunity legislation. Moreover, the amount of resources involved in public education is substantial—approximately $23 billion in federal funds were authorized for education, training, and employment activities in fiscal 1986 (Executive Office of the President 1987b).[13] Considering what is at stake individually and collectively for women who need education and training assistance, there is a strong need for accountability in the distribution of those resources.

Training as a Cause and Effect of Gender Inequality

Public support for training grows in part from the American tradition of providing people with an equal chance to compete for economic success. The specific form of the relationship between training and opportunity, usually measured by earnings, has been cast in recent years by labor economists in terms of human capital theory. Human capital theory claims that greater investments in training yield higher wages in a marketplace that rewards the greater productivity of skilled, better-educated workers. Since the sixties, federal training policy has been crafted by intellectuals and politicians who subscribe to this model of economic attainment. Their assumption is that economic opportunity (higher earnings) can be created by a government-sponsored training system. This assumption is at the center of a debate with others who believe in training

Table 1-5/Labor Force Participation and Unemployment for Civilian Women, Ages 25–64, March 1984

		EDUCATION				
	Elementary	*High School*		*College*		
WOMEN	*8 years or less*	1–3 YEARS	4 YEARS	1–3 YEARS	4 YEARS OR MORE	*Total*
Civilian non-institutional population (N × 1,000)	5,059	7,068	26,310	10,100	10,368	58,901
Civilian labor force (N × 1,000)	1,917	3,472	16,709	7,050	8,086	37,234
Labor force participation (%)	37.9	49.1	63.5	69.8	78.0	63.2
Unemployment rate (%)	11.8	11.5	6.3	5.3	2.7	6.1

Source: Young 1985 (Current Population Survey, March 1984).

but argue that training alone is insufficient without direct intervention in the labor market.

Education and the Labor Force Experience of Women
In a very basic way, the human capital premise appears to be correct: the more education women have, the more likely they are to be advantaged in the labor market. We can see this illustrated in the relationships of educational attainment with employment rates, occupational attainment, earnings, and poverty rates. Women ages 25 to 64 with four-year college degrees in 1984 had the highest participation rate (78 percent) and the lowest unemployment (2.7 percent) of any educational group (see Table 1-5). At the very bottom of the educational attainment ladder, only about 38 percent of women who never attended high school were in the labor force. Of those women, one of three was unemployed. Unemployment was even higher among young women, aged 16 to 24, who were not in college. Female 1983 high school graduates (not enrolled in college) had a labor force participation rate of 80.5 percent and an unemployment rate of 25.4 percent in October 1983 (USED 1986, 209). During the same period, the labor force participation rate was 48.1 percent and unemployment was 29.5 percent for female high school dropouts (USED 1986, 210).

The distribution of women among occupations also varies greatly ac-

Table 1-6/Educational Attainment and Occupations for Employed Civilian Women, Ages 25–64, March 1984

| | EDUCATION | | | |
| | LESS THAN 4 YEARS OF HIGH SCHOOL (%) | 4 YEARS OF HIGH SCHOOL ONLY (%) | College | |
OCCUPATIONAL CATEGORY			1–3 YEARS (%)	4 YEARS OR MORE (%)
MANAGERIAL AND PROFESSIONAL SPECIALTY	4.6	11.6	27.1	70.4
Executive	2.7	8.0	12.8	15.4
Professional	1.8	3.6	14.9	55.2
TECHNICAL, SALES, AND ADMINISTRATIVE SUPPORT	20.9	54.0	55.8	24.0
Technicians	0.8	3.0	6.4	4.3
Sales	9.5	12.8	10.5	6.7
Administrative support, including clerical	10.7	38.3	39.0	13.0
SERVICES	37.1	18.7	10.2	3.3
Private household	5.9	1.3	0.8	0
Protective	0.4	0.4	0.4	0.2
Food	12.4	6.3	2.8	0.7
Health	5.6	4.0	2.7	0.7
Cleaning and building	8.4	2.2	0.8	0.2
Personal	4.3	4.3	2.8	1.4
PRECISION PRODUCTION, CRAFT, AND REPAIR	4.7	2.9	1.5	0.7
OPERATORS, FABRICATORS, AND LABORERS	30.6	11.7	4.0	1.0
FARMING, FORESTRY, AND FISHING	2.2	0.9	0.7	0.4

Source: Young 1985 (Current Population Survey, March 1984).
Note: The percentages are based on the following total numbers (N × 1000) of women: less than 4 years of high school, N = 4,754; 4 years of high school only, N = 15,659; 1–3 years of college, N = 6,676; and 4 years or more of college, N = 7,864.

cording to educational attainment (see Table 1-6). Seventy percent of college-educated women work in managerial and professional specialty occupations. More than half of those women with a high school diploma or some college are in technical, sales, or administrative support occupations, with most of them working in clerical jobs. As we noted above, two-thirds of the women who have not graduated from high school work in service and blue-collar factory operator occupations.

Educational attainment is strongly related to women's income: among year-round, full-time workers, median annual income rises steadily at each

Table 1-7/Median Annual Incomes of Full-Time, Year-Round Workers, 25 Years Old and Over, 1985

| | INCOME AMOUNT | | INCOME RATIO | |
EDUCATION	Women	Men	Women to Women College Graduates	Women to Men
LESS THAN 8 YEARS	$ 9,736	$14,766	.46	.66
8 YEARS	11,377	18,645	.53	.66
HIGH SCHOOL				
1–3 years	11,836	18,881	.55	.63
4 years	15,481	23,853	.72	.65
COLLEGE				
1–3 years	17,989	26,960	.84	.67
4 years	21,389	32,822	1.00	.65
5 years or more	25,928	39,335	1.21	.66
TOTAL	17,124	26,365	.80	.65

Source: USED 1987a. Based on the Current Population Survey.

level of education (see Table 1-7). There are particularly large dollar differ-ences between women with a college degree and others, and between women who graduated from high school and women who did not. The ratio of women's earnings to the earnings of women college graduates ranges from .46 for women with less than eight years of education to .84 for women with one to three years of college. Female college graduates are better equipped than other women to earn enough to support themselves.

By contrast, low educational attainment often relegates women to poverty. When we look at the percentages of white and black women living below the poverty level by educational attainment and age in 1981, we observe that for white women, poverty was much more likely to occur among women who were not high school graduates (see Table 1-8). For black women, the percentage in poverty was two to four times higher than for white women in the same educational and age categories. Educational attainment makes a difference in the likelihood of poverty among female-headed families as well: half of all families headed by a female high school dropout live in poverty (Earle, Roach, and Fraser 1987, 13), compared to 34 percent of all families headed by women (U.S. Bureau of the Census 1987, 72).

Women with lower educational attainment thus have higher unemploy-ment, work in lower-status occupations, earn less money, and have a higher risk of being poor than do college-educated women. However, when one com-pares the effect of education on earnings for women and men, human capital

Table 1-8/Percentages of White and Black Women in Poverty, by Educational Attainment for Selected Age Groups, 1981

| | AGE | | | | | | | |
| | White | | | | Black | | | |
EDUCATION	18–21	22–34	35–44	45–54	18–21	22–34	35–44	45–54
ELEMENTARY								
1–5 years	42.0	38.6	37.5	59.4	—	—	—	—
6 and 7 years	46.5	33.9	36.5	17.9	—	—	—	46.7
8 years	39.1	36.3	24.5	15.3	—	—	42.6	49.3
HIGH SCHOOL								
1–3 years	22.2	28.0	18.9	13.5	56.9	62.2	41.6	35.3
4 years	11.6	10.7	7.8	4.5	33.6	30.9	24.9	22.1
COLLEGE								
1 year or more	9.5	5.9	4.4	4.0	21.3	18.3	10.1	10.4
ALL LEVELS OF EDUCATION	14.2	11.3	9.6	7.4	38.5	33.4	29.0	30.0

Source: USDOL 1983.
Note: Dash (—) indicates base less than 75,000.

theory does not work as smoothly as its proponents insist. Human capital theory fails to account fully for the wage gap between women and men based on differences in the amount of their education and training. No matter how much education women have, they do not earn as much as comparably educated men (see Table 1-7). The dollar gap between women's and men's average earnings is larger at each successively higher level of education. Research has consistently shown that women get lower economic returns than men on their training investments and that even among men and women with the same labor force attachment, the life-time earnings profile of women is flatter than men's (Treiman and Hartmann 1981).

Occupational Segregation and Earnings
To understand why women do not get as much economic return for their education as do men, we must look at the range of occupations available to them. Pervasive occupational segregation by sex and race in the labor market mediates the effect of education and training on earnings. One major study estimated that 35 percent to 40 percent of the wage gap between women and men can be accounted for by occupational segregation, even when analyzing occupational categories that combine many specific occupational titles (Treiman and Hartmann 1981).

To illustrate the association between female-dominated occupations and low wages, consider the rankings of women's annual earnings in the 20 occupations that employed over half of all full-time, year-round women workers in 1980.[14] Only five occupations—managers and administrators (not elsewhere classified), registered nurses, elementary school teachers, general office supervisors, and accountants and auditors—fell in the upper half of the earnings rankings for all full-time women in 421 census occupational categories. In contrast, 12 of the 20 occupations employing the most full-time, year-round male workers were in the top half of the earnings rankings for full-time men. Thus, fewer of the most common women's occupations rank high in earnings even when they are compared to other women's occupations. Women's average 1979 earnings of $11,051 in the top 20 female occupations can be compared to men's average 1979 earnings of $19,943 in the 20 most common male occupations (Taeuber and Valdisera 1986, 19).

Occupational segregation is an important issue for women of all social classes, but the degree of sex segregation is higher in the major occupational groups where women without a college education work than in managerial and professional specialty occupations.[15] While overall occupational segregation declined somewhat between 1970 and 1980, the two most significant drops in the index occurred in managerial and professional occupations (56 percent to 43 percent) and in service occupations (68 percent to 55 percent). However, two-thirds of the net employment growth for women in the managerial occupational group was in male-dominated occupations compared to just under one-third of the growth in the service occupational group.

The economic consequences of occupational segregation are also more severe for women who do not pursue higher education to prepare for professional or managerial careers. Take, for example, women in secretarial occupations where the average salary for full-time workers in 1986 was only 130 percent of the poverty-level income for a family of four. In service occupations, where about half of female dropouts work, 33 percent of white female family heads and 47 percent of black female family heads earned wages that left them below the poverty level (USDOL 1983, 103) in jobs such as nursing aides, child care workers, and waitresses. Yet, many higher-paying jobs in maintenance, repair, crafts, construction, and protective services are performed by male high school graduates and even by male high school dropouts.

Occupational segregation in the labor market limits the options of the average woman, ensuring that she will get less return for her education than men and, thereby, undermining her capacity to be self-sufficient. This places important restrictions on the ability of training to decrease labor market inequalities between women and men. Although the theoretical justification for training assumes a competitive market in which qualified workers receive opportunities, in practice, the market is not impartial to sex and race in allocating jobs. The result is that training does raise women's wages, but only within the limited set of female-dominated occupations available to them.

Occupational Segregation in Job Training

Education and training occupy a crucial position in the chain of events between childhood gender-role socialization and later institutional barriers and domestic responsibilities that lead to the separation of women and men in the job market.[16] From early experiences in public schools, which tend to magnify gender-role stereotypes, through career counseling, tracking, and underrepresentation of women in math and science courses, most educational experiences tend to perpetuate sex segregation. Vocational education and other job-related training programs, themselves highly partitioned by sex, provide some of the most direct evidence of linkages between the educational system and occupational segregation. Rather than counteracting sex segregation, training reinforces it by overwhelmingly preparing women for lower-paying, sex-typical occupations.

One of the fundamental characteristics of job training in the United States is that it is a different experience for women and men. At the most general level, women and men are funneled into completely different programs—in particular, welfare-related work programs are usually populated by women. Other programs—in particular, apprenticeship and the military—are in male institutions. It will come as no surprise to anyone that apprenticeships and the military offer far superior job and earnings opportunities to participants. Some other organizations in the training system, such as vocational education, are shared more equally by women and men, but even in these programs, there are still many important differences in the training they receive.[17]

Training demands are not the exclusive province of either female- or male-dominated occupational categories. For example, 57 percent of administrative support (clerical) and 62 percent of health service workers, traditionally female occupations, require entry-level training according to the survey results reported in table 1-3 above. This is about the same as traditionally male areas, such as protective service (56 percent) and crafts (65 percent). But *what* women and men are trained for and *where* they receive their training is quite different. In addition to separating women and men by major institution, the training system sorts them on two other dimensions, with the result that they are prepared for separate and unequal labor markets. First, classroom training is relatively more important for female-dominated occupations than for male-dominated ones. Second, even training for occupations within classrooms is highly segregated by sex.

Vocational education (school-based training) is a major training ground for the pink-collar ghettos described in Howe's (1977) book. The Census survey reveals that 16 percent (or 2.7 million) of administrative support workers were trained in high school vocational education programs. For the detailed occupational titles of secretaries, stenographers, and typists, the percentage trained in high school vocational education was 35 percent.[18] Public secondary and postsecondary vocational education also trains many women in the health field. For example, 25 percent of the licensed practical nurses are products of public postsecondary vocational education. Community colleges are prominent sources of training for health services: registered nurses (29 percent), inhalation therapists (46 percent), dental hygienists (38 percent), radiologic technicians (39 percent), and clinical lab technicians (24 percent). These fields are heavily dominated by women. Under the personal services occupational category, 45 percent of hairdressers and cosmetologists reported receiving job training in private vocational education programs.

Thus, the survey results reported in table 1-3 indicate that training for many women's occupations takes place in school classrooms. This is true, in part, for some male occupations. For example, 13 percent of auto mechanics, 16 percent of tool and die makers, and 10 percent of metal workers reported receiving training in high school vocational education. Approximately 25 percent of electrical and electronic technicians and drafters were trained in community colleges. But one of the most evident distinguishing features between men's and women's training in nonprofessional occupations is that male jobs are much more likely to be learned outside of school.

Formal company training programs are an important source of qualifying training for several kinds of technicians, over 40 percent of protective service workers, and between 20 and 40 percent of many industrial and construction crafts. Presumably, many workers in the crafts served formal apprenticeships to learn their trades. Few women, however, are trained in this system. The armed forces also trained 17 percent of engineering technicians, 6 percent of protective service workers, such as police, firefighters, and guards, and 45 percent of aircraft engine mechanics. Yet, enlisted men outnumber women nine to one.

Not only is school-based training more important for women's occupations, but even within schools, women and men are segregated into different occupational fields. In 1981–82, a total of 399,717 associate degrees and other awards were conferred on participants in occupational curriculums, and 54 percent of those awards were to women (see Table 1-9). While not all participants in occupational programs receive such credentials, the wide variety of specialties represented here is illustrative of substantial differences in the fields for which women and men are trained.

The awards women received from postsecondary programs of both longer and shorter duration are concentrated in just two areas that accounted for 78 percent of women's total: health services and business. Registered nurses and secretaries accounted for 33 percent of the awards in longer programs, while practical nurses and secretaries accounted for 44 percent of the awards in shorter programs. Men received 65 percent of their awards in mechanical and engineering technologies. There were only a few fields in which the number of awards to women and men were approximately equal. The largest of these were general data processing, computer programming, general busi-

Table 1-9/Associate Degrees and Other Awards Based on Occupational Curriculums, 1981–82

| | AWARDS BASED ON ORGANIZED OCCUPATIONAL CURRICULUMS | | | |
| | At Least 2 Years but Less Than 4 Years | | At Least 1 Year but Less Than 2 Years | |
OCCUPATIONAL CURRICULUMS	MEN	WOMEN	MEN	WOMEN
DATA PROCESSING				
Data processing general	5,464	6,087	590	886
Keypunch operator and other input preparation	30	55	65	790
Computer programmer	4,044	4,478	727	777
Computer operator and peripheral equipment operator	218	270	218	508
Data processing equipment maintenance	1,314	139	286	80
Other	13	43	1	2
Total	11,083 7.8%	11,072 6.8%	1,887 4.4%	3,043 5.8%
HEALTH SERVICES AND PARAMEDICAL				
Dental assistant	15	1,227	9	2,121
Dental hygiene	78	3,630	0	82
Dental laboratory	350	313	2	13
Medical or biological laboratory assistant	531	2,657	40	340
Radiologic	863	2,761	31	100
Nurse, R.N.	2,516	34,081	38	833
Nurse, practical	145	2,042	611	12,245
Occupational therapy	154	743	1	0
Optical	293	333	31	83
Medical assistant and medical office assistant	161	2,073	119	2,949
Inhalation therapy	834	1,618	245	797
Psychiatric	389	1,322	25	95
Other	1,625	4,962	1,272	2,726
Total	7,954 5.6%	57,762 35.7%	2,424 5.7%	22,384 42.4%

Table 1-9/Continued

OCCUPATIONAL CURRICULUMS	AWARDS BASED ON ORGANIZED OCCUPATIONAL CURRICULUMS							
	At Least 2 Years but Less Than 4 Years				At Least 1 Year but Less Than 2 Years			
	MEN		WOMEN		MEN		WOMEN	
NATURAL SCIENCE								
Agriculture	3,817		1,769		2,011		776	
Forestry, wildlife	1,049		322		138		26	
Food services	2,112		1,454		525		429	
Home economics	89		1,661		42		611	
Other	1,543		801		759		82	
Total	8,610	6.0%	6,007	3.7%	3,475	8.1%	1,924	3.6%
MECHANICAL AND ENGINEERING								
Aeronautical and aviation	4,861		246		1,205		43	
Engineering graphics	3,695		891		1,286		314	
Architectural drafting	2,476		683		482		144	
Automotive	5,128		149		4,437		174	
Diesel	1,840		18		1,668		20	
Welding	1,342		33		3,562		150	
Civil	1,820		211		160		21	
Electronics and machines	18,465		1,421		4,661		634	
Electromechanical	2,770		160		283		52	
Industrial	2,228		262		659		121	
Mechanical	3,226		216		1,925		103	
Construction and building	5,549		200		5,572		255	
Other	9,236		1,501		1,873		322	
Total	62,636	44.0%	5,991	3.7%	27,773	64.9%	2,353	4.5%
BUSINESS AND COMMERCE								
Accounting	4,181		9,107		431		2,015	
Marketing, distribution, purchasing, business, and industrial management	14,844		14,513		1,068		1,263	
Secretarial	171		20,383		333		11,140	
Personal service	204		1,090		297		2,689	
Communications and broadcasting	1,334		872		137		86	

	AWARDS BASED ON ORGANIZED OCCUPATIONAL CURRICULUMS						
OCCUPATIONAL CURRICULUMS	At Least 2 Years but Less Than 4 Years				At Least 1 Year but Less Than 2 Years		
	MEN		WOMEN		MEN		WOMEN
Printing and lithography	583		421		441		184
Hotel and restaurant management	1,353		963		77		142
Applied, graphic, and fine arts	2,113		5,119		231		802
Other	13,440		13,946		1,446		2,462
Total	38,223	26.8%	66,414	41.1%	4,461	10.4%	20,783 39.4%
PUBLIC SERVICE RELATED							
Education	919		4,665		26		905
Police, law enforcement, correction	7,941		3,255		1,679		376
Recreation and social work related	890		2,654		123		393
Fire control	2,066		74		548		39
Other	2,087		3,851		366		601
Total	13,903	9.8%	14,499	9.0%	2,742	6.4%	2,314 4.4%
TOTAL	142,409	100%	161,745	100%	42,762	100%	52,801 100%

Source: USED 1986.
Note: Percentages may not add to exactly 100 because of rounding.

ness and commerce, and marketing. A handful of smaller specialties, such as dental laboratory, optical, food services, photography, or hotel and restaurant management, also awarded a similar number of degrees. (See also Vetter, Chapter 3, for sex distributions of students in secondary and postsecondary vocational education.)

Despite the overwhelming evidence of pervasive sex segregation in publicly sponsored training programs, the relation between training and occupational sex segregation in the labor market is complicated. On one hand, the training system is a *source* of occupational segregation. Training programs influence the occupational preferences of millions of women who participate in them each year (Waite and Berryman 1984) and prepare most of them in a few traditional female-dominated occupations. On the other hand, the training system *reflects* the demands of the labor market by providing the skills it requires.

Training programs respond to the high labor demand in low-paying clerical and service occupations with the result that women (and men) are channeled into the paths of least resistance. Giese (Chapter 13), for example, explains that state subsidies are calculated to allow local districts in Michigan (and elsewhere) to expand vocational training in areas of high labor demand, such as secretarial and health, thus insuring a steady supply of female workers. This both enables employers to keep wages low in those fields and relieves them of the cost of educating workers. Thus, the training system and the labor market mutually reinforce the barriers that keep women in segregated occupations.

Job Training and Equal Employment

Because training programs influence occupational preferences, they could conceivably be a major federal "lever" to reduce occupational sex segregation (Waite and Berryman 1984) and thereby have an impact on the single most important source of earnings inequality between men and women. The training system also has the capacity to train women for a wide variety of occupational fields. Both capacities are central to an effective equal employment strategy. What better way to educate women about the economic advantages of historically male work than through counseling and in-take interviews. And, where better to provide them with the skills to fill these significantly higher-paying jobs than in the many nontraditional training programs operating throughout the country.

There are thus a number of ways that training policy can compensate for and reduce the institutional barriers to equal opportunity. These barriers take the form of discriminatory practices and are maintained by gatekeepers in schools and firms which control the conditions under which women prepare for and enter the labor market (Steinberg-Ratner 1980). While training programs cannot be faulted for shortcomings in the regulation and enforcement of federal equal employment policies generally, they do bear a measure of responsibility to carry out their own legislative mandates and to monitor the actions of organizations that receive federal training funds.

Training programs are not living up to their potential: sex stereotyping remains prevalent as the majority of women are being trained for a small number of traditionally female jobs. This in itself is a chief institutional barrier to creating gender equality in the labor market. In addition, the lack of counseling and support services constitutes a serious shortcoming that limits women's ability to enroll in training programs and to make an informed occupational choice.

Another important limitation of the public system, as we noted above, is that training is usually confined to teaching occupational skills that are suitable for entry-level positions in secondary labor markets. To be sure, there are labor markets, such as craft apprenticeships, computer programming, and accounting, for which one can be trained and enter primary labor markets. However, most jobs do not require the kinds of skills that the occupational education system provides, and most entry positions linked to career ladders in primary internal labor markets do not require occupational preparation (Thurow 1979; Vermuelen and Hudson-Wilson 1981, 83). Instead, primary-sector employers are looking for individuals who are "trainable," motivated, and who fit their image of good employees. As both Osterman and Goldstein note in their chapters, an important aspect of training policy that could improve the employment opportunities of women, but is often ignored, is how to establish linkages to the organizational labor markets of large, corporate employers.

In this broader context, then, equal employment in training becomes *teaching women to qualify for jobs* that provide a living wage and other amenities. To fulfill this purpose training programs should enable participants to gain access to good jobs with mobility potential in either occupational or organizational labor markets. Such programs ought to provide women with whatever they need to accomplish that goal and to ensure that the disadvantages of race, gender, and class are minimized. The chapters in this book discuss several ways that training can achieve this goal: expanding occupational options through counseling; increasing awareness and helping to build confidence; providing basic education; teaching job skills, especially in nontraditional occupations; providing financial support for needs, such as child care and transportation; providing instruction on how to search for jobs; and providing assistance in job placement. Training programs can also be used as vehicles to work with employers to change their hiring practices so that they do not unfairly screen women out (Doeringer 1981). Finally, training programs must find ways to hold employers accountable for their records on hiring and placing female participants. As Haignere and Steinberg emphasize in their discussion of nontraditional training programs (Chapter 14), without federal enforcement of affirmative action, women trained for jobs historically performed by males will be unable to find employment.

This last point is extremely important. Training policy by itself can change neither the occupational structure of the labor market nor the low wages attached to the jobs in which most women work. Other strategies are clearly needed in conjunction with training to insure equal employment opportunity for women. One is affirmative action policies. Another important reform is comparable worth, a concept that would ensure that the majority of women who are trained for historically female work will be paid on the basis of their skills and responsibilities rather than on the basis of their sex (Remick 1984).

It is essential as well to raise the minimum wage, because women are much more likely than men to be placed in minimum wage jobs. Under the

Reagan administration, the minimum wage deteriorated so that it is the lowest it has been in decades. In 1988, the U.S. Senate considered a proposal to increase the current federal minimum wage rate of $3.35 an hour by $.30–$.40 an hour in each of the next three years, while Democrats in the U.S. House of Representatives supported an increase to $5.05 an hour by 1992. However, neither bill was passed. Even the more generous House proposal to raise the minimum wage to $5.05 an hour would have been seriously inadequate, if the standard of adequacy is a living wage, or even an improvement over welfare. For example, the income level that is a break-even point (earnings equal welfare benefits) for a typical Massachusetts AFDC family of a mother and two children is $12,000 a year or $5.75 an hour in a full-time job (Werner, Chapter 17). Nonetheless, a minimum wage of $5.05 would be a major improvement, allowing an employee who works 40 hours a week for 52 weeks a year to earn $10,500 before taxes. This is still below the poverty level for a family of four but would represent approximately a 30-percent wage increase for women working in minimum wage jobs.

Finally, equal employment requires that the labor market accommodate family life. As currently implemented, a woman is entitled to equal opportunity as long as she is able to compete on the labor market as if she were a man. In other words, she is penalized for her family responsibilities. This standard places a double burden on women and continues to justify discriminatory treatment of working mothers. One way that the labor market could accommodate family life is through a policy enabling both men and women to work on a schedule of flexible hours. Parental leave policies with pay would also provide the protection men and women need to build their families. And, it requires universal, federally funded day care, national health insurance, and a social security system that provides adequate retirement benefits to employed women.

Training by itself is not a solution to gender inequality in the labor market, but within the broader framework of restructuring the labor market, it is critical for women. Throughout this book, authors have examined the social forces that sustain occupational segregation in training programs and what changes would lead to increased job integration.

Job Training: Goals and Outcomes

Before job training policy can become part of an effective equal employment strategy, its treatment of poor women and women on welfare must change. Over the past 20 years, public training policy for the economically disadvantaged has been driven by the goal of transforming participants into self-supporting workers. As the participant profile in these programs has shifted from unemployed male householders to women who are often rearing children alone supported by public assistance, the rhetoric of self-sufficiency has changed very little. As women's labor force participation rate has steadily increased, so too have the public's expectations that women should contribute to the economic support of the ever-larger number of families they head. For example, in the *Congressional Record*, Senator Daniel Patrick Moynihan invoked the self-sufficiency rhetoric in listing the goals of what was then the Family Security Act of 1988(S. 1511) (now passed as the Family Support Act [FSA] of 1988). He called for "a 'social contract' that obligates State agencies to provide opportunities to become self-sufficient and obligates recipients to take advantage of such opportunities" (*Congressional Record*, 100th Cong., 1st sess., 1987, vol. 133, no. 120).[19]

What has undergone a subtle shift, however, is the meaning of self-sufficiency. The definition of this term appears to be different for men and women. For men, self-sufficiency means economic independence: a job that pays a wage high enough to support a family at a decent standard of living, based on the assumption that he is the sole breadwinner. Self-sufficiency is what a male worker has when he has been trained for a skilled or semiskilled male-dominated occupation. To the extent that there is any consensus on the meaning of self-sufficiency for women, under current welfare and training policies, it has come to be defined not in relation to women's living standard, but in relation to the program's capacity to reduce the burden female-headed families place on society. In short, it means getting women off the welfare rolls. Some suggest tightening the standards for AFDC eligibility so fewer women qualify for assistance. Others suggest having welfare programs provide economic supports to women during a period of transition from welfare to work, leaving unanswered what happens when the transition supplement runs out. Still others would make women long-term members of the "working poor"—those who work but still require public assistance in order to get by. Thus, while not totally "independent," these women and their families are less of a burden than they might otherwise be.[20]

This redefinition is reflected in recent legislation. As we have said, the 1981 changes in welfare legislation (OBRA) authorize states to link work obligations to the receipt of AFDC benefits. The 1982 passage of JTPA aims to reduce welfare dependency among participants. It is also the centerpiece of the 1988 FSA, which, to quote Senator Moynihan (major Senate sponsor of the Act), "turns the present family welfare system on its head. Rather than beginning with a public assistance payment that is supplemented with sporadic child support payments and occasional earned income, the Family Security Act places the responsibility for supporting children where it belongs. With parents. Both parents."[21] Thus, even as it declares self-sufficiency as a goal for women, the welfare system assumes that a female-headed family with a full-time working mother cannot approach economic independence. Instead, the mother needs the father's wage to support her family. Given current employment opportunities for women, this assessment is accurate.[22]

Differing definitions of male and female self-sufficiency lead to differing expectations about what training is supposed to do for men and women. For men, training is supposed to raise wages. For women, its primary purpose is to get them into the labor market and replace transfer payments with earned income, regardless of how small the gain or how short-lived the transition.

In general, training programs as they are currently designed are often not adapted to working-class and lower-class women, whose needs may extend beyond job search and even skill development to career counseling and support —financial, child care, transportation, flexible schedules, and the like. These are the components that would enable these women to participate in training on an equal footing with others. Occupational and personal counseling, for example, can shape their aspirations by broadening awareness of the available options and the consequences of choices.

The negative implications of designing narrow training programs are especially strong for women. With an emphasis limited to getting a job, or even to job skill development, the provision of these other training functions and support services is either devalued, or worse, prohibited by training institutions. Too often, women are simply regarded as less desirable participants than men for conventional programs because they require costly "special" services that are not "legitimate" training functions. Quick turnaround and cheap placements are allowed to substitute for a chance of longer-term stability and higher earnings capacity for women.

These limited objectives are reflected as well in the narrow approach used to evaluate the effectiveness of training programs. As Harlan elaborates in Chapter 2, results measuring employment gains and net earnings impact are offered without placing them in the context of family or economic well-being. When we look beyond the claims of positive benefits for women, however, we find that the vast majority still do not earn enough on which to live. The Manpower Demonstration Research Corporation's evaluation studies of workfare and job search, reported in Chapters 15 and 16 by Gueron and Goldman, are especially important to examine because the results were directly relied upon to justify the employment and training approach taken in the 1988 FSA. In contrast to the carefully balanced presentations of these authors, which stress the limitations as well as the modest accomplishments of demonstration programs, FSA sponsors make grandiose claims about its potential to "reform" the welfare system. Yet Goldman reports, for example, that after two quarters, 49 percent of those enrolled in group job search programs in Louisville, Kentucky, had found jobs, as compared with 34 percent of the comparison group. This means that even with job search experience, over one-half of program participants were unable to find jobs. Moreover, results for the five sites reported by Gueron show that the average difference in earnings between those women enrolled in demonstration programs and the comparison groups ranged from no difference in West Virginia to approximately $700 in San Diego over five quarters. Who benefits from these modest earnings gains? While the small amount of extra earnings may not do much for the individual women involved, they add up to substantial savings for government, which is the real policy agenda.

One can conclude from this and other evidence that, when legislation contains language about self-sufficiency, it has more to do with the political expediency of assuring the public that welfare mothers will be required to work than it does with guaranteeing them the training that will lead to a job paying them a wage on which they can live. As Gueron says,

arguments for and against workfare . . . involve . . . questions about the values attached to the AFDC program. Some will argue . . . that even if workfare costs more up front, it represents a sounder design for AFDC because it fits with the nation's values and will thus improve the image of welfare among recipients and the public.

Some suggest that job search and workfare programs should be used to identify individuals who need a more intensive investment of employment and training resources. Those resources, however, are not forthcoming from the federal government. Indeed, despite the sweeping boilerplate attached to the FSA about employment and training opportunities, monies appropriated for this function are estimated to cover the cost of skills training for about 53,000 of the approximately 12.5 million women living in poverty (Block and Noakes 1988, 18–19).[23] More promising are a few state programs, such as the one in Massachusetts, discussed by Werner (Chapter 17).

Thus, economically disadvantaged women suffer either way: as recipients of AFDC, they are stigmatized and blamed for their poverty and for living within the terms of the societal gender division of labor. They are not provided with the types of training and support programs that would enable them to pull themselves out of poverty. Then, as participants in training programs, they are often viewed and treated as second-class citizens. While they are not perceived as the "real" breadwinners, they require additional resources not necessary to train disadvantaged and unemployed males who either do not have children or have a wife at home assuming primary responsibility for their care. Much of this suffering could be avoided by policies that recognize training's broader functions in a society stratified by class and gender.

Self-sufficiency for women in its true sense—a decent standard of living —should indeed be a goal of training policy. But it can only be a meaningful goal within an equal employment opportunity framework which says that women should be capable of supporting themselves and their families. To achieve this policy goal would require modifying traditional attitudes about women's family responsibility. At the core, domestic policies reflect ambivalence toward women and their roles in the family and the workplace. It is never quite clear whether we, as a society, want women to be economically independent. Poor women and women on welfare pose a special dilemma because many of them are single mothers who perform the dual responsibilities of rearing children and supporting them—alone. Ambivalence is in large measure responsible for the failure of training policy to comprehend women's needs and deal with them.

The executive director of Wider Opportunities for Women, writing from 12 years of experience in developing training programs for women, has felt the contradictions between policy and poor women's reality, and she has been frustrated by the inability of policies to go to the heart of the matter:

There exists profound resistance in our society to confront the causes of female poverty, to tackle the real problems presented, and to take steps in program and policy design which would address these problems directly. More often, we have developed programs and policies embedded with our societal conflicts about women's appropriate roles, the appropriateness of spending and designing programs for females, and fraught with uncertainty about whether we believe women should work as men do, earn as men do, and head families as men do. . . . Real success in addressing the employment needs of low income women will require confrontation with a number of entrenched public norms and beliefs, significant investment of resources, and a lengthy national commitment. To date, none of these three has been the priority of any political party, nor has it been the prime concern of *any* constituency with political power. The result, therefore, has been a patchwork of programs, flawed from the get-go with inconsistent and often contradictory goals, always suffering from a lack of resources needed to get the job done had the goals been clear or consistent. (Marano 1987, 2–3)

This ambivalence is not only cultural but also economic. Playing on this ambivalence can be very profitable for service-sector and some manufacturing employers who justify paying low wages to and withholding benefits from women employees on the assumption that they have a husband at home who is bringing in a family wage and a benefits package (Block and Noakes 1988). Yet as Smith (1984) indicates, the women most likely to work at these jobs are also most likely to be primary earners for their families.[24]

Economic independence for women, however, requires even more than providing a job that pays at least enough to bring women and their families above the poverty line. As the Institute for Policy Studies (1987, 1) has argued, it requires the opportunity to earn a "family wage," one that enables a woman to provide quality child care and to cover transportation to and from work. It also requires some provision for health insurance for her and her family, whether through the employer or through a national health insurance program such as the one enacted in Massachusetts. Finally, in our view, self-sufficiency must also involve the possibility of upward mobility on the job so that the living standard of employed women will improve.

Beyond these economic objectives, self-sufficiency involves teaching women to think and act in ways that can increase their power in the labor market. This more sophisticated definition is offered by both Greenbaum and Watson (Chapter 8) and by Lilly (Chapter 10). Empowerment may mean changing the way individual women make occupational choices or broadening skill training so that women master concepts, as well as task-specific skills. This would allow them more flexibility. It may also mean working collectively with other women to change the institutional structures that discriminate against them. Ultimately, empowerment is teaching women about the limitations of personal options and the necessity of community action in the stark realities of local and regional economies that provide an inadequate supply of jobs that pay a living wage. The chapters that follow illustrate in much more detail both how training programs facilitate economic independence and women's equal employment and the instances in which they have failed.

Notes

1. With the exception of Gittell and Moore (Chapter 18), who discuss the benefits of sending women on welfare to college, all the chapters deal with training for occupations that do not require a four-year college degree. The distribution of employed women 16 years old and over in 1982 among occupational categories was: clerical (34 percent); service (20 percent); blue-collar (13 percent); sales (7 percent); farming (1 percent); and managerial and professional occupations (25 percent) (U.S. Department of Education 1983, 184–85).

2. See for example, a small sampling of monographs: Athena Theodore, ed., *The Professional Woman* (Cambridge, Mass.: Schenkman, 1971); Alice Rossi and Ann Calderwood, eds., *Academic Women on the Move* (New York: Russell Sage Foundation, 1973); Margaret Hennig and Anne Jardim, *The Managerial Woman* (New York: Pocket Books, 1977); Cynthia Fuchs Epstein, *Women in Law* (New York: Basic, 1981); Judith Lorber, *Women Physicians: Careers, Status, and Power* (New York: Tavistock, 1984).

3. The rates of high school completion and college attendance appear to have stabilized over the past 10 to 20 years, suggesting that young women soon to enter the labor market will not be better educated, on average, than their mothers. The national high school completion rate has remained at about 75 percent of the 17-year-old population each year for the past 20 years (U.S. Department of Education 1986, 69). Since 1975, the national rate of enrollment in four-year colleges for all female high school graduates between the ages of 18 and 24 has fluctuated right around 30 percent (U.S. Bureau of the Census 1986, 149). Added to this, there will be a smaller influx of young workers into the labor market in the future because of the decline in the youth

population (USDOL 1987, 8). Thus young, better-educated workers will replace the oldest workers at a slower rate than they have in the past.

4. Dropout rates in urban schools are much higher. The New York City Board of Education found that students in the class of 1987 had the following dropout rates over a four-year period by race and ethnic group: Hispanic (31.1 percent), black (24.3 percent), American Indian, Pacific Islander (23.9 percent), white (18.0 percent), and Asian (12.7 percent) (*New York Times*, 21 June 1988, Sec. A).

5. Data on common occupational titles are from Taeuber and Valdisera (1986) and data on 1986 earnings are from Mellor (1987). One should bear in mind that the earnings data are national averages for full-time, year-round women workers without regard to the educational attainment of women in the occupational title. Less well educated women may have lower-paying jobs within an occupational title, and thus, have lower than average earnings for the occupation. In addition, part-time women workers and those with intermittent labor force participation earn less than the full-time average. As a basis for comparison with these earnings figures, the 1986 federal poverty level income threshold for a family of four was $11,203 (U.S. Bureau of the Census 1988). The 1987 poverty threshold for a family of four was $11,612 (U.S. Bureau of the Census, personal communication, 1988).

6. At elite schools, such as Harvard and the University of Chicago, black enrollments have declined between 30 and 50 percent in the last ten years (Staples 1986). Staples suggests four reasons why fewer blacks are going to college now: (1) the worsening quality of education in inner-city public schools, (2) cuts in federal funds for compensatory education and aid programs for economically disadvantaged students, (3) the necessity for students to take out loans to cover costs once covered by grants, and (4) stiffer admission standards in state colleges that cannot be met by students from poor-quality schools. Some also believe that the Reagan administration's neglect of affirmative action enforcement is, in part, responsible for the decline in black student college attendance.

7. The survey was conducted as a supplement to the Current Population Survey in January 1983. The results were analyzed by the U.S. Bureau of Labor Statistics and reported in Carey and Eck (1984). Table 1-3 is derived from Carey and Eck's tabulations and gives a reasonably good overview of the training options available in the United States.

8. JTPA enrollments were classified as follows: 786,400 in training programs for economically disadvantaged youth and adults, 106,700 in training programs for displaced workers, 748,000 in summer youth programs, and 40,500 in Job Corps.

9. Based on a USGAO (1987b, 52) survey, at least 714,448 individuals participated in all AFDC work programs during fiscal 1985. Most of them were in WIN Demonstrations, but community work experience programs, job search, and work supplementation also enrolled participants.

10. The indirect costs of education and training in industry include wages and salaries paid to teaching and learning workers, equipment use, and lower worker productivity during training, all of which are extremely difficult to estimate separately from other business costs (Lusterman 1977).

11. Three chapters deal with private-sector training. Chertos and Phillips (Chapter 12) describe a physical training program for municipal jobs that was funded by

private foundations. In Part V Goldstein (Chapter 19) analyzes the training decisions of private firms and both Goldstein and Osterman (Chapter 20) examine how public training policy interfaces with private sector firms.

12. Participation rate is defined as the estimated number of individuals who ever participated in any of the work programs during the year divided by the number of adults who ever received AFDC at any time during the year, regardless of the amount or length of time spent in the work program (USGAO 1987b, 52; Block and Noakes 1988, 26).

13. The U.S. Department of Education estimated that in fiscal 1985, federal funds for education and related activities in all federal departments and agencies totaled $38.5 billion. The figure of $23 billion used in the text comes from the Office of Management and Budget's analysis of federal authorizations for elementary, secondary, vocational, and higher education and training and employment programs. In this book we cover a subset of the programs included in this budget figure, as shown in Table 1-4.

14. Taeuber and Valdisera (1986, 18), from whom these data are drawn, list the following occupations employing the largest number of women: secretaries; book-keepers, accounting, and auditing clerks; managers and administrators (not elsewhere classified); general office clerks; registered nurses; nursing aides, attendants, and orderlies; assemblers; cashiers; textile sewing machine operators; teachers (elementary); typists; sales workers (other commodities); supervisors (general office); supervisors (sales occupations); accountants and auditors; machine operators (not specialty); bank tellers; waiters and waitresses; production inspectors, checkers, examiners; data entry keyers.

15. In 1980, the sex segregation indexes for clerical, service, and blue-collar major occupational groups were all more than 50 percent compared to 43 percent for managers and professionals (Taeuber and Valdisera 1986, 21). The index of sex segregation measures the proportion of employed women "that would have to be redistributed among occupations for the occupational distribution to reach complete equality between the sexes" (Beller 1984, 12).

16. The causes of occupational segregation in the labor market are manifold. Relevant explanations, most of which can demonstrate empirical support, cover psychological, cultural, economic, and institutional theories (Reskin and Hartmann 1986; England 1984). Human capital theory offers its own explanation of occupational segregation (Polachek 1979). The theory assumes that most women have intermittent labor force participation because of child-bearing and child-rearing responsibilities, and that female occupations do not penalize women for noncontinuous employment. Therefore, women "rationally" choose female-dominated occupations in order to minimize skill depreciation while they are out of the labor force. Women earn less than men both because their job skills depreciate while they are not working and because the skills fail to appreciate when they are working. England (1982) has largely refuted this theory by showing that: (1) women in traditionally female jobs are not penalized less for intermittent employment than are women in nontraditional jobs, and (2) continuous labor force participation has no relationship to whether women work in predominantly male occupations.

17. Using the National Longitudinal Survey of Youth, Crowley, Pollard, and Rumberger (1983, 139) report the following sources of postsecondary education: busi-

ness college (women 20 percent, men 2 percent); nursing program (women 12 percent, men 1 percent); apprenticeship (women 2 percent, men 19 percent); vocational or technical institute (women 35 percent, men 39 percent); barber or beauty school (women 10 percent, men 1 percent); flight school (women 2 percent, men 6 percent); correspondence course (women 3 percent, men 3 percent); company training (women 14 percent, men 26 percent); remaining 3 percent not reported for either sex.

18. Percentages for detailed occupational titles are not shown in Table 1-3 but are available in Carey and Eck (1984).

19. The Family Support Act, signed into law by President Reagan in 1988, resulted from years of debate about reforming the welfare system and attaching work requirements to the receipt of AFDC benefits. Among the act's provisions is the requirement that states operate a "job opportunity and basic skills training program" for the purpose of reducing long-term welfare dependency through employment and job skills development. Many AFDC recipients, notably those who are single parents of children under 3, are exempt from participation requirements. Of the eligible AFDC families, however, 20 percent are required to participate in the programs by 1995.

20. Our thinking about the meaning of self-sufficiency for women benefited from a presentation by Saundra Rice Murray Nettles at the policy seminar "Occupational Segregation and Its Roots in Education" sponsored by the Center for Women Policy Studies, Washington, D.C., May 1988.

21. The Family Support Act calls on both parents to support their children. It backs up this commitment by establishing a procedure for collecting child support from fathers through social security numbers and provisions for withholding a portion of the father's wages. While this is a desirable principle, as a practical measure, it is fraught with difficulties, especially for the poorest female-headed families. There are issues of identifying paternity and locating the workplaces of fathers, assuming the fathers are employed at jobs that pay sufficient wages to enable adequate withholdings. More problematic for the women and children involved, however, is the fact that much of the child support payments will go directly to the government in repayment for welfare benefits. Thus, these payments will not bring many women and their children above the poverty line. In effect, then, while the act calls for both parents to take responsibility, the act will continue to penalize and stigmatize the mother for her welfare dependence while denying her a job that will enable her to achieve economic independence from both government and a father unwilling to contribute to the support of his children.

22. Of the 12.2 million women living in poverty in 1986, 4.4 million were in the work force. Half of these working women in poverty have full-time jobs when they are at work. Fully 17 percent worked full time, year-round. The median income for a woman in poverty who was maintaining a family alone and working full time, year round was $7,056 in 1986 (National Commission on Working Women of Wider Opportunities for Women 1987, 1).

23. This estimate is based on a training cost of $5,000 a program enrollee. According to Block and Noakes (1988) the Congressional Budget Office has estimated that the job training component would cost $266 million in 1991. Even with the more generous House bill (H.R. 1720), which proposed double the actual appropriations for the FSA, the number of individuals that could be trained fell overwhelmingly short of the eligible population of women. Indeed, the appropriations are so inadequate, that

even with the more limited job search programs which offer no job skills, programs will cover only a small proportion of welfare recipients.

24. One of the motivations for the employment and training provisions of the FSA are the predictions of labor shortages in the 1990s. Many of the jobs projected will be minimum-wage jobs. Without establishing a minimum wage that allows women workers to move out of poverty, the FSA becomes nothing more than a glorified workhouse proposal, where employers are guaranteed a supply of labor at wages below what they would have to pay under free market conditions.

References

Beller, Andrea H. 1984. "Trends in Occupational Segregation by Sex and Race, 1960–1981." In Barbara F. Reskin, ed., *Sex Segregation in the Workplace: Trends, Explanations, Remedies*, pp. 11–26. Washington, D.C.: National Academy Press.

Block, Fred, and John Noakes. 1988. "The Politics of New-Style Welfare." Paper presented to the Seminar on Work and Welfare, University of Pennsylvania, January.

Carey, Max, and Alan Eck. 1984. "How Workers Get Their Training." *Occupational Outlook Quarterly* 28 (Winter): 3–21.

Crowley, Joan E.; Tom K. Pollard; and Russell W. Rumberger. 1983. "Education and Training." In Michael E. Borus, ed., *Tomorrow's Workers*, pp. 103–48. Lexington, Mass.: Lexington Books.

Doeringer, Peter B. 1981. "Occupational Education and Training for the 1980s." In Peter B. Doeringer and Bruce Vermeulen, eds., *Jobs and Training in the 1980s: Vocational Policy and the Labor Market*, pp. 1–18. Boston: Martinus Nijhoff.

Earle, Janice; and Virginia Roach; with Katherine Fraser. 1987. *Female Dropouts: A New Perspective*. Washington, D.C.: National Association of State Boards of Education.

England, Paula. 1982. "The Failure of Human Capital Theory to Explain Occupational Sex Segregation." *Journal of Human Resources* 17 (Summer): 358–70.

———. 1984. "Socioeconomic Explanations of Job Segregation." In Helen Remick, ed., *Comparable Worth and Wage Discrimination: Technical Possibilities and Political Realities*, pp. 28–46. Philadelphia: Temple University Press.

Executive Office of the President. Office of Management and Budget. 1987a. *Budget of the U.S. Government, Appendix, Fiscal Year 1988*. Washington, D.C.: Government Printing Office.

———. 1987b. *Special Analysis Budget of the U.S. Government, Fiscal Year 1988*. Washington, D.C.: Government Printing Office.

Grasso, John T., and John R. Shea. 1979. *Vocational Education and Training: Impact on Youth*. Berkeley: The Carnegie Council on Policy Studies in Higher Education.

Howe, Louise Kapp. 1977. *Pink Collar Workers: Inside the World of Women's Work*. New York: Putnam.

Institute for Policy Studies. Working Seminar on Employment, Welfare and Poverty. 1987. *Women, Families and Poverty: An Alternative Policy Agenda for the Nineties*. Washington, D.C.: IPS, March.

Kolstad, Andrew J., and Jeffrey A. Owings. 1986. *High School Dropouts Who Change*

Their Minds About School. Washington, D.C.: Office of Educational Research and Improvement, U.S. Department of Education, 16 April.

Lusterman, Seymour. 1977. *Education in Industry.* Report no. 719. New York: The Conference Board.

――――. 1985. *Trends in Corporate Education and Training.* Report no. 870. New York: The Conference Board.

Marano, Cynthia. 1987. "Systemic Contradictions: A Practitioner's View of Public Employment and Training Policies for Low Income Women." Wider Opportunities for Women. Typescript, February.

Mellor, Earl F. 1987. "Weekly Earnings in 1986: A Look at More Than 200 Occupations." *Monthly Labor Review* 110 (June): 41–46.

National Commission on Working Women of Wider Opportunities for Women. 1987. "Women, Work and Poverty: A Fact Sheet." Washington, D.C.

Polachek, Solomon. 1979. "Occupational Segregation Among Women: Theory, Evidence, and a Prognosis." In C. Lloyd, E. Andrews, and C. Gilroy, eds., *Women in the Labor Market*, pp. 137–57. New York: Columbia University Press.

Remick, Helen, ed. 1984. *Comparable Worth and Wage Discrimination: Technical Possibilities and Political Realities.* Philadelphia: Temple University Press.

Reskin, Barbara F., and Heidi I. Hartmann, eds. 1986. *Women's Work, Men's Work: Sex Segregation on the Job.* Washington, D.C.: National Academy Press.

Rumberger, Russell W. 1983. "Dropping Out of High School: The Influence of Race, Sex, and Family Background." *American Educational Research Journal* 20 (Summer): 199–220.

Shaeffer, Ruth G., and Edith F. Lynton. 1979. *Corporate Experiences in Improving Women's Job Opportunities.* Report no. 755. New York: The Conference Board.

Smith, Joan. 1984. "The Paradox of Women's Poverty: Wage-Earning Women and Economic Transformation." *Signs* 10 (Winter): 291–310.

Staples, Brent. 1986. "The Dwindling Black Presence on Campus." *New York Times Magazine*, 27 April.

Steinberg-Ratner, Ronnie, ed. 1980. *Equal Employment Policy for Women: Strategies for Implementation in Western Europe, Canada, and the United States.* Philadelphia: Temple University Press.

Taeuber, Cynthia M., and Victor Valdisera. 1986. *Women in the American Economy.* Current Population Reports, Special Studies Series P-23, no. 146. Washington, D.C.: U.S. Department of Commerce, Bureau of the Census, November.

Thurow, Lester. 1979. *Vocational Education as a Strategy for Eliminating Poverty.* Planning Papers for the Vocational Education Study. Washington, D.C.: National Institute of Education.

Treiman, Donald J., and Heidi I. Hartmann, eds. 1981. *Women, Work, and Wages: Equal Pay for Jobs of Equal Value.* Washington, D.C.: National Academy Press.

U.S. Bureau of the Census. 1986. *Statistical Abstract of the United States, 1986.* 106th ed. Washington, D.C.: Government Printing Office.

――――. 1987. *Poverty in the United States: 1985.* Current Population Reports, Series P-60, no. 158. Washington, D.C.: Government Printing Office.

――――. 1988. *Statistical Abstract of the United States, 1988.* 108th ed. Washington, D.C.: Government Printing Office.

Federal Training Initiatives

Introduction to Part I/*Sharon L. Harlan*

In Chapter 1 we sketched an outline of job training and occupational education in the United States. The three chapters in Part I, as well as two later chapters, expand the description of several separate training systems and elaborate general themes of Chapter 1. They convey in carefully detailed analyses the extent and diversity of needs among women. They synthesize and evaluate research findings on women's enrollment opportunities, occupational options, and the relationship between training and labor market outcomes. Finally, they indicate the improbability of achieving the policy goals of self-sufficiency and equal opportunity for women with the current inadequate levels of available resources. Included in Part I are accounts of federal employment and training policy, vocational education, and the military. Glover's discussion of apprenticeship (Chapter 11) and Gueron's discussion of welfare-related work programs (Chapter 15) complete the set of overviews which offers critical assessments of the recent history and current status of major federal training initiatives and their effects on women.[1]

In Part I, Harlan analyzes the shortcomings and contradictions in 15 years of policy efforts to train economically disadvantaged women through programs under the Job Training Partnership Act (JTPA) and its predecessor, the Comprehensive Employment and Training Act (CETA). Vetter discusses public vocational education and emphasizes the efforts that have been undertaken to reduce or eliminate gender stereotyping in occupational programs and the progress that has been made in that regard. Devilbiss looks at job training in the armed forces and explores the deeply rooted social and cultural barriers to integrating women into one of the most traditionally male work places. The parallels among these three very different training environments are striking.

The history of each program is characterized by either de jure or de facto exclusion of women, or both. Real progress in women's enrollments was not made until the 1970s, and it happened as the result of women's increasing participation in the labor force and the emergence of advocacy organizations out of the women's movement which pressed for equal opportunity legislation and the protection of women's rights. Women's enrollments have been increasing ever since. Despite the progress, however, women today are not equitably represented in many JTPA programs, occupational areas of vocational education, and branches of the armed service. Moreover, there are institutional rules that continue to favor men. For example, JTPA performance standards, which regulate program costs and placement levels, discourage the enrollment of women who may require intensive investment of training and support resources. Restrictions on women's occupational assignment to noncombat specialties in all the services mean that men can be utilized more flexibly than women and are therefore more desirable recruits.

Remarkably, the Reagan administration's neglect of equal employment policy and affirmative action did not reverse the national trend toward increasing enrollment for women. JTPA is inferior to CETA in its targeting to women generally, but the legislative focus on welfare mothers has kept female enrollments at previous levels. Vocational education legislation passed during Ronald Reagan's first term actually stipulated more specific provisions for women than did its predecessor, thereby strengthening women's position. Also, a review of the restrictive actions of individual states and branches of the armed forces makes it clear that Congress has played an indispensable role in maintaining women's opportunities throughout changing political tides. Without specific federal protections, the progress made to date would almost certainly not have occurred. Yet, there is much need for expansion in the federal role and this was out of step with the eighties' emphasis on reducing federal oversight.

All three training initiatives have attempted to reduce occupational segregation, but the power of cultural norms and labor market structure to prescribe limited occupational roles for women has undercut desegregation efforts. There has been much less progress in placing women in male-dominated jobs than in increasing women's overall enrollment. This is most clearly evident in the military where Devilbiss attributes the "noncombat" restrictions on women to a contemporary version of the "separate spheres" notion of men's public and women's private societal contributions. She says that even though women are allowed to perform some occupational roles in the military, they must be of a certain type that are commensurate with socially acceptable female activities. Similarly, Vetter claims that vocational education evolved from a "men-at-work, women-at-home" model, which explains why women were largely limited to participation in consumer home economics before 1968. Harlan suggests that on-the-job training positions under CETA and JTPA are "rationed" to men because of the widely held belief that men need jobs more than women do.

Women have been trained successfully for nontraditional occupations (NTO) in all three policy areas, but most women in vocational education and JTPA are in traditionally female fields. Half of all the girls and women in vocational education, for example, are training for office occupations. Both JTPA and vocational education respond to financial incentives to train women to meet the demand for clerical and health service workers in the labor market. Even in the military, which offers extensive NTO options, women are disproportionately in clerical and administrative positions.

Support services are an issue for women everywhere in the training system. Women's unique roles in bearing and rearing children present a real dilemma for a training establishment which, like the labor market, is designed to accommodate the male life cycle of continuous, full-time participation with inflexible hours. Rules allowing the provision of support services in JTPA and vocational education are slow to be enacted, even when a substantial target group of the programs is single mothers. Funding to offer adequate levels of support services is not available. For members of the armed forces, making child care arrangements on a daily or longer-term basis in the event of deployment is the responsibility of individual parents, and most often, the mother.

A substantial amount of federal money has been directed to research designed to measure program impact, but what stands out most clearly in these reviews is how little we know with any certainty about their impact on women. Most of the chapters question what are the appropriate outcome criteria and who are the relevant comparison groups. Ten years of evaluation research on federal employment and training programs, for example, has shown that participation increases women's average earnings by a few hundred dollars a year over nonparticipant comparison groups, but this tells us nothing about the effects of training on improved living standards, movement out of poverty, or reduction in the wage gap between men and women. Evaluations of vocational education also indicate that students who obtain training-related jobs have an earnings benefit, but women graduates in office occupations still find low-paying clerical jobs. Pay scales in the military are much higher than women can command in the civilian labor market, but there is some evidence that military experience does not successfully parley occupational training for women into either nontraditional civilian jobs or higher civilian pay. For all three training initiatives, the paucity of research on the effects of NTO training and the utter lack of support for conducting such studies is evident.

In contrast, Gueron's chapter on welfare-related work programs in Part IV takes a more positive and traditional stance on measuring program success. She provides a sensible overview and analysis of the lessons learned from the most rigorous evaluation research that has been done on any training policy. Her conclusions suggest that job search and workfare programs for public assistance recipients *save governments money* and, therefore, are cost-effective to operate—an important point in establishing credibility with policy makers. Nevertheless, she finds that these programs have quite limited impact on the employment and earnings of most individual participants, and she stresses the need to provide services beyond job search programs in order for women to escape welfare.

Job training policies of all types are constrained by a lack of resources in offering women the kinds of services they need, by the labor market's segregation of women into low-paying jobs, and by inadequate efforts to make training part of a larger economic agenda to create self-sufficiency and equal opportunity for women. We need to work toward obtaining more resources and successful models of how to use them to meet the diversity of women's needs. The future research agenda ought to include support for a greater variety of topics in order to determine if women (and men) benefit from training. Studies should consider the institutional contexts of the firms, schools, and other educational facilities in which participants are trained. We need studies not only of impact but also of access: How are female and male applicants selected and assigned to programs? Under what circumstances are women trained in occupations with opportunities for advancement? Moreover, studies of program impact should relate employment and earnings outcomes to the effects of occupational segregation and different training strategies. More attention is needed to occupational mobility, wage rates, and job quality after participation.

Note

1. We chose to include apprenticeship and welfare-related work programs in later sections because they introduce important substantive topics to which we have devoted separate parts of the book: training women for traditionally male jobs and the welfare/work policy debate. The substantive dimensions of Glover and Gueron are discussed in the introductions to Parts III and IV, respectively. One should bear in mind, however, that the themes in Part I are relevant to them as well, with the exception that women's participation level in welfare-related work programs is not an issue, since women represent by far the majority of public assistance recipients who qualify for these programs and who therefore are the target group for enrollment.

2/Women and Federal Job Training Policy

Sharon L. Harlan

For the past several years, women have been a slight majority of participants in those training programs that are targeted to the economically disadvantaged.[1] The enrollment gains for women are relatively recent and they reflect a change in the population that is being served. Nevertheless, the cumulative effects of designing and operating programs for men over a long period has created a system full of contradictions where women's needs are neither understood nor fully met. In fact, the Job Training Partnership Act (JTPA) of 1982 is widely regarded by women's organizations as having reversed the trend toward greater opportunities for women that began in the late seventies under previous legislation.

JTPA has historical roots in two decades of federal employment and training legislation that has attempted to alleviate the problems of unemployment and low wages among individuals who lack basic educational credentials, job skills, or the means of looking for work. The goals of JTPA are to prepare participants for jobs, increase their earnings through training, and get them off welfare.[2]

JTPA is a small program compared to the magnitude of the problems it is supposed to address. Although it enrolls approximately three-quarters of a million new participants annually in Title IIA training programs, it is estimated that this is only 4 percent of the population eligible to participate. Yet JTPA's significance for women extends beyond the programs it funds directly and even beyond the disadvantaged population. JTPA programs are an integral part of the whole institutional network that provides occupational education and training for people who do not attend college. The way JTPA functions is therefore illustrative of how women's enrollment opportunities and training options are structured in a large number of public and private vocational programs. By examining JTPA, we can learn about the institutional barriers that make it difficult in general for women to participate in training and the mechanisms that segregate working- and middle-class women into educational tracks that lead to low-paying jobs in traditionally female occupations.

JTPA is also important to women because of its particular mission. Unlike most other vocational education and training programs the federal government funds, JTPA is targeted to the poor. Under the current regulations, at least 90 percent of all participants in JTPA Title IIA must qualify as economically disadvantaged. This is important because women are now far more likely than men to be poor. Sex differences in poverty ratios (proportion of poor women divided by proportion of poor men) have increased substantially between 1950 and 1980 such that "in 1980 women were about fifty percent more likely to be poor than men regardless of race" (McLanahan, Sorensen, and Watson 1986, 8). Among working-age women between 18 and 64, sex differences in poverty ratios increase with age. Moreover, changes in welfare programs during the 1980s have increasingly emphasized work obligations for recipients. This has resulted not only in new employment initiatives targeted specifically to mothers on Aid to Families with Dependent Children (AFDC) (see Gueron, Chapter 15), but also in a greater emphasis on serving them in JTPA.[3]

Thus, one of the major issues confronting federal employment policy is that millions of women need jobs—not just jobs that supplement the earnings of husbands or other family members, but jobs that pay female householders enough to support them and their families. A decline in marriage and increases in marital dissolution and births to never-married women have meant that the proportion of women who currently head families and the proportion who will ever head families have grown rapidly, from the 1960s to the present (Wojtkiewicz, McLanahan, and Garfinkel 1988).

Women who maintain families have a higher incidence of poverty than others. Half of all female-headed families with children under 18 have incomes below the official government poverty threshold. Seventy percent of young women (15 to 24 years old) who maintain families are poor. Female-headed families are far more likely to be poor if they are black or minorities of Spanish origin rather than white. Although the poverty rate is much higher among female-headed families in which the woman does not work, even among those who are employed, approximately one of five white women and one of three black women are poor (all statistics are from the U.S. Department of Commerce 1984).

The number of families headed by women with inadequate living standards, however, includes many of those who are not officially classified as poor. Several years ago in Massachusetts, for example, it was estimated that a sufficient annual income for a mother supporting two children was $18,512 (Massachusetts Executive Office of Economic Affairs 1984). By comparison, the national median income for all female-headed families was $10,802 in 1981 (U.S. Department of Labor [USDOL] 1983).

The poverty statistics clearly indicate that women need the services federal job training programs have to offer, ostensibly in order to gain more skills and earn higher income. As women spend less of their lives in families with male breadwinners, the importance of their own earnings to their economic well-being increases. Therefore, the training needs of women should be instrumental in shaping the priorities of JTPA.

This chapter critically reviews the impact of federal job training policy on economically disadvantaged women. It focuses on JTPA and its immediate predecessor, the Comprehensive Employment and Training Act (CETA) of 1973, which JTPA replaced. Early comparisons of the two programs tended to emphasize their differences and these are also discussed here. However, there is enough continuity between CETA and JTPA to examine common themes with respect to their treatment of women. The chapter deals with the creation of national policy and the carrying out of that policy by communities, educators, and employers on four issues that affect women: enrollment, types of training, occupational sex segregation, and post-program impact. To set the stage for that analysis, I first discuss the origins of federal employment and training policy that have in large measure shaped the current contradictions and the dilemmas that federal policy entails for poor women.

Origins of Employment and Training Policy

The economic rationale for employment and training policy is to match the supply of workers to available jobs, thereby reducing the unemployment rate and improving the efficiency of the nation's economy. Sometimes job creation in the public sector has served as that vehicle. At other times skill development for individual workers has been deemed more appropriate, depending upon the perception of the unemployment "problem." The precise focus of federal policy has shifted several times in the past, always with clear consequences for the distribution of employment and training resources among the population in need of assistance. Nevertheless, reviewing these programs shows that from the earliest policy initiatives 50 years ago until the reauthorization of CETA in 1978, men—unemployed men, male household heads, and male teenagers—were the targets. With the exception of specific programs to employ public assistance recipients, women were not a priority.

In response to the general economic crisis of the 1930s, the Work Projects Administration (WPA) created training programs and public service jobs for the unemployed. The legislative intent of WPA, which limited enrollment to one person per household, reflected both a concern for preserving the intact (male-headed) family during a time of massive unemployment and strengthening the responsibility and authority of the family head by maintaining his status as the principal wage earner. Another program, the Civilian Conservation Corps, enrolled young, unmarried men in a residential program to work on public conservation and construction projects. (For a fuller discussion of these early programs, see Haignere and Steinberg [1984] and references cited therein.)

Publicly sponsored employment and training programs vanished as the World War II economy absorbed all available labor, both men and women, and unemployment did not enter the public consciousness again as a pressing economic issue until 20 years had passed. The Manpower Development and Training Act (MDTA) of 1962 provided institutional (classroom) training for selected occupations and living allowances to "unemployed family heads with strong labor force attachment" (Levitan and Mangum 1969, 10). In its focus on educated, skilled men the law reflected the current belief that high unemployment was being caused by the disappearance of jobs that was due to increasing automation. The policy goal was to retrain workers for jobs newly created by emerging technologies (Ulman 1974).

The original MDTA was a small program (only 200,000 individuals had completed training by mid-1965), and it was short-lived as unemployment began falling steadily in response to major tax cuts (Ulman 1974). Another reason was that MDTA program operators could not find enough skilled workers suitable for retraining. With its eligibility requirements, MDTA could not reach a substantial proportion of the unemployed because they were so poorly educated that they did not qualify for training (Sundquist 1969). As a result, policy makers turned their attention to teenage unemployment, which was twice the general unemployment rate. The youth component of MDTA was enlarged. Literacy and basic work skills were added to the occupational training, somewhat changing the profile of participants to younger, less educated, and black males (Sundquist 1969, 17, 18; USDOL 1969, Table F-3).

At the same time, a much larger transformation of domestic policy to alleviate poverty was being developed that would have far greater consequences for future employment and training policy. The "discovery" of illiteracy, the rise of violent youth crime in the black inner-cities, increasing welfare caseloads, and the failure of urban renewal programs coalesced to provide the rationale for the Johnson administration's War on Poverty (Sundquist 1969). The Economic Opportunity Act of 1964 embodied an ambitious antipoverty strategy centered on organizing poor communities in the cities and opening up opportunity structures for inner-city youth. Of the act's five titles, two dealt specifically with the problem of unemployment. The larger of these titles authorized two youth employment programs, the Job Corps and the Neighborhood Youth Corps. The smaller was the short-lived Work Experience and Training program, one of a series of programs for welfare mothers.

The administration task force that engineered the Great Society programs had several motivations for focusing on youth. Certain academics, acting on the poverty-cycle theory popular at the time, wanted to "save" young people "before they continued the poverty cycle through yet another generation" (Yarmolinsky 1969, 39). Others saw the focus on black urban youth as politically expedient. Moynihan (1969, 63) noted the connection between the Civil Rights Movement and high unemployment among blacks: "the 1963 March on Washington was for '*Jobs* and Freedom.' " The instability of the large city slums and the increase in violent crime among black youth were perceived as political liabilities by the administration. The strong Civil Rights Movement, which gathered momentum in the sixties, was a major force in determining where employment resources would be spent.

Although the antipoverty legislation created a separate employment program for welfare mothers, it did not target women in general. Yet women workers had high unemployment rates during this time period, and in fact, the "feminization of poverty" had already occurred (McLanahan, Sorensen, and Watson 1986). Enrolling women in employment programs, however, was not perceived as the solution to the problem of poverty. Instead, an influential theory of the time held that poverty (and a host of other family problems) was caused by the joblessness of black men who left their families because they could not support them (see, for example, USDOL 1965).[4] Therefore, improving the education and employability of black male youths was a critical goal of the employment programs. There was no popular concern for women's issues during the sixties, nor was there any substantial organized advocacy group for women's employment (Haignere and Steinberg 1984; Marano 1987; McLanahan, Sorensen, and Watson 1986).[5]

Before the 1960s were over, the War on Poverty had changed from the task force's original conception of community action to a far-flung network of self-contained programs. Subsequent amendments to the Equal Opportunity Act resulted in a proliferation of categorical employment and training programs, each with its own target group and set of regulations. Some of these (in addition to the youth programs) were work experience for rural adults, paraprofessional training for poor adults, training for adults in target poverty areas, and the employment program for welfare recipients. Overall, women were less than half the participants (45 percent) from 1965 through 1972 (Sexton 1978, 53).

The activities of this period left important legacies for the future of employment and training policy. First, the amount of resources devoted to employment and training increased precipitously, from about $200 million in 1963–64 to $1.4 billion in 1970. Second, a large number of diverse organizations became involved in federally funded employment and training, including public schools, local governments, public and nonprofit agencies, and newly created community-based organizations (CBOs). Third, while the content of most job programs was not new (work relief, public works, and rural conservation centers, for example, had their origins in the 1930s), the Great Society also expanded MDTA's institutional and on-the-job training, focusing it more on remedial help for the disadvantaged. Fourth, it preserved the preference for enrolling male household heads, although the target group shifted from skilled white male workers to unemployed young black men. Fifth, it initiated the focus on job readiness training for youth, especially high school dropouts, that is evident in job training policy today.

The Comprehensive Employment and Training Act of 1973: Repudiation of the Great Society

With the election of Richard Nixon in 1968, the repudiation of the Great Society's approach to solving social problems, which had already begun, was official: "For the past five years we have been deluged by government programs for the unemployed, programs for the cities, programs for the poor, and we have reaped from these programs an ugly harvest of frustration, violence, and failure across the land" (Nixon's 1968 presidential platform quoted in Levitan and Taggart 1976, 3, 4). The Nixon administration's concept of New Federalism was the ideological basis for legislation that replaced the detailed specification of categorical grant programs with broad, comprehensive grants in several policy areas. In the process, substantial decision-making authority shifted from the national to local governments. Employment and training policy was seriously affected by this change in political philosophy.

The Comprehensive Employment and Training Act of 1973 consolidated the majority of categorical programs into a single administrative structure operated by city and county governments (called Prime Sponsors). Title I was a block grant: money allocated by formula for expenditure on training activities, but with local freedom to choose programs, administrative structures, and participants. Other titles authorized a few categorical programs and public service employment.[6] Although CETA began as a modest program, its resources and enrollments for all titles increased by 1979 to a budget of approximately $10 billion and over three million new participants annually (USDOL 1980, Table F-1).

CETA turned full circle from the War on Poverty philosophy of targeting funds to the most disadvantaged. Although the legislative intent of Title I was to help the structurally unemployed and those seeking skills for initial or re-entry into the labor force, the eligibility requirements were unrestrictive: "A person who is economically disadvantaged, unemployed, or underemployed may . . . participate" (*CFR* [*Code of Federal Regulations*], 1976, Sec. 95.32). Any individual who had been unemployed at least one week was eligible for

Title I. Thirty percent of those who had worked during the year, or 27 million persons, were eligible to participate in CETA in fiscal 1977 (Barnes 1978).

Early Experiences of Women in CETA

Under CETA, women's enrollment in employment and training programs increased, continuing a secular, upward trend in both women's labor force participation and training program enrollments that predated CETA. Despite the progress in women's enrollment levels, women were still underrepresented in CETA compared to their proportion of the population eligible to participate. Women were 55 percent of those eligible for Title I (training) and Title II (public service employment) but were only 48.5 percent and 40 percent, respectively, of participants in those titles (Barnes 1978; USDOL 1978, 42).

This underrepresentation was attributable in part to federal eligibility requirements that favored men, such as veteran's preference, means tests based on family income instead of individual earnings, and upper age limitations in apprenticeship positions (see Miller, Chapter 5, and Haignere and Steinberg, Chapter 14) for discussions of the negative impact of eligibility criteria on women's enrollment levels). In public service employment, particularly, the social norms governing job "rationing" to those with the most "need" meant that male breadwinners were more desirable participants. Also, most of the available jobs in public service employment and on-the-job training were in traditionally male occupations (Nathan et al. 1978, 5–8). Finally, the enforcement of federal affirmative action requirements under CETA was cumbersome, requiring a lengthy process of administrative complaint to the Labor Department (National Congress of Neighborhood Women 1979; USDOL 1981b).

Other analyses of women's enrollment opportunities have scrutinized the ways legislative and regulatory provisions encourage or discourage women's participation in training programs (for example, Underwood 1979; National Commission for Employment Policy 1981). The identification of sex bias in federal laws is important, but this perspective alone defines the barriers to women's participation too narrowly, because CETA introduced the element of local control into the delivery of employment services. Decentralized authority under CETA, and its successor JTPA, gave communities considerable leeway in how they define and serve the population in need of job training.

Studies of the implementation of CETA at the local level have found wide variation across communities in the proportion of women enrolled (Baumer, Van Horn, and Marvel 1979; Mirengoff and Rindler 1978; Harlan 1979; Levitan and Mangum 1981). The proportion of women among the local eligible population was not the decisive factor in determining women's enrollment level. Instead, some communities offered women greater opportunities than others because of differences in programmatic decisions, training resources, and local labor markets.

Enrollment patterns were influenced by the preferences of local decision makers who control job training policy. Under CETA, professional employment and training staff, who had the greatest influence on selecting target groups, were influenced by their own backgrounds and by the strength of various interest groups represented on local advisory councils, including politicians, social service organizations, schools, CBOs, labor groups, and private employers.

Communities also influenced enrollment patterns through their choices of contractors to run training programs, particularly contractors responsible for client intake and referral (Mirengoff and Rindler 1978). Local contractors might include, among others, the U.S. Employment Service, vocational schools, CBOs, community action agencies, and private employers. These organizations have diverse functions in the community and different motivations for involvement with job training. Because they typically established their own recruitment and selection criteria for applicants (Baumer, Van Horn, and Marvel 1979), their ability and commitment to serve women was reflected in the local enrollment profile. The choice of contractors was related to the kinds of training offered to participants, and the type of locally available programs, in turn, helped to determine the characteristics of participants. Communities that devoted more resources to on-the-job training programs enrolled fewer women, while the use of classroom training was associated with higher female enrollments (Baumer, Van Horn, and Marvel 1979; Harlan 1979).

Thus, both national and local priorities have affected the level of women's enrollment. To guarantee women equal access to job training programs, the federal legislation must not be discriminatory. But each of the institutions involved in the process—local governments, firms, vocational and technical schools, community colleges, CBOs, and social service agencies—must also be committed to serving women equitably. Once this connection is established between access to job training programs and educational and labor market institutions, a much wider range of research and theory can be used to explain the barriers to women's participation.

Reauthorization: Short-Lived Victory
By the time Congress considered CETA for reauthorization in 1978, the political and economic environment had changed once again. There was a Democratic administration which was more favorably disposed toward targeting training resources to the poor and more sympathetic to women's issues. Moreover, CETA was embattled by public scandals charging misuse of funds by localities, and this also made tightening the eligibility requirements seem desirable. The lower unemployment rate allowed Congress to substantially reduce the public service employment component of CETA, which had underserved women and which had grown explosively to account for 68 percent of total federal funds in fiscal 1977 (USDOL 1978, Table F-1). The 1978 reauthoriza-

tion began to shift the emphasis to training and employment assistance for the poor and structurally unemployed.

Importantly, the reauthorization of CETA also coincided with an era of increasing strength in the Women's Movement. Steinberg (1988) points out that the Women's Movement began to acquire in the 1970s the same legitimacy and political muscle that the Civil Rights Movement had in the 1960s. The political process that brought about increased enrollment opportunities for women and legislative changes favorable to women in the 1978 reauthorization of CETA reflects the efforts, advocacy, and lobbying capabilities of groups such as Wider Opportunities for Women, the League of Women Voters, the Women's Bureau in the U.S. Department of Labor, and many grass-roots women's organizations.

Regulations issued by the U.S. Department of Labor pursuant to the reauthorization contained many provisions that were favorable to women, much more so than any previous program. In fact, this was the apex of reform for women in employment and training policy at the federal level. Prime Sponsors were required to provide enrollment opportunities to women equitably (676.54a).[7] The regulations also targeted welfare recipients and displaced homemakers, of whom women are the majority. Primes were directed to establish affirmative action plans designed to achieve objectives within specific time frames; to take positive steps to ensure that planned levels of service were realized; to take corrective action if service levels to women differed by more than 15 percent of the eligible population; and to eliminate "artificial barriers" (such as sex, race, parental status, or absence of part-time work schedules) to enrollment (676.52–676.54). The regulations were also progressive in other ways, such as authorizing payments for child care and encouraging training in nontraditional jobs for women.

Even before the regulations were officially implemented, the Labor Department began to assign a high priority to increasing women's enrollments (Haignere and Steinberg 1984). By fiscal 1980, women were 53 percent of the participants in CETA Title IIB, which had replaced Title I as the training component (USDOL 1981a, Table F-10.3). Some important steps had been taken toward recognizing women's needs and defining sex discrimination as part of the poverty problem. However, before the reforms got fully under way or the impact of the legislative changes on the complex nature of sex bias in the employment and training system could be evaluated, CETA was being dismantled.

From CETA to JTPA: New Federalism Revisited

CETA, which had begun on the principle of decategorizing and decentralizing employment policy, was, ironically, characterized by reformers in 1980 as having too much central control. The Reagan administration's job training legislation embodied its own version of New Federalism, altering once again the course of federal policy. Under the Job Training Partnership Act of 1982, the federal government delegated most of its oversight and administrative authority to the executive branch of state governments, which now act as intermediaries between the federal government and localities. The rationale for decentralization was the same as it had been under CETA: to increase the efficiency of program delivery and place the authority nearer to daily operations.

The Structure of JTPA

Unlike CETA, which left control of local programs to elected officials and social service administrators, JTPA created a much more active role for private sector employers in initiating and approving policy decisions and controlling access to training resources at the state and local levels. Each local Service Delivery Area (SDA) must create a Private Industry Council (PIC) that selects organizations to receive training grants, approves plans for services, and decides policy direction in conjunction with elected officials (Secs. 102, 103). Representatives of private industry are required to be a majority of local PIC members and at least one-third of the members on the State Job Training Coordinating Council (Secs. 102a1, 122a3). Moreover, public service employment no longer exists; only private-sector jobs can be subsidized through increased use of on-the-job training programs.

Reducing costs and simplifying the federal role outweighted all other considerations in framing the JTPA legislation. Although the major cuts in job training were made in CETA soon after Reagan's election, JTPA further reduced the available funds. In fiscal 1982 the total CETA budget was reduced to $4.1 billion, compared to a total of $3.6 billion for JTPA program year 1984 (first full year of operation). Since fiscal 1982, the annual budget for the basic training component (JTPA Title IIA and CETA Title IIB and C) has remained at slightly less than $2 billion (all budget figures from the U.S. General Accounting Office [USGAO] 1985, 1987).

JTPA requires localities to serve the population most in need of training and to "make efforts to provide equitable services among substantial segments of the eligible population" (Sec. 141a). Forty percent of the funds must be spent on youth ages 16 through 21 (Sec. 203a1, b3).[8] As I mentioned above, Title IIA eligibility requirements specify that 90 percent of its participants must be economically disadvantaged. Women as a group are not targeted by the legislation but AFDC recipients are mentioned specifically as a target group (Sec. 203b3). AFDC mothers are singled out because Congress hoped to use JTPA as a vehicle for reducing the number of recipients (Marano 1987). Thus, JTPA, much more so than previous employment and training policy, is identified with the AFDC population. Among the 10 percent of enrollees who are exempt from the economically disadvantaged requirement, displaced homemakers and teenage parents are mentioned as two of many groups who may participate (Sec. 203a2).

Women's advocates fought hard to retain the provisions that CETA had made for all women, but there was no political support for doing so because policy makers had very specific goals for the categories of individuals who should be eligible. JTPA prohibits discrimination against women (Sec. 167a2), but neither the act nor the regulations contains specific affirmative action guidelines for state or local plans, and the extensive provisions of CETA that recognized special barriers to women's enrollment are absent in JTPA. JTPA's lack of specificity about affirmative action is a problem in two respects. First, the absence of blatantly discriminatory practices does not guarantee that women will have access to enrollment opportunities because, as Haignere and Steinberg discuss in Chapter 14, many of the barriers to women's participation are the subtle factors in training program outreach and design and in support options. Second, progress in equal employment opportunity for women and minorities has usually depended upon strong federal leadership in establishing goals and enforcing standards for meeting those goals. The lack of specific guidelines and decentralization of oversight makes it more difficult to keep the issue of female enrollment at the forefront of the political agenda in each state.

The Coalition on Women and JTPA, an umbrella group based in Washington, D.C., reviewed the program year 1985 and 1986 state plans with respect to how well they addressed women's issues, including: adequacy of targeting to women mentioned in the legislation; support services; representation of women's interests on PICs and state councils; and sex stereotyping in training programs. The "reviewers were distressed by the general lack of concern with women's needs evidenced in the plans, by their poor quality overall, and by the failure of the U.S. Department of Labor to call states to task in cases of obvious inadequacy" (Center for National Policy Review 1985). Thirty states had plans that paid minimal or no attention to any issue concerning women specifically. Only 10 states were rated as having a good plan for addressing women's needs.

The Coalition disbanded shortly after completing the study because it did not have the resources to monitor a block grant program in 50 states. Members also believed that nothing would be done about the problems even if they went on with their research because federal policy makers were not responding to their concerns (Paula Roberts, Center for Law and Social Policy, personal communication, 1988). The Labor Department was quite clear that it would not make the regulations more specific. In hopes of becoming more effective advocates, some members of the Coalition began to work individually with the states and localities that seemed to have a commitment to serving women.

Women's Enrollment: A Priority on Welfare Recipients

Because women are a majority of the poor, and a majority of AFDC recipients, they are eligible for training assistance in larger numbers than ever before. Even without targeting and strong enforcement of standards, women's national enrollment in JTPA has remained essentially the same as under CETA—about 53 percent of the total participants in Title IIA compared to 56 percent of those eligible (USDOL 1987b, 6). Thus, women's participation level has remained stable when many feared it would decrease.

This stability is due to both national and local factors. The federal government's emphasis on reducing welfare dependency and the resulting priority placed on enrolling AFDC recipients may be the single most important reason that women's enrollments have not fallen. National enrollment figures show that 37 percent of Title IIA female enrollees receive some form of cash public assistance (compared to 18 percent of men) (USDOL 1986a). AFDC recipients are somewhat overrepresented among JTPA participants compared to their proportion of the eligible population (see n. 3).

Solow and Walker's (1986) study of 25 SDAs found that JTPA enrollments for women were a continuation of the CETA experience at the local level, probably because there was a great deal of continuity between CETA and JTPA service providers. Although major changes in federal priorities can occur rapidly, the largely fixed local employment and training assets necessitate a more gradual adaptation among localities. Thus, local history, as well as close coordination with the local AFDC program and having a large percentage of enrollees in classroom training, were the primary factors associated with high local female enrollments. The decentralized administration of JTPA increases the variability of what goes on in states and localities, making it difficult to generalize about the experiences of women or any other group. It is also difficult to change or control inequities as the experience of the Coalition on Women and JTPA illustrates.

Despite the stable female enrollment level, there are deep problems in current employment and training policy which potentially depress women's enrollment below what it should be. With the federal role in JTPA limited to fiscal oversight, the program accountability of states and SDAs to meet legislative requirements now relies on short-run indicators of program performance. The Labor Department has established seven performance standards which encourage SDAs to maximize the number of people served and to minimize costs. Performance standards measure things such as participants' entered employment rate, cost per placement, and placement wage. Although the tighter cost/benefit accounting is supposed to eliminate problems that occurred under CETA, it has disadvantages when it comes to enrolling groups who typically require more services. It encourages program contractors to "cream" the applicants that are easiest to serve. The most disadvantaged women often require support services, such as child care, which complicate the program and raise its cost, detracting from the SDA's performance record.[9] The existence of performance indicators has also been used as a reason not to require states and localities to collect more detailed data on the socioeconomic characteristics of participants or on longer-term outcomes. The Office of Management and Budget has denied several requests from the Labor Department to collect such data (USGAO 1986; USDOL 1985). There are no separate performance indicators for women or other groups.

In its study evaluating block grant programs, the Coalition on Human Needs (Bennett and Perez 1987, 12) found:

> JTPA contains an inherent contradiction that burdens the implementation of the program . . . While there is some targeting, . . . the paucity of funding, together with the need to meet performance standards insensitive to these groups' needs creates disincentives for providers to serve them. *The program as currently funded can serve only 4 percent of those individuals eligible to participate.* Under these circumstances, with at-risk groups being more expensive and more difficult to serve, significant shortfalls in service to those who need it most can be expected. The system further discourages service to these groups by generally failing to reward providers for training hard-to-serve populations.

Moreover, the study found that contrary to the hypothesis advanced by New Federalists, public program accountability at the local and state levels was generally poor. Of the seven states in its study, six had held no public hearings on JTPA and six did not have adequate representation of the eligible population and community-based organizations on their state councils.

The contradictions in federal training policy between what is offered and what women need to get them out of poverty extend beyond enrollment opportunities to that small minority of women who are fortunate enough to participate. The problems of sex bias in the operation of job training programs did not originate with JTPA, but in each case JTPA has either sustained or added new conditions which create separate and unequal experiences for women and men even as women's enrollment has increased. The next three sections examine women's experiences during the recent history of CETA and JTPA.

On-the-Job and Classroom Training

Although federal programs have engaged in a variety of employment-related activities, such as job placement, work experience, or public service employment, actual training programs take place either on the job or in the classroom. Participants in on-the-job training (OJT) work for private sector employers during their period of program enrollment. In exchange for a federal wage subsidy for participants, employers provide training in a specific occupation. OJT offers participants skill development, the opportunity to earn while learning, and a chance to continue in unsubsidized employment with the same firm. It results in the highest immediate job placement rates for program completers, thus providing income continuity. The proportion of participants in OJT was 22 percent of the initial JTPA program assignments in program year 1986 compared to 11 percent in CETA in fiscal 1980 (USDOL 1987b, 3; Levitan and Mangum 1981, 25).

Classroom training (CT) takes place in community colleges, vocational schools, or other specialized training facilities. It can be either general education (high school equivalency programs or English language instruction) or job skills training in specific occupations. CT participants lack direct employer contact during enrollment, and unlike OJT participants, their training is not employer-specific. While CETA paid stipends to enrollees, classroom trainees usually do not receive financial assistance from JTPA while they are enrolled (Sec. 108).[10] In fiscal 1986, CT accounted for 36 percent of JTPA initial program assignments, compared to half in CETA during fiscal 1980 (USDOL 1987b, 3; Levitan and Mangum 1981, 16).[11]

Neither CETA nor JTPA imposed regulations that prescribe the sex distribution of participants in OJT and CT, but fewer women have always been enrolled in OJT. In program year 1984, 45 percent of women participants (compared to 30 percent of men) were initially assigned to CT, whereas only 18 percent of women (compared to 27 percent of men) were initially assigned to OJT (USDOL 1986a, 11). Proportionately more black women than white women enroll in CT and proportionately fewer in OJT.

The "qualifications" and "preferences" of women are often cited as reasons for sex differences in enrollment patterns, but not a single study can be cited that adequately defines "qualifications" or shows that they determine program assignments. Nor has anyone demonstrated that women prefer classrooms over OJT. In fact, Berryman, Chow, and Bell (1981) found that being a woman increased the probability of placement in CT rather than OJT independently of characteristics such as labor force experience, education, age, poverty status, or desired CETA services.

In my view, the structure of the training system is a more important determinant of program assignment than the qualifications and choices of individual participants. OJT positions involve paid work and are in short supply. Therefore, administrators of job training programs may be responding to deeply ingrained social attitudes about the inappropriateness of giving jobs to women rather than to unemployed men.

Occupational segregation and sex stereotyping by program administrators and employers contribute to sex differences in OJT and CT enrollments.

OJT contains the highest proportion of blue-collar, traditionally male positions, whereas CT is used most often to train for traditionally female clerical and health care jobs (Levitan and Mangum 1981; Waite and Berryman 1984). The reduced level of CT in use under JTPA is even more concentrated in this narrow range of female occupations (Solow and Walker 1986). The association between type of training and occupational category reflects how women and men prepare for sex-typical occupations. For example, a business office where tasks involve typing, filing, and other clerical work can easily be simulated in a classroom. Some training for blue-collar jobs is also available in vocational schools (for example, in electrical circuitry or drafting), but the large and expensive equipment used in many operative jobs is in factories or on construction sites. Skilled crafts are traditionally learned through formal apprenticeship programs and "hands-on" training. These sex differences in training at least partially reflect employers' willingness to invest in training for men but not for women. For the most part, women's jobs require them to acquire skills before they are hired.

Thus, the underrepresentation of women in OJT could reflect sex discrimination in the hiring practices of private sector firms. OJT positions are in short supply because the creation of subsidized jobs depends upon administrators' abilities to convince local employers to hire participants. In order to insure employers' cooperation, they must respond to the employers' demands for workers with certain characteristics. Although we lack research on the employer selection process for OJT workers, a report on OJT in the Work Incentive (WIN) Program indicates that employers preferred men and were reluctant to hire women (U.S. Commission on Civil Rights 1979).

Social norms and occupational sex discrimination are powerful forces that affect program assignments, but the reduced use of stipends for JTPA participants also contributes to the enrollment of more women in CT: "Because women were more likely to be receiving AFDC, they were better able to afford participation in CT" (Solow and Walker 1986, 17). Men (and presumably non-AFDC women) usually do not have a source of income that will sustain them during training. National figures show that 57 percent of female welfare recipients compared to 44 percent of other women were enrolled in CT during program year 1984 (USDOL 1986a, 14). Welfare payments are a convenient subsidy for JTPA and provide a rationale for limiting women's options. Yet Solow and Walker report that the distribution of men and women in types of training was not a JTPA policy concern in any state they studied.

Different methods of training men and women contribute to inequalities in short- and long-term benefits. Women are less likely to earn wages during the period of training; they have lower rates of immediate job placement; they have fewer opportunities to develop employer-specific skills that contribute to later job advancement; and they are trained in traditionally female occupations that will pay lower wages when they leave the program. These aspects of federal job training programs reflect the institutional linkages between the educational system and the labor market for poor women.

Occupational Segregation

Sex stereotyping is an important factor in how women and men are directed to different kinds of training programs, but occupational segregation also occurs within each type of program. Berryman, Chow, and Bell (1981, 33) found that 76 percent of the women in classroom programs and 47 percent of the women in OJT were preparing for female-dominated occupations in fiscal 1978. By contrast, only 10 percent of the women in CT and 14 percent of those in OJT were in male-dominated occupations. (The rest were in sex-neutral occupations.)

Based on national data for fiscal 1976 CETA participants (Continuous Longitudinal Manpower Survey [CLMS] unpublished data), approximately 50 percent of the white women and 60 percent of the minority women in OJT, vocation-specific CT, and work experience were training for lower-skill white-collar jobs. The most common were typists, bookkeepers, keypunch operators, and (unspecified) clerical. Service occupations, the second largest female category, included practical nurses, health care workers and other aides, hairdressers, cooks, and food service workers. About 40 percent of the men (all races) were in semiskilled blue-collar jobs such as welders, machine operators, construction laborers, and groundkeepers. Another 40 percent of the men were in blue-collar crafts, such as machinists, carpenters, automobile mechanics, and equipment repair persons.

After the reauthorization of CETA in 1978, federal regulations were amended to confront directly the problem of occupational segregation by sex. The revised regulations stated that, "all programs, to the maximum extent feasible, shall contribute to the elimination of sex stereotyping" (676.52c). They directed local administrators to "recruit for, and encourage, female entry, through such means as training, into occupations with skill shortages where women represent less than 25 percent of the labor force" (676.52c1). Using national data for CT and OJT participants in the fiscal 1976 to 1978 cohorts (prior to reauthorization), Berryman, Chow, and Bell (1981, 33) found very slight increases in the percentages of women trained in traditionally male and sex neutral occupations. However, the occupational distribution of post-1978 CETA cohorts was not analyzed, so we cannot determine the effect of regulatory changes on occupational desegregation.

The JTPA legislation states that, "efforts shall be made to develop programs which contribute to . . . development of new careers, and overcoming sex-stereotyping in occupations traditional for the other sex" (Sec. 141d2). However, this is less forceful than CETA's mandate, and the Labor Department has not further articulated the topic of sex segregation in its regulations. The absence of strong affirmative action guidelines for SDAs reduces the pressure on states and localities to innovate.

Very little is known about the occupational distribution of women in JTPA. Solow and Walker (1986) found a paucity of data on occupation and sex available from SDAs in their field study. However, of the nine SDAs that could provide it, seven reported that between 50 percent and 90 percent of job placements for women were in clerical and service occupations. This is consistent with their finding that most female participants were enrolled in clerical and health care CT programs.

Federal performance standards act as a disincentive to desegregate programs because contractors view innovative training in nontraditional occupations as too expensive to operate and too risky because it may be difficult to place women in jobs (Zornitsky and McNally 1980; Solow and Walker 1986). Yet short-term indicators are not valid measures of lasting program effects (Gay and Borus 1980), and so the potential long-term cost effectiveness and benefits of training are ignored. Moreover, many programs are successful and Solow and Walker (1986) found that women in nontraditional jobs had substantially higher wages than other women in the four SDAs in their study which made such placements.

Walker and colleagues' (1984) study of early JTPA implementation plans found that most SDAs were expecting to operate programs of lower cost and shorter duration than those under CETA in order to keep costs per participant down while enrolling the maximum number of participants. National statistics bear out this expectation, indicating that the average length of stay in JTPA programs was 14 weeks in program year 1985 compared to 20 weeks for CETA in fiscal 1980 (USDOL 1986b, 11; Bloom and McLaughlin 1982, 8). The median stay is longer for classroom programs (18 weeks) than for other JTPA activities, but programs of this short duration are virtually assured to be offering training for low-skill, entry-level occupations. Given past experience with the intensive investments necessary to break down barriers for women in nontraditional jobs, these priorities of JTPA are unlikely to advance progress toward occupational integration.

To fully understand occupational segregation in federal job training programs, one must look again to systemic barriers in the educational and employment establishments that operate the programs. Most of these institutions lack the expertise and the will to recruit and train women for nontraditional jobs.

JTPA continues CETA's policy of close cooperation with the vocational education system (see Sec. 107c, Selection of Service Providers, and Sec. 123, State Education Coordination and Grants). Yet, the curriculum of public vocational schools is highly segregated by sex (see Vetter, Chapter 3; National Commission for Employment Policy 1981). Although vocational schools are entitled to receive JTPA funds to operate CT programs, the JTPA legislation makes no requirement that the vocational programs it supports must promote training for nontraditional occupations.

In OJT programs, a disproportionate number of employers are small, marginally profitable firms for which the federal wage subsidy is attractive (see Mirengoff and Rindler 1978; Levitan and Mangum 1981). (Larger, more profitable firms are reluctant to deal with government red tape and less willing to tolerate workers with employment problems.) High labor turnover and thin profits among the small firms mean that they are unlikely to expend scarce resources for the intensive training required to integrate women into unfamiliar work environments. Moreover, they have less reason to do so than other companies have because they are less likely than large corporate employers to be the targets of federal efforts to enforce equal opportunity legislation (O'Farrell and Harlan 1984).

Economic conditions do not provide incentives for training program administrators to make educators and employers adhere to regulations regarding occupational desegregation in federal programs. The obvious demand for workers in entry-level clerical and health jobs provides a steady source of placements for female trainees in traditionally female occupations. At the same time, changes in the economy that eliminate jobs and cause high unemployment in manufacturing industries make it harder to identify traditionally male blue-collar occupations in which there are labor demands (Levitan and Mangum 1981). Available jobs are filled by an oversupply of men.

Given the meagerness of federal job training resources compared to the immensity of the educational system and the labor market, it is unrealistic to expect great strides in occupational desegregation without profound institutional changes beyond the job training system. One study, for example, found that although women trained in nontraditional occupations were significantly more likely than women trained in traditional fields to be in male-dominated jobs after CETA, the nontraditional women were also significantly *less* likely than similarly trained men to be in male-dominated jobs (Streker-Seeborg, Seeborg, and Zegeye 1984). Thus, merely increasing nontraditional training for women without eliminating other barriers to equal opportunity will not solve the problem.

CETA reflected the overall pattern of sex segregation in the labor market, but there were also important exceptions in which CETA funds provided essential seed money that helped to stimulate institutional change. Aggregate statistics do not tell the whole story of CETA in that many successful programs had the single purpose of recruiting and training women for nontraditional, skilled blue-collar jobs (Haignere and Steinberg, Chapter 14; Lilly, Chapter 10;

National Commission for Employment Policy 1980). Marano (1987) reports that over 350 women's employment and training programs were funded under CETA in 1981. For example, the Women's Technical Institute in Boston, the first nationally accredited technical training school for women, originated with support from CETA in the 1970s. The director says that the school has "trained and placed more women as electronic technicians than has the city's largest technical school in its 75 year history" (Women's Technical Institute 1981, 4). Deaux and Ullman's (1983) account of job integration in the steel industry after the 1974 consent decree includes a description of how one mill used a local CETA program to recruit women applicants for a company-operated craft training school. "Many [of these women] . . . would not otherwise have found their way to the blue-collar jobs of the steel industry" (Deaux and Ullman 1983, 158). The experimentation of programs like these has created a base of knowledge about the kinds of institutional changes that are necessary to integrate women into higher-paying, skilled jobs.

In some cases, then, CETA programs acted as catalysts for change in a sex-segregated employment and training system. JTPA funding for many innovative programs for poor women, however, was diminished or completely eliminated under budget reductions that began in the early 1980s. No states and only one SDA in Solow and Walker's (1986) study set training in nontraditional occupations as a policy priority. One-third of the SDAs had special contracts for training, but the maximum spent on them was 2 percent of the SDA training budget. Wider Opportunities for Women in Washington, D.C., which is nationally recognized as an outstanding training organization, had JTPA funding for only 25 training positions in program year 1985. This was the single JTPA program specially designed for women in the whole city (Center for National Policy Review 1985).

Much of the information available about sex segregation in occupations is from early in JTPA's history. Although it is possible that the record may have improved after the initial implementation issues were settled, and while it is virtually certain that exemplary programs in some SDAs can be located, the national picture does not indicate that JTPA will perform even as well as CETA in providing opportunities for innovative solutions to reduce occupational sex segregation.

Support Services

Research on employment and training programs (CETA, WIN, vocational education) consistently shows that the availability of public resources for child care assistance is a critical factor in determining whether women are able to enroll in and complete programs (U.S. Commission on Civil Rights 1981; see also Gittell and Moore, Chapter 18). The CETA regulations of 1978 authorized localities to use CETA funds to pay for child care and other support services (676.25-5c), and employers of CETA enrollees could be reimbursed for the costs of child care (676.25-2). No ceiling was placed on the proportion of funds that could be spent for support services, but local program administrators faced difficult choices concerning how to apportion their limited resources. On the one hand, federal regulations encouraged enrollment opportunities for groups that required an intensive investment of resources. On the other hand, diverting funds away from the central mission of training meant that fewer participants could be enrolled.

JTPA makes it even more difficult for service deliverers to provide support because it places a ceiling on the proportion of allowable costs that are not directly related to training (Sec. 108b1). SDAs can spend a combined total of 30 percent of their budgets on administration and support. Since the full allowable amount of 15 percent is typically spent on administration, about 15 percent of the budget is available for support costs that are estimated to have ranged from 30 to 40 percent under CETA (Walker et al. 1984, 73). These support costs are transportation, health care, services for the handicapped, child care, meals, temporary shelter, and financial counseling (Sec. 4[24]).

In a survey of all 594 SDAs early in JTPA's implementation, the U.S. General Accounting Office (1985) found that 95 percent provided some type of support for participants with JTPA funds, and that transportation and child care were provided most often. However, fully 80 percent of the SDAs spent less than the allowable 15 percent on all services: the average planned expenditure for program year 1984 was 8 percent of the budget. JTPA spending on child care was also very low in Solow and Walker's (1986) small sample of SDAs, averaging only 1 percent of the budget.

A strategy used by SDAs in both studies was to secure support services for participants from other state and local agencies. AFDC mothers, for example, are often eligible for child care assistance through social services departments. But as JTPA was being implemented, the Children's Defense Fund reported that budget cuts in domestic programs had significantly reduced other sources of child care aid for low income families (*New York Times*, 25 September 1984, Sec. A).

One other support service that especially benefits women is pre-employment counseling that educates them about and encourages them to consider nontraditional occupational choices. Solow and Walker (1986) reported that only two of 25 SDAs offered such counseling. Shorter time spent in the enrollment in-take process was one reason given for discontinuing counseling.

JTPA permits SDAs to request waivers of support cost limits under certain conditions, thereby releasing them to spend a larger portion of their resources on support. Only 6 percent of SDAs requested waivers in program year

1984 and they spent somewhat more on services and needs-based payments to participants to offset individuals' costs associated with training (USGAO 1985). (There was little difference in type of expenditures between SDAs that requested waivers and those that did not.) SDAs that did not request waivers reported that either they were able to meet participants' needs within allowable costs or they had made policy decisions to limit support costs, or spending more on support would leave too little funds for training. When viewed within the context of federal performance standards, which clearly serve as a disincentive to spending on support services by emphasizing low placement costs, these reasons are plausible. Under the circumstances, "creaming" the least needy JTPA applicants or categorically denying support services seem reasonable options for SDAs.

Perhaps even more important, the active involvement of the private sector in JTPA contributes to a climate that is unfavorable to serving eligible people who require more resources. A survey of 57 local PICs indicates that more than half believed JTPA expenditures for support services should be kept to a minimum. Reflecting the majority view that JTPA's primary mission is to serve the needs of employers, not specific target groups, one PIC chair said:

With as little money as we've got and so many people eligible for JTPA, who in his right mind would try to bring into our programs the people hardest to train? Our job is to make this JTPA system serve employers quickly and at the lowest possible cost. (Walker et al. 1984, 41)

Research on Program Impact

Attempts to evaluate the effectiveness of employment and training programs are as old as the programs themselves. Studies during the sixties generally either did not evaluate the impact of programs on women or did not separate data on women and other participant groups (see Perry et al. 1975; Sexton 1978 for reviews). Moreover, those early studies are regarded as methodologically flawed in light of today's more sophisticated evaluation techniques (Bloch 1979).

The federal government has taken a very keen interest in job training program evaluation. The Employment and Training Administration (ETA) in the Department of Labor has exercised a strong influence on the design and focus of evaluation research by funding the collection of large national data sets and paying economists to analyze them. Under ETA's sponsorship, the goal of evaluation research is to measure reliably *how much better off* participants are for having participated in programs (USDOL 1985). This follows directly from the legislative mandate of job training programs under CETA and JTPA. The JTPA legislation states that job training is an investment in human capital and not an expense. In order to determine whether that investment has been productive . . . the basic return on the investment is to be measured by the increased employment and earnings of participants and the reductions in welfare dependency. (Sec. 106a)

To do this, ETA says, one must find out how much participation causes individuals' earnings to increase by measuring what is called "net earnings impact." Net impact studies measure change in participants' preprogram and postprogram earnings taking into account change in the earnings of nonparticipants with similar characteristics during the same period. Ideally, this method of calculating impact separates the component of earnings change due solely to program participation from change that, theoretically, would have occurred anyway, even without the program. Earnings gains attributable to programs can be compared to program expenditures to determine the cost-benefit ratio.

Under CETA, ETA and its analysts adopted an evaluation strategy that relied exclusively on longitudinal data from a large national sample of program participants and comparison groups of similar individuals constructed from existing data sets by "matching" them to the participant sample on variables such as sex, race, and age. (These surveys did not contain many social or attitudinal variables that might be used to measure empirically whether or how participants and nonparticipants differed.)

The most reliable and carefully designed evaluations of CETA training programs show that female participants made statistically significant earnings gains in the approximate range of $500 to $1,300 a year relative to comparison groups of nonparticipant females (Westat 1981; Bloom and McLaughlin 1982; Bassi 1983). Within this range, there is disagreement about whether earnings gains were greater for minority women than for white women and whether OJT or CT produced greater gains. All the studies that evaluate both women and men agree, however, that female participants gained more compared to other females than male participants gained compared to male nonparticipants. In a comprehensive review of the CETA research, Barnow (1987) says it is fairly certain that the programs had positive impacts on women's earnings and small positive or zero impacts on men's earnings. Yet he concluded that it is impossible to choose the dollar value of the best impact estimate for technical reasons. Because of the need to justify the cost effectiveness of training programs, this finding has caused ETA to rethink its evaluation methodology for JTPA. (More on this below.)

It is important to place in its proper context the finding that training programs improve women's earnings more than men's. Even though CETA programs seemed not to be responsible for any significant *earnings gain* for men, male participants still had *higher job placement rates, wages, and earnings* than female participants in the postprogram period of CETA (Bloom and

McLaughlin 1982; Westat 1981). Moreover, as Zornitsky and McNally (1980) point out, the sex differential in participants' earnings changed hardly at all between the pre- and post-CETA enrollment period (see also Simeral 1978, on the Public Employment Program). Too often, these facts have been ignored by analysts and policy makers, leading to overly optimistic conclusions about the impact of training programs on women. The measures used in the comparison group studies are too restricted and the concept behind the net impact methodology is too narrow to answer the complex question of what it means for women to be better off because of the training experience. The seriousness of these shortcomings warrants further elaboration in the three points below.

First, these studies fail to place earnings gain in a meaningful context of family or individual economic well-being. Let us consider whether an increase of several hundred dollars a year in a woman's earnings is large enough to make a difference in family economic status. In the year after leaving CETA, the fiscal 1975 and 1976 female cohorts earned an average of $4,300 (Bloom and McLaughlin 1982, 27; estimates based on the CLMS and reported in 1980 dollars). Thus, the average absolute level of female earnings was barely high enough to support a single individual at the official poverty line, and not nearly enough for a woman with one or two children to be self-sufficient. More recently, figures based on a national sample survey of SDAs show that the average wage for JTPA Title IIA female terminees *who entered employment* between April and June 1987 was $4.51 an hour (compared to $4.94 for men) (USDOL 1987b, Table B-36). Even on a full-time, year-round schedule this would mean women earn only $9,380 a year, still below the poverty level for a family of four.

These simple calculations call into question whether it is worthwhile to invest so much in research that exclusively measures net earnings impact, unless the purpose is to obscure how difficult it is to meet standards of self-sufficiency through training alone. The principal contribution of each successive generation of studies has been to increase the precision of earnings estimates by improving the quality of nonparticipant comparison groups. But more precise, unbiased estimation techniques have not changed the basic conclusion of the research nor has it made substantial new contributions to knowledge about individual and family economic well-being. To illustrate, suppose new studies show that instead of gaining an average of $500 to $1,300 a year, women really gain twice that amount. This might be because of better measurement or because JTPA participants may have higher job placement rates or earnings than CETA participants. In the rare event that the estimates did change this much, the "returns" on job training expenditures would improve markedly, but we would not know why. And, the improvement for most poor women and their families in general living standard would still be slight.

Because welfare recipients are a target population for enrollment in job training programs, it is important to consider the effect of earned income on welfare benefits. Studies of a variety of training programs, including CETA, have found "a negligible impact on the number of recipients and small impacts on the size of welfare grants" (Burbridge 1987, 110). Moreover, Goodfellow (1979) found that in job training programs prior to CETA, women lost transfer income after participation, which offset their gains in earnings. The loss or reduction of AFDC, and other benefits such as health insurance, child care assistance, or food stamps, could actually reduce the total income of participants and their families even if a larger proportion of family income is earned. In order to arrive at meaningful substantive conclusions about women's economic status, the absolute level of postprogram earnings and the effect of earnings on the family's total income must be considered.

Second, consider whether earnings gain is a sufficient indicator of program impact. Job training programs can influence average postprogram outcomes by increasing the number of people working or the number of hours worked, creating greater employment stability, or raising wage rates. The extent to which each of these factors contributes to earnings gains in the postprogram period has implications for how program benefits are distributed among participants and for the *quality* of their employment.

In the comparison group studies, which focus on average earnings of participants and nonparticipants, it is easy to lose sight of the fact that some employed women have higher earnings when they leave, but others still earn nothing because they do not have jobs. A majority of CETA applicants were not employed when they entered training programs and between one-half and one-third of the participants left without jobs (Harlan and Hackett 1985). For JTPA Title IIA terminees who left between April and June 1987, 45 percent of the women and 39 percent of the men did not leave with a job (USDOL 1987b, Table B-29). The PIC in Milwaukee, Wisconsin, reports that of the JTPA participants in their SDA who left *with* jobs, only 51 percent were in those same jobs three months later. "Of the rest, some get promoted, some move to new jobs, and some return to the unemployment lines, but . . . no one knows how many" (*Milwaukee Journal*, 16 December 1987).

For participants who have jobs, do women's average earnings gains represent primarily an improvement in the quantity or the quality of employment? Bloom and McLaughlin (1982, 21) estimated that 78 percent of women's earnings gain was due to factors that increased the amount of time women were employed, whereas only 22 percent was due to increased wage rates. Increases in the amount of employment may mean that training programs help women to enter the labor force for the first time (or re-enter after an absence), improve their ability to hold a job, or facilitate a shift from part-time to full-time employment. The relatively small component of women's earnings gain due to rising wages suggests that their human capital is not much improved by the programs: either training may not upgrade women's job skills (Bloom and McLaughlin 1982, xvii) or the skills women acquire are not in high-paying occupations. Certainly the limited research available on women's occupational distribution in CETA and JTPA programs and placements support the latter conclusion.

The findings about the causes of women's earnings gains in CETA also contain clues as to why the net earnings impact methodology shows that women gain more than men gain. Women, as a group, can increase their time spent in the labor market more than men can because women are less likely to be full-time, year-round workers. Thus, women "benefit" from a program that helps them get a job, even though the job is low paying. But the employment service function of CETA was less useful to men, many of whom were in CETA because of temporary unemployment (Burbridge 1987). Another explanation is that CETA shifted women out of jobs in the service sector by training them for clerical occupations that are slightly better paying. In contrast, the male-dominated jobs available in CETA were neither particularly well paying nor in great demand so that men might have taken wage cuts (see Durbin and O'Brien, Chapter 7, and also Burbridge 1987).

Third, let us consider whether female participants should be compared to women who do not participate in job training programs. Quite apart from the problem of identifying comparable populations from which to select nonparticipant samples, evaluations that use comparison groups raise the question of whether nonparticipants who are equally disadvantaged as participants are the proper standard by which to judge the success of a program. I have indicated above that compared to an absolute criterion, such as the poverty line, the average earnings of female participants would not provide even a minimally acceptable standard of living. In addition, the focus on similar nonparticipant groups deflects attention away from comparisons between men and women. As we have seen, if program benefits for women are defined as decreasing labor market inequalities between women and men, then the training programs do not contribute to this goal. Yet it is only by decreasing this gap that women will have a minimum decent standard of living.

Neither do the participant/nonparticipant comparisons tell us if different treatments—types of training, occupations, supportive services—have lasting effects on inequality in labor market outcomes. Do women in OJT or those few trained in nontraditional occupations get jobs with faster-rising wages or more employment stability than their counterparts in CT and clerical occupations? Could the employment and earnings benefits be greater for women if they were distributed proportionately to white men in programs and occupations? From a policy standpoint, these are important questions that have not received much attention.

In a study that compared the effects of CETA program assignment on participants' postprogram employment, Harlan and Hackett (1985) found that, overall, white men were more likely than women or black men to be employed immediately upon leaving CETA. White men who left CETA without a job also entered employment more rapidly than other sex/race groups. Their average spell of unemployment lasted 6.2 months compared to 9.4 months for black men, 11.8 months for white women, and 16.4 months for black women. Part of the differences in employment across sex and race groups could be attributed to the type of training in which these groups were enrolled, independently of differences in participants' backgrounds and labor force participation in the year prior to training. Within each group, persons in OJT were between two and four times more likely to leave CETA with a job than those in CT. OJT participants who left CETA without a job also found employment more quickly compared to those of the same sex and race.

Much more extensive analysis is needed about the relationship of program experience to job stability and job quality. So far, ETA's evaluation strategy has produced higher quality studies of a certain type, but it also limits the information and funds available for other research. Data needed to address issues other than earnings impact either were not included in the CLMS or were of poor quality. The technically sophisticated literature that emerged from federally sponsored evaluations of CETA has increasingly narrowed to a methodological debate over how comparison groups can be constructed to eliminate selection bias in the calculation of earnings gains for participants.[12] The issue of selection bias and competing ways of statistically controlling for it have come to overshadow completely the substance of the research and to reduce the audience to fewer and fewer specialists who are technically competent to evaluate the evaluations. Worse, the entire debate obscures the fact that federal policy makers have set for themselves a deceptively simple definition of program impact that might, if accurately measured, give a cost-benefit accounting of the returns on job training expenditures but would never be able to answer the complex question of whether participants are actually better off because of training.

Many valid questions about program outcomes have disappeared from the research agenda. The broad scope of the CLMS prevented it from capturing the nuances and diversity in program strategies and local labor markets. Lacking the community and institutional context, analysts had no choice but to adopt a "black box" approach to comparing general program categories rather than analyzing specific internal differences among programs.

In response to recommendations from an advisory panel, ETA adopted a different evaluation plan for JTPA. The agency followed the panel's advice to conduct a set of classical field experiments in 20 carefully selected SDAs for five years and to dispense with plans for a longitudinal national survey of JTPA participants. In the experiments, JTPA applicants are assigned randomly to participant and nonparticipant (control) groups and interviewed at enrollment, 18 months, and 30 months after enrollment (USDOL 1985). The experiments are modeled closely on previous studies of other employment and training programs (such as Supported Work and WIN Demonstrations), and they are widely acclaimed in the research community because they produce unbiased estimates of net program earnings impact (see, for example, Gueron, Chapter 15, and Goldman, Chapter 16).

While the JTPA evaluations will provide a more precise and reliable dollar estimate of participants' gains under a new program using a better methodology, from a policy standpoint, they will not represent a step forward if they continue to ask the same limited questions about program outcomes. The study of 20 localities in the JTPA experiments provides an opportunity to incorporate multiple research questions by focusing on some different issues within each site. It is necessary to know much more about the effect of training programs on employment rates and stability, the wage gap between men and women, future wage increases, and changes in living standards in order to fully assess their impact on women. However, the legislation does not specifically authorize any broad research initiatives, nor has ETA established this as an explicit goal.

Conclusions

Today women are slightly over half the participants in JTPA training programs for the economically disadvantaged. Past research has shown that participation increases women's average earnings above those of their nonparticipating peers. But these facts are not enough to conclude that federal training policy serves women well.

The history of employment and training policy has been shaped by perceptions of poverty and unemployment among men. Years late, the feminization of poverty was finally acknowledged, and later still, training programs began enrolling more women. Now, when the focus is ostensibly on women, it is only on women as welfare recipients—those whose dependence on public assistance, not their poverty, is the primary concern. Training policy reflects that narrowness of definition and concern in its targeting, its accounting, and its evaluation standards.

Not only is the focus on women belated and restricted, but the political timing is bad. In the late seventies women were beginning to win some small but significant victories in the struggle for recognition. The long, hard-fought battles over the 1978 CETA reauthorization resulted in substantial improvements on paper for women (such as clauses pertaining to enrollment opportunities, occupational desegregation, affirmative action). But we learned how ephemeral these sorts of changes can be as the reforms were abruptly swept away by a change in legislation under a new administration with different priorities. The priorities of the eighties have been marked by human resource policies that are only grudgingly included in the federal budget, always with the necessity of cutting costs, delivering the bare minimum, and reducing federal management responsibility. Federal training policy is now poised awkwardly between its mission of helping the most disadvantaged and its mandate to deliver acceptable workers to the private sector within strict budget limitations.

Worse, the focus on women in employment and training policy may have come too late, the time for women already passed. Academics are recycling old theories that link the poverty of women and children to *male* unemployment (Wilson 1987). The spotlight is turning away from women once again as discussions of the feminization of poverty yield to concern about programs for the "male partners" of poor women.

Many JTPA programs are the training equivalents of fast food restaurants: the needs of individuals take a distant second place compared to the importance placed on the number of them who are served and how much (or rather, how little) it costs. This is a system that takes people who are already disadvantaged and have been passed over by the educational system and gives them, on average, three and a half months of training or job search assistance. There is no leeway here to focus on "special interests," because what drives the system is crushing need pitted against the meager resources the system has to offer. The end result is that about half the female participants enter jobs (tenure unknown) that pay average wages below $5.00 an hour. Moreover, it is not a policy that recognizes poverty and unemployment as institutional problems. It tells individuals to develop skills, motivation, and independence, and it ignores discrimination, inadequate compensation, and the lack of job opportunities on the margins of the U.S. economy.

Fortunately, this is not a wholly accurate characterization of all JTPA training. Indeed, it may be too pessimistic because federal priorities and national averages do not tell the entire story of training programs. One might say there are really two policies. The "official" policy has, over the past 15 years, channeled billions of dollars through CETA and JTPA to nearly every local government in the 50 states, but has largely failed to address women's problems, such as sex differences in program assignments, occupational segregation, support systems, and low wages. The "unofficial" policy, however, has produced hundreds of small successes brought about by dedicated program administrators who have developed models of innovative programs. From the unofficial policy, we have learned how training can be used to full advantage in helping women, as well as what its limitations are.

There is no mystery about what should be done. Program priorities should be: recruitment targeted to women, occupational counseling, individualized assessment of needs ranging from child care assistance to confidence building, job skills, job search assistance or placement, and follow-up help for new employees. In addition, training staff must work with employers, and sometimes use the legal system, to change work environments.

Each level of government has an important contribution to make in providing a framework within which programs can operate effectively. First, opportunities for poor women in job training programs ultimately depend upon the enforcement of federal laws that guarantee equality of educational and employment opportunities in the institutions that operate these programs. This is because JTPA funds for training economically disadvantaged individuals are only a small part of the public and private resources that these institutions control. Although there are possibilities for JTPA programs to act as catalysts for change, most of them tend to reflect rather than to remove barriers to women's labor market equality with men. The entire infrastructure of the training and employment system must be the object of efforts to eliminate discrimination against women because limited reform in individual programs cannot prevent the reproduction of existing patterns of inequality. This requires that the federal government exercise its authority in a role beyond fiscal accountant. Most important, it means committing considerable resources over a long period.

Second, state and local governments have a responsibility to manage the involvement of the private sector in JTPA. On one hand, the participation of business in setting policy and operating programs can be a stumbling block for enrolling women. On the other hand, governments can help women capitalize on training strategies that forge closer ties between schools and employers. To do this, they should establish women's issues as policy priorities and insure the representation of women's advocates on policy-making bodies. Equal employment policies and demonstrations of concern for female workers should be used as criteria in selecting business representatives for PICs. Governments should monitor the enrollee selection process to see that it complies with affirmative action requirements. They should use training subsidies for new and developing firms in which chances for achieving job integration are better than in industries with slow or declining employment.

The task of ensuring that employment and training policy makes women better off is not easy in a decentralized system with a national agenda that is ambiguous in its message to women. However, as I have shown above, decentralization is not necessarily detrimental to women. Women fare much better in some localities than in others and it is important to find out why and to transfer those strategies to other places. Moreover, the economic problems of poor women are becoming more important within the women's movement —nationally, statewide, and locally (Marano 1987). There is a growing consensus among women's advocates about how training policy should function and a sustained effort to keep the unofficial policy alive even after years of discouragement. One can hope that in the coming decade these ideas will find broader support in the employment and training establishment.

Notes

Acknowledgment: Part of the research for this chapter was supported by a grant from the National Science Foundation. Sections of the chapter draw on Sharon L. Harlan, "Federal Job Training Policy and Economically Disadvantaged Women," in Laurie Larwood, Ann H. Stromberg, and Barbara Gutek, eds., *Women and Work: An Annual Review*, 1: 282–310 (Beverly Hills, Calif.: Sage, 1985). I gratefully acknowledge Ronnie Steinberg's many helpful suggestions on earlier drafts of this chapter.

1. This chapter focuses on programs authorized under Title IIA of the Job Training Partnership Act and formerly operated under Title IIB of the 1978 reauthorization of the Comprehensive Employment and Training Act. These are training programs in which all economically disadvantaged youth and adults are eligible to participate. JTPA also authorizes programs for specific groups of workers, for example, Title IIB Summer Youth Programs, Title III Employment and Training Assistance for Dislocated Workers, and Title IVB Job Corps. The term "economically disadvantaged" applies to individuals or members of families who receive public assistance and individuals or members of families who have a total family income that is either less than the poverty level set by the Office of Management and Budget or less than 70 percent of the lower living standard income level.

2. There is a change between the language of JTPA's statement of purpose, which calls for preparing participants for "entry into the labor force" and "obtaining productive employment," and the expansive language of JTPA's immediate predecessor, the Comprehensive Employment and Training Act, which stated its purpose as leading to "maximum employment opportunities" for participants and the enhancement of "self-sufficiency." The more modest goals of JTPA and the direct reference to eliminating welfare dependency reflect the conservative political agenda and fiscal restraint exercised by its framers.

3. Many economically disadvantaged women receive AFDC, a cash public assistance program for single-parent households. AFDC recipients accounted for 17 percent of the JTPA Title IIA–eligible population and 23 percent of the enrollees in program year 1986 (U.S. Department of Labor 1987b, 6). Historically, federal employment and training policy has been developed, administered, and funded separately from welfare-related work programs. However, the current political support for tying the receipt of welfare benefits to employment and training is blurring the distinction between JTPA training and welfare employment programs.

4. A contemporary version of this theory says that high rates of black male joblessness reduce the pool of marriageable black men, leading to the increase among blacks in poor, never-married women who are single heads of households (Wilson 1987).

5. For example, support for the operation of residential Job Corps centers for

disadvantaged girls was decidedly unenthusiastic (Levitan and Mangum 1969). Eventually, in 1967 Congress set the minimum female enrollment at 50 percent, but that goal was never reached. Female enrollment in Job Corps has remained between 25 percent and 30 percent of the total. (The JTPA legislation of 1982 again set a goal of 50 percent enrollment for women in Job Corps.)

6. Title II of CETA, also locally operated, was limited to public service employment in areas of substantial unemployment. This part of the act continued public employment programs that had begun some years earlier in response to rising unemployment rates. Later, Title VI was added, which greatly expanded the public service employment program to deal with higher national unemployment (see Durbin and O'Brien, Chapter 7). Titles III and IV, smallest of the titles, continued a few categorical programs for special target groups which the U.S. Department of Labor administered directly: assistance to youth, criminal offenders, persons of limited English-speaking ability, migrant workers and Native Americans, and Job Corps.

7. Regulations issued by the U.S. Department of Labor pursuant to the 1978 reauthorization of CETA Titles I, II, VI, and VII are codified at 20 *CFR*, parts 675–79. I will cite only the numbered parts in the text. For JTPA, I will cite the relevant sections from the act itself (PL 97-300, 1982). The JTPA regulations are much less extensive than CETA's. In the preamble to the proposed JTPA regulations, the Labor Department states, "The Secretary believes that the Act is sufficiently clear and, therefore, requires only limited and selective interpretation via regulations" (*Federal Register*, 18 January 1983, p. 2292).

8. Like prior job training legislation, JTPA is highly oriented toward youth. Youth (under 22 years of age) were between 20 percent and 50 percent of pre-CETA training and employment programs, between 48 percent and 62 percent of CETA Title I participants (Simms 1985), and 42 percent of JTPA Title IIA in 1986 (USDOL 1987b). For evaluations of the effects of employment and training programs specifically for youth, see Hahn and Lerman (1983) and Simms (1985).

9. "Creaming" also encourages the selection of the applicants who are best qualified in educational attainment. Persons with a high school education *or more* have been overrepresented in JTPA since its inception. Comparing JTPA Title IIA enrollments in the April-to-June quarter of program years 1984 through 1987, persons with at least a high school education accounted for between 53 and 59 percent of the enrollees compared to 49 percent of the eligible population (USDOL 1987a, Table B-1, 1987b, Table B-1; see also USGAO 1985, 10, for comparison with CETA).

10. A national survey of SDAs determined that approximately 40 percent of SDAs offered need-based payments to at least some participants during the transition year from CETA to JTPA. Approximately 75 percent of those SDAs paid $40 a week or less (USGAO 1985, 22–24).

11. Under CETA, a substantial proportion of participants were enrolled in work experience programs that were temporary jobs, usually in public or nonprofit organizations. JTPA discourages the use of work experience by limiting the proportion of costs that the federal government will reimburse (Sec. 108b2). Work experience accounted for 9 percent of JTPA enrollments in program year 1986; job search assistance accounted for 19 percent, and other activities accounted for 14 percent (USDOL 1987b, 3).

12. Selection bias in the calculation of net earnings gains for participants may occur when there are undetected (unmeasured) differences between participants and the nonparticipant comparison groups against which their earnings are compared. For example, to the extent that participants might be more capable, more motivated, more "work-oriented," or more desirable enrollees from an administrator's or employer's perspective, the component of earnings gains due to program participation will be overstated relative to the comparison group. Selection bias is a problem for estimates of programs impact only when the unmeasured determinants of program participation are related to unmeasured determinants of labor market outcomes, such as employment and earnings (see Bloch 1979; Westat 1977, 1981; Moffitt 1987 for relevant discussions). Although selection bias is one concern in doing program evaluation, there is reason to question how important it is in reality. For selection bias to occur, the process of choosing participants from the applicant pool would have to be structured so that administrators were able to discern applicants' ability and underlying motivation to succeed at work. Yet, administrators do not conduct an in-depth psychological evaluation of each potential participant: the time applicants spend in in-take procedures is short, and has grown shorter, allowing little time for appraisals. Even when applicants are screened for their employability, the judgments often turn out to be wrong as Goldman says in Chapter 16.

References

Barnes, William. 1978. "Target Groups." In National Commission for Manpower Policy, *CETA: An Analysis of the Issues*, pp. 63–94. Special Report no. 23. Washington, D.C.: Government Printing Office, May.

Barnow, Burt S. 1987. "The Impact of CETA Programs on Earnings: A Review of the Literature." *Journal of Human Resources* 22 (Spring): 157–93.

Bassi, Laurie J. 1983. "The Effect of CETA on the Postprogram Earnings of Participants." *Journal of Human Resources* 18 (Fall): 539–56.

Baumer, D. C.; C. E. Van Horn; and M. Marvel. 1979. "Explaining Benefit Distribution in CETA Programs." *Journal of Human Resources* 14 (Spring): 171–96.

Bennett, Maybelle Taylor, and Leticia Perez. 1987. *Block Grants: Beyond the Rhetoric*. Washington, D.C.: Coalition on Human Needs.

Berryman, Sue E.; Winston K. Chow; and Robert M. Bell. 1981. *CETA: Is It Equitable for Women?* Prepared for the National Commission for Employment Policy. Santa Monica, Calif.: Rand, May.

Bloch, Farrell E., ed. 1979. *Research in Labor Economics: Evaluating Manpower Training Programs*. Greenwich, Conn.: JAI Press.

Bloom, Howard S., and Maureen A. McLaughlin. 1982. *CETA Training Programs: Do They Work for Adults?* Washington, D.C.: Congressional Budget Office, July.

Burbridge, Lynn C. 1987. "Black Women in Employment and Training Programs." In Margaret Simms and Julianne Malveaux, eds., *Slipping Through the Cracks: The Status of Black Women*, pp. 97–114. New Brunswick, N.J.: Transaction Books.

Center for National Policy Review. Catholic University of America. 1985. *Jobs Watch Alert*. Washington, D.C., 9 January.

Deaux, Kay, and Joseph C. Ullman. 1983. *Women of Steel: Female Blue-Collar Workers in the Basic Steel Industry*. New York: Praeger.

Gay, Robert S., and Michael E. Borus. 1980. "Validating Performance Indicators for Employment and Training Programs." *Journal of Human Resources* 15 (Winter): 29–48.

Goodfellow, Gordon P. 1979. "Estimates of the Benefits of Training for Four Manpower Training Programs." In Farrell E. Bloch, ed., *Research in Labor Economics: Evaluating Manpower Training Programs*. Greenwich, Conn.: JAI Press.

Hahn, Andrew, and Robert Lerman. 1983. *The CETA Youth Employment Record*. Waltham, Mass.: Center for Employment and Income Studies, Brandeis University.

Haignere, Lois, and Ronnie Steinberg. 1984. *New Directions in Equal Employment Policy: Training Women for Non-Traditional Occupations through CETA*. Working Paper no. 13. Albany: Center for Women in Government, Summer.

Harlan, Sharon L. 1979. *Participation of Disadvantaged Groups in Employment and Training Programs (CETA) in New York and Pennsylvania*. Final Report, prepared for the Office of Research and Development, Employment and Training Administration, U.S. Department of Labor. Washington, D.C.

Harlan, Sharon L., and Edward J. Hackett. 1985. "Federal Job Training Programs and Employment Outcomes: Effects by Sex and Race of Participants." *Population Research and Policy Review* 4: 235–65.

Levitan, Sar A., and Garth L. Mangum. 1969. *Federal Training and Work Programs in the Sixties*. Ann Arbor: Institute of Labor and Industrial Relations, the University of Michigan and Wayne State University.

———. 1981. *The T in CETA: Local and National Perspectives*. Kalamazoo, Mich.: W.E. Upjohn Institute for Employment Research.

Levitan, Sar A., and Robert Taggart. 1976. *The Promise of Greatness*. Cambridge, Mass.: Harvard University Press.

McLanahan, Sara; Annemette Sorensen; and Dorothy Watson. 1986. "Trends in Sex Differences in Poverty: 1950–1980." Center for Demography and Ecology Working Paper 86-12, University of Wisconsin-Madison.

Marano, Cynthia. 1987. "Systemic Contradictions: A Practitioner's View of Public Employment and Training Policies for Low Income Women." Wider Opportunities for Women. Typescript, February.

Massachusetts Executive Office of Economic Affairs. Welfare Task Force. 1984. "Proposed Recommendations of the Program Strategies Subcommittee." Boston.

Mirengoff, William W., and Lester L. Rindler. 1978. *CETA: Manpower Programs Under Local Control*. Washington, D.C.: National Academy of Sciences.

Moffitt, Robert. 1987. "Symposium on the Econometric Evaluation of Manpower Training Programs: Introduction." *Journal of Human Resources* 22 (Spring): 149–56.

Moynihan, Daniel P. 1969. *Maximum Feasible Misunderstanding*. New York: The Free Press.

Nathan, R. P.; R. F. Cook; J. M. Galchick; and R. W. Long. 1978. *Monitoring the Public Service Employment Program*. Washington, D.C.: The Brookings Institution.

National Commission for Employment Policy. 1980. Papers presented at Conference on the Experience of Women in Employment and Training Programs, by S. Gilbert, S. Carruthers, and B. Jacobus. Washington, D.C., September.

———. 1981. *Increasing the Earnings of Disadvantaged Women*. NCEP Report no. 11, Washington, D.C., January.

National Congress of Neighborhood Women. National Organization for Women. New York City Chapter. 1979. *Administrative Complaint Against the City of New York Before the U.S. Department of Labor, Employment and Training Administration*. New York, November.

O'Farrell, Brigid, and Sharon L. Harlan. 1984. "Job Integration Strategies: Today's Programs and Tomorrow's Needs." In Barbara F. Reskin, ed. *Sex Segregation in the Workplace: Trends, Explanations, Remedies*, pp. 267–91. Washington, D.C.: National Academy Press.

Perry, C. R.; B. E. Anderson; R. L. Rowan; and H. R. Northrup. 1975. *The Impact of Government Manpower Programs*. Philadelphia: University of Pennsylvania Press.

Sexton, Patricia C. 1978. *Women and Work*. R and D Monograph no. 46. Prepared for Employment Standards Administration, U.S. Department of Labor. Washington, D.C.

Simeral, Margaret H. 1978. "The Impact of the Public Employment Program on Sex-Related Wage Differentials." *Industrial and Labor Relations Review* 31: 509–19.

Simms, Margaret. 1985. "The Participation of Young Women in Employment and Training Programs." In Charles Betsey, ed., *Youth Employment and Training Programs: The YEDPA Years*, pp. 462–85. Washington, D.C.: National Research Council.

Solow, Katherine, with Gary Walker. 1986. *The Job Training Partnership Act Service to Women*. New York: Grinker, Walker and Associates.

Steinberg, Ronnie. 1988. "The Unsettled Revolution: Women, the State and Equal Employment." In Jane Jensen, Elisabeth Hagen, and Ceallaigh Ready, eds., *Work and Politics: The Feminization of the Labour Force*. New York: Oxford University Press.

Streker-Seeborg, I.; M. C. Seeborg; and A. Zegeye. 1984. "The Impact of Nontraditional Training on the Occupational Attainment of Women." *Journal of Human Resources* 19 (Fall): 452–71.

Sundquist, James L. 1969. "Origins of the War on Poverty." In James L. Sundquist, ed., *On Fighting Poverty*, pp. 6–33. New York: Basic Books.

Ulman, Lloyd. 1974. "The Uses and Limits of Manpower Policy." *The Public Interest* 34: 83–105.

Underwood, Lorraine A. 1979. *Women in Federal Employment and Training Programs*. The Urban Institute, Paper 5074-1, Washington, D.C., January.

U.S. Commission on Civil Rights. 1979. *Women: Still in Poverty*. Clearinghouse Publication no. 60. Washington, D.C.

———. 1981. *Child Care and Equal Opportunity for Women*. Clearinghouse Publication no. 67. Washington, D.C., June.

U.S. Department of Commerce. Bureau of the Census. 1984. "Characteristics of the Population Below the Poverty Level: 1982." In Current Population Reports, Consumer Income, Series P-60, no. 144. Washington, D.C.: Government Printing Office, March.

U.S. Department of Labor. Office of Policy Planning and Research. 1965. *The Negro Family: The Case for National Action.* Washington, D.C., March.

————. 1969. *Statistics on Manpower, A Supplement to the Manpower Report of the President.* Washington, D.C.: Government Printing Office.

————. 1978. *Employment and Training Report of the President.* Washington, D.C.: Government Printing Office.

————. 1980. *Employment and Training Report of the President.* Washington, D.C.: Government Printing Office.

————. 1981a. *Employment and Training Report of the President.* Washington, D.C.: Government Printing Office.

————. Office of the Secretary. 1981b. *Final Determination National Congress of Neighborhood Women et al. v. The City of New York.* Washington, D.C., January.

————. Bureau of Labor Statistics. 1983. *Handbook of Labor Statistics.* Bulletin no. 2175. Washington, D.C.: Government Printing Office, December.

————. Employment and Training Administration. 1985. "ETA's JTPA Evaluation Plans." Washington, D.C., 8 November.

————. 1986a. "Female Participants in JTPA Title IIA: New Enrollees and Terminees During the Transition Year and Program Year 1984." JTLS Special Paper no. 3. Washington, D.C., May.

————. 1986b. "Summary of JTLS Data for JTPA Title IIA and III Enrollments and Terminations During Program Year 1985 (July 1985–June 1986)." Washington, D.C., November.

————. 1987a. "Review of Participant Characteristics and Program Outcomes for the First Eleven Quarters of JTPA Operation (October 1983–June 1986)." JTQS Special Paper no. 5. Washington, D.C., February.

————. Division of Performance Management and Evaluation. Office of Strategic Planning and Policy Development. 1987b. "Summary of JTQS Data for JTPA Title IIA and III Enrollments and Terminations During FY 1986 (July 1986–June 1987)." Washington, D.C., December.

U.S. General Accounting Office. 1985. *The Job Training Partnership Act: An Analysis of Support Cost Limits and Participant Characteristics.* Washington, D.C., November.

————. 1986. *Job Training Partnership Act: Data Collection Efforts and Needs.* Washington, D.C., March.

————. 1987. *Job Training Partnership Act: Summer Youth Programs Increase Emphasis on Education.* Washington, D.C., June.

Waite, Linda J., and Sue E. Berryman. 1984. "Occupational Desegregation in CETA Programs." In Barbara F. Reskin, ed., *Sex Segregation in the Workplace: Trends, Explanations, Remedies*, pp. 292–307. Washington, D.C.: National Academy Press.

Walker, G.; W. Grinker; T. Seessel; R. C. Smith; and V. Cama. 1984. *An Independent Sector Assessment of the Job Training Partnership Act, Phase I: The Initial Transition.* MDC, Inc.

Westat, Inc. 1977. *Continuous Longitudinal Manpower Survey: Methodology*. Technical Report no. 1. Rockville, Md., March.

————. 1981. *Impact on 1977 Earnings of New FY 1976 CETA Enrollees in Selected Program Activities*. Net Impact Report no. 1. Rockville, Md., March.

Wilson, William J. 1987. *The Truly Disadvantaged*. Chicago: University of Chicago Press.

Wojtkiewicz, Roger; Sara McLanahan; and Irwin Garfinkel. 1988. "The Growth of Families Headed by Women: 1950 to 1980." Center for Demography and Ecology Working Paper 88-31, University of Wisconsin–Madison.

Women's Technical Institute. 1981. Annual Report. Boston.

Yarmolinsky, Adam. 1969. "The Beginnings of OEO." In James L. Sundquist, ed., *On Fighting Poverty*, pp. 34–51. New York: Basic Books.

Zornitsky, Jeffrey, and Margaret McNally. 1980. "Measuring the Effects of CETA on Women: Issues in Assessing Program Performance." Paper presented at Conference on the Experience of Women in Federal Employment and Training Programs, National Commission for Employment Policy. Washington, D.C., September.

3/The Vocational Education Option for Women

Louise Vetter

Nearly 17 million students were enrolled in public vocational education in the United States in 1981–82, making it the largest occupational training program in the country (U.S. Department of Education [USED] 1984). A little over half (51 percent) of those students were girls and women. Approximately 35 percent of the total enrollment in vocational education, or 5.8 million students, were enrolled in occupationally specific instructional programs. Forty-seven percent of the students enrolled in occupationally specific programs in 1981–82 were girls and women.

What is public vocational education? Many adults have some notion of "shop" classes or typing classes or something of that nature. However, vocational education programs cover a very broad range of programming at the high school, postsecondary, and adult levels. The federal definition of vocational education is as follows:

"Vocational education" means organized educational programs which are directly related to the preparation of individuals for paid or unpaid employment, in such fields as agriculture, business occupations, home economics, health occupations, marketing and distributive occupations, technical and emerging occupations, modern industrial and agricultural arts, and trades and industrial occupations, or for additional preparation for a career in those fields, and in other occupations requiring other than a baccalaureate or advanced degree and vocational student organization activities as an integral part of the program. For purposes of this definition "organized education program" means only—

(1) Instruction, including career guidance and counseling, related to the occupation or occupations for which the students are in training or instruction necessary for students to benefit from that training; and

(2) The acquisition, including leasing, maintenance, and repair, of instructional equipment, supplies, and teaching aids. The term does not mean construction, acqui-

sition of initial equipment or buildings, or the acquisition or rental of land. (USED 1985, 33235)

States implement vocational education in different ways. Some states have chosen to concentrate on high school–level programs, others on postsecondary (two-year college or technical institute) programs. Still other states offer a fairly even mix of high school and postsecondary programs. Adult programs are offered both at high schools and at postsecondary institutions.

Vocational education in high schools takes place in several different settings. The school may be a "vocational high school" that offers vocational programs and the other courses needed for high school graduation. It may be a "comprehensive high school" that offers both vocational programs and a pre-college academic program. Or it may be an "area vocational school" where students attend half days for the vocational program and the other half day at their home high school for the other courses needed to complete high school graduation requirements. States may choose to implement any or all of these options, and so may local school districts.

A study of the high school transcripts of a nationally-representative sample of youth (Campbell, Orth, and Seitz 1981) indicated that 85 percent of the young women had taken at least one vocational education course in high school. Fewer of the young men (approximately 70 percent) had taken at least one vocational education course. However, only 47 percent of the young women and only 30 percent of the young men who were enrolled in vocational education had taken enough credits to be considered to have developed salable skills.

In 1981–82, 70 percent of agriculture students in occupationally specific programs were enrolled in high school programs. High school enrollments in other service areas were as follows: technical, 7 percent; trade and industrial, 46 percent; marketing and distribution, 52 percent; health occupations, 20 percent; occupational home economics, 61 percent; and office occupations, 56 percent (USED 1984).

At the postsecondary level, vocational education programs may be two-year programs that result in an associate of arts degree. The program may be shorter than two years and result in the student's earning a program certificate, rather than a degree or a diploma. Students may enter the postsecondary programs directly out of high school or at any point later in their careers. Some postsecondary programs are made available to students who have not graduated from high school.

Programs labeled "adult vocational education" have tended to be very short-term programs and very specific to one skill (for example, typing or welding). These programs may be offered in the evenings at high schools, area vocational centers, or postsecondary institutions. However, some states have expanded their adult programs by moving to enroll displaced homemakers and other adults in the high school daytime vocational education programs (Frantz, Strickland, and Elson 1986; see also Miller, Chapter 5). Postsecondary institutions also offer some "adult vocational education" programs during the day.

This description should demonstrate that there is no single national program of vocational education. As stated by Lotto (1986, 56), "It is not an organized national system for creating pools of trained workers in key areas of labor market demand. It is part of a complex, decentralized structure for delivering public education in this country." While there is federal vocational education legislation and funding, states and local educational districts have always overmatched the federal dollars in implementing vocational education. (Currently, states and local districts provide $9–$10 for each federal $1.) Given our system of local control in education as provided by the Constitution, this situation will continue to prevail.

This chapter will examine the participation patterns of girls and women in vocational education and assess the impact of vocational training on their employment, occupations, and earnings after they leave the programs.

Historical Development of Policy in Vocational Education

There has been federal legislation relating to vocational education at the secondary level since 1917. While a number of states had developed programs of vocational education prior to the passage of the Smith-Hughes Act of 1917, passage of the act brought these programs into public view and facilitated similar development in other states.

Financial support for vocational education from the federal government was first regarded as temporary, "stimulating" legislation. However, it is clear that vocational education advanced more rapidly with federal funds than would have been true without them. States that had lagged in developing vocational education programs were stimulated to take action. Over the next 50 years, the federal government continued to enact legislation that broadened the scope of vocational education by adding occupational areas to be included in the curriculum. (See Table 3-1 for a chronological summary of the legislation.)

As pointed out by Vetter (1985), vocational education for girls and women developed from the model of "men-at-work, women-at-home." Home economics was the first service area in vocational education that offered courses to girls and women, whereas the wage-earning agriculture and trade and industrial areas were offered to boys and men. As other service areas, such as health occupations, were added to vocational education, opportunities for girls and women were expanded. The consumer and homemaking aspects of home economics were also expanded to include programs in "wage-earning"

Table 3-1/Federal Vocational Education Legislation Before 1976

Act	Year of Passage	Provisions
Smith-Hughes	1917	Programs in: Agriculture Trades Home economics Industry Teacher training
George-Reed	1929	Expanded agriculture and home economics programs
George-Reed	1934	Programs in: Agriculture Home economics Trades and industries
George-Deen	1936	Added distributive education as a program Continued agriculture, home economics, trades, and industries
George-Barden	1946	Added guidance Continued agriculture, home economics, trades and industries, and distributive occupations
Health Amendments	1956	Added health occupations
Manpower Development and Training	1962	Added technical occupations
Vocational Education	1963	Shifted emphasis from occupational categories to groups of people to be served (individuals with academic, socioeconomic, or other handicaps) Added business education (office occupations)
Vocational Education Amendments	1968	"Set-asides" for emotionally and physically disabled, academically and economically disadvantaged, dropouts, bilingual

Sources: Mobley and Barlow 1965; David 1980; and Taylor 1982.

or "gainful" or "occupational" home economics. However, the patterns of enrollment of girls and women in home economics, office occupations, health occupations, and distribution were based on stereotypes of what was "appropriate" for women to be involved in and reflected their involvement in the home and the provision of services to others in the marketplace.

The Vocational Education Act of 1963 (and its subsequent amendments) brought about major social-policy changes in the administration of vocational education and significant increases in federal monies to implement these changes. The central purposes of Public Law 88-210 were to provide vocational education for all persons and all occupations, except those identified as professional occupations or as requiring a baccalaureate or higher degree. The policy emphasis, however, shifted from defining occupational categories to defining groups of people to be served. Specific provisions were made for the special needs of those with academic, socioeconomic, or other handicaps that prevented them from succeeding in regular programs. The 1963 act also added the category of business and office occupations to vocational education. Federal funds had not previously been available for business education but the program had already been developed on a large scale by the public schools.

The Vocational Education Amendments of 1968 expanded vocational education to provide equal opportunities for enrollment of even larger segments of the population. Funding "set-asides" were provided for programs for the emotionally and physically disabled, programs for the academically and economically disadvantaged, consumer and homemaking courses in economically depressed areas, residential schools and work-study programs in areas with high dropout rates and youth unemployment rates, bilingual training and research, and experimental programs for the disadvantaged. In these amendments, however, there was still no mention of specific concerns for preparing women to compete in the labor market, beyond the provisions for the funding of programs in the traditionally female areas (occupational home economics, office occupations, health occupations, and distribution).

Policy Changes Related to Girls and Women

With the reemergence of the Women's Movement, beginning in the 1960s, concerns about education for girls and women began to change. Federal legislation was not enacted, however, until the 1970s. Title IX of the Education Amendments of 1972 prohibited discrimination on the basis of sex in any education program, including vocational education, that received federal assistance. Sex discrimination was defined as "any action that limits or denies a person or a group of persons opportunities, privileges, roles, or rewards on the basis of their sex" (U.S. Department of Health, Education, and Welfare [USDHEW] 1977, 53831). (The same definition was used for vocational education legislation that followed in 1976.)

Before the passage of Title IX, little attention was given to providing women with the whole range of occupational preparation offered by vocational education. Girls and women could be, and were, excluded from some vocational programs simply on the basis of their sex.

Regulations implementing Title IX were not issued until 1975. During the intervening three years, advocacy groups looked hard at where girls and women were being served in vocational education. As a result of such activity, Title II (Vocational Education) of the Education Amendments of 1976 addressed not only overcoming sex discrimination but also overcoming sex bias (behaviors resulting from the assumption that one sex is superior to the other) and overcoming sex stereotyping (attributing behaviors, abilities, interests, values, and roles to a person or group of persons on the basis of their sex). Title II provided a mandate for vocational education to develop programs to overcome sex bias, stereotyping, and discrimination and authorized the states to use federal monies to do so (USDHEW 1977).

Specific administrative requirements of Title II for state vocational education programs were:

- designating full-time personnel to eliminate sex discrimination and sex stereotyping in vocational education programs (expending not less than $50,000 from each state's basic grant funds to support the personnel)
- representing women's concerns on the state advisory council for vocational education
- including in the state's five-year plan for vocational education a detailed description of the policies and procedures that would be followed to insure equal access to programs by both women and men
- reviewing annual program plans for compliance with state policies regarding eradication of sex discrimination
- evaluating vocational education programs for service to women

Title II required that states expend funds for programs for (female or male) displaced homemakers, single heads of households who lacked adequate job skills, persons who were currently homemakers and part-time workers but who wished to secure a full-time job, and persons who were in jobs that have been traditionally considered appropriate for persons of their sex and wished to seek jobs in areas that traditionally have not been considered appropriate for persons of their sex. However, no dollar amounts were attached to this requirement and there was enormous variation among the states in the funding provided for these programs.

Title II also contained many optional provisions for expenditures related to women. States could use basic grant funds for support services for women and for day care services for children of students. States could use program improvement and supportive services funds for research, exemplary and innovative programs, and curriculum development related to overcoming sex stereotyping. States could support vocational guidance and counseling activities and in-service training to assist teachers and other staff in overcoming sex bias and stereotyping in vocational education programs. Again, there was enormous variation among the states in whether any funding was provided for these optional provisions.

With the election in 1980 of a president who appeared not to be concerned about the provision of a broad range of opportunities to women, many people within and outside vocational education felt that the "sex equity" provisions would be dropped from the federal vocational education legislation when it was reauthorized. Work on the new bill began in 1980, as Title II was due to expire in 1981. However, Title II was extended by Congress until the Carl D. Perkins Vocational Education Act of 1984 was passed. Because of the continuing work of advocacy groups and the work of the people in the sex equity coordinator positions, the sex equity provisions of Title II were strengthened in the Perkins Act.

The sex equity coordinator (one individual to work full time) provision is retained and each state that chooses to receive federal vocational education funding must reserve at least $60,000 to carry out the eight functions assigned to the coordinator. The use of the term "reserve" rather than the term "expend" allows the states a period of up to 27 months to use the funds for sex equity, as is true for the use of other funds under the Perkins Act (Vetter and Richey 1985). This means that new efforts under the Perkins Act may not have begun immediately when the funds became available.

Two funding set-asides are to be administered by the sex equity coordinator. The set-asides are 8.5 percent of the allotment (based on population) that the state receives from the federal legislation for the single-parent and homemaker program and 3.5 percent for sex equity program.

The Perkins Act went into effect on 1 July 1985. Programs for girls and women may be completely funded with federal monies (and most likely will be until states and local districts are willing to designate funds for such programs), although in vocational education in general, only about 10 percent of the funding is from the federal legislation. The other 90 percent of the funding for vocational education comes from state and local sources.

Enrollments

Vocational education has been operating under federal mandates to expand opportunities for girls and women since 1972 (Title IX) and specific programming mandates since 1977 (Title II). What have been the effects of these mandates on the enrollment of girls and women in vocational education programs?

Table 3-2 provides information on enrollments in occupationally specific vocational education instructional programs by service area. Enrollment figures are for the 1971–72 school year (predating Title IX) and for the 1981–82 school year (the most recent figures available). Students enrolled in consumer and homemaking programs and in industrial arts programs are excluded.

Table 3-2/Changes in Enrollment of Women in Vocational Education, Occupationally Specific Programs from 1971 to 1981

| | 1971–72[a] | | 1981–82[b] | | 1971–81[c] |
| | Women Enrolled | Percent Women | Women Enrolled | Percent Women | PERCENT + OR − |
PROGRAM					
AGRICULTURE	48,163	5.4	82,610	21.7	+16.3
Agricultural production	22,581	4.0	34,194	18.5	+14.5
Agricultural supplies/ services	1,172	4.8	4,562	22.4	+17.6
Agricultural mechanics	1,408	1.1	3,203	5.3	+ 4.2
Agricultural products	736	7.8	829	20.6	+12.8
Horticulture	15,157	26.9	29,142	43.9	+17.0
Natural resources	1,863	7.6	2,336	23.5	+15.9
Forestry	527	2.9	2,973	17.0	+14.1
Other agricultural programs	4,719	6.6	5,371	31.5	+24.9
TECHNICAL	33,007	9.8	93,384	22.3	+12.5
Architectural technology	1,151	8.1	5,174	22.1	+14.0
Automotive technology	60	0.8	738	5.1	+ 4.3
Civil technology	799	4.0	2,168	13.8	+ 9.8
Electrical technology	222	1.4	862	7.0	+ 5.6
Electronics technology	1,350	2.1	11,814	11.7	+ 9.6
Environmental control technology	210	4.5	491	8.7	+ 4.2
Industrial technology	1,143	9.8	2,512	15.6	+ 5.8
Mechanical technology	905	3.4	2,606	11.9	+ 8.5
Scientific data processing	5,397	31.8	11,756	55.7	+23.9
Commercial pilot training	389	6.6	371	18.8	+12.2
Fire and safety technology	78	0.9	1,293	8.1	+ 7.2
Police science technology	4,180	9.5	17,942	30.7	+21.2
Water and waste water technology	188	13.3	573	14.8	+ 1.5
Other technology	16,935	17.7	34,084	33.5	+15.8
TRADE AND INDUSTRY	279,510	11.7	296,702	18.5	+ 6.8
Air conditioning	2,664	3.9	1,568	3.3	− 0.6
Appliance repair	507	2.9	634	6.6	+ 3.7
Auto body and fender repair	1,082	1.9	1,943	3.1	+ 1.2
Auto mechanics	5,299	2.3	11,012	5.1	+ 2.8
Other automotive	1,640	4.1	1,184	8.7	+ 4.6

Program	1971–72[a]		1981–82[b]		1971–81[c]
	Women Enrolled	Percent Women	Women Enrolled	Percent Women	Percent + or −
Aviation occupations	2,187	6.9	2,063	10.8	+ 3.9
Commercial art occupations	15,766	50.1	20,725	57.5	+ 7.4
Commercial photography occupations	3,756	25.7	7,983	44.1	+18.4
Carpentry	1,451	1.5	4,302	5.2	+ 3.7
Electricity	590	1.0	900	3.6	+ 2.6
Masonry	236	0.8	652	2.9	+ 2.1
Plumbing/pipe fitting	34	0.1	461	2.9	+ 2.8
Other construction	1,566	2.0	4,907	7.4	+ 5.4
Custodial services	2,547	15.7	1,115	15.8	+ 0.1
Diesel mechanic	185	1.4	834	3.3	+ 1.9
Drafting occupations	6,892	5.4	20,940	20.6	+15.2
Electrical occupations	909	1.1	1,846	5.7	+ 4.6
Electronic occupations	4,412	4.5	11,833	12.5	+ 8.0
Foremanship, supervision, and management development	22,562	18.7	4,906	40.4	+21.7
Graphic arts occupations	8,290	12.1	23,976	39.1	+27.0
Instrument maintenance and repair	107	3.5	485	17.9	+14.4
Maritime occupations	202	3.0	321	10.4	+ 7.4
Metalworking occupations	3,081	1.1	11,212	4.7	+ 3.6
Metallurgy occupations	43	0.8	48	8.7	+ 7.9
Cosmetology	45,870	94.0	70,092	94.1	+ 0.1
Other personal services	11,300	65.2	6,923	61.7	− 3.5
Plastics occupations	1,153	22.5	250	10.8	−11.7
Fireman training	3,321	2.1	1,502	9.2	+ 7.1
Law enforcement training	5,943	7.9	12,589	24.4	+16.5
Other public services	22,483	38.4	9,462	57.2	+18.8
Quantity food occupations	14,094	37.6	15,343	47.4	+ 9.8
Refrigeration	814	7.3	348	10.3	+ 3.0
Small engine repair	605	2.3	804	3.8	+ 1.5
Stationary energy sources occupations	274	3.7	186	10.0	+ 6.3
Textile products	42,210	82.4	7,913	70.7	−11.7
Upholstering	7,605	46.0	3,268	38.9	− 7.1
Woodworking	5,373	6.3	2,387	9.2	+ 2.9
Other trade and industry	32,457	18.6	29,785	28.1	+ 9.5

Table 3-2/Continued

	1971–72[a]		1981–82[b]		1971–81[c]
PROGRAM	*Women Enrolled*	*Percent Women*	*Women Enrolled*	*Percent Women*	PERCENT + OR −
MARKETING AND DISTRIBUTION	290,028	45.3	290,744	57.4	+12.1
Advertising services	7,933	45.2	10,108	59.5	+14.3
Apparel/accessories	16,603	67.0	20,855	84.9	+17.9
Automotive	1,391	14.4	798	13.7	− 0.7
Finance and credit	11,828	42.2	23,089	72.5	+30.3
Floristry	3,616	69.1	5,180	80.8	+11.7
Food distribution	10,899	37.5	11,968	44.1	+ 6.6
Food services	21,139	61.9	18,304	58.5	− 3.4
General merchandise	104,582	51.1	95,079	59.8	+ 8.7
Hardware and building materials	1,276	22.3	671	23.2	+ 0.9
Home furnishings	3,516	59.9	1,497	60.4	+ 0.5
Hotel and lodgings	5,218	41.1	5,007	47.2	+ 6.1
Industrial marketing	2,501	29.0	8,244	46.6	+17.6
Insurance	3,551	27.0	2,586	50.3	+23.3
Personal services	9,161	51.4	3,919	66.6	+15.2
Real estate	26,165	31.9	24,067	45.7	+13.8
Recreation/tourism	6,108	47.8	11,051	65.7	+17.9
Transportation	4,197	33.7	6,496	51.3	+17.6
Other distribution	50,344	43.4	41,825	54.8	+11.4
HEALTH OCCUPATIONS	285,241	84.7	380,229	84.8	+ 0.1
Dental assisting	14,406	93.1	16,364	95.5	+ 2.4
Dental hygiene	4,584	96.4	6,167	96.4	0.0
Dental laboratory technician	1,221	41.4	1,836	53.5	+12.1
Medical laboratory assistant	8,176	77.7	5,568	80.1	+ 2.4
Other medical laboratory technicians	2,676	84.8	3,987	75.6	− 9.2
Nurse, associate degree	58,474	90.1	93,283	91.2	+ 1.1
Practical (vocational) nurse	78,302	94.5	72,678	94.2	− 0.3
Nursing assistant	53,308	90.5	48,616	89.7	− 0.8
Rehabilitation therapy	2,267	75.4	5,402	83.9	+ 8.5
Radiologic technology (X-ray)	3,543	61.4	7,749	73.7	+12.3
Mental health technician	2,880	73.9	6,258	78.7	+ 4.8
Inhalation therapy technician	3,206	55.7	6,953	66.8	+11.1
Medical assistant	9,539	92.4	18,579	92.0	− 0.4

PROGRAM	1971–72[a]		1981–82[b]		1971–81[c]
	Women Enrolled	Percent Women	Women Enrolled	Percent Women	PERCENT + OR −
Medical emergency technician	—	—	8,743	36.1	—
Other health occupations	42,659	66.1	78,046	81.3	+15.2
HOME ECONOMICS (OCCUPATIONAL)	241,239	86.1	188,061	79.6	− 6.5
Care and guidance of children	71,586	92.8	91,426	92.4	− 0.4
Clothing management, production, services	56,818	95.5	22,483	89.6	− 5.9
Food management, production, services	58,359	75.2	47,772	62.0	−13.2
Home furnishings, equipment, services	18,698	87.9	6,528	80.7	− 7.2
Institutional and home management	7,193	89.2	5,194	69.7	−19.5
Other home economics occupations	28,585	78.0	14,658	75.5	− 2.5
OFFICE OCCUPATIONS	1,797,205	76.4	1,342,527	73.8	− 2.6
Accounting and computing	210,255	59.8	244,193	68.8	+ 9.0
Business data processing systems	76,763	49.0	180,250	57.1	+ 8.1
Filing/general office	327,454	82.2	238,732	82.4	+ 0.2
Information communication occupations	17,241	72.4	13,175	72.7	+ 0.3
Materials support	5,324	51.7	2,287	47.3	− 4.4
Personnel training	8,671	63.3	8,444	65.1	+ 1.8
Stenographer/secretary	528,863	96.0	322,925	93.5	− 2.5
Supervisory and administrative management	21,481	27.6	80,551	53.3	+25.7
Typing	500,517	79.6	192,926	80.5	+ 0.9
Other office occupations	100,636	71.2	59,044	68.2	− 3.0

[a] Information from USDHEW 1973. Figures include high school (grades 9–12) and postsecondary enrollments.
[b] Figures and percentages calculated from enrollment figures in USED 1984, Table 1206. 525,294 "Status Unknown" students were excluded from the calculations. Figures include high school (grades 11–12) and postsecondary enrollments.
[c] These percentages must be interpreted with extreme caution. The National Center for Education Statistics has indicated that the accuracy of the figures for their tables is dependent on the reporting of the states and inaccuracies in the reporting from only one state can cause major changes in the total figures. Additionally, ninth and tenth graders are included in the 1971–72 data and are not included in the 1981–82 data, so that the data bases are not the same.

The information in Table 3-2 provides an indication of the extent of change in the enrollment patterns of girls and women. However, because it is difficult to collect statistics on vocational education enrollments, there are some caveats. Conclusions based on the data must be considered somewhat tentative, and the 10-year percentage of change must be interpreted with extreme caution.

Procedures for collecting enrollment data have changed over the 10-year time span. The 1971–72 figures include grades 9–12 and postsecondary enrollments. The 1981–82 figures are for grades 11–12 and postsecondary enrollments. Approximately 525,000 students whose sex was not reported are excluded from the table.

There are also problems with the accuracy of enrollment data. The National Center for Education Statistics (NCES) asks states to ask school districts reporting for the Vocational Education Data System (VEDS) to count each student enrolled in vocational education only once, even though the student may be taking more than one vocational course or program. However, schools do not necessarily follow this procedure. As a result, some students may be counted in more than one place in the national aggregations. In addition, as NCES points out, VEDS data are dependent on the reporting of the states, and inaccuracies in the reporting of only one state can cause major changes in the total figures (Vetter and Hickey 1985).

Given these caveats, what can be tentatively said about the progress in broadening opportunities for girls and women in vocational education?

In the traditionally male programs of agriculture, technical, and trade and industry, both the numbers and the percentages of students who are women have increased. Agriculture showed the highest overall percentage increase in female enrollments. The largest number of women enrollees in agriculture is not in the horticulture programs, as is sometimes suggested, but in agricultural production programs. These programs typically lead to employment on farms or with farm-related businesses. More recent data (1984) from 1,786 area vocational centers showed that 32.1 percent of agriculture students were women (PEER [Project on Equal Educational Rights] 1986). (The data used in the PEER study do not include information from vocational high schools and comprehensive high schools. It is likely that enrollments of women have also increased in these schools; however, no data are currently available to confirm this.)

The two technical programs that showed the largest increases in enrollment of women are scientific data processing—possibly because of the program's close relationship to office occupations—and police science technology. The growth of female enrollments in police science technology is perhaps a result of the growth of affirmative action programs in the public sector. The 1984 data from area vocational schools showed that 42.6 percent of students in protective services were women (PEER 1986). Programs in the technical area are concentrated at the postsecondary level; only 7 percent of technical students are enrolled in high school programs.

The increased enrollment of women in the traditionally male trade and industry area is primarily accounted for by cosmetology (a traditionally female program), where the numbers but not the percentage of women enrolled increased; commercial photography; drafting; graphic arts; and law enforcement programs. Additionally, there are over 10,000 girls and women enrolled in auto mechanics, commercial art, electronics, metalworking, and quantity food occupations. Although the total number of students enrolled in foremanship (*sic*), supervision, and management has apparently decreased considerably, women's share of the enrollment has increased more than 20 percent. The national data show that women are still only a very small percentage of students in craft and repair occupations. PEER (1986) reported that 1984 enrollments at area vocational schools remained low for women in the construction trades (4.1 percent) and in mechanics and repairers programs (4.1 percent).

In marketing and distributive education, which has traditionally had sex-balanced enrollments, the number of women enrolled remains about the same, but the percentage of women has increased. (This may be the result of changes in the data collection procedure.) Approximately one-third of the women in marketing and distributive education continue to be enrolled in one program, general merchandise, which typically leads to retail sales positions.

The number of women enrolled in traditionally female health occupations has increased, but their share of the total has remained steady at 85 percent. (Because 80 percent of the health occupations programs are at the postsecondary level, the elimination of ninth and tenth graders in the data collection procedure probably has not had much effect on the figures.) With the exception of two programs, dental laboratory technician and medical emergency technician, all of the programs have over 70 percent enrollment of women.

Both occupational home economics and office occupations, the other two traditionally female programs, show an increase in male student enrollment. The apparent change could be a result of the change in data collection procedures, but it is also likely that efforts to recruit nontraditional students are responsible for the changes.

The most noteworthy advance for women within office occupations is in supervisory and administrative management. Over 50 percent of the students now enrolled in this program are women; in 1971, only about 25 percent of the students were women. Over the 10-year period from 1971–72 to 1981–82, the concentration of women vocational education students in office occupations decreased from 60 percent to 48 percent (see Table 3-3). Although women are still highly concentrated (and segregated) in clerical training programs, this change indicates that women are beginning to take advantage of the broad range of options available to them through vocational education.

Now that the beginnings of changes in enrollment patterns of girls and

Table 3-3/Distribution of Female Students in Vocational Education Service Areas

PROGRAM	1971–72[a] PERCENT	1981–82[b] PERCENT
Agriculture	1.6	3.2
Distribution	9.8	11.3
Health occupations	9.6	14.7
Home economics (occupational)	8.1	7.3
Office occupations	60.4	48.4
Technical	1.1	3.6
Trade and industrial	9.4	11.5
Total	100.0	100.0

[a] Percentages calculated from enrollment figures in USDHEW 1973.
[b] Percentages calculated from figures in USED 1984, Table 1206.

women in vocational education programs can be seen, what can be said about the female nontraditional students in vocational education programs?

Female Nontraditional Students

What are the reasons that women enroll in nontraditional vocational education programs? Kane and Frazee (1978) surveyed over 1,000 women enrolled in nontraditional high school vocational education programs across the country. They found that the most important reason stated by the high school women for enrolling in the nontraditional program was that they were interested in the program. The second most often given reason for enrolling in a nontraditional program was that the women felt that they had the ability to do the work that the program required. The third most important reason given for enrolling in a nontraditional program was that the earnings that could be obtained from the nontraditional occupation that the program would prepare them for would be higher than the amount they could earn in a traditional occupation (this reason was especially important for black women and low-income women).

The high school women indicated that their parents were the most influential people in determining their decision to enroll in nontraditional programs. Women friends were the next most influential. School personnel were less influential, with counselors being cited more often than teachers. When teachers were mentioned, they tended to be the men who taught the nontraditional vocational education courses.

Houser and Garvey (1985), in studying California women in vocational education programs, found that nontraditional students differed from traditional students primarily in the support they received from female friends and family members. Additionally, compared to a group of students who had considered nontraditional programs, but then enrolled in traditional programs, the nontraditional students reported more encouragement from school personnel.

Kane and Frazee (1978) found that nontraditional students were more likely to be enrolled in vocational education programs in metropolitan areas and that a greater proportion of black women were enrolled in the nontraditional programs. PEER (1986) confirmed this finding in reporting on 1984 data from area vocational centers. In transportation programs, where women are 14 percent of the students, Asian American women were 31 percent of Asian American enrollees, and black women were 25 percent of black enrollees. Asian American, black, and Hispanic women were 21.4 percent, 27 percent, and 28 percent of Asian American, black, and Hispanic students in engineering programs where 13.7 percent of the students were women. In mechanics and repairers programs, where only 4 percent of the students were women, Asian American women were 10.6 percent of Asian American students, black women were 5.2 percent of black students, and Hispanic women were 4.7 percent of Hispanic students. The authors pointed out that "while women of all racial and ethnic groups and men of color remain seriously underrepresented in vocational training leading to higher-paying jobs, PEER is encouraged to note that women of color are leading the way into these fields" (p. 4).

Sixty-five percent of the female students in nontraditional high school vocational education programs studied by Kane and Frazee (1978) reported that they had encountered problems in their schooling. The largest single problem identified by the students was that of harassment by their male classmates. Fewer problems were reported as being related to the teachers. The problem of harassment was much diminished for the women who were in classes where there were at least four women in the class. This finding has obvious implications for policies of class assignment. When few women are enrolling in a nontraditional program, it would be helpful to assign them to the same class. Where only one or two women are enrolling in a program, support groups for women in different programs could be helpful. Teachers must be made responsible for combatting the "turfism" that is being expressed by the traditional male students. When the women are no longer a novelty in the class, as by now is the situation in some nontraditional programs, this problem will fade, because the male students will expect the women to be there.

This has occurred in the New York City high schools. Schulzinger and Syron (1984) report:

Many female students enrolled in predominantly male vocational schools and programs have noticed a significant reduction in discriminatory treatment and harassment by teachers and students. . . . It appears that the reduction in discriminatory treatment and harassment is the result of two major factors: (1) the increased number of female students in some male schools or (2) the presence of a principal who has taken a leadership role to improve the school environment for young women. (pp. 49–50)

Outcomes

What are the outcomes of vocational education? Mertens (1981) has remarked, "The effects from participation in vocational education are probably the most debated policy issue questions relevant to vocational education" (p. 1). Fitzgerald (1985) points out:

Even a cursory review of the literature reveals lively debate concerning the appropriate outcome criteria (earnings, status, unemployment status, advancement versus or in addition to student satisfaction, employer satisfaction, additional education completed, attainment of basic skills, and so forth); the appropriate comparison group (academic graduates, general curriculum graduates, nongraduates); and even the appropriate procedures for identifying a vocational education student for further study (self-report, administrator report, or curriculum transcript). (p. 14)

It is important to point out that tabulations of the NLS (National Longitudinal Surveys) New Youth Cohort data (Campbell 1986) indicate that 60 percent of vocational graduates do go on to postsecondary education: 30 percent to four-year colleges, 13 percent to two-year colleges, and 17 percent to technical schools. (In comparison, of the high school graduates from academic programs, 70 percent went to four-year colleges, 11 percent to two-year colleges, and 6 percent to technical schools. Of the graduates from the general curriculum, 35 percent went on to four-year colleges, 12 percent to two-year colleges, and 13 percent to technical schools.) Thus, there is a better than even chance that one of the outcomes of a high school vocational education program is that the graduates will go on to further education. Although the figures cited above include both men and women, it is likely, given the current enrollment trends, that more of the women than of the men are going on to postsecondary education.

Fitzgerald (1985) reports that vocational education students appear satisfied with their training and seem to feel good about themselves. However, in light of the Kane and Frazee findings about the problems faced by the women enrolled in nontraditional programs it may be that these students find less satisfaction in some aspects of their training.

Does vocational education help to retain potential dropouts in school? Fitzgerald finds the evidence unclear on this point. Lotto (1986) indicates that it seems likely but has not been clearly demonstrated. Given that pregnancy is one of the most common causes of women dropping out of high school, the designation of funds through the Perkins Act for single-parent and homemaker programs will assist in enabling pregnant young women and mothers to complete their high school education. Ferguson and Reed (1987) report that the Ohio vocational home economics program designed to help pregnant students and young parents graduate from high school has enabled 88 percent of the students to graduate or continue to be enrolled. This is a quite different picture from the national figures that indicate that 80 percent of teenage mothers drop out of high school.

There appear to be no differences in unemployment rates between vocational and nonvocational high school graduates (Fitzgerald 1985). Desy, Campbell, and Gardner (1984) reported that "vocational education has a positive, if moderate influence on employment" (p. 39). They attributed this influence to the school-supervised employment part of most high school vocational programs. However, as pointed out by Lotto (1986), gender, ability, ethnicity, and region of the country make a greater difference in a person's rate of employment than does high school course of study. It is important to remember that unemployment rates are higher for women than for men and that more women than men are out of the labor force.

Well over 50 percent of secondary vocational education graduates find employment in areas related to their vocational training (Mertens et al. 1980) and those who do enter training-related employment have higher earnings than otherwise comparable graduates of the academic and general curricula (Gardner 1984). However, despite some of the changes reported in the enrollment figures earlier in this paper, too many female vocational education graduates work in the office occupations area where low-paying positions abound. Campbell et al. (1986) summarize the situation as follows:

To what extent this results from subtle discrimination, from inadequate counseling and/or from the culturally conditioned choices that young women make cannot be ascertained from the data, but there is not much question about its effect. The training that women get channels them into lower paying jobs relative to those of men. (P. 103)

Several national database studies (using class of 1972 and NLS-Labor Market Experience data sets) have shown significantly higher earnings (hourly and weekly) for women who took vocational courses in the business/office area when compared to other women high school graduates in the general curriculum (Grasso and Shea 1979; Meyer 1981; Gustman and Steinmeier 1981; Mertens and Gardner 1981). However, women who took traditional home economics courses were found to be at a disadvantage in earnings, compared to general curriculum graduates (Meyer 1981).

A study of one community followed the high school graduating class of 1969 (Olszewski 1983). Since this class predated Title IX, the community still had "Boy's Trade" and "Girl's Trade" high schools. The vocational courses of study offered to the young women were the traditional ones: home economics and cosmetology. Entry jobs (obtained between 1969 and 1971) were very different for the "vocational" students (N = 26) compared to the female students from the academic curriculum (N = 39), the business curriculum (N = 33), and the general curriculum (N = 17). A majority of the general, business, and academic graduates were all employed in clerical occupations reflecting the limited opportunities open to women in the labor market at that time. However, 78 percent of the women in cosmetology and in the foods or clothing specializations in home economics entered the labor market as hairdressers, cooks, or sewers. The other students in those programs became either clerical workers, operatives, or service workers. The women in the general home economics program had the most difficulty in finding viable employment. Although a few managed to find jobs as teacher's aides or health aides, most accepted jobs as factory assemblers or retail clerks. Thus, for the most part, the entry employment experiences of the vocational graduates were closely associated with the training they had received prior to labor market entry. Vocational and business graduates did not receive higher entry wages compared to general and academic graduates.

Eight years after high school, 61 percent of the business curriculum women were still working, compared to 46 percent of the vocational curriculum women, 47 percent of the general curriculum women, and 44 percent of the academic women. The business curriculum graduates who were still working were primarily employed (80 percent) in clerical jobs in 1977, with 67 percent of them being secretaries or typists. Of the cosmetology graduates, all of those who had both an entry and a final job were employed as hairdressers during both time periods. The female graduates of the home economics programs showed a shift away from operative and sales occupations and a movement toward clerical occupations.

Olszewski (1983) found that enrollment in the traditional vocational curriculum (cosmetology or home economics) during high school had a negative impact on the wages women received after eight years in the labor market, when compared to the earnings of business, academic, and general curriculum graduates.

With the exception of the Olszewski study, these outcome findings are based on analyses of national longitudinal databases and are, for the most part, based on women who were enrolled in traditionally female vocational education programs. There typically are not enough women with vocational education in the traditionally male programs in the national databases to conduct analyses on the outcomes of such training.

There is one study of women and men enrolled in nontraditional programs in Oklahoma where Smith (1982) found that only 11.3 percent of the women exiting (either as dropouts or as graduates) nontraditional programs were employed in jobs related to their training, whereas 23.1 percent of the men exiting nontraditional vocational programs were employed in jobs related to their training. Women exiting from traditional programs were almost three times more likely than women exiting from nontraditional programs to be employed in the field for which they had trained (Smith 1982). However, the women who were working in nontraditional occupations earned significantly higher wages than women employed in traditional female occupations, although they earned significantly lower wages than men employed in those occupations. Smith found that negative effects (unemployment, working in jobs unrelated to training) were least pronounced for female nontraditional students trained in urban areas, those trained in area vo-tech schools, and those over 24 years of age.

Conclusions and Policy Implications

The strong federal legislative mandate in the Perkins Act may not be sufficient to provide the opportunities young women need to obtain vocational education preparation for nontraditional occupations, but it is imperative that such legislation remain in place. Nothing would have changed, in terms of vocational education opportunities for women, without the passage of Title IX and the two federal vocational education acts that included provisions aimed at overcoming sex discrimination, bias, and stereotyping. When it was believed that the sex equity provisions would be dropped from the federal legislation (during the reauthorization process that led to the Perkins Act), many states and local education agencies simply did not expend any further effort to encourage young women to enroll in nontraditional vocational education programs. However, once the Perkins Act was in place, it again became important to encourage nontraditional enrollments and to provide programs specifically for single parents and homemakers (see Miller, Chapter 5, for examples of programs under Perkins).

Federal funding will continue to be needed for implementation of the sex equity provisions in vocational education until all states and local education agencies are willing to designate funds for such programs. The federal funds are especially important for the states and school districts that do not have the tax base to generate the funds needed for such efforts.

Yet, Reskin and Hartmann (1986), while indicating that sex segregation across the major vocational program areas has declined significantly, conclude that a legislative mandate coupled with federal money is not enough. This is suggested by the differential success of various states in implementing the 1976 Vocational Education Amendments. They point out that active monitoring of schools, particularly the administration of pre- and in-service courses for teachers and counselors, seems to be important. "Vocational educators cannot assume that opening traditionally male programs to female students will neutralize family and peer group pressures; rather, affirmative programs will be necessary to attract women to these programs" (Reskin and Hartmann 1986, 112).

Reskin and Hartmann point out as well that the 10 percent decline in the sex segregation index during the 1970s was most pronounced among younger workers. They further point out that it is likely that if more women were trained for occupations that men currently dominate, their representation in such occupations would increase. This is encouraging to those who are concerned with encouraging women at the high school level to consider a broad range of options.

State legislation similar to Title IX and the Perkins Act can be very helpful in providing opportunities for young women to obtain the vocational education they need to pursue higher-paying occupations. Additionally, experimentation with state policies, such as Michigan's system for rewarding local schools for nontraditional enrollments (see Giese, Chapter 13), should be encouraged.

Local educational policies can assist young women in enrolling in nontraditional vocational education programs. Programming should focus on the interests and abilities of the young women and the rewards of working in the nontraditional occupations. Parents of the young women should be alerted to the benefits that their daughters can receive from such education.

School policies can place female nontraditional students in classes together, so that one female student will not be the possible subject of harassment by the male students. If, to begin with, very few women enroll in the nontraditional programs, support groups can be set up across the vocational programs. Administrators and teachers can prevent harassment of female nontraditional students. After it has become the norm that women are enrolled across all vocational education programs, "turf" will have been established and students will probably assume that "that's the way it's supposed to be" just as students now sometimes believe that women should not be in some vocational education programs.

Research by the League of Women Voters Education Fund (Sherman 1982) has documented a "passing the buck" syndrome regarding opportunities for girls and women in vocational education. Interviews conducted with students, families, educators, and employers during a five-state monitoring project indicated that each group of respondents tended to blame other groups for creating barriers to nontraditional enrollments. For example, counselors blamed peers and parents; teachers blamed counselors, administrators, and members of the business community, and so on. Thus, for opportunities for women in vocational education to continue to expand, school professionals will have to take the responsibility to provide the opportunities.

Given the data on the importance of obtaining employment in a training-related job, placement services are a must if young women are to derive earnings benefits from their high school educations. According to Reskin and Hartmann (1986), for training to effectively increase earnings, programs must have placement provisions, provide a broad base of support for women by setting up orientation programs, and provide connections with potential employers. Whether young women go on to postsecondary education or directly to work, such assistance is needed.

State governments have taken the lead in the "comparable worth" effort to assist women in traditional occupations to obtain the rewards that their education and job duties should provide them with. This is important because the Bureau of Labor Statistics (Carey 1981) projects substantial growth in jobs in many heavily and historically female occupational categories, such as professional and practical nurses, nursing aides, secretaries, bookkeepers, typists, and waitresses/waiters. Reskin and Hartmann point out that if the proportions of these occupations that are female remain approximately constant, their growth will represent a demand for an additional 3.3 million female workers.

Finally, it needs to be said that some progress has been made in the vocational education option for women. However, to continue the progress, all of us (social scientists, educators, employers, students, parents) need to continue to support federal, state, and local efforts and initiatives to provide the best possible options to women.

References

Campbell, Paul B. 1986. "Comment." *Journal of Vocational Education Research*: 95–96.

Campbell, Paul B.; Karen S. Basinger; Mary Beth Dauner; and Marie A. Parks. 1986. *Outcomes of Vocational Education for Women, Minorities, the Handicapped, and the Poor*. Columbus: The National Center for Research in Vocational Education, The Ohio State University.

Campbell, Paul B.; Mollie N. Orth; and Patricia Seitz. 1981. *Patterns of Participation in Secondary Vocational Education*. Columbus: The National Center for Research in Vocational Education, The Ohio State University.

Carey, Max L. 1981. "Occupational Employment Growth Through 1990." *Monthly Labor Review* 104 (August): 42–55.

David, Henry. 1980. *The Vocational Education Study: The Interim Report*. ERIC Document Reproduction Service no. ED 195 743. Washington, D.C.: National Institute of Education.

Desy, Jeanne; Paul B. Campbell; and John A. Gardner. 1984. *High School Vocational Education Experiences: In School and in the Labor Market*. Columbus: The National Center for Research in Vocational Education, The Ohio State University.

Ferguson, Judy, and Joan Reed. 1987. "Programs for Teenaged Parents." *Vocational Education Journal* 62 (March): 40.

Fitzgerald, Louise F. 1985. *Education and Work: The Essential Tension.* Columbus: ERIC Clearinghouse on Adult, Career, and Vocational Education, The National Center for Research in Vocational Education, The Ohio State University.

Frantz, Nevin R., Jr.; Deborah Strickland; and Donald Elson. 1986. *High School Graduation Requirements and Enrollment Patterns in High School Vocational Education Programs in the United States.* Blacksburg, Va.: Division of Vocational and Technical Education, Virginia Polytechnic Institute and State University.

Gardner, John A. 1984. *Influences of High School Curriculum on Determinants of Labor Market Experiences.* Paper presented at the annual meeting of the American Educational Research Association, New Orleans.

Grasso, John T., and John R. Shea. 1979. *Vocational Education and Training: Impact on Youth.* Berkeley: The Carnegie Council on Policy Studies in Higher Education.

Gustman, Alan L., and Thomas L. Steinmeier. 1981. *The Relationship Between Vocational Training in High School and Economic Outcomes.* Cambridge, Mass.: National Bureau of Economic Research.

Houser, Betsy Bosak, and Chris Garvey. 1985. "Factors That Affect Nontraditional Vocational Enrollment Among Women." *Psychology of Women Quarterly* 9 (March): 105–17.

Kane, Roslyn D., and Pamela E. Frazee. 1978. *Women in Nontraditional Vocational Education in Secondary Schools.* Arlington, Va.: Rj Associates, Inc.

Lotto, Linda S. 1986. "Expectations and Outcomes of Vocational Education: Match or Mismatch." *Journal of Vocational Education Research* 11 (Winter): 41–60.

Mertens, Donna M. 1981. *The Effects of Vocational Education on Participants.* ERIC Document Reproduction Service no. ED 198 398. Paper presented at the annual meeting of the American Educational Research Association, Los Angeles.

Mertens, Donna M., and John A. Gardner. 1981. *Vocational Education and the Younger Adult Worker.* Columbus: The National Center for Research in Vocational Education, The Ohio State University.

Mertens, Donna M.; Douglas McElwain; Gonzalo Garcia; and Mark Whitmore. 1982. *The Effects of Participating in Vocational Education: Summary of Studies Since 1968.* Columbus: The National Center for Research in Vocational Education, The Ohio State University.

Meyer, Robert H. 1981. *An Economic Analysis of High School Vocational Education: IV. The Labor Market Effects of Vocational Education.* Washington, D.C.: The Urban Institute.

Mobley, Mayor D., and Melvin L. Barlow. 1965. "Impact of Federal Legislation and Policies upon Vocational Education." In Melvin L. Barlow, ed., *Vocational Education: The 64th Yearbook of the National Society for the Study of Education,* pp. 186–202. Chicago: University of Chicago Press.

Olszewski, Donna E. 1983. "Educational Preparation and Career Development in a Local Labor Market." *Dissertation Abstracts International* 44: 1532A. University Microfilms no. DA8320006.

PEER [Project on Equal Education Rights]. 1986. *The 1986 PEER Report Card: A State-by-State Survey of the Status of Women and Girls in America's Schools.* Policy Paper no. 5. Washington, D.C.: PEER.

Reskin, Barbara F., and Heidi I. Hartmann, eds. 1986. *Women's Work, Men's Work: Sex Segregation on the Job.* Washington, D.C.: National Academy Press.

Schulzinger, Rhoda, and Lisa Syron. 1984. *Inch by Inch: A Report on Equal Opportunity for Young Women in New York City's Vocational High Schools.* New York: Center for Public Advocacy Research, Inc.

Sherman, Ruth. 1982. *Achieving Sex Equity in Vocational Education: A Crack in the Wall.* Washington, D.C.: League of Women Voters' Education Fund.

Smith, Paula A. 1982. *The Labor Force Behavior of Sex Nontraditional Vocational Students: A Follow-up Assessment of Training for Nontraditional Occupations.* Stillwater: Office of Business and Economics Research, College of Business Administration, Oklahoma State University.

Taylor, Robert E. 1982. *S.v.* "vocational education." In Harold E. Mitzel, John Hardin Best, and William Rabinowitz, eds., *Encyclopedia of Education Research,* 5th ed. New York: Macmillan.

U.S. Department of Education. 1984. Unpublished data, Tables 1206, 1221. National Center for Education Statistics, Vocational Education Data System, Washington, D.C., 4 June.

U.S. Department of Health, Education, and Welfare. Office of Education. Bureau of Adult, Vocational, and Technical Education. Division of Vocational and Technical Education. 1973. *Summary Data Vocational Education Fiscal Year 1972.* Washington, D.C.

————. Office of Education. 1977. "Vocational Education, State Programs and Commissioner's Discretionary Programs." *Federal Register* 42 (Monday, 3 October): 53822–91.

————. Office of Vocational and Adult Education. 1985. "State Vocational Education Program and Secretary's Discretionary Programs of Vocational Education; Final Regulations." *Federal Register* 50 (Friday, 16 August): 33226–305.

Vetter, Louise. 1985. "Stability and Change in the Enrollment of Girls and Young Women in Vocational Education: 1971–1980." *Youth & Society* 16 (March): 335–56.

Vetter, Louise, and Delina R. Hickey. 1985. "Where the Women Are Enrolled." *Vocational Education Journal* 60 (October): 26–29.

Vetter, Louise, and Marsha L. Richey. 1985. *Update: A Guide for Vocational Education Sex Equity Personnel.* Columbus: The National Center for Research in Vocational Education, The Ohio State University.

4/Job Training Opportunities for Women in the U.S. Armed Forces

M. C. Devilbiss

The decision to enter a particular occupation has many accompanying consequences. Choosing an occupation means choosing the training that will be necessary to prepare for that occupation, the opportunities that that occupation affords, and the lifestyle that it represents. These consequences are especially evident when a young person chooses the military as a career. Military service is different from other kinds of training programs and employment opportunities because, upon enlistment, each servicemember accepts a voluntary and conscious personal risk of injury or even death in the line of duty.

OATH OF ENLISTMENT

I, ——————— , do solemnly swear (or affirm) that I will support and defend the Constitution of the United States against all enemies, foreign and domestic; that I will bear true faith and allegiance to the same; and that I will obey the orders of the President of the United States and the orders of the officers appointed over me, according to regulations and the Uniformed Code of Military Justice. So help me God. (Title 10, *United States Code*, Section 502)

Since the 1970s, young women have been entering the U.S. armed forces in ever greater numbers. "The percentage of women in the military has [also] increased dramatically, from less than 2 percent at the beginning of the All Volunteer Force in 1973 to 8 percent in 1980. By 1987, the percentage of women in the military had risen to 10.2 percent" (Becraft 1988, 2). During this time, additional career fields and related training opportunities were opened to women.

There are many different types of jobs in the armed forces. The Department of Defense identifies approximately 2,000 separate military job special-

114

ties, which it classifies into ten major occupational areas, using its standard numbering system (U.S. Department of Defense 1986):[1]

0. Infantry, gun crew, and seamanship
   a. Infantry
   b. Armor and amphibian
   c. Combat engineer
   d. Artillery/gunnery
   e. Air crew
   f. Seaman
   g. Installation security
1. Electronic equipment repair
   a. Radio/radar
   b. Fire control electronic system (nonmissile)
   c. Missile guidance, control, and checkout
   d. Sonar equipment
   e. Nuclear weapons equipment
   f. Computers
   g. Teletype and cryptographic equipment
   h. Other electronic equipment
2. Communications and intelligence
   a. Radio and radio code
   b. Sonar
   c. Radar and air traffic control
   d. Signal intelligence/electronic warfare
   e. Intelligence
   f. Combat operations control
   g. Communications center operations
3. Medical and dental
   a. Medical care
   b. Technical medical service
   c. Related medical services
   d. Dental care
4. Technical specialist
   a. Photography
   b. Mapping, surveying, drafting, and illustrating
   c. Meteorology
   d. Ordnance disposal and diving
   e. Musician
   f. Technical specialist, general
5. Functional support and administration
   a. Personnel
   b. Administration

    c. Clerical
    d. Data processing
    e. Accounting, finance, and disbursing
    f. Functional support, general
    g. Morale and welfare
    h. Information and education

6. Electrical, mechanical equipment repair
    a. Aircraft
    b. Automotive
    c. Wire communication
    d. Missile, mechanical and electrical
    e. Armament and munitions
    f. Shipboard propulsion
    g. Power-generating equipment
    h. Precision equipment
    i. Other mechanical and electrical equipment

7. Crafts
    a. Metallurgy
    b. Construction
    c. Utilities
    d. Lithography
    e. Industrial gas and fuel production
    f. Fabric, leather, and rubber
    g. Other craftsmen

8. Service and supply
    a. Food service
    b. Motor transport
    c. Material receipt, storage, and issue
    d. Law enforcement
    e. Personal service
    f. Auxiliary labor
    g. Forward area equipment support
    h. Other services

9. Individuals
    a. Patients
    b. Students/trainees
    c. Other

Despite the fact that increased opportunities for women in the armed forces have come about in the last two decades,[2] training and career opportunities for military women are still limited. Training restrictions are related to the types of job (military "occupational specialties" or "career fields") now available to women, and, in turn, the types of job available to women are determined both by law and by separate policy decisions in each of the service branches (Army, Air Force, Navy, and Marine Corps).[3]

Three major factors account for the restrictions on training and career opportunities for women in the armed forces: (1) the "separate spheres" philosophy, (2) combat exclusion laws and policies, and (3) differences in selection and training requirements that stem from the combat exclusion. These factors are examined in detail below.

Factors Affecting Training and Career Opportunities: The "Separate Spheres" Philosophy and the Combat Exclusion

The twentieth century marks the first time that large numbers of women have been utilized by the U.S. armed forces. Their limited use in the past was due to the availability of *man*power and to the belief that military service was the domain—and even the obligation—of men; thus women could and should serve their nation in other ways.[4] This "separate spheres" argument rests on the idea that men by nature are suited for military service and that women by nature are not. A more contemporary interpretation of this notion allows for women to make contributions to the labor market in general—and to the military in particular—but only in certain limited and prescribed ways.

The "separate spheres" argument forms the philosophical basis for the types of training opportunities and job assignments available to women in the military today. Yuval-Davis (1981) suggests that jobs in the armed forces are assigned according to a division of labor by sex. Others contend that, although certain restrictions apply, "military personnel policies provide for [the] full utilization of women" (U.S. Department of Defense 1986, 54). However, the reality is that men as a group are fully utilizable by the military (that is, job training, job assignment, and career choice for men are the result of individual ability, aptitude, and preference), whereas women as a group are not fully utilizable by the military since certain restrictions apply to their training, job assignments, and career choices because of their gender and regardless of individual ability, aptitude, or personal preference. The restrictions that govern the utilization of women in the military are the combat exclusion statutes contained in Title X of the *United States Code* and the combat exclusion policies of each of the individual services. These laws and policies are described below.

Statutory provisions on the utilization of women in the military are contained in Title X of the *United States Code*:

- Section 8549 prohibits the permanent assignment of women in the Air Force to duty in aircraft engaged in combat missions. (In Section 8067, however, exceptions are made for women who are medical, dental, chaplain, or other "professionals.")

- Section 6015 prohibits the permanent assignment of Navy women to duty on vessels or aircraft that engage in combat missions.
- Section 3012 gives the authority to the secretary of the Army to assign, detail, and prescribe duties to all members of the Army.

Service policies also limit the utilization of military women:

- The Marine Corps, under the Department of the Navy, follows the restrictions placed on the utilization of women in Section 6015. Also, its policies further restrict women in the Marine Corps from serving in either combat units or combat "situations."
- The Army has no statutory restrictions on the utilization of women (see above). However, in 1977, the Army developed and adopted the Combat Exclusion Policy, which prevents women from serving in certain jobs designated as "combat" military occupational specialties, and in 1983, it developed the "Direct Combat Probability Code" (DCPC), which restricts the assignment of women according to battlefield location. Positions coded as "P1" (representing the highest combat probability) are closed to women.

What is the source of these exclusionary rules?

- "On 2 June 1948, by a vote of 206 to 133, Congress passed the Women's Armed Services Act of 1948 (P.L. 625, 80th Congress) . . ." (Holm 1982, 113). This law provided for the permanent (rather than temporary) assignment of women to duty in the armed forces. But the act also contained restrictions: on the rank that women could attain (colonel), on the percentage of women who could serve in the armed forces (an upper limit of 2 percent), and on the kinds of military duties and assignments that women could perform. The third restriction came to be known as the "combat exclusion." Since 1948, laws have lifted the rank limitations and percentage quotas (P.L. 90–130 in 1967) but —with only minor modification to Section 6015—the combat exclusion provisions have remained the same.

Of importance for military women is the fact that what constitutes a combat job is determined by each branch of the armed forces and is often subject to change.[5] For women in the military, one implication of this continuing controversy has been that certain jobs in the different branches have been variously opened and closed to them as the definition of combat, as interpreted by each separate branch of the service, has been modified.[6] For example, in the Air Force, women who are medics and chaplains may serve aboard aircraft engaged in combat missions. (These professional categories are exempt by law from the Title X restriction.) Air Force women who are pilots, however, may not serve aboard aircraft engaged in combat missions. The Air Force now designates offensive fighters, bombers, and certain reconnaissance aircraft as combat aircraft, and this means that Air Force women who are pilots may fly only certain types of airplanes, primarily tankers and transports.[7] (Air Force women may be assigned, however, to ICBM launch crews, because this is not designated as a combat specialty.)

In the Navy, women may go to sea—in medical, administrative, and deck specialties, or to fly Navy aircraft—but they may be permanently assigned only to certain types of ship, that is, those classified by the Navy as noncombat ships. This now means research, repair, training, salvage, and support ships, and fleet tugs and tankers. The Navy designates submarines and surface warfare ships as combatant ships and prohibits the assignment of women to *any* job aboard them. All pilot and navigator positions in the Marine Corps are considered combat jobs and are closed to women (Women's Equity Action League 1987b).

Another implication for military women of this changing definition of combat is career selection ambiguity and the possibility of reassignment in certain occupational specialties. For example, in 1982 as a result of a policy review by the Army (U.S. Department of the Army 1982), 23 job categories that had been open to women were closed. "This decision, which directly affected 1,200 women, also had adverse impact on the career progression of over 15,000 women. Almost immediately, the Army came under heavy criticism for the hypotheses and methodology used in the policy review. "In 1985, after a review directed by the Secretary of the Army, many of the job categories in 1982 were reopened" (Becraft 1988, 4) (see, for example, Devilbiss 1983, 90–106). Another recent example was the transfer of many of the 250 women assigned to P1 combat units in Germany. Women continued to be assigned to these (theoretically closed to them) units even after the DCPC System went into effect. "The reason was that the unit commanders wanted them. A personnel officer explained that commanders 'didn't have enough men to fill vacancies' " (*Minerva* 1987e, 39).

Thus, it can be seen that, just because women are theoretically excluded from "combat" roles, they may still be put in combat environments or be required to perform combat missions when military need dictates it. Becraft (1988, 2) writes:

Currently (1988) over 220,000 officers and enlisted women serve in the military, many in nontraditional "combat type" jobs, such as pilots, security police, truck drivers, and missile gunners. They have participated actively in military missions, as well. In the 1983 Grenada invasion, Air Force women flew aircraft that delivered supplies and equipment to U.S. forces, and Army women, serving in a variety of combat support roles, were present from the second day of the invasion. In 1986, Navy women pilots performed carrier landings as a part of the antiterrorism operation against Libya, and Air Force women pilots were a part of the crews that provided combat support to the fighter planes that attacked Libya. In 1987, when the *U.S.S. Acadia* was sent to the Persian Gulf to repair damage done to the frigate *U.S.S. Stark*, 25 percent of [the] crew of the *Acadia* were women.

Other sources also note that the evacuation of military women from combat zones in the event of war—a popular fiction resulting from the combat exclusion provisions—is a highly unlikely event (*Minerva* 1987b).

The Selection and Training Requirements

Despite these realities of situation and environment, the selection and training requirements of military service for women continue to be governed by combat exclusion laws and policies. This happens right from the beginning in initial entry screening for military service. For example, "recruiting quotas are still relatively small for women and, as a result, recruiters can be more selective. . . . In general, women recruited between 1973 and 1976 tended to be older than men, as likely as men to be married, but less likely than men to be black" (U.S. Department of Labor 1983, 78).

We can see more of what the initial entry screening means for women when we closely examine the four categories of enlistment criteria: moral, medical, educational, and aptitude. Moral eligibility includes a background check for an arrest record, membership in certain specified antigovernment organizations, drug use, and engagement in certain forms of sexual activity. Moral eligibility standards are the same for both male and female recruits.

It can be argued that medical eligibility is not the same but is similar for men and women. Basic physical standards for enlistment are the same, with the exception of height and weight guidelines, which vary by gender and also by branch of service.[8] All applicants (male or female) must meet or exceed minimal qualifying physical standards (for example, hearing and eyesight must meet certain standards, and there can be no history of certain types of diseases).

The third area of enlistment standards—necessary educational credentials—varies by branch of service. The standards may either be the same for men and women (Navy and Air Force) or require that women have better educational credentials than men to be eligible for enlistment. The Army and the Marine Corps now require a high school diploma for women but not for men (Women's Equity Action League 1987a). Because occupational restrictions (the combat exclusion) mean that all the services can take fewer women than men, they are thus able to choose from "the cream of the crop" and are able to fill the available demand ("goal") for women recruits from among women high school graduates.

The final general enlistment standard is aptitude. Aptitude test scores are seen as measures of trainability for military jobs. The enlistment test now used to measure this for all services is the Armed Services Vocational Aptitude Test Battery (ASVAB). The ASVAB—"the military's entrance and placement exam" (Marrs and Read 1984, 32)—consists of 10 subtests: arithmetic reasoning, numerical operations, paragraph comprehension, word knowledge, coding speed, general science, mathematics knowledge, electronics information, mechanical comprehension, and automotive-shop information. The different branches of the armed forces combine these subtest scores in various ways to form "aptitude composites." These aptitude composite scores determine the potential recruit's eligibility for different jobs and training programs in the armed forces.[9]

As a criterion for *general* enlistment eligibility, four of the ASVAB subtests (word knowledge, paragraph comprehension, arithmetic reasoning, and numerical operations) yield an Armed Forces Qualification Test (AFQT) score. There are five AFQT categories, corresponding to percentile scores (sometimes called "mental categories"): AFQT I (93–100), AFQT II (65–92), AFQT III (31–64), AFQT IV (10–30), AFQT V (1–9). Category III is sometimes divided into two parts—IIIa and IIIb. The services do not enlist any Category V males or females. Almost all of the female enlistments come from Categories I, II, and IIIa; males are enlisted in Categories I, II, IIIa, IIIb, and IV.[10]

The ASVAB is important because it is taken only once and it determines an applicant's eligibility for military service and for training and career field opportunities that are available. Nevertheless, because of the statutory and policy restrictions on women as a group, an individual woman may meet all of the physical, moral, educational, and aptitude qualifications for enlistment into a particular job but still be denied entrance to a particular job and to the training associated with it.

One final note on enlistment criteria is of interest here. An Army and Air Force policy forbidding the enlistment of non-prior-service single parents faced court challenge recently because it was argued to have a disproportionate impact upon women and especially upon minority women. The court, however, upheld the policy ruling (*Minerva* 1986).

Even after a woman is accepted into the military, however, she will find her training opportunities, her job assignment possibilities, and even her career progression (in certain fields) all affected by the combat exclusion (see, for example, Becraft 1988). As we have noted, in the armed forces, job training and job assignment are linked. If a career field is defined by the services as a "combat" one (and therefore closed to women), then the job training opportunities for that career field will also be closed to women. There is another, implicit aspect of this reality.

This "hidden" implication is that there is a dual occupational identity in the U.S. armed forces. One element is the servicemember's occupational specialty—the particular job that he or she performs. All servicemembers have an occupational specialty. The other element of the dual occupational identity in the military is that of being a member of the *armed* (that is, *combatant*) forces. However, since women cannot be assigned to combat jobs, this supraordinate occupational identity (member of the armed forces) cannot fully apply to them. Women thus form a particular subclass of service personnel: they wear the uniform and perform certain types of military jobs, but they are neither fully admitted to nor expected to aspire to full membership in this occupation.

This dual occupational identity is reflected in the dual track nature of training in the various military services: training opportunities that are directed at acquiring or developing specific job knowledge and career specialty skills can be made available to women. However, training opportunities to acquire or develop general military (read "combat") knowledge and skills are closed to women. Such a system affects women at two places in their careers: during basic military training (where fundamental military/combat skills are learned) and in later elite or specialized training ("leadership development") courses often helpful, or even necessary, for promotion and retention.[11] Opportunities for women to participate in such training (for example, senior service schools, U.S. Army "Ranger," or U.S. Navy "Seal" programs) may be limited or precluded by service policy.

Causes of Occupational Segregation in the Military

We have seen that women cannot be assigned to certain "combat" occupational specialties, variously designated by the different service branches. But does this mean that, as Yuval-Davis (1981) suggests, the armed forces represent a highly sex-segregated occupation?

One way to approach this question is to examine the percentage of women in each of the occupational classifications listed above. Table 4-1 provides this information for the years 1972, 1976, and 1980. Table 4-2 examines this question using 1987 data and also provides the occupational distribution for males as a comparison.

Although caution is urged in making comparative percentage evaluations here (since the number of men greatly exceeds the number of women), Tables 4-1 and 4-2 do in fact show a high concentration of women in support and administration; medical and dental; communications and intelligence; and service and supply occupations. The data also indicate that the percentage of women is much lower, but is increasing, in the other occupational classifications. This increase is due in part to the fact that certain types of occupations have only recently been open to them.[12]

Table 4-1/Percent of Military Women in Enlisted Occupational Categories: 1972, 1976, 1980

OCCUPATIONAL CATEGORY	1980	1976	1972
0. Infantry, gun crew, and seamanship	0.7	0.2	0.2
1. Electronic equipment repair	6.1	4.3	1.2
2. Communications and intelligence	13.1	15.0	4.2
3. Medical and dental	13.5	18.6	23.8
4. Technical specialist	3.2	2.7	2.8
5. Functional support and administration	39.1	41.3	66.8
6. Electrical, mechanical equipment repair	9.8	6.7	—
7. Crafts	2.2	1.4	0.1
8. Service and supply	12.0	9.9	0.9
Total employment	99.7	100.1	100.0

Source: Defense Manpower Data Center 1987.
Notes: Percentages may not add to exactly 100 because of rounding.
The official data did not include category 9 (Individuals) in these years.

Two basic factors may be involved in occupational segregation: individual factors and structural factors. On the individual level, it is possible that women are not qualifying for or do not want to go into certain types of occupations. Women may often fail to qualify for certain types of military jobs (most likely those jobs referred to as "nontraditional" for women)[13] because of the particular composite of ASVAB subscores that are required for entry into those occupations. However, if a woman fails to qualify for a nontraditional job, she may still qualify for another type of job (usually a "traditional" one) that requires a different set of ASVAB subscores, and she may enter it if positions are available.[14]

But even if women do qualify (have the aptitude scores) for nontraditional jobs, will they go into these fields? There is at least some evidence to indicate that military women working in nontraditional jobs often experience isolation, ridicule, or resentment on the part of their male colleagues and also report frequent instances of sexual harassment, ranging from sexual jokes to verbal and physical advances (Rustad 1982; Rogan 1982).[15] To the extent that potential female recruits are aware of this possibility, it may be a factor negatively influencing their decision to "go the nontraditional route."

An even more important consideration in occupational segregation than individual factors are structural factors, specifically, the availability of nontraditional military occupations to women, and this availability is largely dependent on the military's definitions of "combat" (as opposed to "combat support" or "combat service support") occupations. Because "combat" roles are considered to be the most important ones to the accomplishment of the military's mission, they are the most valued, most central, and most rewarded

Table 4-2/Distribution by Occupational Category of All Active-Duty Enlisted Personnel: 1987

| | | WOMEN | | | |
| | | MINORITY | | | |
ENLISTED OCCUPATION	*White*	*Black*	*Total Minority*	*Total Women*	TOTAL MEN
0. Infantry, gun crew, and seamanship	1,649	439	572	2,221	259,141
1. Electronic equipment repair	7,219	1,359	1,860	9,079	161,687
2. Communications and intelligence	13,929	6,179	7,409	21,338	154,868
3. Medical and dental	15,954	7,498	9,375	25,329	77,086
4. Technical specialist	3,122	1,021	1,245	4,367	38,793
5. Functional support and administration	35,982	26,890	32,023	68,005	221,119
6. Electrical, mechanical equipment repair	11,210	3,440	4,440	15,650	367,901
7. Crafts	2,744	702	935	3,679	71,971
8. Service and supply	10,122	5,980	7,039	17,161	149,022
9. Individuals	14,361	5,655	7,658	22,019	165,016
Unknown	11	3	21	32	299
Total	116,303	59,166	72,577	188,880	1,666,903

Source: Defense Manpower Data Center 1987.
Note: The category "Total Minority Women" includes black women.

of military occupations. Because women are precluded from taking on "combat" roles, they can therefore perform only the peripheral, less valued and less well rewarded, military occupations. Combat exclusion laws and policies thus result in occupational segregation.

The Impact of Military Service on Women

A final important issue to analyze when examining job training and related career opportunities for women in the armed forces is the question, What are the effects of this training and military service on the lives of women? While there can be intangible costs and benefits of military service, we will focus our discussion here on tangible costs and benefits of military training and career opportunities in three areas that are important to women: income, education, and job skills.

Income and Related Issues

A characteristic of the military that makes it a special type of occupation is that military pay is based on rank and time in service, not on gender. Thus today, women and men of equal rank and time in service receive equal pay. On the surface, this means that a male truck driver and a female typist who hold the same rank and have the same number of years in the military will draw the same salary. But there are other aspects to this situation that may make it a little less equitable than it appears. For example, there are some exceptions to this general "equal pay" rule: certain hazardous duties, critical skill areas, and assignments in dangerous locations receive special additional pays. Many of these occupations are designated as "combat" specialties, which women are barred from entering.

What are some other consequences for women of the military's "equal pay" scale—frequently mentioned as a "high drawing card" encouraging young women to consider the armed forces as an occupational choice? The answer to this question raises the issue of selecting appropriate comparison groups. A comparison of civilian earnings with military earnings shows that wages are similar in these two sectors for men but not for women (Binkin and Bach [1977], using 1975 wage data, and DeFleur and Warner [1983, 4], using 1980 wage data). For women, and particularly for minority women, military pay scales represent higher wages than they can typically command in the civilian labor market because of the latter's gender- and race-segregated occupational structure.

Some other points about salaries for military women are important here. One is the question, are military women (more likely to be high school graduates than are military men) "getting less return for their education or job skills than men?" (Sharon Harlan, personal communication, 1988). This could be answered in the affirmative, as discussed above, supported by evidence of the comparable educational "investments" of men and women, or it could be answered in the negative, supported by a comparison of military wages that high school graduate women can expect and civilian labor market wages that non–high school graduate men can expect to command.

The conditions of employment for women in the military have income consequences for women. As members of the armed forces, servicemembers are salaried, not hourly, workers who are expected and required to work on their jobs as military need dictates. In some military occupations where there are severe personnel shortages, this means that hours are longer and thus servicemembers are working for a lower "hourly wage" than they could obtain doing the same job in a civilian environment. This problem has recently affected military nurses, who may work alongside civilian nurses, doing similar jobs, in military hospitals (*Navy Times* 1988).

Finally, income in the military is tied to rank, which is tied to promotion.[16] Overall, it appears that servicewomen are promoted at about the same time or even slightly sooner than are servicemen. (U.S. Department of Defense 1986, 78) However, because there are more men in the military than there are women, far greater *numbers* of men get promoted than do women.

There are also the issues of what rank women attain and, within that rank, what kinds of positions they hold. Until recently, there were legal limitations on the military rank that women could achieve, which stemmed from the Women's Armed Services Act of 1948. Since the passage of Public Law 90-130 in 1967, however, there is theoretically no limit on the promotion potential of military women. However, because an individual servicemember is considered for promotion based in part on previous duty assignments and record of achievement, women may be at a disadvantage relative to men since women cannot hold combat jobs, often a necessary prerequisite for promotion to the highest ranks. This has the effect of severely limiting—or even virtually denying—the entrance of women to the military's supergrades. All of these structural limitations on career advancement may be one reason that some women, especially those in certain occupational specialties with career progression opportunities limited by the combat exclusion, leave military service once they attain the "middle-management" level.

Education and Training
The opportunity for education and training is available to servicemembers both while they are still in the military and once they become veterans. A servicemember who is still in uniform may be able to enroll in, either in residence or through correspondence courses, both military-sponsored job training programs and courses offered by civilian schools. Job skill training programs offered by the military are paid for entirely by the military and successful completion of these programs is required for entry (and in some cases, continued duty) in a military occupational specialty. These programs are typically a combination of classroom and practical instruction. Skills may also be acquired through direct on-the-job training (OJT). Many job skill training programs are offered after initial basic training and just before the first duty assignment.[17] Formal job skill training (skills updating) can continue, however, throughout the servicemember's career.

It is not clear whether, in general, military service has a different impact on the training and educational opportunities for servicemen than it does for servicewoman. On the one hand, the pursuit of civilian educational courses while in the military is generally a matter of personal choice, although the availability of the particular courses of interest to the individual and the amount of time that can be devoted to the pursuit of these educational interests, given an often very demanding work schedule, are also factors to be considered. On the other hand, variation in military training and educational opportunities exists by branch of service and is also related, as we have seen, to a "dual track" system: (1) general military ("combat") training, knowledge, and skills and (2) specific ("technical") programs to develop the knowledge and skills necessary to perform a particular kind of military job.

That basic training is not gender integrated in most of the service branches is important, because in basic training servicemembers are given instruction in basic military skills. Again, the combat exclusion is one reason why this training and courses of instruction for women and men are separate and somewhat different. Basic military training at the enlisted level is considered by the services to be basic combat training, that is, it is intended to give fundamental training in soldiering, seaman, or airman skills necessary in this type of occupation. This distinction is maintained despite the fact that, in reality, many women serve in combat environments where such knowledge would be valuable to them. Thus this utilization-based approach, although seemingly rational, has the effect of gender segregation of the fundamental military skill and knowledge base (supposedly common to all military members) at the initial entry level.[18]

This situation, however, changes somewhat when we examine military training beyond the enlisted basic level and look instead at advanced training for enlisted personnel. These programs (the "technical" track) are more likely to focus on the development of specialized job skills; and if a servicewoman just coming into the military has been assigned to a particular military specialty, she needs to have this base of technical knowledge to perform the job. Most enlisted advanced training schools have gender-integrated classes.

Servicemembers who have completed their military obligation become eligible for educational benefits under the G.I. Bill. As veterans, men and women differ in educational outcomes.[19] A recent study by the Veterans Administration found three important differences: (1) female veterans have lower G.I. Bill eligibility rates than do male veterans, (2) female veterans have lower G.I. Bill participation rates than do male veterans, and (3) of those who use their G.I. Bill benefits, female veterans use a greater percentage of their entitlement than do male veterans (Feitz 1985, 12).

The reasons for these gender differences are not entirely clear. Statistical manipulations such as adjusting participation rates by eligibility rates and controlling for such factors as time of separation did not affect the comparative results (Feitz 1985, 7–11). Prior educational level may be one possible explanation for some differences (Feitz 1985, 3–4). As a group, servicewomen are better educated than servicemen because higher standards are required of them as a condition for their service in the first place, and therefore most servicewomen would be unlikely to use G.I. Bill benefits for high school equivalency training as many servicemen do. A survey conducted for the Veterans Administration by Louis Harris and Associates uncovered three major reasons why female veterans did not use their educational benefits: not needing it, not being eligible for it, and not being aware that such assistance was available (Harris and Associates 1985, 167–68, 181).

It is possible that, for female veterans, the last two reasons may be related. Eligibility requirements for G.I. Bill educational benefits stipulate only that six months active duty have been served during specified periods and that the veteran received a discharge other than dishonorable. It is possible that some, especially older, female veterans may believe that their service does not qualify them for these benefits when in fact it does. The debate over which women are veterans, that is, what kinds of service qualifies women for veterans benefits (Willenz 1983, 168–69), and historical differences in educational benefits given to servicewomen and servicemen (Willenz 1983, 193) add to the confusion in this area. The question of educational benefit usage by veterans is an example of an issue where more research is needed to assess why gender differences exist.

Job Skills

In the third category of tangible outcomes of military service, specific job skills, there are two pertinent debates. One is whether military service affords the opportunity to learn skills that transfer to civilian jobs at all. Second, if we assume that military skills are transferable, are servicemen and servicewomen similarly affected?

Important to this argument is the idea of military service as a "bridging environment" (see, for example, Browning, Lopreato, and Posten 1973; Lopreato and Posten 1977). This is the notion that the military is an environment that may provide, through work experience, "the conditions and opportunities for movement from one occupation or cluster of occupations to another." (Broom and Smith 1963, 322). Thus the question: Is service in the military a vehicle for social mobility?

There is evidence to suggest that young women may at least perceive that the military offers them a chance to get ahead, to advance to a more responsible position, and to have a more fulfilling job, and there is evidence to suggest that black women are likely to have more positive perceptions than white women (Segal, Bachman, and Dowdell 1978). Furthermore, "military groups provide opportunities for women to acquire skills for traditionally male jobs that are not easily attainable in other settings" (DeFleur and Warner 1983, 21). However, whether women can actually use these job skills to economic advantage—that is, whether the military functions as a "bridging environment" for women—is questionable. A 1986 pilot study of a small sample of women veterans placed by public employment offices found that:

the women veterans studied were in the lower end of the earning spectrum despite the fact that almost all were high school graduates; the women who had nontraditional military training did not seem to seek out [or] to obtain employment commensurate with their backgrounds . . . [and that] having a nontraditional job in the military did not seem to lead to a similar job in the civilian sector. . . . Most surprising were the relatively low wage rates of women placed by the employment service, and the apparently limited recognition of their military training and experience. (Willenz 1987, 6)

While these findings were from a small sample and can only be considered preliminary (Willenz 1987), it is still necessary to be aware that when examining the "bridging environment" of the military with regard to women, it may be necessary to consider other related factors in order to get an explanation of how and why this bridging environment works the way that it does for female veterans. It may be necessary not only to take into account the particular woman's military background, skills, and experience but also to consider the gender-stratified civilian labor market that she is entering or re-entering and other factors that may differentially impact upon the employment of male and female veterans, such as marriage and family responsibilities (see, for example, DeFleur and Warner 1983, 22). In an extended analysis of the bridging environment hypothesis as it applies to servicewomen, Warner (1985) found that: (1) military service has a negative effect on the hourly wages of a woman's first job, (2) veteran's status does not have a significant effect on wages for men and women,[20] (3) civilian wages are not significantly affected by military training (even in jobs least likely to be affected by the career discontinuity that the interruption of military service and other contingencies may cause), and (4) military service does not increase the likelihood that women will enter nontraditional civilian jobs early in their careers. Based on these findings, Warner (1985) argues that it is important to reconceptualize "military service as an occupation rather than an educational or occupational training experience in future research on the occupational attainment process."

Family-Related Variables
The differential impact of military service on men and women would not be complete without at least a mention of family-related variables. This is an area that affects both servicemen and servicewomen, but one in which servicewomen experience more of a potentially adverse impact. Two examples are the issues of dual careers (both husband and wife are in the military) and child care. Teplitsky (1987) shows that most often the servicewoman's assignments, promotions, and possibly even her military career are subordinated or sacrificed in a dual-career military marriage. Moreover, because in accepting a military obligation, both spouses accept a worldwide duty commitment, the issue of making arrangements for competent child care (on a day-to-day basis, or designating a legal caretaker for minor children in the event of a deployment) is an important, and organizationally necessary, one. Particularly

when it comes to finding adequate child care and designating a legal sponsor for minor children in the event of deployment, the burden of decision and responsibility falls on the servicewoman in a dual-career military marriage (Teplitsky 1987).

In summary, the effects of military service on women are very complex and not entirely understood. Outcomes of military service for women vary according to the group to which they are compared, such as civilian women, or military men, and are affected by several organizational realities regarding women's service, such as higher enlistment criteria, career progression and promotion determinants, the combat exclusion, family variables and the effects of being a member of the token group in an occupation that is 90 percent male.

Conclusion

What can be done to better address the issue of job training and career opportunities for women in the armed forces? Simply targeting women in the military and women veterans as definable subpopulations worthy of study (see, for example, Willenz 1983) on these issues would help. Related to this is the necessity of expanding the research models in this area beyond the traditional single-sex (male only) perspective in order to increase the scientific utility of these frameworks. A third suggestion pertains to the explanatory and predictive power of these conceptual frameworks and models. This is the awareness that "tangible" and "intangible" aspects of military service may be interrelated. For example, because of the several consequences of women's token status in a military environment, positive tangible outcomes of military service for them may be exacerbated by some of the environment's intangible negative effects. These same effects may serve as mitigating, or even empowering, circumstances, however, in the military environment for servicemen. They include the combat exclusion and its effects on training opportunities, career field selection, job assignments, and promotion potential. Another, and equally sensitive, illustration is the question of whether sexual harassment (as one manifestation of dominance, control, and dehumanization) is actually functional rather than dysfunctional to military systems and operations (see, for example, DePauw 1988).

Sorting out these questions thus becomes one of looking for both manifest and latent sociological consequences. This is not an easy task because, as such effects come to light, and particularly if these effects are seen as adverse, the issue then becomes one of whether these are organizationally intended or unintended consequences. This speaks to the very basic assumptions underlying the organizational culture of the military itself (see Schein 1985). Research on issues such as these and, in particular, on their consequences for women in the military goes to the very heart of the basic belief system of the armed forces as a social institution.

Notes

Acknowledgments: I am particularly indebted to Sharon Harlan and Ronnie Steinberg, the editors of this book, for their many hours of work and patient critique. I benefited immensely from their insights and their unfailing belief that the perspective of this chapter was an important one to include in this book. I would also like to express my appreciation to Linda Grant DePauw, who read and commented on an early version of this chapter, and to Debra E. Morgenstern, who provided word processing support throughout the several evolutions of this manuscript.

1. The focus of the chapter is on job training and career opportunities for enlisted women. These generally require a high school education rather than the college degree required of women officers. For classification purposes, the Department of Defense also lists a tenth area of enlisted occupational categories "entitled 'non-occupational,' [which] includes those billets filled by pipeline personnel, for example, patients, prisoners, students, and trainees" (Binkin 1986, 133).

2. See Holm (1982) and Becraft (1988) for discussions of many of the important events that led to the opening of additional career fields to women. Devilbiss (forthcoming) analyzes the importance of six major factors in this process: legislation, court decision, lobby and advocacy groups, key individual military decision makers, military need (resulting from organizational, structural, and functional changes), and pressure from "within the ranks" by military women themselves.

3. Within the U.S. Department of Defense, there are four branches of military service: the Army, the Air Force, the Navy, and (organized under the Department of the Navy) the Marine Corps. Each of these four service branches has an active duty (full-time) and reserve (part-time) personnel force. In addition, there are National Guard units of the Army and Air Force. (These are state administered rather than federally administered programs as the reserve forces are but, like the reserves, afford opportunities for part-time military service.) The U.S. Coast Guard operates under the Department of the Navy in wartime and in time of national emergencies, and under the Department of Transportation (not a Department of Defense agency) in peacetime. Thus, the Coast Guard is not subject to the Title 10, *U.S. Code* exclusions on the utilization of women listed in the next section except presumably during time of war or emergency. This eventuality has been a point of contention between the Navy and the Coast Guard, since all positions in the Coast Guard were opened to women in 1978.

4. See DePauw (1981) for an analysis of the large and active part played by women in the American Revolution when manpower was in short supply and all available resources were drawn upon.

5. In the past, whether one was in combat or not was more clearly defined than it is now. Combat was defined by the environment: if you were in a situation where there was fighting going on between two opposing forces, you were in combat. (Furthermore, even if you were a cook, for example, when the fighting started, you

became a combatant.) Gradually, there arose the definitional demarcation between those in a combat environment who specialized in fighting skills ("combat"), those in a combat environment who possessed other operational skills (such as communications or intelligence-gathering) that were necessary to assist large armies in the field ("combat support"), and those with skills necessary to sustain the combatants ("combat service support"). The distinction between combat and other-than-combat jobs has essentially boiled down to three elements: Did or can you fire (not just provide locating and aiming "support" for) a weapon at a hostile force? Did or can you do so offensively? (The defensive use of deadly force by, for example, military police, is classified as "combat support.") Are you an operational part of a weapons system or platform (such as a ship or an aircraft) that can fire offensively at an enemy target? If so, then your job is a combat one. At this writing, "Defense Secretary Frank Carlucci has approved a new standard for judging which military jobs should be closed to women, a standard that will apply to all services. From now on, jobs will be closed to women only when they carry a risk of exposure to direct combat, hostile fire or capture, that is 'equal to or greater' than the risk for similar units in the same theatre of operations" (*Minerva's Bulletin Board* Spring 1988: 4).

6. It must be stressed that what is or is not combat is subject to very frequent reinterpretation and definition by the services. Local recruiters should have updates on the latest information pertaining to that service branch. Two other excellent sources are the Women's Equity Action League (e.g., 1987b) and the Minerva Center in Arlington, Va. (e.g., *Minerva* 1987a; 1987c).

7. Recently, women who are pilots in the Air Force have been allowed to fly fighters as instructor pilots because these aircraft were engaged in training—not combat—missions. U.S. Navy women, however, can fly aircraft without restriction if these same women are not permanently assigned to combat ships.

8. Some Department of Defense analysts argue that weight rules discriminate against women, since men can exceed the insurance industry's standard for good health and still qualify for enlistment, but women cannot (*Minerva* 1987d).

9. See Binkin (1986) for a discussion of how aptitude composites—the particular combinations of ASVAB subtest scores that qualify the individual for types of training and career fields—may result in differential qualifying rates depending on gender and race. (Presumably this is a function of the knowledge base provided or not provided by the kinds of courses and specific subject matter the applicant has taken.)

10. Congress has limited the number of Category IV recruits to 20 percent of all new enlistments (Women's Equity Action League 1987a).

11. Basic military training is gender segregated in the Army, Navy, and Marine Corps and gender integrated in the Air Force (and Coast Guard).

12. When examining the issue of training and job opportunities for women in the military, it is important to distinguish between actual number of job openings (available "slots" or positions) and the number of occupational categories open to women. This is a crucial distinction to make since a small percentage of closed occupations may actually represent a large *number* of closed positions. In 1988, 50 of the 368 enlisted job titles and 268 of 284 officer and warrant officer job titles were open to women in the Army (Becraft 1988, 4). However, the 318 enlisted and 16 officer job specialties closed to Army women represent a large *number* of jobs. In 1988, only 3 percent of all

Air Force job categories were classified as "combat" jobs (Becraft 1988, 4), but this 3 percent represents a significant number of actual slots.

13. Although women have historically served in many different military jobs, those most likely to be called "traditional" military occupations are those in which women have participated since the 1950s: predominantly those of an administrative or medical nature, with some communications and service-and-supply occupations as well. Other types of jobs are considered "nontraditional," even though military women have performed such jobs in the past. (See especially, DePauw 1981 for a discussion of women in the American Revolution, Holm 1982 and Treadwell 1954 for a history of women's occupational contributions in World War II.) The terms "traditional" and "nontraditional" military occupations apply exclusively to military women, however, since there are no military roles that are considered "nontraditional" ones for men. Military "nurse" comes closest to being defined as a "nontraditional" occupation for military men, since it was only opened to men in the 1950s. However, as increasing numbers of men perform this job—and also as men of increasingly higher rank do so —it comes to be seen as less of an exceptional role for males. Men have frequently performed the job of "medic" in the military, but this is not a professional occupation and it requires less training than nursing.

14. Yet a third possibility is that the aptitude scores necessary for entry into certain military jobs are not being achieved by women recruits—and other military jobs for which they do qualify are not available to them because these types of job are already filled.

15. As the number of women in nontraditional occupations increases (and their presence is thus much less of a curiosity or an anomaly), it is possible that instances of sexual harassment may lessen.

16. In fact, even retention—staying in the occupation itself—is tied to promotion in the military. This is referred to as the "up or out" policy.

17. It is the usual practice for the armed forces to recruit young people who have not acquired a large base of job skills in the civilian labor market. (Some exceptions are made to this, but they are primarily for officer specialties, such as lawyer, chaplain, nurse, or physician.) This eases the ability of the armed forces to train individuals in whatever particular jobs are needed. (The military training and job assignment model is thus a demand-based, no-prior-skills-assumed, model.) "Stripes for skills" (in effect, advanced placement) enlisted programs in the military vary by service, are infrequent, and are subject to changing service policies.

18. The ultimate consequence of being left out of the fundamental knowledge base is, as discussed previously, less than full membership in the military profession. It is important, to note, however, that most women *and most men* do not serve in combat. However, men are trained and receive the knowledge of this eventuality while women do not (Linda Grant DePauw, personal communication, May 1988).

19. In March 1986 there were 1,003,000 women veterans. This figure includes 250,000 female Vietnam veterans (Roca 1986). (For comparison purposes, there were approximately 27,000,000 male veterans at the time.)

20. Warner (1985) found that the only group to see a positive economic return for their military service was minority males, but this effect was not statistically significant.

References

Becraft, Carolyn H. 1988. "Women and the Military: Organizational Stress and Politics." Paper presented at conference, Women and Work, University of Texas at Arlington, May.

Binkin, Martin. 1986. *Military Technology and Defense Manpower*. Washington, D.C.: The Brookings Institution.

Binkin, Martin, and Shirley J. Bach. 1977. *Women and the Military*. Washington, D.C.: The Brookings Institution.

Broom, L., and J. H. Smith. 1963. "Bridging Occupations." *British Journal of Sociology* 14 (December): 321–34.

Browning, Harley L.; Sally C. Lopreato; and Dudley L. Posten, Jr. 1973. "Income and Veteran Status: Variations Among Americans, Blacks and Anglos." *American Sociological Review* 38: 74–85.

Defense Manpower Data Center. 1987. "Distribution of Active Duty Forces by Service, Occupation, Sex and Ethnic Group." Report no. 3694. Washington, D.C., September.

DeFleur, Lois B., and Rebecca L. Warner. 1983. "The Impact of Military Service on Women's Socio-Economic Status and Social-Psychological Well-Being: Some Unanswered Questions." Paper presented at the biennial meeting of the Inter-University Seminar on Armed Forces and Society, Chicago, October.

DePauw, Linda Grant. 1981. "Women in Combat: The Revolutionary War Experience." *Armed Forces and Society* 7 (Winter): 209–26.

———. "Gender as Stigma: Probing Some Sensitive Issues." 1988. *Minerva: Quarterly Report on Women and the Military* 6 (Spring): 29–43.

Devilbiss, M. C. 1983. " 'Women in the Army Policy Review': A Military Sociologist's Analysis." *Minerva: Quarterly Report on Women and the Military* 1 (Fall): 90–106.

———. Forthcoming. *Women and Military Service: A History, Analysis, and Overview of Key Issues*. Montgomery, Ala.: Air University Press.

Feitz, Robert H. 1985. "Female Veterans' Usage of the Post-Korean Conflict G.I. Bill." Washington, D.C.: Veterans Administration, March.

Harris, Louis, and Associates. 1985. *Survey of Female Veterans: A Study of the Needs, Attitudes, and Experiences of Women Veterans*. Washington, D.C.: Veterans Administration.

Holm, Jeanne. 1982. *Women in the Military*. Novato, Calif.: Presidio Press.

Lopreato, Sally Cook, and Dudley Posten, Jr. 1977. "Differences in Earnings Between Black Veterans and Nonveterans in the United States." *Social Science Quarterly* 57: 750–66.

Marrs, Texe, and Karen Read. 1984. *Everywoman's Guide to Military Service*. Cockeysville, Md.: Liberty.

Minerva: Quarterly Report on Women and the Military. 1986. "Ban on Single-Parent Enlistments Upheld" 4 (Summer): 49–50.

———. 1987a. "Army Opens Two Engineer Specialties to Women" 5 (Winter): 39–40.

————. 1987b. "Evacuation of Women from Combat Zones 'Possible but Not Probable' " 5 (Spring): 39–40.

————. 1987c. "Services Revise Exclusionary Policies Affecting Women" 5 (Spring): 40–42.

————. 1987d. "Weight Rules for Recruits Discriminate Against Women, Says Defense Department" 5 (Spring): 54–55.

————. 1987e. "Women in Army Combat Units to Be Reassigned" 5 (Winter): 38–39.

Navy Times. 1988. "Hardship of Longer Shifts Taken in Stride to Finish Job" 23 May: 4, 20.

Roca, Maria L. 1986. *Monthly Labor Review* 109 (December): 30.

Rogan, Helen. *Mixed Company.* 1982. New York: Putnam.

Rustad, Michael L. 1982. *Women in Khaki: The American Enlisted Woman.* New York: Praeger.

Schein, Edgar H. 1985. *Organization Culture and Leadership.* San Francisco: Jossey-Bass.

Segal, David R.; Jerald G. Bachman; and Faye Dowdell. 1978. "Military Service for Female and Black Youth: A Perceived Mobility Opportunity." *Youth and Society* 10: 127–34.

Teplitzky, Martha L. 1987. "Dual Army Career Couples: Factors Relating to the Career Intentions of Men and Women." Paper presented at the American Psychological Association Annual Meeting, New York City, August.

Treadwell, Mattie E. 1954. *The Women's Army Corps.* Washington, D.C.: Office of the Chief of Military History.

U.S. Department of the Army. Office of the Deputy Chief of Staff for Personnel. 1982. *Women in the Army Policy Review.* Washington, D.C., November.

U.S. Department of Defense. Office of the Secretary of Defense. 1986. *Military Women in the Department of Defense.* Washington, D.C., April.

U.S. Department of Labor. Office of the Secretary, Women's Bureau. 1983. *Time of Change: 1983 Handbook on Women Workers.* Bulletin no. 298. Washington, D.C.: Government Printing Office.

Warner, Rebecca Lynn. 1985. "The Impact of Military Service on the Early Career: An Extension of the Bridging Hypothesis to Women." Ph.D. dissertation, Washington State University, Pullman, Washington.

Willenz, June A. 1983. *Women Veterans.* New York: Continuum.

Women's Equity Action League. 1987a. "Recruitment Statistics and Policies: Women in the Active Armed Services." Washington, D.C.

————. 1987b "Women and Combat: A Comparison of the Services' Laws and Policies." Washington, D.C.

Yuval-Davis, Nira. 1981. "Sexual Division of Labour." In Wendy Chapkis, ed., *Loaded Questions: Women in the Military*, pp. 30–35. Washington, D.C.: Transnational Institute.

PART

II

Targeted Groups and Program Experiences

Introduction to Part II/*Sharon L. Harlan*

The occupational education and training system is alternately regarded as a monolith created by federal legislation and evaluated by national averages, or as a chaotic maze of local programs with seemingly no central design or accountability. In fact, neither image is correct, as the six chapters in Part II demonstrate. A more accurate characterization is one in which dedicated local program administrators, educators, and advocates work within a broad national policy framework to develop and deliver effective services to particular populations that need training.

In Part II, we have brought together descriptions of a diverse set of training strategies, which reflect the needs of different groups of women in different parts of the country who seek training. These chapters provide a more focused examination of important issues raised in Part I. Some of the chapters highlight the experience of participation in training and others highlight its outcomes. However, they are all attuned to the context in which training takes place and whether the training was likely to make a difference in the economic well-being, living standard, or life chances for participants. The common thread is that each chapter analyzes a small segment of the education and training system in relation to issues of broader economic, social, and political significance.

Certain categories of women encounter special circumstances which qualify them as unique populations with special needs. Miller and Polit describe two such populations in their respective chapters on displaced homemakers and teenage mothers. Miller examines vocational education and the Job Training Partnership Act (JTPA) from her perspective as director of the Displaced Homemakers Network, a national umbrella organization for 1,000 local displaced-homemaker programs. She argues that program performance standards, cost cutting, and programmatic limitations act as disincentives to serving populations with special needs. Polit's chapter on teenage mothers is a cautiously optimistic review of the potential for developing programs to help young women overcome a very serious drawback to completing their education and becoming employed. In her analysis of Project Redirection, a comprehensive education, employment, health, and social services program for teenage mothers, she finds "modest, but significant, effects on several employment-related outcomes," which are encouraging, given the young age of the population. Only 15 percent of Redirection participants were working at follow-up time, but many others were in school or had gained some job experience or both.

The similarities between displaced homemakers and teenage mothers are noteworthy: neither group has much experience in the labor market; they have few salable skills; and they must maintain families and deal with parenting responsibilities alone. Age is an employment barrier to both, although for opposite reasons. Finally, these women have recently undergone important life transitions, either the loss of a spouse or the birth of a child.

In many ways, their training needs are similar as well. Neither fits the image of the full-time student who is both unencumbered by financial and family responsibilities of her own and often the beneficiary of support from others. Both authors point to this as a primary reason why so many of these women fail in traditional training programs for youth and adults. Miller is adamantly opposed to "mainstreaming" women, and Polit also claims that it does not work. The training needs of displaced homemakers and teenage mothers encompass a wide range of comprehensive services, including personal, social, and job-related assistance in addition to skill training. The authors suggest that community-based organizations, which are generally multi-service, antipoverty agencies, have successful track records as service deliverers for these populations and that they deserve support as alternatives to school-based training.

Despite these similarities, there are two important differences between teenage mothers and displaced homemakers. Teenage mothers usually require assistance for a long time and because of their youth, employment is seldom the immediate goal. Instead, these young women need to complete basic schooling and gain an understanding of work. Displaced homemakers, on the other hand, do have a pressing need for income, which makes short-focused training programs (especially on-the-job training) appropriate for them.

Miller believes that the Comprehensive Employment and Training Act (CETA) was helpful in targeting employment and training resources to displaced homemakers, but that JTPA is not, even though they are eligible as a group for JTPA assistance. Both Miller and Polit point to the inflexibility of JTPA's performance standards and the resistance of JTPA Private Industry Councils to enrolling disadvantaged women as being detrimental to establishing the kinds of training strategies and support services that women need. Vocational education, while viewed more positively and potentially as more useful in meeting these women's needs, has made less federal money available than JTPA for teen mother and displaced-homemaker programs. Moreover, there is variability among states in commitment and quality of service to both groups in JTPA and vocational education.

The next four chapters in Part II are examples of innovative training programs (or, in the case of Durbin and O'Brien, an innovative evaluation of a standard national program) that have developed and are largely funded out of vocational education and federal employment and training legislation. In a unique attempt to evaluate CETA programs by measuring the skills participants acquired, Durbin and O'Brien find that about 45 percent of the women in Connecticut public service employment (PSE), compared to 30 percent of the men, got jobs that were higher in skill requirements than the jobs they had held previously. However, men still earned more than women in PSE. Greenbaum and Watson describe a vocational education program in data and word processing which helps unemployed and underemployed minority women to move up in their companies, or at least to stay employed in New York City's technologically changing clerical labor market. Gould, Stern, and Lyman document efforts all across the country to bring low-income women into the growing entrepreneurial economy through individual training and building community support for their business activities. And finally, in a chapter that analyzes the historical roots of present conditions that divide the southern work force by gender and race, Lilly concludes that skills training programs are useful to women only in the context of larger movements for political change and economic justice. Lilly points out that the retreat of the federal government's commitment to equal employment opportunity for women really does matter in the South because of the way states use their power to repress women and blacks.

Nearly all the authors echo the theme that successful training strategies are more than vehicles for delivering specific job skills. Women's poverty and their status as single householders have an impact on their ability to benefit from training. Programs also need to deal with women's confidence, self-esteem, social awareness, and job placement in a personalized format for an

extended time. These are empowerment goals that enable women to negotiate the labor market, not just get a job. Greenbaum and Watson's program at
Laguardia Community College, for example, runs for nine-month cycles one
night a week and Saturdays. They stress that upward mobility in office work
requires more than typing and computer skills. In fact, the ability to reason
conceptually and communicate are essential in performing clerical work. The
Institute for Community Education and Training described by Lilly offers
programs that last one year and encompass leadership skills, economic relief,
and community-building.

Another theme the chapters share is the importance of linking training
with policies for economic development in the communities where women
live. Gould, Stern, and Lyman discuss ways to mobilize community resources in order to secure financing for women-owned businesses and to
bring women out of isolation to share experiences and start business networks. Lilly's description of a depressed local island-based community in the
South shows the futility of training women for deadend, low-wage jobs in a
tourist-based economy. Mobility is possible, she argues, only if women gain
some decision-making power regarding development policies on the islands.
Durbin and O'Brien offer dim prospects for training women in skilled crafts
in local labor markets where men are losing those jobs and being forced into
less skilled blue-collar positions. These analyses suggest that there is a crucial role for intelligent local planners in carrying out broad federal mandates.

Evaluations of Project Redirection (Polit) and Connecticut public service employment (Durbin and O'Brien) indicate that these program interventions modestly increase the employability of teenage mothers and enhance
the "skill opportunities" of women in PSE. With the exception of this research, however, outcome evaluations are sadly lacking for the innovative
programs described in Part II. The other authors tell us that the subjective
reactions of women to the programs are highly positive and most can provide some evidence to suggest that jobs and wages are improved, at least
for some participants. However, it is unfortunate that the arguments in support of their programs cannot be buttressed by more rigorous research. The
blame for this must be placed partly on the federal policy makers who control research funds. While they have relentlessly pursued answers to a few
questions on mainstream national policies, the resources which might show
the impact of innovative programming have not been forthcoming. There is
also a need, however, for greater awareness by program administrators about
the kind of evidence that is necessary to validate their claims about program
effectiveness.

Nontraditional occupational (NTO) training for women is an issue in
several of these chapters, none of which draws optimistic conclusions about
the availability of such jobs and the amount of resources necessary to secure

women's opportunities. Lilly's account of institutional reform in the coal and highways industries, spurred by CETA in conjunction with women's advocacy organizations, is encouraging. But the availability of such jobs is limited and in rural areas they may be the only high paying jobs around. Gould, Stern, and Lyman hold out self-employment as a potentially new NTO option for women, one that developed in a labor market full of employers that resist hiring women in nontraditional fields. Not surprisingly, they report that many women-owned businesses are in traditionally female-dominated service industries. Nevertheless, the fastest growth rates for women's businesses are in nontraditional areas such as wholesale trade and manufacturing.

Relatedly, Durbin and O'Brien present some new information that may be relevant for explaining why CETA earnings impact studies found that participation increased women's earnings (compared to nonparticipant women), whereas men's earnings actually declined in some studies. The authors argue that men's earnings loss is due to their displacement from craft jobs in the private sector into laborer and service jobs in the public sector, and their analysis indicates that women's previous levels of educational attainment helped women to get higher-status white-collar jobs in the public sector. About 90 percent of the women in Connecticut remained in white-collar public service employment, with a substantial shift out of former clerical and sales positions into higher status education and social services positions provided by the program.

Durbin and O'Brien provide an interesting counterpoint to Greenbaum and Watson on the viability of training women in traditionally female jobs. Because women's public service jobs yielded a greater increase in job skill requirements than men's compared to their former jobs, Durbin and O'Brien conclude that the pursuit of higher white-collar jobs may be a more widely useful strategy for women than NTO training for diminishing blue-collar jobs. Yet, although women gained more than men, their earnings and skill levels were still less than men's, indicating that public service employment certainly did not eliminate gender inequalities. Greenbaum and Watson point out as well that relying on clerical jobs to employ women is no panacea for their employment difficulties. Office automation, reorganization of work processes, and migration of firms to the suburbs are making it more difficult for minority women and older women to find and keep such jobs. Public programs, they say, have been sluggish in responding to the new training needs created by electronic information processing.

These chapters in Part II corroborate our conclusion from Part I that federal training policy is dysfunctional for women in certain ways. Nevertheless, a variety of strategies help individual women to do better in the labor market than they might without training. In general, better evaluations of local programs for specific populations, perhaps modeled on the Project Redirection example, are needed. The most important lesson of these chapters, however, is the futility of trying to use job training alone to overcome individual deficiencies and social problems. Women, such as teenage mothers or South Sea Island residents, who lack basic educational competencies cannot aspire to training for good jobs without first completing at least a high school education. Still more important, the local and regional labor markets of many communities do not provide enough good jobs or entrepreneurial opportunities, especially for poor women, who are needed by employers to fill their least desirable, lowest-paying positions.

5/Displaced Homemakers in the Employment and Training System

Jill Miller

Since 1975, when employment and training programs first became available for displaced homemakers, two facts have become clear. First, displaced homemakers are a unique population with special needs. Unlike many single parents, they are generally mid-life and older women who may have not been in the paid labor market for 10, 15, or 20 years, if ever. Unlike many returning adult students, they are in the midst of a major transition in their lives while they are also attempting to enter the labor force. Second, because of displaced homemakers' special circumstances, for them, traditional approaches to employment and training programs fall short of the mark. This chapter evaluates the legislation and training programs that target displaced homemakers. Specifically, it examines state displaced-homemaker legislation, federal employment and training legislation (the 1978 reauthorization of the Comprehensive Employment and Training Act and the Job Training Partnership Act of 1982), and federal vocational education legislation (the Vocational Education Act of 1963 as amended in 1976 and the Carl D. Perkins Vocational Education Act of 1984).

Who are Displaced Homemakers?

Bernice Campbell and Hillyer Engel are two displaced homemakers whose stories capture the situations in which many other women find themselves.

> *Bernice Campbell, a 55-year-old black woman in Baltimore, had nearly given up hope. In her six years as a displaced homemaker, she had gone back to school and earned an associate's degree in human services. But she had not worked full time in more than 20 years and,*

even with her degree, could not find full-time work. She could not make ends meet with her two part-time jobs. Then she saw a television announcement about Baltimore New Directions for Women, a displaced-homemaker program offering to help women in situations like hers. That was seven years ago. Today, Bernice Campbell works full time, recruiting and counseling other displaced homemakers.

Hillyer Engel's husband of 28 years died suddenly at the age of 51. Engel, like many other women, found herself one of America's "new poor." In the midst of her grief, she began to look for work "in an environment where 35 years of age was considered elderly." Her experience is much like that of other homemakers suddenly forced to re-enter the job market. "While it sounds sensible to say that homemaking skills employed by a wife in organizing her home and managing her budget should be transferable to the business world, employers are slow to accept the idea. In job interviews this was too vague a concept to wrestle with. The employer wanted something more specific. If this or my age didn't prove to be an obstacle, then I was told I was overqualified. Crazy!" How can you lack skills one minute and be over-qualified the next? Building on the assistance of her local displaced-homemaker program, Engel was able to put her communication skills to work directing volunteers in a hospital.

What happens when a homemaker loses her job? She becomes a displaced homemaker—one of millions of middle-aged and older women who have worked in the home for many years caring for their families and have lost their primary source of income because of divorce, separation, the death or disability of their husbands, or loss of long-term public assistance. In an era when women have entered the paid labor force in record numbers, the stories of those who stayed home and raised their families have too often been overlooked. These women, who are forced to seek paid employment, often have outdated training and few marketable skills.

Displaced homemakers are black, white, Hispanic, Asian, and Native American. They live in cities and small towns. A study based on 1980 Census data shows that there were more than 11 million displaced homemakers in the United States in the late 1970s. More than five million of these displaced homemakers were under the age of 65, with the majority between the ages of 35 and 64 (Displaced Homemakers Network [DHN] 1987c). While some may have been middle class, upon displacement, 40 percent lived below the poverty level and another 21 percent were above the poverty level but below the Bureau of Labor Statistics lower living standard. (The lower living standard is defined as 150 percent of the poverty level—an income at which it is estimated one can meet day-to-day living expenses [DHN 1987c].) Many of these women still have dependent children, yet the number and amount of child and spousal support awards in this country is appallingly low. Women and children suffer a 73 percent decline in their standard of living the first year after divorce, while men experience a 42 percent rise in their standard of living (Weitzman 1985). However varied their situations may be, all displaced homemakers have one characteristic in common—the need for jobs that will lead to economic self-sufficiency.

Displaced homemakers face multiple barriers to entering the labor force, including a lack of recent skills training, education, or work experience, as well as age, sex, and race discrimination.

Often, displaced homemakers feel isolated and that they are the only ones in their situation. This feeling, sometimes further complicated by feelings of guilt or humiliation, prevents them from searching out or having knowledge of programs that exist to serve them. This means that programs that exist to serve displaced homemakers must make special efforts to reach them so that they are aware of the services that are available. Programming must include counseling and opportunities to interact with other women who face similar situations. Through support-group activities women realize that they are not alone and that other women are struggling with many of the same issues.

Having spent a considerable number of years outside the paid labor force, many displaced homemakers also lack the confidence needed to engage effectively in job search activities. They often express the sentiment "I've never been anything but a housewife" and cannot comprehend how that experience could be of value in the paid work force. They may have little knowledge of their own career interests or the kind of jobs that exist and what the salary levels are for various jobs. Thus, programs must be able to assist displaced homemakers in making career choices and ensure that they understand the salary implications of their choice. Programs must also take the time to assess the skills an individual has developed while a homemaker and to translate those skills into the terms and language that an employer can understand.

Many displaced homemakers while seeking to enter the paid work force also maintain families. For them to pursue training and employment, adequate child and dependent care must be available. Displaced homemakers often face concerns about child support nonpayment, lack of health insurance coverage, or lack of housing, among other legal concerns. These issues are normally beyond the perview of traditional employment and training programs. For displaced homemakers to overcome their barriers to employment, programs must be prepared to address these concerns.

The Displaced Homemakers Movement

The Displaced Homemakers Movement began in the mid-1970s in California when two middle-aged women found themselves suddenly displaced from their roles as homemaker and in need of employment. One of the women, Tish

Sommers, coined the term "displaced homemaker" to describe women who, like refugees, were forcibly exiled from their homes and into the labor market. At the time, there were no services or programs targeted to these women who were re-entering the work force or entering it for the first time.

Sommers, joined by Laurie Shields, formed the Alliance for Displaced Homemakers for the purpose of advocating for state legislation that would authorize programs for displaced homemakers. In 1975, the Alliance was successful in getting California to pass legislation to fund a two-year pilot displaced-homemaker center in Oakland. As a result of their success in California, leaders of the Alliance began receiving requests for information about state displaced-homemaker legislation from across the country. Laurie Shields, assisted with travel funds contributed by church organizations, the NOW (National Organization for Women) National Action Center, and others, traveled throughout the United States during 1976, informing, organizing, inspiring, and nurturing grass-roots displaced-homemaker advocacy. By the end of 1977, displaced-homemaker bills had been introduced in 28 states and passed in 16 of them (Shields 1981; 1982).

As Shields traveled, she found women throughout the United States eager to talk about their own experiences. The term "displaced homemaker" struck a nerve, and national attention was focused on the growing phenomenom of long-time homemakers who fell through the cracks of government social service and income support systems—too young for Social Security, ineligible to receive welfare because of the absence of dependent children, and ineligible for health and disability insurance. Media coverage, including magazine articles, television talk-show appearances, and the production of an hour-long film, *Who Remembers Mama?*, attested to the fact that displaced homemakers were a national issue.

In 1979, the Displaced Homemakers Network was established in Washington, D.C., as a national umbrella organization for displaced-homemaker programs and advocates. It provides technical assistance, resources, and information on public policy that affects displaced homemakers. By 1987, nearly 1,000 local displaced-homemaker programs were served by the Displaced Homemakers Network.

Programs for Displaced Homemakers

One of the primary goals of the Displaced Homemakers Network is to increase employment and training opportunities for displaced homemakers. People who have worked in displaced-homemaker programs over the last 10 years agree that the best training programs offer a wide range of services, tailored to the special needs of displaced homemakers and putting foremost the goal of job placement. A well-rounded program would offer the following services: outreach, intake and orientation, personal counseling, assessment and testing, career and education counseling, life skills development, skill training, pre-employment preparation, supportive services, referrals (to legal aid, for instance), and job development and placement services (DHN 1982).

Unfortunately, most programs cannot make all of these activities available. The typical displaced-homemaker program is operated by only one or two full-time staff and one or two part-time staff. Furthermore, these programs have low funding levels: most operate on less than $40,000 a year, while serving 200–250 displaced homemakers a year (DHN 1982).

How has this situation arisen? The answer is at once both simple and complex: federal and state policies on employment and training of displaced homemakers have unfulfilled potential. A look at the recent state and major federal training systems reveals that they meet the special needs of displaced homemakers in a limited and imperfect fashion.

State Displaced-Homemakers Legislation

One must first look at state-legislated and state-supported programs to understand how federal displaced-homemaker programs evolved. After California passed its law in 1975, Maryland, Florida, and Oregon soon followed with their own laws. By 1987, 26 states had displaced-homemaker legislation on the books, but only 23 of those states supported the laws with appropriations (DHN 1987a).

The strength of these laws is that they authorize activities designed with displaced homemakers in mind. Unlike the federal programs discussed below, state laws target displaced homemakers and address their specific needs by authorizing the provision of services generally available at displaced-homemaker centers and programs. Every statute may not mention each of the services or use the same language to describe them, but there is considerable commonality among laws. The activities include outreach, referrals, counseling, life skills workshops, pre-employment activities, job search assistance, training, and supportive services.

State-funded programs, however, have some problems. First, the level of funding is low. A survey of states conducted by DHN (1987a) in 1987 reveals that the range in allocated funds is considerable, with the lowest figure at slightly under $100,000 while the highest is over $2 million. The majority of states appropriate between $200,000 and $800,000 a year. Thus, it must be understood that to the extent commitment is measured in dollars, states' commitments do indeed vary and are modest, compared to federal dollars.

Another perspective on funding levels is available through an analysis of the number of programs supported by each state's appropriation. Dividing a state's total appropriation for a given year by the number of programs that receive a portion of the money, one finds that while a few states provide over $100,000 a program, most appropriate less than $80,000 a program, and over 50 percent allocate less than $60,000. Even these figures must be considered high, because many states appropriations are also used to support an administrative entity at the state level.

The second problem is the uncertain nature of funding. When states need to "tighten their belts," they sometimes look to displaced-homemaker programs to absorb the cuts. Programs are particularly vulnerable when states experience economic difficulties, seek balanced budgets, or look for ways to make up federal dollars lost from other programs. In 1985, for example, the farm state of Nebraska eliminated its displaced-homemaker funding. Oklahoma, suffering from the drop in oil prices, ceased state support of programs, and economically depressed Alabama attempted to cut displaced-homemaker funding from the budget. In other words, while states may do an excellent job of designing programs, the programs are subject to the vagaries of the states' economies. Funding is also uncertain when it is derived from marriage and divorce fees, rather than from general revenues, because the number of marriages and divorces varies each year.

Historically, state displaced-homemakers legislation strengthened the case for federal legislation. As the Alliance for Displaced Homemakers brought its message to state legislatures, and as national attention was given to displaced-homemaker issues, it became conceivable that a federal law targeting displaced homemakers be introduced. The state laws supplied precedence and provided models that could be adopted at the federal level.

Federal Employment and Training Programs

Comprehensive Employment and Training Act
A goal of displaced-homemaker advocates was to obtain federal legislation for displaced homemakers. The credibility of this goal was strengthened not only by the existence of state displaced-homemakers legislation but also by feminist advocates in the field of education who had worked to have displaced homemakers included as a group eligible for programs under the Vocational Education Amendments of 1976. Displaced-homemaker legislation was introduced in 1977 in both the House of Representatives and the Senate. It soon became clear, however, that displaced homemakers were not a high priority on Capitol Hill and that it was unlikely that a displaced-homemaker bill would pass.

At the time, Congress was focusing on the reauthorization of the Comprehensive Employment and Training Act of 1973 (CETA), which was designed to provide federal dollars for job training for the nation's economically disadvantaged population. Strategists decided that the best chance of passing displaced-homemakers legislation was to include it as part of the CETA reauthorization. When CETA was reauthorized in 1978, it did strengthen the system's ability to meet the needs of those with the most serious barriers to employment—including displaced homemakers.

The reauthorization targeted $5 million of national Title III funds in fiscal 1980 to support employment-related services for displaced homemakers. Of this, $3.5 million went to local prime sponsors and governor's offices, which sponsored 41 displaced-homemaker projects. Another $1 million was awarded to six projects by direct grants from the Department of Labor to community-based organizations. Some funds went to the Displaced Homemakers Network to provide technical assistance to the Title III displaced-homemaker projects as well as technical assistance to other local programs interested in obtaining CETA funds to serve displaced homemakers.

Title II funds for Comprehensive Employment and Training Services were also used to train displaced homemakers. In fact, local prime sponsors were required to describe the services being provided for individuals facing "severe handicaps" to employment; the law names displaced homemakers, individuals 55 years old or older, single parents and women, among others, as individuals in this category. Finally, Title VI of CETA, which authorizes public service employment, was used to hire displaced homemakers to staff centers.

The impact of CETA was considerable. From 1978 to 1981, the number of displaced-homemaker programs grew from less than 50 to more than 300. The growth in the number of programs came with support not only from CETA but also from vocational education and state-legislated programs. However, it was CETA's positive impact that taught the employment and training community, as well as policy makers, that specialized programs for displaced homemakers can be effective. While some CETA programs for women enrolled a mix of populations, the more effective programs were those that recognized the special needs of displaced homemakers and provided: opportunities for support groups and counseling; time to examine homemaking skills and life experiences; and structured activities to build self-confidence and knowledge of the job market. The more effective programs also recognized that, to prepare them to enter the job market, a 55-year-old widow has very different needs than does a 25-year-old single parent.

The CETA projects demonstrated what program components and service delivery strategies work for displaced homemakers, important lessons for the architects of future displaced-homemaker programs. Specifically, the projects illustrated the value of employing as staff displaced homemakers and other individuals who could identify with participants because of their similar experiences, who were themselves mature and stable, and who had particular skills in employment, training, counseling, and local community resources. Further, the projects showed what program design is successful. A good service mix includes outreach and recruitment, intake process, the core training program, counseling services, job development activities, and post-termination services (Berkeley Planning Associates 1981).

While on the surface these program elements resemble the components of standard employment and training programs, their implementation strategies responded specifically to the circumstances being faced by displaced homemakers. Life skills services included self-assessment, confidence-building, life management skills, career assessment and exploration, community resources information, and basic educational review. The peer support and interaction that occurred in the job-readiness workshops were considered an essential aspect of the service strategy, because the supportive group structure provided a safe place for displaced homemakers to share their problems, fears, strengths, and experiences with one another. It allowed them to overcome feelings of personal blame or failure for their situation, thereby enabling them to move toward constructive action in becoming self-supporting.

The final program component that contributed to the effectiveness of the CETA projects was the availability of supportive services. CETA illustrated the absolute necessity of providing supportive services if displaced homemakers are to participate in training.

CETA was instructive in another respect. Before these projects were undertaken, displaced homemakers were thought to be only middle-class, well-educated women. The Title III projects debunked this myth by demonstrating the existence of low-income displaced homemakers who fit CETA's eligibility requirements and needed training to enter the labor force.

Although CETA did indeed lay important groundwork by leveraging the federal employment and training system for displaced homemakers, it was not without problems. Some service providers attempted to "mainstream" displaced homemakers by designing projects that served them as well as other populations. This meant necessarily that displaced homemakers would not have access to some of the special services or service delivery strategies they needed and that the staff would not be appropriately trained or suited to working with displaced homemakers, particularly for intake and peer counseling. Also under CETA, displaced homemakers, like other women served by the system, were more frequently placed by CETA counselors in classroom training, while men tended to be clustered in on-the-job training. This placement pattern seemed to reflect the stereotypic notion that men have a more immediate need for "jobs" and that women need more "schooling" to prepare for work. Although under CETA most participants who were enrolled in classroom training received a stipend while in training, the overall immediate placement rate in an unsubsidized job was higher for those who received on-the-job training (OJT) than for those who received classroom training. More men than women found employment through CETA.

Furthermore, classroom training tended to be in traditionally female jobs where CETA counselors often felt women "should be." OJT experiences were more likely to be in male-dominated occupations. Thus, displaced homemakers, like other women in CETA, were clustered in training for clerical positions, health aide positions, and other "helping jobs." The majority of the jobs obtained were entry-level jobs paying minimum wage or only slightly above minimum wage.

Finally, CETA projects rarely made a concerted effort to recruit and serve mid-life and older women, women whose special needs make them harder to serve than some other populations. The percentage of displaced homemakers among those enrolled in CETA programs was very low compared to the percentage of displaced homemakers in the population of CETA-eligible persons.

Even given these drawbacks, CETA's value cannot be diminished. It showed that displaced homemakers are in fact eligible and in need of services, it made training opportunities available to many displaced homemakers, and it documented how specially designed programs can be effective.

By 1980, however, the progress was curtailed. Budget cuts resulted in fewer services; of the 47 displaced-homemaker programs funded by Title III, only 11 continued to receive CETA funds. The others either obtained funding from other sources or closed their doors.

Job Training Partnership Act

When the Job Training Partnership Act (JTPA) was enacted in 1982, it held considerable promise for displaced homemakers, promise that has gone unfulfilled. Displaced homemakers are named as a group that is facing barriers to employment and is therefore eligible to be served under Title IIA, the largest pot of money. (See Harlan, Chapter 2, for a description of the legislation.) In 1985, DHN surveyed its programs to determine how displaced homemakers and displaced-homemaker programs were faring under JTPA (DHN 1985). The survey findings, augmented by information gathered at state and regional displaced-homemaker conferences and through individual contact with program operators from across the country, support the conclusion that certain characteristics of the JTPA system function as disincentives for administrators and service providers to design programs that meet the needs of displaced homemakers and help them achieve economic self-sufficiency.

At least three characteristics distinguish JTPA from its predecessor, CETA, and combine to form a system that does not address the training needs of displaced homemakers. First, unlike CETA, JTPA establishes a partnership between the private and public sectors, giving them shared authority over local decision-making. The influence of private-sector representatives on the Private Industry Councils (PICs) has been to encourage a "bottom line" approach in determining what kinds of service are provided (discussed in more detail below).

Second, JTPA limits the expenditures for administration and supportive services to 30 percent and reserves 70 percent of program funds for direct training costs. This is significant because it places a 15 percent cap on administrative costs (down from CETA's 20 percent), which effectively limits to 15 percent the funds available for supportive services, including needs based payments (that is, stipends).

Although these two characteristics affect seriously the shape of JTPA programming, neither exerts the influence of JTPA performance standards. Under CETA, performance measures were introduced but not fully implemented or required. Under JTPA, the performance standards, which are issued by the secretary of labor and can be adjusted by governors in light of state and local conditions, are these: the entered employment rate of participants, the cost per entered employment, the average wage at placement, and the welfare entered employment rate.

The emphasis on performance standards creates a "performance-driven" system. From the level of the individual training provider on up, JTPA professionals are keenly aware that their performance must look good. Service delivery areas (SDAs) strive not just to meet performance standards but to exceed them; in fact, SDAs often receive incentive grants from the governor's office for their successful performance.

While there is nothing wrong with wanting a job training system to produce results measured by performance standards, a grievous error is made when those results serve exclusively as a gauge of how well the system is working. The specific problem with JTPA as it is put into practice is its heavy emphasis on one performance standard—the entered employment rate, or placement rate. The SDAs' interest in achieving high placement rates dictates to whom they provide services and what services they provide. This means that they naturally want to serve people who are close to being job-ready, easily placed in jobs and not in need of an array of services. This does not mean displaced homemakers. The weight given to placement rates results in poor services to displaced homemakers.

SDAs use OJT because its participants have a much higher immediate job placement rate than do other participants. (Although it should be understood that an OJT experience is not the same as, and does not necessarily result in, employment after the program.) Furthermore, OJT satisfies the criterion of low cost per placement rate. It is a shorter activity than classroom training (an average of 16 weeks compared to 26), and less time means less money invested in the training—Walker, Feldstein, and Solow 1984, 19). Moreover, it is less costly than providing additional services that do not, on the surface, seem to contribute directly to job placement. In addition, OJT provides income for participants during their training period.

Although OJT has much to recommend it, a problem arises when such a high proportion of the available JTPA dollars goes to OJT that there are few resources left for other important support services. OJT is of value, but so are the "pre-OJT" services that many displaced homemakers need.

Limited Supportive Services

Nationally, SDAs spend much less on supportive services than the law allows, only 7 or 8 percent of their funds (U.S. General Accounting Office [USGAO] 1985, iii; Walker, Feldstein, and Solow 1984, 12). Furthermore, few SDAs (7 percent) seek waivers on support cost limitations (Walker, Feldstein, and Solow 1984, 15). DHN's own survey of programs that serve mostly women found that almost one-third of the JTPA contracts made no provision for supportive services (DHN 1985).

Basically, JTPA performance standards are the reason that support services to participants are limited. Any money spent on supportive services cannot be put toward training costs—and training, not supportive services, is seen to lead directly to job placements. Also, a contract's cost per placement rate will be higher if supportive services are included than if not. Consider this example: Programs A and B both have contracts that stipulate their placing 60 percent of their clients, or 100 people. Program A uses $3,000 to train each client but provides no supportive services. Its cost per placement, then, will be $3,000. Similarly, program B provides training that costs $3,000, but it also makes $500 worth of supportive services available to each participant, so that the associated cost per placement is $3,500. In a system that is focused on performance standards and "the bottom line," there is no incentive to provide supportive services. Displaced homemakers, who need supportive services to participate in a job training program, will not find that the JTPA system is responsive to their needs.

A GAO study asked JTPA officials about the impact of the limitation in support costs on the type of clients served and training offered. A majority believed JTPA participants to be more motivated and less economically disadvantaged than their CETA counterparts. A majority also believed that some training programs were shorter than they should have been and that other programs could not be offered (GAO 1985, iv). Another report highlighted the influence of the business-oriented PICs: "Their judgment was that the provision of support services often promoted dependency or duplicated resources that could be provided by other means, public, private, or personal. One PIC chair said: 'We are not setting up a program to deal with the unmotivated.'" The local government officials surveyed believed allowable expenditures for supportive services would limit their ability to serve many people, such as displaced homemakers, who needed subsidized training to find employment (Walker, Feldstein, and Solow 1984, 20).

The overall impact of JTPA's performance standards is to encourage PICs, whose members are already predisposed to concentrating on the "bottom line," to award contracts for programs and clients that should guarantee "good numbers." Programs that meet the needs of special populations, such as displaced homemakers, are less attractive than programs that can serve the more easily placed populations. The fewer the services and activities needed, the more desirable the applicant for JTPA enrollment. This is referred to as "creaming," or serving clients who are most easily and cheaply placed in jobs. The JTPA system, which serves an estimated 4 percent of the eligible population, has no trouble locating such clients.

Displaced homemakers can seldom find in JTPA the breadth of services, including supportive services, that they need. DHN found that many displaced-homemaker service providers are too discouraged with the JTPA system even to bid on a request-for-proposal. They report that they do not have contracts because their PICs are not targeting displaced homemakers for services. Instead, PICs are "mainstreaming" their clients and awarding contracts for skills training, which is not the primary focus of displaced-homemaker programs.

Short-Term Skills Training

What happens to those displaced homemakers who do manage to make it through the JTPA system to the point of job placement? These "survivors" are probably not on their way to economic self-sufficiency. In a game in which winning is making many job placements at the lowest possible cost, program operators are naturally interested in providing short-term training, and the result is training for occupations that do not lead to high earnings.

DHN's survey revealed that most training for women was in either the clerical or the health field. The administrators of one displaced-homemaker program that did not have a JTPA contract identified the inherent problem: "We referred very few clients because even with the training they could earn little more than AFDC [Aid to Families with Dependent Children] and in one case a woman was worse off than being on welfare. Presently clients are referred but the approach is traditional jobs for women (low pay)—clerical, food service, retail, etc." An Indiana displaced-homemaker program encountered a similar situation: "Some of the training is for jobs which turn out to be minimum-wage and part-time, such as a recent one in telemarketing and telecommunication—phone solicitation, in other words!"

Anecdotal evidence and DHN's survey findings combine to sound a cautionary note. If displaced homemakers receive training for entry-level, low-paying jobs with little opportunity for advancement—that is, for jobs that will not allow them to support themselves and their children—then the training is of little value to them. In one sense, JTPA's short-term training is desirable, because displaced homemakers need an income as soon as possible. The solution, then, appears to be to offer training that takes longer and has a stipend attached to it.

In summary, performance standards are not in and of themselves objectionable, but they can be used to keep a job training system from serving high-risk populations, such as displaced homemakers. Some argue that the long-term impact of JTPA will be limited because those who were placed in jobs would have found employment anyway. If this is true, then the nation is wasting billions of dollars on a job training system that serves the easily served, not those "most in need."

Federal Vocational Education Programs
Vocational Education Act of 1963 as Amended in 1976
Historically, the vocational education system has segregated men and boys in traditionally female occupational programs and women and girls in traditionally female occupational programs. Research in the 1970s documented that this situation had not changed even though increasing numbers of women were entering the paid labor force (Vetter, Chapter 3; Kane and Frazee 1976).

Primarily through the efforts of women's advocates and organizations, and in particular the National Coalition for Women and Girls in Education, the 1976 amendments to the Vocational Education Act of 1963 contained the first sex equity provisions for vocational education. The law directed states to assign a person full time whose responsibilities would focus on assisting the state in achieving equity in vocational education. The responsibilities of the sex equity coordinator included broad authority to gather information, to review and monitor program activities and distribution of grants, to provide technical assistance, and to develop plans and submit recommendations related to sex equity. The state was required to reserve $50,000 each year to support this position.

The law specifically provided that funds from the basic grant allotted to the states could be used for vocational education for "persons who had solely been homemakers but who now, because of dissolution of marriage, must seek employment" (Sec. 120(b)(L)(i)). Along with the other equity provisions contained in the law, this represented a major advance for women and girls in vocational education and held much promise toward reversing the patterns of sex stereotyping and bias that existed in vocational education.

How did displaced homemakers fare as a result of this initiative? While the law defined broad responsibilities for the sex equity coordinator, it did not define how the responsibilities were to be implemented. As a result, the implementation of the 1976 amendments varied greatly among the states, and because the law did not require that basic grant funds be used to support equity activities, some states chose to do nothing.

The extent to which states chose to fund displaced-homemaker programs ranged from token support of a few small projects to more substantial efforts. Arizona, for example, funded six programs to provide educational programs to prepare displaced homemakers for seeking employment. Maryland funded New Directions for Women, a center for displaced homemakers that reported providing support services to more than 4,000 women over the age of 35. Michigan established three displaced-homemaker centers throughout the state. In Missouri, six displaced-homemaker centers were funded jointly out of vocational education and CETA funds. Twenty-six displaced-homemaker centers were funded in Ohio with cooperative dollars from the Ohio Department of Education and CETA. The State Board for Community College Education in Washington elected to provide 3 percent of their basic grant for displaced-homemaker programs and 2 percent for support services.

While funded programs tended to be small, existing on very modest resources, they provided a valuable training ground for the development of approaches and strategies for serving displaced homemakers. Counseling materials, assertiveness training techniques, skills transfer methods, and support group procedures were developed and refined. Moreover, the experience with the 1976 amendments increased the number of displaced-homemaker programs nationally and legitimatized the support of displaced-homemaker programs under vocational education.

Carl D. Perkins Vocational Education Act
The passage of the Carl D. Perkins Vocational Education Act in 1984 introduced a new and expanded emphasis on sex equity in vocational education in general and for displaced homemakers in particular. The law, which is in effect until 1989, requires states to target 8.5 percent of their basic state grant to single parents and homemakers. The law also requires that state plans for vocational education ensure that in supporting programs under the 8.5 percent provision, special consideration be given to "homemakers who because of divorce, separation, or the death or disability of a spouse must prepare for paid employment," that is, displaced homemakers. At the same time the law makes a major shift by requiring that federal vocational education funds be used exclusively for program improvement and not be used for the maintenance of on-going vocational education programs.

In serving single parents and homemakers under the 8.5 percent set-aside, states are authorized to provide: (1) vocational education and training activities; (2) grants to expand vocational education services; (3) child care, transportation, and organization and scheduling of programs so they are accessible; and (4) information about vocational education and support services. States may, but are not required to, make grants to community-based organizations that have demonstrated effectiveness in providing services to single parents and homemakers.

The Perkins Act strengthens the position of the sex equity coordinator by requiring that the coordinator be assigned responsibility for administering the 8.5 percent set-aside for single parents and homemakers, as well as a 3.5 percent set-aside for eliminating sex bias and stereotyping. Funds for these two set-asides exceeded $100 million nationally in fiscal 1985, which represents the largest amount of vocational training funds targeted to women and girls in the history of this country. While these funds represent a landmark in efforts to provide equitable vocational services to women and girls, the total amount of federal funds allocated for vocational education were less than one-third of those allocated to employment and training programs under JTPA in 1986.

How were such gains accomplished? In 1983 and 1984, when Congress was deliberating renewed legislation for vocational education, there was substantial divisiveness on the value of the sex equity efforts under the 1976 amendments. Some vocational educators wanted the whole sex equity issue to "go away" and lobbied strongly against any special provisions for women and girls. Advocates seeking to improve the situation for women and girls in vocational education argued forcefully about the need for access to vocational training, articulating the link between the lack of adequate training, women's severe disadvantage in the labor force, and the feminization of poverty.

The sex equity advocates were able to do this successfully because of their own organizing efforts. Not long after the passage of the 1976 amendments, which established a sex equity coordinator in each state, those individuals who filled the coordinator positions formed their own professional association under the administrative section of the American Vocational Association called the Vocational Education Equity Council (VEEC). During the early years of its formation, VEEC provided a "safe place" for sex equity coordinators to share their frustrations in trying to implement the mandate of the legislation. It quickly evolved into a forum where materials, programming, and strategies were exchanged and where valuable training took place.

As the vocational education reauthorization process got under way, VEEC developed reports and documentation of the progress that had been made with the limited investment under the 1976 amendments. At the same time, the National Coalition for Women and Girls in Education (NCWGE), a Washington-based advocacy group representing more than 60 organizations, worked daily with Congress, using the information that VEEC had generated. DHN, an active member of the NCWGE, provided further support through information from displaced-homemaker programs across the country, which at that time numbered nearly 400.

The reauthorization process and the opposing views about sex equity programs were being played out at the same time that the value of vocational programs was being questioned. Although vocational education, which has been around since 1907, has always enjoyed widespread Congressional support, members of Congress began asking hard questions about the impact of the programs, the outcomes for those who participated, and the ability of the programs to keep pace with the rapid changes in the labor force. The women advocating for fairer treatment in the system were in a very real sense also arguing about the importance and value of the system. And while it is doubtful that their efforts were recognized by the vocational education lobby, the two groups shared the goal of strengthening overall vocational programming.

The mandated set-aside of funds in the Perkins Act have benefited displaced-homemaker programs. A survey of programs serving displaced homemakers conducted by DHN in late 1986 showed an increase in the number of programs from 423 in 1984 to more than 900. However, not all areas of the country have benefited equally. There are indications that the intent of the law is being circumvented and that the requirement to target funds to displaced homemakers has not been met.

In Pennsylvania, for example, programs funded through the 8.5 percent set-aside for single parents and homemakers are not allowed to focus specifically on displaced homemakers but must include a broad service population that includes all single parents and homemakers. Nothing in the federal law, however, prohibits the use of the 8.5 percent set-aside to support programs specifically focused on displaced homemakers. In fact, other states have interpreted the requirement that the state "give special consideration" to displaced homemakers to mean that displaced-homemaker programs are warranted.

New York, North Carolina, and California, among other states, have chosen to allocate all or part of the 8.5 percent set-aside funds to schools and community colleges using a formula allocation to ensure that every school district or community college gets a portion of the set-aside funds. Formula distribution of federal vocational funds based on economic, social, and demographic factors was required prior to the Perkins Act, although the Perkins Act has refocused the purposes for which federal funds can be used. Formulas are popular because state vocational administrators who make decisions about allocating funds and who have come up through the ranks feel closely aligned with the local vocational directors. They resist changing from the formula funding method to a request-for-proposal approach that can ensure that programs funded with set-aside monies have adequate resources to serve displaced homemakers and single parents. Under formula funding, schools can carry on as usual and ask students at the end of the year, "How many of you are single parents or homemakers?" By taking a head count the school can report that they have "targeted" the funds as required by the law. However, this defeats the purposes of the Perkins Act, which are to improve vocational programs, to correct patterns of underservice, and to increase access to vocational education among populations previously underserved. Another problem inherent in the formula funding approach is that some schools receive so few dollars that it is not feasible to mount any special effort to serve the needs of displaced homemakers or single parents. The ability to provide special programming as intended is thereby circumvented.

An important feature in the Perkins Act is the ability to provide vocational education services with the 8.5 percent funds through community-based organizations (CBOs). This is particularly useful in serving displaced homemakers, who are often intimidated by or reluctant to go to an educational institution. However, some states have ruled that community-based organizations are ineligible to receive funds, or have required that CBOs subcontract with a local school or college. These kinds of limitation are evidence of a desire on the part of vocational educators to keep the programs and dollars "in house" even though the policy may result in unnecessary duplication of services and lack of support for programs with long-term experience.

There is also a reluctance by some states to use vocational education funds for support services, even though it is clearly allowable under the law and necessary for some women to be able to participate in programs. Additionally, the employment and training needs of older displaced homemakers are not being addressed, because it is easier to serve younger women with more recent educational and employment experience. Unfortunately, there is no requirement to insure services to older women.

Another issue is that in some states the sex equity coordinator does not have administrative authority for all or part of the 8.5 percent set-aside. While the law is explicit in requiring that the coordinator have this authority, states have been inventive, creative, and sometimes devious in preventing the intended implementation. Internal politics and organizational structures within state education departments can partially explain this situation. When sex equity coordinators were established under the 1976 amendments, there were no program dollars assigned to the position—states were required only to expend $50,000 to support the position. Within state education department structures, the sex equity coordinator often was located low on the organizational chart, layers below the state vocational education director and other decision-making managers. Changes brought by the Perkins Act gave sex equity coordinators administrative authority for large numbers of program dollars, thereby shifting the authority away from others who may have been in a supervisory or higher managerial position to the sex equity coordinator. However, the supervisors still maintain authority over the coordinators and, therefore, can make decisions about the sex equity programs. They also have close professional ties to local vocational directors who have been funded in the past and are expecting continued funding.

The sex equity coordinator's authority is also diminished by the way most states administer their educational programs. A common structure places educational programs involving kindergarden through twelfth grade in one agency (usually a Department of Public Instruction) and houses programs dealing with postsecondary and higher education in another. Although vocational educations programs are delivered at both the secondary and the postsecondary levels, the sex equity coordinator's position is almost always located in the agency dealing with public instruction (K–12). A proportion of the 8.5 percent funds are controlled by the postsecondary department, and the sex equity coordinator has no input about how local postsecondary institutions expend the funds and little or no responsibility for monitoring what is occurring with the funds. (Almost uniformly, these postsecondary funds are allocated according to a formula.) Some states have designated a person in the postsecondary agency to work cooperatively with the sex equity coordinator, though usually there is no explicit decision-making authority over the designee. Wisconsin has developed an alternative that seems to work well by creating two sex equity coordinator positions—one at the secondary level and one at the postsecondary level—each having administrative authority over their agency's set-aside funds.

The Perkins Act has had a negative impact in some of the states that have displace-homemaker legislation. Some state legislators or governors have tried to cut back or cut out state-funded displaced-homemaker programs, because they feel that with the Perkins Act "the job is being done." A cutback did occur in Oklahoma, and efforts to make a cutback were averted only at the last moment in Iowa. The assessment that the Perkins Act alone is enough is made without an understanding of its limitations.

Although the Perkins Act is theoretically an excellent vehicle for providing the vocational services needed by displaced homemakers, it has not been implemented to its full potential. In part this is because the traditional model for vocational education assumes that participants are young people attending school full time. As a consequence, displaced homemakers who need to have income within a reasonable amount of time might be faced, for example, with enrolling in a full-time training program that lasts a year or longer without any financial compensation. Also, because of the traditional approach to vocational education, displaced homemakers are placed with other populations in programs that do not provide for their special needs. Many vocational educators are ill-prepared to respond to older women, particularly those with immediate needs. Furthermore, the supportive services that displaced homemakers also need are limited because vocational educators are not used to participants who must have the services.

A final example of how implementation is wrongly influenced by the orientation of traditional vocational education is the limited use of community-based organizations, which have a good record of providing effective services for displaced homemakers. Yet, the education system prefers to give funding to educational institutions exclusively. In sum, while the law makes provisions for services and service delivery strategies that meet the needs of displaced home-makers, the vocational education system continues to assume falsely that it is serving only young students without families. Its lack of commitment to older students, with and without families, has prevented the full implementation of the law.

Policy Recommendations

Displaced homemakers are not just women, not just single parents, not just mid-life and older individuals. They are a special population with special needs, and education and training programs that seek to serve them must respond to this fact. What follows are policy recommendations that address the problems discussed above and present goals that advocates must work toward implementing if they are to help displaced homemakers receive appropriate training.

State Displaced-Homemakers Legislation

State displaced-homemakers legislation has authorized good programs for dis-placed homemakers that are specially designed to meet their needs. About half of the states in the United States now have displaced-homemaker legislation on the books; those states with legislation but no appropriations should appro-priate funds, and those states with no legislation should pass a law authorizing services to displaced homemakers. Planning and staffing any employment and training program—and a displaced homemaker-program in particular— requires a revenue source that is adequate and stable. Therefore, appropria-tions for state displaced-homemaker legislation should be a line item in the state budget or a line item in combination with revenue generated by special fees or taxes.

JTPA

Program participants should be preparing themselves for jobs that will allow them to achieve economic self-sufficiency. This means that six weeks spent learning to do telephone solicitation does not constitute an acceptable training program. More comprehensive training is needed—training that leads to good jobs. A related issue is the need to pay stipends during training so that partici-pants can engage in longer training that will result in jobs with higher wages. Furthermore, training programs should not reinforce occupational segrega-tion, which puts women in poorly paying jobs. Although the larger solution is to raise the minimum wage so that all jobs provide a living wage, at least for now programs must be designed to channel women into better jobs.

The income eligibility requirements of programs that are developed to serve the economically disadvantaged must reflect the use of common sense. Under JTPA, the Title II programs often exclude displaced homemakers whose family income six months ago, when the spouse was present or employed, was much higher than at the time of application. One solution that has already been adopted in some states is to define "family" at the time of application so that "family income" for the last six months will not incorrectly account for a spouse who is no longer contributing to the family income. A second solution is to allow Title III funds for dislocated workers to support programs for displaced homemakers. Clearly, the displaced homemaker has lost her long-time job: she is displaced from her former job as a homemaker, and it is unlikely she will be a full-time homemaker again. Already this approach to Title III has been adopted in some states, but it needs to become national policy.

Performance standards, as they are currently used, promote "creaming" and are a disincentive to enrolling the hard-to-serve. Performance standards should be adjusted for populations with special needs. Furthermore, performance standards should include measures of long-term performance so that service providers will focus on securing job placements in good jobs—that is, jobs that can lead to more than minimum wage.

Programs should not emphasize skills training to the exclusion of other services. For many displaced homemakers, obtaining employment that can lead to genuine economic self-sufficiency requires remedial education, pre-employment preparation, and other services. Service delivery areas should, at the minimum, spend the 15 percent of funds allowable for supportive services and, where appropriate, request a waiver on the 15 percent cap. Providing good training without providing the supportive services that displaced homemakers need in order to participate in the program completely negates the value of the program for them.

Vocational Education
Special programs for displaced homemakers should be permitted that provide the support and counseling needed to ensure that displaced homemakers will succeed in education and training programs. Record keeping needs to be implemented that will reflect how well displaced homemakers are being served.

Community-based organizations should be used more extensively. They have proven their special ability to work with displaced homemakers, and they provide an alternative to the "college" setting, which is intimidating to many middle-aged and older women.

Training opportunities of less than one or two years should be considered so that displaced homemakers can begin to earn an income in a reasonable amount of time. The dilemma for displaced homemakers is that they often have to provide immediate support for their families, but in the longer run they would benefit from more long-term training that would provide a job with higher income. Therefore, stipends, loans, and scholarships are necessary for displaced homemakers to take advantage of vocational training programs that extend beyond a year.

Child care expenses and transportation expenses may prevent a displaced homemaker from participating in needed training. Vocational education must respond by providing support to cover these costs for individuals in financial need.

States need to think about formula-funding in a new way so that funds intended for a targeted population are in fact used for that population and are allocated in amounts that can reasonably support a program. Local agencies must be given explicit guidelines about the allowable use of targeted funds, and local agencies must be required to submit plans or proposals in order to receive their "allotments." The state must also be prepared to work with the local agencies whose plans do not meet specific guidelines, to provide adequate staff to monitor the programs, and to deliver technical assistance where needed.

Other Recommendations

Three recommendations apply to state displaced-homemaker legislation, JTPA, and vocational education. First, funding levels must be higher. The funding levels for state legislation, mentioned above, are very low. Even though JTPA has three times the amount of funding as vocational education programs, its funds, it is estimated, can serve only 4 percent of the eligible population. There must be a national commitment to backing up laws with decent appropriations.

Second, services to displaced homemakers available through state legislation, vocational education, and JTPA must be coordinated. While each system has its own special focus and delivery system, all allocate significant public dollars to meeting employment and training needs. Their coordination can lead to better services for displaced homemakers.

Finally, all education and training systems must collect data routinely. It is the only way to monitor whether laws are being implemented as intended. Under both of the current federal education and job training programs, data collection requirements are meager, and so it is difficult to assess the extent to which the laws' intents are being fulfilled and whether the needs of displaced homemakers are being met.

For this reason, the DHN initiated a project designed to collect data about displaced homemakers and other female populations at the point of intake, during enrollment, and after services have been received. A major goal of the project is to facilitate the national standardization of data so that it is possible to develop a national perspective on job training programs for women.

Employment and training services for displaced homemakers do not occur in a vacuum. There are many other factors that affect whether displaced homemakers can successfully participate in available training programs. Access to affordable housing, after-school care, and health services affect their ability to participate in training and consequently in the work force. Because of these considerations, a displaced homemaker's decision is often whether to pursue training and education leading to higher wages or to take the first job offered, no matter what the wage, in order to survive. These issues must be addressed as well by advocates and policy makers.

It is true that the availability of services has improved dramatically in the years since the term "displaced homemaker" was first used. But many displaced homemakers still do not have complete access to the array of training and supportive services needed to become economically self-sufficient. Advocates and policy makers must continue to push for reforms in state and federal employment and training systems that will ensure that middle-aged and older women entering or re-entering the labor force receive appropriate services.

Note

Acknowledgment: Assistance in preparing this article was provided by Rubie Coles and Abby Spero.

References

Berkeley Planning Associates. 1981. *Assessment of the National Displaced Homemaker Program.* Vol. 5, *Summary of Research Findings: Conclusions and Recommendations.* Berkeley.

Displaced Homemakers Network. 1982. Program Policy Statement. Washington, D.C.

———. 1985. *Is the Job Training Partnership Act Training Displaced Homemakers?* Washington, D.C.

———. 1987a. *A Handbook on State Displaced Homemakers Legislation: 1987 Update.* Washington, D.C.

———. 1987b. Planning Papers for the Second Annual National Conference on Displaced Homemakers, Pittsburgh. Typescript.

———. 1987c. *Status Report on Displaced Homemakers and Single Parents in the United States.* Washington, D.C.

Kane, Roslyn D., and Pamela Frazee. 1978. Women in Non-Traditional Occupations in Post-Secondary Area Vocational Training Schools. Final Report to the U.S. Department of Health, Education, and Welfare, Office of Education. Arlington, Va.: RJ Associates, Inc.

Shields, Laurie. 1981. *Displaced Homemakers: Organizing for a New Life*. New York: McGraw-Hill.

U.S. General Accounting Office. 1985. *The Job Training Partnership Act: An Analysis of Support Cost Limits and Participant Characteristics*. Washington, D.C.: Government Printing Office.

Walker, Gary; Hilary Feldstein; and Katherine Solow. 1984. *An Independent Sector Assessment of the Job Training Partnership Act*. New York: Grinker, Walker, and Assoc.

Weitzman, Lenore J. 1985. *The Divorce Revolution: The Unexpected Social and Economic Consequences for Women and Children in the United States*. New York: The Free Press.

6/Employment Services for Teenage Mothers

Denise F. Polit

Teenage parenthood has emerged as a major social problem of the 1980s in the United States. Each year about half a million babies are born to women under age 20, accounting for about one-fifth of all babies born. By the time they turn 20, 41 percent of black females and 19 percent of white females have become mothers. An especially troublesome issue is the dramatic increase in out-of-wedlock births among teens. The birth rate to unmarried teenage women was 30.2 per 1,000 in 1984, compared to 22.4 per 1,000 in 1970 (Hayes 1987).

Teenage pregnancy has captured the interest of policy makers at the federal, state, and local levels, and action agendas are increasingly being demanded. Most states have organized teen pregnancy task forces to develop both preventive and ameliorative strategies. Teenage parenthood has become an important policy issue not only because our society is concerned with the moral and sexual development of our youth but also because early childbearing has been shown to result in a host of personal and societal costs. Among the best-documented consequences of adolescent parenthood are diminished educational attainment (Moore et al. 1979; Mott and Marsiglio 1985); adverse health outcomes for the mother and infant (Makinson 1985; Strobino 1987); high rates of divorce and illegitimacy (Mott and Moore 1979; Bahr and Galligan 1984); and poor lifelong economic prospects (Ellwood 1986; Haggstrom et al. 1981; McLaughlin 1977).

The educational attainment of teenage mothers is a key determinant of their poor financial prospects. Pregnancy is the leading cause of dropping out of school among teenage girls. By age 18, 60 percent of all teen mothers have not completed school, and by age 19, the rate is still 40 percent (Alan Guttmacher Institute 1981). Nine months after delivery, only 17 percent of white school-age mothers and 39 percent of black school-age mothers were in school in 1979 (Mott and Maxwell 1981).

The economic costs of teenage parenthood have attracted particular concern in this era of fiscal restraint. According to a recent projection (Burt 1986), the public cost associated with babies born to teenagers in 1985 alone will total $6.04 billion dollars. This estimate includes projections for costs to be incurred over a 20-year period and includes only those births for a single year. The same report estimated that in 1985 alone, the public outlay for all teenage childbearing—that is for women who at some point in the past first gave birth as teenagers—was $16.65 billion for three major programs: Aid to Families with Dependent Children (AFDC), Food Stamps, and Medicaid.

These figures reflect the fact that women who give birth during their teenage years are at substantial risk of becoming public welfare recipients. During their lives, nearly two-thirds of all teenage mothers will require AFDC at some time. Furthermore, it has been estimated that over a third of the women who become AFDC recipients when they are 21 years old or younger will have over nine years in a single spell of welfare dependency (Ellwood 1986). Developing strategies to overturn these estimates has become a major challenge of the 1980s.

Welfare mothers have two primary routes to exiting the AFDC rolls: through employment earnings or through marriage. For the majority of unmarried teenage mothers, the more common path is through employment (Bane and Ellwood 1983), yet the obstacles these teens face in securing employment are enormous. They bring to the labor force little in the way of human capital: they lack educational credentials, have little prior work experience, have few marketable skills, and have parenting responsibilities. Furthermore, they are competing in a difficult youth employment market. Early work experience and job training appear to be critical to the future employability of young mothers. Programs are needed to help young mothers complete their basic schooling, to acquire a basic understanding of the world of work, and to develop marketable skills.

The Social Response

During the 1970s and early 1980s, programs serving young parents and pregnant teens proliferated in this country under many different auspices— community-based organizations, youth-serving agencies, schools, hospitals, and so on. The emergence of these special programs generally reflected the conviction that, despite the availability of many social, educational, and health services, young mothers do not usually have ready access to them. Early studies showed that teenagers in general, and teenage parents in particular, are not sufficiently experienced or aggressive in seeking out needed services, particularly from multiple service providers (Cannon-Bonventre and Kahn 1978).

While many of these special teen parent programs began with a focus on one or two specific problems (for example, retaining pregnant teens in school or providing prenatal health care), program operators began to recognize the desirability of offering *comprehensive* services. This movement gained momentum because of a growing awareness that programs that were in operation in the early 1970s were inefficient and nonresponsive to the multiple needs of young mothers. Fragmentation of effort and lack of coordination were continuously cited as obstacles to effective service delivery to this needy population.

Thus, the late 1970s witnessed the burgeoning of comprehensive teen parent programs, hundreds of which are now in operation (Polit 1986b). These programs typically offer (or broker, through arrangements with other service providers in the community) such services as prenatal education, parenting education, nutrition education, life management education, educational counseling or services, family planning education, personal counseling, recreational activities, and peer support groups. Relatively few of these programs, until recently, have offered or brokered employment-related or vocational services to their clients. This gap in the provision of "comprehensive" services stemmed, in part, from the staffs' lack of familiarity with the delivery of employment-related services. Program operators in teen parent programs generally tried to work with the existing employment-service-delivery system (that is, with available CETA [Comprehensive Employment and Training Act] and JTPA [Job Training Partnership Act] programs) for those young mothers who were ready for some type of vocational preparation.

Within the past few years, however, staff in teen parent programs have become increasingly concerned about the inability of the existing service-delivery system to meet the employment-related needs of young mothers. Many service providers are now challenging traditional training programs by adding employment-related components to their own operations. The major criticisms being leveled at traditional training programs are that (1) teenage mothers are not recruited or enrolled, because of anticipated failure or absenteeism; (2) the programs are too short, rigid, and nonindividualized; and (3) the programs do not provide adequate support services, most notably child care. Thus, as a result of a variety of changes in our society since the early 1970s, teen parent programs are now beginning to recognize the need for vocational and employment-related services for this target population, and many are beginning to offer them.

The Project Redirection Experience

The evolving interest in including employment-related services in comprehensive teen parent programs probably reflects, to some degree, the recognition that such a program design is feasible. This feasibility was documented in an innovative demonstration known as Project Redirection, which was designed and managed by the Manpower Demonstration Research Corporation, a non-profit organization that focuses on policies relating to employment, training, and social welfare. The overall goal of Project Redirection was to "redirect" the lives of young mothers onto a path of long-term self-sufficiency. It was among the earliest efforts to directly confront the issue of economic self-sufficiency in this target population. Although training was not a part of the program model (program participants were no older than 17 years), the program had several objectives related to long-term economic stability, including the attainment of a high school diploma or General Educational Development (GED) certificate, the acquisition of skills and experiences that would enhance participants' employability, and a delay of subsequent pregnancy.

Project Redirection was originally implemented in community-based organizations in four sites. Program participants were pregnant or parenting teens who were economically disadvantaged; the vast majority were unmarried and members of an ethnic/racial minority. The Project Redirection programs offered (or brokered through collaborative arrangements) a comprehensive mix of educational, health, employability, and social services. Three mechanisms were used to help teens to better use the program's services: (1) community women, or mentors, who served as role models and supports; (2) Individual Participant Plans, which specified the services and activities needed by each teen; and (3) peer support groups. A further description of the Redirection model is provided by Branch et al. (1981) and Branch, Riccio, and Quint (1984).

Nationally, Project Redirection was a closely scrutinized teen parent program not only because of the ambitiousness of its goal and the comprehensiveness of its service-delivery model but also because it was evaluated more thoroughly and rigorously than other teen parent programs. The implementation analysis revealed that the community-woman component worked very successfully, and that the staff was able to provide teens with the promised comprehensive services. However, the brokerage approach to service delivery made it difficult, in some areas, to insure appropriate services. One of those areas was in the vocational and employment arena. The programs ran into obstacles locating suitable employability services for these young teens, and the result was that such services had to be organized and provided directly by the programs. Activities related to employability tended to focus on career awareness and job-readiness, usually offered through individual vocational counseling or group workshops. Job placement assistance was also offered to interested teens, usually for summer jobs. About two-thirds of all program enrollees obtained some services related to employment.

The impact analysis portion of the study was a carefully controlled evaluation of the program's effects on employment, education, and fertility.[1] (Polit,

Tannen, and Kahn 1983; Polit, Kahn, and Stevens 1985). In the impact analysis research, longitudinal data were collected from a sample of 305 program participants (experimental teenagers) and 370 nonparticipants (comparison-group teenagers) three times: at baseline (the time of program enrollment for experimental teenagers), and 12 and 24 months later. Comparison-group members were young women who met the program eligibility criteria but who resided in carefully matched communities that did not offer the program.

Descriptive data obtained in the impact analysis interviews indicated that these young women had a fairly positive orientation toward work. For example, the overwhelming majority of teenagers in both groups (92 percent) reported that they would rather work than be on welfare. Nearly 75 percent of the sample expected to be employed for most of their adult lives. When presented with a list of different types of service and asked what their needs were, the teenagers rated job and employability training highest.

The impact analysis results suggest that it is possible to capitalize on these young women's positive work attitudes. Table 6-1 presents some of the findings on employment outcomes. In this table, Redirection teenagers are compared with comparison-group teenagers, after statistically controlling important background factors (including work experience prior to the initial interview). The first outcome in this table takes the teenagers' school and work status at the final (24-month) interview into account simultaneously. That is, the outcome indicates either a positive school status (either still enrolled or completed) or a positive work status (either employed or actively seeking employment). Seventy-four percent of the Project Redirection participants, compared with 65 percent of the comparison-group teenagers had a positive work/school status 24 months after the initial interview. A further analysis revealed that this program effect was especially powerful among school dropouts and those teenagers who had no work experience prior to the baseline interview. For example, among those teenagers with no prior employment, 54 percent of the experimental compared with 29 percent of the comparison teenagers had a positive school/work status at the end of the study, a difference significant at the .01 level.

Table 6-1 shows that actual employment rates at both the 12- and 24-month interviews were low for both groups, and differences were small and nonsignificant. This result is not surprising in light of the fact that the teenagers were only 18 years old, on average, at the end of the evaluation, and most of the interviews took place between September and May, when school programs were in session. However, subgroup analyses revealed an interesting outcome: experimental teenagers who were on welfare at baseline were significantly more likely than similar comparison teenagers to be employed two years after entry into the study (16 percent compared with 10 percent).

Although for the aggregated sample the program did not appear to affect the teenagers' employment at two discrete times (at the two follow-up inter-

Table 6-1/Summary of Adjusted Employment Outcomes in Project Redirection Demonstration

	RESPONDENTS, BY GROUP		
	Experimental	*Comparison*	*Difference*
EMPLOYMENT OUTCOME	*(370)*	*(305)*	
	PERCENT		
Either in school, completed school, or in the labor force[a] 24 months postbaseline	74	65	9***
Employed 12 months postbaseline	14	12	2
Employed 24 months postbaseline	15	15	0
Ever employed, baseline to 12-month interview	49	38	11***
Ever employed, baseline to 24-month interview	61	54	7*
	ADJUSTED MEAN		
Number of jobs held, 12 months postbaseline	1.47	1.25	.22***
Number of jobs held, 24 months postbaseline	2.16	1.90	.26**

Source: Polit, Kahn, and Stevens 1985.
Notes: The means and percentages in this table have all been adjusted through analysis of covariance for ethnicity, age, school status at baseline, and baseline work experience. Various other covariates were also controlled, but different covariates were required for different outcomes.
The figure in parentheses below each respondent category represents the number of respondents in that group.
[a] A teen was considered to be in the labor force if she was currently employed or reported that she was actively seeking employment.

*p ≤ .10
**p ≤ .05
***p ≤ .01

views), participation in the program was found to be related to cumulative employment experience. Table 6-1 shows that at the 12- and 24-month interviews, the Project Redirection teenagers had held significantly more jobs than had comparison teenagers after adjusting for baseline work experience and other background characteristics. In an adult sample, a result such as this one might be difficult to interpret, since holding more jobs could reflect greater employment instability. However, in a sample of teenagers whose employment occurs primarily during the summer, this finding suggests that the experimental teenagers were accumulating more (and more varied) work experience than the comparison teenagers were. This experience was mostly in low-paying unskilled jobs such as in fast-food restaurants, but given their youth this is not surprising. Inasmuch as disadvantaged youth often face obstacles in obtaining any work experience, the program's effect on the teenagers' ability to get jobs is noteworthy.

Finally, Table 6-1 shows that participation in Project Redirection was associated with an increased incidence of employment after the baseline interview. In the 12 months following baseline, 11 percent more of the experimental (49 percent) than comparison (38 percent) teenagers had worked for pay. The difference at the final interview, though diminished, was still significant. The subgroups that appeared to have benefited most from Project Redirection were teenagers who had no initial work experience and those who had been on welfare. For example, among teenagers who were AFDC recipients at baseline, 63 percent of the experimental group but only 48 percent of the comparison group held a paying job during the two-year study period.

Overall, the results of the impact analysis suggested that Project Redirection had some modest, but significant, effects on several employment-related outcomes. The effects appeared to be especially strong among certain subgroups that can be characterized as bringing relatively greater disadvantage to the program experience—school dropouts, teenagers with no prior work experience, and those living in a welfare-dependent household. This finding is consistent with the findings from other studies of employment interventions aimed at welfare recipients (for example, Masters and Maynard 1984; Friedlander 1988) and presumably reflects the fact that the highly disadvantaged are especially in need of intensive, coordinated programs.

Despite evidence of some positive effects, the impact analysis revealed that many program impacts gradually diminished over the two years of the study.[2] That is, the experimental/comparison groups' differences were more substantial at the 12-month than at the 24-month interview. Because of this fact, and because the comparison group turned out to have received substantially more services in their own communities than had originally been anticipated (making the test of program effectiveness relatively conservative), supplementary analyses were performed.

In an attempt to identify what a teenage parent might look like in the absence of special programs, the comparison group was divided into two subgroups—those who had ever participated in a special ameliorative program for teen parents (N = 201) and those who had not (N = 167). Two subgroups of program participants were also constructed—those who were enrolled in Project Redirection for fewer than 12 months (N = 172) and those who were enrolled for 12 months or longer (N = 129). Table 6-2 compares some of the employment-related outcomes at the end of the study for these four groups. The results of such analyses must be interpreted cautiously, because differ-

Table 6-2/Adjusted 24-Month Employment Outcomes in Project Redirection Demonstration, For Four Service-Defined Groups

	RESPONDENTS, BY GROUP			
	Experimental		Comparison	
EMPLOYMENT OUTCOME	ENROLLED ≥ 12 MOS. (129)	ENROLLED < 12 MOS. (172)	EVER IN TEEN PARENT PROGRAM (201)	NEVER IN TEEN PARENT PROGRAM (167)
	PERCENT			
Either in school, completed school, or in the labor force 24 months, postbaseline	79	71	67	62
Ever worked, postbaseline	69	59	57	50
	ADJUSTED MEAN			
Number of jobs ever held	2.40	2.10	1.82	1.96

Source: Polit, Kahn, and Stevens 1985.

Notes: The means and percentages in this table have all been adjusted through analysis of covariance for ethnicity, age, school status at baseline, and baseline work experience. Various other covariates were also controlled, but different covariates were required for different outcomes. The figure in parentheses below each respondent category represents the number of respondents in that group. There are fewer respondents in this table because of missing data on teen parent program participation. All group differences were significant at or beyond the .05 level.

ences in outcomes could reflect variations in individual characteristics such as motivation that might lead to different service-utilization behaviors, rather than the effect of actual receipt of services. However, important background characteristics (including several that could be considered proxies for motivation, such as baseline school status) were statistically controlled, so many major initial differences among teenagers in the four groups were presumably eliminated.

The results indicate that comparison-group teenagers who had never enrolled in a special program generally had the least favorable employment-related outcomes, while teenagers enrolled in Project Redirection for at least 12 months had the most favorable ones. For example, 69 percent of the long-term Project Redirection participants but only 50 percent of the control teenagers who had never enrolled in a special teen parent program had worked for pay between baseline and the end of the study. This 19 percentage point difference represents a nearly 40 percent rate of improvement for the long-term Redirection participants. These analyses suggest that the "typical" teenage mother—who is generally receiving routine, but uncoordinated, services from several different social service agencies—has a substantially more difficult time in the area of employment than her peers who enroll and stay in specially designed programs like Redirection.

The original Project Redirection demonstration provided many important lessons about targeting the teen parent population with programs designed to enhance their self-sufficiency. The first is that the program model was feasible, attractive to the teen parent population, and capable of affecting a broad range of outcomes, including ones in the employment arena. Considering the young age of the participants, and the program's relatively modest emphasis on specific employment-related skills, these findings are encouraging. The second lesson is that such programs can be effectively targeted to young mothers who are extremely disadvantaged. In fact, the biggest gains were experienced by those who entered with the greatest degree of disadvantage. The third lesson is that, in order to be especially effective, such programs must be designed to provide services for a relatively long time. Although it seems sensible to expect that longer programs can have more impact on a person's life than short-term ones, it is noteworthy that most employment programs for youth are programs of relatively short duration.

The evaluation revealed some disappointing results as well. For example, when one looks at *absolute* outcomes, such as the percentage of teenagers in both groups who were employed, who were in school, or who had a repeat pregnancy at the end of the study, it is clear that comprehensive programs do not eliminate all the problems associated with adolescent pregnancy. Nevertheless, given the very serious degree of disadvantage among these teenagers, the results are not totally discouraging. All of the teenagers in this study were receiving some services from human service agencies, and thus the evaluation question was whether intensive programs such as Redirection are incrementally more effective than what is normally available. The impact analysis suggests that the answer is a modest yes. Small gains are inevitable and should not discourage efforts to improve the life prospects of young mothers.

The Project Redirection demonstration was later replicated in an additional seven sites. Although this replication was not evaluated as extensively as the original demonstration (there was no impact analysis), an implementation analysis did confirm and extend some of the earlier findings (Riccio and Council 1985). In the replication, several program components were strengthened, including employment-related services. The new sites offered employability classes that were better organized and more structured, and they helped field test an employability curriculum designed specifically for the teen parent population (McGee 1985). Additionally, two of the seven sites offered skills training. Overall, over 80 percent of the participants in the second demonstration received some kind of employability service.

As in the first demonstration, program operators learned that their communities offered few employment-related programs suitable for the young Redirection population. The program operators therefore became more actively involved in the delivery of employment-related services, despite relative inexperience in this area. Research during their second demonstration also revealed that the age of participants had an important bearing on service delivery. Among younger teenagers (those 15 years old and younger), employment was a distant concern. Although it was possible to include these younger girls in world-of-work seminars, activities that focused more directly on preparation for jobs were not considered appropriate. Finally, program staff learned that, although these young mothers were generally positively oriented toward employment, few made the critical connection between future job success and good academic performance and credentials. To address this problem, the programs actively recruited community women with professional backgrounds and positive school and work experience to serve as role models.

Manpower Demonstration Research Corporation has more recently completed a pilot test of a new demonstration—called New Chance—that builds upon the lessons gained in Project Redirection. New Chance also targets economically disadvantaged young mothers but focuses on a slightly older group, 17- to 21-year-olds. This program offers a substantially strengthened employment component, including work experience and skills training, as well as on-site GED instruction. As in the earlier project, New Chance offers comprehensive programming and an array of support services. The New Chance program model is designed to offer program services for 18 months, and follow-up services for up to one year after leaving the program. The New Chance demonstration operated its pilot phase between 1986 and 1988 in six sites. A full demonstration of New Chance, including a random assignment evaluation, will be launched in about 15 sites nationwide beginning in mid-1989.

Teen Parent Employment Program Models

In the years since the Project Redirection demonstration, many teen parent programs have either expanded their comprehensive programming to include an employment-related component or have emerged with this specific focus in mind.[3] In this section, brief summaries of five such programs are presented to illustrate several different program models, operated under the auspices of different types of agencies. While impact information is generally not available, all five programs appear to be operationally successful. These and other programs offering employment-related services are described in more detail in a recently published handbook (Polit 1986a).[4]

Comprehensive Skills Training Program in an Urban
Community-Based Organization
The Via de Amistad Program, operated by Chicanos por la Causa in Phoenix, Arizona, was one of the four original Project Redirection sites. During the ini-

tial demonstration, the Via/Redirection program developed the most extensive employment-related component of any of the sites, and this component is now the core of Via's comprehensive program. The program services are available to pregnant and parenting teenagers 21 years old or younger. Each participant is tested upon entrance for both academic skills and vocational interests. A case manager then works with the teenager to develop an employability development plan, which designates the services the teenager is to receive in pursuit of both short-term and long-term goals. This plan is reviewed and updated monthly to ensure that the teenager is progressing and to determine new service needs.

All program participants receive vocational counseling and employability instruction. GED instruction, offered at an individualized pace, is also available directly from the program. Teenagers who are ready and interested in business skills are enrolled in the Via's business education program, which teaches business English, bookkeeping, typing, clerical skills, computer literacy, and word processing. Teenagers interested in other vocational areas are referred to a Skills Center, where the program has a fixed number of slots for its participants. Training in entrepreneurship is also being planned. An in-house job developer helps with job placements and work experience opportunities. On-site child care is available for program participants. A needs-based stipend of $6.00 a day is offered, and bus tickets are distributed to those with transportation needs. Over 100 teenage mothers are served each year, and 40 of these can be trained in the business education program. Recruitment into the program has been highly successful, and the retention rate is nearly 100 percent.

Funding for the Via program is richly diversified. The program has two JTPA contracts, as well as funding from the Carl D. Perkins Vocational Education Act, the Arizona Department of Health, the Arizona Department of Economic Security, the Social Services Block Grant, and private foundations. The annual operating expenses for the program are about $450,000. The Via program was included in the pilot phase of the New Chance demonstration.

Comprehensive School-Based Program
The Teen Parent Assistance Program (TPAP) is operated by the Oakland (California) School District and is co-located in one of the city's alternative schools. It is an open-enrollment, competency-based instructional program offering (or brokering) educational, health, psychosocial, employment preparation, and job placement services to both pregnant and parenting teenagers. To be eligible, an applicant must be at least 15 years and 9 months old. The majority are high school dropouts, behind in grade level by one or more years when they enroll. The program operates on a regular school calendar, which is five days a week for nine months.

The program offers individualized computer-aided instruction in remedial education (in preparation for the GED examination); courses in career exploration, life skills, and job readiness; and a business education program. The business education curriculum includes typing, computer literacy, word processing, and office skills. The program also offers job placements, work experience, pairing with a community mentor, and a series of seminars on sex-role stereotyping that involves lectures and discussions about gender rights and nontraditional jobs. Although efforts to secure funding for on-site child care have not yet proved successful, the project case manager works with the students to help them find suitable arrangements.

The program has had good success in attracting and keeping teenage mothers enrolled, with only a 29 percent dropout rate. Each year about 30 percent of the students graduate. Each year about 67 percent of the enrollees master entry-level job skills, and 30 percent get nonsubsidized jobs. The program has two JTPA contracts, as well as funding from the Carl D. Perkins Vocational Education Act, the Maternal and Child Health Block Grant, and private foundations.

A Nontraditional Job Training Program
Expanding Options for Teen Mothers is a nontraditional vocational training program offered by New York City Technical College. It is a comprehensive training, counseling, and placement program for young mothers aged 17 to 21. Each program cycle runs for 20 weeks and serves between 20 and 30 young mothers in each cycle. Classroom activities are scheduled for 20 hours a week.

About half the time in the program (roughly two months) is spent in basic skills and remedial education instruction, designed to prepare trainees for a GED certificate. The program tries to offer a broad, humanistic education designed to expand the young mothers' world views. The remaining half of the program is spent on vocational skills that are nontraditional for women. The curriculum is divided into four parts: carpentry, plumbing, electricity, and basic building maintenance. In each section, students learn how to use the basic tools. Each student works on one personal, hands-on project, such as making a bookcase, and one group project. The vocational curriculum is supported by a mentoring program, visits to places where women are employed in nontraditional jobs, and videos on nontraditional work. Counseling includes weekly group workshops on personal/family issues and job readiness skills. Free on-site child care is provided for infants at least 6 months old, and a weekly stipend of $30 is offered to offset transportation costs. A job developer helps to find appropriate placements for program graduates.

In the program's third year of operation, 100 percent of the participants were able to complete training. About 33 percent of the students had received their GEDs through the program, 10 percent had entered college, and 50 percent of the program graduates had been placed in training-related jobs.

The program has a JTPA contract and is also supported by other local and state public funds, as well as by grants from foundations. The program has an annual operating budget of $255,000. The Expanding Options program is one of the sites included in the pilot phase of the New Chance demonstration.

Comprehensive State Agency Program

The Illinois Department of Public Aid operates the Young Parents' Program in Chicago. The aim of the program is to help young mothers aged 20 and under obtain skills needed for self-support. The program is available to young mothers who are recipients of AFDC, but it is a completely voluntary program. Each participant must have an approved "self-support plan"—a plan for education or employment or both that signifies progress toward personal self-sufficiency. Each client must agree to participate full-time in one of three areas: education, vocational training, or employment.

The program has four core components: Return to School, English as a Second Language, Vocational Training, and Job Club/Independent Job Search. The program itself does not offer skills training or job placement but works closely with other agencies that do. Employability skills and career planning are central to the program, augmented by instruction in parenting, health, nutrition, and birth control. Services include group and individual counseling, home visits, advocacy, information and referral, and payments for child care and transportation. The Young Parents' Program operates on an open-enrollment format; on average, the participants are enrolled for nearly 2.5 years. Follow-up is provided for six months after program completion, and staff attempt to work with dropouts for 90 days. The program serves over 1,000 teenage mothers each year.

At the end of two years of operation, 15 percent of the young parents enrolled in the program had completed their component, and about 70 percent were actively pursuing an approved plan of self-support. At the end of May 1986, over one-third of the participants were enrolled in school and nearly 20 percent were enrolled in employment training programs. This program is one of several concerted efforts in Illinois to address the problem of teenage pregnancy. It is funded through the Social Services Block Grant.

A Rural Comprehensive Work Experience Program

The Parent/Child Center in Middlebury, Vermont, operates a 20-hour-a-week work and parenting training program for teenage parents (mothers and fathers). The participants and their infants (from birth to 3 years of age) are transported by van to the Center three days a week. The children are cared for in the Center's developmental day care center, while the parents participate in the program.

Most of the parents' time is spent actually performing a specific job under the close supervision of a core staff person. The jobs include child care, office clerk, food service, building maintenance, transportation clerk, and play group organizer. The goal is to give participants actual work experience, a work reference, and opportunities to learn some pre-vocational and interpersonal skills that will help them to be successful in a regular job. The participants earn $1.00 an hour plus a daily bonus linked to attendance and promptness. In addition to the work experience component, each participant is involved in one formal class of their choice (academics, sewing, assertiveness training, mechanics, and so on). The program has offered courses in such areas as typing, word processing, carpentry, auto mechanics, and journalism, all dictated by the interests of the clients; this individualization has required the flexibility of tutorials and small-group workshops. The program serves about 200 young mothers each year, though only 25 are enrolled in the work experience component.

About 80 percent of those who enroll in the work experience component complete it. Although full evaluative data are not available, program records indicate that about 80 percent of the program graduates are currently employed, including the first group that graduated four years ago. The Center obtains funding from a diversified funding base, including JTPA, the federal Office of Adolescent Pregnancy Programs, the Vermont Department of Education, and the United Way.

Strategies for Training Teenage Mothers

There are several dozen programs in existence that offer employment-related services to teenage mothers. Most serve economically disadvantaged young women in urban areas. Since most programs serve under 100 young mothers each year, it is clear that only a small percentage of teenage mothers are now being served through comprehensive programs offering employment services.

Although existing programs differ in auspices, specific services, and funding sources, they have some common elements that are worth attending to in designing new interventions and expanding the number of young women served. In this section we consider the lessons that have been gleaned from such programs about program design and funding.

Program Design
The five models briefly described above illustrate that teen parent programs that offer employment-related services and training can operate under a variety of auspices, including ones that have not traditionally been involved with operating a youth employment program. Community-based organizations (CBOs) are the most common agency settings for such programs, but several schools for parenting teenagers have expanded their programs to offer vocational ser-

vices. The Department of Public Aid program in Illinois was the first of its kind and illustrates how a state agency can effectively operate teen parent employment programs. The following discussion synthesizes the collective experience of exemplary programs by highlighting features that many of them have in common.

COMPREHENSIVENESS

A key feature of programs that have been successful in delivering employment services to young mothers is that they are comprehensive. They are not just training programs—they are a complex array of educational, vocational, social, and health services designed to address the multiple needs of young women who are generally too inexperienced to aggressively pursue available community resources. Most programs offer or broker such services as remedial education, family planning, parenting education, health services, life skills instruction, recreational events, individual counseling, and advocacy. Program directors feel strongly that the success of their programs hinges on this comprehensiveness. According to their view, it is because traditional youth and women's training programs are *not* comprehensive that teenage mothers so often fail in them. Program staff also feel that by providing a broad array of services they are better able to reinforce overall program goals, which often focus on helping the teenagers to become better parents and to take control of their lives.

SUPPORT SERVICES

Another feature of these programs is that they have all had to deal with the issue of support services, most notably child care. Those programs that are able to provide on-site care feel that they are at a tremendous advantage because the potential for high absenteeism and dropping out is greatly reduced. Young mothers tend to be reluctant to leave their children in a nonfamilial arrangement or with someone they do not know or cannot monitor personally; hence, an on-site arrangement is well-suited to reducing their anxieties. Those without on-site child care have to work with the teenagers to help them overcome these anxieties and to help them find reliable, affordable arrangements. Some programs, like the Oakland TPAP program described above, offer a mini-course to teach young mothers how to choose suitable child care. In addition to child care, many exemplary programs have made some provision to assist teenage parents with transportation.

PROGRAM ATMOSPHERE

These teen parent programs are also similar in the atmosphere they try to create and the philosophies that guide their programming and methods of handling clients. In virtually all the currently available employment-related programs for teenage mothers, program staff strive to create a caring, family-like environment. The staff tend to work as a team and to assume a high degree of professional accountability for the success of each client. Opportunities are sought to reward individual achievement, and achievement is defined in such a way that every participant can attain some measure of it. Staff tend to be sympathetic and supportive and often are engaged in advocacy activities on behalf of the young mothers. At issue in the creation of such an environment is the teenagers' self-esteem. There is a strong belief among staff that the young women in these programs—almost all of whom are economically disadvantaged and have had negative school experiences—will never attain self-sufficiency if they do not improve their sense of personal efficacy. In the words of one staff person, "The goal is to help teens to like themselves, to take control of their lives, to open up and see that there *are* opportunities for them, and that their lives are not predestined."

INDIVIDUALIZATION

The most successful programs are also generally structured to maximize opportunities for individual progress. Classroom size tends to be small, with generally only 10 to 20 students in a class. Basic skills instruction is often individualized, using either a tutorial approach or computer-aided instruction. Another aspect of individualization is that almost all programs develop individual service plans and offer an extensive program of individualized counseling.

PROGRAM SCHEDULE

Most smoothly functioning programs schedule activities on a less than full-time basis. Project directors stress that the special circumstances of teenage mothers make it virtually impossible to run a program that requires 40 hours a week attendance. Another aspect of program schedule is that most of these programs are not designed to be short-term interventions. The programs that are of a fixed length tend to run at least six months, but many programs are open-ended and participants are sometimes enrolled for a year or more.

CASE MANAGEMENT

Most of the successful teen parent employment programs have a case management system. That is, at least one person on the staff, such as the counselor, project coordinator, or a special case manager, has the responsibility for ensuring that each participant has access to, and is availing herself of, needed services.

In conclusion, the best of the programs that have emerged to target the teen parent population with employment-related services have been designed to acknowledge the multiple needs of young mothers. They offer a range of remedial and employability services, combined with a full complement of support services designed to enhance the teen mother's ability to make a successful transition to adult roles.

Funding

Most teen parent employment programs share a common feature with respect to funding: diversification. These programs rely on a complex mix of funding arrangements from the local, state, and federal governments, and from private sources. Procuring monies from these multiple funders is time consuming and difficult, because each funder requires separate proposals and final reports, establishes different eligibility criteria for program participants, and requires different monitoring, evaluation, and record-keeping procedures. Nevertheless, in order to offer a comprehensive array of services, these programs must be resourceful in obtaining funds from many different public and private agencies.

The need for diversification underscores another fact: these programs are expensive to run. Given the range of services provided in these programs, their small-scale, long-term structure, and their commitment to providing extensive individual attention, staff needs are usually considerable. These programs generally cost between $3,000 and $6,000 for each enrollee; costs are generally even higher if there is on-site child care.

The two major sources of funding for employment-related services are the Job Training Partnership Act and the Carl D. Perkins Vocational Education Act. Program operators have reported different experiences with JTPA, but most have a fairly negative reaction. Common complaints include the lack of responsiveness of Private Industry Councils (PICs) to this population, the lack of flexibility associated with performance standards, the bureaucratic red tape associated with eligibility and reporting, and the difficulty of working with a performance-based contract with this hard-to-serve population. Program operators of teen parent programs who are interested in expanding their programming in the area of employment-services often insist that their lobbying efforts on behalf of this population meet with considerable resistance. Even in communities where the PIC has implemented a youth competency system, there is often resistance to funding a program for teen mothers because of anticipated high costs and low performance, both of which would adversely affect the PIC's overall record. However, the situation is improving because of the JTPA mandate to serve disadvantaged groups.

Funding from the Perkins Act is more easily accessible to community-based organizations than under the vocational education act that it replaced. CBOs must, however, work in concert with their local educational agencies. Although in theory the Perkins Act has many provisions that permit funding for services to teenage parents, in practice relatively small amounts of funding come from this source. However, several states have developed plans for targeting special interventions for teenage parents using Perkins dollars, and so funding through vocational education is likely to expand in the next few years.

Conclusions

There is a growing interest in the development and implementation of employment programs for teenage mothers in this country. Most of this interest has, until recently, developed at the local level, especially within community-based organizations and local school districts. However, that picture is rapidly changing, as policy makers at all levels have begun to question whether this population needs special interventions—and whether they should be *required* to engage in activities designed to promote their economic self-sufficiency. The Family Support Act of 1988, national welfare reform legislation, reduces the age-of-youngest-child exemption for participation in work-oriented programs from 6 to 3, and states have the option of lowering this age limit even further. Under such reforms, young mothers could, in some states, become "mandatory" cases for welfare-to-work programs soon after giving birth.

Of special interest to those concerned with welfare reform issues is a demonstration that was initiated in late 1986. The U.S. Office of Family Assistance selected the states of New Jersey and Illinois to operate a special demonstration of "innovative approaches to decrease long-term AFDC dependency among teenage parents." The states have received a waiver of the usual exemption under the Work Incentive (WIN) Program for the registration of young women with children under age 6. Teenage parents who are AFDC recipients are being required to participate in a combination of education and work activities, and they are also provided with support services. This demonstration will be rigorously evaluated using an experimental design and will involve a sample of over 7,000 teenage mothers.

Many state governments are further ahead in policy development and program implementation than the federal government. For example, in 1985 Pennsylvania launched a coordinated, multi-agency initiative, several components of which address the vocational and employment needs of teenage parents. One component involved a competitive grant program to fund over 20 comprehensive teen parent programs for in-school youth through the Perkins Act and state funds; the budget for the fiscal 1985–86 program was nearly $1.5 million. A second component, aimed at school dropouts, provides funds to Private Industry Councils to establish employment programs for pregnant and parenting teenagers. Thirteen programs were funded through JTPA and state funds, for a total program budget of $1.6 million. Other exemplary multi-agency state initiatives have been launched in Illinois, Massachusetts,

Wisconsin, and Maryland, and agencies in many other states have initiated some activity designed to improve the self-sufficiency of young parents.

These efforts represent important steps in the development of program design and policy direction. It must be acknowledged, however, that offering vocational and employment-related services to young parents will not be a panacea to the problems associated with early childbearing. The population of teenage mothers is one that overlaps considerably with two traditionally hard-to-serve groups: disadvantaged youth and disadvantaged female heads of household. Like other disadvantaged youth, many teenage mothers bring to an employment training program a number of barriers to successful program participation: they are young and inexperienced, they often have poor basic skills, they have few working adult role models, they have low self-esteem, and they may have attitudinal or motivational problems. In addition, however, they share a burden with other female heads of household: they have to worry about child care, and they have parenting responsibilities whose demands may make them exhausted and highly stressed. Given the difficulty of designing successful interventions for disadvantaged youth and female heads of household, it is to be anticipated that these difficulties will be compounded for teenage mothers.

Besides the constraints that arise from the characteristics of the teen parent population, there are structural barriers to contend with. For example, Weatherley and his colleagues (1985) have recently described how difficult it often is to convince "male gatekeepers" of the need to serve a population that in many communities is politically unpopular. Furthermore, it may be unrealistic to expect that young mothers will make an easy transition to the world of work, even with extensive remedial education and skills training. In particular, the loss of Medicaid benefits shortly after the termination of welfare benefits may make it impossible for young mothers to do as well working as they would do on welfare, unless they have jobs with health benefits.

Nevertheless, despite these obstacles, it is clear that efforts must be made to invest in the futures of young mothers through programs that will assist them in getting a high school diploma, or GED certificate, and some specific job training. The lessons from both Project Redirection and from the extensive history of program efforts for disadvantaged youth (see, for example, Betsey, Hollister, and Papageorgiou 1985; Hahn and Lerman 1985) do suggest that some strategies might be especially effective in developing self-sufficiency. These strategies include the integration of remedial education and job training and the provision of services for an extended time. The exemplary programs described in this chapter are, in fact, using models that are consistent with these lessons.

Providing teenage parents with the means to enter the labor force should increase their self-sufficiency and should therefore be a cost-effective measure, if well-designed interventions can be implemented. The *average* public cost per teenage mother for the three major entitlement programs has been estimated to be about $14,000; for the teenage mother who receives AFDC benefits during her teen years, the average cost is over $40,000 over the mother's lifetime (Burt 1986). These costs are considerably higher than the cost of providing employment and vocational training to disadvantaged teenage mothers. Clearly, further impact and benefit/cost data are needed. Information from both the New Chance and the Office of Family Assistance demonstrations is expected to provide critical guidance in the years to come. It is also clear, however, that if our society is committed to eliminating poverty among young mothers, we must also examine a broad range of policies that affect the young mothers' capacities to be self-sufficient, including policies affecting the abilities of their partners to secure employment and contribute to the support of stable family units.

Notes

1. Only employment-related outcomes are reported here. For a discussion of outcomes in other areas and for more details on the study methodology, see Polit, Kahn, and Stevens 1985.
2. Results from a recent five-year follow-up of the Redirection sample, however, indicate significantly better outcomes among the experimental group than among the comparison-group mothers in work experience, earnings, and welfare dependency. The group differences were especially pronounced for women who had been AFDC recipients at baseline. The results of the five-year follow-up study are published in Polit, Quint, and Riccio 1988.
3. Most current programs are for teenage mothers rather than teenage fathers. Several teen mother employment programs, such as those in the New Chance demonstration, have attempted to serve teenage fathers or the current partners of teenage mothers, but relatively few of those programs have been successful in attracting large numbers of men.
4. The following program descriptions are based on my first-hand observations of them, interviews with staff, and agency documents.

References

Alan Guttmacher Institute. 1981. *Teenage Pregnancy: The Problem That Hasn't Gone Away.* New York: Alan Guttmacher Institute.

Bahr, S. J., and R. J. Galligan. 1984. "Teenage Marriage and Marital Stability." *Youth and Society* 15: 387–99.

Bane, Mary Jo, and David T. Ellwood. 1983. *The Dynamics of Dependence: The Routes to Self-Sufficiency.* Cambridge, Mass.: Urban Systems and Engineering, Inc.

Betsey, Charles L.; R. G. Hollister; and R. Papageorgiou. 1985. *Youth Employment and Training Programs: The YEDPA Years.* Washington, D.C.: National Academy Press.

Branch, Alvia; J. Quint; S. Mandel; and S. Shuping-Russell. 1981. *Project Redirection: Interim Report in Program Implementation.* New York: Manpower Demonstration Research Corporation.

Branch, Alvia; J. Riccio; and J. Quint. 1984. *Building Self-Sufficiency in Pregnant and Parenting Teens: Final Report of Project Redirection.* New York: Manpower Demonstration Research Corporation.

Burt, Martha. 1986. *Estimates of Public Costs for Teenage Childbearing.* Washington, D.C.: Center for Population Options.

Cannon-Bonventre, Kristina, and Janet Kahn. 1978. *The Ecology of Help-Seeking Behavior in Pregnant Adolescents.* Cambridge, Mass.: American Institutes for Research.

Ellwood, David T. 1986. *Targeting "Would Be" Long-Term Recipients of AFDC.* Princeton: Mathematica Policy Research.

Friedlander, Daniel. 1988. *Subgroup Impacts and Performance Indicators for Selected Welfare Employment Programs.* New York: Manpower Demonstration Research Corporation.

Haggstrom, Gus W.; T. J. Blaschki; D. E. Kanouse; W. Kisowski; and P. A. Morrison. 1981. *Teenage Parents: Their Ambitions and Attainments.* Santa Monica, Calif.: Rand Corporation.

Hahn, Andrew, and Robert Lerman. 1985. *What Works in Youth Employment Policy?* Washington, D.C.: National Planning Association.

Hayes, Cheryl. 1987. *Risking the Future: Adolescent Sexuality, Pregnancy, and Childbearing.* Vol. 1. Washington, D.C.: National Academy Press.

McGee, Elizabeth. 1985. *Training for Transition: A Guide for Training Young Mothers in Employability Skills.* New York: Manpower Demonstration Research Corporation.

McLaughlin, Steven D. 1977. *Consequences of Adolescent Childbearing for the Mother's Occupational Attainment.* Washington, D.C.: U.S. Department of Commerce.

Makinson, C. 1985. "The Health Consequences of Teenage Fertility." *Family Planning Perspectives* 17: 132–39.

Masters, S., and Rebecca Maynard. 1984. "The Impact of Supported Work on AFDC Recipients." In R. Hollister; P. Kemper; and R. Maynard, eds., *The National Supported Work Demonstration.* Madison: University of Wisconsin Press.

Moore, Kristin A.; Sandra L. Hofferth; Steven B. Caldwell; and Linda J. Waite. 1979. *Teenage Motherhood: Social and Economic Consequences.* Washington, D.C.: The Urban Institute.

Mott, Frank L., and William Marsiglio. 1985. "Early Childbearing and Completion of High School." *Family Planning Perspectives* 17: 234–37.

Mott, Frank L., and N. L. Maxwell. 1981. "School-Age Mothers: 1968 and 1979," *Family Planning Perspectives* 13: 287–92.

Mott, Frank L., and S. F. Moore. 1979. "The Causes of Marital Disruption Among Young American Women." *Journal of Marriage and the Family* 41: 355–65.

Polit, Denise F. 1986a. *Building Self-Sufficiency: A Guide to Employment Services for Teenage Parents.* Jefferson City, Mo.: Humanalysis, Inc.

————. 1986b. *Comprehensive Programs for Pregnant and Parenting Teens*. Jefferson City, Mo.: Humanalysis, Inc.

Polit, Denise F.; J. R. Kahn; and D. Stevens. 1985. *Final Impacts from Project Redirection: A Program for Pregnant and Parenting Teens*. New York: Manpower Demonstration Research Corporation.

Polit, Denise F.; Janet Quint; and James Riccio. 1988. *The Challenge of Serving Teenage Mothers*. New York: Manpower Demonstration Research Corporation.

Polit, Denise F.; M. Tannen; and J. R. Kahn. 1984. *School, Work and Family Planning: Interim Impacts in Project Redirection*. New York: Manpower Demonstration Research Corporation.

Riccio, James, and Delia Council. 1985. *Strengthening Services for Teen Mothers*. New York: Manpower Demonstration Research Corporation.

Strobino, Donna M. 1987. "The Health and Medical Consequences of Adolescent Sexuality and Pregnancy: A Review of the Literature." In Sandra L. Hofferth and Cheryl Hayes, eds. *Risking the Future: Adolescent Sexuality, Pregnancy, and Childbearing*. Vol. 2. Washington, D.C.: National Academy Press.

Weatherley, Richard; S. Perlman; M. Levine; and L. Klerman. 1985. *Patchwork Programs: Comprehensive Services for Pregnant and Parenting Adolescents*. Seattle: University of Washington.

7/Women and Public Service Employment: A Case Study in Connecticut

Elizabeth Durbin and Roger J. O'Brien

In 1973 the United States Congress passed, and President Richard M. Nixon signed into law, the Comprehensive Employment and Training Act (CETA). Title I provided for a wide range of employment and training activities, while Title II authorized the creation of transitional public service employment jobs for unemployed and underemployed people in areas with substantial structural unemployment. As national unemployment worsened over the next two years further legislation added Title VI to provide a program of countercyclical public service jobs. By 1978, 755,000 men and women nationwide were enrolled in Public Service Employment (PSE) under Titles II and VI, and the program accounted for 60 percent of total CETA expenditures.

The PSE component of CETA explicitly excluded any formal training; however, it was expected to help increase the incomes of the economically disadvantaged.[1] First, the government would act as employer of last resort in the short run. Second, the program had the potential for increasing skills, both of the unemployed, whose jobs had become technologically obsolete, and of the underemployed, who had been unable to find jobs commensurate with their training, because they could be placed in positions that allowed them to maintain or improve their skills. But there were some limits to PSE as a vehicle for enhancing long-run earning ability. Public-sector jobs are predominantly white collar with few openings for skilled craftworkers or operatives. Only lower-skill entry jobs in clerical, maintenance, and laboring occupations were available in significant numbers to make an impact on unemployment. Nevertheless, the expectation was that such positions would provide better opportunities for many of the disadvantaged.

By the mid-1970s when PSE became operative, women had become a large proportion of the poor population eligible for the program. Thus, it was hoped that PSE could become a tool for enhancing the employment skills of poor women by opening up access to jobs and career ladders from which they had been excluded. This could happen in two ways: women could be placed in higher-skill positions within traditionally female occupations; or they could be placed in better-paid nontraditional occupations, thus breaking the barriers of occupational segregation. It has long been argued that if the wide and continuing wage gap between women and men is to be reduced significantly, or if poor women's wages are to be raised above the poverty level, then women must move into nontraditional occupations. To accomplish either of these goals, many women will also require further training and support services, such as day care.

Before the PSE program was finally eliminated by the Reagan administration in September 1980, several studies were completed by the National Commission for Employment Policy (NCEP), which analyzed CETA's performance from the perspective of women and suggested various ways in which it could be made more effective at increasing the earnings of disadvantaged women (National Commission for Employment Policy 1981). CETA required prime sponsors to identify the significant segments of their population, as defined by sex, race, national origin, and age, and to serve them equitably. However, it was not until the 1978 amendments and later regulations that the prime sponsors were also required to overcome sex stereotyping and to place women in nontraditional jobs. Examining both the quantity and the quality of jobs available for women on CETA, the NCEP recommended (1) improved access to CETA jobs, (2) special training for nontraditional jobs, (3) more services to support work efforts, and (4) a broader definition of eligibility to include recently separated wives.

Researchers assessing the impacts of CETA on participants have disagreed about whether the legislation was more helpful for men or for women. One group of studies have argued that women were underrepresented in federal employment and training programs for several reasons (Underwood 1979; Berryman, Chow, and Bell 1981; Harlan 1985). Policies often explicitly favored male heads of family or limited jobs to one a family and usually gave preferential treatment to veterans. At the same time, programs neglected the needs of potential women participants by concentrating on developing job slots for which few women were qualified. Local CETA programs tended to assign women more frequently to the Title I classroom training programs, where they were often overrepresented relative to their eligibility, and less frequently to the PSE programs, where they were usually underrepresented. Finally, CETA tended to place women in traditional female occupations and failed to open new opportunities in mixed or traditional male occupations. In general, CETA jobs reflected the same sex/wage differences observed in local job markets as a whole. A systematic study of occupational segregation on CETA, before the prime sponsors were required to overcome it, also found that female CETA participants were concentrated in female-dominated occupations; however, there was less segregation on the training programs, but more on PSE (Waite and Berryman 1984).[2]

In contrast, early research of the impact of CETA on earnings had concluded that the earnings of participants were raised significantly above the earnings of a nonparticipant comparison group (Ashenfelter 1979; Kiefer 1979), and that women had benefited more than men (Bassi 1983; Westat 1981). Bassi reported that disadvantaged white women on PSE increased their earnings by more than $1,000 a year compared to $300 for similar white men; minority women of the same status increased their earnings over $1,600 a year compared to less than $200 for similar minority men. Subsequent studies reported a much smaller increase in women's earnings and in some cases a significantly *negative* impact on men's earnings (Dickinson, Johnson, and West 1986).

In a recent review of this literature, Barnow found that the studies had used different models and methodologies, which affected their findings significantly, that they were all subject to selection bias, and that they had ignored the complex interactions between participants and administrators in the placement process (Barnow 1987). He concluded that there were no strong reasons to "accept the findings from one study over those of another." It is important to note that although these studies agreed that PSE had a larger impact on women's wages than on men's (comparing them each with nonparticipant groups), women were still earning considerably less than men. Indeed, a study of the earlier 1971 Public Service Employment Program revealed that the jobs that participants had on that program were even more sex-typed than those they held before; also, although the wage differential was smaller between men and women participants in their public-sector positions, it reverted to the preprogram levels after they left (Simeral 1978).

One of the problems in evaluating the impact of PSE has been the lack of data about the kinds of jobs that participants held before, during, and after entering the program. The earnings studies compared earnings before and after but did not include information on specific occupations and skill levels. The occupational studies used very broad occupational categories, and no measures of skill levels or earnings. Thus, we know very little about the actual skills required for PSE jobs, or the kind of job transitions that participants experienced. Were participants given access to higher-skill jobs than they had held before, despite the lack of formal training? Were there significant occupational shifts? What characteristics increased or decreased the likelihood that participants would hold higher-skill positions? What, if any, were the significant differences between the PSE experiences of women and of men?

A recent study of the Public Service Employment Program in three Connecticut towns from 1974 to 1978 has attempted to fill the information gap and to answer some of these questions. By collecting information on the jobs that participants held before they came on the program, we are able to explore systematically the changes in occupations that PSE afforded men and women. Then, by assigning skill values to prior jobs and PSE job slots, we are able to test the extent to which PSE provided increased skill opportunities, and to estimate which factors contribute most to increasing skill opportunities. Thus, we believe that this study provides a unique opportunity to examine the experience of women in public service employment and to compare it with men's. Furthermore, one of the authors has added insight from having served as a regional director for the program.

Three Connecticut Cities and Their Public Service Employment Program

The three study communities in Branford, East Haven, and West Haven are adjacent to New Haven, Connecticut. The mayors and first selectmen of 12 of the 13 cities and towns in the New Haven labor market area, acting as the chief executive officers of their municipalities, formed the New Haven Labor Market CETA Consortium in 1974.

The population of the New Haven labor market area in 1975 was 445,546. The largest city, New Haven, had 132,300 residents, a decline of 5,000 from 1970; West Haven had 54,000 residents, a gain of 1,200 from 1970; East Haven had 24,800 residents, a loss of 400 since 1970; and Branford had 21,300 residents, a gain of 800 since 1970. The labor force totaled 195,000 workers, which represented 50 percent of the population over 16 years of age. Labor force participation rates were 81 percent for white men and 51 percent for white women, both slightly higher than the national levels. Nonwhite labor force participation rates were 82 percent for men and 59 percent for women, both considerably higher than the national averages. Unemployment rates in the New Haven labor market area averaged 7 percent for both white men and white women during the study years but were twice as high for nonwhites, 14 percent for men and 15 percent for women.

In 1978 the United States labor force was about 12 percent black, while blacks and Hispanics represented about 23 percent of the unemployed. Blacks were 38 percent of the New Haven labor force in 1980 but only 11 percent in West Haven, 2 percent in Branford, and 1 percent in East Haven, for an average of 6 percent in the three study communities. Thus, the study area is predominantly white, and the conclusion we draw with respect to women and the comparisons we make of women to men refer in large part to whites. The data do not enable us to draw any useful conclusion about blacks in general, or to compare the experiences of black and white women.

In 1974 when CETA was inaugurated, unemployment in the New Haven labor market area was very close to the unemployment level in Connecticut and nationally, that is, around 6 percent. Unemployment in Connecticut and in the New Haven labor market area rose to 9.9 percent in 1976, more than national unemployment, but it also recovered better; in 1978 the unemployment rate was 5 percent compared to 6 percent in the United States.

For the fiscal years 1974 through 1978, the New Haven labor market area received almost $26 million for Public Service Employment programs. West Haven, East Haven, and Branford received over $7 million or 28 percent of the funds made available to the area. The three towns accounted for about 25 percent of the unemployed in the labor market area; 13 percent of the area unemployed were residents of West Haven, 6 percent were residents of East Haven, and 6 percent were residents of Branford.

The main function of the Public Service Employment Program was to develop jobs with the municipalities and nonprofit agencies in the three towns. These openings were then posted at the work site and at the office of the State of Connecticut Employment Service. Periodic newspaper advertisements and mailings to community-based organizations were also used to recruit applicants. A special intake unit at the State of Connecticut Employment Service Office in New Haven interviewed applicants to determine their eligibility for the CETA-PSE positions, and referred them to a hiring interviewer.[3] Most of the hiring interviewers were the supervisors or department heads in the municipality or agency job sites. Most applicants were not given pre-employment skills tests, although some were given language or physical tests. The hiring interviewer would select from the pool of referrals the applicant whom they believed best met their needs within the confines of hiring guidelines and goals. PSE positions were allocated town by town for residents of that town. Of the 601 participants in this study, 54 were residents of Branford, 161 were residents of East Haven, and 386 were residents of West Haven. The job sites were usually in the city or town where the participant lived.

Actual hiring for PSE positions was decentralized at each job site,[4] so that applicants were not interviewed for the full range of available jobs at a particular time or "placed" in the most appropriate opening for them. Once hired, a participant was subject to the same probationary period as other employees of the hiring department or agency. Some PSE participants were dismissed before completing this period. But this does not mean that those who were kept were necessarily competent for the positions they held; their actual competence cannot be judged, because participants were not pretested for skill level. The skills of clients were not tested during their participation either, so that there are no precise measures of individual skill levels.

There were 601 study participants enrolled under the Public Service Employment Program in the three study communities between 1974 and 1978 for which complete information was available (only 19 participants were omitted overall). Table 7-1 provides the participant characteristics of men and women in the three Connecticut towns. Of the total, 433 were men and 168 were women; thus women were less than 30 percent of total enrollment. Aggregate national data show that women comprised between 30 percent and 38 percent of new enrollments in PSE Title VI during the study years and between 34 percent and 45 percent of new enrollments in PSE Title II, and that women averaged between 32 percent and 39 percent of all PSE enrollments. Thus, women were even more underrepresented on PSE in the three Connecticut towns than in the United States as a whole. Although the labor force participation rate of women in the New Haven area was somewhat higher than the national level, it is possible that it was lower in the primarily white working-class towns studied, which would account for some of this discrepancy.

Almost half the men in the Connecticut study were veterans, far higher than the national level.[5] There were 40 blacks among these participants, 21 men and 19 women, too few to make statistically significant comparisons. There were roughly two economically disadvantaged participants for every advantaged one; women were found in virtually the same proportions in each group.

In the three Connecticut towns, men enrolled in PSE were on average about three years older than the women in the program. This was mainly due to a much higher proportion of men over the age of 40; about 30 percent of both men and women were between 18 and 24. Women enrollees were better educated than men; they had 12.7 years of schooling on average compared to 11.7. More important for job qualifications, more than 90 percent of the women, compared to less than 70 percent of the men, had completed high school. Finally, on average, both men and women had been unemployed for a substantial period of time before being enrolled on the program; only about 40 percent were unemployed for less than six months, while 33 percent of men and 38 percent of women had been unemployed for more than a year. The median length of unemployment for men was 32 weeks, for women 34 weeks. The reader should note, however, that if an individual was unemployed for more than a year, the CETA intake would simply record an unemployment length of 52 weeks or more. Thus, the actual mean and median values for length of unemployment were certainly somewhat higher.

Information on the program status of PSE participants at the end of the study period reveals little difference in the proportion of men compared to the proportion of women who had left the program during the study period of four years and four months. Somewhat more than half were still enrolled in PSE job slots as of 30 September 1978 and slightly less than half had left. (See Table 7-2.) However, among those who had left there were some significant differences. Roughly the same number, 22 men and 19 women, were hired as regular workers by their public service employers. However, the

Table 7-1/Characteristics of Men and Women in Public Service Employment in Three Connecticut Towns, 1974–1978

	MEN	WOMEN	TOTAL
SOCIOECONOMIC CLASSIFICATION			
White	412	149	561
(%)	(72)	(28)	(100)
Black and Hispanic	21	19	40
(%)	(53)	(48)	(101)
Total (participants)	433	168	601
(%)	(72)	(28)	(100)
Economically disadvantaged	333	128	461
(%)	(72)	(28)	(100)
Economically advantaged	100	40	140
(%)	(71)	(29)	(100)
Total (participants)	433	168	601
(%)	(72)	(28)	(100)
Veterans	196	4	200
	(98)	(2)	(100)
AGE			
Distribution			
18–24 (%)	(28.6)	(28.6)	
25–40 (%)	(29.6)	(37.5)	
40+ (%)	(41.8)	(33.9)	
Total (participants) (%)	(100.0)	(100.0)	
Average in years	36.8	34.0	
EDUCATION			
Distribution			
Less than high school			174
(%)	(37.4)	(7.1)	
High school			259
(%)	(36.7)	(59.5)	
More than high school			168
(%)	(25.9)	(33.4)	
Total (participants)			601
(%)	(100.0)	(100.0)	
Average level in years	11.7	12.7	
UNEMPLOYMENT			
Time unemployed in weeks			
Mean	32	31	
Median	32	34	
Mode	52	52	
Distribution			
Less than 4 weeks (%)	(2.1)	(6.0)	
4–26 weeks (%)	(42.3)	(36.3)	

Table 7-1/Continued

	MEN	WOMEN	TOTAL
27–51 weeks (%)	(22.6)	(19.6)	
52 weeks or more (%)	(33.0)	(38.1)	
Total (participants) (%)	(100.0)	(100.0)	
Average time unemployed before			
PSE in weeks	32	31	

Source: O'Brien 1985.

Table 7-2/Program Status of Men and Women in Public Service Employment in 1978 in Three Connecticut Towns, 1974–1978

	MEN	WOMEN	TOTAL
NUMBERS BY PROGRAM STATUS IN 1978			
Participants terminated			
Hired by PSE employer	22	19	41
(%)	(54)	(46)	(100)
Found own job	44	13	57
(%)	(77)	(23)	(100)
Other terminations	119	42	161
(%)	(74)	(26)	(100)
Total (terminations)	185	74	259
(%)	(71)	(29)	(100)
Participants in public service employment	248	94	342
(%)	(72)	(28)	(100)
Total (participants)	433	168	601
(%)	(72)	(28)	(100)
TIME ON PROGRAM IN MONTHS			
Mean	15	17	
Median	12	12	
Mode	7	12	
Distribution			
Less than 6 (%)	(15.9)	(11.3)	
6–12 (%)	(41.1)	(41.1)	
13–18 (%)	(22.0)	(18.4)	
More than 18 (%)	(21.0)	(29.2)	
Total (participants) (%)	(100.0)	(100.0)	

Source: O'Brien 1985.

19 women represented more than 25 percent of all women who left subsidized employment, while the 22 men represented only about 11 percent of the men who left. In contrast, 44 men compared to 13 women were able to find jobs in the private sector, or almost 25 percent of the men, compared to 18 percent of the women.

Public Service Employment and Occupational Change for Men and Women

Earlier research emphasized that PSE jobs for women were predominantly in traditional occupations. It has been suggested that the emphasis on quick placement and turnover reduced the likelihood that women would be placed in nontraditional jobs (NCEP 1981). Furthermore, women themselves often asked for traditional placements. For example, of CETA women sampled nationally in 1976, only 31 percent expressed the desire for a nontraditional job; of these only 67 percent received nontraditional slots, while 33 percent were placed in traditional jobs. By 1978 when the program was much larger, 45 percent wanted nontraditional jobs, but almost 50 percent were placed in traditional jobs. Thus, as more women wanted to get out of their traditional occupations, it became even harder to find opportunities for them. The possibilities for altering the occupational distribution are also limited by the nature of jobs in the public sector; they are more likely to be for clerical and service workers and less likely to be for skilled operatives, compared to the private sector.

Although we did not attempt to identify PSE jobs as male or female dominated, the information on PSE participants in the three Connecticut towns enables us to compare their previous occupational distribution with their PSE experience. Before entering the program in the three towns, 25 percent of the men were in white-collar jobs, almost 50 percent in blue-collar, 12 percent in service occupations, and the rest in occupations included in the miscellaneous category, usually maintenance workers. (See Table 7-3.) In contrast, 91 percent of the women were in white-collar jobs, 75 percent in clerical and sales alone; of the rest, 8 percent were service workers, 2 percent in blue-collar jobs, and 1 percent miscellaneous.

PSE employment scarcely changed the distribution of male occupations, the biggest change being an increase in service workers and a decline in miscellaneous. However, with white-collar occupations, there was a significant decline in the less-skilled clerical and sales, and an increase in the more-skilled professional, technical, and managerial positions. Examples of professional, technical, and managerial positions held by women include teacher, teacher's aide, instructional aide, media aide, program worker, counselor, counselor's

Table 7-3/Occupational Distribution of Jobs Before and on Public Service Employment, by Percentage of Total Men and Women, in Three Connecticut Towns, 1974–1978

	MEN		WOMEN	
	Prior Jobs	*PSE Jobs*	*Prior Jobs*	*PSE Jobs*
WHITE COLLAR				
Professional/technical/managerial	12.9	18.9	13.7	29.2
Clerical and sales	12.7	5.3	75.0	62.5
Total (white collar)	25.6	24.2	88.7	91.7
BLUE COLLAR				
Agriculture	0.9	0.2	—	—
Processing	1.8	—	—	—
Machine trades	9.5	3.9	0.6	—
Bench work	2.1	0.2	1.2	—
Structural	30.3	39.7	—	0.6
Total (blue collar)	44.6	44.0	1.8	0.6
SERVICE WORKERS	12.3	28.6	8.3	7.7
MISCELLANEOUS	17.5	2.2	1.2	—

Source: O'Brien 1985.

aide, librarian, outreach worker, insurance coordinator, fire dispatcher, administrative assistant, crisis worker, recreation supervisor and recreation leader, project coordinator, tutor and draftsman. The proportion of white-collar jobs for women actually increased slightly on PSE and a shift took place, as it did for the men, from the lower-skill positions to the higher skill. Indeed, PSE placed almost 30 percent of women enrollees in positions classified as professional, technical, and managerial. There were fewer women in blue-collar and service occupations on PSE. This finding supports the contention that women were not placed in nontraditional jobs.

It is interesting to note that the occupational distribution of men and women in public service employment in the three Connecticut towns was similar to the national picture (NCEP 1981); indeed, male jobs were practically identical at the local and national levels. In fiscal 1981, 28 percent of the men on PSE were in white-collar positions nationally, 52 percent in skilled blue-collar jobs, and 19 percent in service occupations. For women, the national data show a lower proportion of women in white-collar jobs and more women in service occupations.

Looking at the Connecticut experience in greater detail, we see that men increased their proportion of construction jobs; although there were almost the same number of skilled painters, carpenters, and masons on PSE as before,

Table 7-4/Job Titles Most Frequently Held by Men and Women Preparticipation and in Public Service Employment in Three Connecticut Towns, 1974–1978

	MEN	WOMEN	TOTAL
PRIOR JOB TITLE			
General clerk	2	49	51
Laborer	45	0	45
Truck driver	34	0	34
Clerk, shipping & receiving	23	1	24
Clerk-typist	0	16	16
Painter	15	0	15
Security guard	14	0	14
Secretary	0	14	14
Carpenter	12	0	12
Mechanic	12	0	12
Cashier	1	11	12
Material handler	12	0	12
Machine operator	1	11	12
Sales clerk	3	7	10
Maintenance assistant	10	0	10
PSE POSITION			
Security guard	92	5	97
Laborer	86	0	86
Clerk-typist	0	45	45
Teacher's Aide/instructional aide	0	19	19
Painter	15	0	15
Maintenance assistant	14	1	15
Custodian	12	3	15
Secretary	0	14	14
Clerk	2	11	13
Maintenance person	12	0	12
Mechanic	11	0	11
Mason	10	0	10
Police or fire dispatcher	9	1	10
Carpenter	9	0	9

Source: O'Brien 1985.

by far the largest increase was as unskilled laborers. (See Table 7-4.) The increase in male service workers was largely due to the number of security guard positions, 97 in all, almost 25 percent of all male PSE jobs. The most noticeable change for women was that 19 were hired as teacher's/instructional aides. Otherwise, the same number were secretaries, and slightly fewer were clerks or clerk-typists. Only 10 women held jobs that might qualify as nontraditional, five as security guards, three as custodians, one as a maintenance assistant, and one as a fire dispatcher.

Public Service Employment and Skill Opportunities for Men and Women

Analyzing occupational changes only provides the most general picture of skill shifts for PSE participants. Indeed, the categories are so broad, it is not always clear that changes were not simply a question of different classifications in the public and private sectors. The new data generated for the three Connecticut towns enable us to gain a much clearer picture of the actual skill differences in jobs held by PSE participants compared to their previous experience.

The New Data
For this study, a special data set was constructed. The average number of months training necessary to do the job was estimated for the position that each PSE participant held before entering the program, and for his or her PSE job slot. Thus, it was possible to discover whether the PSE job slot for each participant required more, the same, or less training time than the previous job. Since training levels were measured in months, it was also possible to obtain a quantitative measure of skill change.

The average training time required to perform specific jobs was calculated using the Specific Vocational Preparation (SVP) analysis published by the U.S. Department of Labor. The SVP values given to each job represent a range of skill-level training times, from a week to 10 years. In order to assign a discrete number of training months to the jobs, specific values were assigned to each of the SVP codes measuring the midpoints of their ranges with the highest set at 48 months. For more general conclusions, jobs with skill levels less than 4.49 months were classified as low skill, jobs with skill levels from 4.5 to 35.9 were classified as moderate skill, and jobs with skill levels over 36 months were classified as high skill.[6] About 75 percent of both the jobs held before public service and the jobs on public service were of a low or moderate skill level.

It is important to emphasize that these measured skill levels apply to the jobs, not necessarily to the people who held them. No skill tests were given to participants. Thus, if a person held a job below his actual skill level before he entered the program, this measure would overstate his personal skill enhancement. Similarly, it would be understated if his PSE job slot required fewer skills than he had already acquired. Therefore, it is best to interpret the changes as measures of skill *opportunity,* not of skill acquisition.

Table 7-5/Estimated Skills for Jobs Held by Men and Women Preparticipation and in Public Service Employment in Three Connecticut Towns, 1974–1978

	MEN	WOMEN	TOTAL
ESTIMATED MONTHS OF PRETRAINING			
White participants			
For prior job	15.0	8.0	13.2
For PSE job	15.2	11.1	14.1
Change in pretraining months	+ 0.2	+ 3.1	+ 0.9
Black participants[a]			
For prior job	10.0	7.9	9.0
For PSE job	8.5	9.4	9.0
Change in pretraining months	− 1.5	+ 1.5	0.0
All participants			
For prior job	14.8	8.0	12.9
For PSE job	14.9	10.9	13.8
Change in pretraining months	+ 0.1	+ 2.9	+ 0.9
DISTRIBUTION OF ALL PARTICIPANTS BY PERCENTAGE CHANGE IN PRETRAINING MONTHS			
PSE more training than prior job	30.4	45.3	34.7
PSE same training as prior job	43.4	39.9	42.4
PSE less training than prior job	26.2	14.8	22.9

Source: O'Brien 1985.
Notes: Calculated using Specific Vocational Preparation analysis compiled by U.S. Department of Labor. See text, O'Brien (1985), and U.S. Department of Labor (1981) for further details.
[a] Black includes 2 Hispanic participants. The results for blacks were not statistically significant.

Changes in Average Pretraining Months for Men and Women
Estimates of changes in the average pretraining months for PSE slots compared to their pre-PSE jobs provide the basis for analyzing more precisely the impact of PSE on men and women. (See Table 7-5.) On average, PSE slots offered opportunities that increased the necessary pretraining time by one month. However, women on average gained almost three months, while men only gained three days.[7] Although women on average gained far more in skill opportunity in the PSE slots, it must be emphasized that this gain still left them far behind men in estimated pretraining months. Thus, while the women's average rose from eight to 11 months, the average pretraining months for men were still 15 months. At the same time, there was also an overall upward shift in the skill-level distribution of jobs held by women. More than 45 percent of the women were hired for positions requiring more training than did their prior positions, compared to 30 percent of the men. More than 25 percent of the men were placed in lower-skill positions on PSE, compared to 15 percent of the women.

Table 7-6/Skill Opportunity Distribution of Men and Women in Public Service Employment in Three Connecticut Towns, 1974–1978, by Estimated Skill Level Before and on PSE

PRIOR SKILL LEVEL	PSE SKILL LEVEL (IN MONTHS)							TOTAL PARTICIPANTS
	1	*2*	*4.5*	*9*	*18*	*36*	*48*	
	MEN							
1 Month	1	7	7	1	1	4	0	21
2 Months	1	56	22	5	10	6	0	100
4.5 Months	0	32	43	13	7	12	0	107
9 Months	0	9	7	7	6	3	0	32
18 Months	0	8	8	2	14	17	4	53
36 Months	0	17	12	2	8	63	6	108
48 Months	0	2	1	0	0	4	5	12
Total (men participants)	2	131	100	30	46	109	15	433
	WOMEN							
1 Month	8	6	15	1	15	1	0	46
2 Months	3	9	15	1	6	0	0	34
4.5 Months	1	2	28	2	6	3	0	42
9 Months	0	0	4	0	2	1	0	7
18 Months	0	2	9	0	12	1	0	24
36 Months	0	1	0	0	3	9	1	14
48 Months	0	0	0	0	0	0	1	1
Total (women participants)	12	20	71	4	44	15	2	168

Source: O'Brien 1985.

A more detailed picture of the distribution of men and women by skill opportunity is provided in Table 7-6. Since there were seven possible skill level values for both prior jobs and PSE slots, each participant fell into one of 49 skill-change possibilities. For example, one male participant held both a prior job and a PSE job requiring one month's pretraining, while 17 men hired for PSE slots requiring 36 months training held prior jobs that required only 18 months of training. Those on the diagonals experienced no change; those to the left and below the diagonals lost skills, those to the right and above gained skill opportunities. Comparing men and women, it is clear that a substantial number of women in very low-skill jobs (three months and less) moved into PSE slots that required longer training. Indeed, as many as 16, whose earlier jobs required only a month's training, held PSE jobs requiring 18 months and more. In contrast, 37 men, whose previous jobs required three years of training, held PSE slots that required less than a year. A Chi-square test found that the skill opportunity distributions represented a significant upward shift in skill level from prior to PSE jobs for both men and women.

Of the 15 women who were upgraded from one month to 4–5 months, the majority were upgraded within the clerical sector from a general clerical job to a clerk-typist position. Of the 15 women who were upgraded from one month to 18, six moved from a general clerical job to a secretarial position, and nine moved from general clerical positions to instructional aides. To check whether these moves increased earnings as well as skill level, we had data to compare the wage rates of seven of the nine women who became instructional aides. Their prior wage rates ranged from $2.10 an hour to $2.59 an hour, of which four were at the then minimum wage of $2.31 an hour. The starting pay rate of the PSE instructional aides ranged from $2.75 an hour to $3.05 an hour. Although still in the low wage category, these PSE jobs did provide an increase in earnings for these women, as well as a change in their classification.

The men, who were hired for PSE positions requiring less skill than their prior jobs, were generally in the skilled construction trades as painters, plumbers, or carpenters, or they were mechanics, leadmen, pipefitters, or toolmakers. Under PSE, these individuals were hired as public works laborers, custodians, or security guards. Many of these workers had become unemployed when their factories closed down, and the public sector did not need these private-sector manufacturing skills. Unfortunately, there is not sufficient information on earnings to make valid comparisons.

Factors Affecting Changes in Skill Opportunities for Men and Women

In the previous section we showed that public service employment slots did provide many program participants, particularly women, with significantly more skilled positions than they held prior to enrollment on PSE. In this last section, we explore the effects of different factors on the determination of changes in pretraining time for men and women. Using regression analysis, the personal characteristics of participants, their age, race, education, pretraining level, and economic status, were related to their measured skill opportunity change to test which factors added to, detracted from, or made no difference to the amount of skill change. The results for all participants together and for men and women separately are reported in Table 7-7, together with the equation used.

Sex was introduced as a separate variable in the equation for all participants. However, its coefficient was not significant statistically. This suggests that *by itself* gender was not important as a determinant of skill opportunity change. The separate equations for each sex were statistically significant, although less than 25 percent of the variance in skill opportunity change was explained by these factors. For both sexes, pretraining skill level was negatively related to skill change and was the most significant determinant of skill

Table 7-7/Determinants of Training-Level Change for Men and Women in Public Service Employment in Three Connecticut Towns, 1974–1978: Regression Results

	MEN	WOMEN	ALL PARTICIPANTS
INTERCEPT	−.8935	−5.7422	−.9473
AGE			
Coefficient	−.0723	−.0982	−.0778
Standard error	.0463	.0565	.0371
T-value	−1.56	−1.738*	−2.097**
RACE			
Coefficient	4.8213	1.8964	3.4139
Standard error	2.84	2.1304	1.9264
T-value	1.697*	.89	1.77*
SEX			
Coefficient			.8189
Standard error			1.1246
T-value			.7281
YEARS OF EDUCATION			
Coefficient	.4474	1.1178	.5254
Standard error	.2633	.4977	.2256
T-value	1.6992*	2.24**	2.3289**
ECONOMIC STATUS			
Coefficient	2.4099	.0003	1.6015
Standard error	1.4607	1.6104	1.1392
T-value	1.6498*	.0001	1.4058
PRETRAINING LEVEL			
Coefficient	−.4537	−.4921	−.4504
Standard error	.0432	.0766	.0365
T-value	−10.50***	−6.42***	−12.3397***
R^2	.2311	.2282	.2339
F value for equation	25.6634***	9.5822***	30.21***

Source: O'Brien 1985.

Note: The equation is:

$$Y = A + b_1x_1 + b_2x_2 + b_3x_3 + b_4x_4 + b_5x_5 + b_6x_6$$

Y = Skill level change (in months)

x_1 = Age (in years)

x_2 = Race (0 = black, 1 = white)

x_3 = Sex (0 = female, 1 = male)

x_4 = Highest grade (in years)

x_5 = Economic status (0 = disadvantaged, 1 = nondisadvantaged)

x_6 = Prior job skill level (in months)

  * $p \leq .10$

 ** $p \leq .05$

*** $p \leq .01$

level change. In other words, those in prior jobs with the lowest skill levels were most likely to have the highest skill level increase, while those in prior jobs with the highest skill levels had the least improvement. Indeed, as noted earlier, many participants were in fact placed in lower skilled jobs, reflecting in part the difficulty of finding skilled jobs in the public sector to match lost private-sector jobs. On the positive side, this result may also reflect the success of the selection and placement processes of the program in helping the least skilled to find better skill opportunities, even if they were in the lowest grades of the public sector.

Otherwise the factors affecting skill level change were significantly different for men and for women. For women, educational level was the next most important factor in accounting for skill level increase. Since we know that several women who had held unskilled positions gained experience as teacher's aides on the program, this suggests that PSE can be of specific assistance to women in their gaining entry into occupations for which they have the appropriate education but which they have not been able to obtain. For men, educational level was also important but had a lower impact and was less significant statistically. For them, being white and being economically nondisadvantaged were also significant, while for women, these factors were unimportant. This may suggest that, when the other factors are held constant, the PSE program affords better skill opportunities to white men who are less economically disadvantaged.

To summarize, these results suggest that it was characteristics other than sex that determined the differences in skill opportunities for men and for women. Education was more important for women, and race and economic status were more important for men.

Conclusions

Our study of PSE in three Connecticut towns cannot be used to extrapolate the program's impact nationwide; it served only a very small area and its clientele was atypically white and older. Nevertheless, we do believe that our findings provide some useful insights into the operation of the PSE program in general, as well as the different experiences of men and women, from which useful policy implications can be drawn.

The primary purpose of the public service employment portion of CETA in the 1970s was to reduce long-term structural unemployment (Title II) and short-term cyclical unemployment (Title VI). For the substantial proportion (40 percent) of men and women in the three Connecticut towns whose PSE slots required no additional skills, and the 26 percent men and 15 percent women whose PSE jobs required *fewer* skills, the program performed its macroeconomic function as employer of last resort. It seems reasonable to conclude that part of the negative earnings impact of CETA for men, which other studies have found, might occur as workers lose high-skill jobs (usually in craft occupations) that do not exist in the public sector and that can no longer be found in the local labor market.

This case study also found that, despite the deliberate exclusion of any formal training from PSE, the program did increase skill opportunities on average, and for women significantly more than for men. However, the average skill levels of PSE jobs held by women were still substantially below those of men. We have suggested that PSE did succeed in helping some women to gain access to jobs for which they already had the necessary education. We have also concluded that the selection and placement processes helped the least skilled the most. But after accounting for these factors, the program tended to give less disadvantaged white men the better skill opportunities.

Therefore, although our study applies only to PSE placements and not to subsequent earnings, our results suggest that women were helped more than men because skill opportunities were opened up. It proved very difficult to find craft jobs for the large numbers of skilled workmen who lost their jobs when a factory closed; the best that could be offered were positions as security guards or public works laborers. In contrast, a number of opportunities existed to enhance the lower clerical and service skills of women by placing them in higher-skill jobs. Today in Connecticut, there are secretaries who started as PSE general clerks, as well as public works foremen who started as PSE laborers and police and fire dispatchers who started as PSE trainees.

Our results indicate that women's skills can be increased through public service employment. Thus, although there is not necessarily a direct relationship between increased skills and higher earnings, PSE also can enhance women's potential income in the long run. However, in the three Connecticut towns, the access to better opportunity was predominantly in traditional occupations, with only a handful of women placed in nontraditional jobs. Traditional male-dominated jobs with good prospects for advancement were difficult to find for men, which made it even harder to allocate such slots to women. Within the local government public sector, there may be little chance of finding well-paid blue-collar opportunities for men or women, unless the uniformed services provide access to their ranks. The loss of skill level which many men faced in PSE only added to the difficulty of placing women in nontraditional jobs. In contrast, public service employment could provide significant progress in advancing the skill opportunities of women within their traditional occupations.

These findings underscore some of the difficult dilemmas in designing public employment programs to improve the economic status of disadvantaged women. First, there will always be stiff competition with disadvantaged men for the relatively scarce number of better-paid, higher-skill jobs available in the public sector. Second, in resource allocation, there will always be a trade-off between the less costly option of helping more women to improve their skills somewhat in their lower-paid traditional occupations, and the more expensive alternative of helping fewer women a lot more by opening up better-paid nontraditional occupations. Finally, such problems will be exacerbated by the limits of public funding for such programs.

On 30 September 1980, Public Service Employment was phased out completely. The Comprehensive Employment Training Act of 1973 as amended was replaced by the Job Training Partnership Act (JTPA) of 1982. Cities and towns under JTPA were replaced as program sponsors by private industry councils comprised of business, education, labor, nonprofit, and government leaders. Despite the fact the PSE is not an allowable activity under JTPA, many youth "work experience" programs function in much the same way as PSE programs. In Connecticut at least these programs have also run into the dilemmas outlined above; a project to train women carpenters had to be discontinued because it cost far more than was allowable. More recently, workfare programs aimed particularly at mothers on welfare have proliferated in many states and are facing many of the same dilemmas in the allocation of scarce job slots and other employment services (Durbin 1986). If there are sufficient jobs available in the local economy, and if the private sector can generate more skilled blue-collar slots for men *and* women, then the new programs can assist the disadvantaged to obtain greater skill opportunities. But in areas of high unemployment or in areas suffering a decline in the manufacturing sector, such programs are likely to provide only short-term relief and little skills advancement. In these instances the best avenue of advancement for women lies in the access, which they can be afforded, to higher-skill jobs within their traditional occupations as well as the development of career ladders within the emerging office technology area.

For the overall earnings of women to match the overall earnings of men, it is necessary for comparable jobs to receive comparable pay and that quality child care programs be instituted by employers and schools. Where public service employment is a significant component of ongoing programs, this study underscores the importance of designing PSE jobs that meet the skill needs of participants as well as the service needs of municipalities and nonprofit agencies. If a state or a municipality creates a preponderance of "laborer" positions, it will not meet the employment needs of women unless it is also committed to training and hiring women for nontraditional jobs. PSE positions must offer at least a moderate skill level in order to function successfully as the doorway to decent standards of living for men and for women.

Notes

1. People defined as economically disadvantaged for CETA purposes were members of families receiving cash welfare payments or whose annual income did not exceed the poverty level established by the U.S. Office of Management and Budget. For a family of four, the poverty level was about $4,000 in 1974 and $6,200 in 1978. In fiscal 1978, individuals meeting 70 percent of the lower living standards of the U.S. Bureau of Labor Statistics were also considered economically disadvantaged.

2. Only 38 percent of women, whose last pre-CETA occupation had been male-dominated, held similar positions on the PSE program. Forty-three percent of the women, who had held positions in male-dominated jobs before coming to CETA, and 45 percent of those in mixed occupations were placed in female-dominated occupations. Ten percent of the women previously in mixed occupations and 7 percent of those in female-dominated occupations were placed in traditional male jobs. In terms of their post-CETA prospects, 75 percent of the women in CETA training and employment were in service and clerical occupations, the lowest paid jobs in the labor market.

3. There were three basic PSE eligibility groups during the study period:

   1. Thirty days unemployed only (original Title VI projects 1974, 1975, 1976)
   2. Thirty days unemployed and economically disadvantaged (original Title II projects 1974, 1975, 1976, 1977)
   3. Unemployed 15 weeks or more and economically disadvantaged (1975 Act Title VI projects 1976, 1977, 1978).

There were participants enrolled in earlier years under the less restrictive criteria who met the more restrictive criteria. There were also participants enrolled in later years who did not meet the requirements for new hires.

   1973 Legislation, Title II, 30 days unemployed or underemployed and economically disadvantaged.
   1974 Legislation, Title VI, 30 days unemployed; no income requirement.
   1976 Legislation, Title VI, 50 percent of positions subject to 1974 criteria, 50 percent of positions subject to new criteria. Unemployed 15 of 20 weeks and economically disadvantaged or an income of not more than 70 percent of Bureau of Labor Statistics Lower Level Living Standard.
   1978 Legislation, 10 weeks of 12 unemployed with family income no more than 100 percent of Bureau of Labor Statistics Lower Level Living Standard. Participation was limited to 18 months within a five-year period.

4. There were significant changes in the criteria for PSE job slots during the study period.

   1973 Legislation, Title II, Public Service jobs in local or state governments providing "unmet local needs"; $10,000 salary limitation from PSE funds.
   1974 Legislation, same as 1973 legislation except without salary limitation.
   1976 Legislation, 50 percent of positions must be project-type positions which will end in 12 months. Average wage limitation of $7,800 imposed with $10,000 maximum salary.

> 1978 Legislation, $7,200 average salary with $10,000 salary limit. New position must be project-type position with 18-month limit.

5. Fewer than 10 percent of eligibles were Vietnam veterans; the older group of Connecticut men may have had several Korean War veterans.

6. There are nine levels of specific vocational preparation included in the classification system of the U.S. Department of Labor. Levels 1 to 4 represent a preparation range from a short demonstration up to and including six months of training. These skill levels represent what one thinks of as low-skill jobs. Levels 5 and 6 represent job preparation of over six months up to and including 24 months. These levels are moderate skill. Levels 7, 8, and 9 represent job preparation of over 24 months up to and including 10 years. In order not to overstate job-skill upgrade opportunity, the author chose to record levels 8 and 9 as 48 months. Levels 7, 8, and 9 were classified as high skill.

7. Using a Z-test, the training level change of 0.1 months for men was determined to be not statistically significant. The Z-value is equal to 0.115. The training level change for women of 2.89 months was statistically significant at the .05 level. The Z-value here is 4.648. The significance of the higher proportion of women (45.3 percent) to men (30.4 percent) being hired for positions requiring higher training levels was determined to be statistically significant. The calculated Z-value was 3.41 allowing us to reject the null hypothesis that the two proportions were actually the same.

References

Ashenfelter, Orley. 1979. "Estimating the Effect of Training Programs on Earnings with Longitudinal Data." In Farrell E. Bloch, ed., *Research in Labor Economics: Evaluating Manpower Training Programs.* Greenwich, Conn.: JAI Press.

Barnow, Burt S. 1987. "The Impact of CETA Programs on Earnings: A Review of the Literature." *Journal of Human Resources* 22 (Spring): 157–93.

Bassi, Laurie J. 1983. "The Effect of CETA on the Post-Program Earnings of Participants." *Journal of Human Resources* 18 (Fall): 539–56.

Berryman, Sue E.; Winston K. Chow; and Robert M. Bell. 1981. *CETA: Is It Equitable for Women?* Prepared for the National Commission for Employment Policy. Santa Monica, Calif.: RAND, May.

Bloom, Howard S., and Maureen A. McLaughlin. 1982. "CETA Training Programs: Do They Work for Adults?" Congressional Budget Office and National Center for Employment Policy Report. Washington, D.C.

Dickinson, Katherine P.; Terry R. Johnson; and Richard W. West. 1986. "An Analysis of the Impact of CETA Programs on Participant Earnings." *Journal of Human Resources* 21 (Winter): 64–91.

Durbin, Elizabeth. 1973. "Work and Welfare: The Case of Aid to Families with Dependent Children." *Journal of Human Resources* 8, Supplement.

————. 1986. "Is Workfare Fair?" *New Society*, 7 November.

Harlan, Sharon L. 1985. "Federal Job Training Policy and Economically Disadvantaged Women." In L. L. Larwood, A. Stromberg, and B. Gutek, *Women and Work: An Annual Review 1.* Beverly Hills, Calif.: Sage.

Kiefer, Nicholas M. 1979. "The Economic Benefits from Four Government Training Programs." In Farrell E. Bloch, ed., *Research in Labor Economics: Evaluating Manpower Training Programs*. Greenwich, Conn.: JAI Press.

National Commission for Employment Policy. 1981. *Increasing the Earnings of Disadvantaged Women*. NCEP, Report no. 11, Washington, D.C., January.

O'Brien, Roger J. 1985. "Public Service Employment and Job Skills: The South Central Connecticut Experience, 1974–1978." Ph.D. diss., New York University, Graduate School of Public Administration.

O'Brien, Roger J., and Irene Marmo O'Brien. 1986. "A Follow-Up Study of 125 Former JTPA Participants." New Haven SDA Private Industry Council.

Simeral, Margaret H. 1978. "The Impact of the Public Employment Program on Sex-Related Wage Differentials." *Industrial and Labor Relations Review* 31: 509–19.

Underwood, Lorraine A. 1979. *Women in Federal Employment and Training Programs*. The Urban Institute, Paper 5074-1, Washington, D.C., January.

U.S. Department of Labor. Employment and Training Administration. 1977. *The Dictionary of Occupational Titles*. 4th ed. Washington, D.C.: Government Printing Office.

————. Employment and Training Administration. 1981. *Selected Characteristics of Occupations Defined in the Dictionary of Occupational Titles*. Washington, D.C.: Government Printing Office.

Waite, Linda J., and Sue E. Berryman. 1984. "Occupational Desegregation in CETA Programs." In Barbara F. Reskin, ed., *Sex Segregation in the Workplace: Trends, Explanations, Remedies*, pp. 292–307. Washington, D.C.: National Academy Press.

Westat. 1981. "Continuous Longitudinal Manpower Survey Net Impact Report No. 1: Impact on 1977 Earnings of New FY 1976 CETA Enrollees in Selected Program Activities." Report prepared for the U.S. Department of Labor under Contract no. 23-24-75-07.

8/Office Automation Training: An Empowerment Approach

Joan M. Greenbaum and Sandra Watson

Training is not enough. It is most commonly used as a stop-gap measure to "retool" current workers in machine or task-specific skills. The retooling metaphor, frequently used in training literature, is symptomatic of the problem of seeing people as things. People are not simply part of a system—components to be inserted or deleted as workplace requirements change. For clerical workers, and women in particular, retooling obscures the need for flexible job preparation and skills development in the midst of the rapidly shifting terrain of clerical work. This chapter takes an in-depth look at one training program at LaGuardia Community College that effectively assisted urban women to re-enter the labor market and gain confidence in their abilities.

Women make up about 80 percent of the 16.7 million clerical workers in the United States. With average salaries around $250 a week, women remain crowded into lower-paying jobs in the clerical and service sectors of the economy (U.S. Department of Labor [USDOL] 1985, 3,9). And as the "office of the future" appears, such an office is not likely to open many magical doors. Between 1982 and 1983, for example, while the overall economy climbed out of a steep recession, jobs in the clerical area did not grow. In fact, traditional ports of job entry such as billing, payroll, and postal clerks were in noticeable decline, and other formerly high-growth positions like bank teller and telephone operator began to fall sharply. And perhaps most disappointingly of all, the job of secretary, which had been expected to be one of the fastest growing occupations, began to see a serious slowdown in its growth rate (USDOL 1984). While some of these changes were strongly influenced by increased output from office automation, others were the result of a general reorganization of work processes. The fact remains that the number and type of office jobs are changing rapidly. Traditional skill-based training can no longer be used to fill in the gaps.

There are still other factors compounding the problem of declining and changing jobs. Unfortunately these factors fall disproportionately on the shoulders of mature women and minority women. During the last half decade there has been a flow of clerical jobs from the cities to the suburbs, as well as a flow of jobs out to rural areas. These trends leave inner city women with diminished choices. Adding to the immensity of the problem is the fact that for jobs remaining in the cities, employers have favored hiring newer out-of-firm workers, who for the most part are younger women with already acquired skills (USDOL 1985, 16).

The Birth of a Training Program

Well over 7 million computers were in office use in 1985 and it has been expected that the number will be over 40 million by the end of the decade (Greenbaum, Pullman, and Szymanski 1985, 1). Access to desktop computers as well as hands-on experience with different software packages has been a growing demand among office workers. Yet existing training programs are limited, expensive, or inaccessible to lower-level clerical workers.

Businesses have been introducing office training, but courses and funding run sadly behind the emphasis on investment in new equipment. In 1982, for example, corporations spent an average of $3,600 a worker on new equipment and facilities, but a mere $300 a worker on training (Greenbaum, Pullman, and Szymanski 1985, 16). And most clerical workers report that the in-house training that exists is either not readily available or too skill-specific to offer any real chance for job enhancement (see Greenbaum, Pullman, and Szymanski 1985). A woman in the program summed it up this way: "Oh sure I got offered a chance to learn the new machine—but it was a four-hour training course, and then when things went wrong there was no one to call. You can't learn anything in a few hours. It's crazy."[1]

Public and private educational institutions are also offering training, but the latter are prohibitive in price (usually over $2,000 for a word processing certificate) and the public programs have been generally slow to respond to technical changes in office requirements, concentrating, still, on machine-specific keyboard training (U.S. Office of Technology Assessment [OTA] 1985).

Even these expensive traditional programs would barely buttress women against the rising tide of problems created by rapidly changing technology, job content, or job location. A course in a specific word processing system or a stab at a computer literacy course would do little to help women stay afloat in these fast-moving waters. We realized that as difficult as the environment was, it was still possible to enable women to gain access and mobility to different and shifting jobs in the office. The issue was to identify realistic job areas and develop careful policies to help steer women into safer waters.

While office employment was not growing, overall office employment was, at least, not shrinking. Its main characteristic was constant change. And since office work has been and continues to be, a comfortable port of entry for many women, we felt that it was realistic to focus our efforts here. Additionally, as the Office of Technology Assessment points out, "at least 75% of adult workers for the year 2000 are already in the labor market," clearly illustrating the need to support the large number of women already experienced (and possibly trapped) in office occupations (OTA 1985, 75).

Out of a sensibility to these issues and in response to the need to provide clerical workers with training to meet constant workplace changes, the Office Automation Training Program grew. LaGuardia Community College (part of City University of New York) is housed in a semi-abandoned industrial area in the Borough of Queens. More than two-thirds of the full-time students are women, and the majority of the community outreach programs are aimed at the same population. Community programs are coordinated by the Division of Continuing Education, and it was through an existing women's program in this division that we designed, built, and housed the Office Automation Training Program.

From the start we sought to create a broad-based program that would reach out to unemployed and underemployed women in the clerical field. After an extensive study of the effects of office automation on clerical occupations, we applied for funding from the New York State Education Department.[2] The program, now in its fifth year, has taken between 40 and 50 students a year through a nine-month part-time course. Attending courses one night a week and Saturdays, the women have rigorously gone through specific computer skills courses, extensive oral and written communication, and job counseling, preparation, and placement. Despite the work, more than 85 percent of the women have completed the course each year, and graduates report results ranging from significant wage increases to greater job mobility and a wide range of intangible benefits—starting, but in no way limited to, heightened self-esteem.

An Empowerment Approach

As we sat down to write our initial grant application we found ourselves drawing up a wish list of support services we knew would be vital to a women's program. The wish list was very much like the kind of education we as women and as educators knew we needed. It included child care, counseling, job placement, flexible and changing skill courses, and supportive written and oral communication practice.

As we developed the list and translated it into specific program requirements, we realized that we had clearly moved beyond the normal range of training programs. Our priorities were simple—to create a supportive environment where women could feel comfortable learning a wide variety of flexible concepts. The emphasis was on the transferability from a conceptual base, rather than on the mastery of specific skills. And since the target population earned well under half the median family income, the program had to be free to participants.[3] The not-so-simple wish list had become the basis for an empowerment approach.

A 1984 National Academy of Sciences study entitled *Microelectronics and Working Women* put the issue of skill clearly:

> Merely replacing a typewriter with a word processor in the classroom will not provide women with the skills they need as electronic systems are introduced into the office. More than providing task-specific skills, training is needed to give a broader understanding of an organization as a system and must lay the basis for the continuous retraining that will be necessary over a career (Werneke 1984, 9).

Our research highlighted the fact that office skills include more than simply using a computer. Personnel department and training programs focus on skills as a quantifiable or technical qualification (How fast can you type?), but most office work also includes abstract thinking and a great deal of communication and interaction. These less technical aspects of skill are often overlooked in analyses of office work, particularly in jobs done by women. While abstract thinking and communication are the backbone of office work, they are sometimes called "invisible skills," because they do not get counted or noticed until they are not done. Empowerment, then, was not simply an issue of giving a new technical skill but of enriching conceptual and communication qualifications as well.

It was important that the program provide marketable skills, but we saw the issue as broader than training a Wang operator or a Xerox microcomputer word processor. Typically, employers demand skills that are hardware or software specific, since this type of training reduces on-the-job costs. But employers also seek adaptable workers—people who can think conceptually and can solve problems creatively.

After an extensive investigation of key hardware and software packages, we integrated the specific technical courses with corresponding courses in organizational behavior and written and oral communication. Students were given, and encouraged to use, lists of vocabulary and concepts that could help them adapt to any new machine or program. We looked at the empowerment approach as a way of helping students say, "Well, I don't know the XYZ machine, but with my experience using word processing programs on the QXR computer, I think that I can pick it up rapidly!"

As courses in technical practice, concepts, and communication became the core of the program, we also focused on helping women look at their lives and their options. The empowerment approach to course design and teaching was viewed as a process to enable students to obtain qualitatively better working conditions and to be in a position to make clearer choices about their lives. The program does not specifically address the problem of declining numbers of jobs, but it does attempt to provide women with confidence in themselves, more awareness of organizations, and greater flexibility in the job market. It also helps them find new jobs and stay in touch with organizational change. A graduate of the program has this to say of her experience:

I've worked as a typist for many years in the same department of a company. I know what people really want and need even if they don't tell me clearly. Now I know that my experience is really useful in understanding how the company works. I'm proud of it and I can use it to help figure out what kind of work I can look for in my next job.

When we were developing our wish list and turning it into program requirements, we were eager to have empowerment education steer clear of the pitfalls of assertiveness training. Many training programs, particularly those offered for women, direct women to get better jobs by asserting or pushing themselves forward. We strongly feel that this individualistic approach is neither good nor successful and often ends up with women putting more responsibility and blame on themselves. Given the nature of the far-reaching changes in offices, it is clear that the problems and choices are social dilemmas, not problems for individual action.

Where the Women Came From

The women seeking out our program were overwhelmingly mature women (40 and over) and minority women. Two-thirds of the applicants were single heads of household, and the majority earned less than the average clerical wage. Few had access to training programs on their current jobs, and fewer still had time or resources to return to a traditional educational program.

Despite the overwhelming odds that most of the women faced in their daily lives, they flocked to announcements about the program. Within two months, in the first year's recruitment, over 500 telephone and walk-in inquiries were received.

Unemployed and underemployed women responded to advertisements placed in local newspapers, program announcements sent to unions, community-based organizations, and social agencies, and flyers that were distributed in commercial areas of Western Queens. Initially, the majority of inquiries came from women who were underemployed. Many worked in such deadend positions as typing or data entry, where they saw the need to develop computer-related skills in order to get some mobility in the job market. Recently, the majority of inquiries shifted from underemployed women to women who have lost their jobs. This development probably reflects the outward movement of lower-level clerical jobs from the city to other areas.

Criteria for acceptance into the program is based on an interview and a typing test. High motivation, the ability to attend classes one night a week and Saturday, and a typing level of 35 words per minute (wpm) are the minimum entrance criteria. Out of more than 1,000 program inquiries during the first three years, about 400 women were interviewed and tested to fill 135 openings in the program.[4]

In the first two years, black women made up between 60 percent and 65 percent of the program. Hispanic women made up about 25 percent, and white women about 10 percent. More recently there have been many more Hispanic women applying, probably because of the Hispanic population in the college's neighborhood and the fact that the recruitment has become primarily word-of-mouth.

The overwhelming majority of women have had long-term commitments to the labor force—almost half have been employed more than 15 years. Most, typically, have worked in the lower end of the clerical spectrum in jobs such as clerk typist, file clerk, or data entry clerk. During the interview they shared their most common job-related problems, which were: feeling underutilized on the job, no or minimal access to on-the-job training, and limited promotional opportunities. The feeling of being underutilized on the job was a strong theme among the women. One expressed it this way: "Oh, I've worked for more than 10 years as a typist. I do a good job and want to do more, but nobody seems to care. I've asked again and again for training on the new machines, but it's as if nobody hears me."

Core Curriculum

The Office Automation Training program is divided into three major areas. These are:

- skills training in word processing and micro-computer operations,
- career exploration and development, and
- internship placement.

In designing the program we felt that its effectiveness would rest on the fact that the focus of all courses should be on the transferability of skills. In exercises, group work, and workshops the students were taught to think about the concepts and vocabulary as well as the specific office skills. They were also encouraged to work together, and as a result, strong friendships developed as women taught each other new software packages or practiced interviewing and vocabulary building.

The skill courses, which include Electronic Keyboarding, Concepts of Word Processing, Word Processing I and II, Oral and Written Business Communication, Introduction to the Automated Office, and Microcomputer Operations I and II, are offered in 10-week course cycles. During a nine-month program over 200 skills training hours are offered.[5] The word processing courses teach at least two different software packages (selected to fit current employment demands) and microcomputer operations courses concentrate on database and spreadsheet applications. Although non–credit bearing, the courses are closely modeled after existing credit courses in various academic departments within the college. Students are exposed to the expectations of the college curriculum within a supportive environment.

To create a supportive environment, the instructors were selected for their commitment to the empowerment of women through support and education as well as for their technical knowledge, familiarity with a wide variety of hardware and software, and awareness of adult education needs. Although the list of creative characteristics seems long, we were successful in recruiting instructors, who, like the students themselves, had worked their way up with practical experience. One instructor, for example, the director of training programs for a large telecommunications company, has enthusiastically supported the program since its inception. Her dedication is, in part, based on her experience as a minority woman who worked her way out of a key-punch pool.

The career development and internship placement parts of the curriculum were developed by a specialist familiar with the changing labor market. Career development seminars were held weekly and covered subjects from resumé writing and interviewing to less traditional topics such as dance and body movement as methods of gaining confidence. Through role play and classroom interaction, as well as videotaped interviews, these career development sessions introduced women to self-assessment tools and techniques. Special sessions were devoted to helping students discover and enhance the image they present to the work world. And particular emphasis was placed on focusing on defining job values, interests, and aptitudes.

Internship placement was accomplished through individual counseling sessions where the internship counselor discussed the student's interests, needs, and abilities. Many students helped develop their own internships after consultation with the placement counselor.

Students and Teachers Evaluate the Program

Recent graduates are in agreement that it was the career development part of the program that gave them their most valuable boost. Admittedly, it was the technical skill and communication courses that opened job opportunities for them, but, they say, it was the increased self-esteem and heightened self-confidence that enabled them to "go for it" or "try their wings."

A graduate who got a job as an administrative assistant to the Vice Chancellor for Education told the others in the program, "I thought I only wanted computer training, but when I finished, I realized that the practice interviews, role-playing, and videotapes really helped me the most. The Office Automation Training Program gave me insights into what kind of person I could be. I was afraid to try anything new. My fear of failure was also a hindrance—I never tried, I never failed, and I never grew. Now I'm willing and eager to try just about anything." Another had this to say: "At first the videotaped interviews really scared me. I thought I would look terrible and stupid. What I really liked was that we helped each other. There wasn't any one right way to do it, and we were all in the same boat."

While the students have been enthusiastic about the program, we have tried to adapt and change to meet shifting student needs and employment situations. This has not been easy, but constant monitoring and evaluation have helped. During each 10-week cycle, we have maintained an evaluation process to monitor student expectations, outcomes, and suggestions. Included in the evaluation procedures are student-instructor evaluation discussions, student evaluation forms, and a final program questionnaire. The questionnaire asks students to rank the effectiveness of the program on a list of 13 specific characteristics, such as: ability to use dbase II and Multiplan, ability to compose business letters using Standard American English, and ability to develop a realistic plan for job mobility. The overwhelming majority of students give the program a high rank on acquisition of technical and business skills. Almost all students give it the highest ratings in achieving nonquantifiable outcomes like self-confidence and motivation.

Again, one student summed it up, saying, "Personally the program has been very beneficial. Not only did I acquire technical skills, I also made friends." Another said simply, "I can say it in one word: TERRIFIC—for my psychological and personal improvement." Reading the students' evaluation reports and talking with the students about the program was an exciting and encouraging process. Some were not able to get the jobs or the results that they thought they wanted, but all seemed pleased with the process.

In general, it has been easier to evaluate the program by the subjective reflections of the participants rather than by any quantifiable, objective data. Our purpose was to develop and deliver a workable program, and therefore data collection was a secondary concern. Admittedly then, the process of evaluating the student salary and title changes was a little harder than analyzing their reactions to the program. And since the women began with many different expectations and needs, no simple statistical measure could give us a general picture of their success. Salary increases were dependent on the original titles and skills of the women as well as the circumstances in their daily lives. For between 10 percent and 20 percent of the women, full-time employment was not possible and job choices had to be made according to proximity to home or availability of family members to watch their children.

Of the women who could look for full-time work, roughly half have been able to find new positions, and slightly fewer than the remaining half have reported upgrading their current jobs to a better title or salary. In a recent class, for example, almost all graduates reported increases in salary—with a wide divergence from $1 an hour (a data entry operator) to $12,000 a year (an office manager).

Title changes were as far-reaching as the salary increases. For some women, upgrading from clerk typist to word processor was a major achievement; for others, movement from secretary to office manager was the desired objective. While some women remained at the lower end of the clerical salary ladder in jobs like data entry operator or office assistant, most evaluated their concluding job titles with some sense of accomplishment. They had set out to "learn the ropes" and this they felt they had achieved.

Student decisions to change jobs for job security, benefits, or mobility were pronounced. As the counseling and career preparation portions of the program emphasized, many women chose to make job changes for these reasons rather than for salary alone. For many women, taking these issues into consideration was a new way to look at job choices and helped them to open doors that they had not previously noticed.

Perhaps the most noticeable outcome was the interest of women in beginning a college education. Although we had thought that this might happen, we had not initially planned for it. In a recent class, about 20 percent of the women are actively planning to start college. Interestingly, while most women had expected to major in office technology or business, there is now a renewed focus on the liberal arts. Some women have chosen to move out of clerical and computer work and to look into college programs in social work and education.

For the women, the bottom line of the program was their re-entry into and maneuverability in the job market. As educators and administrators we are proud of this. But we are also proud of the financial bottom line of the program. Our yearly funding has been approximately $50,000 for 45 students a program. Thus, the intensive and comprehensive course averaged a little more than $1,000 a student. With an 85 percent retention rate, the direct program costs were under $1,500 a student. (Indirect expenses included LaGuardia Community College's contribution of classroom space, equipment, and one-third funding of the director's salary.)

We feel that the program, in concept and practice, is clearly replicable for other community colleges and learning centers. As four years of pilot operation have shown, a flexible curriculum, embedded in an empowerment approach to learning, can produce a solid and relatively inexpensive model.

The Changing Clerical Workplace and Its Implications for Training

In December 1985 the Office of Technology Assessment highlighted the broad impact of changing office work in a study called *Automation of America's Offices*. We found the study useful in helping us focus on developing specific parts of the program. For us, the changing nature of office work represented a challenge. A challenge that our small program could only begin to address.

Specifically, we used some of the main points in the OTA report (as well as other research reports) to look for ways that women could overcome and bypass barriers within the office. In particular, barriers that affected women in our program included changes in: productivity and pace of work, quality and job content, mobility, work flow and organization of work, and equal opportunity. We present here an overview of significant changes in office work so that they might be useful for others in planning training programs.

Productivity and Pace of Work
Managers and economists are quick to note that office technology is introduced as a labor-saving investment. Managers who requisition new equipment are usually asked to cost-justify their orders by increased productivity or output per worker. In a recent study of New York City municipal workers, managers reported increased output among clerical workers using computers (Greenbaum, Pullman, and Szymanski 1985, 1.4). This is evident across the board as the volume of business transactions has risen much faster than the number of workers needed to handle them (Werneke 1984, 7).

For clerical workers this can mean increased competition for declining or slow-growth occupations. This problem is compounded by the fact that managers expect greater output and often intensify the pace of work to get it. Jan Zimmerman, in her book *The Technological Woman*, reports on a secretary who explained it like this:

Bosses get ridiculous expectations of increased productivity; . . . they expect major increases in output and put more pressure on you to produce; and . . . they start to see you as an extension of the machine. They forget there's any operator skill involved. My bosses used to ask, "When can you do this?" Now they ask, "When can your machine do this?" (Zimmerman 1983, 7)

Clearly, a comprehensive training program is needed to address these issues. In our experience, such a program can be framed within a supportive and cooperative environment. Staying competitive in a slow-growing field does not necessarily mean being aggressively competitive or having a need for "assertiveness." Instead, we found that women who are accurately and supportively counseled can seek out positions and organizations where their flexible skills will help them gain mobility as some jobs become phased out.

In our program, the issue of increasing intensity of work was addressed by specific keyboard practice courses. Initially, we expected women to achieve keyboard speeds of 50 to 60 wpm, but as we analyzed employer demands we found that we had to help the participants develop speeds of up to 80 wpm. Since not all women want or can adapt to this increased pace, the program counseled the participants to develop other skills such as database management and computer spreadsheet applications. This will remain a serious consideration for office training programs.

Quality and Job Content

There is an increasing polarization in the way clerical work is being done. Some say that a clericalization of professional work is occurring, while others argue that professionalization of clerical work is the trend. Both are happening (Greenbaum, Pullman, and Szymanski 1985, 5.2–5.4). While some clerical workers are getting stuck in back-office functions where they perform more routine work, others are in positions where they can "upskill" their jobs with more professional tasks. Secretaries who have knowledge of database operations, for example, may get to take on more professional responsibility. And those who can combine this knowledge with their experience and understanding of an organization might be able to use these skills to move within an organization.

While the majority of clerical jobs are in the lower-paying, repetitive back-office operations, many of these jobs, like data entry, are slated to be eliminated within the next half-decade with the introduction of inexpensive optical scanning equipment. We felt it essential that our program steer women clear of these deadend job traps.

Mobility

Many training programs mistake technical training as the only key to job mobility. Several European studies have found, however, that success in clerical work is equally dependent on the invisible skills that enhance a worker's ability to perform. Indeed, as mentioned earlier, invisible skills are the ones that most successful secretaries thrive on, for they involve tasks like prioritizing work, "gatekeeping" for their boss, being sensitive to others, and knowing what is happening in the office (see Lei and Rassmussen 1985; see also USDOL 1985). We feel that it is useful to help women recognize that they have these skills. Training is, in part, a matter of reinforcing qualities like these and helping women learn to take credit for their strengths.

But job mobility is a complicated issue, for it rests on both the range of skills and on existing job ladders. Several studies have reported that the introduction of office technology is resulting in shortened job ladders and cut-off career paths (see Working Women Education Fund 1981; see also OTA 1985). Obviously, office training programs need to stay in touch with these changes and help women realistically assess the traps. We found that this is not easy, and sometimes we felt quite helpless because we were not in a position to change the situation. The question of career ladders is now being addressed by unions such as Service Employees International Union local 9 to 5 and United Automobile Workers District 65, who are actively organizing clerical workers. Hopefully, unions, community groups, and training programs can play a joint role in pointing out the problems and working together toward creating viable paths to mobility.

Work Flow and Organization of Work
A word processing operator in a large pool generally has less job mobility and far less freedom than an operator in a small group or team, because the operator in a large pool is less visible to the organization. The way work is organized clearly opens or limits both the ways technology is used and the opportunities for the workers involved.

Many management journals are reporting increased job satisfaction and increased efficiency with a team approach rather than a pool organization. *Fortune* magazine, for example, in 1986 (26 May), ran a cover story on ways that managers should look at decentralized work organization. And IBM, one of the creators of the pool or centralized approach, has become an advocate of teams or smaller working groups.

Management's swing to decentralized office organization is something clerical workers have long pushed for. It may now be more possible for office workers to use their informal knowledge of organizational work flow and behavior to their advantage. Decentralized workplaces and teams are possible starting places for clerical workers to make their invisible skills more visible.

Equal Opportunity
In a 1985 report, the Women's Bureau of the U.S. Department of Labor spelled out the seriousness of the problem for minority women:

Studies suggest that there is a tendency toward tracking black and other minority women into centralized back office "transaction environments" in industries like banking, insurance, and finance, where they may work at high stress factory-like jobs characterized by low pay, poor benefits, electronic monitoring, and productivity quotas. (USDOL 1985, 21)

The issues of job mobility, work organization, and pay equity are compounded for minority women. As previously mentioned, the movement of jobs out of urban areas continues to turn the heat up on this problem.

Training programs clearly need to address these issues, but like other resources, training alone cannot unravel the complexity of a society stratified by race and gender bias. While we feel that our program is a successful pilot project, it remains but one step of many that need to be taken. An empowerment approach to training is useful in setting the stage to prepare women for changes in office work, but other joint efforts are necessary. Pay equity legislation, union-created viable job ladders, government-supported flexible training, and further research are a few of the necessary ingredients for change. Training, even empowerment training, is not enough.

Notes

1. Quotations from students in the LaGuardia Community College training program that appear throughout this chapter were obtained from students who completed the program during 1984–85.

2. The New York State Education Department funds vocationally oriented training programs. Our initial grant was for 1983–84, and through continuing grant applications we were funded through 1987.

3. Median family income for a family of four was $29,300 for 1984 according to the Bureau of Labor Statistics, U.S. Statistical Abstract; entrants to our program had average incomes of approximately $11,000 a year (USDOL 1984).

4. Many people who inquired about the program were not able to make the time commitment or were not able to follow through for other reasons.

5. The courses were organized in 10-week cycles to fit into the existing La Guardia Community College term schedule. Skill training hours were arranged to meet standard employment expectations in the area.

References

Greenbaum, Joan; Cydney Pullman; and Sharon Szymanski. 1985. *Effects of Office Automation on the Public Sector Workforce: A Case Study*. Washington, D.C.: Office of Technology Assessment.

Lei, Merte, and Bente Rassmussen. 1985. "Office Work and Skills." In *Women, Work, and Computerization*, ed. L. Schneider. New York: North Holland.

"The Puny Payoff of Office Computers." 1986. *Fortune*, 26 May.

U.S. Department of Labor. Bureau of Labor Statistics. 1984. *Employment and Earnings*. Washington, D.C., January.

———. Women's Bureau. 1985. *Women and Office Automation: Issues for the Decade Ahead*. Washington, D.C.

U.S. Office of Technology Assessment. 1985. *Automation of America's Offices, 1985–2000*. Washington, D.C., December.

Werneke, Diane. 1984. *Microelectronics and Working Women: A Literature Summary*. Washington, D.C.: National Academy Press.

Working Women Education Fund. 1981. *Race Against Time*. Cleveland, Ohio.

Zimmerman, Jan, ed. 1983. *The Technological Woman*. New York: Praeger Press.

9/Supporting Women's Self-Employment: A New Training Option

Sara K. Gould, Deborah Stern, and Jing Lyman

The United States is experiencing an unprecedented increase in the number of self-employed persons—a 50 percent increase between 1970 and 1984. During this period, the rate of growth in self-employment exceeded that of wage and salary employment (U.S. Department of Commerce [USDC] 1986b, 105, 107).

This widespread entrepreneurial activity has motivated a growing number of state and local economic development officials to create programs that cultivate and nurture local entrepreneurs and small business owners within the community. Many of these programs offer technical and financial assistance and opportunities to obtain government contracts to existing local business owners and to new owners whose employment experience and relatively high level of education enable them to "break into the system." A growing number of programs, however, are targeted to nontraditional entrepreneurs—people of color, dislocated workers, underemployed people, and women.

During the last decade, women have entered self-employment in overwhelming numbers. Between 1976 and 1983, the number of self-employed women increased five times faster than the number of self-employed men, and more than three times as fast as women wage and salary workers (Becker 1984, 16). According to data from the Internal Revenue Service, there were 3,254,248 female-owned nonfarm sole proprietorships in 1983, representing an average annual increase of 9.4 percent over the 1,900,723 businesses

Parts of this chapter were taken from "A Working Guide to Women's Self-Employment," by Sara K. Gould and Jing Lyman, published in February 1987 by the Corporation for Enterprise Development, Washington, D.C. Used with permission of the Corporation for Enterprise Development.

recorded in 1977.[1] These firms comprised 27.6 percent of all proprietorship businesses, and contributed 11.5 percent of receipts (USDC 1986a, 2). The trends indicate that women are creating a growing share of employment opportunities for themselves.

Women-owned sole proprietorships are engaged in all kinds of business activities. In fact, the share of such businesses increased in each major industry division between 1977 and 1983 (USDC 1986a, 8). They registered strong growth in industries like retail trade and services where they have always held a large share. The highest rates of growth occurred, however, where self-employed women are relative newcomers—wholesale trade, manufacturing, and agricultural services.

The share of receipts of women-owned sole proprietorships also increased steadily from 1977 to 1983. The 13.1 percent average annual increase in sales from women-owned businesses from 1977 to 1983 was significantly higher than that for sales of all nonfarm sole proprietorships during the same period (USDC 1986a, 9). However, the 1982 Census reports that only 11.2 percent of all women-owned firms had total receipts in excess of $50,000 (USDC 1986a, 5).

While not a panacea, self-employment is a viable option for some low-income women, particularly those who are already engaged in part-time, marginal business activity. This chapter will examine how low-income, less-educated women are being trained successfully for self-employment. It begins by taking a closer look at the characteristics of self-employed women. The chapter then reviews the experience of selected entrepreneurial training/consulting programs that serve low-income, unemployed, and underemployed women and men. Finally, it discusses a few key issues in the field that require further attention.

Characteristics of Self-Employed Women

An examination of selected characteristics of self-employed women and women wage and salary workers in 1970 and 1980 (Table 9-1) and of the median earnings of year-round, full-time workers in 1982 by occupation, class of worker, and sex (Table 9-2) reveals an interesting portrait of self-employed women. They are somewhat older, on average, than women wage and salary workers, and smaller proportions of them are black and urban dwellers. Self-employed women also earn relatively less income than their wage and salary counterparts. This reflects two main factors: the wage gap between self-employed women and men, and the generally lower earnings of self-employed persons compared to their wage and salary counterparts.

The wage gap between self-employed men and women is partly accounted

Table 9-1/Characteristics of Self-Employed and Wage and Salary Women 1970 and 1980

	SELF-EMPLOYED WORKERS		WAGE AND SALARY WORKERS	
	1970	*1980*	*1970*	*1980*
Age[a] (years)	47.1	44.1	41.0	38.3
College educated (%)	12.2	16.4	16.9	18.6
Veteran (%)	—	1.7	—	1.3
Black (%)	3.6	4.2	12.5	12.5
Urban (%)	69.3	78.5	78.4	84.4
Immigrant (%)	6.2	8.2	5.6	6.2

Source: Evans, 1985.
[a] Arithmetic average age. All other variables are percentages of population with given characteristics.

Table 9-2/Median Earnings of Year-Round, Full-time Workers in 1982, by Occupation, Class of Worker, and Sex

	MEN		WOMEN	
OCCUPATION	*Self-Employed*	*Wage and Salary*	*Self-Employed*	*Wage and Salary*
Managerial and professional specialty	$24,720	$28,637	$10,366	$17,955
Technical, sales, and administrative support	15,841	21,694	7,468	12,897
Service	10,913	14,632	4,837	9,185
Precision production, craft, and repair	13,890	21,432	7,557	14,024
Operator, fabricator, and laborer	12,015	17,167	5,918	11,047
Farming, forestry, and fishing	6,584	11,323	238	7,958
Total	14,360	21,542	6,644	13,352

Source: Becker 1984.

for by the fact that more than half of self-employed women work in the relatively low-paying sales and services occupations. But the earnings differential exists within occupational categories as well. In these cases, women's businesses may generate less income because they are conducted less than full time. Women are much more likely to conduct their businesses in addition to fulfilling traditional obligations, such as child care, dependent care, and housework, thus reducing the time available for business activities. In addition, women's businesses may be severely undercapitalized because of their limited access to all kinds of financing, and, in many instances, their lack of control over shared personal assets.

In comparing self-employed income to wages and salaries, one must remember that the figures do not include implicit income that self-employed workers often enjoy, such as the use of the business car for personal travel or feeding the family from a store owner's own stock. Moreover, self-employed persons are entitled to numerous federal income tax deductions that may let them keep a higher proportion of their gross income. For example, owners of home-based businesses can deduct percentages of rent, utilities, housecleaning bills, and use of the family car for business purposes.

On the other hand, self-employed workers do not enjoy the range of fringe benefits that may be available to wage and salary workers. Self-employed people forego such benefits as paid sick and personal time, annual leave, and employer contributions to health insurance plans. For this reason, providing national health insurance, developing a comprehensive federal child care policy, and making available affordable business liability insurance are particularly important policy issues for small business owners, both women and men.

Unfortunately, many women wage and salary workers, particularly those who work part time or who work in low-paying service occupations, receive few or no fringe benefits. Given that the majority of women now work in marginal jobs as employees, it is crucial that women's self-employment activities not be marginalized as well. Experience shows that women's business activities can be strengthened and their income increased through participation in well-designed training, technical assistance, and lending programs.

Entrepreneurial Programs for Low-Income, Less-Educated Women

As noted above, many states and localities have developed programs to cultivate and nurture local entrepreneurs and small business owners. The goal of this new activity is to create an entrepreneurial economy—an economy of problem solvers and doers—that is flexible, diverse, dynamic, and able to adapt to new shocks and changes.

Several stereotypes about the characteristics of successful entrepreneurs have constrained the development of such programs for less-educated women, but recent research and program experiences indicate that the stereotypes are largely inaccurate. A recent analysis of the 1980 U.S. Census data found that educational attainment was not significantly related to the propensity of women to choose self-employment or to their entrepreneurial success as measured by earnings (Evans 1985, 9–10). These findings are supported by the experience of entrepreneurial training and consulting programs whose clients include low-income, unemployed men and women who are not college educated. The Hawaii Entrepreneurship Training and Development Institute (HETADI), which has conducted entrepreneurship training programs for low-income, less-educated clients since 1977, reports that they have found "no significant differences in entrepreneurial capability due to ethnicity, religion, gender, income or education. In short, . . . such factors . . . should not determine whether training is provided, but should be taken into consideration in designing the specific program" (Kennedy 1986, 11–12).

Not surprisingly, organizations serving low-income, less-educated women were the first to recognize that many such women participate actively in the entrepreneurial economy. To supplement income from a low-wage or part-time job, or income received through a transfer payment program, many provide products or services on a small scale in their neighborhoods. The terms "entrepreneur of necessity" and "creative survivor" fit these women well. Most often, their business-related activity is carried on "underground" and without the benefit of outside technical or financial assistance.

While recognizing that small business ownership is no panacea for women's unemployment and underemployment, a few women-serving organizations or community-based development groups with large numbers of low-income women constituents have initiated direct service programs to strengthen existing income-generating activities and assist the entry of other low-income women into self-employment. Such programs offer a new option to women who are seeking ways to provide economically for themselves and their families. Although most are less than five years old, they are achieving significant results.

The goal of entrepreneurial assistance programs is to help women move toward economic self-sufficiency by teaching first-rate planning, decision-making, and managerial skills. In addition, participation in a well-designed entrepreneurial training/business consulting program can help women identify and access appropriate sources of start-up capital. This section examines performance objectives and program designs of entrepreneurial programs for low-income, less-educated women.

Performance Objectives of Entrepreneurial Training/Consulting Programs
To set realistic performance objectives, entrepreneurial training/consulting programs must first determine their overall goals and then define what is meant by successful placement of participants. Some programs set the same goal —business start-up—for all participants and conduct pretraining workshops designed to identify those applicants who are the most suited and well prepared for business ownership. Such programs consider a participant to be placed only when he or she has secured the necessary financing for business start-up according to the needs outlined in their completed business plan.

Business financing can come from many different sources, including personal savings, loans or investments from family members and friends, or loans from conventional lenders.

Other programs set more than one goal for participants—while half are projected to start in business, for example, the other half are projected to secure unsubsidized employment with others. Such programs consider a well-reasoned decision not to start in business to be a valid and positive outcome of program participation. In addition, the training enhances participants' overall work-related skills, strengthening their ability to obtain well-paying employment for someone else.

A growing number of entrepreneurial training programs are wrestling with another issue related to performance objectives: Will a business activity generate sufficient surplus (owner's draw) to support the participant and his or her family? In this case, the performance objective is not simply business start-up, but start-up in business activities that will enable participants to become economically self-sufficient. If self-sufficiency is not viable through a particular business idea, then program operators assist the client to modify the idea, if possible, or to secure decently paid unsubsidized employment.

Program Design

Entrepreneurial training programs assist the participant to accomplish those tasks that lead to successful business start-up—developing a business plan, learning business-related language, sharpening decision-making and personal effectiveness skills, and learning systems, such as record keeping, that are crucial to setting up business operations.

Their training methods are tailored to fit the business start-up approach of people who are new to ownership and who have very limited access to mainstream sources of assistance. Such people begin in business with the skills, time, and money they have at hand. They develop the business step by step, growing as their resources and the demand for their product or service allow. In addition, because women are the primary caregivers, they must determine how they can best balance their family and business responsibilities. Often this leads to starting a business at home.

The design of entrepreneurial training programs is typically based on either a classroom training or individual consulting model, although a program may combine elements of both approaches. Under a classroom training model, participants attend a series of sessions held over a period of 12 to 20 weeks. Classroom training programs use various instructional techniques, such as lectures, resource speakers, group exercises and case studies, and videotapings of participants' public speaking and business plan presentations. Classroom training may be followed by a period of individual consulting as participants start their business activities.

Under an individual consulting model, clients work one-on-one with professional consultants to develop the business plan and discuss issues related to business start-up. Business plan preparation is often accomplished as clients complete a series of homework assignments to which the consultant reacts with feedback and suggestions for revisions. In addition, small groups may be formed to meet for a short term to address common start-up problems and to offer mutual support.

Many entrepreneurial training programs focus initially on "self-assessment"—providing a framework through which each participant can assess her own ability to become successfully self-employed. Self-assessment training enables a woman to know herself—her motivations for seeking self-employment, her personality traits and how they may help or hurt her business, and her ability to organize her personal responsibilities and establish priorities (Hisrich and Brush 1986, 36). Through this process, she identifies her strengths and weaknesses, pinpointing areas that need further development. Self-assessment training usually makes use of both formal written exercises and informal discussion techniques. It may be the first part of an entrepreneurial training program, or it may be a prerequisite for entry into the formal training program itself.

Those participants who choose to pursue self-employment must then define and describe their business and chart its future direction. These tasks are accomplished by preparing a business plan. A well-prepared plan is a working tool with a dual purpose: to attract the financial resources necessary for business start-up and to guide the business owner in the ongoing operation of the business.

A business plan includes a description of the business concept and product or service to be offered, a market analysis, production plans, a marketing and distribution strategy, a description of the organizational design and the management team, multi-year financial projections, and plans for acquiring financing. It provides a wealth of information within a framework that the business owner can utilize to make effective decisions as the business moves forward in its development. Business plans are usually prepared piece by piece, beginning with a concise definition of the business concept. An entrepreneurial training program may make use of existing business plan preparation handbooks, or design its own materials to facilitate the planning process. Classroom or office-based work is usually augmented with field work to do research and gather information.

Finally, entrepreneurial training programs introduce the potential business owner to the community's array of business assistance resources, financial institutions, and business-owner networks. Participants come into contact with many such community resources in the process of gathering information for their business plans, while others are invited into the classroom to discuss a particular topic related to starting up and operating a business.

Three key issues affect the design of both classroom and individual consulting-based programs aimed specifically at low-income women: building personal self-confidence, effectiveness, and support; gaining access to financing; and overcoming barriers faced by women receiving AFDC (Aid to Families with Dependent Children) or unemployment insurance benefits.

The first key program design issue is the sense of isolation and lack of self-confidence experienced by many women, and particularly low-income women, pursuing business ownership. Too often, low-income women must attempt business start-up within a hostile environment. Many influential institutions fail to see that such women can transfer their survival skills and creative energy to become successful entrepreneurs. Even the families and personal support networks of these "creative survivors" may meet their aspirations for business ownership with discouragement and derision.

Among the strategies used by entrepreneurial training/consulting programs to increase the personal effectiveness and meet the personal needs of these women are:

- Affirming a woman's decision to pursue self-employment
- Establishing a focus on the woman's own positive vision of her business idea, minimizing the negative messages too often conveyed by outside people and institutions
- Providing skill-building that enables a woman to assess realistically the personal, technical and financial resources at hand, or potentially available, and to use such resources effectively
- Assessing a woman's needs for day care and transportation and identifying ways to meet those needs

The second program design issue is women's lack of access to financing. In attempting to secure conventional financing, women who are new to business ownership and who have limited financial resources face the following obstacles:

- Their businesses often require outside financing in amounts well under $25,000. Conventional lenders shun such small loans because of their high transaction and information costs.
- Their work experience is predominantly in the service sector, making it less likely that they will start manufacturing or other kinds of businesses with fixed assets that can serve as collateral.
- They are less likely than men to own personal assets outright, or to control shared assets, such as a house or a car, which can be used as collateral.
- They have comparatively limited personal or family savings to use as equity and have not been in the networks of friends and colleagues who have resources to invest.
- They seldom have a credit history in their own name, or if they do, they may have a poor credit record.

Responding to these obstacles, entrepreneurial training/consulting programs have designed such creative financing mechanisms as:

- Revolving loan funds that make small loans with flexible collateral and equity requirements
- Guarantee pools that reduce the exposure of conventional lenders
- Use of a bank's consumer lending "window" to obtain small loans with flexible collateral and equity requirements
- Holding companies that can keep the business assets of a woman receiving assistance through the Aid to Families with Dependent Children program until her business earns sufficient income for her personal or family support
- Group lending mechanisms, under which program participants form into groups to receive small initial loans. Subsequent, larger loans are contingent on the clear credit record of the group. Such schemes often include a "forced savings" component through which a contingency fund is created to meet the emergency personal and business needs of group members

Finally, many low-income women are dependent on benefits from transfer payment programs such as AFDC and Unemployment Insurance. Anticipated loss of family medical benefits, in particular, keeps many women from attempting to leave welfare. Unfortunately, in most cases, making an earnest effort to become self-employed will result in the loss of program benefits because of certain program policies and regulations. Such restrictive AFDC policies and regulations include:

- Limitations on the business assets of recipients because no distinction is made between business and personal assets
- Prohibitions, varying from state to state, against deducting from income certain expenses that are recognized as legitimate business costs, such as depreciation, transportation, and the purchase of certain supplies and capital equipment
- Requirements that AFDC recipients participate in training or other activities
- Loss of Medicaid benefits when a recipient leaves the welfare rolls
- Effective high marginal taxation of the business income of recipients, due to limited income disregards, high benefit reduction ratios, and work-hour limitations
- Limitations on eligibility for certain supports (for example, child care slots and transportation subsidies) to recipients enrolled in training or other activities

A few consulting-based programs that work with low-income women entering self-employment are experimenting with approaches to limit the effects of one or more of these policy and regulatory barriers. Following a two-year advocacy effort led by Women and Employment, Inc., in Charleston, West Virginia, for example, the state legislature passed a bill in March 1987 that authorizes a pilot entrepreneurship project for a small group of women and men on welfare. During the pilot project, state payments will substitute for program participants' federal AFDC benefits. This strategy will free the participants from restrictive federal regulations for the period of the project. The Women's Economic Development Corporation (WEDCO) in St. Paul, Minnesota, has developed a nonprofit holding company, which will avoid asset limitation problems by enabling women receiving AFDC benefits to lease their business inventory, supplies, and equipment during a start-up period. While neither approach solves all of the policy and regulatory problems, they can demonstrate that many women on welfare can use a self-employment option to become self-sufficient if certain barriers are removed and the right kind of help is provided.

Both of these approaches are illustrations of "transfer payment investment," which aims to lower policy and regulatory barriers by using transfer payments, alone or in combination with other mechanisms, to support the self-sufficiency efforts of recipients. In 1986, the Corporation for Enterprise Development (CfED), initiated a multi-state demonstration project to test the viability of self-employment as a route to economic self-sufficiency for welfare recipients. Each of the participating states agreed to establish a pilot program in which welfare regulations that impose barriers to business development are waived for program participants. Participants retain their benefits and receive technical assistance, counseling, and some form of modest seed capital to help launch their self-employment enterprises.

This demonstration is modeled on programs in Europe that pioneered the concept of allowing recipients to use their transfer payments to become self-employed or start small businesses. Examples of such programs include:

- France's "Chomeur Createurs d'Enterprises" (Unemployed Entrepreneur) program, initiated in 1979, under which French citizens entitled to unemployment compensation or supplementary (income maintenance) benefits can collect a lump sum payment of up to 43,000 francs (approximately $6,500), instead of their monthly benefit to start a business. Recent evaluations of the 24,606 businesses started during 1981 and 1982 found that, on average, they created one job in addition to that of the owner. Approximately 30 percent of program participants were able to leverage their lump sum payment with a bank loan. Between 60 and 80 percent of the businesses survived at least one year, and more than half of those participants who closed their businesses were able to find a new job or start a second business. Over 175,000 individuals have been in the program since it began.

- Great Britain's Enterprise Allowance Scheme (EAS), initiated as a pilot program in five areas in 1982 and made into a national program in 1983, is available to those who have been unemployed for eight weeks (formerly 13 weeks, until April 1986) and are eligible to receive unemployment or supplementary (income maintenance) benefits. Instead of these benefits, participants receive weekly EAS payments of about £40 (approximately $65) for one year while they attempt business start-up. Data from an 18-month survey of the nationwide program (begun in August 1983) showed that 76 percent of businesses that completed 12 months on the scheme were still operating. For every 100 businesses surviving, 91 new jobs had been generated. Of these, 37 were full time and 54 were part time. Later surveys showed a survival rate of 52 percent after three years, with somewhat better job creation rates. Approximately 200,000 people entered the program from 1982 through 1986, and 100,000 are projected to participate in 1987.[2]

These and other transfer payment investment program models in Europe are being closely observed for their applicability in this country.

It is also possible to use transfer payments in creative combinations with other efforts to promote self-sufficiency without encountering regulatory problems. For example, the Save the Children Federation has combined federal nutrition program funds with its efforts to help low-income women become home-based child care providers for other working mothers. In its Southern States Office in Atlanta, Georgia, Save the Children offers a training program on how to develop and run such a service business. To help finance this program and stabilize the family day care providers' income, Save the Children administers a U.S. Department of Agriculture child care food program which reimburses the family day care providers for meals served to children in their care. Save the Children receives modest administrative fees for managing the program and the women have certain costs of providing meals underwritten. Save the Children also promotes women's child care businesses by referring women clients in training programs funded by the Job Training Partnership Act (JTPA). Coordinated efforts such as this break the cycle of dependency by using transfer payments to help create new employment options for low-income women.

Experience of Selected Entrepreneurial Training/Consulting Programs

Entrepreneurial training/consulting programs that serve low-income, less-educated women fall into two broad categories: training directed to both women and men, and training and business consulting services designed specifically for unemployed and underemployed women. This section reviews the design and experience of selected programs of each type.

PROGRAMS FOR WOMEN AND MEN

Programs in this category focus on disadvantaged workers—low-income, long-term unemployed and underemployed women and men whose prior work experience is in relatively low-paying, often part-time or temporary jobs—and on dislocated workers—people with long work histories who suffer lay-offs from relatively well-paying jobs in declining industries. Such programs are now funded primarily through the federal JTPA and were previously funded through the Comprehensive Employment and Training Act (CETA). Their development within the traditional employment and training system reflects a growing acceptance of self-employment as a viable employment option, particularly in areas experiencing high unemployment in traditional local industries.

HETADI. Founded in 1977, HETADI conducts entrepreneurial training programs in the United States and several countries in the Third World.[3] HETADI performs its services under contract to both public and private agencies, including the Small Business Administration of the U.S. Department of Commerce, refugee resettlement agencies, and the Veterans Administration. Because of the burden of excessive administrative regulations, however, HETADI no longer operates programs with traditional federal job training resources, such as JTPA funds.

In its 10 years of operation, HETADI has provided training of some kind to approximately 2,500 people. Of these, nearly 1,000 people have participated in HETADI's full program of entrepreneurial training. The vast majority of businesses started by program participants are retail or service enterprises.

HETADI's entrepreneurial training programs typically enroll approximately 25 participants and extend for three months (100–200 hours). Classroom training is often followed by a period of individual consulting as the business begins operation. The training is conducted by one or two full-time instructors and several consultants and guest speakers who provide information on specific topics (such as taxes, legal requirements, and bookkeeping).

HETADI's entrepreneurial training is designed around the preparation of a business plan. The organization's founders believe that the process of business plan development lays a solid foundation for business start-up. The participant learns a range of skills through business plan preparation that will guide her or him in starting up and operating the business. Personal motivation and achievement are emphasized throughout the process. HETADI's program does not train participants extensively in specific business operation or management skills but encourages them to acquire such knowledge through standard training courses offered through community colleges and other institutions.

HETADI's training exposes program participants to the available options for financing their businesses. Participants are assisted to make a realistic assessment of funds available from their personal savings, as well as from their family members, friends, and associates. Representatives of local lending institutions participate in the training as guest speakers and resource people. In addition, HETADI involves bank loan officers on the panels of professional people that it organizes to respond to business plan presentations made by program participants. In some cases, this method of introducing hopeful entrepreneurs to lenders leads to a bank loan.

Early in its development (January 1978), HETADI contracted with the Office of Human Resources of the City and County of Honolulu to conduct six cycles of entrepreneurial training over a two-year period with CETA-eligible participants—men and women who were unemployed or underemployed and had incomes below a specified poverty level. They selected participants whose businesses required relatively small amounts of capital and worked with them to secure conventional financing when necessary. HETADI projected that 50 percent of these program participants would become self-employed, and 40 percent would find unsubsidized employment with existing firms.

To evaluate the degree to which the six cycles of training achieved their objectives, HETADI gathered information on the status of HETADI graduates and nongraduates in 1982. Approximately 40 percent of participants were female, 20 percent of all participants had less than a high school education, 60 percent had the equivalent of a high school education, and all were low-income people who met CETA eligibility requirements. Arthur Young and Company, an international accounting firm, performed an independent analysis of the data. They found that 66 percent of program graduates became self-employed, compared to 10 percent of a selected control group. Eighty-four percent of these graduates were still in business after four years and had generated 94 new positions in addition to their own jobs. In total, 94 percent of program graduates either became self-employed or found unsubsidized employment with others.

EDIT, Inc. Founded in April 1985 in Brice, Ohio, EDIT, Inc., provides training to people who have the desire to start their own businesses.[4] The organization was started by two women entrepreneurs, one of whom is not college educated. She started her first business when, as a divorced, single mother, she was displaced from a low-paying but highly responsible position in the construction industry. She and her partner started EDIT to share what they had learned about entrepreneurship, particularly for moderate income people.

Shortly after their own start-up, EDIT received a $60,000 grant from the Ohio Bureau of Employment Services, JTPA Division, to train dislocated workers in starting and managing their own businesses. The contract was precipitated by a serious decline in the local construction and transportation industries. The dislocation of many skilled and semiskilled workers and the lack of alternative employment opportunities led to the bureau's interest in funding entrepreneurial training. Launched in December 1985, EDIT enrolled 20 participants in its pilot cycle. Following completion of this cycle, EDIT received continued funding from the bureau to run a second cycle for 37 participants.

The training is structured around business plan development and conducted by two full-time instructors with entrepreneurial experience. Many guest speakers augment the formal training.

At the outset of training, participants set realistic personal income goals. As business plan development proceeds and they determine how much income their proposed business can generate, this figure is compared to their initial goal. If it falls short, they are assisted to restructure the business plan whenever possible.

EDIT's program consists of 12 weeks of classroom training and a follow-up period during which one-on-one consulting is provided at no cost. During the first six weeks, the group meets three days each week for four hours each day. This time commitment shortens to one or two days a week during the second six weeks, depending on the group's needs. Participants often form into small groups to offer mutual support in developing parts of their business plans and to engage in problem solving about certain aspects of business start-up and operation.

Most of EDIT, Inc.'s clients' businesses require a minimum amount of start-up capital, which is provided by the clients themselves. Since most clients had sufficient previous income to purchase their own homes, they are encouraged to obtain a home equity loan for any additional business financing that may be required. EDIT, Inc.'s female clients without such collateral can access a mini-loan guarantee program sponsored by the State of Ohio. In addition, EDIT, Inc., staff is in the process of organizing a "last resort" loan fund to be capitalized through private contributions.

A total of 57 participants, 38 men and 19 women, enrolled in EDIT's first two training cycles. Of these participants, 47 were white, 9 black, and 1 Hispanic. Three were college graduates, 16 had one or more years of postsecondary education, 40 had a high school diploma or General Educational Development (GED) diploma, and one had not completed high school. Of the 19 female participants, only two had some postsecondary education.

All participants were dislocated workers (as defined under Title III of JTPA) from hourly wage, blue-collar jobs in the telephone, trucking, and construction industries. Their willingness to commit substantial amounts of time and effort to both the training program and business start-up served as a major participant selection criteria. The median pretraining income for men was $22,332; the comparable figure for 16 women was $10,245 (three women had held jobs paying more than $20,000).

Examples of the types of businesses launched by participants in the pilot cycle included in-home word processing services, telephone sales/installation and service, custom glass sales and installation, in-home companionship care for the elderly and handicapped, custom baking, and a catering business.

PROGRAMS FOR UNEMPLOYED AND UNDEREMPLOYED WOMEN

Programs in this category assist the transition of low-income, unemployed and underemployed women into economic self-sufficiency through self-employment. For the most part, programs like these have been developed by women-serving organizations or by community-based development groups with large numbers of low-income women constituents. Many of these groups have extensive track records in providing nontraditional job training to low-income women. By initiating entrepreneurial training/consulting programs, they are extending themselves further into the economic development arena. They are offering another nontraditional option to women—that of creating their own jobs.

For the most part, entrepreneurial training/consulting programs focused on women have relied heavily on private-sector resources, including private and corporate foundation grants and, when appropriate, client fees. A few have accessed Carl D. Perkins Vocational Education Act monies or state-level JTPA funds. Formal eligibility requirements vary depending on the source of funding, but most programs require participants to have a business idea and target their resources to women who do not have sufficient income to support themselves and their families.

The Women's Economic Development Corporation (WEDCO). WEDCO provides comprehensive services to women engaged in the start-up or on-going operation of their own businesses in the State of Minnesota.[5] Clients are assisted in pursuing business opportunities that will increase their economic self-sufficiency and provide a balance between their personal and economic goals.

The organization emerged from an extensive planning process funded by local foundations and jointly sponsored by the Humphrey Institute of Public Affairs at the University of Minnesota; Chrysalis, A Center for Women located in Minneapolis; and Mainstay, a displaced-homemaker program operating in rural Minnesota. Incorporated in October 1983, WEDCO began program operations in January 1984.

WEDCO builds an ongoing relationship with each client by providing a range of individual consulting, group training, finance, and information and referral services. To insure a businesslike relationship with its clients, WEDCO charges fees for its services on a sliding-scale indexed to client income.

WEDCO assists individual women in business plan preparation through a "teaching/consulting" model in which responsibility for moving forward rests with the client. Following an initial intake session, clients contract for individual consulting sessions with WEDCO staff, as well as for group training workshops as needed. Clients prepare sections of the business plans in advance of each session and receive feedback and homework assignments until their plans are complete. This self-paced, self-motivated process requires, on average, six to eight sessions (over a period of two to eight months) to complete a plan.

WEDCO also offers "workgroups," which bring together four to six women for intensive training in marketing, record keeping, or personal effectiveness. The groups usually meet for approximately five training sessions, scheduled within a two-month period.

To provide better service to its clients who receive benefits under AFDC, WEDCO incorporated a nonprofit subsidiary, Self-Employment Training Opportunities, Inc. (SETO), in 1986. SETO is a holding company that is authorized to make leasing agreements for the inventory, equipment, and supplies needed by women on AFDC who are pursuing business start-up. WEDCO clients wishing to structure a leasing arrangement with SETO must complete a formal, six-month training component that addresses issues related to personal effectiveness, the choice of self-employment or employment by others, and business plan preparation. They must also be pursuing a viable business idea that can return sufficient income to allow them to leave AFDC within one year of receiving financing.

A key element in WEDCO's structure is its comprehensive approach to improving women's access to capital. Depending on a client's needs, WEDCO offers access to financing through conventional lenders or through its own loan funds, which are designed to meet the needs of both new and expanding businesses. In addition, WEDCO assists a small number of businesses to obtain private financing, venture capital, or government-sponsored loans.

In the area of conventional financing, WEDCO and the First Bank system in Minneapolis/St. Paul have carefully developed a unique relationship. The bank has assigned loan officers from within its consumer lending division to work with WEDCO staff and clients. These loan officers actively negotiate the collateral and equity requirements of each loan.

Through its in-house seed fund, WEDCO promotes the idea of "stepping loans"—small, short-term loans that assist a new business to establish a credit history and move a step forward in its development. Clients approaching this fund must first be refused a loan by a conventional lender.

During its initial three years, WEDCO assisted over 2,000 women to assess their business ideas, develop business plans, or operate ongoing businesses. Its efforts resulted in the start-up of 564 new businesses and the expansion of an additional 300 businesses. Approximately one-third of the businesses WEDCO assists create jobs in addition to their owner's job.

WEDCO's clients engage in many different kinds of business activities, including pest exterminating, hairdressing, snow plowing, designing and manufacturing jewelry and clothing, upholstering furniture, manufacturing plastic food containers, filling mail order gift requests, word processing, manufacturing fishing lures, designing cartoons, and teaching dance.

WEDCO has assisted a substantial number of low-income, less-educated clients. During its first three years, 75 percent of WEDCO's clients reported personal incomes of less than $15,000, with 45 percent reporting less than $7,000. Twenty-four percent of the women assisted supported themselves with some type of transfer payment, and 65 percent were single or the head of their household. Approximately 26 percent had no formal education beyond receiving a high school diploma.

WEDCO's operations are funded through three main income sources. Ten percent of its budget is generated from client fees, 70 percent comes from contributions from private and corporate foundations, financial institutions and individuals, and 20 percent from contracts for services.

Maine Displaced Homemakers Project: New Ventures. Transitions: A Displaced Homemakers Project (DHP) has been serving displaced homemakers in Maine since 1978 and currently operates eight centers throughout the state. The project assists economically dependent homemakers, forced to re-enter the job market because of separation, divorce, or the death or disability of a spouse, to become job ready.

In the fall of 1985, DHP staff piloted New Ventures, an entrepreneurial training program, in the mid-coast region of Maine. Several factors contributed to their decision to introduce a small business skills training component. First, Maine's primarily rural economy relies heavily on small business activity, much of which is home-based. Second, national statistics revealed the startling growth of new and successful women-owned businesses. Finally, an increasing number of the project's own constituents expressed interest in exploring the option of self-employment. They had business ideas but lacked the technical skills and personal confidence to pursue them.

As of early 1987, two cycles of training had been completed with a total of 27 enrolled participants. The New Ventures staff aim their recruitment efforts at single parents and homemakers who have a specific business idea and are seeking start-up assistance. Applicants are required to submit a three-page written application form, attend a three-hour orientation session, and participate in an individual interview.

Through this self-selection process, 12 women were enrolled in the pilot training session and 15 in the second session. Of the original 12, four had a high school diploma or the equivalent and eight had some postsecondary education. In the second session, five participants had a high school diploma or the equivalent and 10 had some postsecondary education, including three with vocational training. In regard to income prior to training, nine participants in the second cycle had incomes below $10,000 annually, three had incomes between $10,000 and $25,000, and three had incomes over $25,000.

The New Ventures staff includes the program coordinator, an assistant, an accountant, and an attorney. An employment and training specialist works with women who choose not to pursue business ownership, or who have other employment-related needs.

Training consists of 90 classroom training hours scheduled within a 10-week period, and a three-month follow-up component. Classes meet three times a week for three hours. The training process focuses directly on participants' business ideas and is highly interactive. Participants hear lectures and panel discussions, share ideas, and engage in mutual support and problem solving.

The curriculum is structured around the step-by-step process of preparing a business plan. While accomplishing this task, participants learn concrete skills in areas such as pricing, financial forecasting, and record keeping, and they participate in exercises to increase their ability to take calculated risks and to trust their own judgment. Primary curriculum materials include *The Business of Small Business*, a handbook published by the Women's Economic Development Corporation in St. Paul, materials adapted from *Entrepreneurship Education*, developed by the Illinois Department of Education, and sections of the *Career/Life Planning Curriculum* of the Maine Displaced Homemakers Project.

New Ventures has not yet developed a capital source through which access to financing can be offered to program participants. The training curriculum, however, incorporates information on capital sources, and representatives from area banks, the Small Business Administration, and local economic development lending agencies present information on their specific programs at various sessions. The majority of the initial 27 New Ventures participants who have started up in business have obtained seed capital through their own personal networks.

During the spring of 1986, 10 of the 12 graduates from the first training cycle opened their businesses or entered the final stages of planning. The businesses include custom sewing and alterations, word processing, payroll and billing services, personalized beauty and fashion services, quilt designs, a greenhouse, custom and specialized metalworks, health insurance claims services, a mail-order crafts catalogue, and housing renewal and refabrication. Twelve of the 15 women who completed the second cycle in December 1986 are in various stages of business start-up.

Funding for the New Ventures training came from the Carl D. Perkins Vocational Education Act, through a grant from the Bureau of Adult and Secondary Vocational Education in the Maine Department of Educational and Cultural Services.

Key Issues: Mobilizing Community Resources and Securing Adequate Funding

The long-standing skepticism about the capabilities of low-income, less-educated women and men to become successfully self-employed is beginning to give way in the face of programs such as those discussed above and ones from abroad that target welfare recipients and the unemployed. The idea of creating programs that will draw upon previously unrecognized strengths of disadvantaged women (including some of those receiving public assistance), create more jobs, and stimulate local economic activity is becoming attractive to an ever-widening circle of individuals and institutions. This increased interest in self-employment, however, highlights two key issues that require further attention: How can a community mobilize its resources in support of the self-employment activities of low-income women? Can adequate and renewable funding be secured?

Mobilizing Community Resources
In most communities throughout the world, women business owners operate with little or no support from the mainstream business, economic development, or financial institutions. Leaders in these sectors too often regard women's business activities as "hobbies" or assume that they will not be successful. Low-income women and women of color are regarded as especially risky candidates for business ownership. Such attitudes spill over into the community-at-large, creating a generally unsupportive climate for women who attempt business development.

To create a positive environment in which direct service self-employment programs may develop, particularly those focused on low-income women, a number of activities must take place. Women, in all their diversity (urban/rural, young/old, rich/poor, and of every race and ethnicity) must be brought out of isolation and encouraged to discuss their experiences related to preparing for and starting up in business. Information must be gathered that can counteract prevailing stereotypes and better describe the business activities in which many low-income women are already engaged in the "informal" economy and the nonprofit sector. A free exchange of perspectives within the community must be encouraged. Influential individuals and institutions must be courted and persuaded that they have something to gain from and something to contribute to establishing new programs.

There are undoubtedly many ways to build local awareness of, information about, and support for women's self-employment activities. One proven way, adaptable to a variety of local and regional settings, is to engage local community-based women's organizations, successful women business owners, women interested in self-employment, and community leaders from all sectors (economic development, business, labor, government, education, and social service) in a needs assessment and capacity-building process. The National Coalition for Women's Enterprise (formerly the HUB Co-ventures for Women's Enterprise), has designed and tested a needs assessment process that is adaptable in a variety of local and regional settings (Gould and Lyman 1987).

A needs assessment process accomplishes, formally or informally, the following objectives:

- To gauge the level of activity and interest in self-employment and enterprise development among local women of all income levels and all racial and ethnic backgrounds
- To explore with local women their experience with business ownership, and to identify the particular barriers they face and opportunities they see in business start-up and expansion
- To learn about the support services (for example, training and technical assistance, sources of financing, and day care) available for self-employed people and small business owners
- To communicate the information gained to key individuals in the community, and to enlist the investment of their resources and expertise in responsive new and expanded strategies

Several kinds of organizations, acting alone or in coalition, can undertake a needs assessment process. Because of ties to a low-income women's constituency, a local women's social service organization or a community-based development group sensitive to women's needs and potential might take the lead. A women's business owners' association, city department of community or economic development, commission on the status of women, or chamber of commerce might take a more limited role, while lending crucial support to the effort. In Philadelphia, Pennsylvania, for example, the Women's Association for Women's Alternatives (WAWA) led a six-month planning initiative that followed the HUB Process. To implement the Process, WAWA formed an advisory council with representatives from a variety of organizations (that is, the Philadelphia Citywide Development Corporation, Fidelity Bank, Wharton Small Business Development Center, and Women Business Owners of Greater Philadelphia) whose participation in the effort was key to its success.

The National Coalition's experience suggests that a needs assessment and capacity-building process can be accomplished in approximately six to eight months. Some localities may require considerably more or, perhaps, even less time, depending on their geographic scope and the existing awareness of and sensitivity to women's self-employment and small business activities.

Securing Adequate and Diversified Funding
Initiating new or expanding existing direct-service programs to assist the entry of low-income women into self-employment requires a high level of financial resources from both the private and the public sectors.

Many of the training and consulting-based programs initiated during the last few years have obtained the majority of their funding from private and corporate foundations. Approximately 70 percent of the WEDCO budget, for example, is contributed by private and corporate foundations. Eager to create new jobs and to create a new employment option for low-income and minority women, such institutions have funded the core operating costs of new programs. They have also contributed to the capital base of revolving loan funds that make available small amounts of start-up debt capital to low-income women. In at least one case (WEDCO), a private foundation has made a program-related investment in the form of a loan to a revolving fund established to provide expansion capital to existing women's businesses.

While funding from private and corporate foundations has enabled the start-up of a few pioneering efforts, it cannot by itself fuel the more widespread development of programs that support women's self-employment. Unfortunately, the level of private-sector resources required to fully fund a women's self-employment program exists in only a few, usually urban areas. In addition, programs that rely primarily on this source of funding place themselves in a precarious position as foundation and corporate priorities change. For these reasons, initiating new and financially stable programs depends on acquiring additional sources of support. Key among new sources are the public sector and income generated through fees or business-related activities of the programs themselves.

Increased public-sector support can come from federal job training and vocational education funds; local, state, and federal economic development programs; and transfer payment programs such as AFDC and unemployment insurance. In a growing number of areas, JTPA funds are supporting self-employment programs aimed at dislocated workers. Such funds were key, for example, in the start-up of the EDIT program. As yet, however, far fewer examples exist of JTPA funds supporting programs to foster self-employment among low-income, disadvantaged women. Using the resources of the traditional employment and training system to create a self-employment option for low-income women will require continued exposure and education of that system's policy makers and practitioners to the successful program models now being developed.

A few programs make use of vocational education funds. Carl D. Perkins Vocational Education Act funds, for example, support the New Ventures program in Maine, which provides entrepreneurial training to single parents and displaced homemakers. In Newark, New Jersey, state vocational education funds provided operating support in the second year of the HUB Program for Women's Self-Employment, initiated by the WISE Women's Center of Essex County College following implementation of the HUB planning process.

The last few years have seen an increase in the level of resources available for self-employment training from federal, state, and local economic development programs. In recent years, the U.S. cities and states that have focused their economic development efforts on a "smokestack chasing" model have experienced serious frustration. This practice—of trying to lure branch plants of large manufacturing firms by promising reduced taxes, low labor costs, few environmental restrictions, or lower welfare benefits—is simply not paying off. As a result, many economic development practitioners have recognized the need to invest public resources in local entrepreneurs and small business owners, and a growing number are interested in supporting the self-employment efforts of low-income people, people of color, and women.

Finally, using transfer payments in innovative ways to support the self-sufficiency efforts of recipients is crucial to releasing the full economic potential of these nontraditional entrepreneurs. Organizations like the Corporation for Enterprise Development have played an important role in bringing the results of transfer payment investment programs in Europe to the attention of policy makers and practitioners in the United States. CfED's demonstration program in this country will be watched with great interest.

Conclusion

Self-employment is not for everyone. It is, however, an important vocational option chosen by a rapidly increasing number of people. This group includes low-income, less-educated women whose often marginal entrepreneurial efforts can be strengthened.

Effective training and technical assistance programs for low-income, less-educated women display several characteristics. They build specific business skills while strengthening participants' general problem-solving abilities. They are practical and "street smart" and are taught by practitioners as well as academics. They combine classroom learning with hands-on experience. In each of these ways, they meet the particular needs of their participants by taking into account their strengths and weaknesses and the scale of their business activities. They enable each woman to make an informed choice about whether to pursue self-employment.

On an individual level, this development of skills, experience, and perhaps most important, confidence brings both economic and personal benefits to women and their families. On a societal level, it contributes to the vitality of local economies and creates a new employment option for low-income women.

Notes

1. According to the 1982 Economic Census of Women-Owned Businesses, 92.3 percent of all women-owned businesses in 1982 were sole proprietorships, 4.6 percent were partnerships, and 3.1 percent were 1120-S (subchapter S) corporations.

2. Information on the British and French programs was obtained in conversations with program staff at the Corporation for Enterprise Development, Washington, D.C. in November 1986.

3. Information on HETADI was obtained from Kennedy 1986 and also from conversations with Richard Kennedy in March 1987.

4. Information on EDIT, Inc., was obtained from Spruill and Sciacca 1986 and also from conversations with Connie Spruill in March 1987.

5. Information on WEDCO and New Ventures is taken from Gould and Lyman 1987, and also from conversations with program staff in March 1987.

References

Becker, Eugene H. 1984. "Self-Employed Workers: An Update to 1983." *Monthly Labor Review* (July).

Evans, David S. 1985. "Entrepreneurial Choice and Success." CERA Economic Consultants, Inc., Old Greenwich, Conn., May.

Gould, Sara K., and Jing Lyman. 1987. "A Working Guide to Women's Self-Employment." Corporation for Enterprise Development, Washington, D.C., February.

Hisrich, Robert D., and Candida G. Brush. 1986. *The Woman Entrepreneur: Starting, Financing, and Managing a Successful New Business*. Lexington, Mass.: Lexington Books.

Kennedy, Richard. 1986. "HETADI: Serving the Poor Throughout the World." *The Entrepreneurial Economy*. Washington, D.C.: Corporation for Enterprise Development, June.

Spruill, Connie, and Patricia Sciacca. 1986. "EDIT, Inc.: Entrepreneurial Training for Dislocated Workers." *The Entrepreneurial Economy*. Washington, D.C.: Corporation for Enterprise Development, June.

U.S. Department of Commerce. Small Business Administration. 1986a. Office of Advocacy. Office of Economic Research. "The Recent Growth of Women-Owned Businesses." Washington, D.C., July.

———. Small Business Administration. 1986b. *The State of Small Businesses: A Report of the President*. Washington, D.C.: Government Printing Office.

10/Training Women for Jobs in Rural Economies: A Southern Experience

Leslie Lilly

The political economy of the South has been distinguished by its political conservatism, its rural and small-town character, its economic history as an agricultural region, and its deep and tragic struggle with issues of equity. These have played no small part in contributing to the persistence of barriers to women's economic opportunity.

The political institutions and social practices of slavery are part of the social fabric of the South. Abolition did not end an economic system that rationalized the exploitation of workers and natural resources as a necessity of competition with more industrialized northern neighbors. After the Civil War, the amount of commerce and manufacturing in the Northeast far exceeded that in the South. Southern promoters, seeking a way to develop the region's economy, wooed labor-intensive industries with offers of land originally reserved for rural homesteading. Eventually the sale of millions of acres displaced a large amount of southern agriculture, leaving a surplus labor force in rural communities. Surplus labor was a further attraction to northern investors who introduced industries that did not require large amounts of capital or a skilled work force.

The economic strategy for southern development was to prepare agricultural products and raw material that would be manufactured and sold elsewhere. Little thought was given to the region itself as a marketplace for indigenous goods. Few residents could actually afford the products that were destined to be made and refined elsewhere. Instead, the vision of development for the South was that of an economic colony for northern capital. Although the South was rich in natural resources and had an abundant labor supply, it did not create a healthy, diversified rural economy.

Industry's accountability to local communities in which it located was made more tenuous by the failure of state and local governments to regulate development in rural areas. Government was more inclined to protect industries than to regulate their practices. Added to these factors were economic policies in which taxes were cut and funds for services—especially public schooling —were slashed. Not surprisingly, the major beneficiaries were corporations, utility companies, and railroad barons. The tale of the carpetbagger has been, in many ways, a smokescreen for the exploitation of the region's resources and peoples by an indigenous privileged class.

These development practices contributed to a caste system of employment that placed greater emphasis on maintaining race and sex discrimination than on educating workers or building their skills. Rural women, both black and white, are underrepresented and segmented in the labor force. Occupational segregation by race and gender continues to have profound effects on their economic opportunities, often limiting them, for example, to peripheral service occupations. Social custom and institutional discrimination have inhibited migration across occupations and industries to jobs that offer better opportunities for women. Historically, the only way oppressed workers could improve their conditions was to move out of the South altogether. Massive migrations, almost always northward, by blacks and poor whites, demonstrate how powerful this system has been.

The interaction of gender and race in shaping the labor force participation of rural southern women has been especially profound. Although almost all jobs that are "women's jobs" are low paid, white women get the "better" jobs in factories, while black women work in agriculture or in white homes. "Better" may mean more status or even a somewhat increased level of compensation, but it seldom means breaking through the barriers to nontraditional employment.

Class privilege, along with race, creates further wedges between southern rural women. "White trash" girls from "Mill Hill" do not socialize with the rich white girls on "Money Street"; nor do they socialize with the black maids of the white girls of "Money Street." Privilege based on racism "worked" because it gave the white working poor some basis for distinguishing themselves from blacks, even though this white working poor remained "white trash" to their class-superior racial peers. It also "worked" because many white "crackers" left the red hills of their upbringing to find better lives elsewhere before reacting against their real subordination by class.

The price this region has paid for its industrial base and its economic and social bigotry has been enormous: despite the slow rise in per capita income that can be tracked over the last 10 years, the South has the lowest per capita income and the highest poverty rate in the nation. The majority of the nation's rural poor resides in the Southeast, as do over 40 percent of all unemployed blacks.

Women constitute the majority of those who are poor in the South.

Among these poor women, over 40 percent have total annual incomes that are less than one-half of the national poverty level. The poverty of children is directly attributable to the inability of women to earn an adequate income as single parents. This is despite the fact that almost 80 percent of single-parent women are in the labor force.[1]

While the economic significance of women as workers and as participants in the economy has earned some recognition in recent years, the needs of most women workers continue to be systematically ignored. Young girls continue to be socialized toward traditional roles and responsibilities. Racism endures. The unevenness of economic development is rarely scrutinized for its effects on rural black and white women. Despite the rhetoric of Sunbelt ascendancy, rural communities suffer severe economic decline, and industries that have traditionally employed women are disappearing, going either overseas or out of business altogether. The jobs lost are not being replaced by industries that characteristically employ women. This loss of economic opportunity for women is occurring at the same time women's economic responsibilities are on the increase. Women's contribution to low-income families remains unacknowledged, even though a woman's pay frequently has meant escape for a two-earner family from poverty.

It is against this backdrop that efforts at occupational training have occurred in the Southeast. Educating women for work traditionally has been tailored to accommodate male dominance and conventional attitudes about appropriate jobs. The result is that women simply have not received education or training for the majority of jobs requiring manual or professional skills. Added to these difficulties is the retreat of federal commitment to policies insuring affirmative action and equal employment opportunity. This is especially serious because the rights of federal citizenship and the guarantee of protection counteract the impact of living in a region where devotion to states' rights has been a hollow deceit for insuring the freedom to systematically discriminate. Finally, the abhorrence of organized labor in the South and the enactment of right-to-work laws have militated against reforms in which women as workers might have benefited from collective bargaining tactics.

These circumstances and conditions underscore the hurdles to be overcome in developing job training strategies for women in rural southern economies. There is a certain amount of ineffectualness in training women for low-wage and limited opportunity jobs that are so rigidly prescribed by a race-, gender-, and class-conscious occupational marketplace. The economic limitations are inherent. In response to these constraints, some programs have a dual focus on training and job advocacy, combining skills training with a strategic analysis of the marketplace in which women must compete for jobs. Moreover, the tyranny of single, predominant industries in rural southern communities has required some experimentation with this approach, especially in the economic arena of nontraditional jobs for women. Nontraditional jobs serve the dual function of providing opportunities for increased skills training, and improving the wage-earning ability of female workers.

This chapter will review the efforts of two organizations whose goals are to help women get training and access to nontraditional jobs. It then examines the uses and limits of training women in a service economy.

Nontraditional Jobs: Coal Mining and Road Building

The diversity of local economies in the South creates some employment opportunities that are highly specific to geographic location. Thus, on the one hand, regional labor markets are an important consideration in planning and implementing successful employment and training programs for women. On the other hand, certain industries that are characteristic of rural economies provide employment opportunities in many southern communities. In both cases the jobs are often in occupations that are nontraditional for women.

Particularly in the coal fields of south and central Appalachia coal mining is the major source of employment. Individuals without access to mining jobs are almost always among the poor of a coal field community. For example, in the state of West Virginia, the coal industry has dominated the state economy for more than a hundred years. Jobs habitually characterized as "women's work" have been extremely scarce. As a result, women who live in West Virginia have the lowest labor force participation rate of any state in the country.

Road building and maintenance is an activity of every local political district, and the jobs associated with it are visible in most rural communities. It is similar to coal mining employment in that the industry tends to pay substantially more than minimum wage. In addition, road building and maintenance is a necessary part of the infrastructure required to develop rural areas, allowing for the exploitation of natural resources and the marketing of goods and services. Coal haul roads are only one example of the government subsidy that supports this development policy. The work force cuts across white- and blue-collar occupational categories.

In regional economies such as these, the greatest challenge for employment and training policy is to improve opportunities for women's employment in very limited occupational labor markets. It meets this challenge by satisfying the performance standards and placement requirements of federally sponsored programs, and by instigating reforms that institutionalize fair employment practices having long-range economic value for women. The coal and highways industries have been the targets of movements that press for institutional reforms of direct economic benefit to women. These efforts have also expanded generally the opportunities available to women in occupationally limited rural labor markets.

The emergence of industrial targeting strategies in the coal and highways industries coincided with organizationally based CETA-funded training programs in the Southeast that focused on training women for nontraditional jobs. Access to nontraditional jobs was a major issue in job placement, and probably in no other industries were the attitudes more hard-bitten against the introduction of female participants. These male-dominated industries were the targets of early efforts at unionization, which depended almost exclusively on a tradition of male leadership. Moreover, labor unions began through building trade associations which affected few occupations where women were employed.

Two organizations that have used a method of industrial targeting to expand opportunities for rural Southern women in these industries are the Coal Employment Project (CEP) and the Southeast Women's Employment Coalition (SWEC). CEP, a private, nonprofit public-interest group, assists women in getting and keeping mining jobs. SWEC is a multi-state coalition of women working as leaders to achieve economic equity for southern women. Both organizations were founded by women who grew up in the Southeast, primarily in small towns and rural communities of the South. Both CEP and SWEC focused on contract compliance provisions required of federal aid contractors, and equal employment opportunity (EEO) laws for the leverage to establish the right of access for women. In 1977, CEP documented that 99.8 percent of all coal miners were men, and 98.6 percent of all workers in the industry—including file clerks and secretaries—were also male (CEP 1977). SWEC conducted similar research on the road building industry in 1979 (SWEC 1980) and documented that 98.8 percent of all jobs were held by men. Because both industries relied heavily on federal contracts, CEP and SWEC undertook legal and administrative initiatives to open the doors for jobs for rural women.

In 1978, CEP filed a complaint against 153 of the country's mines and companies that produced 50 percent of the nation's coal. Two years later SWEC followed suit and filed administrative complaints with the U.S. Department of Labor and the U.S. Department of Transportation, charging 33 of the nation's largest road builders with sex discrimination. These private contractors performing federal aid road work counted for 80 percent of federal aid road contracts in the Southeast. In addition, SWEC named all 50 state departments of transportation (DOTs) in a complaint charging blatant patterns of discrimination in recruitment, training, hiring, and employment of women in "internal" state DOT work forces. CEP's original advocacy resulted in millions of dollars in backpay awards to women who had applied for coal mining jobs but who were never hired, and mandatory hiring and recruitment goals for female applicants.

Independently conducted investigations by the U.S. Department of Labor's Office of Federal Contract Compliance (OFCCP), and the U.S. Department of Transporation's Federal Highway Administration (FHWA) found blatant patterns of discriminatory practices in the industry among state DOTs and private contractors performing federal aid road work. Major private contractors found out of compliance were forced to enter into conciliation agreements that contained numerous remedial steps designed to aggressively recruit, train, and employ women in highway work. The 50 state DOTs were subjected to a national investigation by the FHWA, which scrutinized each state DOT's hiring and employment practices with regard to women and minorities. Those found out of compliance were forced to institute initiatives similar to those required of private contractors by the OFCCP.

The provision of training support to rural women was a crucial ingredient in the larger strategy to open up access to the jobs in these industries. The training objective was provided in part by collaboration with many CETA-funded women's programs in the region. Both CEP and SWEC recognized the critical necessity of training women for nontraditional jobs, not only because lack of knowledge is an invitation to bodily harm in these industries, but also because once doors began to open to the employment of rural women, continued support was an important factor in women's moving beyond the "pioneering" that characterized their entrance into these occupations. The goal was to have the industries acknowledge women as permanent members of their work forces.

CEP pioneered its own approach to training because of the lack of knowledge concerning the appropriate content of training for women in coal mining. According to CEP literature, nonsexist training programs were developed in explicit recognition that attitudes must change in a work force in which it was unprecedented for men and women to work together. Two training programs were developed by CEP. The first dealt with new miners "to complement and enrich federally-required mine safety training." The orientation of this training was toward tool identification and use, physical conditioning, legal rights, mine safety, assertiveness training, and support group development. Women miners were recruited as participants in the training process to help would-be miners assess work and family-related issues affecting their employment in the industry. The second training program was developed to work with mine management personnel who had never worked with women in underground mining. The training was geared to insure effective management of the transition that would be required to successfully integrate women into coal mining occupations.

By contrast, SWEC contracted with CETA programs that used several different approaches to train women for blue-collar jobs in road construction. These included skills and physical fitness, job orientation, and education efforts related to sexual harassment and racism, trade unions, the structure and administration of the federal aid road building program, EEO law, tool identification, and job safety. SWEC's work with CETA programs was a marriage of both convenience and necessity. Confrontation was an integral element of SWEC's access strategy, and CETA-funded entities could not visibly challenge employers on discrimination issues because of the sensitivity of their funding to political pressure. At the same time, training support was critical to preparing new female candidates who hoped to become the first to break the barriers to women entering the blue-collar trades. SWEC perceived its role from the outset more as an advocate than as a provider of direct services. As a regional organization, SWEC could perform this needed function.

In both the coal and highways industries, the scope of reforms sought by CEP and SWEC created a situation in which training was one objective but securing a permanent job was the goal. This was because rural areas, which by definition are more isolated and have fewer resources, could not sustain a recruitment, training, and job placement capacity indefinitely. Neither could they sufficiently alter the composition of these industrial work forces so that rural women could get jobs without the support of several programs. Thus, the goal of advocacy was to reform industry employment practices to institutionalize and sustain entry level access and training to female applicants. These strategies depended on the empowerment and leadership of the rural women who wanted the jobs enough to fight for the rights of access and training for themselves and other women. In addition, CEP began developing local support groups for coal mining women that subsequently became the basis for a national network of coal mining women. This network internalized its own training "curriculum" through local support groups and an annual national conference.

In both industries, efforts were undertaken to focus specifically on attitudinal barriers held by the co-workers and employers of women in nontraditional occupations. CEP began that process within the locals of the United Mine Workers of America (UMWA). The UMWA was, initially, as adamant in its opposition to women in the mines as were the coal producers. But CEP encouraged coal mining women to participate in UMWA activities. Historically, women had always been active in UMWA but only as wives and family members of miners in UMWA auxiliaries. In testament to CEP's success with the UMWA, in 1978, UMWA's governing board passed a resolution unanimously supporting "their sisters who are working to widen opportunities for women in mining." Rural women in coal mining subsequently have been elected by their locals as delegates to the national UMWA convention, as representatives on mine safety committees, and other committees actively working to improve the status of miners. In the February 1986 edition of the *United Mine Workers' Journal,* a member of the International Executive Board of UMWA cited the UMWA position on maternity/paternity leave as "one more step forward, and entitling working parents to be with their children in time of need." This change has resulted, in large part, because CEP was successful in challenging and overcoming institutional barriers and the negative attitudes that women workers experienced in the coal industry. Ten years ago, such changes would have been inconceivable.

CETA-based women's programs working with SWEC also attempted to develop more favorable attitudes among co-workers and employers of women on road construction sites. Tactics used with employers included asking for cooperation in making placements, visiting with and informing employers of female-oriented placement programs, advising employers of the availability of the pool of female candidates, identifying procedures that could be used to match potential female candidates with available jobs, following up on employer contacts, and regularly communicating and educating about CETA nontraditional job placement goals for women. Similar work was done with union locals in the construction trades.

Private contractors and the leadership of local building trade unions in rural areas of the South have proven, on the whole, to be much more entrenched in their opposition to women than is implied by the official rhetoric of company management or the national institutions of the building trades. The negative attitudes of Southern white men toward working with women and blacks seem to predominate overwhelmingly among private contractors and the trade unions of the region. Even in cases where many of the contractors performing road maintenance and construction were nonunion, these attitudes are prevalent.

Overall, the participation of women in coal mining and highways has been steadily increasing despite their grudging acceptance by employers and co-workers. Although women in 1983 were only about 4 percent of the work force of federal contractors nationally, the hiring gains appear far more dramatic when examined at the state level. Where advocacy has been most effective, some states have increased their hiring of women 500 percent to 1,000 percent since 1980. Nearly 4,000 women were in underground mining in 1985; government records from prior to the founding of CEP show no women in coal mining. As in most rural jobs, the gains made by rural women are somewhat vulnerable because of the susceptibility of rural economies to fluctuations occurring in the industry nationally and the erosion of federal commitment to EEO. In both industries, however, women have made substantial gains in increasing their participation in on-the-job training because the combination of advocacy and training have created a more favorable climate for female work force participation.

Rural women retain the major responsibility in advocating their rights to these jobs, in seeking and making successful application to on-the-job training programs, and in finding employment in entry-level positions. However, the structural reforms that have been achieved and that continue to be sought in attitude and issues of access provide the basis of a systemic approach in which the industries themselves bear the burden of integrating women as permanent additions to their work forces. In rural economies, the provision of training alone could not provide systemic relief. Ultimately, the training and skills acquired by women in the mining and road construction industries, and the knowledge gained by an industry-wide, industry-based approach to the training and employment of women, has provided the potential for a crossover effect in other industries and occupational sectors. For example, a next step may be to target municipal "uniform" jobs for rural women as police officers, firefighters, and sanitation workers. In rural southern economies, the present reality suggests that the responsibility for training women must be largely sustained by the industries providing the employment, even as industries utilize public resources to accomplish this objective. This does not, however, preclude the importance of accountability as the decisive factor in whether, in fact, these objectives are met.

Training Women for Service Jobs: Gain with Pain

Fundamental shifts in the nation's economy have had a devastating effect on the job status of rural women, and especially minority women, in rural communities in the southeast. The restructuring of the manufacturing sector, a nationwide trend, strikes at the heart of the employment opportunities most traditional to the employment of rural southern women. For most rural women the service sector is the only field of employment where job opportunities are certain to increase in the future. According to the Southeast Women's Employment Coalition report, *Women of the Rural South: Economic Status and Prospects*,

> Far more than their urban counterparts, rural women in the South (and throughout the United States) are dependent for their livelihoods on unskilled production jobs in manufacturing industries. Nearly one-fourth of employed rural women in the South work as operatives. Among rural black women, dependence on the manufacturing sector is even greater: one-third are employed in textiles, furniture and low-wage rural industries.
>
> All too frequently, rural women do not find job opportunities in the new manufacturing plants that are locating in the South. . . . Approximately 70% of the workforce in emerging southern industries is male, as compared to only 55% in the traditional sectors. . . . Rural women remain concentrated in labor-intensive production where they were first employed 100 years ago, precisely the sector where employment is declining. . . . It is the services industries that are recording the highest growth rates and that are projected to offer the greatest number of new jobs in the foreseeable future. . . . Nearly two-thirds of services workers in the South are women. (Smith 1976, 12)

Tourism, the report goes on to note, is one service industry that is growing rapidly in selected rural areas. But tourism creates seasonal, low-wage employment. The pay scales of jobs in service industries are even lower than those of manufacturing jobs in the Southeast. This fact emphasizes the enormous price that race and privilege routinely exact from rural minority women who are trapped in low-wage servitude with little hope of upward economic mobility. Even so, training strategies for the employment of women in jobs generated by the kind of development associated with tourism cannot be ignored.

Innovative approaches to job training in this sector suggest that these jobs could increase the wage earning capacity of rural women beyond minimum wage if they were viewed as one stage in rural women's economic development. Training initiatives with this orientation need to meet several objectives: to encourage personal and cultural development; to insure the achievement of basic workplace competencies; to make provisions for educating rural women about workers' rights, including workplace health and safety; and to provide program support to women so they can make intelligent choices about how to conduct their own job search within the existing structure of a rural economy. Occupational mobility can be built into training by providing a progression of different work experiences encompassing a diversity of skills. Women generally are not offered the opportunity to progress to another, higher-paying level of development once they have become gainfully employed. Most training programs are geared toward placement as an end in itself.

It is worth emphasizing as well that despite the disadvantages associated with service employment, these jobs represent the only source of economic opportunity for the many rural women who are chronically underemployed. Yet if the South is to ever overcome its poverty, the empowerment of rural women is especially critical, since it is they who suffer the worst of the inequities that grow out of southern economic development. Some job training programs in the South are working to go beyond the imposed limitations of the labor market by both increasing the earning and purchasing power of their constituents, and encouraging them to participate in decision making about development in the communities in which they live. This distinctive approach to job training is illustrated in the response by the Institute for Community Education and Training to the employment opportunities created by the economic development that has taken place in the Sea Islands of South Carolina.

The Reform of Industrial Education: An Old Paternalism Turned on Its Ear

Back in 1890, blacks owned over 75 percent of the land in Beaufort County, which includes Hilton Head Island.[2] The fact of black landownership alone set the island residents of this area apart from all other southern blacks.[3] Yet it was also the site of a famous post–Civil War experiment in which a group of northerners attempted to prepare the freed and former slaves with "an education for life."

The freedmen education movement that found its way to the Sea Islands began in Fortress Monroe, Virginia, in 1861 under the tutelage of Mary Peake, who was herself a free black. During that year, thousands of slaves sought refuge in Union-held territory. Under military law, runaway slaves were "contraband of war" in the North and thus entitled to protection. The school begun by Mary Peake was an attempt to provide religious education and basic academic training to the refugees. Similar schools soon spread to 17 states and the nation's capital.

Industrial schools of the type that located in coastal South Carolina proliferated all over the South following the Civil War. Penn Center on the then-isolated St. Helena Island represents the most important of these institutions on the Sea Islands. The schools followed the basic pattern of industrial education found in the northern schools, teaching trades such as knitting, braiding straw, sewing, and manual labor to the freed slaves. The missionaries and educators who became part of the industrial education movement saw in it an opportunity to give freedmen alternatives to the overcrowded fields of education, the ministry, or domestic service.

Northern educators representing the Bureau of Refugees, Freedmen, and Abandoned Land attempted to convince southern whites that the education of freedmen would promote community stability and, not coincidentally, make them patient and moderate in their pursuit of equality. The function of education became a means to instill character through the teaching of industrious work habits and by creating dependable, efficient, and contented workers. Vocational and moral training for blacks was put forward as the means for ensuring that the presumably backward and dependent Negroes would attain their place—a process that, according to the view of most whites, would likely take centuries. Conservative white southerners supported these views and remained justified in their prejudice and discrimination toward blacks. What was absent from this vision of industrial education was the possibility of achieving the social, economic, or political independence of blacks.

Almost a century later, the racist paternalism that led to the founding of Penn Center has seen the ultimate implications of its philosophy amplified in the deteriorating status of the black community in Beaufort County. Indeed, economic development occurring on Hilton Head Island carries with it the historical thread of the old oppression, without the benefit of the good, paternalistic intentions of the northern whites engaged in the original Penn Center "experiment." Once again, the development of the sea islands economy is occurring without regard for native black economic, social, or political self-sufficiency.

Tourism has displaced agriculture and fishing as the major source of employment in Beaufort County. The occupational history of the island residents does not readily lend itself to a transfer of skills appropriate to the service sector where maids, food service workers, and chauffeurs predominate.[4] The tourist economy on Hilton Head Island offers a job market that is largely geared to services, dominated by seasonal, low-wage work.

In Beaufort County, where Hilton Head Island is located, black women constitute the largest segment of the population. Thirty-eight percent of those who are employed work as maids, cooks, and health aides, and in other related service occupations. Only 17.5 percent work full time year-round. Their unemployment rate, at 14.9 percent, is the highest of any group. The average Beaufort County black women lives on $579.00 a year less than the state per capita median income.[5]

Women in the coastal region also face the economic difficulties associated with underemployment. In resort communities, the work is seasonal, attracting south-bound vacationers during the winter months. The demand for service workers thus ebbs and flows with the climate. In addition, much of the work is part time, allowing employers to avoid paying those benefits generally associated with full-time employment such as health insurance and retirement. Service work also offers few opportunities for upward mobility. Because of the barriers associated with dead-end, service-sector employment, additional education and skills training is necessary to prepare women to move into more sophisticated and more responsible positions associated with tourism. Rural women also need programs that emphasize basic education and academic skills to prepare them for available opportunities in higher education.

In this context, the Institute for Community Education and Training started as a nonprofit community organization located on Hilton Head Island. A group of community residents founded the Institute in response to their concern over the employment options in a community in which over half of the high school graduates are functionally illiterate. Foundations provide the primary source of financial support for the Institute. It also receives some church monies and some training funds from the Job Training Partnership Act. In 1980, the Institute conducted a survey of employers, which revealed that employers perceive rural women as having poor academic backgrounds, few job skills, poor job attitudes, and "unrealistic" job expectations. In general, employers regard the skill level of the available pool of labor as inadequate (White 1980). The Institute also conducted a self-assessment of program participants, which echoed the employers' concerns.

In training rural women for employment and insuring their mobility once employed, the Institute had to overcome several obstacles unique to the sea islands. Local public schools have not adequately prepared their graduates in basic academic and vocational skills; graduates are thus unprepared for employment. Potential employees lack knowledge of available opportunities, are unclear about their individual talents and goals, and possess little self-confidence. Rural women, especially black women, lack the financial resources, public transportation, and child care services that would enable them to pursue even traditional education and training opportunities that are available. Even in the Hilton Head resort area, with its reputation as a multi-billion-dollar playground of the rich, the economic conditions of black women and others living less than a mile away from the center of the resort community can only be described as bleak and hopeless.

The Institute provides economic relief to the poor, black women who represent the majority of its program participants as well as training in basic employment skills. The project's training program lasts for one year. Approximately 50 women are enrolled in each cycle. The Institute's goal is to raise the standard of living among black residents and to reverse the erosion of the black community that happened as a by-product of the island's development. In addition to its employment training, the Institute works to develop strategic leadership skills in its participants which enables them to participate in the economic development of the area. Distinct from the past goals of industrial education in the area, their vision is to foster social, economic, and political independence in the black community. This vision includes helping rural women learn to articulate their needs and to develop appropriate strategies for not only their own but also community problems.

The training curriculum of the Institute educates participants on the characteristics of different jobs or occupations available in the Hilton Head area. Their curriculum begins with information about the physical and psychological working conditions of certain occupations. Instructors provide job applicants briefings on entry-level requirements and the basic skills and credentials needed for certain kinds of employment. Participants are familiarized with the employee benefits, compensation policies, advancement opportunities, career ladders, and industrial outlook of certain sectors in the rural economy of the area. In addition, the Institute works with each woman analyzing the costs and benefits of working—evaluating both economic and personal benefits, examining the availability of certain jobs as part of an overall job search strategy, researching personnel policies and practices, and, ultimately, finding and maintaining employment. Increasing the confidence and assertiveness of rural black women is seen, in general, as essential to building the participants' awareness and understanding of the relationship between developing their employment potential and improving the economic community they live in.

The Institute's training focuses on an individual learning plan in which rural women begin at their own level and work toward goals appropriate to themselves. Basic skill development includes language skills—vocabulary development, reading comprehension, and written and oral communication skills, because one of the greatest barriers to employment in the Sea Islands is that schools have failed in teaching Standard English as both a spoken and a written language.[6] The Institute's approach to teaching language skills is meant to be both fun and educational. Instead of using textbooks, the Institute uses stores based on the life experiences of the women, working with program participants to learn the standard pronunciation. The use of tapes, newspapers, magazines, textbooks, workbooks, and the resources of the community library are integral to this approach.

The Institute also provides training appropriate to the development of basic skills in math—addition, subtraction, multiplication, division, and the use of percentages, decimals, and fractions. The emphasis in the training program is on the practical and everyday application of these skills—balancing a checkbook, comparing prices in the stores, determining correct measurements and quantities, understanding deductions made on paychecks, and learning to fill out income tax forms.

The training prepares women for job seeking by helping them set some career goals. A primary goal is to develop women's ability to search for employment. Classes give individual women a forum to practice and reinforce their mastery of job search skills, which include such tasks as filling out job applications, developing resumes, perfecting job interview techniques, learning strategic personal presentation in the interview process, and developing proficiency in the management of a job search plan. Early in the training, the Institute hosts a job/career fair featuring the participation of prospective employers from the private sector who provide a briefing session on the characteristics they seek in employees and the skills required in certain job categories. The job preparation classes also serve as a support group to individual women as they begin their job search activities.

Centuries of oppression take their toll in ways that are less visible than the outward manifestations poverty may suggest. "Internal" barriers—negative attitudes and beliefs that individuals hold about themselves and others—create low self-esteem, lack of confidence, feelings of powerlessness, and behavior that can result in the oppression of others. Most of the rural black women interviewed during the preparation of the SWEC report (1986) described their economic problems as being the result of race, not gender (Smith 1986). The depth of the resignation and pessimism in attitudes expressed by rural black women hoping to change their economic circumstance is a seriously debilitating attitudinal barrier. Racism, and its role in structuring economic opportunities, presents a difficult challenge in training programs working to unite women. Yet economic inequalities in rural economies are the result of both racism and sexism, and they will be overcome only by challenging both forms of oppression. In response to these and other issues, the Institute includes consciousness raising, assertiveness training, values clarification, and exercises designed to help women begin making personal assessments that can lead to more positive attitudes about themselves and others. Personal assessment focuses on past work experiences of the women and identification of the positive values of these experiences.

Finally, cultural arts of the Sea Islands are important parts of the Institute curriculum, including dance, music, drama, arts and crafts, folklore, and exposure to non-indigenous cultural events. Rural women develop familiarity with their unique cultural heritage and are encouraged to preserve these traditions. As a living and growing entity, the black culture of the Sea Islands is used as a means to build self-confidence and pride. A community newsletter has been developed by the Institute for the publication of stories, poems, songs, and other community events pertinent to the experience of the program participants.

The success of the Institute's efforts cannot be measured in job placements alone, although over 80 percent of participants did secure employment in service occupations, such as hotel cleaning and food preparation. Perhaps ultimately more important, two women's organizations, one black and one interracial, have been founded in the Hilton Head area as a result of the training program. The interracial group's goal is to begin eliminating the barriers that have historically divided black and white women on the island. The black women's group serves as a leadership training and support organization to preserve and promulgate the cultural traditions of the black community while also organizing the black community on issues of community development in which it has a stake.

A leadership training program has also been fostered by the Institute for parents of children in the Beaufort County school system. The goal of the parents' program is to create more awareness about the issues confronting the education system in the county and to increase the system's accountability to the parents. In addition, the Women's Economic Development Project has been initiated. It will provide outreach and economic development assistance to rural low-income women in both the Piedmont and coastal regions. Its goal is to foster women's leadership on economic issues especially affecting women in South Carolina. Community and statewide discussions on the economic status of women in the state have begun, and as a result, economic strategies are being proposed that will encourage more accountability and responsiveness to the needs of women and families. Community women are taking on roles of policy and decision making in state and local entities concerned with issues of development. A participatory research project utilizing the skills and leadership of local women is currently in progress, which hopes to document the economic status of women in the coastal areas. The study will be used as a tool to influence policy making and to advocate job equity and economic opportunity for female workers. It is too soon to tell what effects these actions will ultimately have in institutional and occupational reforms that will benefit women. Without these initiatives, however, the hope for change will be nonexistent.

Conclusion

Training programs for women in southern rural economies face an especially difficult challenge in preparing women for employment, not only because of occupational segregation, but also because of the low pay in most jobs where women are employed. A strategy that relies exclusively on training as an exercise in skill development and job placement will likely miss the more critical issue of the occupational segregation of women in the work force and the racism that divides those opportunities among women even more stringently. Even if the goal of job placement is sufficient to claim success, the economic rewards most women reap are not. The majority of women remain only one step ahead of poverty, even though they may have gained other material and personal benefits as a result of participating in training programs. The benefits of training women for nontraditional employment are apparent because both the jobs and the income provide satisfying results by moving women closer to economic equity and to more opportunity for self-determination. However, training some women for nontraditional jobs provides only a limited solution to the problem of occupational segregation. If the bleak outlook for women's employment is to be substantially altered, other programs and policies must come into play.

The economic importance of comparable worth to working women is all the more obvious in view of an occupational future that offers little change. Job training cannot be a policy solution created in a vacuum that ignores the historical, political, and economic context of women's work. Nor can job training be effective as an alternative to unemployment and poverty if the jobs that training is designed to fill offer no more than working-poor wages. Ultimately, the failure of job training to effectively alleviate the poverty of the underemployed and unemployed will erode its public support and credibility. Training is but once piece of a broader strategy that can focus on what a job ought to provide economically. It is also an opportunity to foster a deeper understanding of the policy issues in a development process that ignores issues of economic equity.

In that context, effective training must do more than build skills and prepare women for work. It must provide a vision of economic and political empowerment. This means not only working with women as individuals and clients, but also incorporating an explicit recognition of the barriers to economic opportunity that women as a constituency will face in their job search. Understanding the role of racism in the oppression of women is fundamental to enabling women to begin to work across the barriers that divide them. Training programs can begin this process, but the women themselves must complete it as a movement for justice. In some rural economies of the South, that process is only just now beginning.

Notes

1. All statistical data in this section are based on the 1980 U.S. Census.

2. The rural area of Beaufort and Jasper counties is bordered on the east by the Atlantic Ocean and on the west by the Savannah River. It is composed of mainland areas and 62 sea islands, which are separated by sounds, tidal rivers, inlets, estuaries, and a vast area of wetlands. Twenty of these islands are uninhabited, and 18 are accessible by bridges and causeways. For more than 100 years after settlers came to the area, there were virtually no bridges to any of the islands, and regular transportation was impossible because of hazardous conditions and the lack of adequate watercraft.

3. The geographical remoteness of the area resulted in several unusual historical developments that make this rural economy unique in the Southeast. Before the Civil War, few whites chose to live on the malaria-infested islands. Instead, they became a safe refuge for runaway slaves, who built their own independent communities. This settlement of freed slaves continued to exist after the Civil War. As a consequence, African cultural patterns have been maintained through the years in the Sea Islands to a far greater extent than elsewhere in the nation. The language of the black residents, Gullah, is a combination of English and African words and speech rhythms, a clear sign of this distinct cultural heritage. The unique geographical composition of the region has created small isolated communities where African culture and language patterns have been maintained by native blacks.

4. Coastal South Carolina, because of the amenities of its climate and coast, is being rapidly developed as a tourist mecca. During the last 30 years, the rural coast-line has become a vacation playground, with resort areas such as Hilton Head Island attracting millions of tourists every year. With the development of Hilton Head into a wealthy retirement and resort area, land values and property taxes have skyrocketed. As a result, the black community is being displaced. It has been predicted that by the turn of this century, there will be no remaining black landowners in the area, a particularly insidious decline, given that blacks have historically owned major land resources in Beaufort County. The land loss being experienced by the black community, the escalation of taxes, and the speculative nature of the development occurring on Hilton Head Island are exacerbated by the fact that most of the higher-paying jobs created by the increased development go to educated, nonindigenous young people from off the island. The indigenous community residents lack the necessary education and skills to acquire the jobs or to negotiate a meaningful share in the economic benefits accruing now to the few in the development of the island.

5. All statistical data in this section are based on the 1980 U.S. Census.

6. Area employers require a degree of proficiency in Standard English usage; thus, local blacks who speak the Gullah dialect must be able to speak and write in

acceptable form in order to be considered for employment. The Institute estimates that although most parents in the black community have completed high school, the average reading capability is only about the fifth grade level.

References

Burstein, Paul. 1985. *Discrimination, Jobs, and Politics: The Struggles for Equal Employment Opportunity in the United States Since the New Deal*. Chicago: University of Chicago Press.

Cashman, Sean Dennis. 1984. *America in the Gilded Age: From the Death of Lincoln to the Rise of Roosevelt*. New York: New York University Press.

Coal Employment Project. 1977. Complaint and Preliminary Statement of CEP v. Department of Labor, Office of Federal Contract Compliance Programs.

"The Coal Employment Project and Coal Mining Women's Support Team." 1980. Informational brochure. Dumfries, Va.: Coal Employment Project.

Cobb, James C. 1982. *The Selling of the South: The Crusade for Industrial Development*. Baton Rouge: Louisiana State University Press.

Haignere, Lois, and Ronnie Steinberg. 1984. *New Directions in Equal Employment Policy: Training Women for Non-Traditional Occupations Through CETA*. Working Paper no. 13. Albany: Center for Women in Government, Summer.

Kacoway, Elizabeth. 1980. *Yankee Missionaries in the South: The Penn School Experiment*. Baton Rouge: Louisiana State University Press.

Manhein, Jarol B. 1976. *Deja Vu: American Political Problems in Historical Perspective*. New York: St. Martin's Press.

Morris, Robert C. 1976. *Reading, 'Riting, and Reconstruction: The Education of Freedmen in the South, 1861–1870*. Chicago: University of Chicago Press.

Oakes, James. 1982. *The Ruling Race: A History of American Slaveholders*. New York: Alfred A. Knopf.

Smith, Barbara Ellen. 1986. *Women of the Rural South: Economic Status and Prospects*. Lexington, Ky.: Southeast Women's Employment Coalition.

———. 1985. "The Job Training Partnership Act and Women: A Survey of Early Practices." MDC, Inc., Chapel Hill, N.C.

Southwest Women's Employment Coalition. 1980. Complaint and Preliminary Statement of SWEC v. Federal Highway Administration, Department of Transportation.

White, Gardenia. 1980. "Rural Women in South Carolina." Paper prepared for The Institute for Community Education and Training, Hilton Head Island, S.C.

III

Training for Nontraditional Jobs

Introduction to Part III/*Sharon L. Harlan*

One of the most important functions of training is to provide participants with job skills. The policy rationale for providing skill training for women in male-dominated occupations is that it will prepare them for a wider range of jobs that pay higher wages. Theoretically, at least, training in nontraditional occupations (NTOs) should eliminate one of the barriers, lack of qualifications, to occupational desegregation in the labor market. Although, as we have seen, training is not a sufficient condition for job integration, there is a direct link between successful NTO programs and providing equal employment opportunity for women.

The chapters in Part III report on the state of knowledge in the field of NTO training. They do not entirely resolve the complex issue of the availability of a sufficient number of good jobs, but they indicate unequivocally the existence of a knowledge base on *how to* train for NTO. Glover's chapter sets the stage by reviewing apprenticeship policy in the U.S. He notes that apprenticeship in its current form, neglected and inefficiently administered by federal and state policy makers, has too few openings to offer men or women. Chertos and Phillips assess the effectiveness of privately funded programs that trained women to pass the physical fitness tests for firefighters and sanitation workers in New York City. Giese, illustrating some of Vetter's themes from Chapter 3, shows how Michigan has struggled with the prob-

lem of increasing sex equity in vocational education at the same time it tries
to accommodate its curriculum to a changing industrial base. By evaluating a wide range of CETA-funded training, Haignere and Steinberg demonstrate that it is possible to design programs that successfully prepare women
to work in NTO. However, they find that excellent programs suffer under
political obstacles and business resistance to hiring women for men's jobs.

Like job training for women in general, NTO became a national issue
in the late 1970s because people began to recognize the significance of occupational segregation in setting and maintaining the low wages of female-dominated occupations. CETA was the most important source of funding for
experimentation in NTO recruitment and training for poor women. In apprenticeship, the other major source of NTO training, some of the program
models for outreach and recruitment were drawn from previous experiences
with minority men, whereas some other program aspects were unique to
women and came about through intensive experimentation with federal and
private funds.

An important function of these chapters is to demystify the process of
obtaining nontraditional jobs for women and to reveal their objective skill
requirements. While it is clear that nontraditional blue-collar jobs usually require some training for job skills that most women do not possess, the jobs
do not require either excessive training time or rare talents. They are ordinary
jobs in crafts, machine repair, or electronics that many people could do, but
from which women have been categorically excluded. Firefighting and refuse
collection are good examples of male-dominated jobs that "require no particular educational background or skills," yet offer excellent benefits and high
starting salaries (the mid-twenties in New York City during 1984, according
to Chertos and Phillips).

Male-dominated occupations require no more training, on average,
than do female-dominated jobs, yet the occupations for which men train pay
higher wages. For example, the 40 percent of Michigan high school students
who are enrolled in wage-earning vocational education programs can train *in
the same amount of time* for computer programming (male-dominated jobs)
as they can for business and office programs (female-dominated jobs). Often,
as in the case of apprenticeship, learning for predominately male occupations
is not classroom based and, thus, it offers a chance to earn a salary while
perfecting skills. Moreover, apprenticeship is usually broad-based training
relevant to an industry and not just for a particular employer, adding a measure of mobility potential and the possibility of higher compensation than
most female jobs.

Nevertheless, there are important barriers that discourage women from
making NTO choices. Interestingly, both Giese in her chapter and Haignere
and Steinberg in theirs note that these barriers are not likely to arise from ac-

tive resistance to NTO by training staff so much as they are from the failure to understand that active measures are needed to eliminate discrimination. In Michigan's experience, state financing for non-gender-biased curriculum materials and staff workshops made little difference in NTO enrollments, largely because these strategies did not include recruitment activities directed at students or active support for nontraditional students. Similarly, in many CETA programs, standard intake procedures simply channeled participants along the paths of least resistance into traditional female occupations.

The barriers that do exist for women in NTO are of two sorts, according to Glover and to Haignere and Steinberg. The first are barriers embedded in past socialization and preparation for careers. These are in the form of attitudes toward women doing "men's work," abilities and knowledge, and life circumstances. In confronting women's own negative attitudes and self-doubts, Haignere and Steinberg point to the need for active strategies in outreach and career exploration that can counteract them and allow women to make informed decisions. Glover presents a well-tested model of effective outreach for women, including craft orientation, peer group support, and child care. However, Chertos and Phillips provide a good example of how women's attitudes are sometimes overplayed as barriers. They report high levels of interest among women for a relatively small number of good municipal jobs. Money was the main reason women wanted them.

Among the other socialization barriers mentioned by Glover and by Haignere and Steinberg are the lack of math skills, tool familiarity, and physical conditioning among women. Once again, Chertos and Phillips demonstrate that it is relatively easy for women to develop the necessary stamina for even the most demanding jobs in a short time. Ninety-two percent of the women who took the firefighter exam after a 12-session physical training program administered over 6 weeks passed it, whereas only 22 percent who took the exam without training passed it. This training for public-sector jobs was funded by private-sector funds.

Whereas program models seem to be straightforward for adult women, apparently vocational education in secondary schools has more difficulty in getting girls to make NTO choices. Part of the difficulty in transferring these models to younger women may be their inexperience with the realities of occupational segregation in the labor market. Program operators often report that older women make better NTO candidates, and in fact, one suggested action that would help increase women's enrollments in apprenticeship programs is changing the upper age limit in entrance requirements. However, another part of Michigan's difficulty may be the absence of communication with NTO experts or the reluctance of the vocational education establishment to accept the systemic changes Giese says are necessary.

The second set of barriers to women in traditionally male jobs is what

Glover calls external barriers and Haignere and Steinberg discuss as the treatment of women once they make NTO choices. These are employers' reluctance to hire women and co-workers' and supervisors' resistance to working with women on the job. They are also the male-biased eligibility criteria and accountability standards of federal programs. As is the case with gender-role socialization, the authors point out that we know how to overcome external barriers to NTO success. They point to the law and federal regulatory agencies that are supposed to provide the oversight and monitoring to insure equal employment opportunity. Haignere and Steinberg also suggest several remedies to insure program accountability without sacrificing NTO enrollments.

Nevertheless, systemic barriers to NTO are not easily overcome. Chertos and Phillips are careful to point out, for example, that physical training as a job integration strategy must be part of a larger strategy for change that affects all of organizational life. The hostility of the city, the unions, and the municipal departments toward women and their willingness to engage in protracted court battles to keep women out are testimony to how much resistance there is to women. On the other hand, there are instances of publicly funded job developers working constructively with employers to create a harmonious working environment for women. Giese points out another dimension of the problem in her look at federal/state vocational education funding policy which tends to maintain a steady supply of workers in predominantly female occupational areas of high demand. Manipulation of the supply of labor in secretarial and nursing programs, she charges, contributes to keeping wages in those fields below market value.

Progress for women in nontraditional jobs can be viewed as a glass half full or a glass half empty. Although much has been learned in the past through experimentation with federal funds, NTO training has not developed into a major vehicle to reduce occupational segregation. Nor is it likely to under present conditions, for as Haignere and Steinberg point out, the political commitment to institute systemic changes are not deeply rooted or reliable.

11/Apprenticeship: A Route to the High-Paying Skilled Trades for Women?

Robert W. Glover

Apprenticeship is a primary training route to the skilled crafts—an occupational category that has remained almost completely a male preserve. In fact, among all the better-paying occupational classifications, women have been least represented in skilled craft jobs. Further, the construction industry—in which the majority of apprenticeships can be found in the United States—has the smallest representation of female workers. Apprenticeable occupations such as bricklayer, carpenter, plumber, electrician, sheet metal worker, or operating engineer have long been dominated by males. For women, these are classic nontraditional jobs—the most difficult to enter.

Apprenticeship not only offers special challenges. It provides special opportunities because apprenticeship is a formalized process of training with regular, standardized entry requirements and procedures. Such formality and regularity makes it an easier target with which to work. The requirements and standards applicants must meet to enter the programs are explicit and reasonably objective.

Finally, there exists a track record of affirmative action success with minority males in apprenticeship. Participation of minority males was raised to parity with their proportion in the labor force as a whole. Further, a considerable amount of action, research, and experimentation was undertaken to move women into apprenticeship in the late 1970s, which demonstrated that changes are possible with women in apprenticeship as well. But these activities were abruptly terminated with the Reagan administration's cutbacks in 1980.

The significance of women in apprenticeship goes beyond numbers. Currently, there are little more than 250,000 active apprenticeships in the U.S., and about 60,000 individuals enter into apprenticeship contacts each year. Apprenticeships in the skilled trades offer women excellent opportunities for employment in jobs that are both personally satisfying and well paid. Further, since apprenticeable jobs have been among the most difficult for women to enter, if an effective means can be found to integrate women into apprenticeable occupations, then any nontraditional blue-collar occupation can be made available to women. Finally, although there are relatively few apprentices in the U.S. today, future reforms of the system could bring a significant expansion of apprenticeship. Women need to be involved before such expansion occurs.

Background on Apprenticeship in America

Apprenticeship is a process through which individuals learn to be skilled craftworkers. For thousands of years, skilled workers have been passing along their skills from generation to generation in some sort of formalized relationship. The earliest reference to apprenticeship can be found in the Code of Hammurabi, written more than 4,000 years ago, which specifies requirements for skilled workers to teach their crafts to youths. Since the Middle Ages, apprentices have been indentured to "master" craftworkers for a specified number of years through a written document in which the master promised to provide food, clothing, and shelter, and to teach the secrets of the trade and the apprentice promised to be a good worker and learner. Apprentices lived in the master's house, and at the end of their indenture, they gained a set of tools and status as a "journeyman" or fully skilled independent worker.

The industrial revolution changed all this. It brought widespread abuse of the indenture system. In response, governments intervened to protect the welfare of apprentices through laws and regulations. Also, in many apprenticeable occupations, the industrial revolution brought an increased need for training in math, practical physics, and other theory applied to the job. Formal related classroom instruction became a standard component of apprenticeship, supplementing training received on the job.

Although apprenticeship has been established in America since colonial times, it currently enjoys widespread use only within a few limited industrial sectors and it remains one of the least understood and least utilized training systems operating in the United States. Fewer than 2 percent of American high school graduates become indentured as apprentices. In contrast, more than 50 percent of school-leavers in Germany, Austria, and Switzerland—both boys and girls—enter apprenticeships.

In the United States, apprenticeship is used across a narrow range of occupations. Although more than 750 occupations are recognized nationally as "apprenticeable," fewer than half of these occupations had active apprentices in 1986 and the bulk of apprenticeships were concentrated among only a few occupations in the building trades, metalworking trades, and various repair

Table 11-1/Female Participation in the Twenty Trades with the Most Numerous Apprentices Nationwide, Ranked by Total Number of Apprentices: December 1986

RANKING	TRADE	TOTAL APPRENTICES	PERCENT FEMALE
1	Electrician	30,139	4.0
2	Carpenter	34,368	4.1
3	Plumber	11,035	2.4
4	Pipefitter, any industry	9,617	4.1
5	Sheet metal worker	9,522	3.7
6	Machinist	6,293	4.3
7	Cook (hotel and restaurant)	5,615	17.4
8	Firefighter	5,332	1.6
9	Tool-and-die maker	5,278	1.9
10	Roofer	4,662	1.4
11	Electrical repair, maintenance	4,352	8.0
12	Painter	3,955	8.8
13	Diesel mechanic	3,494	3.6
14	Structural steel worker	3,471	3.4
15	Automobile mechanic	3,248	3.0
16	Millwright	2,923	2.3
17	Construction equip mechanic	2,896	2.2
18	Airframe and power plant mechanic	2,893	1.9
19	Bricklayer—construction	2,892	2.0
20	Operating engineer	2,585	17.3

Source: Calculated from U.S. Department of Labor, unpublished information from National Apprentice Statistics series, December 1986.
Note: Data are *not* included for California, District of Columbia, Puerto Rico, Hawaii, Rhode Island, Virgin Islands, and Vermont. Data include both military and civilian apprentices. Females accounted for 2,812 or 6.2 percent of the 45,285 military apprenticeships counted, whereas females were found in 5.9 percent of the civilian apprenticeships (9,966 of 168,506).

occupations. Two-thirds of all apprenticeships nationally were found in only 20 trades in December 1986 (see Table 11-1).

Apprenticeship is underutilized in America for several reasons, including its identification with trade unions, the perception of many employers that apprenticeship is expensive and not cost-effective, and perhaps most of all, ineffective promotion and administration of apprenticeship by the federal and state governments. Only 26 states have any apprenticeship agency and the level of effort and cooperation varies considerably among states. At the national level, there is no clear agreement about what the federal role should be. Although technically apprenticeship training is a joint responsibility of the U.S. Department of Labor (for the on-the-job training portion) and the U.S. Department of Education (for the classroom-training portion), neither department communicates about apprenticeship matters. In fact, apprenticeship has been largely neglected by both departments.

American apprenticeship is best established in unionized building trades such as carpenter, plumber, electrician, bricklayer, sheet metal worker, structural steelworker, operating engineer, painter, and roofer. More than half of all registered apprentices are in the unionized building trades. For a variety of reasons, nonunion employers do not typically use registered apprenticeship to train their employees. Only about 5 percent of all registered apprentices in the construction industry are in the nonunion sector. Rather, nonunion employers tend to try to hire already trained staff or rely on informal or task-specialized training.

A second major area where apprentices are trained is major manufacturing firms, in such maintenance trades as millwright, machinist, or pipefitter. Manufacturing accounts for perhaps 20 percent of all registered apprentices.

Entry to apprenticeship differs significantly between manufacturing and construction. In most manufacturing enterprises, apprenticeships are reserved for incumbent employees and allocated on the basis of a bidding and seniority system, whereas in the building trades, apprentices are typically new hires. There are other significant differences as well. In construction, crews are constantly being formed and re-formed as the job progresses and as the job site changes. Most construction workers expect to be seasonally unemployed for at least part of the year. Skilled craftworkers in manufacturing work more consistently and with the same co-workers.

An apprenticeship program may be sponsored unilaterally by a single employer or by a group of employers, or jointly by a single employer with a union or by a group of employers with a union. In all cases, employers are involved as apprenticeship sponsors. Of the more than 40,000 active apprenticeship programs operating across the United States, about 85 percent are operated unilaterally by employers, but most of these are small—offering only one or two apprenticeships.

The programs jointly operated by a group of employers and a union are the largest programs. They contain more than 80 percent of the nation's apprentices. Most of these so-called group-joint programs are administered by a Joint Apprenticeship and Training Committee, composed of equal numbers of employers and worker representatives. These committees are responsible for administering the apprenticeships and making sure that quality training is provided. In most cases, they also select the apprentices through a formal process, involving tests and interviews (Egan 1978).

The term of an apprenticeship contract is established in national standards for each occupation. The minimum term of apprenticeship must be one year. However, the most common apprenticeable trades involve training in all aspects of the trade over a period of three to four years. Credit may be obtained for relevant prior work experience or training to shorten the period of apprenticeship.

Advantages of Apprenticeship
Several features of apprenticeship make it especially attractive:

- Apprenticeship offers the opportunity to earn while learning, according to a progressive pay scale that increases as skills improve. This feature is particularly desirable for individuals—such as single female heads of household—who cannot afford to leave the labor force to enter full-time training in a school or institution.
- Apprenticeship emphasizes broad training in all aspects of the trade. This encourages flexibility among apprentices, who become more able to adapt to changes in technology or the labor market.
- As a training scheme combining work and study, apprenticeship offers the pedagogical advantages of blending theoretical and practical learning. Apprentices are taught both how to do a task and why it is done that way.
- By offering applied learning in a paid on-the-job setting, apprenticeship can motivate individuals who may not respond well to traditional classroom settings.
- Because 90 percent of the time in training is spent on the job, apprenticeship ensures that training is conducted on up-to-date equipment actually in use on work sites.
- By design, apprenticeship trains for the industry rather than for the individual firm. Apprenticeship is conducted only in occupations recognized throughout an industry and according to prescribed national standards. This helps ensure that transferable skills are taught.
- Apprenticeship is entry training to a high-paying job. Since apprenticeship covers a broad range of skills used across an entire industry, it prepares one for a career rather than just a single job.
- In many building trades—in which apprenticeships are widely used —apprentice-trained craftworkers commonly work as supervisors and have opportunities to start their own businesses.

Because of the advantages apprenticeship offers, there is often considerable competition for apprenticeship positions. In fact, it is quite common for the better apprenticeship programs to attract four or more applicants for each available apprenticeship.

Equal Access to Apprenticeship for Black Men
Although the focus of this chapter is on gaining access to apprenticeship for women, it is useful to review the history of black males in apprenticeship

because the strategies taken by black males contain lessons that are applicable for integrating women into apprenticeable trades.

Equal opportunity in apprenticeship entry has been a special concern of public policy in the United States since the early 1960s, when blacks in New York City, Chicago, Pittsburgh, and other major metropolitan areas demonstrated at various construction projects, successfully shutting many down. Unlike most unions, in which blacks were well represented, most of the skilled building trades unions had few black members. And the presence of all-white construction crews working in predominantly minority neighborhoods was particularly galling.

Civil rights activities and public concern about the issue prompted several government actions. In 1960, the first Congressional hearing on apprenticeship was held since the 1930s; it resulted in promulgation of special regulations for equal opportunity in apprenticeship in 1961 (29 *Code of Federal Regulations [CFR]* 30). Throughout subsequent years, a series of imposed or "voluntary" or "hometown" metropolitan plans for affirmative action setting goals and timetables for government contractors in Philadelphia, Chicago and 68 other cities were initiated under Executive Order 11246 (Rowan and Brudno 1972; Rowan and Rubin 1972; Glover and Marshall 1977) and numerous court cases brought under Title VII of the Civil Rights Act of 1964 and other statutes (Marshall et al. 1978, 26–60), increased pressures for affirmative action. Simultaneously, research and demonstration projects sponsored primarily with funding from the U.S. Department of Labor were initiated.

Research documented the problem of the paucity of blacks in apprenticeship programs (Marshall and Briggs 1967). According to the best information available in 1960, blacks represented only an estimated 2.2 percent of all apprentices in the United States (Marshall and Briggs 1967, 28). The study concluded that limited exposure to information about apprenticeship as well as outright discrimination hindered the admission of black males into apprenticeship. Marshall and Briggs went beyond the research to identify and publicize promising techniques for solving the problem of underrepresentation through specialized community-based outreach programs focused on apprenticeship (Marshall and Briggs 1968). The original apprenticeship outreach program grew out of efforts in 1963 by the Workers Defense League (WDL), a human rights organization founded to fight the economic and political exploitation of workers in New York City. WDL joined a coalition protesting against the exclusion of minorities from the building trades unions in the city. Through a series of demonstrations, the group successfully shut down several major construction projects. In the midst of the demonstrations, WDL staff realized that, if the unions suddenly acceded to their demands to admit minorities, the protesters could provide the names of only a few youths who were interested and qualified to become apprentices. At first, WDL staff thought that minority candidates were unavailable because they simply lacked information about apprenticeship. So WDL compiled a booklet on apprenticeship trades in New York City, including information on entry standards and the timing of class openings, and distributed it widely in the minority community.

But the pamphlet did not solve the problem. Minority candidates did not appear. Merely providing information was not enough. Thus, WDL decided to actively recruit minority youngsters. With a small grant from the Taconic Foundation, WDL opened a storefront office on 1 June 1964 in the predominantly black Bedford-Stuyvesant section of Brooklyn, marking the beginning of the first apprenticeship outreach program. An intensive campaign was begun to recruit through schools, parents' groups, YMCAs, and community organizations, and on street corners.

Recruiting alone proved to be insufficient. In the first admissions test given by Sheet Metal Workers Local 28, the highest scoring black ranked 68th and the union admitted the first 65. As a result, the apprenticeship outreach staff embarked upon a program to maximize the minority applicant's chances for admission. It went far beyond the counseling available through the employment service or other agencies. First, a program of tutoring sessions lasting several hours a day over the course of several weeks was begun, designed to teach the basic mechanical and mathematical skills that applicants had never learned or had forgotten since leaving school. Applicants also were coached through a series of simulated interviews to teach them how to make a favorable impression in interviews with JATC members. Finally, apprenticeship outreach staff took a personal interest in the youngsters, helping them find temporary jobs until the apprenticeships opened, making sure that they showed up for the interviews and exams, and providing general encouragement.

The efforts showed dramatic results. In the admissions tests of the Sheet Metal Workers Local 28 given in 1965, 12 of the applicants sent by the apprenticeship outreach program placed among the top 30 taking the examination. The following year, 75 percent of the blacks taking the exam passed, compared with only 31 percent of the whites. Indeed, the apprenticeship outreach program was so successful in preparing its applicants that the union brought charges, subsequently proven false, that the staff had prior knowledge of the apprenticeship exams.

The strategy taken by apprenticeship outreach was not to demand lower standards but instead to seek minority youths who could meet existing standards with some tutoring and preparation. It also was a pragmatic approach; namely, to do what was needed to get black youths into the apprenticeship programs. It was developed in incremental fashion—overcoming obstacles as they appeared. And though the apprenticeship outreach staff sometimes were confrontative, they did not take an adversarial approach to the employers and unions with whom they were working.

Some recalcitrant unions and employers did not work voluntarily with apprenticeship outreach programs. In these cases, legal action was needed. For example, Sheet Metal Workers Local 28 faced court battles for several years. The outreach program generally did not take an active role in bringing such legal action; instead, staff referred those with grievances to attorneys and other agencies who could take action. While the court battles themselves were costly, time-consuming, and uncertain as to outcome for the aggrieved parties, they provided an effective threat to encourage union locals and employers to work cooperatively with apprenticeship outreach programs (Marshall et al. 1978).

For their part, outreach programs worked with cooperative elements and individuals within the system to institutionalize changes in the behavior of unions and employers. In 1968, the A. Phillip Randolph Institute—an organization of black trade unionists—was invited to co-sponsor the original apprenticeship outreach program. In September 1969, the 55th Convention of the Building and Construction Trades Department (AFL-CIO) endorsed affirmative action, especially as embodied in the apprenticeship outreach concept.

The prod of administrative and legal remedies, including affirmative action, goals, and timetables, and the threat of court action helped generate a willingness to cooperate by employers and unions on the demand side of the labor market. At the same time, outreach organizations were able to locate, interest, and prepare a supply of appropriate applicants for the newly available jobs. The combination produced results. By 1967, a total of 245 individuals (almost all of whom were black) had been placed into the building trades in New York City (Marshall and Briggs 1968, 48).

Prompted by the research recommendations and documented success in New York City, the U.S. Department of Labor (USDOL) funded the program to replicate its effort in several other cities. The outreach model also was adopted by other organizations such as the National Urban League, the Human Resources Development Institute of the AFL-CIO, and funded by USDOL in other locations. While the initial focus of these outreach efforts was to help black males to enter apprenticeships, efforts were soon extended to include all minority males.

By 1980, nationally funded outreach programs had been established in 114 locations and had helped to register over 45,000 apprentices. In 1967, minorities had been less than 6 percent of all apprentices. By the beginning of 1973, they accounted for 14 percent of all apprentices and 17 percent of all new indentures over the previous year. By 1979, minority apprentices constituted 17.4 percent of all registered apprentices.

Like the two blades of a scissors, the combination of prodding and assisting worked to bring progress. On one hand, pressures for affirmative action brought by the advocacy of civil rights groups and government regulations created a demand for minority apprentices. On the other, outreach organizations were there to provide suitable candidates to fill that demand. These outreach organizations used a systematic, pragmatic methodology for recruiting and preparing individuals for apprenticeship that included specialized efforts to (1) disseminate information, (2) recruit, (3) tutor to pass entry requirements (tests, interviews) for apprenticeship, and (4) provide supportive counseling and assistance to the applicants.

Women in Apprenticeship
The lack of women in apprenticeship did not become an issue of public policy until the 1970s. In large part, this was because the women's movement lagged behind the civil rights movement, and the initial focus was on getting women into nontraditional white-collar occupations.

Female apprentices were indeed a rarity before the 1970s. For example, as of 1 July 1968, among apprenticeship accounts serviced by the U.S. Bureau of Apprenticeship and Training (BAT) nationwide, only 2 women were reported among 77,151 apprentices across the entire construction industry. There were no women at all among the 6,105 apprentices in mining, public utilities, and transportation. And only 100 apprentices out of 43,386 in manufacturing were women (BAT 1968). Three years later in 1970, there were only 5 women apprentices in construction, and still zero in public utilities, transportation, and mining, and only 24 in metal manufacturing (BAT 1971).

Because of difficulties with apprenticeship reporting systems, a consistent data series on the total number of women in apprenticeship is impossible to obtain for the 1960s and 1970s, but what is available is shown in Table 11-2. The participation of women in apprenticeship grew from 0.3 percent to 5.9 percent from 1971 to 1986. For purposes of comparison, the percentage of entrants to college engineering programs who were women grew from 2.6 percent in 1971 to 16.5 percent in 1985 (Dix 1987, 62, citing data from the Engineering Manpower Commission). Less access for women to apprenticeship training for blue-collar skilled trades has been achieved than in engineering—the area of college study with traditionally the least participation by women.

But much has been learned about how to get women into apprenticeships. A pathbreaking project begun in 1970 in Wisconsin attempted to demonstrate ways in which obstacles to fuller utilization of female workers in apprenticeship could be identified and overcome. The project's initial concerns were to develop methods of influencing employers and unions and of motivating women. As it proceeded, it found barriers in the attitudes and procedures of government agency staff and the educational system. The project began by questioning the Wisconsin state apprenticeship agency staff about the dearth of women in apprenticeship. It then surveyed trade and industry coordinators in vocational-technical schools and documented and investigated the paucity of

Table 11-2/Female Participation in Apprenticeship

YEAR (AT DECEMBER 31)	FEMALE APPRENTICES		TOTAL APPRENTICES
	Number	*Percent of Total*	
1967	880	0.4	178,376
1968	650	0.4	166,374
1969	880	0.4	201,712
1970	722	0.4	199,928
1971	620	0.3	186,236
1975	3,198	1.2	266,477
1976	4,334	1.7	254,968
1977	5,777	2.2	262,586
1978	8,997	3.1	290,224
1979	13,279	4.1	323,866
1986[a]	9,960	5.9	168,506

Source: Figures for 1967–71 include federally serviced workload only data from internal "Summary Management Reports" at the U.S. Bureau of Apprenticeship and Training.
[a] Includes only a partial count of apprentices nationwide and excludes apprentices in the military (as consistent with data in previous years).

women training in drafting, welding, electronics, and other male-dominated occupations. Project staff interviewed apprenticeship sponsors in the Fox River Valley of Wisconsin and distributed questionnaires to both female apprentices and the employers who trained them. The project served effectively as a consciousness-raising device, producing several conferences, a film entitled *Never Underestimate the Power of a Woman*, and a monograph entitled *Women in Apprenticeship: Why Not?* (Briggs 1973)—both designed to explode myths about the alleged unsuitability of women for work in a wide range of industrial jobs filled by men, and to motivate attitudinal changes in employers to encourage them to women apprentices. The project recommended the extension of apprenticeship into traditionally female occupations in the fields of day care and health care. Through the consciousness-raising efforts and through working with the Work Incentive (WIN) Program and Manpower Development and Training Act (MDTA) programs for the disadvantaged, the project was able to broaden participation of women in apprenticeship somewhat. But no women were placed into apprenticeships in the building trades, and generally only one or two "breakthrough" women were admitted to traditionally male apprenticeships. "Consciousness-raising" alone produced limited results. The project concluded with an appeal to establish apprenticeship outreach programs for women, to require affirmative action for women in apprenticeship through governmental regulation, and to influence guidance counselors and the educational system to eliminate practices that reinforce sex stereotypes.

By 1977, efforts to get women into apprenticeships were gathering momentum. A few local women's organizations had successfully adapted the apprenticeship outreach methodology to recruit and prepare women for apprenticeship. When Ray Marshall became secretary of labor in January 1977, he brought into the department several individuals who were familiar with apprenticeship outreach strategies, including Ernest Green as assistant secretary of labor for employment and training and Alexis Herman as director of the Women's Bureau. Under new leadership, the Women's Bureau made gaining access to apprenticeship for women a major goal. The Bureau undertook an advocacy campaign to spread information about apprenticeship to women (Hernandez 1980). It identified and publicized selected model outreach programs for women in Boston and Denver (USDOL 1979b and 1979c). It encouraged local sponsors under the Comprehensive Employment and Training Act (CETA) to establish programs to recruit and prepare women for apprenticeable jobs not traditionally held by women. It advocated the use of apprenticeship in federal prisons for women (USDOL 1980). It established a task force with the Bureau of Apprenticeship and Training to educate staff about the issue of women in apprenticeship. The Women's Bureau urged that better information on women in apprenticeship be developed through research. The Women's Bureau also campaigned for the establishment of specific goals and timetables for women in apprenticeship and for women on federally contracted jobs.

In the spring of 1978, facing two legal suits advocating affirmative action for women in apprenticeship, Secretary of Labor Ray Marshall acted against the recommendations of union and industry officials and established goals and timetables for hiring women on federally financed construction projects as well as goals and timetables specifically for apprenticeship. In April, goals and timetables were set under regulations (41 *CFR* 60.4) enforcing Executive Order 11246 for female participation in federally financed construction projects where contracts exceeded $10,000. The goals for employment of women were set to increase as follows: from 1 April 1978 through 31 March 1979 there was to be an increase of 3.1 percent; from 1 April 1979 through 31 March 1980, 5.1 percent; and from 1 April 1980 through 31 March 1981, 6.9 percent. Additionally, goals and timetables were prepared specifically for apprenticeship and published for comment in September 1977. In May 1978, with promulgation of final regulations for "Equal Employment Opportunity in Apprenticeship and Training" (29 *CFR* 30), the U.S. Department of Labor established the goal of enrolling women in apprenticeships in numbers equal to half of their proportion in the general labor force. Since women constituted 40.5 percent of the work force in 1976, the regulations effectively set a goal of making one out of every five entrants to registered apprenticeship a female. In April 1979, the Department of Labor raised the goal for women apprenticeship entrants to 25 percent or one out of four persons by 1980.

Industry officials complained that these goals were unrealistic and impossible to meet because there were not enough women with the ability or interest to enter the skilled trades. But Labor Department officials familiar with the apprenticeship outreach experience for black males simply counted on outreach programs to do the job.

Apprenticeship Outreach for Women
Rather than establish an additional set of outreach organizations specifically for women, the Labor Department adopted the strategy of expanding the performance goals of existing outreach organizations to include women. Most existing outreach organizations were based in minority communities; and some raised the concern that these organizations would tend to recruit minority women rather than white women (Kane and Miller 1981, 94–95). Wanting to avoid apparent duplication of effort under budget restraints, feeling pressure to reduce nationally funded programs and turn more employment and training programs to local prime sponsors under CETA, and confident that existing outreach organizations could do the job, Labor Department officials provided national funding to only a handful of new apprenticeship outreach projects operated by women's organizations. In addition, the Labor Department urged local CETA prime sponsors to consider funding pre-apprenticeship programs for women (USDOL 1979a). As a result of this strategy, only a few local projects were funded among the women's groups.

A few innovations to the original outreach model used for minority males were added by the women's organizations, including the following:

- *More complete orientation* to give the women a realistic picture of the jobs they would be applying for. Because of their traditional views of sex roles in childhood and inadequacies in school counseling, most women were not prepared to consider a career in the skilled trades. These orientations aimed to present both the favorable and the unfavorable aspects of the jobs so that an informed choice could be made. The Women in Apprenticeship project in San Francisco, for example, began its program with several hours of group orientation to introduce the skilled trades to women. The program then worked only with women who remained seriously interested. Many programs learned early that if women did not make knowledgeable choices, they were less likely to stick with their apprenticeships.
- *Pre-apprenticeship training*, including tool identification and often some "hands on" experience in working with tools. This component was needed to make up for the lack of vocational preparation and experience many females brought to the programs. If female apprentices could perform well on the job, it was reasoned, their male colleagues were more likely to accept them.
- *Physical conditioning* to help prepare women for the physical demands

of the jobs and to teach women safe practices in lifting, bending, and using their bodies as leverage.

- *Assistance in arranging child care* for apprentices who were on the job or in related classroom training two evenings a week.
- *Organization of peer support groups* composed of women apprentices designed to facilitate their helping one another in apprenticeship and on the job. Such support groups can often help a woman deal with harassment she may encounter on the job. It can also help her distinguish between the normal hazing apprentices encounter on the job and sexual harassment.
- *Training and technical assistance for supervisors* of women in traditionally male jobs. Supervision can have a major impact on the success of integration. For example, supervisors who cater to their female employees by giving them easier assignments do not help the women gain acceptance from male co-workers as equals on the job. Supervisors can also eliminate or minimize harassment on the job.

In addition, outreach programs encouraged employment practices such as assigning more than one woman to a job (to avoid isolation). They also negotiated entry for women who were beyond maximum age limitations for apprentices.

The Results of Activities for Women in Apprenticeship During the 1970s

Under pressure to achieve goals and timetables and with the assistance of publicity campaigns and a few outreach programs seeking to generate suitable and informed female applicants for apprenticeship, the percentages of women apprentices finally began to rise in the late 1970s. In 1976, the year prior to initial publication of regulations for goals and timetables for women, females comprised 1.7 percent of all apprentices. The percentage moved up to 3.1 percent in 1978—the year after publication of the regulations—and to 3.7 percent in 1979.

Unfortunately, no major, nationally networked organizations were established for women's apprenticeship outreach. Such nationally networked organizations had always been a strength among outreach organizations for minority males. The fact that organizations such as the National Urban League's LEAP (Labor Education Advancement Program) program, the Human Resource Development Institute of the AFL-CIO, and the Recruitment and Training Program (RTP, Inc.) operated national programs helped to maintain quality control among local groups and to create a national presence that helped to preserve the discretionary national funding apprenticeship outreach received from the Labor Department.

No national organization was funded or formed among the women's organizations. In fact, though attempts by the Women's Bureau were made, no effective coalition or even alliance was developed among existing women's apprenticeship outreach organizations. Part of the reason that the sponsoring organizations for these local programs were very different and could not reach agreement. But the primary reason was that Labor Department staff found it difficult to justify the creation of a national outreach organization for women that apparently operated parallel to other outreach organizations during a period of fiscal constraint.

Thus, by the end of the Carter administration in 1980, a well-developed national apprenticeship outreach movement for women had not been established—though a few local outreach programs for women did exist. Further, since the apprenticeship outreach movement relied almost completely on funding directly from discretionary national Labor Department accounts, it was an easy target for cutbacks at the beginning of the Reagan administration. National funds for outreach programs were one of the first cutbacks made by the Reagan administration; all were defunded. Likewise, pressure for affirmative action was relaxed. Thus, just as the campaign to place women into apprenticeships was beginning to show results, it was wiped out.

Also a victim of the Reagan cutbacks was the State and National Apprenticeship System (SNAPS)—the Labor Department's major information system on registered apprenticeship. It was closed down in January 1980—and with it went evidence on national progress made by women in apprenticeship.

A resurrected computerized "National Apprentices Statistics" series showed that for the year 1986, 5.9 percent (or 9,960) of 168,506 apprentices outside of the military were women. However, as of 1986, the new information system did not include data from California, the District of Columbia, Puerto Rico, Hawaii, Rhode Island, the Virgin Islands, and Vermont. Thus it appears that progress has improved only slightly over the past six years—certainly not at the same rate as achieved for minority males in the late 1960s and early 1970—nor has progress occurred at the same rate that was achieved under affirmative action pressures and outreach efforts for women in the late 1970s. Eight years after promulgation of goals for women in apprenticeship, the original goals were little over one-fourth met. At the current rate, it will be well into the twenty-first century before women achieve representation in apprenticeship in numbers equal to even half of their proportion of the labor force.

Record keeping on registered apprentices is slowly being improved and computerized in many states, with the result that a much better picture of apprenticeship activities is beginning to emerge. The new computerized information system can display apprenticeship activity by occupation, industry, individual program, and geographic area, and by characteristic of apprentices.

Further, new information elements are being added, such as data on attrition, including the reasons for leaving apprenticeship.

Documenting the performance of women apprentices is important for several reasons. First, with new, more comprehensive, reliable, and accurate information systems, much can be learned from a close examination of detail. Such information can be a motivating force for action as well as help to target and shape effective action. Aggregate numbers hide much interesting variation. For example, while nationally 5.9 percent of apprentices were women in December 1986, in some states the percentages were higher. Washington State (including Seattle, where a goal of 12 percent or more for female employment on construction contracts had been in place since 1974), the percentage of female apprentices was 8.7 percent. Likewise, significant variations exist across the trades, as illustrated in Table 11-1. For example, how is it that women have been able to gain 17.3 percent of all operating engineer apprenticeships—a construction trade that involves driving or operating heavy construction machinery? (One spokesperson from the international union explained to the author that several of the union's locals "took a beating in court" over the issue of admitting black males into their union and they want to avoid becoming vulnerable again over the issue of affirmative action for women.)

A second reason for documenting the performance of women in apprenticeship is to check the accuracy of widely held myths about the performance of women in apprenticeable occupations traditionally occupied by men. Relying on opinions rather than objective evidence is often misleading.

What Has Been Learned and Where Do We Go From Here?
First and foremost, from experience we know that success is possible to achieve in integrating women into apprenticeable skilled trades that have been traditionally occupied by men. But the achievement will come only with effort. Enforcement of the law and regulations are not enough. Women face two types of barriers to entering the trades: external and internal. To a certain extent, legal or regulatory tools can remedy such external barriers as discrimination by employers in the selection and hiring process or harassment from co-workers. However, the internal barriers imposed by socialization lead women not to consider such work.

Even if enforcement of equal opportunity laws were dramatically increased, there would still be an insufficient flow of female applicants into skilled trades jobs. Specialized programs for recruitment and preparation of women are needed to generate female applicants for jobs in the crafts. We know a lot about how to design these programs and we even have written program models to follow (Lyndon B. Johnson School of Public Affairs 1979; USDOL 1979a, 1979b, and 1980). Rather than simply promoting the skilled trades to women, these programs should provide a full orientation to both the attractive and the unattractive features of the jobs. Women need to make fully informed decisions about entering such jobs or many will not last through the period of training—just confirming the preconceptions that women cannot or will not do this work.

Specialized recruitment programs need to be focused at the entry points to the training pipeline for these jobs. These programs should involve industry participation and be nationally networked and based on standardized models that are sufficiently flexible to meet local conditions.

Getting women into vocational preparation and training in the skilled trades in schools is important. But once trained in school, women must still find a job. Apprenticeship is an attractive entry point because it provides the job and training all in one package. Further because it is formally established with written standards and procedures, it is an easier target for specialized recruitment programs to aim at.

Beyond entry, women in these nontraditional jobs need encouragement and support. Peer support groups have proven to be very useful to many women, once on the jobs. Several such groups have been formed spontaneously by women apprentices.

Resistance, disapproval, and even harassment from co-workers have been major problems in skilled blue-collar jobs. It is important to understand that even though many skilled blue-collar jobs pay well, they are not valued highly by American society because they involve manual work. This "anti-manual" bias affects the men who work in these trades and the job cultures in important ways. Often lacking social status, such workers draw dignity from pride in their craftsmanship, which can become closely associated with manliness. In this context, the entry of women to their jobs can be threatening in many ways.

Experience has demonstrated that problems from co-workers can be alleviated by good, sensitive supervision. However, supervisors themselves can be part of the problem. Supervisory staff—especially foreman—often need specialized training to deal effectively with this situation; and action by top management is needed to prevent problems from co-workers.

How have women performed in apprenticeship? Much research has been conducted on the problems encountered by individual female apprentices (Briggs 1973 and 1974; Kane, Dee, and Miller 1977; Green 1979; Wesley and Pinston 1982). However, despite all the well-publicized problems of female apprentices, a growing body of evidence demonstrates that women who have entered apprenticeships are more likely to complete their training than are men apprentices. A study of female apprentices in Wisconsin (Briggs 1973) found a dropout rate of 24 percent, as compared with an overall dropout rate for Wisconsin apprentice programs (which were over 90 percent male) of 50 percent (Barocci 1972). More recently, in New York State over the nine-month period from January through September 1986, 69 percent of the women who exited apprenticeships were completers, as compared with only 65 percent of the men. Further, among those exiting, the proportion of women who quit was slightly lower than for men (22 percent for women, 23 percent for men). It appears that contrary to stereotype views, women have a stronger attachment to their apprenticeship training than do men.

The experience with apprenticeship has been an important crucible for developing techniques for effectiveness in equal opportunity. A significant body of knowledge has been accumulated over the past 20 years, which has important implications for the future of apprenticeship as well as other training programs.

Beyond apprenticeship, how have women fared as journeymen craft-workers? Although several case studies are available of individual female apprentices who have succeeded (Wheat 1978; Hernandez 1980; Peace, Love-lace, and Englebrecht 1986), unfortunately, to date we have no comprehensive longitudinal studies of women who completed their apprenticeships. This re-mains a primary gap in our research base.

It is unclear what the overall retention and career patterns are for female craftworkers as compared with those for men. Further, once numbers be-come available, it is important to understand what they mean. For example, if retention rates are found to be lower for women than for men, is this due to problems with the jobs or to characteristics of the women? It could be that since the first few breakthrough women were so highly selected, their exceptional qualifications enabled them to move to even better positions.

Whatever the case, better information on female journeymen is needed. In the meantime, the available case studies demonstrate that women can perform well working in the trades.

American Apprenticeship: Limited Reality But Great Potential
While apprenticeship remains a good training route to higher-paying jobs for those without college degrees in the United States, in its present atrophied state, apprenticeship can offer limited promise for women. Excluding appren-tices in the military, there were approximately 250,000 apprentices in training in 1987—down by more than one-fourth from the peak number of apprentices in 1979. Each year about 60,000 individuals enter apprenticeships nationwide. If the goal of 25 percent of apprenticeships going to females were reached, this would mean a total of 15,000 apprenticeships annually for women nationwide. While this number is significant, expanded use of the apprenticeship concept could offer much greater potential for women.

Apprenticeship provides an excellent entry route into the skilled trades; but directing more women into apprenticeship without also expanding the number of apprenticeships itself is a limited strategy. A "funnel problem" already exists in apprenticeship—too many applicants competing for too few positions. In some locations and some trades, where the best apprenticeship programs are established—such as electricians, sheet metal workers, plumbers, and pipefitters—the competition for apprenticeships is often intense. Applicant/acceptance ratios commonly reach 4 to 1. Many who are accepted into the mechanical trades have some college training or are collge graduates.

American apprenticeship today faces a triple challenge to (1) maintain and improve the quality of training offered, while (2) expanding its use and (3) providing access to the disadvantaged, women, and minorities. Failing to rise to these challenges will result in gradual atrophy—with apprenticeship becoming a less and less significant part of occupational training in America. Achieving any of these goals without all the others will lead to failure. Providing access to an apprenticeship system for women and minorities is important for its economic implications as well as equity considerations. Fully 80 percent of the net increase in the American work force to the year 2000 will be women and minorities. And from 2000 to 2020, women and minorities will account for almost all of the growth of the U.S. labor force.

The need for revitalizing American apprenticeship is becoming increasingly obvious, and the calls for it are becoming more numerous (Carnegie Council on Policy Studies in Higher Education 1980; Taggart 1981; Glover 1986; National Conference of Catholic Bishops 1987; Berlin and Sum 1988; William T. Grant Foundation Commission on Work, Family and Citizenship 1988; Children's Defense Fund 1988). During the past decade, a dozen attempts have been made to amend the three-paragraph National Apprenticeship Act passed in 1937. None has yet succeeded, largely because none has achieved consensus from all the major participant groups in apprenticeship. But someday, new national legislation on apprenticeship will pass and apprenticeship reform will be spawned.

From the experience of the past two decades, we learned how effective equal opportunity in apprenticeship can be achieved—and we learned many lessons that need not be repeated. With some modifications, the strategy for integrating black males into apprenticeship can work for females as well. Where there is gross underrepresentation of women in occupations that have formalized processes for entry, specialized outreach programs can work effectively to identify and prepare interested, suitable applicants for integrating these occupations. Such programs work best in combination with the real threat of administrative and judicial pressures for affirmative action. Without the motivating threat of such pressures, outreach may yield only token changes. Likewise, administrative and judicial pressures for affirmative action without outreach efforts may produce only frustration.

These lessons from experience and objective research should be incorporated into any new apprenticeship legislation that is developed, so that the full measure of apprenticeship's potential can be realized for American workers—both men and women.

References

Barocci, T. 1972. *The Drop-out and the Wisconsin Apprenticeship Program: A Descriptive and Econometric Analysis.* Madison: Industrial Relations Research Institute, University of Wisconsin.

Berlin, Gordon, and Andrew Sum. 1988. *Toward a More Perfect Union: Basic Skills, Poor Families, and Our Economic Future.* Occasional Paper no. 3. Ford Foundation Project on Social Welfare and the American Future. New York: The Ford Foundation.

Briggs, Norma. 1973. *Women in Apprenticeship: Why Not?* Manpower Research Monograph no. 33, U.S. Department of Labor. Washington, D.C.: Government Printing Office.

————. 1974. "Women Apprentices: Removing the Barriers: Project Challenges Stereotypes of Sex Roles in the Workplace." *Manpower* 6, no. 12 (December): 2–8.

————. 1979. *Women and the Skilled Trades.* Columbus, Ohio: Educational Resources Information Center.

————. 1981. "Overcoming Barriers to Successful Entry and Retention of Women in Traditionally Male Skilled Blue-Collar Trades in Wisconsin." In *Apprenticeship Research: Emerging Findings and Future Trends*, ed. Vernon M. Briggs, Jr., and Felician F. Foltman, pp. 106–32. Ithaca: New York State School of Labor and Industrial Relations.

Carnegie Council on Policy Studies in Higher Education. 1980. *Giving Youth a Better Chance.* San Francisco: Jossey-Bass.

Children's Defense Fund. 1988. *A Children's Defense Budget FY 1989: An Analysis of Our Nation's Investment in Children.* Washington, D.C.: Children's Defense Fund.

Dix, Linda S., ed. 1987. *Women: Their Underrepresentation and Career Differentials in Science and Engineering.* Washington, D.C.: National Academy Press.

Egan, Christine. 1978. "Apprenticeship Now." *Occupational Outlook Quarterly* 22, no. 2 (Summer): 3–17.

Glover, Robert W. 1980. *Apprenticeship in the United States: Implications for Vocational Education Research and Development.* Occasional Paper no. 66. Columbus: National Center for Research in Vocational Education, Ohio State University.

————. 1986. *Apprenticeship Lessons from Abroad.* Information Series no. 305. Columbus: National Center for Research in Vocational Education, Ohio State University.

Glover, Robert W., and Ray Marshall. 1977. "The Response of Unions in the Construction Industry to Antidiscrimination Efforts." In *Equal Rights and Industrial Relations*, pp. 121–40. Madison, Wis.: Industrial Relations Research Association.

Green, D. A. 1979. "Women in Apprenticeship for Non-Traditional Occupations."

Final Report. Center for Vocational, Technical and Adult Education, University of Wisconsin-Stout-Menomonie, Menomonie, Wis.

Hernandez, R. B. 1980. *A Women's Guide to Apprenticeship*. Pamphlet no. 17. Washington, D.C.: U.S. Department of Labor, Women's Bureau.

Kane, Roselyn D., and Jill Miller. 1981. "Women and Apprenticeship: A Study of Programs Designed to Facilitate Women's Participation in the Skilled Trades." In *Apprenticeship Research: Emerging Findings and Future Trends*, ed. Vernon M. Briggs, Jr., and Felician F. Foltman, pp. 83–105. Ithaca: New York State School of Labor and Industrial Relations.

Kane, Roselyn D.; Elizabeth Dee; and Jill Miller. 1977. *Problems of Women in Apprenticeship*. Arlington, Va.: R. J. Associates.

Latack, Janina C.; Susan L. Josephs; Bonnie L. Roach; and Mitchell D. Levine. 1984. "Women Carpenters: The Union's Role in Successful Transition to a Non-Traditional Career." Working Paper Series 84–49. College of Administrative Science, Ohio State University, Columbus.

Lyndon B. Johnson School of Public Affairs. 1979. *Preparation for Apprenticeship through CETA*. Austin: Lyndon B. Johnson School of Public Affairs, University of Texas at Austin.

Marshall, F. Ray, and Vernon M. Briggs, Jr. 1967. *The Negro and Apprenticeship*. Baltimore: The Johns Hopkins University Press.

————. 1968. *Equal Apprenticeship Opportunities: The Nature of the Issue and the New York Experience*. Policy Papers in Human Resources and Industrial Relations no. 10. Ann Arbor: Institute of Labor and Industrial Relations, the University of Michigan—Wayne State University and the National Manpower Policy Task Force.

Marshall, F. Ray; Charles B. Knapp; Malcolm H. Liggett; and Robert W. Glover. 1978. *Employment Discrimination: The Impact of Legal and Administrative Remedies*. New York: Praeger.

National Conference of Catholic Bishops Conference. 1987. "Economic Justice for All: Catholic Social Teaching and the U.S. Economy." In *Building Economic Justice: the Bishops' Pastoral Letter and Tools for Action*, paragraph 159, p. 36. Washington, D.C.: National Conference of Catholic Bishops, U.S. Catholic Conference.

Peace, Betty; Bill Lovelace; and Jo Ann Engelbrecht. 1986. *A Woman's Guide to Apprenticeship Programs in Texas*. Denton: North Texas State University, Division of Occupational and Vocational Education.

Poyo, Gerald; Karen Rowlett; and Sue Mutchler. 1981. *Combating Labor Market Underrepresentation Through a Targeted Outreach Program (TOP)*. Austin: Center for the Study of Human Resources, University of Texas at Austin.

Rowan, Richard L., and Robert J. Brudno. 1972. "Fair Employment in Building: Imposed and Hometown Plans." *Industrial Relations* 11 (October): 394–406.

Rowan, Richard L., and Lester Rubin. 1972. *Opening the Skilled Construction Trades to Blacks: A Study of the Washington and Indianapolis Plans for Minority Employment*. Philadelphia: Industrial Research Unit, the Wharton School, University of Pennsylvania.

Taggart, Robert A. 1981. *A Fisherman's Guide: An Assessment of Training and Reme-*

diation Strategies. Kalamazoo, Mich.: W. E. Upjohn Institute for Employment Research.

Ullman, Joseph C., and Kay K. Deaux. 1981. "Recent Efforts to Increase Female Participation in Apprenticeship in the Basic Steel Industry in the Midwest." In *Apprenticeship Research: Emerging Findings and Future Trends*, ed. Vernon M. Briggs, Jr., and Felician F. Foltman, pp. 133–49. Ithaca: New York State School of Labor and Industrial Relations.

U.S. Bureau of Apprenticeship and Training. 1968. "Summary Management Report." Washington, D.C., 17 September.

———. 1971. "Summary Management Report." Washington, D.C., March.

U.S. Department of Labor. Employment and Training Administration. 1979a. *Apprenticeship and CETA Technical Assistance Guide*. Washington, D.C.: Government Printing Office.

———. Women's Bureau. 1979b. *Women in Nontraditional Jobs: A Program Model —Boston Nontraditional Occupations Program for Women*. Washington, D.C.: Government Printing Office.

———. Women's Bureau. 1979c. *Women in Nontraditional Jobs: A Program Model— Denver: Better Jobs for Women*. Washington, D.C.: Government Printing Office.

———. Women's Bureau. 1980. *The Women Offender Apprenticeship Program: From Inmate to Skilled Craft Worker*. Pamphlet no. 21. Washington, D.C.: Government Printing Office.

Wesley, L. A., and G. Pinston, Jr. 1982. *A Territorial Issue: A Study of Women in the Construction Trades*. Washington, D.C.: Wider Opportunities for Women and the Center of National Policy Review.

Wheat, Valerie. 1978. *Apprenticeship and Other Blue Collar Job Opportunities for Women*. San Francisco: Women's Educational Equity Communications Network, Far West Laboratory for Educational Research and Development.

William T. Grant Foundation Commission on Work, Family and Citizenship. 1988. *The Forgotten Half: Non-College Youth in America*. Washington, D.C.: The William T. Grant Foundation, January.

12/Physical Training as a Strategy for Integrating Municipal Uniformed Services

Cynthia H. Chertos and Sarah C. Phillips

There are relatively few occupations left that are held exclusively by men. Although occupational segregation persists, slowly and often in small numbers, women have begun to enter almost every occupation for which sex is not a bona fide occupational qualification. The uniformed municipal services of firefighting and sanitation appear to be among the last occupations to begin to accept women.

In firefighting, only recently has women's participation been great enough even to measure on a national scale. In 1982, the International Association of Firefighters reported that there were 420 full-time female firefighters, in a national force of about 180,000 (*New York Times* [NYT] 2 November 1982). That means that less than 0.3 percent of all paid firefighters were women. At that time, there were only 42 women out of approximately 10,000 New York City firefighters. This is slightly above the national average, but still an extremely small number.

The job of firefighter is a very desirable one for many women. It involves on-the-job training, great responsibility, and some autonomy. It is well respected and, in most cases, it is well remunerated. In New York City, firefighters receive starting salaries of almost $26,000 a year and have extra pay for shift work, four weeks of vacation after only three years, unlimited sick leave benefits, and generous employee insurance packages (*NYT*, 19 April 1984, New York City Department of Personnel, personal communication, 1985). Many women would be interested in such a job that requires no special education or experience prior to hiring.

Although no national statistics are available on sanitation workers, it is obvious that women are only beginning to make inroads into this occupation.

In New York City government, until 1986 there was not one woman sanitation worker in a work force of approximately 7,000. Yet, sanitation work also may be a desirable employment option for many women. Working in an essential municipal service typically provides employment security. In addition, like firefighters, New York City sanitation workers receive excellent pay and benefits. Starting salaries are over $23,000, plus premiums for working shift work, on weekends, and on an assigned day off. Sanitation workers receive 25 vacation days, as well as paid holidays. As for firefighters, sick days are unlimited and employee health insurance packages are generous (*NYT*, 19 April 1984, New York City Department of Personnel, personal communication, 1985). Women might well choose either firefighting or sanitation work as a good way to earn a middle-income salary with excellent benefits, without having to obtain additional education or experience prior to hiring.

In this chapter we explore New York City's efforts to integrate these two work forces. In particular, we review the difficult process of gaining acceptance of women in the city's firefighter and sanitation worker roles. We then outline in some detail the efforts of the Center for Women in Government to assist in the initial integration of women into each of these departments through the use of physical training. This training helped women to develop and demonstrate their competence to join the most masculine of municipal occupations. We conclude with a discussion of the integration lessons common to both of these departments and recommendations for other employers seeking to integrate women into their nontraditional work forces.

Women in Firefighting

Firefighting in New York City, as in all American cities, has long been an exclusively male occupation. Since the beginning of recorded firefighting history, women were excluded from both the volunteer and paid firefighting forces. In the early 1970s, this began to change. Title VII of the Civil Rights Act of 1964 was extended to government employers, and for the first time, women were to be admitted into nontraditional municipal jobs. This admission did not occur easily, however.

The History of Firefighting in New York City

As New Amsterdam, which later became the City of New York, expanded in the early 1600s, so did the risk of fire. Funds received through fines levied against those who created fire hazards were used to purchase equipment, including hooks, ladders, and, most important, buckets, for the technology of firefighting was changing and the need for buckets increased dramatically (New York City 1965). Earlier fires had been fought by all able-bodied men in town, who dipped a bucket into the canal or river and ran to the fire. After flinging the water onto the fire, a man would run back to refill his bucket, and so on. This was not very effective.

A better method was developed, which involved the formation of "bucket lines" from the river to a fire. Two lines were formed—one passed full buckets from man to man from the river to the fire; the other passed the empty buckets back from the fire to the river. The hands passing empty buckets in this second line usually were those of women and children (Dunshee 1948). Along with the need for more buckets had come a need for more hands, and thus women (and children) were, for a short time, incorporated into the firefighting forces in the City of New York. Later, "bucket brigades" were added, which allowed two men simultaneously to carry many buckets attached to two parallel poles. Women's participation was no longer needed.

In 1737, the Volunteer Fire Department of the City of New York was founded. The act creating the department provided for "the appointment of able, discreet, and sober *men* who shall be known as Firemen of the City of New York, to be ready for service by night and by day and be diligent, industrious, and vigilant" (Dunshee 1948; emphasis added). Thus, very early in its history women were excluded from formal participation in firefighting in New York City. With one recorded exception, this practice was to continue for more than two centuries.

The single exception occurred approximately 50 years later. In the 1780s, there was reported to be one woman firefighter in New York City. A member of the Oceanus Company No. 11, she was recorded for history only as "Molly." We know little about her except that she was a black slave. Although she fought fires with the volunteer force, we do not know under what circumstances this lone woman participated in the company or whether she was an officially appointed member. The only available account suggests that she participated willingly and quite capably, because it contains a drawing of her smiling as she pulled the pumper and it reports she was "often seen running at the sound of an alarm in her calico dress and checkered apron, a clean bandana kerchief neatly folded over her breast, and another wound about her head" (Dunshee 1948, 53). Perhaps it is because volunteer firefighting in the 1780s usually was exclusively the domain of men that Molly's physical appearance and dress seemed so important to describe, while her role in the volunteer force goes without further comment. With this single exception, no women are known to have participated in the volunteer or paid firefighting forces in New York City until the 1980s.

The Occupational Culture of Firefighting

Firefighting is, without a doubt, one of the most "masculine" occupations in the American work force. By this we mean that the cultural environment of the firefighter and the firehouse is dominated by traditional notions of men and masculinity. Moreover, the New York City Fire Department has a well-known and "long tradition of sons joining fathers in the [firefighting] ranks" (*NYT*, 2 September 1982). Thus, the introduction of female firefighters challenges tradition on two important counts.[1]

From the beginning, the masculine culture of the occupation has raised questions about whether women could do the job. When women were trying to obtain jobs as New York City firefighters, for instance, bumper stickers reading "Don't hire a girl to do a man's job" were widespread.

In Seattle, which has one of the most sex-integrated fire departments in the country, a male firefighter indicated to a reporter that "There have been very few women who have come across as real aggressive firefighters. When somebody is hanging from a window, it's *my* job to get them out" (*NYT* 2 November 1982; emphasis added). This suggests that female firefighters are considered unprepared to fully participate in the effort, to do their share of the job.

Women's behaviors have been used as evidence that women are unfit. For instance, court testimony reveals that when New York City female firefighters cried, they were accused of being mentally unstable for the job (Berkman v. City of New York, 580 F. Supp. 226 [1983]).

The need for acceptance in order to perform one's job especially is critical for firefighters. Fighting fires is team work, where every member of the team must be trusted to do his or her job. The solidarity of a company then, is of great importance—and solidarity is dependent on the acceptance of and trust between every member. Building solidarity may take years, and social scientists studying this process have noted that "the presence . . . of one individual officer may radically alter the solidarity that has been achieved" (McCarl 1984, 412–13).

In New York City it has been very difficult for women to be accepted into the firefighting team. An example is provided in a report concerning one woman's difficulty in handling the hose nozzle. The supervisor demonstrated "apparent niggardliness in volunteering the kind of detailed criticism and training which any probationary firefighter is entitled to in order to learn the trade" (Berkman v. City of New York, 580 F. Supp. 226 [1983], 238).

In U.S. District Court Judge Charles P. Sifton's first finding of sex discrimination in the Fire Department, he found that female firefighters were subjected to substantial psychological trauma. His decision cites that there was

extensive sexual abuse in the form of unimpeded hazing. . . . [C]rude sexual comments appeared regularly in the form of graffiti and cartoons containing blatant sexual mockery. . . . These included a bra marked with [a female firefighter's] name, a teeshirt mocking her, and crude graffiti questioning her sexual preference and courage. . . . In the case of [another female firefighter], prophylactic devices and a wet vibrator were placed in her bed; her earrings, underwear, and badge were stolen from her locker . . . and her air hose had been disconnected from her tank. (Berkman v. City of New York, Memorandum Decision and Order of District Judge Sifton [8 December 1983], 10–11)

The masculine culture of the occupation extends in other ways into the day-to-day life of these workers, because they virtually live together at the firehouse. Another example of how the culture can be used to deny acceptance involves life at the firehouse. For instance, Robert McCarl, writing on the occupational culture of firefighting, argues that mealtime is "an integral and revealing aspect of firefighting life, . . . a microcosm of the day-to-day canon of technique performance." Thus, "participating in a firehouse meal, like fighting a fire, is an acceptance of a participatory role in a standardized performance activity" (McCarl 1984, 394–95).

However, women do not easily break into such participatory rituals. Judge Sifton found that two women

met with extraordinary difficulties in achieving integration into the unique forms of communal living that are characteristic of the firefighters' workplace. [One woman's] bed was not made by the firefighters assigned this task as a part of their regular duties. She received little help on cooperative tasks in the firehouse. A meal prepared by [another woman] was thrown into the garbage by the men in her firehouse. Both were, in the language of the Department, "put out of the meal," meaning they were denied the opportunity to share in the traditional communal effort to use the cooking facilities of the firehouse to enjoy a common repast. (Berkman v. City of New York, Memorandum Decision and Order [1983], 12)

The New York City Integration Experience

In the mid-1970s, when women were beginning to see the doors of many nontraditional occupations open to them, New York City announced an upcoming examination for entry level firefighters. Many women were interested in and took the test in 1976–77; but in the final analysis no women passed. In 1982, a revised test was offered to these women and 51 eventually passed. New York City was about to begin integrating its firefighting forces.

THE 1976–77 EXAMINATION

The 1976–77 firefighter examination was given in two parts—written and physical. Only those who passed the written test were eligible to take the physical test. The demonstrated skills necessary to pass that physical test included lifting and carrying a 120-pound dummy up and down stairs, squeezing a dynamometer, broad jumping, hanging from a bar, running an obstacle course that included scaling a eight-foot wall, and walking a simulated building ledge. Although records are unavailable on how many women applied to take or took the written test in 1976, we do know that 410 women passed it. Moreover, although we do not know how many of those 410 women chose to continue in the process, we do know that not one woman passed the Fire Department's physical test given in 1977. Almost 8,000 men passed that test.

Based on a claim of disparate impact, a group of women brought a class action suit against the Fire Department in 1979.[2] They claimed that the physical test was discriminatory, that it unfairly excluded women from becoming firefighters. Moreover, they argued that many of the tasks on the examination were not job related. The Federal District Court agreed with the plaintiffs and demanded that the city create a special qualifying examination, revise its physical test to be job related, and then retest the women. The ruling further required that later tests for both men and women be revised to be more job related. In addition, it mandated that the department hire up to 45 female firefighters (Berkman v. City of New York 1985).

This decision was protested by the Uniformed Firefighters Association, which represents the more than 10,000 firefighters in the City of New York. The union's position was that the test did not specifically discriminate against women, but instead it kept both unqualified men and unqualified women out of the job. They feared a new test would lower the standards, endangering not only other firefighters but the public as well. It is important that tests be job related, screening out candidates who are not capable, and that at the same time they be nondiscriminatory.

THE 1982 TEST FOR FEMALE FIREFIGHTER CANDIDATES

In compliance with the court order, the city revised its physical test for the women who failed the 1976–77 test. The new test was to be more job related and included dragging a 145-pound dummy; dragging a heavy 50-foot hose; carrying a 46-pound folded hose up four stories; raising a 20-foot, 58-pound ladder; climbing a ladder and entering a second-story window; carrying a 16-pound tool for forcible entry up five stories; and simulating a forcible entry using an eight-pound sledgehammer. Each candidate had four minutes and nine seconds to perform the test, with a timed rest midway through. Eighty-seven women chose to take this revised test. Of these, 51 passed for a pass rate of nearly 59 percent. Forty-two women obtained positions as firefighter 4th Grade, the probationary grade, in September 1982.

The difficulties of the 42 women who entered the Fire Department in the 1982 class were not over when they were hired. In fact, for many, their problems had only begun. The usual cultural problems of entering an all-male occupation were only magnified by the fact that these women entered under special circumstances, having passed a different test than any of the men had taken. On 4 March 1983, the *New York Times* reported that the "friction between men and women in New York City's Fire Department since women were admitted . . . has broken into the open." The newly appointed fire commissioner was quoted as saying that the relationship between male and female firefighters was one of the biggest problems he faced. The Uniformed Firefighters Association president was quoted as saying, "It's like a time bomb out there. There's a lot of resentment that favoritism is being shown to the women" (Dunlap, 1983b).

Of the 42 women appointed, five were dismissed for poor performance and three resigned during the first year. At the end of their one-year probation, only 34 women remained. Of these, two more were fired, 10 were assigned to an extended probation for up to six months, and 22 were promoted to firefighter 3d grade, for a promotion rate of 65 percent. At that time, 93 percent of the men from the same class were promoted (Dunlap 1983a).

The two women who were dismissed filed suit against the city, charging discrimination. Judge Sifton ruled that they be reinstated to an extended probation, charging that the department had "failed lamentably to prepare its officers and members for the extraordinary task of integrating women into its previously all-male ranks" (Berkman v. City of New York 1983). Testimony and evidence produced by the plaintiffs and later comments by their attorneys documented the extreme kinds of harassment faced by these women, some of which was cited earlier in our discussion of the occupational culture of firefighting. Additional examples include the tires of a woman's car were punctured; men intruded on women in firehouse washrooms; some men refused to speak with women; and women's buttocks, breasts, and hair were touched by male co-workers (Shenon 1983). The court ordered that the two women be restored as probationary firefighters 4th grade.

While a large portion of the harassment undoubtedly resulted from the fact that the Fire Department had not done a good job in preparing its uniformed work force for the introduction of women, the problem must have been exacerbated by the men's notion that the women came in with special treatment. If at all possible, the department needed to eliminate that situation in its next entry examination.

THE 1983 REVISED PHYSICAL TEST FOR FIREFIGHTERS
In response to Judge Sifton's 1983 ruling, the Fire Department was required to create a new bias-free test. The New York City Fire Department and the Departments of Personnel and Law, therefore, jointly designed a new physical examination that they believed would follow federal uniform testing guidelines. They also believed that it would insure their ability to create the best firefighting force possible. There were three special concerns: to ensure that the examination was job related; to ensure that it would control for possible adverse impact against women; and to ensure that it would not dilute standards, endangering the safety of citizens and firefighters. It also seemed clear to city

officials that women's integration into the force would be easier if they passed the same test that men passed. As before, the physical test was preceded by a written examination. Over 550 women passed the written component of the test. Of these, 139 took the physical component and 66 passed it, for a pass rate of slightly over 47 percent.

We will never know how many of the 552 women who passed the written test would have been interested in taking the physical test if the previous lawsuits and the recent dismissal of two women had not had their chilling effects. Clearly, women did not feel welcome in the Fire Department. In a subsequent ruling in 1985, Judge Sifton found an "extraordinary fall off of interest on the part of women candidates who passed the written exam when called on to present themselves for physical testing." He projected that if men and women who passed the written test had responded at the same rate, 432 women would have taken the physical examination instead of 165. He concluded that "the highly publicized events . . . served to discourage women applicants" (Berkman v. City of New York, Memorandum and Order [1985], 29).

The revised New York City firefighter physical exam is a timed, competitive test, which is divided into three major segments—an engine simulation, a rest period, and a ladder simulation. The engine simulation requires a candidate to drag a 3.5-inch-diameter hose 150 feet, then place a folded hose onto his or her shoulder and carry it up three flights of stairs and a distance of 85 feet. He or she must place this hose on a bench and then pull a length of weighted 50-foot hose in through a simulated window. From the moment the hose-pull segment of the test is completed, the candidate begins a 100-second mandatory rest period. During this rest, the candidate must walk down three flights of stairs and proceed approximately 370 feet to the start of the ladder simulation. At the end of 100 seconds, the signal for the ladder simulation begins, regardless of whether the candidate is at the starting point and ready to proceed.

The candidate begins the ladder simulation by scaling a 4.5-foot wall and immediately proceeds 75 feet to the ladder raise. After raising the 20-foot ladder, he or she ascends and descends another 10-foot ladder. At the foot of this ladder, the candidate picks up a 15-pound weight and ascends three flights of stairs. At the top of the stairs, he or she puts down this weight and performs a forcible-entry simulation, hitting a 77-pound weighted tire down a 12.5-foot metal-topped table with an eight-pound mallet. This is followed by a crawl through a U-shaped tunnel, approximately 25 feet long and 2.5 feet wide at the center. The final event involves pulling a 145-pound dummy around the table used in the forcible-entry simulation.

Throughout the entire test, the candidates must wear a weighted vest, the weight being concentrated on the hips and lower back, and an air tank on his or her back. The 40-pound weight simulates the weight of the gear worn by firefighters on the job. The entire test must be completed in under seven minutes for a minimum passing score and in four minutes or less for a perfect passing score.

The Model Training Program

When the 1983 revised physical examination for firefighters was announced, a variety of independent training schools throughout the city began offering prospective candidates instruction and training for the test. These training schools regularly offer test preparation for major city and state tests. A Fire Department survey of the schools showed that very few of the women who had passed the written portion of the firefighter exam were attending the private training programs. In part, women reported that they did not feel welcome in these courses and they were not comfortable training with men who did not make them feel welcome. It was clear that if women were to compete successfully there was a need for training especially targeted to the eligible female candidates.

The Center for Women in Government, with cooperation from the Fire Department, decided to provide physical training for eligible women.[3] The objectives of the training were three-fold:

1. to provide the women taking the firefighter physical test with a program designed to train them for successful completion of the examination;
2. to assist the women to develop the discipline and dedication they need to attain their goals; and
3. to produce women applicants who could compete successfully with men on the same examination and ultimately could get on the single competitive list to become firefighters for the City of New York.

While the revised test required physical fitness and strength, the most important features of the training were technique, pacing, and efficiency of motion.

The majority of the eligible women were untrained and not physically strong or fit. They quickly realized that their participation would require hard work and intense motivation. In addition to teaching the participants physical skills for the examination, the training also gave them information on nutrition, discipline, and training habits for use at home.

The Center for Women in Government sent letters to the 552 women who had passed the written firefighter exam. The letters described the physical training program and invited them to participate at no cost. One hundred thirteen women registered to participate in at least one of the physical training sessions. Of these, 50 women completed the course.[4]

The program was designed to take place in three phases of four sessions each, totaling 12 sessions. Sessions averaged three hours in length and were held twice a week. Each four-session phase consisted of the graduated performance of certain tasks and pieces of the total test, leading to the performance of the entire examination as it would be during test conditions. All phases of the training program included a warm-up stretching and exercising period. Phases I and II also included aerobic training, strength exercises, and weight training.[5]

In *Phase I* participants learned each task of the revised test. In addition, weight training began. Each task of the test and the weights were set up as a separate station. Trainees were divided into groups and moved through the stations where they were taught the techniques behind each skill. Participants were rotated in their small groups from station to station to allow them to develop each new skill separately before trying to put it all together. Participants wore no equipment or weights and were not timed during this phase.

In *Phase II*, only two stations were set up. The first station was the engine simulation of the revised physical examination. The second station was the ladder-and-rescue simulation of the revised test. Thus, in this phase, the trainees practiced the tasks of Part I of the test as a whole, and Part III of the test as a whole. During the first sessions, they were not timed and carried no weights or equipment. In the second session, participants were timed for both parts of the examination but carried no weights or equipment. In the third session, performance on Parts I and III of the examination were timed and participants wore a 20-pound vest. In the final session of this phase, participants walked through Parts I and III wearing the 20-pound tanks and the 20-pound vests, but they were not timed.

Phase III most closely approximated the actual examination. During all four sessions, trainees were timed through Parts I, II, and III, continuously wearing full equipment. This meant that they performed the engine simulation, had a 100-second rest period, and performed the ladder simulation under test conditions. A total score for the test was calculated and recorded. For safety reasons, the trainees were closely monitored for any physiological problems such as dizziness, nausea, hyperventilation, and lack of stamina.

Occasionally, during Phases I and II, new participants would join. In these instances, they started with Phase I activities to learn the appropriate techniques before joining the rest of the group. Many late-starters worked additional time with instructors to develop their skills so that they could catch up to the larger group. Once their techniques were developed, late-starters walked through the test with no equipment and were not timed. If the trainers judged that the trainee could handle it, she walked through with equipment on the third session, still with no timing. By their fourth session, most late-starting trainees were able to assimilate with the group.

Participants and Results

Unfortunately, the age, race/ethnicity, and occupational status of each participant was not formally recorded. Informally, however, it was easy to see that the participants represented a broad spectrum of women in age and race/ethnicity, and they described themselves as representing a broad spectrum of occupational statuses, including unemployed, welfare recipient, construction laborer, military reserve personnel, nurse, and teacher. A few of the participants had firefighters in their families and had been encouraged by relatives to apply, perhaps building a new cultural tradition, expanding from "father and son" to "father and daughter."

Physical training as a strategy for integrating women into nontraditional jobs such as firefighting has proved to be extremely successful. This program demonstrated that, with proper training, women are capable of performing well on the same tests of strength and endurance that men have to pass to enter these occupations.

Fully 92 percent of the women who completed the training passed the physical examination. This is in contrast to an overall pass rate of 47 percent for women. Only 22 percent of the women who did not participate in the training passed the test (see Table 12-1). It seems reasonable to conclude that training women in lifting techniques, pacing, and efficiency of motion had a positive effect on their ability to perform on the physical examination. However, it is important to note that without a comprehensive evaluation we cannot be sure whether there were other differences between women who were trained and those who were not that might have contributed to their differential pass rates. Unlike the process of integrating the first women into the Fire Department, the women who enter based on the 1983 test will have demonstrated the same competencies as men who come into the department. We expect this to improve greatly the cultural process of integration. No longer will female firefighters have to carry the stigma of not having met the "men's standards."

Unfortunately, few of the women passed the combined tests with scores high enough to insure their hire in large numbers. Therefore, once again litigation ensued, suggesting that the physical test remained more difficult than necessary to screen out unqualified candidates. The physical test scores were divided into three ranges with all those in the same range treated equally—as though they had obtained the average score for the range. In addition, Judge Sifton ruled that the written examination discriminated against women and ordered that new written test scores be assigned according to a normal curve distribution. The written and physical examination scores each count as 50 percent of the overall score. A new hiring list then was established (Claffey 1986). This entire process was intended to increase the number of female firefighters appointed. The city opposed the ruling and filed an appeal. The

Table 12-1/Results of the 1983 Physical Training Program for Female Firefighter Candidates in New York City

	WOMEN WHO TOOK EXAM FOR NYC FIREFIGHTER	
	Number	*Percent of Total*
PROGRAM PARTICIPANTS		
Passed exam		
90 or greater	6 (13%)	
85–89	14 (31%)	
80–84	10 (22%)	
75–79	14 (30%)	
70–74	2 (4%)	
Total (passed exam)	46 (100%)	92
Failed exam	4	8
Total (took exam)	50	100
OTHER WOMEN WHO TOOK THE SAME EXAM		
Passed exam		
90 or greater	0 (0%)	
85–89	2 (10%)	
80–84	4 (20%)	
75–79	8 (40%)	
70–74	6 (30%)	
Total (passed exam)	20 (100%)	22
Failed exam	69	78
Total (took exam)	89	100

Source: Center for Women in Government 1983.

Note: Program participants are defined as those women who attended more than half of the sessions offered, that is, those who attended seven or more training sessions.

Uniformed Firefighters Association, with intervenor status, joined the city in its efforts to overturn the decision. This solution was overturned by the Appeals Court for the Second Circuit. Subsequently, the Supreme Court let stand a lower court ruling that New York City's test based largely on speed and strength was valid (*NYT*, 6 October 1987). The impact of the ruling was that at most, only one or two women would qualify from the current list.

In September 1987, another written test for firefighter was given. The Fire Department made an effort to reach female applicants (and minority applicants as well). Nevertheless the percentage of women applying to the Fire Department remains lower than women applying to any other municipal uniformed service. The Fire Department is currently investigating the establishment of a physical training program for the women who pass the written test. This time the physical training will focus on enhancing the speed with which candidates complete the test.

Thus, while physical training undoubtedly was beneficial in promoting the sex integration of the New York City Fire Department, it is not enough. Physical training helped the women to demonstrate their competence to do the physical parts of the job as well as men do them. However, until the department solves the larger social and cultural problems involved in bringing women into a nontraditional occupation, women will continue to suffer disadvantages. The Department of Sanitation in New York City has learned from the Fire Department's difficulties. It has approached the integration challenge from a different perspective, to which we now turn.

Women in Sanitation

Sanitation worker is the last all-male job in New York City's uniformed services. The most important function of a sanitation worker is to pick up the city's garbage and transport it to a transfer station. On an average day a collection truck crew picks up between seven and 15 tons of garbage. Until August 1986, the job had never been done by a woman.

In 1983, the city began to recruit applicants for a new sanitation worker examination. One of the objectives of the recruitment drive was to encourage women to apply. As with the firefighter examination, the test had two parts—the first was written, the second was physical. Almost 3,000 women passed the written section and were eligible to take the physical examination.

As preparation of the physical test began, there were serious questions being asked about any woman's ability to pass a job-related test for the position. Staff at the Center for Women in Government, based on our experience with the Fire Department, were convinced that providing physical training would increase female applicants' chances of passing the physical test and subsequently being hired as sanitation workers.

The Recent History of Sanitation Work in New York City
In 1937, when Fiorello LaGuardia was re-elected mayor, sanitation men earned between $5.00 and $6.00 a day, worked six days a week, and had only two paid holidays. These men tried to improve their status through benevolent associations, but the associations were unable to improve the workers' conditions. This provided the impetus for unionization. In 1956, after almost 20 years of conflict over union jurisdiction, sanitation men voted to become a Teamsters local. They immediately won a wage increase, a 40-hour workweek, and the unification of all related positions into the official title of "sanitation man." In 1961, a full grievance procedure was established. In 1962, the

Table 12-2/Applicants Taking the Physical Examination for New York City Sanitation Worker

DATE	MEN	WOMEN	TOTAL
1957	11,728	0	11,728
1961	8,521	0	8,521
1965	25,156	0	25,156
1970	17,462	0	17,462
1974	68,784	60	68,844
1984	43,229	1,822	45,051
Total	174,880	1,882	176,762

Sources: Perry 1978 (Statistics for 1957–74); New York City 1984a (Statistics for 1984).

men were allowed to retire after 25 years of service. In the mid-1960s, this was reduced to a 20-year retirement policy and salary parity with firefighters, police officers, and correction officers (New York City 1984a).[6]

Between the 1956 unionization and 1974, five civil service examinations for sanitation worker were given. Although over 130,000 people took the physical examinations, only 60 were women, and all of these were in 1974.[7] (see Table 12-2). There was no test given between 1974 and 1984 because of the city's fiscal crisis and its resulting inability to hire any additional workers.

A Male-Dominated Environment
Within the uniformed field operation in the Department of Sanitation there is surprising homogeneity. Almost 80 percent of the current job holders are white and a large percentage have Irish and Italian surnames. Until about 10 years ago, the sanitation garages were a totally male environment—even the clerical jobs were performed by male sanitation workers. The first time women were introduced into the garages was through a program called "civilianization." This program replaced male uniformed personnel performing clerical functions with lower-paid nonuniformed clerical staff. The clerical replacements almost always were women.

The fact that employees often shared common characteristics of sex, race, and ethnicity has had an important impact on the development of the organizational culture. For example, these men tend to have very traditional family lives. According to an unpublished department survey comparing New York City sanitation workers to the general population, proportionately more New York City sanitation men maintain a family where their wives do not work outside the home than do married men in the general population of the city, the state, or the nation.

Collegiality in the garages centers on shared work. There is considerable socializing on the job, during breaks, and after the day's work has been completed. "The shared on-the-job socialization is a large part of worker gratification" (Jervis 1985). Moreover, sanitation workers often are proud of their jobs and defensive about negative public attitudes toward their work.

The introduction of women represents a major disruption in the culture of the workplace. Because the organization prides itself on being "New York's strongest," women doing the job of "the strongest" is a threat to the mythology of the workplace. Women's entry is a source of male resentment, mostly focused on women's presumed inability to do the job. Many men assume that women will not be able to perform the collection part of the job and that if they can, then they are not "real women."

In the early stages of discussing the potential introduction of women as sanitation workers, typical comments around the garages included: "A woman can't keep up with my pace"; "She'll get the easy assignments"; "If a woman can do the job, it may be that she has a woman's body, but there is a man inside"; "They water down the test for the women" (Jervis 1985; Center for Women in Government 1983).

Because women had passed the written and physical tests and because management was committed to women's integration, men in the field eventually realized that women were going to become sanitation workers. At that point the tone of some of their conversations changed to include phrases like, "But if she can do the job, it's O.K. with me." This change in tone represented a major and a critical shift. The men began to realize that performance is the only appropriate test for the introduction and retention of women. It does not focus on sex, sexual preference, or favoritism. The focus is where it should be —on their ability to do the job.

The New York City Integration Experience

The entrance of women into the New York City sanitation force in 1986 signified the end of major and complete occupational segregation in the city. However, as the negative quotations cited above demonstrate, integration is not happening without considerable resentment on the part of the members of the previously all-male sanitation work force. To understand some of the resentment toward women, it is important to be able to compare the city's experiences with its two most recent sanitation worker tests.

A COMPARISON OF THE 1974 AND 1984 SANITATION TESTS

The 1974 test was the first one open to women as a result of the 1972 amendment to the Civil Rights Act. The primary recruitment strategy was not aimed at women but instead was aimed generally at all graduating high school students. There were age and height requirements: to be eligible to take the test, individuals had to be at least 18 years old at the time of appointment and no more than 29 by the application date. Also, eligible candidates had to stand at least 5 feet 3 inches without shoes. There were two parts of the 1974 examination, a written test and a physical test. The written test was given first and only candidates who passed that were allowed to take the physical test.

The 1974 physical test required the candidate first to pick up a garbage can from a shelf, carry it 35 feet, and place it on another shelf. Second, the candidate had to pick up another can and return it to the first shelf. This was done eight times. Third, the candidate had to lift and carry six cans weighing 60 pounds each and 16 cans weighing 40 pounds each. Each candidate was rated on how many cans were carried in three minutes. Fourth, the candidate was required to carry a 40-pound can through a maze, which included climbing a six-foot wall. Finally, in 70 seconds, the candidate was required to lift a 60-pound can up 36 inches and return it to the floor three times. This was increased to 70-, 80-, 90-, and 100-pound cans lifted three times each until the limit of strength and endurance was reached. Almost 69,000 men and 60 women took the physical test; while approximately 50 percent of the men passed, 59 of the women failed the physical test, for a pass rate of less than 1 percent.

Although this test was given in 1974, appointments were not made from the list until 1980, because of the city's fiscal crisis. By 1976, the actual number of sanitation workers had declined from 10,800 to 8,626. As a result of citywide layoffs, supervisors were "bumped down" to sanitation workers and sanitation workers were let go. Another economy move that kept the number of sanitation workers from returning to pre-fiscal-crisis levels was the introduction of a new vehicle program that reduced the number of workers on a truck from three to two. Since all laid-off workers were called back to work before any vacancies could be filled by new employees, it was not until 1980 that vacancies could be filled with candidates who had taken the test in 1974.[8]

The 1974 list contained the names of the over 30,000 people who passed the written and physical examinations. Naturally, by 1980, since such a long time had passed between the testing and the first hire, many people had already found other employment. Nevertheless, the list produced a sufficient number of candidates. These candidates now were considerably older than those produced by previous lists. Although there was a maximum age requirement for taking the test, there was none for appointment. Thus, it was not unusual for new employees hired in 1985 to be nearly 40 years old. While this provided the benefit of more mature men with more work experience, it also presented problems for some of the older men who had difficulty entering such a physically demanding job at their age.

In preparing for the 1984–85 test, the Department of Sanitation made a concentrated effort to expand its minority representation. This recruitment effort was important because there was a great underrepresentation of minority employees among the sanitation workers. Women were totally unrepresented. Although the recruitment efforts were not targeted directly at women, public relations efforts did include pictures of women and men, white and minority, in subway and bus recruitment posters. The recruitment drive resulted in the distribution of over a quarter of a million applications. Of these 86,845 people applied for the job of sanitation worker.[9]

In total, 64,833 men and women took the written test. Of those for whom race/ethnicity was recorded, 47 percent were white, 34 percent were black, and 19 percent were Hispanic. The sex breakdown was 95 percent male, 5 percent female.

The test used multiple-choice questions and was scored either pass or fail. Of those who took the test, approximately 95 percent passed. The percentages of those who passed reflect the applicant pool almost exactly: 95 percent were male and 5 percent were female; the racial composition was 46 percent white, 34 percent black, 19 percent Hispanic, and 1 percent Asian. Once the written test process was completed, the City of New York, like all municipal employers, was grappling with the question of what constitutes a job-related physical test.

In light of the experience of the Fire Department, the Sanitation Department was eager to test correctly and to retain control over its own testing procedure, rather than to have to deal with court intervention. After review, the city determined that previous tests were unrelated to the actual job. In previous tests sanitation worker candidates had been required to broad jump, scale walls, and run endurance and speed tests.

In 1984, there would be great effort expended to create a test that reflected the duties and skills of the actual job and to communicate the relevance of the new test to existing sanitation workers. In "The Open Door," a publication of the Department of Sanitation, the commissioner stated that,

> in order to construct a fair and "job-related" exam, we sent a team of measurement experts, along with sanitation workers and supervisors, to a district where the workload is heavy . . . because most new sanitation workers . . . must be ready to perform under the most difficult circumstances from their first day on the job. (Steisel 1985)

Test design experts were sent with sanitation workers to measure the actual weights of garbage bags, the average number of bags loaded, the distance usually walked from the curb to the truck, and the average distance from one set of garbage cans to the next.

DESCRIPTION OF THE REVISED PHYSICAL TEST FOR SANITATION WORKERS

The revised sanitation worker physical examination was a timed test. Each candidate had one minute to lift a series of weighted bags from the floor to a hopper that duplicated the height of a garbage truck (38 inches). This was followed by a 30-second interval. At the end of the interval the candidate moved to the next group of weighted bags. There were 18 stations with a total of 147 bags, each weighing between eight and 65 pounds.

A candidate's score was based on how well he or she performed the physical test. To get 100 percent, all 147 bags must have been loaded into the hoppers within the allotted time. Initial hiring was to be done through a random selection from among all those who scored 100 percent. The next score is 70 percent. A candidate who loaded at least 132 bags within the allotted time received 70 percent. After everyone who scored 100 was offered a position, the people in the second score band would become eligible for appointment. Candidates who loaded fewer than 132 bags failed the test.

The Model Training Program
The Center for Women in Government, after its success in raising the pass rate of female firefighters, wanted to offer similar training for female candidates taking the sanitation test. Getting this program going in the Sanitation Department initially was a more difficult task than in the Fire Department. The Fire Department had called to request assistance, whereas the Sanitation Department was not convinced that any special efforts for women were required or desirable.

The task first required convincing the Department of Sanitation that training the women candidates, even by an outside group with private funding, would not jeopardize the test or make it more vulnerable to legal challenge. The best example was the success of training on the firefighter examination. Second, the Center for Women in Government encouraged the department to pilot test the examination to determine whether *any* women would be able to pass. Finally, for this program to work, it also required convincing the city to manipulate the order of calling women to take the examination so that they would have time to be trained before their test. Once convinced of the benefit of training women, the Department of Sanitation supported efforts to delay the testing of any woman until after they were trained. The Department of Personnel also was convinced of the merit of this plan and agreed to hold off calling any women until their initial training with the Center was complete.

Based on the test designed by the New York City Department of Personnel and described above, the Center developed a six-week physical training program that emphasized the techniques needed to do the job coupled with actual development of upper body strength.[10] This required individualized instruction. In addition, simulated test equipment had to be designed and built, which meant significantly higher capital costs than for the firefighter training, for which the equipment was provided. The Center's funds were limited. Therefore, the initial physical training program for sanitation worker candidates had to be viewed as a small pilot, to assess whether physical training could significantly increase women's pass rate on the physical test.

The Center sent a recruitment letter to every woman on the list of eligible candidates. The letter described the training program and the process of candidate selection. Each woman who wished to be included in a lottery to select program participants was instructed to fill out and return a postcard.[11]

The Center sent letters to 2,200 women. Although 2,800 had passed the written test, 600 women were "lost" in the two-year period between the written examination and the physical examination. This loss rate is typical and is attributed to candidates' moving without filing a change-of-address form or losing interest in the test.

The return rate for the postcards indicating interest in physical training exceeded expectations. On the basis of the return from the firefighter training, the Center had expected about 400 to 500 women to reply. Instead, over half of the 2,200 women responded. Because the initial training program could accommodate only 100 women, the Center randomly selected 125 names, assuming there would be some dropouts. There were fewer dropouts than anticipated, and 116 women participated in the initial training.

Participants took part in intensive physical training in preparation for the sanitation test. Each woman participated in three training sessions a week, two hours a session. Training sessions met on Mondays, Tuesdays, and Thursdays in the early evenings. The women were divided into three classes of approximately 40 participants and each class was assigned two highly qualified instructors allowing for a ratio of one instructor for every 20 women. This provided close supervision for all training programs.

The program had three components: strength and muscular endurance, cardiovascular and aerobic fitness, and specific training for the New York City sanitation test.

The strength and muscular endurance component had two subcomponents —weight training and circuit weight training. Weight training involves standard techniques of progressive resistance. Weight training at approximately 70 percent of the 1-RM (one repetition maximum, determined prior to training) of the major muscle groups was used. Special emphasis was placed on the specific musculature required for the sanitation test and for subsequent sanitation work. The standard training techniques of six to eight repetitions an exercise and two to three sets an exercise were used with progressive increases in the amount of weight lifted for each of the major muscle groups. Circuit weight training involves relatively recent developments in weight training. In circuit training one lifts lighter weights (30 to 40 percent of 1-RM) at higher repetitions (16 to 22 repetitions) during timed exercise periods in order to engage both the muscular and cardiovascular system in moving specific weights. Usually eight to 10 exercise or circuit weight stations are employed, with each station providing exercise of a different major muscle group. Individuals made two or three trips around the total circuit to complete an exercise session.

The cardiovascular and aerobic fitness component used research-proven techniques of interval training to provide general aerobic training of the major muscle groups. Special emphasis was placed on interval techniques that simulate the energy requirements of intermittent and paced sanitation work. Training intensity was governed using target heart rates (THR) at 70 percent to 85 percent of the age-predicted maximum heart rate for each individual in order to insure sufficient cardiovascular stress to produce fitness improvements. Participants learned how to select exercise intensities based on THR and how to monitor pulse rate during training. Since exercise heart rates decrease with training, the participants learned how to adjust their training intensities so that heart rates are maintained in the appropriate zone.

Over half of each training session was spent on activities specifically related to the sanitation test. The activities in this third component included lifting simulated refuse containers of varying weights, carrying several refuse bags, and lifting and throwing refuse bags into simulated dumpsters. All tasks were practiced within the constraints of the specific time limits set by the New York City Personnel Department. Participants used the training principles of progressive overload during practice and were instructed in the proper techniques of lifting, carrying, and throwing in order to be successful and avoid injury. All aspects of a realistic testing environment were maintained.

The First Training: Participants and Results

The Center learned from its experience in the Fire Department to gather more background information from the participants. During the first week of the sanitation training, the Center distributed a survey to the candidates. Eighty-three of the women responded. According to their responses, 72 percent of the women were black or Hispanic. This compares with a 44 percent black or Hispanic rate for the male sanitation examination applicant pool. The women were primarily within the age range of 26 to 35; more than 50 percent were 30 years old or older, two were over 60, and several were in their fifties.[12] It is interesting to note the age distribution in light of the fact that the age restriction had been removed for the first time for this test. Previously candidates could not be over 29 years old when they applied. Eighty-two percent of those responding had responsibility for children. Six percent of the respondents were college graduates and 41 percent had attended some college. A little over one-third (36 percent) of the women had performed manual labor; 19 percent of the women had worked outdoors on construction or other projects.

The respondents reported wanting the job of sanitation worker primarily for economic reasons. Forty-three percent were unemployed at the time of the survey. Most indicated that being a sanitation worker would be an advancement in their career, salary, or benefits. One of the surprising facts that emerged about the group was the apparently high number of women who were recipients of Aid to Families with Dependent Children (AFDC). Most respondents expected to like the job "a lot."

The participants were encouraged to work together and a remarkable sense of comradery and mutual support developed over the life of this program. After the women in the first session took their physical tests they organized a celebration in the park.

The participants who trained through this program passed at a higher rate than their untrained counterparts. Based on unofficial data from the Department of Personnel, the pass rate for trainees was 92 percent, compared with an 84 percent pass rate overall.[13] Once again, it is reasonable to conclude that physical training had a positive effect on women's ability to pass the test. However, without conducting a comprehensive evaluation, controlling for women's characteristics, there is no way to determine whether other differences between trainees and other women contributed to their differential pass rates.

The first group of women to seek entrance to the job of sanitation worker was newsworthy. The class received an enormous amount of media coverage. More than 20 articles appeared in local and national newspapers. The *New York Times*, the *Wall Street Journal*, and the *Christian Science Monitor* ran articles. Local television news programs covered the training and two of the participants were featured on an award-winning focus segment of the "MacNeil/Lehrer News Hour."

The Second Training: Participants and Results
The combination of the attention from the media, the success of the training program, the hundreds of additional women who had indicated they wanted to be part of the training program, and the interest of funders in continuing to support this effort, resulted in the Center's putting together a second round of training.[14]

In consultation with the trainer consultants and based on experience with the first training, the Center decided that the program could be run in four weeks instead of six, thus reducing the cost. The second program began four months after the first one. During that period, men and women had been taking the physical test.

The 100 women who participated in the second training were selected from among those who had not yet taken the physical test. The participants did not show up as regularly as the first group, perhaps because of the winter weather, the fact that it was light outside when the first group began training, or the days of training—instead of a Monday, Tuesday, Thursday schedule, the second group met Monday, Wednesday, and Friday. The reduced four-week training period did not appear to diminish the effectiveness of the training. By the last week, participants were picking up the weighted bags in the allotted time.

In many ways, the survey of this second group indicates that they were similar to the earlier trainees. they were overwhelmingly minority (91.8 percent) and most were employed. They worked in clerical, sales, and hospital occupations for the most part. Twenty-nine percent were receiving AFDC. Thirty-three percent of the respondents had friends or relatives working for the Department of Sanitation and almost 50 percent had friends or relatives in the other uniformed services (fire, police, or correction). The women reported wanting the jobs for career advancement, job security, and the opportunity to work outside; 66 percent anticipated that they would enjoy the work "a lot."

One of the most rewarding aspects of the second training group was the Center's ability to assist a large number of women who were AFDC recipients. The program offered an opportunity to help these unemployed women become employable in relatively high-paying jobs and thus enhance the city's ability to provide employment opportunities for female heads of household.

Like the first group, the participants in the second training passed at a higher rate than those who did not receive training. The actual pass rate was collected through a telephone follow-up survey of participants. Of those contacted, 98 percent passed the physical test, with 90 percent receiving a score of 100.

The Department of Sanitation physical test did not turn out to be as difficult to pass as was first imagined, although the trained women did pass at higher rates than the untrained women. The training demonstrated clearly that women can take and pass the sanitation physical test, and it fostered a sense that they would be able to stand "toe-to-toe" with the men in the department.

Conclusions and Final Recommendations

The success of the Sanitation Department and the failure of the Fire Department to recruit, hire, and integrate women is the result of a variety of considerations. These considerations include the leadership of each agency during the transition, the political environment in the city, and the perceived status of firefighters and sanitation workers. A full discussion of these issues falls outside the perview of this discussion. However, we did learn some important lessons.

The Center's experience with physical training of female candidates is singular. Training works. The pass rate of the women who participated in the firefighter training far surpasses women in an untrained group. Similar relative pass rates are indicated in the sanitation worker examination.

If admission to these high-paying uniformed jobs requires demonstration of physical capabilities, then training for women must continue. However, we do not believe sex-segregated training must continue indefinitely. Private training companies and ethnicity-based fraternal organizations currently provide training only to men. When and if they are willing and able to provide training to women, we believe the need for special training will be over.

While physical training proved successful in assisting women to gain entry into firefighting and sanitation work, successfully integrating women into previously all-male occupations requires more than just physical preparation of women candidates. It involves change throughout the entire organization. We have identified six additional areas that need attention in order to enhance the integration process.

1. *Agency Support*. It is critical that the head of the agency go on record as being supportive of the integration of women. The agency head must publicly support integration as often as possible. Without such explicit top-level support, managers and supervisors may feel the message is ambiguous at best and therefore discourage or even sabotage successful integration.

2. *Facilities*. Agencies must make appropriate accommodations in their facilities. At a minimum, fire and sanitation women need toilet and changing facilities. In the New York City Fire Department, this was accomplished by putting locks on the inside of doors in firehouses so that both men and women had privacy when using the same facilities. In the Department of Sanitation separate toilet, shower, and changing areas are being constructed in garage facilities.

3. *Policies and Procedures*. Some new policies such as those covering pregnancy must be created, others such as those covering paternity/maternity leave must be examined to be sure they do not have an unanticipated and negative impact on women. For example, light duty positions should be reviewed to ensure that women and men are assigned light duty fairly and without regard to their sex. In addition, sex-neutral language must be introduced in job titles and job orders. For example, the term "foreman" should be changed to "supervisor," "fireman" to "firefighter," and "sanitation man" to "sanitation worker."

4. *Training*. Top to bottom training in managing, supervising, and working in a changing environment is needed to prepare the work force for the change.[15] In the first stages of integration, the firstline supervisors are the most critical since they are responsible for the day-to-day operations.

5. *Sexual Harassment*. Sexual harassment must be stopped. It is endemic in the traditional workplace. And, when an all-male work force is

integrated, it should be assumed that sexual harassment will occur there too. The form sexual harassment usually takes is the creation of a "hostile, intimidating work environment" (Equal Employment Opportunity Commission 1980). Whether intentional or unintentional, sexual harassment is illegal under Title VII of the Civil Rights Act. If action is not taken to stop sexual harassment, management can be held liable.

6. *Communication.* It is imperative to keep lines of communication open within the agency. The New York City Fire Department established a special liaison. He is a high-ranking officer who has regular contact with the commissioner, the women, and the women's co-workers to ensure that lines of communication are kept open, complaints are heard, and responses are immediate. In addition, public attention will be focused on any agency that is integrating for the first time, which means the women may receive special attention which the men do not get. This can result in a sense of unfairness among the men. Agencies must be sensitive in handling this situation.

The Sanitation and Fire departments in New York City share some common characteristics. They both have jobs that have been held exclusively by men. They both use physical tests as gate-keeping devices. They both select recruits from a list that ranks individuals on the basis of physical prowess. In these agencies and other agencies similar to them, there is an acute need to continue to provide physical training for women applicants in order to increase the pool of eligible female candidates. However, the job does not end at increasing the pool of candidates. Organizations sincerely interested in successful integration will use training as one part of their strategy and will also give attention to the other aspects of organizational life that affect the integration process.

Notes

Acknowledgments: We wish to thank the New York City Fire Department and the Departments of Personnel and Sanitation for their cooperation in the efforts reported here. We especially thank Deputy Assistant Chief Anthony DeVita at the Fire Department, and Vito Turso, Director of Public Affairs at the Department of Sanitation. In addition, we are grateful to Norma Ricucci, Fredda Merzon, Diane Strock-Lynskey, Audrey Seidman, and Nan Carroll, as well as to Sharon Harlan and Ronnie Steinberg, for their helpful comments.

1. Firefighting is also largely a white occupation. In New York City, white men constitute approximately 92 percent of all firefighters, black 5 percent, Hispanics 2 percent, and Asians, Pacific Islanders, American Indians, and Alaskan Natives combined 1 percent (New York City 1984b).

2. A 1972 amendment to Title VII of the Civil Rights Act of 1964 extended the act to municipalities and resulted in increased interest in ensuring that employment tests are job related. Most important, the courts had ruled that an employer must be able to justify as job related any employment selection procedure that has a disparate impact on women as job related. The "Four-fifths Rule," commonly used as a guide by those enforcing the law, stipulates that if women (or any protected class) do not pass at least at four-fifths the rate of men (or a nonprotected class), that is evidence of a disparate impact ("Uniform Guidelines on Employee Selection Procedures" 1978).

3. The funds for this training were supplied by the Edna McConnell Clark Foundation, the Fund for the City of New York, and the Hugh Hefner Foundation.

4. Participants who completed the course are defined as those women who attended more than half (seven) of the training sessions.

5. The training was subcontracted to the Boone Training Program. For the previous 18 months its director, Maureen Boone, had provided physical training for firefighter candidates both through the New York City Fire Department and private training schools. The staff for this project consisted of 29 firefighters, civilians with degrees in physical education, and civilians with college physical education backgrounds and coaching experience.

6. During the fiscal crisis the 20-year retirement was increased to 30 years for new hires.

7. Of these 60, 59 failed the physical test. See section entitled "A Comparison of the 1974 and 1984 Sanitation Tests."

8. The one woman who passed was not offered a position.

9. Ironically, even with the outreach recruitment program, 70 percent of the women who answered a Center for Women in Government survey said they heard about the test through the Civil Service newspaper or through a friend or relative.

10. The funding for the initial training program came from the Edna McConnell Clark Foundation, Tambrands Corporation, and the Fund for the City of New York. The program consultants were Dr. John Magel and Dr. William McArdel of the Physical Education Department at Queens College, City University of New York. They designed the actual training and equipment.

11. The postcard requested only name, address, and day and evening telephone numbers. In hindsight, it probably would have been helpful also to have collected Social Security numbers because these were used to identify candidates by the Department of Personnel, and age, race/ethnicity, and AFDC status for research purposes and for securing additional funding from social services agencies.

12. This resulted in the additional requirement of a physician's note for women over 35. Two visibly pregnant women were also required to get their physician's permission to participate. Both pregnant women voluntarily dropped out of the program.

13. This information was reported by the Department of Sanitation in a meeting held in October 1985.

14. The funding for the second training came from the New York State Department of Social Services, the Tortuga Foundation, and New York Community Trust, sources interested in employment potential for women receiving Aid to Families with Dependent Children and young women.

15. The Center has prepared such a curriculum for the New York City Depart-

ment of Sanitation. Using the curriculum, the department is in the process of training its own work force.

References

Center for Women in Government. 1983. "Training of Female Candidates for New York City Firefighter Physical Exam." Final Report. Center for Women in Government and Boone Training Program, Albany.

Claffey, Michael. 1986. "FDNY Won't Buy 'Lotto' Rescoring for Firefighters." *The Chief-Leader*, 28 February.

Dunlap, David W. 1983a. "City Fire Department to Give 22 of 34 Women Full Status." *New York Times*, 7 September.

————. 1983b. "Fire Department Friction on Women Goes to Court." *New York Times*, 4 March.

Dunshee, Kenneth Holcomb. 1948. *As You Pass By*. New York: Hastings.

Equal Employment Opportunity Commission. 1980. "Guidelines on Discrimination by Sex." *Federal Register* 45 (10 November).

Goodwin, Michael. 1982. "Fire Department's First 42 Women Take Oath as Probationary Firefighters." *New York Times*, 22 September.

Jervis, Nancy. 1985. "Sanmen and Sanwomen: Problems and Perspectives." Report prepared for the New York City Department of Sanitation, 23 December.

McCarl, Robert S. 1984. "You've Come a Long Way—And Now This Is Your Retirement: An Analysis of Performance in Firefighting Culture." *Journal of American Folklore* 97, no. 386: 393–422.

McDonnell, Vincent D. 1968. "Nine Days That Shook New York City." *USA Record*, 29 February.

New York City. Fire Department. 1965. *History of Firefighting in New York City: 1865–1965*. New York.

————. Department of Personnel. 1974. Notice of Examination, Amended Notice (4 January) no. 3090, Sanitation Man, Official Number 1.2.74 70112.

————. Department of Sanitation. 1984a. EEO Report.

————. Fire Department. 1984b. Uniform Workforce EEO-4 Forms. August.

New York Times. 1982. "Female Firefighters an Issue in Seattle." 2 November.

Perry, Stewart E. 1978. *San Francisco Scavengers*. Berkeley: University of California Press.

Shenon, Philip. 1983. "2 Women Win Bias Suit Against Fire Department." *New York Times*, 9 December.

Steisel, Norman. 1985. "The Open Door." Report prepared for the New York City Department of Sanitation, January.

"Uniform Guidelines on Employee Selection Procedures." 1978. *Federal Register* 43: 38290, 40223.

13/Expanding Occupational Choices in Michigan's Secondary Vocational Education

Elizabeth H. Giese

Vocational education is going through a period of upheaval. Its appropriateness at the high school level in the post-industrial age is being questioned, funding is being reduced, and people are increasingly concerned about the segregation by sex in occupational training programs that is common in vocational education. The goals reflected in the Carl D. Perkins Vocational Education Act of 1984 to change secondary vocational education address these concerns: to reduce the occupational segregation reflected in its present structure and content, and to develop in society the skills needed to respond to economic change and technological development. In particular, vocational education must change in order to train adequately the large number of future workers who will require math and computer-related skills. Whether those changes will reinforce or reduce occupational sex stereotyping in vocational education is a crucial issue for women living and working in industrial states.

Michigan, automobile capital of the world and frontier of the industrial heartland, has endured the highest unemployment since the Great Depression. In the wake of this industrial decline, Michigan has decided to get down to what it knows best: building on its heavy manufacturing base to become a leading center of durable goods manufacturing. The rationale for this new economic strategy grows out of the state's economic history:

We possess, [says a state- and university-sponsored report,] some of the largest manufacturing firms in the world in a variety of industries, including automobiles, steel, machinery, office equipment, chemicals, pharmaceuticals, appliances, and office furniture. Our management and labor skills are concentrated in manufacturing firms to a degree perhaps greater than any other state in the nation. We have a vast indus-

316

trial infrastructure, highways, railroads, airports, water and related resources, physical plant, equipment, labor—created expressly to support manufacturing. (Ross 1984, 53)

Michigan plans to become the "factory of the future"—developing a world-wide business expected to generate over $30 billion a year in sales by 1990 just for automated factory robots, computer controls, and materials-handling systems (Ross 1984, 56).

This economic strategy has two major tenets that have implications for vocational education:

1. In Michigan's emergence as a center of complex manufacturing, "new technology" will not be a separate industrial sector; it will be at the heart of every industrial sector. . . .
2. Brain power will replace back and hand power for most employees in plants with complex manufacturing processes. (Ross 1984, 58, 59)

Thus, traditional skill training and a strong physique will no longer be enough to get a well-paid job in Michigan. The need for skills in dealing with the complexities of new technology will go far beyond the robotics and computer-related manufacturing industry. For example, the auto industry is becoming deeply involved in the technology of robotics, in computer-aided design and computer-aided manufacturing. According to the president of General Motors, Roger B. Smith, worker brain power will be needed for workers to participate actively in decision-making areas formerly the territory of management (Smith 1985, 4).

It is not clear how vocational education will be modified to meet the state's new labor needs. Some suggest a "Tech Prep" approach involving a clearly articulated program that provides two years of high school and two years of postsecondary training in technical fields. Others propose a kindergarten through twelfth grade technology curriculum. Still others propose a realignment of vocational program offerings and curriculum changes. For instance, some suggest adding training in entrepreneurial skills to office-related vocational programs. Also, proposals have been made to change clerical programs to emphasize administrative support and management skills, providing the skill-basis for redesigning clerical job ladders. Another suggestion is to add a grade thirteen, to provide a concentrated high school vocational education experience after the twelfth grade.

Yet, a third trend that will affect Michigan's economic strategy is not even in the "Path to Prosperity" report: the increasing numbers of women joining the workforce. According to a report by the University of Michigan Institute for Social Research, in the last decade women accounted for 61 percent of Michigan's labor force growth and nearly 65 percent of women between 18 and 64 were working or seeking work in 1984 (Sarri 1984, 3). Will women be trained and prepared to take part in this complex manufacturing industrial society—or is this economic strategy primarily being designed by men for men?

To insure women's full participation in Michigan's economic strategy requires that women be educated for the work of the future. This shift to brain power in manufacturing industries could benefit women, but they must have the required math and science background. And, to obtain these job-related skills, they must enroll in trade and industry vocational training programs at both the high school and postsecondary levels.

Michigan is attempting to address the need for math and science education in general. Following a study that found fewer than 50 percent of Michigan students were taking math beyond the ninth grade (Giese 1982, 2), a 1984 State Board of Education plan for educational improvement set voluntary standards for local school districts that require two years of math and two years of science for high school graduation (Michigan State Board of Education 1984). The new requirements may put females and males on a more equitable footing, at least in course preparation, because many technical jobs now require high school algebra and geometry and some biological and physical science.

Despite this attempted shift in curriculum, many researchers and practitioners are increasingly concerned that even when a young woman takes and does well in a course, it does not translate into new occupational choices. Although things are changing slowly, about 80 percent of women continue to work in a mere 20 out of 420 occupations (Linn 1982, 7). Connected to this occupational choice and opportunity structure, many of the traditional vocational education programming areas for women remain in clerical, sales, service, and health fields, areas that constitute the limited occupational sphere of most working women. Because the Michigan State Advisory Council on Vocational Education views career choices as "among the most crucial that a person ever makes," helping to determine economic security, job mobility, and life satisfaction (Dietrich, Atkinson, and Foote 1985, 2), it has tried to increase sex equity in vocational education. This chapter reports on this experience.

Michigan's Record on Sex Equity in Vocational Education

Forty percent of Michigan's eleventh and twelfth graders are in wage-earning vocational programs. The distribution of girls and boys in different areas of study is quite unequal in Michigan, as it is nationwide. The state's largest program is Trade and Industry, with 42,345 students. It has a 15 percent female enrollment (Dietrich, Atkinson, and Foote 1985, 6). An analysis of Michigan vocational enrollment data over a three-year period from 1981 through 1983 found the small gains of females in Trade and Industry cannot be traced to females entering courses that lead to apprenticeship opportunities. In fact, the number of females in cosmetology courses always exceeds the number of females who are enrolling in all other Trade and Industry courses.

Even within programs, the sexes cluster extensively in different courses. For example, females are 85 percent of the 21,376 students in the Business/ Office program. Males in this program disproportionately cluster in business data processing. Gains in the overall enrollment of males in the Business/ Office program are attributed in great part to the inclusion of high tech and computer-related courses in the curriculum. The wage-earning Home Economics Related Occupations program, 10,523 students, is 65 percent female with the greatest number of males enrolled in food management. The Agricultural program, 9,282 students, is 28 percent female, with the greatest number of females taking horticulture. Health Occupations, 8,616 students, is 85 percent female with the greatest number of males concentrated in a health occupations cluster course.

The problem with where girls are enrolled is that vocational education is training large numbers of them for relatively low-paying historically female jobs with few opportunities for advancement out of occupational ghettos. For example, even in relatively new fields like computer sciences, girls make up 59 percent of Michigan's computer data processing classes and 60 percent of the computer operations classes. By contrast, girls are only 36 percent of computer math courses. What follows is that girls disproportionately enter a narrow selection of lower-paying computer jobs involving clerical and administrative support while computer math students (largely male) strengthen their options for jobs in a wider range of science and technical occupations and in higher paying fields (Giese 1982, 1).

The Health Program's curriculum focus is on entry-level lower-level jobs in the medical field, rather than on preparing young women for leadership and upward mobility in the health professions. On the other hand, agricultural students, most of whom are boys, learn leadership and entrepreneurial skills as a part of their training, even though they may enter the job market as farm laborers. Similarly, in Trade and Industry classes, boys train for jobs that can lead to apprenticeships or to self-employment in an industry.

Secondary vocational education is, unfortunately, the training ground for subsequent occupational segregation in the labor market. According to the National Center for Research in Vocational Education:

- Among males, twice as many vocational concentrators as nonvocational graduates worked in craft occupations (33 percent compared to 15 percent).
- Among females, 61 percent of vocational concentrators worked in clerical occupations, whereas 37 percent of nonvocational graduates did.
- Male secondary students who enroll in vocational education are ap-

proximately eight times more likely to be self-employed than are males who did not take vocational education. However, the experience for women is the opposite—seldom are women who took secondary vocational education self-employed. (National Commission on Secondary Vocational Education 1984, 30, 31)

Student enrollment patterns, the content of the curriculum, and vocational education outcomes all reflect the lack of a commitment to and successful strategies for increasing the number of girls trained in nontraditional fields. Michigan has experimented with some approaches for improving sex equity but has had difficulty.

Sex Equity Assessed by State Council

In the fall of 1983, the Michigan State Advisory Council on Vocational Education (SAC-VE) decided to assess Michigan's progress in expanding occupational options for boys and girls at the secondary level. Their study evaluated Michigan's sex equity program, a strategy designed by the state Vocational-Technical Education Service (V-TES) and implemented over seven years, beginning in 1977 (Dietrich, Atkinson, and Foote 1985). The V-TES strategy was to fund local school districts (101 of 570 during the peak year of 1981) to conduct staff workshops on sex bias, to operate pilot activities, to review vocational and career materials for evidence of sex bias, and to promote the use of nonbiased resources. Local grants were limited to one year and in some cases there was little correlation between size of the district project, population served, and amount of money awarded. V-TES also established a Michigan Vocational Education Resource Center for sex equity materials at Michigan State University and funded two intermediate school districts to provide technical assistance to the local grant recipients.

The State Council's study found that over three years, September 1981 through June 1984 the enrollment of nontraditional students at the state funded sites was no better than the progress of local school districts that did not receive sex equity grants. Thus, technical assistance and state financing of local sex equity activities, by themselves, do not appear to have contributed significantly to balancing enrollments in vocational education. This finding is especially surprising since Michigan has tried to be actively responsive to the mandates of sex equity in the Vocational Education Act of 1976. For example, during 1982–83 Michigan spent $425,390 for this targeted program, more than eight times the federal requirement of $50,000 (Michigan Department of Education 1984b, 3).

The State Council concluded that to meet the goal of increasing girls' enrollments in nontraditional program areas the scope of activities must be expanded and focused more precisely upon the student. The Council stated unequivocally: "The direction we would like to chart is one where, with conscious design, vocational enrollment patterns begin to shift as an indicator of our commitment to allow each student to find the career best suited to that person regardless of gender" (SAC-VE 1985, 1).

Barriers to Occupational Choice: Findings from a State Survey
If Michigan's experience can be used as a guide, it shows that developing materials and training teachers around issues of sex bias are not enough to achieve sex equity. At the least, more active interventions targeted directly at girls must be a central part of any sex equity program. Specifically, because girls enroll in vocational education with traditional job goals, the whole system of recruiting, counseling, admitting, and supporting students in nontraditional programs must change to increase their job options. These traditional attitudes are shared by vocational educators. Their influence and action further inhibits expanded occupational choice. Therefore, sex equity may also necessitate active intervention to change the attitudes of educators as well as curriculum structure and content.

In an attempt to understand further the barriers to increased nontraditional enrollments, the Michigan State Advisory Council on Vocational Education commissioned the Michigan League of Women Voters to conduct a survey on sex equity. This state study replicated an earlier national survey to determine the extent to which state and local school districts were responding to the sex equity provision in the 1976 amendments to the Vocational Education Act.[1] The Michigan League conducted 429 interviews at 20 vocational education sites in a sample representative of the state schools and skill centers. Respondents included 149 vocational education teachers and counselors, 41 administrators, 175 students, and 64 local representatives of business and labor.

The League's survey found that vocational educators (teachers, counselors, administrators) held a narrow view of what sex equity means. They associated it with doing activities funded by the state, such as participating in workshops, reviewing vocational materials, and the like. Forty-six percent of the administrators and 31 percent of the teachers and counselors thought of these activities as strategies for recruitment of nontraditional students. Students, however, differed. They did not think that these activities of vocational educators were either support for or encouragement to enroll in nontraditional programs. Students were more likely to mention job placement and co-op placement in nontraditional fields, rather than counseling or the distribution of printed material, as support for nontraditional enrollment.

The survey also revealed that only 27 percent of vocational administrators had ever received sex equity training and only 37 percent have evaluated their sex equity programs. Thus, there are three problems that need to be addressed in designing an effective sex equity program: First, all vocational administrators should be trained in sex equity. Second, as part of that training, they should learn that workshops and materials are a means to an end, not an end in themselves. Third, students need to receive both active encouragement to choose a nontraditional career and support that is meaningful to them.

Educators view open access to courses as a key strategy for guaranteeing equity in school programs. In other words, as long as programs and courses preparing girls for nontraditional jobs are open to girls, educators are meeting their sex equity obligations. But are educators accurate in assuming equal access policies alone can effectively remove barriers to occupational choice? Are school policies, procedures, and counseling practices subtly discouraging some students from choosing vocational education courses in nontraditional fields? As Haignere and Steinberg suggest in Chapter 14, even though educators in the survey acknowledge there are strong pressures on students to make only traditional choices, they continue to conclude that enrollment in a course is itself evidence of interest in the subject as a vocation. And rather than expanding the range of options being considered by a student, the strong emphasis on job placement results in closing off options by seeming to prefer that students demonstrate an interest in a vocational education course before they are even admitted. While we cannot tell from the survey results whether admission criteria are actually applied uniformly from student to student and program to program, fully 40 percent of the teachers and counselors said students are required to provide evidence of vocational interest in a subject, such as test scores or having taken prerequisites, before they are allowed to enroll. Indeed, 70 percent of the students surveyed had taken a standardized test to identify their career interest, and 44 percent of the teachers and counselors said interviews were required before students could enroll in vocational education. And, 59 percent of the students pursuing nontraditional vocations felt there were admission criteria for entering a vocational education school or courses, compared to only 36 percent of the traditional students who perceived such admission criteria.

Prior knowledge of the career and subject area thus seems to be a critical factor in choosing a nontraditional training program. After all, few students are likely to choose a course in an unfamiliar area, especially one associated with the opposite sex. Not surprisingly, then, the survey found that 74 percent of the traditional students said they had never received information on nontraditional programs and courses. And, although educators may feel tests are useful for determining vocational education interest, only 23 percent of the students felt tests had influenced their plans for an education or career. Based on these findings, programs designed to make students more aware of nontraditional options may be more effective in influencing vocational choice than formal assessments of vocational interests or aptitudes.

Two-thirds of the administrators acknowledged that students were under a lot of pressure to take traditional courses, yet indicated that little effort went into dealing directly with those pressures in influencing occupational choice. Schools do not counsel young women about the likelihood of needing to work and the possible need for financial independence, whether or not they plan to marry and to have children, despite the fact that a recent study shows that dealing with this life role issue is critical to considering a nontraditional career. (Waite and Berryman 1985, 22.)

According to administrators, the majority of counselors inform students about opportunities in nontraditional jobs only if students request such information. Thirty-five percent of counselors mentioned "encouraging students" to consider such choices. Counselors also provide information about nontraditional careers to individuals or groups at "career day" programs or in connection with classes in career planning. But only 34 percent of counselors judged this to be an effective method of increasing the enrollments of girls in nontraditional programs.

Other data support these results:

- Somewhat fewer students who made nontraditional choices had contact with counselors (59 percent) than did students who made traditional choices (66 percent).
- Thirty-seven percent of the administrators reported that some counselors are reluctant to enroll students in courses nontraditional to their sex.
- Only 31 percent of the counselors and teachers said they had conducted recruitment programs to attract females and males into nontraditional occupational programs.

Not only must recruitment become a more active process, but also it must include active encouragement of nontraditional occupational choices. According to student survey respondents, they are not receiving such support:

- Sixty-six percent of the traditional students said they were encouraged to enroll in the vocational education program they were taking, while only 23 percent of the nontraditional students said they were encouraged.
- Only 3 percent of the nontraditional students said they were discouraged. Counselors and vocational education teachers agree, saying students mention encouragement more often than resistance as influencing them to choose a nontraditional course.

In addition to changing recruitment and admission policies, there may also be a need for changes in the vocational education curriculum to attract nontraditional students and to provide training for those in traditional programs that will improve their long-run career opportunities. Support within

Table 13-1/Attitudes Toward Changing Vocational Education Programs

RESPONDENTS	YES (%)	NO (%)	NOT SURE (%)	TOTAL RESPONDENTS
	Could restructuring provide a base for a wider range of occupational opportunities?			
Counselors and teachers	56	22	22	149
Administrators	49	24	27	41
	Would women's earning opportunities be increased if the curriculum were changed to emphasize small business/ entrepreneurial skills?			
Business and labor representatives	57	14	29	64
Counselors and teachers	51	18	31	149
Administrators	29	22	49	41
	Is such a change feasible?			
Business and labor representatives	60	8	32	64
Counselors and teachers	61	12	27	149
Administrators	37	10	53	41

Source: Michigan League of Women Voters 1984.

the vocational education community, especially from administrators, is the key to educational improvement, especially in changing institutionalized programs and practices. While the League's survey found that almost one-half of all educators agreed that program restructuring would increase occupational choice, it also found that many educators did not believe that changing the structure would broaden the range of occupational opportunities for students (see Table 13-1).

For example, educators sometimes blame business and labor for the lack of students entering nontraditional training programs, saying business does not want to employ nontraditional students. However, when asked about changing the curriculum of office education to emphasize small business or entrepreneurial skills, business and labor survey respondents appeared to be much more likely than administrators to see the potential such a change would have on improving women's earning power and to see such change as feasible. Interestingly, counselors and teachers appear to be closer to business and labor than to administrators in their answers to these questions (see Table 13-1).

Changing the curriculum and the program structure of vocational education at the secondary level is the least tried sex equity strategy. Administrators in Michigan seem reluctant to consider it. Emphasis has been on other, less disruptive, approaches. Despite administrators' skepticism, such changes in program design may be needed. And, these changes not only may meet the goals of sex equity but also become increasingly necessary as programs are changed to meet technological changes and demands for innovation. The adoption of applied physics or entrepreneurial programs, for example, could provide an opportunity to implement a sex equity approach that would ensure that girls and boys enroll in equitable proportions. These opportunities may be missed if administrators fail to explore the potential for improving nontraditional enrollments as curricula content and structure are shaped.

Open access of girls to nontraditional programs without active encouragement as a sex equity strategy is simply not enough. Educators instead must examine the vocational education system as a whole, including its structure and content, school policy and procedures, as well as their own attitudes and actions.

Vocational Education Policy and Occupational Choice
Another barrier to sex equity in vocational education is federal and state vocational education policy designed to insure an adequate labor supply in some predominantly female fields. The federal government, for example, establishes policy through vocational legislation. Even though the Carl D. Perkins Vocational Education Act of 1984 goes further than any prior vocational legislation toward supporting sex equity, the focus continues to be primarily on meeting business and work force needs. And the sex equity provisions may soon be weakened during the reauthorization process. States are required to evaluate vocational program quality only in terms of workplace and technological concerns (Sec. 113(a) (3) (D)) and not on sex equity. State subsidies to local districts in Michigan and elsewhere supplement federal monies to reinforce federal priorities: using funding formulas based upon occupational supply and demand, states insure continued training in some occupations by allowing local districts to maintain vocational classrooms, teachers, and equipment through upturns and downturns in the business cycle.

In Michigan, for example, the state vocational education department encourages program expansion in areas of highest employment demand. Funds are allocated according to student hours and an added cost factor for each vocational program. The added cost factor range for 1988–89 was $58 to $488 a student hour. Sixty percent of added cost funds are distributed according to statewide employment demand, placement, and the demand/supply relation, and the remaining 40 percent are distributed according to local/regional employment needs. Above and beyond state and federal monies, local districts must provide 25 percent of the money for the added cost of vocational education above other general education programs.

Programs are ranked according to the demand formula and are funded going down the list till the legislated allocation runs out. Vocational programs preparing girls to enter historically female occupations do very well with this method. In 1983, the Secretarial and Related Program received $4.9 million, more than twice as much as most "full funded" programs. The runners up in terms of large allocations were Food Production ($2.6 million) and Business Data Processing ($2.3 million). Nursing and marketing and distribution always make the list. This is how the supply of clerical, health, and sales workers is maintained.

Yet, the fact that these programs are well funded is not the same as saying that women do well on the labor market once they enter the historically female occupations for which they have been trained. The fact that labor supply is manipulated in these fields, indeed, is one reason why employers can keep wages low. Because vocational education programs maintain an adequate supply of trained labor, employers do not have to raise wages to attract workers as they would in a free market system. Nor do they bear the training costs.

While funding according to labor market factors is accepted practice in vocational education and federal training programs, without adequate provisions to achieve sex equity, it perpetuates occupational segregation by locking programs into meeting short-term funding requirements rather than focusing on the educational needs of and long-run employment options of its students. This shortsightedness has been particularly detrimental to women, in that programs seem to fare well when they take the occupational stereotyping of the labor market as given and provide sex-appropriate employees to businesses in their local labor markets.

To correct the influence of market bias in rewarding vocational education programs requires innovative approaches. One proposal by a vocational administrator suggests setting a nontraditional student enrollment balance level of 35 percent.[2] Any program with enrollments of students of the nontraditional sex above the 35 percent cutoff would receive 100 percent added cost funding for each student, and thus districts making successful efforts to recruit and train nontraditional students would receive a bonus. The state would pick up the local district's share of funding for the nontraditional students, so instead of paying 75 percent of the cost under the full funding formula the state would pay 100 percent (see Table 13-2). For those programs, such as cosmetology, that do not receive added cost funding, the state could set a dollar amount incentive.

This example is provided to show that there are ways to direct funding that will reduce rather than reinforce occupational segregation. At present Michigan is using a version of this plan. Michigan's state council on vocational education recommended a study be made of the effects of the state's current funding formula, labor market demands on curriculum, and the cur-

Table 13-2/Proposal to Create an Incentive for Enrollment of Nontraditional Students

	STATE'S SHARE OF THE FULL-FUNDED FORMULA		LOCAL INCENTIVE FOR NONTRADITIONAL STUDENT
	75%	*100%*	
Construction	$210	$253	$53
Automobile mechanics	156	195	39
Health occupations	153	191	38

riculum content of vocational education on the enrollment patterns of males and females. Such a study should also ask how students at the secondary level can best be prepared for work in a new, technological society.

Michigan's New Strategy

Beginning in the 1985–86 school year, V-TES initiated an innovative approach to sex equity we hope will correct deficiencies described earlier as part of SAC-VE's assessment of the previous program. The new program provides incentives based upon the number of nontraditional students who successfully complete one year of training in a nontraditional experience. Grants the first year were $150 a nontraditional student, determined by estimates of nontraditional enrollments at the beginning of the fiscal year (adjusted as actual enrollments become known). The second year the participating districts received $350 a nontraditional completer.

The purpose of the grants is to eliminate sex-role stereotyping in 34 vocational education programs identified as having 75 percent or more of one sex enrolled.[3] Twenty of the programs are in Trade and Industry. Long-range planning is facilitated by identifying the targeted vocational education programs every three years, rather than every year. Grants are for one year, but all districts who participate are eligible for renewal, since grants are not competitive. According to the V-TES grant guidelines, program activities must be aimed at promoting successful experiences for nontraditional students with objectives stated "in measurable terms for evaluation purposes."

Forty-one local education agencies and intermediate school districts participated in 1985–86, including, in one case, an intermediate school district that combined the money from four districts to develop a recruitment program all four can use. In the 1986–87 school year, 58 school districts or consortia of school districts participated. Eventually the program plans to fund over 100 incentive grant sites, twice the number of sites funded under the previous grant program, and to designate a vocational education sex equity coordinator in each district.

Although funding is not based on increasing nontraditional enrollments (and thus runs a slight risk of maintaining the status quo), it is linked to the size of the nontraditional population in the local agency. The project will need to be carefully monitored both to determine whether enrollments of nontraditional students increase more in the funded agencies than in the nonfunded agencies and to identify successful recruitment models.

The results of the first year of the program showed nonfunded sites doing as well as or better than funded sites. The second year resulted in a 42 percent increase in males in nontraditional programs and of a 0.5 percent increase of females in nontraditional programs. The increase in male nontraditional students was attributed to the development of an office cluster program that requires office/clerical classes along with computer and accounting classes for all students in the program.

Michigan's incentive program is an interesting and innovative approach, but it is too soon to tell whether it will result in increased nontraditional enrollments. Much will depend on the kind of technical assistance provided, the strength of the evaluation process, the quality of activities at the local level, and how vocational education activities are coordinated with the entire educational program of the local school. Nonetheless, state initiatives have provided guidance in designing more effective equity strategies. The framework is there to make great strides forward.

Conclusions

The major challenge confronting vocational education is the need to increase nontraditional enrollments. We have several recommendations for doing so, based on the SAC-VE study.

First, the high school sex equity recruitment model to be developed and implemented should aim for a high level of active local commitment to ending occupational segregation.

The recruitment model would include components such as: the student awareness program (ASETS—Achieving Sex Equity Through Students), resource center materials at Michigan State University, and the nontraditional role model bank and the Expanding Career Opportunities awareness models, but only if the component had been tested for effectiveness. It would involve targeted public information programs. New components that have to be developed include:

- strategies for providing support services and programs for nontraditional students,

- junior high nontraditional student recruitment programs linked with prevocational classes, and
- financial incentives/formulas for local agencies based on increases in nontraditional vocational enrollments.

Second, forces outside of vocational education such as business people, labor, legislators, and state officials, and the State Council on Vocational Education must provide leadership. The Council should examine structural and policy issues that may impede progress, that is: the impact of the current state vocational education funding formula based on supply/demand factors and on sex equity efforts, the impact of labor market demands on curriculum and sex equity, and the impact of curriculum content on enrollment patterns of females and males.

Third, a decade of laissez-faire strategies has not worked. Both perceptual and institutional barriers to expanding occupational choice must be removed and innovation must be encouraged.

- Strategies to end occupational stereotyping should include recruitment efforts that actively encourage students to explore and try nontraditional career choices/classes. Nontraditional co-op and job placement programs must be instituted.
- Students should be made aware both of the pressures that exist to choose sex-stereotyped vocational education classes and of specific information about the subject matter and careers that are nontraditional for their sex.
- Educators should examine procedures for gaining admittance to vocational education classes. Requirements for recommendations, interviews, and proof of career interest may be unfair to students who must "justify" their nontraditional career choice.
- Vocational administrators must participate in sex equity training and become actively involved in the change process.

Women must move beyond the limited number of occupations for which they are now educated. In vocational education we must train women in Trade and Industry programs. Such jobs increasingly depend less on physical strength and more on brain power as technology continues to transform all phases of manufacturing. This transformation may be favorable to women if they have the necessary math, science, and vocational background.

To truly open these opportunities to women means to provide support and encouragement for nontraditional choices, to actively recruit women into the programs and to take a hard look at the structure, curriculum, and state funding strategies of vocational education. Here is where issue management in vocational education, which often treats sex equity as separated from the mainstream of planning and management activity, becomes a problem. And, the commitment of vocational administrators becomes crucial. Without the support of the top leadership, the sex equity coordinator cannot have an authoritative voice in matters of funding, curriculum, and structure. Yet achieving sex equity in occupational education is more than just recruitment and training of students in programs as they exist today, although even that would constitute a major accomplishment. It must be dealt with according to the changing demands of the workplace and the long-term needs of the students, which means that the entire vocational education system must undergo change to achieve sex equity.

Notes

1. The 1982 report, "Achieving Sex Equity in Vocational Education: A Crack in the Wall," was based on a monitoring study conducted by Renee Sherman, Jane Murray, and Anne Sheeron and sponsored by the League of Women Voters Education Fund. The study was conducted in Iowa, Massachusetts, Pennsylvania, Idaho, and Wisconsin to determine the extent to which the state and local school districts were responding to the sex equity provisions of the 1976 amendments to the Vocational Education Act. The researchers used trained members of the League of Women Voters to conduct interviews using survey questionnaires developed for each respondent group.

2. The following list indicates those Michigan programs by the United States Classification of Instructional Program (CIP) code that in 1983–84 reported statewide completers of less than 25 percent of one sex. The letter *f* or *m* in parentheses indicates whether females or males are eligible for incentive dollars under the V-TES program.

01.0201 Agricultural Mechanics (f)
01.0301 Agricultural Production (f)
03.0101 Renewable Natural Resources (f)
07.0601 Secretarial and Related Program (m)
07.9999 Business and Office Cluster (m)
12.0408 Cosmetology (m)
17.0000 Dental Occupation Cluster (m)
17.0508 Medical Office Cluster (m)
17.0600 Nursing Occupation Cluster (m)
17.0800 Laboratory Occupation Cluster (m)
17.9900 Health Occupation Cluster (m)
20.0201 Child Care Services (m)
20.0301 Clothing and Textile Production and Services (m)
20.0601 Building and Home Maintenance (f)
46.0301 Electrical and Power Transmission Installation (f)
46.9999 Construction Trades (f)
47.0101 Electrical and Electronics Repair (f)
47.0102 Business and Vending Machine Repair (f)
47.0106 Major Appliance Repair (f)

47.0201 Heat, Air Conditioning, Refrigeration Machines (f)
47.0301 Industrial Equipment Maintenance and Repair (f)
47.0401 Hydraulics and Pneumatics (f)
47.0602 Aircraft Mechanics (f)
47.0603 Automotive Body Repair (f)
47.0604 Automotive Mechanics (f)
47.0605 Diesel Mechanics (f)
47.0606 Small Engine and Related Equipment Repair (f)
48.0101 Drafting (f)
48.0503 Machine Tool Operation/Machine Shop (f)
48.0506 Sheet Metal (f)
48.0508 Welding, Brazing, and Soldering (f)
48.0604 Plastics (f)
48.0701 Woodworking and Furniture Making (f)
49.0101 Air Transportation (f)

3. This proposal was submitted as a recommendation for revision of "The Annual and Long Range State Plan for Vocational Education in Michigan" in 1983 by Jay Johnson, a career education planning specialist.

References

Dietrich, Allene; Karla Atkinson; Alice Foote. 1985. *Analysis of Michigan's Sex Equity Efforts in Vocational Education with Recommendations.* Lansing: Michigan State Advisory Council on Vocational Education.

Giese, Elizabeth H. 1982. "Michigan PEER Math Report." A report prepared for the Project on Equal Education Rights, Washington, D.C.

Linn, Leslie Y. 1982. *The Research News: Bringing Women to Science* 33, nos. 9–10 (September–October). Ann Arbor: Division of Research, Development and Administration, University of Michigan.

Michigan Department of Education. 1984a. "Secondary Vocational Education, Added Cost Program, 1985–86." Lansing.

————. 1984b. "Sex Equity in Michigan Vocational Programs." Annual Report. Lansing.

Michigan League of Women Voters. 1984. "A Survey of the Status of Sex Equity in Michigan's Vocational Education Programs." A report prepared for the Michigan State Advisory Council on Vocational Education, Lansing.

Michigan State Board of Education. 1984. "Better Education for Michigan Citizens: A Blueprint for Action." Lansing.

Michigan State Advisory Council on Vocational Education. 1985. "How to Change the World: Eliminating Sex Role Stereotyping in Michigan Vocational Ed Programs." Lansing.

The National Commission on Secondary Vocational Education. 1984. "The Unfinished Agenda; The Role of Vocational Education in the High School." The Ohio State University, The National Center for Research in Vocational Education.

Ross, Doug. 1984. *The Path to Prosperity: Findings and Recommendations of the Task Force for a Long-Term Economic Strategy for Michigan*. Lansing: Michigan Department of Commerce.

Sarri, Rosemary C. 1984. "A Look at the Socio-Economic Status of Women in Michigan and the United States—1984." A report prepared for The University of Michigan Institute for Social Research and the School of Social Work, Ann Arbor.

Sherman, Renee; Jane Murray; and Anne Sheeron. 1982. "Achieving Sex Equity in Vocational Education: A Crack in the Wall." A report prepared for the League of Women Voters Education Fund, Washington, D.C.

Smith, Roger B. 1985. "Business and the Liberal Arts." *Michigan Today*, December.

Waite, Linda J., and Sue E. Berryman. 1985. *Women in Nontraditional Occupations: Choice and Turnover*. Santa Monica, Calif.: The Rand Corporation, March.

14/Nontraditional Training for Women: Effective Programs, Structural Barriers, and Political Hurdles

Lois Haignere and Ronnie J. Steinberg

The substantial increase in the proportion of women in the labor force since the early 1960s has not resulted in a more integrated labor force.[1] Over 80 percent of all employed women work in just 71 out of 400 detailed occupations. Furthermore, almost two of every five female workers are employed in just 10 occupations (U.S. Department of Labor [USDOL] 1983, 54). This persistent occupational segregation has been estimated to account for over one-quarter of the wage gap between the average earnings of full-time working men and women (Chiswick et al. 1974, 219–28). Moreover, this labor market differentiation of men and women has been linked to the perpetuation of poverty in many female-headed households (Wider Opportunities for Women 1981).

The persistence of occupational segregation and the female-male wage gap has defied more than two decades of concerted equal employment enforcement of the Equal Pay Act of 1963 and Title VII of the 1964 Civil Rights Act and has challenged equal opportunity advocates into expanding and diversifying previously limited approaches. For example, the equal pay prong of EEO (equal employment opportunity) policy traditionally conceptualized as equal pay for *equal* work, has been reconceptualized as equal pay for comparable worth or pay equity. Likewise, an earlier, and quite successful emphasis on promoting women's entry into professional and managerial occupations has extended to a focus on increasing the opportunities for women to enter high technology and blue-collar, traditionally male occupations. The advantages of nontraditional jobs are evident. They do not require a college degree, they have above-average growth projections over the next decade, and they offer good salary and advancement potential.

Increasing the opportunities for women to enter male-intensive occupa-

333

tions involves more than just providing equal access. Moving into entry-level jobs with some career ladder prospects often requires prior training. Because of cultural bias and sex-role socialization, many women do not possess the same skills and knowledge of tools and machines as do most men. Since equal employment does not, and should not, require hiring the unqualified, women must be provided with special training and support services. Such training is necessary for women who do not desire (given class background) or cannot realistically expect to enter elite occupations requiring graduate or professional education. These women could qualify for skilled trades and an increasingly broad range of technical occupations.

This chapter examines the effectiveness of training programs that prepare women to enter nontraditional occupations (NTO) and the structural barriers that block fuller development of these programs.[2] There are four primary sources for funding occupational training—public vocational education, private vocational education, apprenticeships, and federal employment and training programs. We focus exclusively on those programs funded federally through the Comprehensive Employment and Training Act (CETA), which was replaced by the Job Training Partnership Act (JTPA) enacted in 1982 and implemented in 1983. Although the three other categories of training are of great importance (and two are treated elsewhere in this book), we focus our discussion on CETA-funded programs for three reasons.

First, CETA, from its inception in 1973, targeted the poor. Given the relation between poverty, female-headed households, and employment in traditionally female jobs, CETA's objective of helping people out of poverty should have led to an equal employment emphasis on nontraditional training for women. CETA legislation was amended in 1978 to target nontraditional training for women. Although no specific goals were set, all programs were directed to contribute "to the maximum extent feasible" to the elimination of sex stereotyping (Sec. 676.526). Moreover, prime sponsors were instructed to recruit women and encourage, through such means as training, their entry into occupations where women represent less than 25 percent of the labor force.

Second, CETA programs included several advantageous features for women. Stipends were paid to trainees, who were also eligible for day care allowances. Programs were usually short term, intensive, and generally located in areas reachable by public transportation. The programs could include special recruitment, pretraining, and job-outreach services.

Finally, we focus on CETA because, between 1973 and 1983, CETA represented a major federal lever for affecting employment patterns in the labor market. In 1978, its relevance to occupational segregation and the male-female wage gap was recognized explicitly through the sections targeting NTO training for women. CETA flowed from the earlier federal employment and training programs of the 1960s and substantially influenced the direction for employment and training programs that are following it. JTPA cites a need to develop training that contributes to overcoming "sex stereotyping in occupations traditional for the other sex." In addition, it specifies that services be provided to those on welfare in proportion to their representation in the eligible population (Wider Opportunities for Women 1982). Given the low salaries of traditionally female occupations, efforts to get women out of poverty should continue to have an NTO emphasis. Recognizing and using the technical know-how in initiating and running effective NTO programs, which was developed during the latter part of the CETA era, is crucial to the success of such programs in the future.

Our assessment of nontraditional training programs draws on several sources. We used an extensive literature evaluating CETA and NTO programs, some published and some unpublished (see especially Kane and Miller 1981; Meyer and Lee 1978; Shuchat 1981; Underwood 1979). We attended a nationwide meeting of NTO program directors and conducted in-depth individual and group interviews.[3] Subsequently, we interviewed by telephone other training directors and people instrumental in the NTO training field, focusing specifically on perceived structural barriers to NTO program success. Finally, some of the material on NTO program effectiveness is based on the insights gained from the Women's Outreach Project, a two-year project examining and building NTO programs.[4]

Background

Employment and training programs have not always been associated with the goal of equal employment opportunity for women and minorities. Instead, longstanding programs designed to meet the crises of high unemployment have been used for new purposes. In 1933, the incoming Roosevelt administration, responding to both public pressure and a Congress ready to support whatever the administration proposed, enacted the first federally sponsored work-relief and work-training program, the Civilian Conservation Corps (Clague 1976, 3). The addition of the Work Projects Administration (WPA) in 1935 indicated the federal government's willingness to assume responsibility for alleviating unemployment. While it fostered job creation and training opportunities for over 2.5 million people a year from 1936 to 1939, it primarily served men because opportunities to participate were limited to one person a household.[5]

Training programs to combat unemployment and to aid the economically disadvantaged grew under the Kennedy Administration and have continued up to the present, largely as a result of sustained political pressures from ongoing interest groups. Initial support for such programs as the Neighborhood Youth Corps and the Job Corps came largely from civil rights organizations (Clague

1976). Large numbers of different programs evolved piecemeal to meet the divergent needs of groups such as youth, the elderly, migrants, and blacks. However, no program was targeted especially to women.

CETA was enacted in late 1973. Again, the unemployed and the economically disadvantaged were targeted. As had been true in previous programs, there was no specific targeting of women although female workers were experiencing high levels of unemployment. The consequence of this was that women made up more than 55 percent of those who were CETA eligible but until the late 1970s, represented less than half of those served by CETA (USDOL 1980). Most likely in response to grassroots pressures from women's groups, the CETA 1978 reauthorization finally specifically targeted women as well as displaced homemakers and public assistance recipients. NTO programs for women were given specific mention.[6]

The typical CETA training process began with outreach activities to attract potential trainees, followed by an intake process, consisting largely of an eligibility check to verify that the unemployment, income, and other qualifications were met. The client was then asked to select from the training programs in which openings were available.

Up to this point, all services were usually provided by a central CETA office, directly associated with a local prime sponsor. Prime sponsors were the agents for administering CETA monies locally. Most prime sponsors were city and county governments with populations of 100,000 or more.[7]

Some "primes" conducted their own training while others contracted with community groups and institutions that had submitted formal proposals. Training programs were held in schools, hospitals, companies, and community-based organizations. These programs ranged from classroom training in basic education and occupationally specific skills, adult work experience providing part-time or temporary jobs in the public and non-profit sectors and on-the-job training (OJT) involving occupationally specific training in an actual work setting, often with a private employer. In addition, there were Public Service Employment (PSE) programs providing full-time subsidized jobs in the public sector, primarily for individuals who were job ready. Once the training program was completed, the training program staff was responsible for assisting clients with job placement and conducting follow-up at 30-, 60-, and 90-day intervals after completion or termination. CETA has been responsible for training many women for traditional female jobs through this process.

Research has shown that the type of training varied by gender, with women more likely to be in classroom training and adult work experience programs and men more likely to be in OJT and PSE (Harlan 1980; Mirengoff and Rindler 1978; Westat 1979: Waite and Berryman 1982; Baumer, Van Horn, and Marvell 1979; Wolfe 1981).[8] In fact, CETA program placement was found to perpetuate segregation. An important study done by Waite and Berryman

(1982) analyzing the record of CETA programs found that OJT assignments increased a woman's chances of being trained in a mixed or traditionally male occupation. The authors concluded that the proportion of traditionally female OJT slots was so small that, if CETA had increased women's OJT participation, there would have been a simultaneous increase in occupational desegregation for women, simply by virtue of their being in OJT. By contrast, relative to OJT, a classroom training assignment increased a woman's chances of being trained in a traditionally female occupation by about 60 percent.

In our experience, it is relatively rare for counselors, intake workers, and trainers to be actively opposed to NTO for women. Instead, problems arise when staff fail to understand the underlying issues and the consequences of past, present, and future inequalities. Without understanding how women are often discouraged from taking math, for example, it is easy to conclude that women are no good at math and to convey this attitude to women.

As a result, the training process for traditionally female and nontraditional occupations differ. NTO programs characteristically provide services designed to counteract potential problems affecting women, such as their lack of background in tools and terminology, or offering suggestions for dealing with potential opposition from co-workers and supervisors. These additional services are needed to bring women to a point that enables them to perform as competently on the job as a man. In sum, NTO training programs differ from ordinary training primarily because they target clients with special needs, and therefore, must include special service components to meet their needs.

Effective NTO Program Components

To succeed, NTO programs must address the functional inequalities that deter or preclude women from entering and remaining in nontraditional occupations. Functional inequalities encompass both unequal preparation and the social and psychological factors that prevent women from making full use of the skills they may already possess. Together, these may undercut the full realization of women's rights to equal employment opportunity.

We shall distinguish two types of functional inequalities: past and future. Past inequality is the sum of the effects of differential socialization and treatment of males and females that are relevant to career choice and preparation. Future inequality is the sum of the effects of the treatment of others, particularly those in the job setting, on the ability of a woman to succeed in a nontraditional occupation once she enters the job setting.

A successful NTO training program, meaning one that enrolls, trains, and places a substantial number of women in nontraditional jobs, has components that are designed to combat both past and future inequalities. As indicated above, these components consist of special activities pertaining to recruitment, support services during training, pretraining, employer outreach, and follow-up programs. In addition, staff development for NTO-trainers cuts across all these components, being necessary for both those who make policy affecting NTO women and those who come into direct contact with them.

Past Inequalities

Inequalities created by differences in how most men and women have been socialized concerning career choice and career preparation produce what we call past inequalities. A short list of such inequalities includes the following:

- *Attitudes:* men's jobs are for men; it is unfeminine for a woman to have a technical job or to work in the skilled trades; women are no good at math; women are too weak (physically and emotionally) for nontraditional jobs; their husbands' masculinity would be threatened by an NTO wife; parents and peers would object to a woman's NTO status; women lack ambition and have a thin skin; women shouldn't work in these fields because they're taking jobs from men who need them.
- *Abilities and Knowledge:* weaker math background; undeveloped muscles and stamina for physical tasks; ignorance of tools and technical terminology; ignorance of the social norms in male-intensive occupations.
- *Life Circumstances:* poverty; responsibility for child care (or elderly parent care) leading to fragmentation, absenteeism, and fatigue.

Most CETA intake and referral processes made no attempt to counteract these past functional inequalities and JTPA has unfortunately followed its predecessor's lead in this. Given the number of clients to be processed and the constraints on staff time, it is understandable that the intake phase consists largely of an eligibility check accomplished as expeditiously as possible. Similar constraints affected the time that job counselors had to spend with clients before referring them to one or more training options. This meant that under normal operating procedures, there was not time—or staff—to actively counter the assumptions and expectations of both staff and female clients. As a result, referrals tended to be to sex-traditional training programs.

Most women did not resist these referrals to sex-traditional programs, in large part because they had been affected by many of the functional inequalities just described. Even one of these is sufficient to discourage consideration of NTO options. Moreover, even if a woman got as far as enrollment in a training program for a male-intensive occupation, these past functional inequalities continued to come into play. Often they caused women to drop out of the training program, in which case, the expectation that "women can't do men's

work" seemed confirmed. Yet, properly understood, these are less an individual failure than a failure of the training process to overcome long-standing
sex stereotypes that create sexual barriers.

To be effective in neutralizing past functional inequalities, training programs must include a component that directly confronts the assumption that
male-intensive jobs are for men. Specifically, outreach messages must be targeted explicitly to women; in some cases going so far as to highlight that the
message is focused on women. For example:

Women: become an auto mechanic and earn good money.
There's no such thing as a man's job.
High paying jobs in the skilled trades for women. (Shuchat 1981)

It is also helpful to emphasize, as these slogans do, jobs and money. Women
know this is what they need and why they are seeking training. As a result,
ads, posters, brochures, public service announcements, and other methods
stressing jobs and money catch their attention. It is best to counteract the anti-
NTO assumption directly, as does a poster headlined "Best Jobs for Women in
the 1980's." It shows a series of women in nontraditional jobs, with positive
quotations from each.

We interviewed one program director in a vocational-technical school
who spoke about her experience with women-oriented and non-neutral outreach messages. After completing a successful recruiting effort aimed explicitly at a female audience, the school's director asked her to revise her
approach: "We don't treat men and women differently here." Her next ads
and posters invited county residents, rather than women, to enroll in several obviously male-intensive training programs. As she expected, only men
responded. Armed with this information, she convinced the school director
to allow her to resume her previous approach, which resulted once again in
attracting women.

The methods and locations need also to be tailored to women. For instance, Women's Technical Institute, located in Boston, Massachusetts, places
targeted advertisements in laundromats, grocery stores, day care centers, and
other places where low-income women can be reached. The Broward Community College program in Fort Lauderdale, Florida, makes extensive use of
public service announcements on radio stations that homemakers listen to, as
well as in newspapers and on television. The program director also frequently
makes personal presentations at churches, PTA meetings, and women's community groups. This same director found another very creative approach to
recruitment. Recognizing that many of the women she wanted to recruit to
NTOs were already employed in traditionally female jobs, she targeted companies with shortages of skilled technical workers in the areas of electronics

and data processing. Four such companies were convinced to sponsor courses that would help to eliminate their skill shortages by upgrading their lower-level employees, largely female clerical workers. Thus, with employer cooperation, this director even used companies' internal labor markets as sources of recruitment. This innovative recruitment technique solved as well the equally difficult training issues of job placement and retention, which are discussed at greater length below.

The purpose of outreach is to interest women in coming to the NTO programs's center to learn more about NTO options. This leads to the next phase, that of career exploration. Despite some progress in breaking down occupation-gender stereotyping, many women still expect to enter female-intensive occupations, largely because they always have and because most of the women they know work at traditionally female jobs. Career exploration is needed to expose women to a broader range of occupational options that might suit them better, and to inform them about what people do in those jobs, what the pay scale is, what training is involved, including the physical or math requirements, and other considerations. Many job counselors have told us that without an explicit focus on nontraditional occupations, women almost invariably choose traditionally female careers.

While career exploration was not often a major element in CETA and is rarely used now in JTPA, it is possible to offer a half-day or full-day workshop. Women's Technical Institute, for example, holds open houses to acquaint potential trainees with what an NTO can offer.

It is most helpful to provide potential female enrollees with an opportunity to observe what is actually done on the job, preferably by female role models. If this is not possible, female occupational experts at a career exploration event profit from good NTO encouragement. The Waukesha County Technical Institute, which called its NTO program TNT—Think Non-Traditional— organized a series of exploratory workshops featuring role models, hands-on tryouts, industry tours, and sex-neutral career interest inventories.

Ideally, career exploration is continued even after women have become NTO trainees, through a continuing series of briefer meetings on selected occupational areas. One such CETA-funded program provided by the Altoona Area Vocational-Technical School offered stipends to trainees throughout an intensive five-phase program, the first of which is a five-week exploratory period. Altoona women trainees spent a week in the shops and laboratories of each of five broad occupational clusters. Not only did such extensive occupational exploration periods assist women in making NTO choices but also, used widely, they might have substantially reduced the revolving door aspect of job training programs. The revolving door imagery attributed to CETA regardless of the sex of the trainee stemmed from the tendency for previous trainees to return to CETA to be trained in different occupations that had just come to their attention or that had subsequently become more attractive to them.

If the career exploration activity is to serve men's needs for job information as well as women's, care must be taken that clients do not take the path of least resistance by attending sessions on occupations that are already familiar to them, or the sex-traditional ones. This could be done by holding one session on NTOs, for women only, followed by another session for men only. It could also be done by requiring clients to attend a given number of sessions from each grouping of occupations, or by featuring occupations from both groups at a single session for men and women.

We emphasize that the purpose of outreach and career exploration is *not* to get as many women as possible to sign up for nontraditional training programs but to enable them to make the most informed career choice they can on the basis of more complete knowledge. Ultimately, a woman's career longevity is the crucial test of program effectiveness, and herding women into NTOs for the sake of EEO statistics or other reasons will not contribute to longevity. However, experience suggests that when women learn—many for the first time—about the advancement and salary advantages of NTOs, the number who are willing to enroll in NTOs is usually impressive.

Once a woman has made an informed choice to seek NTO training, her readiness for training should be considered. If the program involves strenuous work, it is often helpful to arrange physical fitness classes so that women can begin to build up the muscles and stamina needed for the job. Advance preparation in math may be needed. If so, it is best to call it "refresher math." "Remedial math" implies they were too stupid to learn it the first time around. At one of the Women's Outreach Project field test sites, for example, several women were about to drop out of an electronics program. Each felt she could not do the work. An alert program coordinator realized, after conversations with each, that math was the problem. She arranged for tutoring sessions, which eliminated the problem. Another example is provided by the Altoona program. The second phase of this program provided a month-long session including physical fitness, refresher math, blueprint reading, continued occupational counseling, and information on women's issues.

A quick summary of technical tools and terminology related to the occupational area they have chosen is useful, since it will reduce the knowledge disparity between the female and male trainees (who have had the opportunity to learn these earlier). Although it is most effective to schedule these support services before the actual training, it may be possible to arrange for it to coincide with training. For example, the Coal Employment Project located in Oak Ridge, Tennessee, offered women miners special training in technical skills, such as tool and safety equipment use. Rather than being conducted before other training, this program was usually added on to the safety training required of all new miners.

Finally, special support services are needed in order to assist women in meeting their home and family responsibilities while being trained. The need for these services is not unique to NTO training; instead, they are very important for women's participation in many job training programs. They include child care, stipends, and transportation to and from training. Without special support in the form of child care facilities or child care allowances, many mothers are prevented from taking advantage of employment and training services. In some cases, assistance in locating child care, including arranging child care pools, is necessary. The TNT program of Waukesha County provided such assistance with child care, as did the Coal Employment Project.

Stipends were necessary for many, if not most, CETA-eligible women, since few could afford to be both out of the work force and out of the home for the time required for training. There is no substitute for financial assistance. Thus, the lack of provision for stipends under JTPA is no doubt a stumbling block to designing effective NTO training programs.

Special transportation assistance may also be needed, particularly where facilities are remote from low-income housing or from the homes of other special target groups. The Trident Technical College NTO program was considered highly successful except for one thing: they had not managed to recruit many black women, although they had done well with white women. The program coordinator had organized a Technology Discovery Week, role model panels, and hands-on tryouts all targeted to black women. However, it was not until she overcame the largest obstacle to the transportation of black women that she was successful in enrolling a substantial proportion of black women in her program. Most of these women lived in downtown Charleston, while the NTO programs were offered at a suburban campus, and public transportation was nearly nonexistent. Because of a shuttle bus operating frequently between the two locations, 31 black women enrolled, an increase of 86 percent over the previous year.

To summarize, past inequalities that affect women's entry into and successful pursuit of nontraditional occupations can be combated through special components of NTO programs. These include recruitment and career counseling designed to convince women that occupations traditionally held by men are excellent occupations for women, pretraining and refresher math programs designed to provide the women with some of the background more common among men, and special support services designed to remove the hurdles placed in women's ways by their home and family roles. Note that the services we have discussed are in addition to the occupational training. Job skills training remains the same for everyone.

Future Inequality

The second kind of functional inequality we discuss is future inequality. A woman and a man meeting all performance standards in their automobile mechanics program might be thought to be equally competent to perform the job ahead of them. Even though both get jobs as auto mechanics after completion of the program, they are not going into the same job environment. The difference is best summarized by this version of the double standard:

He's new. Let's see if he can do it.
She's new. I'll bet she can't do it.

Particularly in the more strenuous or "macho" occupations, women are often (although not always) resented. Their presence makes men feel awkward and uncomfortable, as the presence of any outsider in an in-group would. To the extent that men base their self-worth on the exclusively masculine image of their jobs, the presence of a "mere" woman who can do their work is ego deflating. Thus, they may act in ways that contribute to the failure of a woman entering their occupation and work setting. This goes far beyond the normal testing period experienced by most new employees (equivalent to "He's new. Let's see if he can do it. . . ."). Rather than a wait-and-see attitude with a little friendly kidding thrown in for good measure, the situation awaiting some NTO women is active resistance and, on occasion, sabotage.

Such is not always the case. We have spoken with NTO women in the skilled trades and other strenuous jobs, who spoke favorably of their co-workers and supervisors. The point is that men and women preparing for the same male-intensive occupations may be, in reality, preparing for two quite unequal job experiences, at least initially. Whether or not the problems will actually occur, most women are aware that they might and are understandably reluctant to take on such a burden—a burden that the men in these occupations do not face.

A second group of components of successful NTO programs takes into account these future functional inequalities. These include: special aspects of training programs designed to prepare women to meet discrimination on the job; employer outreach programs designed to increase employer receptivity to women NTOs and sensitivity to minimizing the ostracism such women may experience; and follow-up programs to help ensure that problems caused by the future functional inequalities do not lead to low retention of women in these occupations.

Special training topics such as sexual harassment, ostracism, tokenism, and racism should be incorporated in the NTO program to prepare the trainees for the eventuality of meeting and handling such problems. NTO program directors often recommend assertiveness training as a basic strategy for dealing with interpersonal conflict problems. They have found that unless attention is given to harassment and how it happens, many women fail to recognize it for what it is and are, therefore, unable to deal with it effectively.

Such a focus has been important for coal mining women. The Coal

Employment Project offered women miners special training to combat co-worker ostracism, such as how to deal with the problems of sexual harassment, what their legal rights are and how to obtain them, and how to form support groups. In addition, two of their staff lawyers were made available to help female miners and to provide information to women trainees.

Special preparation for the placement process is also needed by many NTO women. They need to be coached in the interview process: the normal stress of a job interview is augmented by the unfamiliarity of the environment and the concern over possible opposition to their presence. The ability to recognize and respond to discriminatory interview questions as well as a basic knowledge of their legal rights is particularly critical for NTO women.

Employer outreach is important to facilitate job placement and break down employer resistance to hiring and promoting NTO women. An effective approach used by Women's Technical Institute and the Altoona Area Vocational Technical School was to have a staff person assigned full-time to job development. This job developer maintained personal contact with a large number of employers, providing education and information about the competence of NTO women, the advantages of bringing women into occupations not traditionally held by women, and effective ways of combating the disadvantages of occupational desegregation. In addition, they encouraged employers to meet with trainees. In some cases, these meetings took place in the training setting where employers may speak about their companies or conduct group interviews. In other cases, site visits as well as formal job interviews were arranged for trainees by the job developer.

Follow-up to promote job retention is a particularly critical component of successful NTO programs, since such programs are fruitless if NTO women do not continue to do the jobs for which they are trained. Job developers are in the best position to be responsible for follow-up because of their ongoing relationship with employers. They collect follow-up data on trainees after placement, giving special attention to the NTO-specific aspects of women's job adjustment. Research indicates that women in blue-collar nontraditional occupations report high levels of job satisfaction (O'Farrell 1982) and higher levels than women in traditionally female jobs (O'Farrell and Harlan 1982), particularly in the first year of work (McIlwee 1982). Although dissatisfaction with male co-workers may not be related to job retention (Walshok 1981), questions need to be asked about interactions with co-workers and supervisors (Schroedel 1985). The job developer may be able to help resolve any conflicts that may have occurred before they escalate. For example, the job developer at the Women's Technical Institute maintained close and ongoing contact with both employers and program graduates. They have found that this helps to ensure that problems that could cause low retention are confronted and resolved. In addition, the Institute is completing a research study that has followed 300 women NTO graduates from the Institute.

The participation of NTO women in networks and support groups of women in their own and similar occupations is an equally important aspect of good follow-up after placement. Women's Technical Institute strongly encouraged graduates to join the Network of Women in Trade and Technical Jobs, which has specific occupational subgroups, monthly meetings, a newsletter, and support groups. Similarly, the Coal Employment Project was closely associated with a Coalmining Women's Support Team, which promotes support groups and publishes a newsletter every month discussing the special problems and current events of concern to female miners.

Finally, staff training is a crucial element of successful NTO programs that cuts across all of the special components of those programs. It is necessary for staff indirectly associated with NTO programs as well as for those directly involved with NTO trainees. For instance, those in the admissions and financial aid offices of educational institutions need to understand the importance of NTO training. As we said above, NTO staff is not often actively opposed to NTO training but does often fail to understand the nature and consequences of past and future inequalities. Staff training is often helpful in orienting them to a different explanation of lower female recruitment and a higher female dropout rate. With such assistance, most staff people become more supportive of NTO women.

Structural Barriers Hindering NTO Success

We know what is necessary to train women effectively to enter and perform competently in nontraditional occupations. Yet the number of CETA programs that incorporated the components necessary for successful NTO programs was small. One important reason was that the CETA guidelines contained many structural barriers both to women's being trained and to the proliferation of NTO training programs. These barriers still exist under JTPA. Two major categories of barriers are discussed below: those that existed because of the way *eligibility* was defined and those *performance criteria for accountability* that provided an incentive for prime sponsors to disproportionately exclude women from training, particularly for occupations not traditionally held by women.

Eligibility

Federal employment and training programs have historically demonstrated an explicit male head-of-household preference. Vestiges remain. Perhaps most notable is the firmly entrenched veterans' preference. Important as well are regulations defining income ceilings and age limits.

CETA legislation specifically stated that prime sponsors should serve the significant segments of their population equitably. However, the regulations also gave both explicit and implicit priority to veterans. In fact, this focus on veterans preceded CETA. The Emergency Employment Act (EEA), of 1971, which was replaced by Public Service Employment (PSE) two years later, had a goal of 40 percent veteran's participation. Women averaged 30 percent of participants; veterans averaged 43 percent. The Department of Labor in its 1973 *Report to the President* attributes the low participation of women to the high goals for veterans.

Although the goals for veterans specified by CETA regulations were less ambitious than in preceding legislation, Wolfe (1981, 109) points out that President Carter directed prime sponsors to have a goal of 40 percent enrollment of Vietnam-era veterans in public service employment programs. Yet, Vietnam veterans were only about 3 percent of those eligible under CETA regulations. While Carter's goal was never reached, Vietnam-era veterans participated at 2.5 times their eligibility rate (Wolfe 1981, 109). Although specific goals for veterans were not included in the last amendment to CETA adopted in 1978, programs were encouraged to increase the participation of veterans. The JTPA legislation also specifies that programs should be conducted to meet the needs of veterans without specifying goals or limits on expenditures (Sec. 441 [a] [1]).

Providing additional evidence, Underwood (1979) demonstrates that as the enrollment of veterans declined, the enrollment of women in public service employment programs increased:

Although women have been about 46 percent of the unemployed and 54 percent of the eligible population during the 1970's, their participation in PSE has ranged from 28 to 40 percent. Veterans have been about seven percent of the unemployed during the 1970's, but their participation in PSE has ranged from 24 to 47 percent. (p. 35)

The inverse relationship noted by Underwood between the enrollment of women and the enrollment of veterans is due in large part to the small number of women veterans. Until 1973, women were less than 2 percent of military personnel (Underwood 1979). Even today they are about 10 percent of new recruits. Thus, women are largely excluded not only from the job training opportunities offered by the armed services but also from the abundance of services provided for veterans, not the least of which is priority access to employment and training programs. To our knowledge, there has been no examination to date of the effect of veterans' preference on the enrollment of women in JTPA. Because veterans' preference is firmly entrenched in our sociopolitical values, it is likely to remain a barrier for women long after other barriers have been surmounted.

Income criteria have constituted a second category of eligibility barriers. In 1976, provisions were added to the CETA legislation designed to ensure that more services were provided to the most economically disadvantaged groups in the population. These provisions for eligibility stated that an individual must be unemployed for 15 weeks or receiving Aid to Families with Dependent Children (AFDC) and be a member of a household with an income that does not exceed 70 percent of the Bureau of Labor Statistics lower-living-standard income level (PL 94-444, Sec. 608).

On face, these provisions do not appear to discriminate against women. And, in fact, a follow-up study done by the National Commission for Manpower Policy indicated that, although these provisions reduced the total eligible population from 23 million to 6.9 million, there was an increase in the proportion of eligible women from 54 to 65 percent (Underwood 1979, 22). However, eligible women were largely drawn from the population of women heads of household, that is, women without husbands present (most notably AFDC recipients). These women, while among the most disadvantaged, represented only one group of lower-income women who could have benefited from CETA training. Another group were unemployed women who lived with their spouses. If their husbands earned any more than 70 percent of the lower living standard, these women were ineligible for CETA training. By contrast, men were much more likely than women to have spouses present who earned less than 70 percent of the lower living standard.

Underwood indicates that those designing this provision understood the impact of maximum family income eligibility limitation on married women with spouses in the household. The National Commission for Manpower Policy report, which recommended this legislative revision, stated:

It is inequitable to have individuals in families with secondary wage earners competing with unemployed family heads without regard to the total financial needs and resources of their respective families. (National Commission for Manpower Policy 1975, 2, as quoted in Underwood 1979).

Moreover, as Miller (Chapter 5) notes, family income barriers also block many newly separated, divorced, or widowed women who have an especially high need of employment and training services. The income determination period is six months, meaning that many women are not eligible until six months after their marital separation. Although these women have little or no income of their own, they are frequently disqualified for eligibility by their former husband's income. In addition, marital assets such as a home may disqualify such women even though their relative need for job training and experience may exceed that of most other unemployed groups.

As with income provisions, regulations targeting youth and setting a minimal percentage for young participants appear on their face to be gender neutral. However, they are likely to produce fewer services for women, because women are a larger proportion of the eligible population over 21 than those under 21. The difference is substantial, in most cases reaching 10 percentage points. (Wolfe 1981, 112)

In addition, there is ample evidence that women were underrepresented relative to their eligibility in many employment and training programs explicitly designed to serve youth. Underwood showed that young women have been underrepresented in Job Corps, the Young Adult Conservation Corps, and the Youth Community Conservation and Improvement Program (Underwood 1979, 40–50). The underrepresentation of women in these programs was, in part, the result of the programs' emphasis on traditionally male occupations such as forestry, carpentry, and electronics. In part, it was caused by a failure to apply focused affirmative action programs on recruitment and retention of women through the appropriate outreach and special services.

Age can be a particularly formidable barrier to nontraditional occupations. Age limits for many apprenticeships are quite low, commonly between 22 and 26. The Equal Employment Opportunity Commission has exempted these limits from the 1978 amendments to the Age Discrimination in Employment Act. Thus, while age discrimination is generally illegal, it is still possible to exclude people from trade apprenticeships because of age. Wolfe (1981, 114–15) points out that these limits are more restrictive to women than to men because:

1. Many women, denied access to an apprenticeship 10 years ago, would reapply now that access is not so limited.
2. Women have more traditional career aspirations before they have worked at a low-paying job for a while. With age and experience, they are more capable of resolving or disassociating from any sex-role conflicts that may be brought about by the cultural overlay of what is appropriately masculine or feminine work.
3. Because of child-rearing, many women do not work or only work part-time in their late teens and early twenties. Their interest in employment and NTO apprenticeships may develop after this time.

Finally, age restrictions can impact women more than men because of the traditional marriage and family system. Women, who have been homemakers during their younger years with little, if any, employment experience, frequently find themselves forced to enter the labor market for the first time because of divorce or the death of their spouse. The average age of these displaced homemakers is 40. They are thus ruled out of any programs serving only the young, and age becomes an unnecessary barrier to this class of women who are particularly in need of services.

Thus, an affirmative action program focused on circumventing this structural barrier for women from 25 to 40 is needed. Such a program might even be modeled after privileges extended to veterans, who are frequently given exclusions from the maximum age restrictions to apprenticeships. For example, women advocates have argued for pregnancy and child-rearing exemptions using as their model veterans' preference. If entry of some older workers is justified for one set of trainees, why not for others? By making this comparison we again see how a privilege extended unquestioningly to an overwhelmingly male group is either not even considered or rejected as unfair when suggested for women.

The situation we have reported concerning income restrictions and age as structured barriers under CETA have been perpetuated in the current JTPA legislation. As with veterans' preference, we know of no systematic examination of their effects under JTPA. Unfortunately, we have no reason to believe that their negative impacts on the participation of women and on nontraditional training are not being perpetuated.

Criteria for Accountability
Despite the eligibility barriers of income, age, and veterans' preference, women constituted more than half of those eligible for most CETA and JTPA services. Nevertheless, women have not been enrolled in proportion to their eligibility by most prime sponsors. Research has shown that prime sponsors were able to actively manage who received their services through the types of programs they emphasized, the selection of contractors, and the structuring of the selection process (Baumer, Van Horn, and Marvel 1979). Some prime sponsors may have consciously used these mechanisms to discourage NTO training programs, while others may have done so inadvertently. This underenrollment of NTO women has been further reinforced by federal accountability criteria.

The Department of Labor assessed the performance of CETA prime sponsors primarily on the basis of the proportion of enrollees placed and the cost per placement, thereby rewarding programs that targeted those who were least expensive to serve and most easily placed in a job. Performance standards emphasizing minimum training cost and rapid placement have continued and been more strictly enforced under JTPA (Solow and Walker 1986). Such standards discouraged the enrollment of women into training programs, especially NTO women. First, it is harder to place women in jobs, because women are traditionally restricted to a narrow range of jobs, while men can be placed in a wider range of jobs. Even for nontraditional occupations, it is frequently easier to place males in occupations that are traditionally female than vice versa (Blau and Hendricks 1979; Schreiber 1979).

This emphasis on rapid job placement goes hand in hand with the cost-per-placement measure. Prime sponsors were encouraged to serve those who are least expensive to serve and, therefore by extension, least in need of services.[9] The cost per placement was substantially greater for persons with little, if any, job experience and persons requiring supportive services such as child care, transportation, and counseling. Most CETA- and JTPA-eligible women fall into these categories. Moreover, we have seen that nontraditional training for women is doubtlessly more expensive than sex-traditional training. Money is needed for active career exploration to counterbalance the weight of women's assumption that men's jobs are for men. Money is needed to provide compensatory individualized instruction in physical fitness, math, technical tools and terminology, and so forth, to enable women to benefit from training on a par with most enrolled men. Money is needed to pay for counselors who are knowledgeable about the issues involved in NTO, including dealing with sexual harassment, social isolation, tokenism, lack of female peers, and others. Money is needed for job developers to spend more time with employers to diminish possible resistance to hiring NTO women. All of this raises the training cost per trainee, which, when compared with a sex-traditional option, undeniably looks bad in the training program's annual report.

However, the catch-22 is that NTO training programs that provide the necessary support services (such as physical fitness, child care, and education about discrimination and harassment) are likely to be among the more costly and lengthy programs. Yet by offering these services they contribute to the NTO women's ability to find a job (placement) and succeed in her new career (retention). Moreover, Solow and Walker (1986) found in their sample of JTPA service delivery areas that in three of the four areas where women were placed in NTO jobs, they earned, on average, substantially more than women placed in traditionally female jobs.

Given performance assessment based on cost per placement, it is not surprising that most of the CETA programs to train women in nontraditional occupations were short-lived pilot projects, many of which were funded through governors' discretionary funds (20 *CFR* 671 [P]). Without the 1978 CETA targeting of NTO training for women, it is unlikely that many of these programs would have been initiated.

Three performance measures stressing outcomes for the trainees have sometimes been used in conjunction with placement and cost.[10] These are the *ability to get off welfare, job retention,* and *income increase.* These measures could be more favorable to women and to NTO programs. For example, when a woman receives training in a high-paying traditionally male field, she is more likely to earn enough to allow her to get off welfare, which would provide an incentive for her to continue in that field of work. In addition, measures of income increases frequently have shown that women profited most from CETA enrollment, since they were most likely to have had no employment income before enrolling.

Unfortunately, however, even these three performance assessment measures can be problematic for women. Removal from welfare roles in many states is immediate for working men, but women are allowed to continue to collect some benefits while working. CETA program directors in these states thus had another motivation to enroll male, as opposed to female, welfare recipients. In addition, projects in states with a high proportion of men on their welfare rolls could receive better reviews on the basis of this standard than could projects in states without this high proportion of men (Wolfe 1981, 112).

The use of job retention as an assessment standard can also work to the detriment of programs serving high proportions of NTO women. Psychosocial processes inherent in being in a small visible minority in a work setting (Kanter 1977) and more blatant employer and co-worker harassment contribute to a high turnover rate for women entering nontraditional occupations. This is especially true in the absence of support services, which can both prepare women for the situations they may meet and counsel them about how to cope with these situations.

An increase in the income of those trained by the program could be a performance criteria favorable to NTO programs. However, because the complexity of long-term follow-up, measures of increases in income were usually taken at the end of only three or six months. Although the potential career ladders of male-dominated jobs are longer and the wages much higher, entry-level jobs in some NTO occupations have salaries similar to those in female-dominated occupations. Measures of increase in income taken at the end of three or six months will not reflect the full income advantages of nontraditional training.

Given that most CETA and JTPA performance measures discouraged the enrollment of NTO women, how could these measures be improved? What new measures might encourage the enrollment of women and the development of nontraditional training programs? Measures of placement, of removal from welfare rolls, and of increases in income could be modified so that they would not discourage nontraditional training for women.

Placement, as a performance measure, could encourage NTO programs if the placement of those in greater need of services is weighted more heavily than the placement of white men with many years of job experience. As a first step, nontraditional placement for women could be given additional value.

Underwood (1979, 52) suggests designing a special point system to determine eligibility and enrollment. Points could be given to potential enrollees on the basis of employment-related factors such as sex, race, age, and economic disadvantage. Although Underwood suggests such a point system for selecting individual enrollees, this system could be used to evaluate prime sponsors. Placement of a person with greater need for services could be given greater value than, say, placement of a white male with many years of job experience.

Similarly, nontraditional placement for women would be weighted to give it additional value.

Likewise, if reductions in welfare payments because of employment are used in conjunction with removal from welfare, the Department of Labor could get a more accurate picture of the success of different programs. Similarly, increase in income measures taken two to five years after placement might also more accurately reflect the mobility gained through training. Since such long-term follow-up is difficult, the average earnings in the occupation in which the enrollee is placed might also be used in combination with short-term follow-up income figures to give a more accurate view of potential income.

Alternatively, more attention could be paid to the demographic characteristics of a prime sponsor's eligible population and incentives provided for serving groups underserved by the present system. Allowing or requiring prime sponsors to report indicators separately for groups that cost more to serve could help alleviate the problem. Process—for instance, the establishment of special outreach programs or support services—rather than outcome measures could be rewarded.

Conclusion

This chapter has focused on CETA-funded programs to train women to enter nontraditional occupations. It has used a study of CETA programs to explore factors that perpetuate occupational segregation and to explore how these factors can be overcome. Some of these factors relate to men's resistance to women entering their occupations, whether active or passive, whether expressed as sexual harassment or as social isolation. Other factors relate to past and future functional inequalities that women bring to the labor market, whether their lesser likelihood of enrolling in high school math classes or their greater likelihood of having responsibility for child rearing and maintaining the family household. Still others point to structural barriers that are the engrained legacy of centuries of channeling women and men into different occupations, for example, the preference for trainees who are male heads-of-household or veterans. These factors taken together so strongly encourage occupational segregation that one is hard pressed to see how meaningful changes can come about unless program directors, interest groups, and concerned government agency officials actively intervene to bring about change. Business-as-usual means the perpetration of what exists.

In the 1978 amendments to CETA, the federal government had encouraged the development of increasingly effective NTO programs through targeting such programs. As a result of its support of pathbreaking NTO training programs, the government, along with those who advocate NTO training as an equal employment opportunity strategy, has gained a body of experience on which it can base recommendations for further improvements in regulations on governing such programs. Perhaps most important are the specifications of the need for changes in performance review criteria that will encourage programs to initiate or expand NTO components, along with thorough enforcement of existing antidiscrimination laws that will create greater employer incentives in hiring NTO women. In both these areas the current situation is less favorable to NTO programming than the situation was under the 1978 CETA amendments. JTPA has put even more emphasis on cost-effectiveness placement performance reviews. In addition, the Reagan administration moved away from enforcement of civil rights legislation and affirmative action quotas.

When energetically pursued, enforcement and oversight of equal opportunity laws encourages the integration of occupations through both a direct impact on employers and an indirect impact on potential NTO trainees. Research indicates that managerial awareness of employment discrimination litigation or consent decrees increases the likelihood that firms will voluntarily implement equal opportunity programs, which identify, encourage, and hire female candidates (Hartmann and Reskin 1982; Meyer and Lee 1978; Shaffer and Lynton 1979). Moreover, women in male-extensive occupations covered by federal contract compliance rules have lower turnover rates and longer job tenure than those in similar jobs not covered by federal rules (Osterman 1981). Enforcement, and the media attention and public awareness it can attract, clearly improves employers' receptivity to integrating their labor force.

Equally important is independent monitoring or outside oversight of training programs. While many special groups have been targeted throughout the decades of employment and training legislation, only rarely are these broad statements of policy translated into regulations providing specific goals and timetables. The current lack of attention to the JTPA legislative mandate to develop programs that overcome "sex-stereotyping in occupations traditional to the other sex" is an excellent case in point. Employment and training program administrators would invest more program resources in NTO programs if an oversight agency provided positive incentives for implementing such programs. If no one is watching, the business-as-usual mentality will hold sway.

Under these circumstances, we can expect little improvement in national targeting and oversight. However, the degree of control invested in state-level councils by the JTPA legislation leaves open the possibility that progressive state jurisdictions can use specific target and oversight mechanisms to increase equitable services to women, especially more NTO training programs. Interest group activity may be a crucial determinant of whether state councils focus on the need for NTO training. Active intervention could provide the encouragement needed to translate NTO objectives into state and local policy.

Enforcement is also important for its secondary impact on potential NTO employees. The publicity surrounding the passage of antidiscrimination laws as well as litigation and formal complaint hearings is a critical facilitator of change, largely because it changes individual women's perceptions of their chances of actually gaining entry to traditionally male jobs. Without such stimulus, few apply, giving the false impression that women are not interested in traditionally male jobs and thereby providing a victim-blaming explanation for continuing occupational segregation.

Finally, programs are needed that demonstrate creative approaches to meshing NTO objectives with the distinctive features of labor markets, especially the types of work available and the changing labor force needs. One especially innovative example is drawn from the CETA Mason City Iowa Door Opener project. Many of those this project served were women. Soil testing was determined to be a regionally unmet need. A soil testing training program for women was developed in conjunction with a nearby university. After being trained, the women opened a successful small business, which continues to provide a much needed service. The Broward Community College program was another example of creatively designing a program to meet specific labor force needs. As indicated earlier, the program coordinator targeted companies she identified as having skill shortages and proposed a joint effort to upgrade their lower-level employees, largely female clerical workers, by providing the technical courses they needed.

Under JTPA the need for more creative program components that educate employers to advantages of hiring NTO women is more acute than ever. These components can address how women can best be integrated into the workforce and how to overcome entry level and career ladder barriers that may disproportionately impact women. As indicated above, employer resistance continues to be a primary factor inhibiting the training and placement of NTO women. Were employers as receptive to training women on-the-job as they are to training men, many more women could be trained for male-intensive occupations than are now being trained under federal employment and training programs. Moreover, if employers' receptivity to women NTOs was clearly demonstrated, project directors, vocational educators, and apprentice program administrators, not to mention women themselves, would begin to supply enough women to meet the demand. Therefore, employer resistance must be addressed not only through enforcement of equal employment opportunity laws but also through NTO program components specifically designed to change employer attitudes.

Support must continue for NTO programs that have proven their creativity and effectiveness in reaching, training, placing, and retaining women in NTO occupations. Such programs should be used as models in the development of other programs. Too frequently training programs are funded as demonstration projects, only to be discontinued at the end of the pilot period regardless of their success. Ironically, the demonstration project approach often results in the very programs that have proven their worth being excluded from continued regular funding. Too often NTO training programs do not have the power or savvy to compete within the old-boy networks of more traditional contractors.

This chapter has documented that the technical know-how to run effective NTO programs exist. It is less clear, however, that the commitment to fund such programs is deeply rooted or reliable. If real needs for equality are to be met, there must be the strong political commitment to fund effective programs.

Notes

Acknowledgments: We would like to thank the following people for their insights on NTO training programs: Julie Armstrong (Non-traditional Job Opportunities, Longview, Wash.); Sharon Bahn (Women's Technical Institute, Boston, Mass.); Betsy Jean Hall (Coal Employment Project, Va.); Sandy Burton (Displaced Homemakers Network); Diana Eli (Displaced Homemakers, N.D.); Jill Miller (Women's Bureau); Jeri Brown (Phoenix Institute, Salt Lake City, Utah); Rosalie Kelly (YWCA Nontraditional Outreach, Indianapolis, Ind.); Georgetta M. Mitchell (Vocational Guidance Service, Houston, Tex.); Betsy Jacobus (Creative Employment Project, Louisville, Ky.); Shirley Sandage (The Door Opener and the Older Women's League, Mason City, Iowa); Susie Suafai (Women in Apprenticeship, San Francisco, Calif.); Jing Lyman (Women in Foundations and Corporate Philanthropy); Judy Joseph (YWCA, Milwaukee, Wisc.); Averal Madison (Wider Opportunities for Women, Washington, D.C.); Vickie Kramer (Options for Women, Philadelphia, Pa.); Julie Newcome (Library of Congress, Washington, D.C.); Janice Powell-Rollins (Displaced Homemakers, Denver, Colo.); Barbara Van Burean (Project Green Hope, New York City); Sue Ferguson (Resource Center, Loveland, Colo.); and Pat Evans (Women Advocacy Bureau, Baton Rouge, La.).

1. Fully 53 percent of women are now employed fulltime compared to 38 percent in 1958. Examined from a different angle, in 1950, women constituted 29.6 percent of the labor force, while today they make up 43 percent.

2. This chapter is drawn from Haignere and Steinberg (1984).

3. Wider Opportunities for Women, Working for Women Workers, National Conference, 19–22 February 1982.

4. This project, under the direction of Jo Shuchat, is among the most comprehensive studies to date on programs that prepare women for nontraditional occupations. Early in the Women's Outreach Project, the directors of 166 NTO programs across the country were interviewed. In addition, approximately 85 women who were about to complete their training or already working were interviewed. The interviews touched on essential features in NTO programs and pitfalls that should be avoided. The interview results were compiled in a manual (Shuchat 1981). In the second phase of the project, the manual and a guide for women were field-tested by five NTO programs established for this purpose. A total of 372 women were recruited and trained for

NTOs. At the end of the field test funding, all five program coordinators were retained by their schools.

5. Early employment and training programs made no pretense about primarily serving men. In 1933, before the WPA, the first program served only unmarried men, 18 to 25 years old. The targeting of divergent groups that began in the 1960s never displaced the male-head-of-household concept. In most cases, targeting means only special mention in the legislation. And, most targeted groups did not conflict with a male-head-of-household focus. For example, Underwood (1979) documents that even the Work Incentive programs, designed for AFDC recipients, gave priority to male heads of household by limiting family income—specifying a limit of one participant from each family—as well as expressing priority for serving male heads of household.

6. The legislative language of JTPA is, in most cases, less specific about services for women than is the 1978 CETA reauthorization. JTPA emphasizes training the population most in need, although it mentions the concern with providing services equitably. It prohibits discrimination but makes no mention of affirmative action. It does, however, target women 14 to 21 years old. For this group, the secretary of labor is directed to take immediate steps to achieve 50 percent enrollment of these women in Job Corps programs. Second, AFDC recipients, a large proportion of whom are women, must be served on an equitable basis, taking into account the proportion they are of the economically disadvantaged in the service delivery area (Wider Opportunities for Women 1982).

7. State government administered only the discretionary funds allocated by the federal government to state governors as well as the funds for rural areas not covered by prime sponsors called "Balance of State Areas."

8. This pattern of enrollment directly impacts women's present incomes and future employability. PSE programs paid higher average wages (Westat 1979). OJT programs paid the highest Title I in-program wages and had the highest postprogram job placement rate of any CETA programs (Mirengroff and Rindler 1978). While we cannot conclude that these disparities are the result of discrimination, they are indicative of structural inequities (Harlan 1980).

9. Thus, existing cost-per-placement performance criteria are consistent with a general pattern of "bottom-line" pressures that encourage the "creaming" of the best off the top of those in poverty.

10. JTPA indicates that "The Congress recognized that job training is an investment in human capital and not an expense. . . . The basic return on the investment is to be measured by the increased employment and earnings of participants and the reduction in welfare dependency."

References

Baumer, Donald C.; Carl E. Van Horn; and Mary Marvel. 1979. "Explaining Benefit Distribution in CETA Programs." *Journal of Human Resources* 14, no. 2.

Blau, Francine D., and Wallace E. Hendricks. 1979. "Occupational Segregation by Sex: Trends and Prospects." *Journal of Human Resources* 14; no. 2.

Chiswick, B. R.; J. A. O'Neil; J. S. Fackles; and S. W. Polachek. 1974. "The Effects of Occupation on Race and Sex Differences in Hourly Earnings." American Statistical Association, *Proceedings of Business and Economic Statistics Section*, pp. 219–28.

Clague, Ewan. 1976. *Manpower Policies and Programs: A Review, 1935–1975*. Kalamazoo, Mich.: The W. E. Upjohn Institute for Employment Research, January.

Haignere, Lois, and Ronnie Steinberg. 1984. *New Directions in Equal Employment Policy: Training Women for Non-Traditional Occupations Through CETA*. Working Paper no. 13. Albany, N.Y.: Center for Women in Government, Summer.

Harlan, Sharon L. 1980. *Sex Differences in Access to Federal Employment and Training Resources Under CETA: An Overview* Working Paper no. 58. Wellesley, Mass.: Wellesley College Center for Research on Women.

Hartmann, H., and B. Reskin. 1982. "Job Segregation: Trends and Prospects. In *Occupational Segregation and Its Impacts on Working Women*, a conference report. Albany, N.Y.: Center for Women in Government.

Kane, R.; and J. Miller. 1981. "Women and Apprenticeship." In V. Briggs and F. Foltran, eds., *Apprenticeship Research*. Ithaca, N.Y.: Cornell University School of Industrial and Labor Relations.

Kanter, R. M. 1977. *Men and Women of the Corporation*. New York: Basic Books.

McIlwee, Judith. 1982. "Work Satisfaction Among Women in Non-Traditional Jobs." *Sociology of Work and Occupations* 29 (August): 299–335.

Meyer, H., and M. Lee. 1978. *Women in Traditionally Male Jobs: The Experience of Ten Public Utility Companies*. R & D Monograph no. 65. Washington, D.C.: U.S. Department of Labor, Employment and Training Administration.

Mirengroff, W., and L. Rindler. 1978. *CETA: Manpower Programs Under Local Control*. Washington, D.C.: National Academy of Sciences.

National Commission for Manpower Policy. 1975. *Public Service Employment and Other Responses to Continuing Unemployment*. Report no. 2. Washington, D.C., June.

O'Farrell, Brigid. 1982. "Women in Non-traditional Blue Collar Jobs in the 1980s: An Overview. In Phyllis A. Wallace, ed., *Women in the Workplace*. Boston: Auburn Press.

O'Farrell, Brigid, and Sharon Harlan. 1982. "Craftworkers and Clerks: The Effect of Co-Worker Hostility on Women's Satisfaction with Non-Traditional Blue-Collar Jobs." *Social Problems* 29 (February).

Osterman, P. 1981. "Affirmative Action and Opportunity: The Impact of Federal Contract Compliance Program upon Turnover of Women Workers." Mimeograph. Boston University, Boston.

Schreiber, Carol Tropp. 1979. *Changing Places: Men and Women in Transitional Occupations*. Cambridge, Mass.: MIT Press.

Schroedel, Jean. 1985. *Alone in the Crowd: Women in Trades Tell Their Story*. Philadelphia: Temple University Press.

Shaffer, R., and E. F. Lynton. 1979. *Corporate Experiences in Improving Women's Job Opportunities*. Report no. 755. New York: The Conference Board.

Shuchat, Jo. 1981. *The Nuts and Bolts of NTO: A Handbook for Recruitment, Training, Support Services and Placement of Women in Non-Traditional Occupations*.

Cambridge, Mass: The Women's Outreach Project, Technical Education Research Centers.

Solow, Katherine, with Gary Walker. 1986. *The Job Training Partnership Act Service to Women*. New York: Grinker, Walker and Associates.

Underwood, Lorraine A. 1979. *Women in Federal Employment Programs*. Washington, D.C.: The Urban Institute, January.

U.S. Department of Labor. Women's Bureau. 1980. *CETA Journey: A Walk on the Women's Side*. Pamphlet no. 19. Washington, D.C.

———. 1983. *Handbook of Women Workers*. Bulletin no. 298. Washington, D.C.

Waite, Linda J., and Sue E. Berryman. 1982. *Occupational Desegregation in CETA Programs: The Record for Male and Female Hispanic, White and Black Participants*. Santa Monica, Calif.: The Rand Corporation.

Walshok, Mary L. 1981. *Blue Collar Women*. Garden City, N.Y.: Anchor Books.

Westat, Inc. 1979. *Continuous Longitudinal Manpower Survey. Follow-up Report #2, Post Program Experiences and Pre/Post Comparisons for Terminees Who Entered CETA During Fiscal Year 1976*. Washington, D.C.: U.S. Department of Labor, March.

Wider Opportunities for Women. 1981. *The Feminization of Poverty*. New York: Wider Opportunities for Women. December.

———. 1982. "The Jobs Training Partnership Act." Typescript. October.

Wolfe, W. 1981. *"The Experiences of Women in Federally Sponsored Employment and Training Programs" in Increasing the Earnings of Disadvantaged Women*. Report no. 11 of the National Commission for Employment Policy, Washington, D.C.

Welfare,
Workfare,
and Training

Introduction to Part IV/*Sharon L. Harlan*

During the last year of the Reagan presidency, the federal government enacted legislation that changes the philosophical underpinnings and the daily
functioning of Aid to Families with Dependent Children (AFDC), the main
cash public assistance program for poor families with children. The Family
Support Act (FSA) of 1988 (described in Chapter 1) was passed for the purpose of overhauling this system which, in 1985, served 3.7 million families,
or 11 million individuals. Almost 90 percent of the recipients were in families headed by a single woman. The number of female-headed families on
AFDC nearly doubled between 1970 and 1985 (all statistics from U.S. General Accounting Office [USGAO] 1987, 19). The desire to stop this precipi-
tous increase, or even to reduce the number of such families on assistance, is
the major motivation for the changes.

The FSA has been marketed to the American public as the result of a
broad-based national "consensus" among liberals and conservatives on welfare "reform." The reform centers on strengthening the tie between work and
the receipt of welfare benefits. However, this portrayal of the issue obscures
a great diversity of opinion that lies underneath the smooth facade of political
consensus. There are voices, though they are seldom heard as part of the debate, who argue that raising children—especially alone—*is work,* as well as
a valuable social contribution. Therefore, mothers of small children ought to

have the option of staying at home to care for them. Proponents of this view reason, much as did the sponsors of the original public assistance programs 50 years ago, that mothers of young children need an income subsidy. If the subsidy is not forthcoming from the children's father—for whatever reason— then they are entitled to it from the government.[1]

The chapters in Part IV take other perspectives that are in general agreement with the notion that women's participation in education, training, and employment programs is a strategy that ought to be pursued as a route to obtaining self-sufficiency. Nevertheless, the contrasts in rationale, methods, and goals among these contributors are striking and further erode the notion of consensus on changes in the welfare system. The most important thing they have in common is their ability to go beyond the rhetoric of global reform and onto a discussion of hard issues and choices.

Gueron, as we mentioned in Part I, provides an overview of the history of training and work programs in the welfare system and explains the evolution of the emphasis on job search assistance and community workfare for AFDC recipients. She also presents results from five of the WIN Demonstrations evaluated by the Manpower Demonstration Research Corporation (MDRC). These programs were designed by individual states and approved by the federal government to offer a variety of work and training-related services to welfare clients. Goldman, also of MDRC, reports moderately positive outcomes from an early (1979) project in Louisville, Kentucky, that tried to help mothers on welfare find employment through job search assistance. As she points out, subsequent programs have benefited from lessons in those early experiments. Werner examines the widely publicized Employment and Training Choices Program (ET Choices or ET) in Massachusetts, which began in 1983. In contrast to short-term, low-cost investments in job search and workfare, ET Choices operates on an alternative model of greater resource investment based on the assumption that it will yield higher returns. Three community case studies of welfare recipients and social services agencies in Boston, Philadelphia, and Baltimore are the basis for Gittell and Moore's dismissal of all current welfare-related work and training programs as "shortsighted public policies that deny to low-income women quality education and work experiences." They argue that in order to be self-sufficient, women require postsecondary education, preferably from four-year or two-year colleges.

As we noted, underlying the so-called consensus are vastly different approaches to getting women on welfare into the labor market, and not all of them involve training. Job search programs, as Gueron and Goldman point out, assume that many women, if they are taught how to look for jobs, can be placed quickly and inexpensively into jobs without skill training. Goldman demonstrates that some of them do indeed find jobs: after an orientation period and several weeks of telephoning prospective employers from the welfare office, significantly more women in the experimental job search program found work than those in the comparison group. (This represented 25 percent of those assigned to the experimental program and 49 percent of those who participated, compared to 34 percent of the comparison group.) Workfare, another low-cost strategy in which participants work in public-sector jobs in exchange for welfare benefits, also usually generates some positive employment results. Fewer states have tried workfare than job search, and workfare is usually limited to a few months. Interestingly, Gueron points out that workfare jobs, despite the criticisms leveled at them, are often the same kinds of entry-level positions in public agencies that were funded under the CETA public service employment program (see Durbin and O'Brien, Chapter 7).

Gueron and Goldman say that a chief rationale for these programs is that they direct scarce resources efficiently, screening out those who can find a job without training. The programs save some money for governments (about an 8 percent reduction in outlays in San Diego) and they provide some limited employment and earnings gains for women. It is quite clear, however, that they neither improve on the kinds of low-paying jobs women get on their own, nor help many of them out of poverty.

Werner argues a different rationale for ET Choices, suggesting that voluntary participation and customized services selected by participants from a "menu" of choices is much more likely to result in a motivated clientele who are able to find higher quality jobs. Whereas job search programs define "need" as the minimum service required to get a job—any job—the Massachusetts program does not screen out job-ready individuals who want to participate in other activities, such as training, postsecondary education, or career counseling. It allows participants to judge for themselves what to pursue. Given Goldman's finding that program administrators cannot accurately predict who will be successful job seekers, this appears to be a sensible approach.

It is, however, an expensive strategy: the fiscal year 1989 budget request for ET Choices was close to $1 billion (nearly double the expenditures for fiscal 1986). Although placement costs across programs cannot be compared precisely, ET spent $3,333 for each participant placed in a job compared to between $77 and $195 for each placement in Louisville job search. Yet, as Werner says, this does not tell us about the relative cost-effectiveness of ET Choices, because an impact evaluation that compares expenditures to welfare savings or earnings gains has not been completed. Neither does it mean that ET participants have better opportunities after the program, although the placement and earnings outcomes suggest that they might (see below). It is interesting to note that the voluntary participation rate for ET Choices—

between 20 and 28 percent of the eligibles—is about average for WIN Demonstration programs, some of which are mandatory (USGAO 1987).

In theory, at least, Gittell and Moore are more sympathetic with the goals of ET Choices than with those of job search. However, they argue that ET does not go far enough and, according to interviews with participants in Boston, that it does not live up to its claims. Most important for Gittell and Moore is the issue of college attendance. Their subjects cited a number of problems that made it difficult for them to take advantage of higher education: ET tardiness in paying tuition bills, no help in interfacing with the college bureaucracy, unfavorable rules on what public assistance they could keep while attending college, and even, not being made aware of the college option. Looking at the data in Werner's chapter we see that only 13 percent of ET participants were enrolled in higher education as of January 1988. The ET rules limit participants to one year of support in the Massachusetts community college system, not what we would usually classify as a college education. Actually, what accounted for a much larger proportion of activities under ET were skills training (31 percent) from JTPA contractors, for example, and job search and placement (39 percent).

These facts point to a very complex picture of what goes on in programs that are apparently predicated on very different assumptions and of what the bulk of participants are capable of doing in a program like ET. Job search, for example, is still an important component in a program that advertises itself as offering a wide range of services (although we do not know how many of those participants also used other ET services). Yet, despite the programmatic barriers to higher education, we cannot forget that fewer than half of AFDC recipients have a *high school* diploma (data reported by Werner and by Gittell and Moore). Thus, programs that enable these women to obtain high school credentials so that they can pursue postsecondary education are essential.

Next to their lack of education, Gittell and Moore's respondents cited the lack of child care as the most significant barrier that prevented them from obtaining a good job. Child care is an area where ET Choices has invested substantial resources: more than half of its fiscal 1989 budget request will pay for day care voucher services that let mothers purchase their own day care from among providers approved by the state. According to Gittell and Moore, mothers with preschool children "rely absolutely" on the voucher, but there are still problems with using it. Some cannot use day care of their choice (friends or relatives) because they are not licensed providers. Others find that centers want payment in advance for voucher children or that training programs want proof of child care before admitting them. Conversely, ET wants evidence of acceptance in a program before authorizing the voucher.

There are other sources of disagreement about ET Choices, such as whether it "creams" participants, the roles and attitudes of caseworkers, and most important, whether the job placements it provides are better than those participants get through job search (or after attending college). Goldman reports that job search participants are likely to find minimum-wage clerical and service jobs. Werner says that 68 percent of ET placements are in jobs that pay more than $5.00 an hour and 80 percent of those have employer subsidized insurance. But Gittell and Moore (and others) point out that ET has done almost nothing toward training women for nontraditional jobs, and they claim that job placements are still in traditionally female clerical fields with little potential for earnings growth.

An issue that one must face in assessing these chapters is the difference in the type and quality of their factual evidence. The strength of the MDRC studies is the rigor of the research design and methodology that yields precise information about the impact of programs. Their weakness is that they do not ask in any detail the questions that would tell us how much they improve women's lives compared to existence on welfare. Werner's data on outcomes, though not based on an analysis that can differentiate program effects from other sources of change, is more informative about the quality of jobs participants get and how it compares to incomes needs. Gittell and Moore add information from the women participants to this debate, which is a vital perspective in formulating better policies. But until evaluations are completed, as Werner says, many of the policy issues regarding the effectiveness of training and education strategies compared to job search and workfare remain unsettled.

There are several concrete points on which these studies agree. First, many women on welfare want to get an education and a job. The women in Gittell and Moore's study specifically wanted good jobs with decent wages and benefits. Many women in the MDRC study accepted less—work is viewed simply as a better alternative than welfare. Often, "situational" factors, some of which might be overcome by proper support services, stand in the way of women's employment. Second, a minority of women on AFDC at any one time participate in work and training programs, perhaps for personal reasons, but also because the system's resources are too meager to handle everyone. Therefore, the notion that public assistance might be eliminated by work-related reforms is unduly optimistic. Third, the demand side of the labor market is important in determining whether and what kinds of jobs women can find. Just as West Virginia's poor economy yielded zero employment and earnings gains for workfare participants, the boom economy in Massachusetts may be in large part responsible for ET's success. Fourth, there is tremendous diversity in what states choose to do about work, training, and welfare. Many, though not all, the states examined in these studies are among the more enlightened, but we should not forget that there are also many that are less progressive. Finally, the mobilization of community resources and the coordination of public agencies, including economic development agencies, is essential in achieving successful training programs for welfare recipients.

These four chapters provide a true sense of the currents of social and political thought that are stirred by the concept of welfare in American society and they illustrate, as Gueron says, that the debate is really over values. But whereas Gueron and many others emphasize the significance of the work ethic in framing the dilemma for the welfare system, Gittell and Moore touch upon another value that is equally firmly embedded in the national consciousness: the value of education and the opportunities for upward mobility that flow from it. Are we, as these authors believe, establishing a different and discriminatory set of values and expectations for poor women than for the rest of society?

Note

1. Using women's high labor force participation rate to justify policies that require welfare mothers to enter the labor force, ostensibly to support themselves, ignores the reality that most white, married, middle-class mothers of young children who work have part-time or part-year jobs that would not support them without a husband's income. Thus, poor single mothers are being held accountable to a standard that few other women in this society could achieve. (These ideas were suggested in commentary by Vilma Ortiz and Cindy Marano at the policy seminar entitled "Occupational Segregation and its Roots in Education," sponsored by the Center for Women Policy Studies, Washington, D.C., May 1988.)

Reference

U.S. General Accounting Office. 1987. *Work and Welfare: Current AFDC Programs and Implications for Federal Policy.* Washington, D.C., January.

15/Work Programs for Welfare Recipients

Judith M. Gueron

The welfare system operates against a background of broad agreement on two points: that society should provide basic support to the needy, and that those who can should work to sustain themselves and their families.[1] Given the diversity of the welfare population, however, consensus breaks down over the question of who can reasonably be expected to hold a job. Opinions are settled for the extremes—for the severely disabled person on one extreme, or for the able-bodied father on the other. For poor single mothers, however, answers have been less clear. The resulting debate has raised important issues about poverty and about the dependency of a group that makes up an ever larger share of the nation's poor.

Over the years, the welfare system has placed increasingly more emphasis on work and self-support for this group and recently has moved decisively in this direction. This chapter first reviews this evolution in public policy. It then examines some of the current welfare reforms that are designed to improve the self-sufficiency of women on welfare and thereby to help reconcile the sometimes conflicting goals that comprise the work/welfare dilemma.

National welfare programs began with the 1935 passage of the Social Security Act, which authorized cash assistance to certain categories of needy individuals and provided for shared federal/state financing and administration. At the time, the categories seemed uncontroversial; they were designed to include individuals who were not expected to work and were thus considered deserving of assistance: the aged, the blind, and dependent children. (This last category was later expanded to include the mothers of dependent children, primarily presumed to be widows or the wives of disabled workers.)

It was expected that aid under these cash assistance programs would be temporary and small. Additionally, the issue of work incentives did not arise because of the consensus that the groups covered by cash assistance programs were unemployable. The relation between welfare and work was largely ignored.

By the 1960s, however, several factors combined to make the program for mothers with dependent children—Aid to Families with Dependent Children (AFDC)—the center of controversy. First, contrary to original expectations, AFDC rolls and expenditures grew rapidly: from 612,000 families and $618 million in 1955, to 2,208,000 families and $4,853 million by 1970 (U.S. Department of Health and Human Services 1981).

A second factor was the dramatic change in the proportion of working women and, as a result, in the public's attitude toward the appropriateness and equity of categorizing AFDC women as unemployable. While in 1935 it was accepted that women with children still at home should not work, this became increasingly less tenable as large numbers of such women took jobs. Persistent questions arose about the appropriateness of classifying some individuals as unemployable, while others, including mothers of school-age children, work and pay taxes.

Findings from research undertaken during the 1970s supported the idea that employment is a realistic and promising alternative for welfare recipients. For example, data on recipients' length of stay on AFDC have suggested that there is substantial turnover. And although the data are less clear on this point, it appears that employment is an important—although not the major—reason why many individuals leave the rolls.[2] Thus, it seemed reasonable to try to encourage this trend among welfare mothers.

Attempts to Solve the Dilemma
The 1960s and 1970s

During the period from the mid-1960s to the early 1970s, most efforts to increase the employment of welfare recipients included the provision of financial incentives to work that were built into the AFDC program itself. Most important, the 1967 amendments to the Social Security Act provided for a "disregard" of the first $30 and one-third of the remaining earnings of the recipient in the computation of AFDC benefits, thereby reducing the implicit statutory tax on earnings from 100 percent to 67 percent. Several studies that used nonexperimental data and findings from federally sponsored income maintenance experiments suggested, however, that more generous work incentives, by increasing the size of the beneficiary population, would reduce, rather than increase, the overall work effort.[3] This evidence and the high cost of a negative income tax approach led to a shift toward direct employment strategies and work requirements.

On the national level, such efforts actually began in 1967 when Congress authorized the creation of a special employment and training program for AFDC recipients: the Work Incentive (WIN) Program. Initially WIN was conceived as a voluntary program to provide support, training, education, and counseling services. In 1971, however, the focus changed. The program became mandatory: that is, applicants and recipients of AFDC (with certain exceptions, primarily for women with children under the age of 6) were required to register with WIN in order to receive AFDC benefits. Further, once on AFDC, a WIN registrant who was found employable, and for whom adequate social services such as child care were provided, could be required to accept an offered job or placement, or be sanctioned, that is, have his or her AFDC grant reduced for a specified time. In addition, the emphasis of the program shifted from preparation for employment and long-term employability development and training to immediate placement.

While WIN registration was mandatory, the cost of WIN services and the program's funding limitations have meant that only a small fraction of WIN registrants have actively participated. Most WIN offices have relegated a large share of the caseload to an inactive or "unassigned recipient" pool. In fiscal year 1978, the national WIN office reported that there were 949,074 unassigned recipients out of 1,553,010 registrants nationwide; in fiscal year 1981, there was an unassigned recipient pool of 826,339 out of 1,566,515 registrants.[4]

Another initiative to provide employment to welfare recipients, and one for which there are extensive and particularly reliable findings, is Supported Work. Originally tested through the multi-site, five-year National Supported Work Demonstration beginning in 1974, the program provided a structured work experience to four groups of individuals with severe employment difficulties: women who had been on AFDC for at least three years, former addicts, ex-offenders, and young school-dropouts. Participants were offered jobs for a limited time under conditions of close supervision, graduated stress, and peer support. After extensive evaluation using an experimental research design by which individuals were randomly assigned to the program or to a control group, Supported Work was found to be an effective method of helping women who were long-term recipients of welfare enter the labor market, while at the same time reducing welfare costs to participants.

AFDC women who took part in the program performed significantly better than did the controls in increased employment and earnings and reduced welfare dependence. Moreover, the differences held up consistently throughout the postprogram period, as reflected in interviews up to 40 months after enrollment. The data also suggest that the program was particularly beneficial for those who were least employable: women who were older, had not completed high school, had been on welfare a very long time, and had no previous work experience.

Women in the AFDC group sought and obtained jobs and remained employed even though their earnings were substantially offset by the loss of welfare benefits. In addition, the cost-benefit analysis for the AFDC group in the Supported Work Demonstration revealed that the program yielded considerable net benefits because of the earnings gains of participants, the value of the work performed, and the reduction in transfer payments received. In other words, a structured work experience for AFDC recipients could have long-term results and prove cost-effective. It should also be noted, however, that the program requires a relatively high initial investment of resources.[5]

The federal government, which was one of the funders of the demonstration, is no longer financing the Supported Work projects, but programs are operating in several states, notably California and Massachusetts, which have passed legislation to institutionalize the program.

In view of the high costs of providing traditional employment and training services to a large number of AFDC recipients, recent initiatives have tended to focus on two other methods of providing employment and improving employability—job search assistance and mandatory work experience.

Job search assistance programs are based on the theory that the main barrier to welfare recipients' finding jobs is not the absence of specific work skills or employment experience but recipients' inexperience in, and lack of effective techniques for, seeking out and obtaining a job. Since job search training, often conducted in a group, appears to be a relatively inexpensive service that can be provided in a short time, this approach is particularly appealing in a period of diminishing resources, when the stress is on the rapid job placement of as many welfare recipients as possible.

Several different models of group job search training were tried during the 1970s. They were similar, however, in that they all: assumed that there is a "hidden job market" of unadvertised jobs that people must be taught how to find; involved participants in a daily, full-time supervised job search; attempted to develop peer support and self-confidence among participants; taught specific job-seeking skills, such as resumé writing and interviewing; required participants to develop their own job leads; and included sessions in which participants, in a group setting, telephoned employers to obtain interviews.

The models of job search programs for welfare recipients evaluated during this period included the WIN-operated Job Finding clubs, studied by Nathan Azrin, the pioneer of group job search techniques; the Employment Opportunities Pilot Project (EOPP), a large-scale demonstration program run under the Carter administration; and two job search programs operated by the Louisville, Kentucky, WIN office between 1979 and 1981 (see Goldman, Chapter 16).[6] Generally, the research on these programs suggests that job search is a useful program to offer to women on welfare. They all resulted in at least modest and statistically significant gains in employment and earnings rates. There is no evidence, however, that they changed the kinds of low-paying jobs typically found by participants.

These findings are suggestive, but they were based on studies conducted before 1981, a watershed year for changes in the welfare system. Pre-1981 studies could not, therefore, describe the feasibility or effectiveness of job search in a changed environment, one that was to be characterized by a different set of rules for the calculation of benefits for working recipients and by an increased emphasis on mandatory, rather than voluntary, participation in such activities as job search.

Furthermore, questions remained about the cost-effectiveness (including the yield and cost of alternative staffing levels) of group job search and about appropriate targeting of the program. Also left uncertain was whether group job search should be mandated across the board or directed to particular groups of welfare women—for example, to women applying for welfare, to women already on the rolls, or to women with some employment experience. Little information existed on the usefulness of job search used in combination with other strategies to assist welfare women. Finally, little was known about the durability or decay of job search impacts.

Another approach to attract interest during the 1970s was the use of programs that require work in return for benefits or support. In some sense, these programs constitute the oldest strategy for tackling the work/welfare dilemma. Since the establishment of the Poor Laws in seventeenth-century Britain and in the American colonies, communities have required work from the able-bodied who do not support themselves or their families.

In the twentieth century, in response to massive unemployment, large-scale work relief programs were established for individuals dislocated by the Great Depression. Many states and counties have also made work a requirement for relief in their state-funded General Assistance programs (typically for single adults and childless couples). In the 1970s, several states—including Utah, California, and Massachusetts—developed work relief programs for all or some of their welfare recipients. Congress in 1977 also mandated a demonstration of work relief in the Food Stamps program.

Evaluations of some of these work relief programs have tended to focus more on how these programs were managed than on their effects, largely because, for several reasons, they floundered operationally, except when only a few participants were involved.

Where there were efforts to measure the effect of work relief, findings varied. Initial impact data for the Food Stamp Demonstration, based on a representative sample of individuals at matched demonstration and comparison sites, found different results for men and women, with possibly atypical results for San Diego (Ketron 1981). The study found that workfare significantly increased the earnings and reduced the food stamp allotment for females over the initial three-month postregistration period, while for males the program led to a reduction in earnings and food stamps. The cost-benefit results varied with the methodology used.

Studies of other programs tended to find that relatively small numbers of welfare recipients actually received work relief job assignments. Moreover, several of these programs gradually shifted the emphasis of work experience from simply working for a welfare grant towards providing well-structured and carefully chosen worksites as a means to assist participants in gaining job skills (Gueron and Nathan 1985). At the end of the 1970s, it was clear that there remained a great deal to learn about the effects, usefulness, and most effective operating techniques of work relief programs.

Post-1981

Even though a wide range of reforms to the AFDC program were adopted, the dilemma persisted. The 1980 election, and the inauguration of another administration interested in welfare reform, marked the beginning of a renewed focus on strategies to reduce the AFDC caseload and increase the transition of recipients to self-sufficient employment.

Under the Omnibus Budget Reconciliation Act (OBRA) of 1981 (with some modifications brought about by the Deficit Reduction Act of 1984), the $30 and one-third income disregard was eliminated after the first four months. In addition, through OBRA, the administration sought to begin a reform in the roles of the federal and state governments in welfare policy by granting the states greater discretion in this area while reducing federal matching funds.

Following the model of the California and Utah programs of the 1970s, the Omnibus Act authorized states for the first time to establish a work requirement for individuals required to register with WIN. States could choose to mandate participation for families with children aged 3 to 5 as well as for those with children over 6. Through this work relief program—the Community Work Experience Program (CWEP), sometimes also called "workfare" —states could require a WIN registrant to accept a public or nonprofit agency work assignment as a condition for receiving AFDC benefits, and to work a number of hours a month equivalent to the family's grant divided by the federal minimum wage.

The CWEP option was based on beliefs and expectations that had characterized the work experience efforts of the 1970s but that now were commanding increased interest. These included the notions that receipt of public assistance should be conditioned on providing useful community work; that work experience will assist people in making the transition to regular work; that some recipients of public assistance will leave the welfare rolls faster and some will not apply at all if faced with a work requirement; and that some recipients will refuse work relief assignments because they are already spending time earning unreported income. Also at this point the concept of work relief was attractive to a public sector that had experienced concurrent cutbacks in staffing when the Comprehensive Employment and Training Act Public Service Employment program was eliminated. In addition, the argument was posed that both recipients and their communities are likely to find that work programs confer greater dignity on the acceptance of welfare benefits.

The Community Work Experience Program also raised anew major questions that had never been answered in the 1970s: whether sufficient numbers of jobs that were publicly useful and not "make-work" could be created; whether participant performance in these positions could be monitored; whether welfare rolls would actually be reduced; and whether public employee groups would accept without complaint the supplementation of their work force by public assistance recipients.

The 1981 Omnibus Act also created the authority for states to propose special WIN Demonstration Projects, which would allow states to restructure the organization of their WIN Programs, divert AFDC benefits as wage subsidies to private-for-profit or other employers, and effect other changes in the operation and rules of their WIN Programs. Compared to WIN, a WIN Demonstration offers states greater flexibility and allows centralization of administration under a single agency.

In all, OBRA gave states much more latitude to design their own work/welfare programs. They could focus on many or all of a group of work-related activities, including a work requirement, job search, education or training; and they could sequence and target services as they saw fit.

Two important facts emerge from a consideration of welfare policy as it stood in the early 1980s:

1. Although the previous two decades had witnessed numerous initiatives to reduce the welfare rolls and help people make a transition to unsubsidized employment, there had emerged, with the exception of a few programs, little reliable information on which programs produce what results and for which groups, which are cost-efficient at what scale, and what kinds of specific operating techniques are most useful under what conditions.
2. Large federal funding cuts, public deficits and the greater emphasis on individual responsibilities and state discretion combined to place considerable pressure on state governments to undertake innovative and cost-effective programs in work/welfare.

It was within this context that the Manpower Demonstration Research Corporation (MDRC) in 1982 undertook a national demonstration of innovative, state-initiated work/welfare efforts. As of this writing, the demonstration is past the midpoint, and final results are now available in five of the programs.

A review of the information that has so far been generated by the study shows what kinds of strategies states are now adopting to improve the employability of women on welfare and suggests some early lessons on effectiveness and targeting of services.

The Demonstration of State Work/Welfare Initiatives

MDRC's 11-state Demonstration of State Work/Welfare Initiatives includes large-scale evaluations of new welfare/employment initiatives in eight states and smaller-scale studies in three additional states.[7] The states are broadly representative of national variations in AFDC benefit levels, administrative arrangements, and program capacity. Demonstration locations include several large urban areas—San Diego, Baltimore, and Chicago—and several multi-county areas that span urban and rural centers in Arkansas, Maine, New Jersey, Virginia, and West Virginia.[8]

The demonstration tests many different strategies. Some of the tested programs are limited to one or two activities, while others offer a wider mix. Most require participation as a condition of benefit receipt, but a few rely on a voluntary approach.

Contrary to some expectations, most states in the demonstration did not respond to the OBRA opportunities by deciding to implement universal workfare. An approach that was even more prominent was required job search. While the reasons are not always clear, the choice appears to have been the result of both practical and philosophical considerations. Job search is noncontroversial, relatively low-cost, and comparatively easy to run.

Among the demonstration states, only West Virginia operated a workfare program with no limit on a recipient's length of participation, and it was directed primarily to unemployed heads of two-parent households, who are mostly male (recipients of Aid to Families with Dependent Children-Unemployed Parent [AFDC-U]) rather than to the mostly female AFDC caseload. In placing more emphasis on work obligations for men than for women, West Virginia was unique among the 11 states.

Arkansas, California, and Illinois established a two-stage program of job search followed by a limited (usually three-month) work obligation for those who did not find unsubsidized jobs. Virginia required job search of everyone but offered CWEP as one option among other mandatory services. Maryland also offered a range of education and training options (including job search and unpaid work experience), with choices tailored to individual needs and preferences. New Jersey and Maine established voluntary on-the-job training programs with private employers, using grant diversion as the funding mechanism.[9]

The projects varied in scale, and although most were directed to women with school-age children, within that category they differed in the groups targeted—for example, welfare applicants or recipients.[10] Five of the programs were implemented in only part of their states (sometimes in only one city or county).

The states also differed in objectives. Some placed relatively more emphasis on human capital development and helping welfare recipients to get better jobs and achieve long-term self-sufficiency. Others tended to stress direct job placement and welfare savings.

As a result, states differed in the extent to which they emphasized and enforced a participation obligation. In each state the program can thus be described as a distinct multi-dimensional "treatment" that includes a specific degree of obligation and provides a certain mix and intensity of services and activities. The program's impact on eligibles can be conceived as a combination of the effect of both factors. The resulting treatment can in some cases be characterized as a work requirement (eligibles had to either get regular jobs or work for their grants) and in other cases as a participation obligation (those who did not find work would have to participate in program activities designed to help them obtain employment but would not necessarily have to work for their grant). For convenience, this discussion characterizes both types of programs as "participation obligations."

The Findings

The MDRC demonstration addresses four questions.[11]

QUESTION 1: *Is it feasible to impose obligations—or participation requirements—as a condition for welfare receipt?*

As noted earlier, pre-1981 initiatives that did seek to impose obligations on welfare recipients generally resulted in low participation rates and implementation failures. The MDRC study tries to determine whether the programs after OBRA repeat this experience or in fact succeed in implementing a broad participation obligation.

One indicator of accomplishments in this area is the "participation rate," defined in the MDRC demonstration as the proportion of registrants in the group under examination who ever showed up at a program activity within a given period.[12] For several reasons—including the fact that many nonparticipants have already left welfare or have had participation deferred for legitimate reasons such as temporary illness—nonparticipation is not synonymous with program failure. All nonparticipants have not been lost in the administrative shuffle of a large program. On the other hand, the participation rates may also overstate achievements, since they count only whether a participant showed up for an activity, not whether that person fully satisfied requirements.

Notwithstanding these caveats, the interim results suggest some tentative conclusions about the limits of participation in the initiatives. In most states, participation rates are running above those in previous special demonstrations or the WIN Program. Typically, within six to nine months of registering with the program, about one-half of the AFDC experimentals had participated in some activity, usually job search. Participation rates were lower in mandatory work programs when that activity followed job search in a sequence.

Findings from the San Diego program for AFDC and AFDC-U welfare applicants suggest that, at least in this program's environment and for the segment of the caseload it serves, it is possible to implement a broad participation obligation. Within nine months after application, all but a small proportion (no more than 9 percent) of sample members had either left welfare, become employed, were no longer in the program, or had fulfilled all requirements (Goldman et al. 1985).

Thus, the findings point to the feasibility of running large-scale mandatory programs for a substantial subset of the AFDC population. There was, however, considerable variation in participation rates across states. Rates were influenced by factors such as staff's degree of past experience in running employment programs, funding levels, the nature of the populations served, program scale, local economic conditions, and, finally, program goals—with the imposition of a participation requirement a primary concern in some states and a secondary one in others. In light of these variations, questions remain about the potential to duplicate this record in other states and about the feasibility of implementing an open-ended participation requirement on the entire welfare case load, as proposed in the Reagan administration "Work Opportunities and Welfare" legislation.

QUESTION 2: *What do workfare programs look like in practice and how do welfare recipients themselves judge the fairness of requirements?*

The workfare concept has engendered considerable controversy, which hinges largely on whether the positions offered to recipients are punitive and make-work and the system coercive or stigmatizing, or whether they produce useful goods and services, provide dignity, and develop work skills. The MDRC study uses an in-depth survey of a random sample of supervisors and work experience participants in six of the states to shed light on this controversy. The number of interviewees ranges from 25 to 94, depending on the state.

Survey findings to date, covering five states, provide a complex picture of how work experience programs look in practice.

- The jobs were generally entry-level positions in maintenance or clerical fields, park service, and human services, and sometimes were slots that had been paid positions under the Public Service Employment program, which Congress eliminated in 1981. On the whole, they did not provide much skill development, because most of the participants had the required general working skills at the time they began the assignment.

- While the positions did not primarily develop skills, they were not make-work either. Supervisors judged the work important and indicated that participants' productivity and attendance were similar to that of most entry-level workers.
- A high proportion of participants interviewed were satisfied with their work sites, felt positive about coming to work, believed that they were making a useful contribution, and felt that they were treated as part of the regular work force. However, many participants felt that the employer got the better end of the bargain, or that they were underpaid for their work. In short, they would rather have had a paid job. Nonetheless, most participants in most states agreed that a work requirement was fair. (Ball 1984; Friedlander et al. 1986; Friedlander et al., *Maryland,* 1985; Friedlander et al., *Arkansas,* 1985; Goldman et al. 1984; Price et al. 1985; Quint 1984b)

While some states placed more emphasis than others on using workfare as a way to achieve welfare savings or extract a quid pro quo for receiving benefits, results from the work site survey suggest that most states did not design or implement CWEP with a punitive intent. The survey results are also consistent with findings from other studies that show that the poor want to work. It has been observed that these workfare programs did not create the work ethic, they found it.

QUESTION 3: *Do the state initiatives reduce welfare rolls and costs or increase employment and earnings?*

In eight of the states, the MDRC study examines the program's effect on welfare and employment behavior. In all cases, the evaluations use experimental designs: program eligibles are randomly assigned to the new test program —the experimental group—or to a control group, which receives no services or limited ones. The differences between the employment and welfare behavior of experimentals and controls provides an estimate of program achievements. In an unusual display of commitment to such a study, the human resource commissioners and their local counterparts in the eight states actively cooperated with the random assignment of over 35,000 individuals.[13]

Assessing the impact results to date is very much like looking at a glass and characterizing it as half full or half empty. Depending on one's perspective, there are real accomplishments or there is a basis for caution. In either case, the findings are complex and require a careful reading.

First, the results dispel the notion that employment and training interventions do not work. In light of the findings for these work/welfare initiatives, it is no longer defensible to argue that welfare employment initiatives have no value. Using a variety of approaches, four of the five programs studied thus far produced positive employment gains for AFDC women. In interpreting these results, it is important to remember that they are averaged over a large segment of the caseload, for example, all applicants, both participants and nonparticipants. Thus, even relatively small changes multiplied by a large number of people have considerable policy significance.

The one exception to the pattern of the positive employment gains was the workfare program in West Virginia, where the state's high unemployment and rural conditions severely limited the job opportunities.

In San Diego, the program of mandatory job search followed by short-term CWEP increased quarterly employment rates by between 3 and 8 percentage points during the 15 months of follow-up. Average total earnings over the same period went up by $700 per experimental, representing a 23 percent increase over the control group's average earnings. (See Table 15-1.) Roughly half of the earnings gains came about because more women worked and half because they obtained longer-lasting jobs or jobs with better pay or longer hours. The employment gains persisted, although at a somewhat reduced level, throughout the almost 18 months of follow-up. In contrast, the program had minimal or no sustained employment effects on the primarily male group receiving AFDC-U assistance (not shown in Table 15-1).

There were relatively more modest changes in welfare dependency and benefit payments, with no evidence that once people had applied for welfare, they were deterred from that process by the work obligation. Over the full follow-up period, average welfare payments to experimentals were $288 below those paid to controls, a reduction in welfare outlays of almost 8 percent. (See Table 15-1.)

The Arkansas program for AFDC applicants and recipients, consisting of mandatory job search followed in some cases by short-term unpaid work experience, led to modest but statistically significant employment gains of between 3 and 5 percentage points per quarter, an increase of one-third over the very low control group level. Impacts on the welfare rolls and benefits were relatively large. (See Table 15-2.) By the third quarter of follow-up, 64 percent of the control group were receiving welfare, compared to 57 percent of experimentals. During the same period, average benefits fell from $289 to $246, for a difference of $43—a 15 percent reduction. Overall, more than three-quarters of the welfare savings occurred because people moved off the rolls.

In Baltimore, where both welfare applicants and welfare recipients were required to participate in any of a broad range of activities, the program led to similar increase in quarterly employment rates of between 3 and 5 percentage points and a 12-month increase in earnings of $176. But in contrast to Arkansas, San Diego, and Virginia, these gains were not accompanied by any notable welfare savings.[14] (See Table 15-3.)

Table 15-1/Summary of Impacts on AFDC Applicants in San Diego

	JOB SEARCH FOLLOWED BY CWEP		
OUTCOME AND FOLLOW-UP PERIOD	*Experimentals*	*Controls*	*Difference*
PERCENT EVER EMPLOYED DURING			
Quarter of random assignment[a]	35.5	33.1	+2.5
Quarter 2	35.6	28.7	+6.9***
Quarter 3	40.2	32.3	+7.8***
Quarter 4	42.4	36.9	+5.5***
Quarter 5	42.9	37.5	+5.4***
Quarter 6	41.9	38.1	+3.8*
AVERAGE TOTAL EARNINGS DURING			
QUARTERS 2–6 ($)[a]	3801.75	3101.63	+700.12***
PERCENT WHO EVER RECEIVED			
ANY AFDC PAYMENTS DURING			
Quarter of random assignment[b]	78.3	80.3	−2.0
Quarter 2	64.2	67.6	−3.4*
Quarter 3	51.8	56.2	−4.5**
Quarter 4	45.8	47.9	−2.0
Quarter 5	39.5	41.1	−1.7
Quarter 6	35.0	36.2	−1.2
AVERAGE TOTAL AFDC PAYMENTS			
RECEIVED DURING QUARTERS 1–6 ($)	3409.32	3696.94	−287.62**

Source: Goldman et al. 1986.

Notes: These data include zero values for sample members not employed and for sample members not receiving welfare payments. There may be some discrepancies in calculating experimental-control differences because of rounding.

A two-tailed t-test was applied to differences between Experimental and Control groups.

[a] For Unemployment Insurance earnings quarters, random assignment may occur in any of the three months of calendar quarter of random assignment. For this reason, quarter 1, the quarter of random assignment, may contain some earnings from a month or two before random assignment, and it is therefore not counted as a complete follow-up quarter for employment and earnings impacts.

[b] The first month of the quarter of random assignment is the month in which an individual is randomly assigned.

*$p \leq .10$
**$p \leq .05$
***$p \leq .01$

The Virginia program for AFDC applicants and recipients, centering on mandatory job search followed by work experience and limited other services, led to modest quarterly employment gains of between 2 and 4 percentage points during the 12-month follow-up. Although the average total AFDC payments over the same period decreased by $84—a 4 percent reduction—there was no change in the number of people leaving welfare. (See Table 15-4.) Unlike most other states in the demonstration, Virginia targeted the entire WIN-mandatory caseload.

Table 15-2/Summary of Impacts on AFDC Applicants and Recipients in Two Counties in Arkansas

OUTCOME AND FOLLOW-UP PERIOD	EXPERIMENTALS	CONTROLS	DIFFERENCE
PERCENT EVER EMPLOYED DURING			
Quarter of random assignment[a]	16.1	11.8	+4.3**
Quarter 2	14.6	9.6	+5.0***
Quarter 3	15.2	12.2	+3.1*
AVERAGE TOTAL EARNINGS DURING			
QUARTERS 2–3 ($)[a]	290.63	212.94	+77.70*
PERCENT WHO EVER RECEIVED			
ANY AFDC PAYMENTS DURING			
Quarter of random assignment[b]	66.6	69.0	−2.4
Quarter 2	65.6	71.4	−5.9**
Quarter 3	56.8	63.8	−6.9***
AVERAGE TOTAL AFDC PAYMENTS			
RECEIVED DURING QUARTERS 1–3 ($)	771.69	864.55	−92.86***

Source: Friedlander et al., *Arkansas*, 1985.

Notes: These data include zero values for sample members not employed and for sample members not receiving welfare payments. There may be some discrepencies in calculating experimental-control differences because of rounding.

A two-tailed t-test was applied to differences between Experimental and Control groups.

[a] For Unemployment Insurance earnings quarters, random assignment may occur in any of the three months of calendar quarter of random assignment. For this reason, quarter 1, the quarter of random assignment, may contain some earnings from a month or two before random assignment, and it is therefore not counted as a complete follow-up quarter for employment and earnings impacts.

[b] The first month of the quarter of random assignment is the month in which an individual is randomly assigned.

$*p \leq .10$
$**p \leq .05$
$***p \leq .01$

The findings are very different in West Virginia, where the relatively straightforward workfare program led to no significant increases in regular, unsubsidized employment or reductions in the AFDC caseload. (See Table 15-5.)

Although there are many possible explanations for the West Virginia results—including the design of the program or the characteristics of the women served—the most likely one was foreseen by the program's planners, who did not anticipate any employment gains. In a largely rural state that recorded the nation's highest unemployment rate during part of the research period, a welfare employment initiative could provide a positive work experience without translating this into postprogram unsubsidized employment gains.

West Virginia's program is a useful reminder that there are two sides to the labor market. Welfare employment programs focus on the supply side. In

Table 15-3/Summary of Impacts on AFDC Applicants and Recipients in Baltimore

OUTCOME AND FOLLOW-UP PERIOD	EXPERIMENTALS	CONTROLS	DIFFERENCE
PERCENT EVER EMPLOYED DURING			
Quarter of random assignment[a]	28.1	26.4	+1.8
Quarter 2	27.2	24.0	+3.2**
Quarter 3	32.4	27.9	+4.5***
Quarter 4	34.7	31.6	+3.1*
Quarter 5	36.5	31.6	+5.0***
AVERAGE TOTAL EARNINGS DURING			
QUARTERS 2–5 ($)[a]	1935.15	1758.74	+176.41
PERCENT WHO EVER RECEIVED			
ANY AFDC PAYMENTS DURING			
Quarter of random assignment[b]	92.5	92.1	+0.4
Quarter 2	87.3	87.5	−0.2
Quarter 3	77.4	76.2	−0.8
Quarter 4	71.7	73.2	−1.5
Quarter 5	68.8	70.4	−1.7
AVERAGE TOTAL AFDC PAYMENTS			
RECEIVED DURING QUARTERS 1–5 ($)	3058.03	3084.12	−6.09

Source: Friedlander et al., *Maryland*, 1985.

Notes: These data include zero values for sample members not employed and for sample members not receiving welfare payments. There may be some discrepencies in calculating experimental-control differences because of rounding.

A two-tailed t-test was applied to differences between Experimental and Control groups.

[a] For Unemployment Insurance earnings quarters, random assignment may occur in any of the three months of calendar quarter of random assignment. For this reason, quarter 1, the quarter of random assignment, may contain some earnings from a month or two before random assignment, and it is therefore not counted as a complete follow-up quarter for employment and earnings impacts.

[b] The first month of the quarter of random assignment is the month in which an individual is randomly assigned.

*$p \leq .10$
**$p \leq .05$
***$p \leq .01$

extreme cases, when the demand is not there, the provision of work experience and a change in the terms of the welfare "bargain" may simply not be enough to affect employment levels. Welfare recipients can be encouraged or required to take regular jobs, but the jobs must be available. The results to date suggest that demand constraints may be particularly acute in rural areas.[15]

A second encouraging piece of information is that the programs were most helpful for certain segments of the welfare caseload. For example, employment increases were usually greater for women receiving AFDC than for men on AFDC-U, and for those with no prior employment compared to those with a recent work history. Although women, and those without recent

Table 15-4/Summary of Impacts on AFDC Applicants and Recipients in Virginia

OUTCOME AND FOLLOW-UP PERIOD	EXPERIMENTALS	CONTROLS	DIFFERENCE
PERCENT EVER EMPLOYED DURING			
Quarter of random assignment[a]	27.2	25.7	+1.5
Quarter 2	28.3	26.4	+1.9
Quarter 3	31.2	27.9	+3.3**
Quarter 4	34.4	30.5	+3.9**
AVERAGE TOTAL EARNINGS DURING			
QUARTERS 2–4 ($)[a]	1119.05	1038.16	+80.89
PERCENT WHO EVER RECEIVED			
ANY AFDC PAYMENTS DURING			
Quarter of random assignment[b]	82.8	82.9	−0.2
Quarter 2	76.3	76.4	−0.0
Quarter 3	65.9	67.5	−1.6
Quarter 4	59.7	59.8	−0.1
AVERAGE TOTAL AFDC PAYMENTS			
RECEIVED DURING QUARTERS 1–4 ($)	1923.28	2006.87	−83.59**

Source: Riccio et al. 1986.

Notes: These data include zero values for sample members not employed and for sample members not receiving welfare payments. There may be some discrepencies in calculating experimental-control differences because of rounding.

A two-tailed t-test was applied to differences between Experimental and Control groups.

[a] For Unemployment Insurance earnings quarters, random assignment may occur in any of the three months of calendar quarter of random assignment. For this reason, quarter 1, the quarter of random assignment, may contain some earnings from a month or two before random assignment, and it is therefore not counted as a complete follow-up quarter for employment and earnings impacts.

[b] The first month of the quarter of random assignment is the month in which an individual is randomly assigned.

$*p \leq .10$

$**p \leq .05$

$***p \leq .01$

employment were still less likely to be working and more likely to be on welfare than women with recent work history and men, employment requirements and services helped narrow the gap.[16]

QUESTION 4: *How do program benefits compare to program costs?*

A benefit-cost analysis measures the programs' outcomes against the resources used to produce them. It shows the net benefits for society as a whole, and it identifies who—the welfare population or everyone else—gains from and pays for the programs.

When benefits were compared to costs, results were generally positive. An examination of the programs' effects on the government budget show that, not surprisingly, such initiatives cost money up front, but in general, the investment pays off in future budget savings in five years or less. In San Diego,

Table 15-5/Summary of Impacts on AFDC Applicants and Recipients in West Virginia

OUTCOME AND FOLLOW-UP PERIOD	EXPERIMENTALS	CONTROLS	DIFFERENCE
PERCENT EVER EMPLOYED DURING			
Quarter of random assignment[a]	8.4	9.2	−0.8
Quarter 2	9.2	9.9	−0.8
Quarter 3	10.9	11.2	−0.3
Quarter 4	12.0	13.1	−1.0
Quarter 5	12.7	13.8	−1.1
Quarter 6	13.4	13.8	−0.4
AVERAGE TOTAL EARNINGS DURING			
QUARTERS 2–6 ($)[a]	712.51	712.20	+0.32
PERCENT WHO EVER RECEIVED			
ANY AFDC PAYMENTS DURING			
Quarter of random assignment[b]	94.2	93.2	+1.0
Quarter 2	87.6	86.7	+0.9
Quarter 3	78.0	79.0	−1.0
Quarter 4	70.9	72.5	−1.5
Quarter 5	65.5	67.8	−2.3
Quarter 6	61.8	63.5	−1.7
Quarter 7	57.8	60.7	−2.8*
AVERAGE TOTAL AFDC PAYMENTS			
RECEIVED DURING QUARTERS 1–7 ($)	2681.37	2721.40	−40.03

Source: Friedlander et al. 1986.

Notes: These data include zero values for sample members not employed and for sample members not receiving welfare payments. There may be some discrepencies in calculating experimental-control differences because of rounding.

A two-tailed t-test was applied to differences between Experimental and Control groups.

[a] For Unemployment Insurance earnings quarters, random assignment may occur in any of the three months of calendar quarter of random assignment. For this reason, quarter 1, the quarter of random assignment, may contain some earnings from a month or two before random assignment, and it is therefore not counted as a complete follow-up quarter for employment and earnings impacts.

[b] The first month of the quarter of random assignment is the month in which an individual is randomly assigned.

*$p \leq .10$

**$p \leq .05$

***$p \leq .01$

an average dollar spent on the program for AFDC women led to estimated budget savings over a five-year period of over $2.00. Programs in Arkansas and Virginia also had estimated budget savings, while in Baltimore and West Virginia, there were some net costs.

The research also offers some unusual findings on the distribution of benefits across federal, state, and county budgets, a question not often addressed in benefit-cost studies. In San Diego, where a detailed study was conducted, all three levels of government ultimately gained under the particular funding formulas and matching arrangements in place. However, the federal government bore more than half of the costs but also enjoyed the greatest net savings. Indeed, had there been no federal funds—or had there been less—the state and county would have had no financial incentive to run these programs. The findings highlight the importance of continued federal support to encourage states to undertake welfare employment initiatives that may ultimately prove cost-effective to operate.

Another way to look at program benefits and costs is to examine them from the perspectives of the groups targeted for participation—that is, those who might have earned more as a result of the program, but who also might have lost money because of reductions in welfare and other transfer payments, such as Medicaid and Food Stamps. In most cases, the AFDC women came out ahead. The exceptions were in Arkansas, where almost any employment, in a state with such low grants, led to case closings, and West Virginia, where there were no gains in earnings. For men on AFDC-U, the story was very different. There were overall losses, not gains, from the programs, because reductions in welfare and other transfer payments exceeded increases in earnings.

Issues and Conclusions

In deciding what kinds of programs should be directed to women on welfare to improve their success in the labor market, policy makers face complicated but not unanswerable questions. Research, both past and current, offers insights that should help them reach decisions on the structure and targeting of services.

The diverse state strategies now being tried constitute one important learning opportunity for those who wish to design better approaches. In examining a group of these state strategies, MDRC's ongoing demonstration already points to several conclusions, which will be explored in more depth as the study progresses. Among other observations, it suggests the feasibility, under certain conditions and at the scale used in those programs, of tying welfare receipt to participation obligations, be they job search, workfare, or a "menu" of activities.

Among all the obligations used by the states, workfare is the one that has engendered the most controversy. Thus far, the interim results do not support the strongest claims of critics. Today's "workfare" is more likely to be designed to provide useful work experience than simply to enforce a quid pro quo, although both objectives may operate. As a result, the positions often resemble public service employment jobs, structured to meet public needs and provide useful work experience. Under these conditions and with the obligation usually limited to three months, welfare recipients generally did not object to working for their grants. Nor, however, do the findings so far justify the more extreme claims of proponents. The work positions provide relatively little skills development. Furthermore, although results from San Diego—where the research design allowed for the separate estimate of the effects of job search and work experience—provided some evidence that adding workfare after job search may increase a program's effectiveness, the West Virginia results are a cautious reminder that at least in certain conditions what is needed is not just workfare positions but regular jobs.[17] Moreover, there was no evidence in San Diego that the work mandate as it was administered deterred individuals from completing their welfare applications or "smoked out" large numbers of AFDC women who held jobs with unreported income.

Thus, arguments for and against workfare may involve not so much a trade-off between welfare savings and fairness as questions about the values attached to the AFDC program. Some will argue, as did the West Virginia human services commissioner, that even if workfare costs more up front, it represents a sounder design for AFDC because it fits with the nation's values and will thus improve the image of welfare among recipients and the public.[18] Others will contend that what is needed are not requirements but jobs and investments in training.

The impact results from the demonstration indicate that many quite different program approaches will lead to increases in employment but that the gains will be relatively modest. For those used to grandiose claims, this conclusion will appear discouraging. The real lesson, however, is quite different. When available, careful impact and benefit-cost studies show that work approaches for welfare recipients can increase employment and be cost-effective. Admittedly, the gains are not likely to be dramatic and the savings are going to be limited.

But programs do not necessarily have to effect dramatic changes to be worthwhile. The small savings achieved through these programs may often be large enough to justify their costs. Furthermore, modest impacts can be significant if they are long-lasting or if they occur for a large number of people. Thus, the research points to an important finding about expectations. In the past, we have had to oversell social programs to convince policy makers that they were useful investments. The data from these state programs suggest that this is not necessary.

The findings also indicate that it may be possible to target resources more carefully and thereby to increase program effectiveness. A lesson that emerges both from the Work/Welfare demonstration and from earlier programs like Supported Work is that impacts are likely to be larger for women who would be considered more disadvantaged or less employable.

This does not mean that these hard-to-employ groups had the highest

384 / Welfare, Workfare, and Training

placement rates and levels of postprogram employment. On the contrary, the data show that these outcomes were generally much higher for the individuals who seemed more able to go to work.[19]

While seemingly contradictory, this pattern is consistent with the dynamics of the welfare population. For many, welfare is only a temporary source of aid. A program achieving high placement rates by working with people who would have found jobs on their own may look more successful but, in fact, may not have accomplished much. In contrast, a program working with those who would do very poorly on their own may have less impressive placement or employment rates but may have made a major change in behavior.

Current knowledge about welfare caseload dynamics also suggests that it makes little sense to target very expensive program services to women who are likely to cycle off welfare with little or no assistance.[20] An alternative strategy —and one used by several states in the Work/Welfare demonstration—is to use job search as a relatively low-cost method of identifying which women will be able to move into jobs with only modest assistance and which will require more extensive help.[21]

One reason to adopt this system is that past research has shown that the a priori judgments of staff in employability programs are poor predictors of whether or not welfare women are ready to work. Thus, using the outcomes of an actual job search appears to be a more reliable way to determine which women can enter the labor market with relatively little assistance. Conversely, programs like Supported Work, which provide more intensive training and work experience, should be reserved for long-term welfare recipients. At this point, administrators should not be deterred from Supported Work by its relatively high cost. Despite the expenses entailed, administrators should remember that Supported Work has been shown to be cost-effective.

The difficulty in applying this last lesson to practice is that the traditional measure of success, program placements, creates incentives and rewards that push administrators toward serving the more advantaged segments of the welfare population. The challenge for policy makers and program administrators is to resist the allure of high placement rates and to concentrate on the more difficult task of reducing welfare dependency. As this discussion has suggested, real changes will necessarily be incremental, but meaningful improvement is nonetheless a realizable goal.

Notes

1. Much of the background information in this introductory section was first presented in Gueron 1983 and in Chapter 1 of Goldman et al. 1984.
2. For a review of the literature on this question see Hutchens 1982. For a recent discussion of welfare dynamics, see Bane and Ellwood 1983 and Ellwood 1986.

3. See Moffitt and Kehrer 1981 for a summary of these results. See also U.S. Department of Health and Human Services 1983.

4. Information, as of September 1978 and September 1981, prepared by the Office of Work Incentive Programs, Division of Program Planning and Review.

5. On the Supported Work Demonstration, see Board of Directors, Manpower Demonstration Research Corporation 1980 and Hollister, Kemper, and Maynard 1984.

6. On Azrin's job clubs, see Azrin 1978, and Azrin, Flores, and Kaplan 1975, 17–27. On EOP see Brown et al. 1983. For a summary of the Louisville demonstrations on which the material in Chapter 16 of this book is based, see Wolfhagen and Goldman 1983.

7. Much of the discussion in this section was originally published as Gueron 1986. Also see Gueron 1987 for a discussion of the findings from the demonstration and implications for national policy.

8. For convenience, this discussion refers to "states" and "state programs," even though many programs in the demonstration cover only parts of states.

9. In all, five of the states required participation in some form of job search and six had a mandatory unpaid work experience component. Of those, four used the CWEP formula (by which work hours were determined by dividing the AFDC grant by the minimum wage) and two used a system in which the number of hours was unrelated to the grant level (WIN Work Experience).

10. MDRC's research identifies these subgroups by their welfare status when they entered the research sample. Thus, applicants who eventually became recipients continue to be designated as applicants.

11. The findings discussed here are presented in the reports thus far released by the Manpower Demonstration Research Corporation, New York City, as part of the Work/Welfare demonstration. They include Auspos 1985; Ball 1984; Bangser, Healy, and Ivry 1985; Bangser, Healy, and Ivry 1986; Goldman et al. 1984; Goldman et al. 1985; Price et al. 1985; Quint 1984a; Quint 1984b; and Sherwood 1984. Except for Goldman et al. 1985, which covers some interim impact findings and presents a process analysis, all of these studies focus on implementation findings. Final reports, containing final impact results, that have so far been published are: Friedlander et al. 1986; Friedlander et al., *Maryland,* 1985; Friedlander et al., *Arkansas,* 1985; Goldman, Friedlander, and Long 1986; Riccio et al. 1986.

12. This measure is not identical to the participation goals set in the Reagan administration's "work opportunities and welfare" proposal, which would require ongoing participation from 75 percent of the eligible caseload in each state.

13. For a description of the process MDRC followed in promoting and implementing random assignment, see Gueron 1985.

14. Several other recent studies of AFDC work programs have found similar gains in employment with smaller or no welfare savings. Part of the explanation probably lies in the benefit calculation rules, which allow deductions from gross earnings of work-related expenses such as documented child care, plus $30 and one-third applied to the balance for four months. The length of follow-up in Baltimore was notably short, given the longer duration of program services for some participants. To ensure that the study did not mistake the program's accomplishments, additional work is now under way to determine whether the measured impacts increase or decay over a longer period.

15. The Virginia and Arkansas studies also showed lower or no employment gains in rural as compared to urban areas. See Riccio et al. 1986; Friedlander et al., *Arkansas*, 1985.

16. This pattern of differences is not as clear for the most disadvantaged recipients. See Friedlander 1988.

17. One unusual feature of the San Diego study was the simultaneous random assignment of AFDC applicants to a control group and to two experimental treatments: job search alone and job search followed by short-term workfare. The results showed that job search alone also had positive impacts (that is, employment gains and welfare savings), but the findings were less consistent and the gains in earnings smaller than for the combined program. This suggests that, under certain circumstances, employment impacts may be greater if individuals who do not find employment in job search workshops are required to meet a short-term work obligation. For further discussion of the findings for the programs in San Diego and West Virginia, see Goldman, Friedlander, and Long 1986 and Friedlander et al. 1986.

18. See the views of Leon Ginsberg (1983) on workfare.

19. In addition, one study of the impact of five welfare employment programs found that when subgroups of WIN-mandatory AFDC women were defined by previous work and welfare experience, the most job-ready and least welfare-dependent groups had below-average program impacts, which were often the smallest impacts. See Friedlander 1988.

20. See Bane and Ellwood 1983; and Ellwood 1986.

21. See Goldman, Chapter 16 of this book, for a fuller discussion of this point.

References

Auspos, Patricia. 1985. *Maine: Interim Findings from a Grant Diversion Program.* New York: Manpower Demonstration Research Corporation.

Azrin, Nathan H. 1978. *The Job Finding Club as a Method for Obtaining Employment for Welfare-Eligible Clients: Demonstration, Evaluation, and Counselor Training.* Anna, Ill.: Anna Mental Health and Development Center.

Azrin, Nathan; T. Flores; and S. J. Kaplan. 1975. "Job Finding Club: A Group-Assisted Program for Obtaining Employment." *Behavior Research and Therapy* 13:17–27.

Ball, Joseph. 1984. *West Virginia: Interim Findings on the West Virginia Community Work Experience Programs.* New York: Manpower Demonstration Research Corporation.

Bane, Mary Jo, and David Ellwood. 1983. "The Dynamics of Dependence: The Routes to Self-Sufficiency." Cambridge, Mass.: Urban Systems and Engineering, Inc.

Bangser, Michael; James Healy; and Robert Ivry. 1985. *Welfare Grant Diversion: Early Observations from Programs in Six States.* New York: Manpower Demonstration Research Corporation.

———. 1986. *Welfare Grant Diversion: Lessons and Prospects.* New York: Manpower Demonstration Research Corporation.

Board of Directors. Manpower Demonstration Research Corporation. 1980. *Summary and Findings of the National Supported Work Demonstration.* Cambridge, Mass.: Ballinger.

Brown, Randall S.; John Burghardt; Edward Cavin; David Long; Charles Mallar; Rebecca Maynard; Charles Metcalf; Craig Thornton; and Christine Whitebread. 1983. "The Employment Opportunities Pilot Project: Analysis of Program Impacts." Princeton, N.J.: Mathematica Policy Research, Inc.

Ellwood, David. 1986. "Targeting 'Would-Be' Long-Term Recipients of AFDC." Princeton, N.J.: Mathematica Policy Research, Inc.

Friedlander, Daniel. 1988. *Subgroup Impacts And Performance Indicators for Selected Welfare Employment Programs.* New York: Manpower Demonstration Research Corporation.

Friedlander, Daniel; Marjorie Erickson; Gayle Hamilton; and Virginia Knox. 1986. *West Virginia: Final Report on the Community Work Experience Demonstrations.* New York: Manpower Demonstration Research Corporation.

Friedlander, Daniel; Gregory Hoerz; David Long; and Janet Quint. 1985. *Maryland: Final Report on the Employment Initiatives Evaluation.* New York: Manpower Demonstration Research Corporation.

Friedlander, Daniel; Gregory Hoerz; Janet Quint; and James Riccio. 1985. *Arkansas: Final Report on the WORK Program in Two Counties.* New York: Manpower Demonstration Research Corporation.

Ginsberg, Leon. 1983. "Ginsberg: Workfare Is Working in West Virginia." *National Association of Social Workers News* 28, no. 4.

Goldman, Barbara; Daniel Friedlander; and David Long. 1986. *California: Final Report on the San Diego Job Search and Work Experience Demonstration.* New York: Manpower Demonstration Research Corporation.

Goldman, Barbara; Daniel Friedlander; Judith Gueron; and David Long. 1985. *California: Findings from the San Diego Job Search and Work Experience Demonstration.* New York: Manpower Demonstration Research Corporation.

Goldman, Barbara; Judith Gueron; Joseph Ball; and Marilyn Price. 1984. *California: Preliminary Findings from the San Diego Job Search and Work Experience Demonstration.* New York: Manpower Demonstration Research Corporation.

Gueron, Judith M. 1984. "The Background of Work and Welfare." *Review of Employment and Employability of Participants in the Food Stamps and Related Welfare Programs.* Hearing before the Subcommittee on Domestic Marketing, Consumer Relations and Nutrition of the Committee on Agriculture, U.S. House of Representatives. Washington, D.C.: Government Printing Office.

———. 1985. "The Demonstration of Work/Welfare Initiatives." *New Direction for Program Evaluation,* no. 28 (December).

———. 1986. "Work for People on Welfare." *Public Welfare* 44, no. 1 (Winter).

———. 1987. *Reforming Welfare with Work.* New York: Ford Foundation.

Gueron, Judith M., and Richard Nathan. 1985. "The MDRC Work/Welfare Project: Objectives, Status, Significance." *Policy Studies Review* 4, no. 3 (February).

Hollister, Robinson J., Jr.; Peter Kemper; and Rebecca Maynard, eds. 1984. *The National Supported Work Demonstration.* Madison: The University of Wisconsin Press.

Hutchens, Robert. 1982. "Recipient Movement from Welfare Toward Economic Independence: A Literature Review." Report prepared for the Council of State Planning Agencies and U.S. Department of Health and Human Services.

Ketron, Inc. 1981. "Food Stamp Workfare Demonstration Project: Report on the Short-Term Impact of the First Year Project." Wayne, Penn.: Ketron, Inc.

Moffitt, Robert A., and Kenneth C. Kehrer. 1981. "The Effect of Tax and Transfer Programs on Labor Supply: The Evidence from the Income Experiments." In Ronald Ehrenberg, ed. *Research in Labor Economics: Evaluating Manpower Training Programs*. Greenwich, Conn.: JAI Press.

Price, Marilyn; Joseph Ball; Barbara Goldman; David Gruber; Judith Gueron; and Gayle Hamilton. 1985. *Virginia: Interim Findings from the Virginia Employment Services Program*. New York: Manpower Demonstration Research Corporation.

Quint, Janet. 1984a. *Arkansas: Interim Findings from the Arkansas WIN Demonstration Program*. New York: Manpower Demonstration Research Corporation.

————. 1984b. *Maryland: Interim Findings from the Maryland Employment Initiatives Program*. New York: Manpower Demonstration Research Corporation.

Riccio, James; George Cave; Stephen Freedman; and Marilyn Price. 1986. *Virginia: Final Report on the Virginia Employment Services Program*. New York: Manpower Demonstration Research Corporation.

Sherwood, Kay. 1984. *Preliminary Management Lessons From the Arizona WIN Demonstration Program*. New York: Manpower Demonstration Research Corporation.

U.S. Department of Health and Human Services. Social Security Administration. 1981. *Social Security Bulletin*. Annual Statistical Supplement.

————. Office of the Assistant Secretary for Planning and Evaluation. Office of Income Security Policy. 1983. *Overview of the Seattle-Denver Income Maintenance Experiment*. Final Report. May.

Wolfhagen, Carl, and Barbara S. Goldman. 1983. *Job Search Strategies: Lessons from the Louisville WIN Laboratory*. New York: Manpower Demonstration Research Corporation.

16/Job Search Strategies for Women on Welfare

Barbara S. Goldman

During the early 1980s, job search programs became a popular strategy for helping women on welfare to enter the labor market. Take, for example, one woman's experience:

> *Nadine, a 23-year-old welfare recipient under the Aid to Families with Dependent Children Program (AFDC),[1] lived alone with her six-year-old daughter. She had completed 11 years of school and worked for a brief period as a cleaner and cab driver; she had also done some construction work.*
>
> *Every day she arrived on time at the Louisville, Kentucky, local Work Incentive (WIN) Program office, the employment program attached to the AFDC program with which she had been required to register when she applied for public assistance. She reported to the Telephone Room of her WIN group job club, where she sat at the center table with other women in her classroom group. Together they talked and made jokes for awhile and then turned to concentrate on writing lists of employers in their log books. Soon, however, Nadine or one of the others would interrupt the quiet with another comment, and the women's conversation would resume. Topics ranged from possible job leads and interview experiences to home life and men. Nadine was the most active participant in these casual conversations. She joked and laughed, encouraging the others to tease her. During the morning, Nadine would not sit quietly for long but fidgeted and talked. Occasionally a counselor reminded her to be quiet, since other women were using the telephones.*
>
> *Although not achieving the quota of 50 daily telephone calls to employers, Nadine did keep calling. She managed to arrange several interviews but was unsuccessful in getting a job. Yet she continued to be cheerful, obviously uplifted by the company of the other job-seekers.*

With encouragement from her group members, she stopped wearing the tightly fitted knitted cap in which she had first appeared. Then, after several weeks in the telephone room, a fellow participant told Nadine about an opening for a cleaner in a medical supply store. Nadine went on that interview and was hired.

The group job search program in which Nadine took part was studied during 1980 and 1981 by the Manpower Demonstration Research Corporation (MDRC), a nonprofit research corporation that evaluates programs designed to help the poor become economically self-sufficient. In an earlier 1978–79 experiment, MDRC examined an individual job search program operated out of the same Louisville (WIN) office, in which women looked for jobs on their own, with the assistance of employment counselors or social workers, rather than in a peer setting, as Nadine did.

Job search programs have strong intuitive appeal. Rather than training welfare recipients or developing specific jobs for them, such programs presume that with instruction, modest financial assistance, and some structure within which to operate, many welfare recipients will be able to find jobs and begin to support themselves through their own efforts. Individual job search programs supply job leads; participants assume much of the burden of job hunting and report back to their counselors on their efforts. Group job search programs generally begin with classes on job search techniques and then place participants in group settings where they make "cold calls" to prospective employers.

It is not surprising that during the mid-1980s state welfare administrators, who were given increased discretion for designing employment programs under the Omnibus Budget Reconciliation Act (OBRA) of 1981, but who are faced with limited resources, have increasingly turned to the job search approach as a low-cost option to help a large number of welfare recipients. Although the Louisville experiments were operated at a different time and under a different set of AFDC work incentives, they illuminate some early lessons for these post-OBRA efforts. More generally, they yield a number of interesting insights about the potential of job search programs to assist women on welfare.

The WIN Research Laboratory Project

The MDRC Louisville studies were themselves part of a larger set of separate evaluations conducted by MDRC in four local WIN offices from 1977 through 1981. Jointly, the evaluations were called the WIN Research Laboratory Project, or the WIN Labs. The Labs were a cooperative venture of the National WIN Office and the Office of Research and Development of the U.S.

Department of Labor, with supplemental funding from the Ford Foundation.[2]

The Labs were designed to nurture a process of innovation in a system more noted for its adherence to procedure than its flexibility or capacity for new program development. As a mandated program for welfare recipients, WIN theoretically required all individuals applying for or receiving AFDC who were not exempt—broadly speaking, people with no preschool-age children —to take part in its employment-related activities. In fact, for most women registration was the only activity they participated in.[3]

WIN had only modest resources to work with its registrants and much was consumed in processing people. Staff determined whether welfare recipients were employable; assigned them to education, training, and other activities —but more often to a "hold" status—and arranged child care for those who were active.

One study of decision making in three local WIN offices found that although workers in each office all collected the same kind of information on their registrants, they processed it differently. Factors like high caseloads and few program resources meant that WIN workers would be inclined to assign people with barriers to employment—for example, little or no work history or particularly low levels of education—to a hold status (see Levy 1981).

In view of such criticisms, officials involved in the development of the WIN Labs wanted to help the system find more streamlined and creative ways of assisting women on welfare. Furthermore, they believed that for innovation to really take hold, it was important to start the process at the local level, rather than to impose new ideas developed outside the system. Thus, the Labs were designed as separate experiments, each initiated at the individual local WIN office and then tested by MDRC.[4]

The Origins of the Louisville Experiments

The Louisville WIN office did not set out to test job search programs. The first interest for staff and managers was a concept they called "immediate services." Louisville workers were concerned about the delays that took place in their office between the time a woman walked in the door and the time that she was actually assigned to an activity—on average, six weeks. These delays reflected the lack of resources as well as the program rules which at that time prevented WIN from serving registrants who had not yet been approved for welfare. During that period, they reasoned, women who initially might have been reasonably enthusiastic about WIN could easily become discouraged. To address this problem, the Louisville office staff decided to find out what would happen to a group of women who were assigned to a WIN activity with as few delays as possible and to have these results compared to those for another group who would be processed at the usual pace.

To infuse the immediacy concept with more content than the typical WIN experience, office staff were urged to assign as many eligible women as possible to a substantive activity, rather than to a "hold" status, even if they had not yet been approved for welfare. (A condition of grant approval is WIN registration. Individuals who do not register with WIN will not have their grant applications approved.) The activity to which they were encouraged to direct women was job search. The choice was not accidental. It was in keeping with a trend in service provision that was beginning to make itself felt at WIN offices around the country in the late 1970s.

During the 1960s the major WIN activities offered to welfare women had been education and training. By the 1970s, however, WIN officials embraced the growing interest in activities that would be of shorter duration, and that could reach a broader group of women by providing them with a less intensive, less costly, and less complex set of services. Job search activities fit this description.

Not surprisingly, then, for its first experiment under the auspices of the WIN Labs, the Louisville office turned to an official WIN activity ("component" in WIN terminology) that involved structured job search. It was called Intensive Employability Services, or IES. Women assigned to IES were given job leads by their WIN counselors and were asked to report back on how their job hunts had progressed. They were provided with stipends for child care, lunch, and transportation, and a small incentive payment for every day that they actively looked for jobs. Unlike many of today's job search programs operated by state welfare systems, the Louisville program was technically a voluntary, not a mandatory, one: that is, although counselors were encouraged to assign experimental women to the activity and although the women were likewise strongly encouraged to take part, they nevertheless had the right of refusal. If they chose not to participate or to drop out, they were not in danger of losing their welfare grants, as they would in a truly mandatory program. (Some of the women may not have recognized this, however. The voluntary nature of the program was not stressed, and they may have assumed that the welfare system required their participation.)

IES had been little used in the Louisville office before the experiment began, but now—with the Lab interest in giving women more structured activities combined with the general WIN enthusiasm for straightforward, low-cost programs—its time had come. In fact, by the end of the first MDRC demonstration, the job search approach had become of equal and even greater interest to staff and researchers than the immediate services idea.

In 1978, the initial year for the individual job search experiment, Nathan Azrin released a study documenting the effectiveness of group job search—a technique he had previously developed for a nonwelfare group—for a welfare-eligible population. Azrin and his colleagues tested his program, known as the Job Finding Club, in five local WIN offices, using an experimental design

(Azrin 1978). Participants were told to treat job search as a full-time job and were encouraged to use friends and relatives to obtain leads. They were trained in interviewing and social skills and used standardized scripts on the telephone to uncover job openings and get interviews. The basic philosophy is that there are many jobs that become vacant and subsequently filled without going through an elaborate job referral network. Frequent telephone calls will locate these vacancies and provide participants with opportunities they would not have had had they relied on job developers or want ads. As part of the program, they were also given regular staff supervision and assistance and were involved in a peer support network.

Azrin's results were highly positive. Compared to a control group, a substantially higher number of experimentals found employment during a seven-month follow-up period. The findings interested WIN in using the group strategy, and by the start of a second WIN Labs test in Louisville, staff had decided to make group job club, rather than an individual search, the focus of IES activities.

The new program brought job seekers like Nadine into the WIN office in a group setting to conduct their activities under direct supervision of WIN staff. The approach assumed that there is a "hidden job market" of unadvertised jobs that people must be taught how to find. Women were given a one-week orientation in job-seeking techniques followed by up to five weeks of making at least 50 telephone calls daily to potential employers. Employers were usually selected from the Yellow Pages of the telephone book, but the women also used other information. They received the same support services and incentive payments that had been offered in the individual job search experiment. Like the earlier program, the group program was nominally voluntary.

Research Design and Samples

Both the individual and group job search programs were analyzed from three perspectives: the WIN Labs looked at their implementation experience, at their costs, and at their effects on employment rates and earnings levels and welfare benefits. Each program evaluation used an experimental design. A group of Louisville WIN registrants who were continuously enrolled over a period of several months were randomly assigned to an experimental or to a control group. Experimentals were immediately eligible for individual job search services; controls were offered normal WIN services with the typical time frames of the Louisville office. The difference between the outcomes of the two groups—that is, the employment and welfare behavior of experimentals net of controls—provides a true estimate of program achievements.

The research sample for the individual job search experiment encompassed 1,619 women—equal numbers of experimentals and controls randomly assigned from November 1978 through June 1979.[5] For the group job search study, there were 750 sample members—376 experimentals and 374 controls—who joined the sample over an eight-month period, beginning October 1980.[6]

The two experiments differed markedly in the rigor of the criteria used for randomly assigning registrants. Experience in Louisville's first experiment had shown that women who were already employed (mostly part time) or in school or training—as well as those with severe personal or family health problems—would not usually take part in job search voluntarily. Thus, such individuals were screened out of the group job search experiment before random assignment.[7] However, these additional criteria were not designed to eliminate registrants simply because they were not likely to find work or counselors initially judged them to be "unemployable."

A greater proportion of WIN volunteers[8] and individuals who were already recipients enrolled during the individual job search experiment (see Table 16-1). As a group, recipients (as opposed to women applying for welfare) are generally expected to have more employability problems than applicants. Volunteers are women not required to register with WIN but on their own seek out the program. They are usually considered a fairly motivated group, although they do have young children. Because of the tighter screening criteria in the second demonstration, the group job search sample were less likely to be handicapped or have received welfare previously. Thus, the group job search sample appeared to be slightly more employable than the individual job search sample.

However, the women in both research samples were a disadvantaged group, one that would be expected to face serious difficulties in the labor market. Only half of the women in the group job search sample and less than half in the individual sample had completed high school or earned a GED. Furthermore, seven out of 10 women in the group job search sample and eight out of the 10 in the individual sample had been on public assistance at least once before they enrolled in the experiment.

Interestingly, upon WIN registration, almost half, 48 percent, of the women in the group job search sample were rated as "not job-ready" by WIN staff. In other words, even under the more restrictive screening criteria characterizing this second experiment, many of the women judged initially as not employable would have probably been placed on a "hold" status in the past.

Implementation: Participation Patterns and Registrant Attitudes

In both of the experiments, the WIN Labs implementation research tracked the flow of participants through the program, and in both cases, the results

Table 16-1/Selected Baseline Characteristics of the Individual and Group Job Search Demonstrations

SAMPLE CHARACTERISTICS	INDIVIDUAL JOB SEARCH	GROUP JOB SEARCH
AFDC STATUS (%)		
Applicant	44.7**	54.5
Recipient	55.3	45.5
WIN STATUS (%)		
Mandatory	56.9**	62.0
Volunteer	43.1	38.0
AGE (%)		
Less than 19 years old	14.0***	10.5
19–23 years old	26.4	23.1
24–34 years old	40.5	49.3
35–44 years old	15.2	14.4
45 years old or more	3.8	2.7
AVERAGE AGE (YEARS)	27.1	27.8
ETHNICITY (%)		
White	40.8	44.7
Black	58.7	55.1
Other	0.4	0.3
DEGREE RECEIVED (%)		
None	54.3*	51.5
GED	7.5	10.1
High school diploma	38.2	38.4
HANDICAPPED (%)	9.0***	5.9
AVERAGE NUMBER OF CHILDREN LESS THAN 6 YEARS OLD	0.7*	0.6
AVERAGE NUMBER OF CHILDREN 6–18 YEARS OLD	1.5	1.5
AFDC DEPENDENCY (%)		
Never on AFDC	17.2***	29.3
Two years or less	27.9	30.2
Greater than two years	54.9	40.5
HELD A JOB IN QUARTER PRIOR TO WIN REGISTRATION (%)	24.1	25.5
AVERAGE QUARTERLY EARNINGS DURING QUARTER PRIOR TO WIN REGISTRATION	218	245
SAMPLE SIZE	1,619	750

Source: MDRC data collection worksheets.

Note: Percentage distributions may not add to exactly 100.00 because of rounding.

The individual job search samples are significantly different from the group job search samples at the .10 (*), .05 (**), and .01 (***) levels, as measured through chi-square or two-tailed t-tests.

suggested that the Louisville WIN office could work actively with a considerably larger group of women than it had in the past. In the individual job search demonstration the research target was for counselors to assign at least 70 percent of the experimental women to job search. This they did not attain, but over an eight-month period they were able to approach a 60 percent rate. (During the same period, with no special efforts made to influence assignment rates, only 16 percent of women in the control group were ever placed in IES.) In the group job search sample—more carefully screened beforehand to exclude women inappropriate for job hunting but still a group with serious disadvantages—over 90 percent of the women were assigned to IES. Not all women assigned to job search actually participated. The rates at which those women attended the activities was 55 percent for the individual job search sample and 65 percent for the group job search sample.

While the implementation analysis of the individual job search program was largely confined to questions about patterns of assignments to activities and participation rates, the study for group job search encompassed a wider range of issues. To find out how women reacted to the program and to get a clearer picture of what it consisted of, the study included 24 in-depth case studies of program participants (Nadine was one of these women) conducted by an ethnographer, as well as structured interviews with 157 experimental women on their experiences with group job search (Gould-Stuart 1982).

The ethnographer found that, in general, women liked the program. They were pleased to learn about job search techniques and welcomed the support of the counselors. Most of all, they valued the interactions with other job seekers. As one staff member put it:

The women check on each other. They confide in each other. They lend money, food stamps, and see each other after they leave here. Some have personal problems and still want to come in because this is a social situation, where they can solve their problems. (Gould-Stuart 1982, 71)

Notwithstanding the women's generally positive reactions, the implementation report also makes it clear that the women felt that the job search was often disappointing and frustrating. All of the women interviewed by the ethnographer about their experience in the program voluntarily brought up the need to make frequent telephone calls and mentioned the rejections—often rude—with which their inquiries were greeted. One participant described her reactions: "Want to know a secret? Nobody's hiring! . . . I dread using the phone." She added that there was no point in even making the calls, since she could just as easily write in her log book, "not hiring, not taking resumes, not hiring . . ." (Gould-Stuart 1982, 58).

Given the demoralization inherent in conducting a job search, peer and counselor support was critical to the women's resolve to remain active. In the words of another staff member, "Everyone knows it's depressing to look for a job. It motivates people to keep at it in a group. Constant support and communication help."

Many women, even when they became discouraged, did demonstrate a good deal of persistence. They would "write down more telephone numbers to call," they said, or "call someone new" or just "keep trying." Nevertheless, the report concluded that maintaining morale is a major challenge for any group job search program.

The women assigned to group job search can be divided into four categories: 34 percent never attended the program at all ("no-shows"); 23 percent dropped out of the program before completing ("dropouts"); a smaller group, less than 20 percent, completed the program but did not find jobs ("completers"); and 25 percent (but 38 percent of those who actually attended some part of the program and 42 percent of those who participated in the telephone room, not just the orientation) found jobs while in the program ("successful job-seekers").

The study took up the interesting question of what factors caused the women to arrive at one of these outcomes. It found that on the whole, there were some significant differences when the socioeconomic characteristics of those four subgroups were compared. For example, women who completed the group job search program with or without finding jobs had more years of education than did either women who never showed up or those who dropped out (see Table 16-2). However, these characteristics can account for only a small variation in program outcomes.

When counselors were asked to assign job-readiness ratings to the women (a numerical rating based on a woman's background and experience and on a perception of her level of motivation), it was discovered that there were virtually no differences among the ratings assigned to the four subgroups (Gould-Stuart 1982, 83).

In other words, neither socioeconomic characteristics nor counselor assessments were adequate predictors of the women's outcomes. Was there a more helpful theory? Based in part on the case studies and other observations made by the ethnographer, the study arrived at an alternative explanation, one that had been recognized by those who worked with women on welfare but that had not found its way into formal theory. Ironically, the factors that could best predict outcomes, according to the study, were themselves unpredictable. The study called these factors *situational problems*.

Situational problems are life difficulties, such as health, transportation, or housing problems, or shifts in marital situations and family responsibilities, which besides being quite difficult to anticipate, are subject to considerable change over time: a child develops a serious illness; a relative who has been

Table 16-2/Selected Baseline Characteristics of Experimental Clients Assigned to Group Job Search, by Subgroup

CHARACTERISTIC	NO-SHOWS[a]	DROP-OUTS[b]	COM-PLETERS[c]	SUCCESS-FUL JOB-SEEKERS[d]	TOTAL ASSIGNED EXPERI-MENTALS
AFDC AND WIN STATUS (%)					
Applicant***	64.8	51.9	39.8	47.7	53.1
Mandatory***	56.1	42.4	27.1	39.0	43.5
Voluntary	8.7	9.5	12.7	8.7	9.6
Recipient***	35.2	48.1	60.2	52.3	46.9
Mandatory*	17.4	12.0	11.0	8.7	12.8
Voluntary***	17.8	36.1	49.2	43.6	34.1
AVERAGE AGE (YEARS)	27.9	26.5	26.1	26.9	27.0
RACE (%)					
White***	58.3	32.3	24.6	37.2	41.0
Black***	41.7	67.7	75.4	62.8	59.0
HIGH SCHOOL DIPLOMA OR GED (%)***	40.9	39.9	55.1	61.6	48.4
AVERAGE NUMBER OF CHILDREN					
Less than 6 years old***	0.4	0.6	0.9	0.8	0.6
6–18 years old**	1.4	1.2	1.0	1.1	1.2
EMPLOYED DURING THE PAST 2 YEARS (%)**	67.4	69.0	56.8	73.8	67.6
JOB-READINESS RATING[e]					
Job-ready	57.4	57.6	57.6	68.0	60.2
Not job-ready	42.6	42.4	42.4	32.0	39.8
TOTAL CLIENTS	230	158	118	172	678

Source: Gould-Stuart 1982.

Notes: "Total Assigned Experimentals" include 302 individuals enrolled during a pilot phase operated from April to December 1980 as well as the 376 experimentals used in the impact analysis.

[a] No-Shows are defined as experimental clients assigned to group job search who did not attend a single day of the program.

[b] Dropouts are defined as experimental clients who participated in the program for up to five weeks but left without finding employment.

[c] Completers are defined as experimental clients who participated in the program into the sixth week but terminated without finding employment.

[d] Successful job-seekers are defined as clients who found employment within the six-week program period.

[e] Job-readiness ratings of clients were recorded by WIN Employment Service counselors during the appraisal interview process. These ratings, on a scale from "1" (not job-ready) to "4" (job-ready), were based on counselors' assessments of clients' willingness and ability to look for employment. For this table ratings "3" and "4" were combined into the category "job-ready"; ratings "1" and "2" were combined into the category "not job-ready."

Characteristics of no-shows, dropouts, completers, and successful job-seekers are significantly different from each other at the .05 (**) and .01 (***) levels, as measured by analysis of variance.

willing to provide child care decides to move; a secondhand car breaks down, and there is no money to fix it; the family is evicted and moves to a location inaccessible to public transportation. Understandably, these kinds of problems are likely to be more debilitating for women on welfare than they are for more advantaged women.

Given their fluidity, situational problems are difficult to capture in the kind of interview to appraise a woman's employability that was typically administered by the WIN program. At that point, a woman might have felt ready for job search, but subsequently, with the appearance or intensification of a problem, she would decide that she was less able to look. Conversely, a situational problem that had precluded job search during the appraisal might resolve itself and the woman would then be more ready for employment. The study found that although women in all four categories faced these kinds of problems, the difficulties were apparently more serious for no-shows and dropouts than for completers and successful job-seekers.

In passing, it should be noted that although the concept of situational problems was developed to explain the outcomes of a group job search program, it may well have wider application. For example, it may be that much of the volatility in patterns of job retention that characterizes poor and near-poor women once they are actually working is likewise driven by situational problems. Furthermore, given that a situational problem is by definition likely to take its heaviest toll on the poor, limited access to services that could ameliorate or solve the problem may have important and often unacknowledged labor market implications. For example, if a woman becomes ill and does not receive adequate care, she is that much more likely to be facing a situational problem that will keep her unemployed.

But if one lesson from the experiments was that the life circumstances of welfare women pose some real difficulties to labor market participation, another equally compelling one was that for many women, it is a mistake to "write off" their potential to work. The fact that a woman had little education, that she had been on welfare in the past, or that she had limited work experience did not necessarily make her inappropriate for Louisville job search activities. All too often, the research suggested, labeling such a woman "unemployable" and sending her home underestimates her capacity to actively pursue a transition from welfare to work. For example, 60 percent of the group job search sample who did not have a high school diploma or General Educational Development (GED) certificate participated and 63 percent of those without any recent employment did so. Further, 56 percent of those women judged by counselors as "not job-ready" took part in the group activities. Participation among the very disadvantaged group, while not universal was by no means negligible.

Impact Findings

In both the individual and group job search experiments, women were randomly assigned to either an experimental group (eligible for job search assistance) or to a control group, eligible for the regular WIN program. After random assignment, information about them was tracked for a set period, and at the end of the follow-up period, outcomes of all experimentals—including those who participated in job search and those who did not, as well as those who were approved for welfare and those who were not—were compared to those of all controls.[9] The discussion of employment, earnings, and welfare outcomes for each program indicates whether differences between the behavior of experimentals and control groups were statistically significant—in other words, whether they were likely to result from program intervention rather than from chance.[10]

Earnings data were collected for two quarters (approximately six months) for group job search sample members, and initially for the same amount of time for individual job search sample members.[11] Later, however, the individual job search follow-up was extended to nine quarters. Welfare outcomes were tracked for four quarters for group job search and for 11 quarters for individual job search.

The impact analysis showed that both programs resulted in modest employment and earnings gains. In the individual job search program, in each of the nine follow-up quarters, employment rates were about 5 percentage points higher for the experimental group than the control group—or about a 15 percent increase in employment rate. (See Table 16-3.) Thus, even as long as two years after WIN registration, experimentals appeared to maintain a significant advantage. By the ninth quarter, 35.9 percent of the experimentals were employed compared to 30.5 percent of the controls as indicated in Table 16-3. These improvements in employment rates were associated with earnings increases of between $35 and $93 a quarter. During the ninth quarter, experimentals were still experiencing statistically significant earnings gains of $77. Increases over time may partially reflect increases in the federal minimum wage in January 1980 and 1981.

While the impacts on welfare grant payments were low during the first six quarters, welfare payments among experimentals dropped considerably during each of the following quarters.

Individual job search, then, appears to have had a statistically significant and durable impact on the employment and earnings and rate of welfare receipt of welfare-eligible women. It is important to emphasize that what appear to be relatively small changes for each registrant can have considerable policy significance when they affect a wide cross-section of registrants and are long-lasting, as is the case for this program.

For group job search, there were immediate and statistically significant

Table 16-3/Percent Employed and Average AFDC Payments for Registrants in the Individual Job Search Experiment, by Quarter of Follow-Up

QUARTER OF FOLLOW-UP	EXPERIMENTAL	CONTROL	DIFFERENCE
PERCENT EMPLOYED (%)			
Quarter 1	35.9	30.0	+5.9***
Quarter 2	39.1	33.6	+5.5***
Quarter 3	37.4	32.9	+4.5**
Quarter 4	34.7	28.8	+5.9***
Quarter 5	38.0	31.5	+6.5***
Quarter 6	38.2	33.0	+5.2**
Quarter 7	38.1	33.6	+4.5**
Quarter 8	36.3	31.3	+5.0**
Quarter 9	35.9	30.5	+5.4***
PERCENT EVER EMPLOYED			
DURING 9 QUARTERS	73.4	69.9	+3.5*
AVERAGE AFDC PAYMENT ($)			
Quarter 1	436.04	442.78	−6.74
Quarter 2	450.05	468.35	−18.30**
Quarter 3	400.74	416.66	−15.92* .
Quarter 4	376.41	388.96	−12.55
Quarter 5	360.04	382.93	−22.89**
Quarter 6	357.51	382.30	−24.79**
Quarter 7	358.81	389.21	−30.40**
Quarter 8	353.14	391.24	−38.10***
Quarter 9	326.92	374.77	−47.85***
Quarter 10	306.21	335.74	−29.53**
Quarter 11	277.28	303.91	−26.63**
AVERAGE TOTAL AFDC PAYMENTS			
DURING 11 QUARTERS	4,003.13	4,276.84	−273.71***
SAMPLE SIZE	802	797	—

Source: Wolfhagen and Goldman 1983, 199.
Notes: These data are regression adjusted using ordinary least squares models. Quarter 1 includes the month of WIN registration.
*One-tailed t-test statistically significant at the .10 level.
**One-tailed t-test statistically significant at the .05 level.
***One-tailed t-test statistically significant at the .01 level.

improvements in employment rates and earnings for the experimental job search sample, although welfare savings were negligible. During the first two quarters after registration, 49 percent of the experimentals were employed as compared to 34 percent of the controls—a 15 percentage point gain in employment. (See Table 16-4.) This was associated with earnings increases of $144 over these two quarters.

Since data on employment and earnings for the group job search sample

Table 16-4/Percent Employed and Average Earnings in the Individual and Group Job Search Experiments, by Quarter of Follow-Up

QUARTER OF FOLLOW-UP	INDIVIDUAL JOB SEARCH			GROUP JOB SEARCH		
	Experimental	*Control*	*Difference*	*Experimental*	*Control*	*Difference*
PERCENT EMPLOYED						
Quarter 1	33.6	25.7	+7.9***	29.2	20.1	+9.1***
	(660)	(666)		(373)	(371)	
Quarter 2	38.8	32.6	+6.2**	38.9	24.7	+14.2***
	(660)	(666)		(286)	(287)	
Two quarters	53.8	44.1	+9.7***	49.0	34.0	+15.0***
	(660)	(666)		(286)	(287)	
AVERAGE EARNINGS ($)						
Quarter 1	199.99	148.60	+51.39***	185.74	149.70	+36.04
	(660)	(666)		(373)	(371)	
Quarter 2	332.21	263.22	+68.99**	373.96	254.75	+119.21**
	(660)	(666)		(286)	(287)	
Two quarters	532.20	411.82	+120.38***	549.91	406.05	+143.86**
	(660)	(666)		(286)	(287)	

Source: Wolfhagen and Goldman 1983.
Notes: These data are regression adjusted. Employment rates are adjusted using logistic models. Individual job search impacts are calculated for the statistically screened individual job search sample. Sample sizes are shown in parentheses. Sample sizes for group job search are lower during the quarter following WIN registration since second quarter follow-up data were not available for women who registered for WIN in April and May 1981.
    There are no significant differences between individual job search and group job search impacts.
    *One-tailed t-test for differences between experimentals and controls statistically significant at the .10 level.
    **One-tailed t-test for differences between experimentals and controls statistically significant at the .05 level.
    ***One-tailed t-test for differences between experimentals and controls statistically significant at the .01 level.

were collected for only six months, it is impossible to know if impacts from this program are as durable as those for individual job search. But analysis of welfare payments for an additional five quarters shows that there continued to be no welfare reductions over a longer period.[12]

Which was more effective: individual or group job search? To answer this question, the researchers first took the individual job search sample and from it, statistically constructed a group that reflected the tighter screening imposed during the group job search experiment (Wolfhagen and Goldman 1983, Appendix D).

Experimental-control differences for employment and earnings for the two samples were similar during the quarter—three-month period—when the women registered with WIN. However, during the quarter following registration—six months after registration and therefore at a point when most women in the experimental group had finished the program—group job search increased the employment rate of experimental women by 14.2 percentage points and improved earnings by $120, while the employment increase for individual job search was only 6.2 percentage points and the increase for earnings, $69. (See Table 16-4.)

One possible explanation for the "bulge" in the group job search impacts could be that group job search, which gives women specific instructions on how to look for a job, leaves them with skills that are useful to them even after they have left the program. Several findings from the demonstration support this hypothesis. When asked more than six months after WIN registration how helpful the program training would be if they were to look for a job, almost 70 percent of participants rated it as "very helpful." [13] Only 2 percent indicated that the experience did not teach them anything currently useful. Women who found employment through the program were the most likely to consider it helpful, but even those who had dropped out were favorable.

Both experimental and control group women were asked if they had looked for work during the six months after they registered with WIN. Those who had were asked how many weeks they had spent. Almost 90 percent of experimental women, as opposed to 78 percent of controls, had looked. Experimental women who worked spent less time on average looking for jobs (11.9 weeks) than did control group women who found employment (13.2 weeks). It is striking that even without the encouragement of the program a substantial proportion of welfare women looked for work. This set of responses, suggesting that the shorter job search activities of experimental women may have been more intensive and effective than the longer efforts of the women who were not exposed to the program, was further evidence that group job search left participants with lasting job-seeking skills.

Neither group nor individual job search programs had much influence, however, on the types of jobs women found. In the individual job search program, most jobs were in clerical and service occupations, and just over half paid no more than the minimum wage. For group job search, the vast majority of jobs found did not pay above the minimum wage. The average wage of the first job for employed experimentals was $3.48—similar to that received by controls—with about half of these jobs involving 35 or more hours a week. This should not be surprising, given that job search programs generally—and this was true of the Louisville programs in particular—place more stress on rapid placements than on the quality of the jobs found. Neither the programs, nor the research associated with them, were in a position to focus on the difficult question of whether and to what extent work was economically more rewarding than welfare to these women.

Initially there was some concern that group job search techniques would actually result in women being encouraged to accept jobs that they would not have otherwise accepted. In fact employed experimentals and controls found similar types of jobs and exhibited similar job retention patterns. Nevertheless, the implementation study of the group job search program noted that for some women, the program meant a downward adjustment of expectations—to employment goals that staff considered more realistic than those they began with. Some women were counseled to start with relatively low-skill positions and to regard training for a better position as a goal to be sought once they had breached the job market barrier with an entry-level job.

Several impact findings from the studies underscore the volatility with which welfare women participate in the labor market. In the individual job search experiment, the contrast between cumulative employment rates and rates for individual quarters for both experimentals and controls shows that there was a substantial amount of movement for both groups. Furthermore, despite the impacts on employment and earnings rates, neither program had much of an effect on the rates at which women left the jobs they found. In the individual job search experiment, for example, roughly one-third of the experimentals and controls who found employment during the three months after they registered with WIN were no longer working in the following quarter. For group job search, there was a difference between proportions of experimentals (73 percent) and controls (61 percent) who found jobs in the first quarter and held them into the second, but the difference was not statistically significant.

The impact analysis for both programs measured outcomes for selected subgroups. Findings for the group job search program indicated that contrary to what staff might have expected, job search assistance may be most helpful to women who would be considered less job-ready as evidenced by less favorable recent work history. Women who have worked recently are more likely to find employment after WIN registration than those who have not worked. That is, while 46.5 percent of controls with recent work history were employed, only 8.1 percent of controls without such experience did find jobs. It is precisely this latter group of women—those less likely to find work on their own—who will benefit the most from a program focused on increasing the effectiveness of their job search. Women who have previously worked are assumed to have more of their own resources (both in terms of prior experience searching for a job and employer contacts) to help them locate another job and thus may not gain as much from a job search assistance program.

Program outcomes were compared for women who had and had not worked in the two years before WIN registration (see Table 16-5). For women with no employment experience, group job search resulted in a significant 23.5 percentage point increase in employment, almost a 300 percent increase over control group employment. These employment rates translated into substantial earnings gains of $350.53. In contrast, group job search resulted in only a 10 percentage point increase in employment and $96.49 in earnings for women with immediate previous employment.

For group job search, WIN volunteers—those with children less than 6

Table 16-5/Cumulative Percent Employed, Earnings and Welfare Payments in the Individual and Group Job Search Experiments, by WIN Status and Prior Work Experience

Subgroup, Outcome, and Follow-up Period	Individual Job Search			Group Job Search		
	Experi-mental	Control	Difference	Experi-mental	Control	Difference
WIN VOLUNTEERS						
Percent employed	55.5	50.3	+5.2	54.1	27.7	+26.4***
(2 quarters)##	(316)	(307)		(111)	(112)	
Average earnings	$514.67	$394.43	+$120.24**	$510.47	$272.36	+$238.11***
(2 quarters)	(316)	(307)		(111)	(112)	
Average AFDC payments	$1,755.93	$1,843.77	−$87.84**	$1,878.93	$1,842.48	+$36.45
(4 quarters)	(313)	(300)		(111)	(111)	
WIN MANDATORIES						
Percent employed	52.1	38.1	+14.0***	46.3	36.8	+9.5*
(2 quarters)	(344)	(359)		(175)	(175)	
Average earnings	$543.52	$431.26	+$112.26**	$578.39	$488.14	+$90.25
(2 quarters)	(344)	(359)		(175)	(175)	
Average AFDC payments	$1,553.64	$1,603.52	−$49.89	$1,555.01	$1,622.77	−$67.76
(4 quarters)	(340)	(357)		(175)	(173)	
WOMEN WITH NO WORK IN LAST 2 YEARS						
Percent Employed	27.8	19.0	+8.8**	31.6	8.1	+23.5***
(2 quarters)##	(244)	(277)		(93)	(89)	
Average earnings	$295.16	$148.11	+$147.05***	$420.76	$70.23	+$350.53**ᵜ
(2 quarters)	(244)	(277)		(93)	(89)	
Average AFDC payments	$1,871.59	$1,947.27	−$75.87	$1,962.04	$1,938.93	+$23.11
(4 quarters)	(241)	(272)		(93)	(88)	
WOMEN WHO WORKED IN LAST 2 YEARS						
Percent employed	68.7	61.8	+6.9**	56.5	46.5	+10.0**
(2 quarters)	(416)	(389)		(193)	(198)	
Average earnings	$687.23	$582.47	+$104.75**	$633.08	$536.59	+$96.49
(2 quarters)	(416)	(389)		(193)	(198)	
Average AFDC payments	$1,502.66	$1,567.86	−$65.20*	$1,548.98	$1,601.48	−$52.50
(4 quarters)	(412)	(385)		(193)	(196)	

Source: Wolfhagen and Goldman 1983.

Notes: These data are regression adjusted. Employment rates are adjusted using logistic models. Individual job search impacts are calculated for the statistically screened individual job search sample. Sample sizes are shown in parentheses. Sample sizes for welfare payment data differ from those for employment and earnings because welfare data were missing for some women.

*One-tailed t-test for differences between experimentals and controls statistically significant at the .10 level.
**One-tailed t-test for differences between experimentals and controls statistically significant at the .05 level.
***One-tailed t-test for differences between experimentals and controls statistically significant at the .01 level.
##Group job search impacts were significantly greater than individual job search impacts at the .05 percent level, measured by two-tailed t-tests.

years old—experienced greater employment effects than WIN-mandatories. Here again, the program was most useful for a group usually considered less employable, because their children were younger and child care arrangements may be more difficult. This group is also considered more motivated than mandatories but yet has less prior work experience. A group setting may provide special encouragement for those women. In the individual job search program, on the other hand, women with at least one school-age child were more successful than the volunteers.

An important question in assessing any employment strategy for women on public assistance is whether it leads to reductions in welfare dependency and creates welfare savings. For the Louisville experiments, the answer is both mixed and complex. Individual job search had a relatively small impact on the proportion of women receiving welfare benefits during the first year following WIN registration—with a significant reduction for only one quarter —but thereafter there were significant reductions for six of the remaining seven follow-up periods, with reductions ranging from 2.6 to 6.3 percent.

For group job search, there were no reductions in the proportions of experimentals who received AFDC benefits during any quarter. On average, experimentals received $1,680 over four quarters of follow-up, only $30 less than controls and this difference was not statistically significant.

Why did a program that led to significant employment and earnings gains fail to produce a commensurate change in welfare rates and savings? To answer this question, it is important to remember that work and welfare are not mutually exclusive categories. Because their jobs were low-paying, some women in the program were able to mix the two and thus did not leave the rolls even though they found employment. Furthermore, the rules governing the amounts of work-related expenses and child care costs that a welfare recipient could deduct from her income in calculating her grant that were in effect at this time meant that many women could continue to receive welfare checks while at work.[14]

In all, the Louisville welfare impacts suggest that it should not be assumed that greater employment and earnings among welfare women will automatically result in welfare reductions of similar magnitude. The possibility of mixing work and welfare, though diminished by the changes in welfare rules in 1981 and afterward, still is a factor that will be taken into account in assessing how a successful employability technique will play itself out with respect to welfare payments. At the same time, helping individuals get into the labor market and helping them understand that they can get and hold jobs may offset this lack of welfare savings.

Program Costs

These modest impacts should be considered in the context of what it costs to operate, since the Louisville experiments were focused on using limited resources to provide a broad range of welfare women job search assistance, a relatively inexpensive program, rather than using the resources to provide a small segment of this population with more intensive services such as training and education. In a period of fiscal constraint, choices on how to distribute limited resources become even more acute. On average, individual job search cost from $77.33 to $115.88 per experimental woman—including those who participated as well as those who did not.[15] Even using the highest cost assumption, costs were more than offset by welfare reductions within two years.

With an estimated cost of $194.92 per experimental, group job search was more expensive than individual job search. However, the group program's staffing patterns were unusually high, and there is evidence that it could have operated just as effectively under more streamlined conditions. The study estimated that by using two full-time counselors, as opposed to the seven funded during the demonstration, the office could have brought the costs of the program to those within the range estimated for individual job search. Nevertheless, with documented welfare reductions of only $30 per three-month period, it would have taken several years before Louisville's group job search program could have paid for itself. This is important since employment and training programs that yield impacts—no matter how modest—and pay for themselves within a reasonable period of time are not a common occurrence.

Conclusions

A relatively small-scale experiment, the Louisville WIN Labs focused on a technique for assisting welfare women that was to earn increasing popularity during the demonstration period and in the years that followed the study. Since they offered insights into a strategy that policy makers and program operators wanted to explore, the experiments proved to be an unexpectedly useful source of information. Current research on large state-mandatory job search programs draws heavily on the understandings and methodologies developed in this one local experiment.

There is still much to be learned about job search, especially as operated under current welfare regulations and as a required rather than a quasi-voluntary activity. But the Louisville experiments offer some working hypotheses about the utility of this technique.

First, there were some interesting findings about the place of job search in an employability program for welfare women. Louisville's solid participation rates clearly told program operators that they ought to consider offering the activity to a broad range of welfare women, not just to a carefully preselected group of "employables." The impact findings even suggested that job search was most useful to the women whom counselors were likely to consider the least employable.

The fact that the program was both relatively easy to operate and inexpensive further recommended that it be widely used—and there was yet another consideration, one that was highlighted by the Louisville insights into the vagaries of predicting "employability" among welfare women. Thus, job search assistance replaced the more traditional assessment techniques and allowed the labor market to identify those women who could not or would not find jobs with minimal assistance. If it was difficult to know in advance which women would find and keep jobs, it might make sense to let the job search process itself operate as a screen for determining those women who can quickly find employment and those who need more intensive and expensive services.

In fact, several current state initiatives have adopted the practice of using job search in this way by sequencing it first in a mix of employability activities offered to people on welfare and reserving other activities for those who fail to find work. Other current state initiatives, however, such as the Maryland OPTIONS program, offer job search as one among an array of program choices to which participants can be assigned at any point in their participation. Final results from MDRC's Demonstration of State Work/Welfare Initiatives will provide some further evidence on the relative utility of these two approaches.[16]

Second, the findings—especially those from the group job search experiment with its ethnographic documentation—made a point that also emerges from numerous other studies of this population: women on welfare want to work. Group job search was a taxing activity. But the women almost universally said they found the program useful and rewarding, and large numbers of them stayed with it, although they were technically under no obligation to do so. Admittedly, group job search did offer benefits—peer support and comradery—but since women who were disposed to enjoy this aspect of the experience under the stress of making 50 telephone calls a day to employers would probably welcome it at least as warmly in a real work setting, there is no particular reason to expect that the commitment demonstrated during the program period would dissipate when women entered the labor market.

The third point suggested by the Louisville experiments was simply that job search, even though a modest intervention, could make a difference in women's employment and earnings rates, and that it could be especially useful to women considered to have the weakest employment history. The impacts of the individual job search program were remarkably durable, and there is reason to suppose that those from the group job search program were at least as long lasting. In all, then, the studies suggested that job search increases the probability of more women entering the labor market and staying there, even if many move back and forth between welfare and jobs.

Job search, however, cannot in and of itself eliminate welfare dependency. There are too many problems that it does not even address—for example, the quality of the jobs found or the stubborn problem of how to improve job retention. Furthermore, for the very reason that the program does succeed on the relatively limited grounds that it established for itself, it may create a climate in which program operators and policy makers are content to limit their efforts to low-cost, low-risk techniques. With the assurance that job search is a feasible and at least cost-effective activity to offer to women on welfare, society may be tempted to reject more ambitious efforts to improve the overall self-sufficiency of these women.

Job search programs may best serve as a self-screening mechanism that allows more comprehensive and expensive services to be targeted to those who face substantial barriers in finding employment. This is especially important in an environment of fiscal constraint where there are not sufficient resources to offer every woman on welfare education and training. Nor may this be desirable, since the analysis suggests that many women will find employment without program intervention, or with minimal program assistance. Unfortunately, training and education options have not been subjected to the same extent to the rigorous research methodology as has been applied to the less-costly, short-term program interventions. The differential effects of various programmatic alternatives—taking into account their costs—are not clear at this time—particularly their effects on key factors such as job quality, wages, and job retention—that short-term job search assistance was not intended to have.

Nevertheless, on the assumption that it is better for many welfare women to be in the labor market where at least they have a chance to build an employment history and improve their economic position, the Louisville experiments suggest that job search programs are a good idea. While further findings from current research may modify or reinforce the conclusion, so far at least job search programs seem to have been a useful addition to the repertoire of program ideas used to help welfare women attain the employment they clearly need and want.

Notes

Acknowledgment: The material in this chapter is based on several reports associated with the evaluation of the Louisville Work Incentive (WIN) Laboratory Project, including Goldman 1981; Gould-Stuart 1982; and Wolfhagen and Goldman 1983; the author acknowledges the contribution of Susan Blank, formerly an editorial assistant at the Manpower Demonstration Research Corporation (MDRC), who assisted in preparing this chapter, and the prior contribution of Carl Wolfhagen and Joanna Gould-Stuart, former research associates at MDRC, and Dr. Judith Gueron, president of MDRC.

1. Her name has been changed to protect her privacy.

2. Along with the U.S. Department of Health and Human Services, the U.S. Department of Labor held federal responsibility for the WIN program.

3. AFDC provides assistance to single-parent heads of household, who are mostly female. In the Louisville experiments, male heads of household were excluded from the analysis. The Aid to Families with Dependent Children-Unemployed Parent (AFDC-U) program provides assistance to two-parent households where at least one of these adults has demonstrated an attachment to the labor market. This demonstration did not include AFDC-U recipients.

4. The WIN Labs experiment ended in 1981. Subsequently, the OBRA legislation gave the states much more authority for designing and managing WIN programs, with the result that states, and not the federal government, are now expected to initiate innovation in the area of work programs for welfare recipients. In fact, a number of states have accepted this challenge and have redesigned and modified WIN services. In a sense the descendant of the WIN Labs in this New Federalism setting is MDRC's Demonstration of State Work/Welfare Initiatives. Like the Labs, the Demonstration examines a series of diverse state innovations in the work/welfare field. It is, however, funded by a combination of state and private resources, not primarily by the federal government, as the WIN Labs were.

5. Several sample members were missing selected key demographic data and were not included in the analysis.

6. An additional 713 had registered for WIN and were randomly assigned during a pilot phase of the experiment, which ran from April to September 1980. These individuals are not included in the analysis.

7. Women who were employed or in school or training on a part-time basis, or had recently given birth or were pregnant, were included in the research sample if they indicated that they were still interested in job search. Women could decline to participate in the experiment prior to random assignment. As part of the final report analysis, a comparison of the effects of the two Louisville projects was made. As part of this comparison, the individual job search sample was modified to exclude individuals who would not have been included in the group job search experiment. (Wolfhagen and Goldman 1983, Chapter 5 and Appendix D.)

8. It should be noted that regardless of WIN status (that is, volunteer or mandatory) participation in job search activities during these demonstrations was voluntary for WIN registrants. Volunteers are individuals who register with the WIN program although they are exempt from mandatory registration under the Social Security Act for the following reasons:

1. under 16 years old
2. enrolled full-time in school and under 21 years
3. sick as determined by the income maintenance unit
4. incapacitated as determined by the income maintenance unit
5. 65 years old or more
6. living in a remote area: located two hours or more away from a WIN office
7. a caretaker of a sick person

8. a mother of a child under 6 years old

9. a mother or female whose spouse is a WIN registrant

9. Given the research design, if impacts on participants alone had been studied, it would have been necessary to single out, within the control group, a similar subgroup of individuals who would have participated if the program had been available to them. This is virtually impossible, since so many unmeasured characteristics, such as motivation and situational circumstances, are usually related to the fact of participation. Thus, the research design combined the groups in the experimental sample.

10. These data are regression adjusted using ordinary least squares regression models, including independent variables measuring age, education, ethnicity, medical barriers, number of children, marital status, prior work history, prior welfare dependency, and AFDC and WIN status.

11. Information on employment and earnings primarily came from the State of Kentucky computerized unemployment insurance earnings records. In Kentucky, all employers, with the exception of the self-employed, must report the earnings of their workers, except domestic ones, to the state unemployment insurance system. Earnings data for these workers are aggregated by calendar quarter (for example, January, February, and March; April, May, and June). These earnings data were used as the best source for information on employed WIN registrants. As with most data sources, however, they posed some difficulties, in this case because quarterly data meant varying lengths of follow-up, depending on whether a woman registered during the first, second, or third month of any given calendar quarter. Another short-coming was that these data were available to researchers only for a relatively short period, because of lags in wage reporting. Information on welfare payments came from the State of Kentucky computerized case files. For compatability in presentation of outcome data, monthly AFDC grant data were also aggregated by three-month periods, where the first month of the first quarter of follow-up was the month of WIN registration.

12. The Mathematica Policy Research in a special study extended the follow-up for welfare savings to an additional three quarters and found slight but not statistically significant welfare savings during this extended period. Slightly different statistical methods were used in the MDRC and MPR studies. (Jean Gossman, Rebecca Maynard, and Judith Roberts, "Reanalysis of the Effects of Selected Employment and Training Programs for Welfare Recipients" [MPR, June 1985].)

13. As part of both projects, interviews were conducted with sample members by telephone or in-person six months after registration.

14. With the passage of OBRA in 1981, these regulations governing allowable deductions became more stringent, and it is not clear what the welfare impacts from the Louisville experiment would have been had it operated in this post-1981 period.

15. Because counselors in this program worked with both experimental and control-group women, it was necessary to estimate the proportions of time they spent with each group. Differences in these estimations account for the range of final cost estimates.

16. MDRC's Demonstration of State Work/Welfare Initiatives includes 11 states. In eight of them a rigorous impact and benefit-cost study are being undertaken: Baltimore, Md.; San Diego, Calif.; Cook County, Ill.; and selected areas of West Virginia, Maine, New Jersey, Arkansas, and Virginia. The final reports for all states have been

completed (see Auspos, Cave, and Long 1988; Freedman, Bryant, and Cave 1988; Friedlander et al. 1986; Friedlander et al., *Arkansas*, 1985; Friedlander et al., *Maryland*, 1985; Friedlander et al. 1987; Goldman et al. 1986; Riccio et al. 1986). In most of these programs, job search assistance is at least one of several component activities and in many cases the first in a sequence of activities. The findings to date indicate that programs involving participation requirements mostly focusing on job search and to a lesser extent work experience result in modest employment and earnings gains and minimal to modest welfare savings.

References

Auspos, Patricia; George Cave; and David Long. 1988. *Maine: Final Report on the Training Opportunities in the Private Sector Program*. New York: Manpower Demonstration Research Corporation.

Azrin, Nathan H. 1978. *The Job Finding Club as a Method for Obtaining Employment for Welfare-Eligible Clients: Demonstration, Evaluation, and Counselor Training*. Anna, Ill.: Anna Mental Health and Development Center.

Freedman, Stephen; Jan Bryant; and George Cave. 1988. *New Jersey: Final Report on the Grant Diversion Project*. New York: Manpower Demonstration Research Corporation.

Friedlander, Daniel; Marjorie Erickson; Gayle Hamilton; and Virginia Knox. 1986. *West Virginia: Final Report on the Community Work Experience Demonstrations*. New York: Manpower Demonstration Research Corporation.

Friedlander, Daniel; Stephen Freedman; Gayle Hamilton; and Janet Quint. 1987. *Illinois: Final Report on Job Search and Work Experience in Cook County*. New York: Manpower Demonstration Research Corporation.

Friedlander, Daniel; Gregory Hoerz; David Long; and Janet Quint. 1985. *Maryland: Final Report on the Employment Initiatives Evaluation*. New York: Manpower Demonstration Research Corporation.

Friedlander, Daniel; Gregory Hoerz; Janet Quint, and James Riccio. 1985. *Arkansas: Final Report on the WORK Program in Two Counties*. New York: Manpower Demonstration Research Corporation.

Goldman, Barbara S. 1981. *Impacts of the Immediate Job Search Assistance Experiment: Louisville WIN Research Laboratory Project*. New York: Manpower Demonstration Research Corporation.

Goldman, Barbara; Daniel Friedlander; and David Long. 1986. *Final Report on the San Diego Job Search and Work Experience Demonstration*. New York: Manpower Demonstration Research Corporation.

Gould-Stuart, Joanna. 1982. *Welfare Women in a Group Job Search Program: Their Experiences in the Louisville WIN Research Laboratory Project*. New York: Manpower Demonstration Research Corporation.

Leiman, Joan M. 1982. *The WIN Labs: A Federal/Local Partnership in Social Research*. New York: Manpower Demonstration Research Corporation.

Levy, Sydelle Brooks. 1981. *The Workings of WIN: A Field Observation Study of Three Local Offices*. New York: Manpower Demonstration Research Corporation.

Riccio, James, George Cave, Stephen Freedman, and Marilyn Price. 1986. *Virginia: Final Report on the Virginia Employment Services Program.* New York: Manpower Demonstration Research Corporation.

Wolfhagen, Carl, and Barbara S. Goldman. 1983. *Job Search Strategies: Lessons from the Louisville WIN Laboratory.* New York: Manpower Demonstration Research Corporation.

17/Work, Training, and Welfare Reform in Massachusetts: The ET Choices Program

Alan Werner

The ongoing policy debate over the future of the American welfare system takes place amidst some points of basic agreement. For example, most observers believe that, given the right reasons to choose work and the right training and other services to become ready for work, many welfare recipients could and should work. This was not always true, as Gueron (Chapter 15) observes. In 1935 when the Social Security Act created a set of grant-in-aid programs to the states for the provision of cash assistance to certain categories of needy citizens, it was expected that these programs would dwindle away as the work-related provisions of the Social Security Act (such as, for example, old age, survivors' and disability insurance) kicked in to provide for the widows and orphans of America's work force. In addition, in 1935, the groups covered by cash assistance programs (chiefly the elderly poor and the children of single-parent families)[1] were both considered to be among the "deserving" poor and were by design cleared out of the labor force in favor of America's underemployed "prime" wage earners.

Since the time of the Social Security Act of 1935, however, much has changed in welfare programming and policy and in American culture and society. The welfare rolls have grown substantially instead of withering away, and the composition of the rolls has changed dramatically. For example, in 1940 about 840,000 children in 349,000 families received cash assistance under the Aid to Dependent Children (ADC) Program, the principal welfare program for poor families with children (now called AFDC, or Aid to Families with Dependent Children); by 1985, the number had grown about tenfold, to approximately 7,198,000 children in 3,701,000 families (U.S. Department of Health and Human Services, 1988). Since the late 1960s, the comparatively large

414

number of welfare recipients has increasingly become an unacceptable political fact for Republican and Democratic administrations and Congresses. In addition, until the 1970s, the vast majority of AFDC recipients were products of "broken" marriages, through death or divorce, while today, most AFDC dependents are children of never-married women. This increase in "permanent" female-headed families on the welfare rolls came at roughly the same time as an important increase in the work effort of women of all backgrounds and the related expectation that women, even single mothers, have an obligation to help support their families through work.[2] One significant political result of these forces has been the development of a broad consensus that the welfare rolls can and ought to be reduced and that some amount of reduction in welfare dependency can be realized through increased work effort among adult welfare recipients.[3]

The current consensus that welfare recipients ought to seek employment in preference to receiving aid ends, however, where practical proposals to help increase work effort among welfare recipients begin. A major source of debate over welfare reform in this decade has centered on the most effective design of the program intended to move individuals off welfare and into jobs. One common set of strategies developed by the states in the 1980s under the stimulus of federal policy have implied relatively short-term and low-cost investments in employment and training services for welfare recipients. For example, many states have implemented job search or job club programs in which the major service provided is training about how to find and obtain employment. Other states have implemented "work experience" programs in which participants are placed usually in public-sector workplaces where they perform tasks (most often without direct compensation for their labor) in the expectation that participants will somehow absorb valuable work skills and habits. In addition, some states have implemented genuine "workfare" programs in which some portion of the AFDC caseload must work in mainly public-sector employment, usually at the minimum wage as a condition for receiving cash assistance.[4]

While there are clearly some important differences among the aforementioned short-term strategies for increasing the employment and decreasing the economic dependency of welfare clients, they all share some central features. First, they are relatively low-cost programs. Second, while these programs typically allow for volunteers, they also subject a group of welfare clients to mandatory participation with the potential loss of all or some benefits as a sanction for failure to abide by program regulations. Third, these programs are most often designed to provide one type of employment and training service to welfare recipients with a wide range of education and employment background, skills, and experience. Fourth, even in those instances where these programs do provide some more intensive educational and vocational training, they do so only after an individual has engaged in some mandatory "upfront" activity (such as job search) without finding employment.

In contrast to the more common approaches to employment and training programming and policy listed above, a few states have recently attempted to develop programs designed around an entirely different set of guidelines. The most important of these guidelines are that the programs be voluntary, and that the programs offer a set of services "customized" to a participant's needs, skills, interests, and aspirations. The first such program and perhaps the most notable is the Employment and Training Choices Program, or the ET Choices Program, operating in the state of Massachusetts since 1983.[5] The ET Program is an employment and training strategy for welfare reform that represents an important alternative to the set of programs developed under the impulse of federal policy in the first half of the 1980s. Unfortunately, while the ET Program is much discussed and often admired, it has not yet been as rigorously evaluated as have some of the other employment and training programs developed in this decade (see Gueron, Chapter 15, and Goldman, Chapter 16).[6] Nevertheless, the ET Program exerts a strong influence on current thinking about welfare reform and remains an important "counterbalance" to the programs that, for example, have been evaluated by the Manpower Demonstration Research Corporation (MDRC) since 1981 (see Gueron).

The Development of the ET Choices Program in the Context of National Work and Welfare Policy

The Omnibus Reconciliation Act of 1981 (OBRA) made some significant changes in national work and welfare policy. The basic thrust of these changes was to allow for more state discretion in the design of employment and training programs for AFDC recipients. (See Gueron, Chapter 15, for an overview.) One of the policy options for states, the WIN (Work Incentive) Demonstration Projects (WIN-Demo), gave states the latitude to redesign their employment and training programs and requirements within a fairly wide range of policy and programming options. Although OBRA allowed for more creativity and flexibility in employment and training policy and programming at the state level, it also cut federal funding for the WIN Program by one-third.

Massachusetts was one of the first states to take advantage of the WIN Demonstration Projects regulations to design a new employment and training program for welfare recipients. In the spring of 1982, the administration of then-governor Edward King used the WIN-Demo provisions to consolidate employment and training programs for welfare recipients within the Massachusetts Department of Public Welfare. (WIN-Demo projects had to have single-agency administrations in contrast to the dual-agency administration of the WIN Program.)

The WIN-Demo project developed in Massachusetts in 1982 was called the Work and Training Program (WTP). WTP embodied many of the policy and programming principles that characterized the short-term, low-cost, compulsory approach to employment and training for welfare recipients. Indeed, WTP was designed in part by staff from the White House domestic policy advisors "on loan" to the Massachusetts Department of Public Welfare. For example, WTP emphasized immediate job placement and the sanctioning of noncompliant mandatory participants. Basically, WTP consisted of a compulsory period of job search for WIN mandatory welfare applicants and recipients during which program participants were required to attend job counseling sessions, contact employers, and take any job offer at the minimum wage or above. Participants who did not cooperate with these program requirements were subject to sanctions that could include the loss of all or part of their welfare benefits. At the end of the compulsory job search period (usually lasting up to five weeks), participants who were not successful in finding jobs were "reappraised" by a WTP worker and were either sent through the job search program again or were given the option of entering more intensive educational and skills training programs. Coordination with other state agencies was poor, and the actual opportunities for vocational and educational skills upgrading were limited. In addition, although the Massachusetts Department of Public Welfare had planned to include a workfare component, that part of the WTP Program was never implemented.[7]

The WTP began operation in April 1982. By the end of the year, however, a new governor, Michael Dukakis, had been elected and a new administration began to make changes in welfare policy and programming. By February 1983, the Massachusetts Department of Public Welfare had suspended the operation of WTP; by April, a Task Force on Work and Welfare was convened by the secretary of human services. This task force was composed of representatives from public employee unions, the human services community, and welfare advocacy groups. In May 1983, the task force submitted a proposal for the "prototype" of the ET Choices Program to the new commissioner of the Massachusetts Department of Public Welfare. During the summer of 1983, the Welfare Department slightly modified the task force's design and submitted a proposal to the federal government under the rubrics of the WIN Demonstration Projects guidelines. The proposal for the Employment and Training Choices Program was accepted by the U.S. Department of Health and Human Services and ET Choices began operation on 1 October 1983.

The ET Choices Program
Administrative Design and Management Structure
The ET Choices Program has been operating for several years and has undergone some evolution in its design and delivery of services. Throughout the

period of its operation, however, the program has been guided by a number of principles in its administrative design and management structure, including: voluntary participation and marketing and outreach to potential participants; a "customized" set of support, education, skills training, and job placement services designed to meet individual needs, aspirations, interests, and aptitudes; a commitment to jobs with sufficient income and benefits to draw welfare clients into the program and to increase the probability that participants who obtain employment will be able to leave the welfare rolls permanently; centralized administration of the program; performance-based contracting with service deliverers; the use of objective, quantifiable goals (including goals for job quality) to drive performance of Department of Public Welfare employees and outside agencies. We review these principles and their practical implications below.

Voluntary Participation

As mentioned above, most of the employment and training programs developed in the states since 1981, as well as the WIN Program, contain provisions for mandatory participation for some portion of the AFDC caseload.[8] In contrast to these approaches, the ET Choices Program does not enforce regulations requiring WIN mandatory welfare recipients to participate (although they must "register" for the program). Instead of stimulating participation through the use of prescriptive regulation, the ET Choices Program must market itself to welfare recipients as though they were consumers of a service. Indeed, almost from the beginning of the program, the Massachusetts Department of Public Welfare has carried on an aggressive advertising campaign for ET that includes direct mailings, posters, special sponsored events, and other marketing techniques. The Welfare Department even has an administrative unit within its Office of External Affairs that is dedicated to marketing ET and other departmental programs to its clients. It is this voluntary aspect of participation in the program that is perhaps its most controversial feature.

The policy of encouraging voluntary participation in the ET Choices Program, rather than making participation a condition of eligibility for receiving welfare, has led to the development of some unique characteristics of the program. First, the program can succeed only by making a positive appeal to potential participants. There is theoretically no reason for a welfare recipient to choose to enroll in the ET Program other than the belief that the program will somehow improve the well-being of her family. In order to sustain this belief, the program must deliver quality services that ultimately do make a difference in the life of its participants and their families. Second, by serving volunteers, the program has the advantage of dealing, in most instances, with motivated individuals. This has had at least two felicitous results. One is that by serving more motivated clients, the program has built into it at least one important concomitant of success, that is, it is dealing with people who by and large want to get jobs (although they perhaps can afford to be more picky about their jobs than participants in mandatory programs). A second result of having motivated participants redounds to the advantage of the service deliverers in ET. In employment and training programs with provisions for compulsory participation, the agencies delivering services must also be "truant officers" who monitor compliance with program rules for the welfare department. In addition, those service providers in programs with mandatory participants must also try to serve recalcitrant clients who are in the program only because they do not want to be sanctioned and not necessarily because they want a job. Presumably the participants in ET are in training to develop skills needed for employment.

A final result of voluntarism in participation is the subtle change in perception of welfare clients both by Welfare Department staff and by welfare recipients themselves. To succeed in their mission of encouraging participation and helping welfare recipients leave the caseload through employment, welfare case managers must learn how to deal with clients as individuals facing choices, rather than as "captives" to a bi-weekly check. Since the introduction of the ET Program in 1983, this particular orientation toward clients as consumers has permeated the Welfare Department and has led to genuine changes in the agency's institutional culture. In addition, welfare clients themselves must understand that they can make some choices about their lives and that such choices exist and are sustained by public institutions.

Customized Services

Another central administrative feature of the ET Choices Program, related to the policy of voluntary participation, is the principle of a "customized" set of services tied to an individual's needs for educational or skills training and support services. This policy is tied to voluntarism and consumerism in the program's approach to welfare clients by allowing for some choice in the menu of services within the program as well as choice in the decision to participate. This policy also distinguishes the ET Choices Program from most other employment and training programs for welfare recipients that include one or more compulsory program components, most often some provision for job search before allowing access to more expensive and longer-range education and training services.

The range of choices in individualized design of program service is, to be sure, somewhat circumscribed by issues of availability, cost, and appropriateness of the service, but the number of different options available to welfare clients is relatively large (see below, "ET Choices Program Services," for a summary of the various ET services). The individualized plan of program services is usually developed by the program participant and a specialized ET worker within the local welfare office. The program also funds professional career assessment services for welfare clients wanting a more thorough investigation of their aptitudes, skills, and career possibilities. In addition, the particular "service plan" that the ET participant chooses may string together many different services and may involve a relatively lengthy stay in the program.

Some critics of the individualized approach to choice of program services have argued that it undermines efficiency in the distribution of program resources. That is, given the fact that participants will sometimes choose the "wrong" options (for example, options that are inappropriate because they require skills the client does not have, or because they offer training that the client does not necessarily need to get a job), program resources may be wasted. In contrast to ET, most employment and training programs for welfare clients attempt to distinguish between "job-ready" individuals and those that require more intensive remedial training. Those other programs usually do not allow job-ready welfare recipients to participate in more expensive program services and channel them into immediate job search and job placement services. The theory behind this policy is simply that resources should be distributed according to need and that "need" be defined in terms of what is required to obtain employment. While the ET Choices Program also provides these immediate job placement services, it does not impose them on clients who may appear to be ready for employment at program application. Although the principle of individualized service planning may sometimes lead to inappropriate or inefficient choices in the distribution of resources, however, this policy is in keeping with the ET Program's underlying philosophy of choice and consumerism in that it theoretically allows for the provision of those services needed to obtain the job that the participant wants and will keep.

Quality Jobs
It has long been recognized by economists and policy analysts that choosing employment over welfare does not always represent a rational choice for individuals seeking to maximize their income and benefits. For those who decide to work part time and remain on welfare, for example, their welfare grant is reduced one dollar for every dollar of earned income after deductions for work-related expenses are taken into account. Those welfare clients who leave the rolls altogether for employment often face the loss of medical insurance and other benefits. For these reasons, many welfare clients either choose not to work or return to welfare shortly after leaving for a job. Indeed, an informal survey by Welfare Department staff of ET job finders who return to the welfare rolls has suggested that loss of Medicaid benefits and an initial decrease in disposable income after leaving welfare are primary reasons cited by clients who return to welfare.

To stimulate participation in the program among welfare clients and to help ensure that the jobs that ET "graduates" do obtain are stable, long-lasting jobs, the ET Choices Program has tried to institutionalize the goal of "quality" jobs in at least two ways. First, when prospective participants first discuss the ET Program with an ET worker or a welfare caseworker, they can use an automated "wage guide" to estimate the hourly wage needed on a job to at least replace the income and benefits afforded by the welfare system.[9] To perform these calculations, several work-related costs are considered, including child care, health insurance, transportation, and others. The wage guide affords each program participant with an estimated salary goal to aim for when seeking employment. A second way in which the ET Program has attempted to institutionalize the goal of stable, quality jobs in the program's administration is through performance-based contracting (see below). By setting standards for the types of job that the Welfare Department is willing to pay its contractors for, it has tried to push the ET Program toward job placements that represent an economic improvement over welfare. In the state fiscal year 1988, for example, the Welfare Department only acknowledged jobs in reimbursing ET service deliverers that were full time, paid at least $5.00 an hour to start, and lasted for at least 30 days.

Performance-based Contracting for ET Services
The WIN Program was characterized by a dual administration at the federal and state level between the U.S. Department of Health and Human Services and the U.S. Department of Labor and their state-level analogues. In contrast to this arrangement, the ET Program has taken advantage of the single-agency administration policy of the federal WIN Demonstration Projects regulations to concentrate all funds, and therefore all budget and policy decisions, within the state Welfare Department.

Through the power afforded the Welfare Department by the single agency administrative structure of the ET Program, it has been able to impose a system of performance-based contracting on its sister state agencies and the private contractors who deliver the variety of services in the ET Program. That is, the Welfare Department has entered into interagency agreements with other state agencies, most notably the agency overseeing the administration of the Job Training Partnership Act (JTPA) programs and the state Division of Employment Security (DES).[10] Through these agreements, the Welfare Department "buys" a specified level of services (participation levels) and outcomes (for example, number and quality of jobs obtained by ET participants) from other state agencies; if these participation levels or job placement rates are not met by the contracted agency, monies for those services may be withheld. The Welfare Department also contracts with private agencies and companies to deliver services in the ET Program on the same performance basis.

The practice of engaging in performance-based contracting with service providers has probably exacted better performance out of the providers than if federal and state monies had gone directly to those other agencies. Although this supposition has not been tested rigorously, it is clear that the JTPA agencies and the DES have an added incentive to serve welfare clients, whereas previously, these agencies were funded directly, regardless of their performance.[11] In addition, the practice of using ET Program funds to contract with other agencies and institutions to deliver services has enhanced the variety of services available to participants and has engendered competition among the various service deliverers in program performance. That is, the performance standards tend to be driven by the agency or institution that has delivered services most effectively as measured by the number and quality of jobs obtained by ET participants.

Performance Standards for Local Welfare Offices
In addition to having control of the monies used to fund ET Program services, the Massachusetts Department of Public Welfare has the advantage of being a state-administered agency (as opposed to being a state-supervised and country-administered agency). The implication of this administrative structure is that the commissioner of the department can dictate department policy to local welfare office directors, since they serve at his discretion. This aspect of centralized administration has helped to strengthen the ET Choices Program by establishing the program's success as a quantifiable goal for each local welfare office. That is, each office has a quota of job placements that it must meet; individual office progress in meeting its annual goals is carefully monitored.

A long-term result of imposing goals for ET placements on local welfare offices has been the change in institutional cultures within the Welfare Department. That is, individual caseworkers have broadened their image of their jobs through the department's emphasis on the ET Choices Program. Previously, welfare caseworkers performed essentially clerical tasks focused on the correct determination of eligibility and benefit amounts. While this aspect of income maintenance work has not been neglected with the advent of the ET Program, the emphasis on moving welfare recipients into the ET Program and providing them with the necessary services to achieve economic independence has been changing the welfare caseworker from essentially a clerical worker to a more traditional "social worker" or even "antipoverty worker." We will discuss this issue in more detail below as we review the broader implications of programs like ET for welfare reform in general.

ET Choices Program Services

As discussed in the preceding section, the principle of individual choice both in the decision to participate and in the menu of services is a cornerstone of the

ET Choices Program. To support a program that attracts participation through the promise of quality services and the ultimate goal of a stable, high-quality job, the Welfare Department has made a relatively large investment in providing a broad range and generous supply of services (see, for example, U.S. General Accounting Office [USGAO] 1988). It is important to note that the individual support, education, skills training, and job placement services available in the ET Choices Program do not represent a particularly new training technology. The novel aspect of the ET Program services has more to do with the number of choices facing the participant. In this respect, the ET Choices Program is attempting to make an appeal to a group of individuals with relatively diverse educational and employment backgrounds. For example, based on a Welfare Department survey of AFDC recipients in the last quarter of 1987, 53 percent of welfare recipients do not have a high school degree, but 12 percent have schooling beyond high school. Similarly, while 23 percent of those surveyed had no work experience outside the home, 52 percent had worked full time at some time in the past. The ET Program has attempted to make available a range of services designed to be helpful to individuals within this broad range of background and skills. In many instances, an individual must "string together" a series of services that will ultimately lead to employment. In this section we review the "menu" of the various services that make up the ET Choices Program; we also present budget information about the resources represented by these services.

Career Planning Services
In accordance with the basic philosophy of choice and individualized services, the ET Program has funded since its inception a career planning and assessment service for welfare clients who want or need professional guidance in their choice of an employment goal. Career planning services are delivered by contracted service providers and include skills testing, evaluation, and career counseling. The ET Program has standardized career planning across the various service providers and has developed a model for the service that integrates assessment with the education and training services available through the program. Surprisingly, relatively few ET participants begin their participation with a career assessment; of those welfare recipients actively participating in the ET Program as of January 1988, for example, only 12 percent had received career planning services (Massachusetts Department of Public Welfare [Mass. DPW] 1988).

Basic Educational Services
Many welfare recipients lack the most basic academic skills required for success in the labor market or even for admission to skills training programs. The particular services made available to participants include English as a second

language, General Educational Development (GED) courses and preparation, adult literacy training, and basic math and reading courses. The Welfare Department has used several different service providers to deliver these basic educational services. For example, the Welfare Department contracts with the JTPA system for basic and adult education services in addition to skills training services; often the JTPA contractor provides the educational upgrading as a preparation for skills training. Besides contracting with the JTPA system for educational services, the ET Program has contracted with numerous independent public and private local education agencies to provide training to ET participants. Very often participation in a basic education course is the first step in a succession of ET Program services that a particular individual may pass through in preparation for employment. Of those individuals participating in ET as of January 1988, approximately 14 percent were engaged in adult basic education; of the remaining participants, however, some had likely received educational services as part of their stay in the Program (Mass. DPW 1988).

Higher Education Services

In an effort to help those welfare recipients who have vocational goals that may require post-high-school education, the ET Program makes exposure to college courses possible in two ways. First, for those welfare recipients who are attending college and receiving aid from a source other than the ET Program (for example, through a Pell Grant or a college scholarship), the ET Program will make support services available (see below). Also, however, the Welfare Department has contracted with the Massachusetts community college system for a voucher system by which ET participants may attend a community college for up to one year and may take up to two courses. In most instances, ET participants enroll in vocational training courses, such as word processing, or accounting, at the community college. As of January 1988, approximately 13 percent of active ET participants were enrolled in a community college course or courses (Mass. DPW 1988).

It should be noted that these courses at local community colleges are more like adult vocational education than "higher education" in the popular sense. They often prepare participants for typical entry-level jobs in service industries or office work rather than as "professionals." Nevertheless, the exposure to the community college afforded by the voucher program has led some ET participants to remain at the college under a Pell Grant or other scholarship arrangement and continue to receive the AFDC grant and support services from the ET Program.

Skills Training Services

Occupational skills training is a traditional means of improving the employment chances of individuals with few marketable skills and little work experience. The primary goal of most skills training programs is to prepare individu- als for work in a specific type of job that requires some specialized knowledge and for which there is demand in the labor market. Usually participants in skills training programs require some level of basic educational competence. In addition to the basic adult education services described above, some ET skills training contractors offer educational upgrading as a preparation for their occupational training courses.

The ET Choices Program has made skills training services available through two types of service delivery systems. First, the program has relied heavily on the JTPA system. JTPA is a federally funded, state- and locally administered employment and training program for disadvantaged individuals. Among those individuals that the JTPA agencies are mandated to serve are a given proportion of AFDC recipients. The ET Choices Program has con- tracted separately with the statewide agency in charge of administering the JTPA program for an extra number of services for ET participants. To qualify for the added ET monies, however, the JTPA program must serve its mandated quota of AFDC clients in addition to the increment paid for through ET Program funds.

In addition to the JTPA program, the Welfare Department has relied on other skills training agencies for ET services. The most notable of these other agencies is the Bay State Skills Corporation, a nonprofit agency funded by monies from private and public sources. The Bay State Skills Corporation contracts out for education and training services with other service delivery agents and enjoys a special relationship with certain industries in the state for which it prepares ET participants. As of January 1988, approximately 31 percent of ET participants were engaged in skills training and vocational education (Mass. DPW 1988).

Job Development and Placement Services
A certain proportion of welfare recipients are skilled and experienced in some occupation and merely want help in finding a job. In addition, other ET participants who have completed their course of education or skills training may need help in locating suitable employment. For these individuals, the ET Choices program has contracted with the state DES to provide help in locating and obtaining available jobs.

The DES is the public agency that maintains a file of available job open- ings. Often, the DES receives "job orders" from companies needing workers with specific skills. Although the DES has a mandate to provide help finding a job for any citizen of the state, the contract with the ET Choices Program "buys" a set of services exclusively for welfare recipients. The performance criteria for the contracted services also provide an incentive to DES to deliver high-quality services to welfare clients and to help provide access to jobs that meet some minimal wage and benefit standards. As of January 1988, approximately 39 percent of active ET participants were engaged in job search under the guidance of the DES (Mass. DPW 1988); it is likely that many individuals now engaged in other ET activities may at some time take advantage of job placement services.

Supported Work

The Supported Work Program in ET is designed to serve individuals with little or no recent employment experience. This option is a variant of an earlier training program that was developed in 1975 as a large national demonstration program.[12] Massachusetts was one of the pilot sites in the demonstration and Supported Work has continued as a resource for AFDC recipients since that time.

The central feature of the approach developed by the Supported Work Program is the emphasis on graduated responsibility in the workplace through on-the-job training and peer support. Participants are placed immediately (or after some weeks of classroom preparation) at an actual work site where they train in job skills and receive counseling in work-related behavior and attitudes. As Supported Work participants learn appropriate skills they are likely to be hired as regular employees by the company or public agency in which they trained. As of January 1988, approximately 3 percent of ET participants were engaged in Supported Work (Mass. DPW 1988).

Support Services

It is a truism in work and welfare policy that welfare recipients require a range of support services in order to participate in employment and training programs and to be able to go to work. Even the most conservative approach to work and welfare policy, for example, must take account of the fact that the vast majority of welfare families are single-parent families and that therefore child care is an absolutely essential support service for many potential program participants. The ET Choices program provides three central kinds of support services for its participants and graduates. These services are: assistance with child care, assistance with training- and work-related transportation costs, and transitional services for participants who leave welfare for a job. We describe the ET program support services below.

When policy experts list the "necessary" support services for work and welfare programs, child care usually tops the list. Even for families with no preschool children, after-school and summertime child care may be an absolute prerequisite to participation in any training and job placement program. Support for participants' child care needs has been a policy priority for the ET Program since its beginning. The program supplies this service through two mechanisms: the voucher day care system and the independent day care system.

The majority of program-provided support is through the ET Voucher Day Care system. This system was developed through an interagency agreement with the Massachusetts Department of Social Services (DSS) exclusively for the ET program. The DSS also manages the state's contracted day care system, which provides day care services for families eligible under Title XX programs. In part, the voucher system draws on the expertise of DSS and its links to the child care provider network. The voucher system differs from the contract day care system in an important way. Under the contract day care system, the DSS buys several slots directly from certified institutional and family day care centers and distributes these slots as they become available to eligible individuals. Under the voucher system, however, the ET participant who has chosen a provider is given a voucher to pay for the service directly. The provider can redeem the voucher through a network of voucher management agencies that administer the system for DSS. One important similarity between the two systems is that they both operate on a sliding fee scale. Clients in both systems must pay a small fee for the service; the fee varies according to the client's income, the type of day care arrangement, the client's family size, and the number of children receiving care. In fiscal 1986, for example, the average ET participant in the voucher system paid $3.85 a week for the service (Mass. DPW, *Budget Request*, FY1987).

The voucher day care system developed for the ET Program is thought to have several advantages over the contract day care arrangement. First, the contract system deals only with licensed institutional and family day care systems (these systems are composed of consortia of family day care centers that receive formal training and technical assistance), while the voucher system also allows access to a greater number of family day care providers (licensed day care in private homes that serve no more than six children). This arrangement increases the potential supply of day care providers for ET participants. A second difference that benefits ET participants is the flexibility in scheduling that the broader range of providers allows. That is, those clients who may have limited day care needs because they are in training or education services that meet several days a week rather than all week find more flexibility in the voucher system, since priority for a contracted slot is usually given to individuals with more full-time child care needs. Finally, the waiting period for voucher day care is usually shorter than that for a contracted day care slot. As soon as an ET participant has chosen a provider and is ready to begin training, a voucher for the service can be provided. In the contract day care system, however, the client has to wait for a slot in the appropriate geographic region and program type to become available.

Besides the voucher day care system for ET participants, the ET Program allows participants to be reimbursed directly for "independent day care." "Independent day care" refers to arrangements that the clients may make with neighbors, friends, or relatives to take care of their children. Participants using this system must establish their costs and are reimbursed for those costs up to $1 an hour for up to three months. The use of "independent day care" is not particularly encouraged and is usually used as a stopgap measure by program participants.

The ET Choices Program has made an increasing commitment to providing resources for child care assistance since the program's inception in 1983. For example, the budget for the voucher day care system, the major source of child care assistance for ET participants, rose from about $8 million in fiscal 1985 to about $35 million in fiscal 1988; the budget request for fiscal 1989 asks for over $50 million for the voucher day care system. The fiscal 1988 budget for voucher day care represents about 43 percent of the entire ET Program budget. (Mass. DPW, *Budget Request*, FY1986–FY1989). Despite the commitment to child care assistance and the relatively generous budget set aside for it, surprisingly few ET participants actually use the voucher system at any given time. For example, as of January 1988, only 29 percent of current ET participants were involved in the voucher system (Mass. DPW 1988). These findings are somewhat deceptive, however, since the voucher system seems to be used disproportionately by ET participants with preschool children. For example, in April 1985, over 80 percent of the children in the voucher system were preschoolers.[13]

The ET Program also reimburses participants for program-related transportation costs up to $10 a day and for various training-related expenses for uniforms or tools.

A third form of support services are transitional services. These are services made available to ET participants who obtain employment and leave the welfare rolls. They are intended to "soften the blow" of losing the benefits associated with being on welfare. In particular, the loss of medical benefits is of great concern to ET graduates. The ET Program has three forms of transitional medical insurance support for individuals who leave the welfare rolls for a job through the ET Program. First, under federal regulations, Medicaid coverage can be extended for four months for any welfare recipient who leaves the rolls for a job that does not have health insurance. Second, under a separate federal regulation, some ET job finders under certain relatively rare circumstances can receive up to 15 months of extended Medicaid coverage. Finally, the Massachusetts Department of Public Welfare has introduced its own variant of extended medical coverage for those ET graduates not covered by the 15-month Medicaid extension. That special transitional service is a year of health insurance coverage for any ET graduate who joins the special "Health Choices Program" as a welfare recipient. Health Choices is a form of managed health care (usually within a health maintenance organization, or HMO) available to welfare clients under the Medicaid Program. The provision of this health insurance for up to one year after leaving the welfare rolls for a job is intended to be an incentive to participate in both ET and the Health Choices Program.[14] In addition to transitional health insurance, the ET Program also extends coverage under the voucher day care system for ET graduates for up to one year after leaving the welfare rolls.

ET Choices Program Budget

The ET Choices Program is expensive when compared to other work and welfare programs. For example, a 1988 report on four state work and welfare programs (Massachusetts, Michigan, Oregon, Texas) by the U.S. General Accounting Office found that in fiscal year 1986 the average cost per program participant in ET was about three times the amount of the next most costly program ($1,257 per participant in ET as opposed to $410 per participant in the Michigan program) and the average cost per placement was about four times the next most costly program ($3,333 per placement for ET as opposed to $810 per placement in Oregon) (USGAO 1988, 21). Another point of reference is the relatively inexpensive job search program described by Goldman in Chapter 16 in which the cost per placement is between $77 and $195. Although the exact proportions of the relative costs of these various programs are deceptive, given differing definitions of "participant" and "placement" (see USGAO 1988, 21), it is clear that the ET Choices Program invests a great deal more in services per capita than do most other work and welfare programs (see Table 17-1).

ET Choices Program Participation and Outcomes

When considering the size of the ET budget both by itself and by comparison to other work and welfare programs, it should be noted that this consideration of raw cost data tells us nothing more than that the ET Choices Program makes a larger investment in human capital than do most other similar programs. By itself this does not mean that the ET Program is "wasteful" or "inefficient." For example, the ET Program may be more cost-effective than less expensive programs if the program impact exceeds the program cost by a greater margin than it does in other programs. The ET Choices Program may be more cost-beneficial than other programs for several reasons. For example, it may lead to more employment among welfare recipients than otherwise would have occurred by a greater amount than other programs have added to the employment of welfare clients. These greater program effects may occur because the ET Program serves "less employable" individuals, or because the ET Program helps clients obtain jobs that last longer and pay more than jobs they would have gotten in the absence of the program. In any event, the determination of

Table 17-1/The ET Choices Program Budget, Fiscal Years 1986–1989, (in thousands of dollars)

BUDGET ITEM	ESTIMATED FY86 EXPENDITURES	ESTIMATED FY87 EXPENDITURES	ESTIMATED FY88 EXPENDITURES	FY89 REQUEST
Career Planning Services	1,375	1,250	964	964
Job Placement Services	6,820	7,050	11,375	11,425
Skills Training Services	5,975	7,360	12,300	12,347
Adult Education Services	2,685	3,900	6,048	6,075
College Voucher Program	600	400	700	700
Supported Work Program	5,500	4,400	4,165	4,195
Programs for Targeted Groups [a]	1,110	1,380	2,743	2,806
Support Services [b]	750	1,600	5,101	5,101
Program Admin. and Support	2,565	2,550	2,559	2,606
SUBTOTAL	27,380	29,890	45,955	46,219
Voucher Day Care Services	17,700	27,600	36,700	53,300
GRAND TOTAL	45,080	57,490	82,655	99,519

[a] Includes, for example, programs for pregnant and parenting teens, displaced homemakers, and so on.
[b] Does not include voucher day care or extended Medicaid coverage.

the ultimate "value" of the ET Program as measured by its cost-effectiveness cannot be made on the basis of raw costs alone but is dependent on the ability to measure the "counterfactual" to the program, or the employment experience of welfare clients *in the absence of the program.*

Unlike the employment and training programs reviewed by Judith Gueron and Barbara Goldman in earlier chapters, the impact of the ET Choices Program has not yet been evaluated. That is, the degree to which the ET Program has added to the employment chances that its participants would have had in the absence of the program has not been measured by rigorous scientific methods.[15] For this reason, we cannot compare the impact of the ET Program with other work and welfare programs that have been evaluated. In this sense, many points of policy debate between those advocating short-term, inexpensive, mandatory work programs and those favoring the voluntary, more expensive, and "customized" approach of programs like ET remain unsettled. There are, however, many interesting findings about participation rates and patterns and about program outcomes (and about trends in those measures) that allow for some assessment of the success of the ET Choices Program.

ET Program Participation
A measure of the success of the ET Choices Program is the extent to which eligible clients enroll and participate in the program's various services. Perhaps of equal importance are questions about how many and which clients are participating in the ET menu of services they are choosing. In this section we review the record of the ET Program in attracting welfare recipients to participate.

How Many Welfare Clients Are Participating in the Program?
From its inception, the ET Program has been characterized by a relatively high participation rate. For example, in the first 20 months of the program's operation (1 October 1983–31 May 1985), the program served about 37,000 welfare recipients, or about one in five of the different adults on the caseload during that time. The USGAO study of four work and welfare programs found that total participation for federal fiscal year 1986 (1 October 1985–30 September 1986) was about 34,000 welfare recipients, a proportionately higher number representing about 28 percent of all potential participants (USGAO 1988). The USGAO (1988, 24) report also points out that the ET Choices Program uses a much more restrictive definition of "participant" than any of the other three states examined, yet still has an annualized participation rate that compares favorably with the other states.

Who Is Participating in the ET Program?
Critics of the ET Program sometimes argue that its voluntary approach to participation invites what is called "creaming." Creaming is the systematic enrollment in a social program of individuals who are more likely to succeed in the program that the average individual who is eligible for the service. Some have argued that the ET Choices Program creams by allowing more job-ready individuals to select themselves for the program. Creaming is sometimes an intentional strategy by program practitioners to insure success in program outcomes. Even where creaming is unintentional, however, it undermines program effectiveness in at least two important ways. First, as we have explained above, a program's effectiveness is a measure of the degree to which it improves its participants' well-being over and above what it would have been without the program. If the ET Program is creaming, therefore, it is merely enrolling individuals who would have gotten jobs anyway and thereby undermining the program's impact. Second, if the ET Program is creaming by enrolling disproportionately those individuals who would have gotten jobs anyway, it may be underserving the welfare recipients of most concern to those interested in welfare reform, that is, the less-educated individuals with little or no work experience who have disproportionately longer spells on welfare.[16]

The most convincing evidence about whether or not the ET Choices

Table 17-2/Characteristics of ET Program Participants and the Massachusetts AFDC Caseload, by Percentages

	1 Oct. 1983–30 Sept. 1984		1 Oct. 1985–30 Sept. 1986	
Characteristic	ET	AFDC	ET	AFDC
SEX				
Male	30	6	8	4
Female	70	94	92	96
RACE/ETHNICITY				
White	72	64	60	60
Black	12	18	19	17
Hispanic	15	17	20	21
Other	1	1	1	2
HAS CHILD UNDER 6 YEARS OLD	41	61	53	60
HIGH SCHOOL DEGREE OR GED	72	50	38	52
EMPLOYMENT BACKGROUND				
Ever worked	87	73	62	82
Worked within past 2 years	69	32	—	—

Sources: Data for 1 Oct. 1983–30 Sept. 1984 from Mass. DPW 1986a; data for 1 Oct. 1985–30 Sept. 1986 from USGAO 1988.
Note: Percentages may not add to exactly 100 because of rounding.

Program has creamed employable individuals from the AFDC caseload would require some knowledge of how well ET participants would do on their own in obtaining jobs. As we discussed above, this type of evaluation has not yet been done for the ET Program. Short of a rigorous evaluation, however, we can make a guess about the issue by looking at the characteristics of ET participants and comparing them to the characteristics of the AFDC caseload as a whole, particularly to characteristics that appear to be associated with the likelihood of obtaining employment (see Table 17-2).

The ET participant pool appears to reflect the diversity represented by the AFDC caseload. Through its emphasis on individualized services, the program appears to have been able to attract individuals with a wide variety of backgrounds and skills. In addition, the composition of the participant pool has changed over the first five years of the program's operation in ways that suggest that if the program was creaming early on in its operation, since then its participant pool has become more reflective of the AFDC caseload as a whole. For example, while in the first year of program operation participants were disproportionately male and white, by fiscal 1986 the sexual and racial distribution of ET participants was very close to that of the AFDC caseload as a whole. Also, the program in later years has been able to attract more

AFDC recipients with younger children. The same trend is true of character-istics representing education and employment backgrounds. For example, the percentage of ET participants with a high school degree or the GED decreased from 72 percent in 1983–84 to 38 percent in 1985–86. In addition, the per-centage of ET participants with work experience decreased markedly over the two periods of measurement.

The change in the composition of the ET participant pool is probably reflective of two related phenomena. First, the most employable part of the AFDC caseload probably volunteered for ET and left the caseload at a greater rate than did less employable individuals.[17] Second, it is likely that the time of participation for individuals more likely to get jobs is shorter than the time required by less employable welfare recipients. Because the rates of flow out of the program are different, therefore, it is possible for the less employable portion of the participant pool to increase over time. On the summary evidence of a few demographic and education and work-related characteristics, however, it does not appear that the policy of voluntary participation has necessarily led to creaming on the basis of employability. Nevertheless, ET participants are more motivated than nonparticipants, and insofar as this motivation influences success in the program, voluntarism can be considered an advantage that programs with provisions for compulsory participation or compulsory services do not enjoy.

ET Choices Program Outcomes

While measuring participation levels and patterns in an employment and train-ing program may be an important first step in assessing its effectiveness, a more important question is the degree to which participants achieve the goal of economic self-sufficiency. When considering these data it is important to remember that we are reporting *outcomes,* or the raw results of ET Program participation, and not *impacts,* or the benefits due directly to the program.

How Many and Which Program Participants Got Jobs?
The question of how many ET participants got jobs is complicated by the fact that the Massachusetts Department of Public Welfare maintains several differ-ent systems for counting placements. For example, the most inclusive measure is the number of all ET participants who got a job (but not AFDC clients who get jobs on their own). By this measure, the ET Program had placed approxi-mately 50,000 individuals into full- or part-time jobs between October 1983 and June 1988, thereby realizing its goal for the first five years of the program. A more restrictive measure of jobs also used by the Welfare Department is the number of so-called "ET priority jobs." As explained above, these jobs

Table 17-3/A Comparison of ET Job Finders, 1983–1984 and 1986, by Percentage

	1983–1984		1986	
	Participants	*Job Finders*	*Participants*	*Job Finders*
SEX				
Male	30	35	8	16
Female	70	65	92	84
RACE/ETHNICITY				
White	72	74	60	65
Black	12	13	19	20
Hispanic	15	13	20	14
Other	1	1	1	1

Source: Mass. DPW 1986a; 1986b.

are full time, pay an hourly wage of $5.00 or more to start, and last for at least 30 days. In state fiscal year 1987 (1 July 1986–30 June 1987), the program had 8,018 priority placements, representing about 68 percent of all ET placements.

Perhaps of equal importance to the raw number of ET participants that obtained employment is the question of who got jobs. That is, did the ET Program place "less employable" individuals at the same rate as more employable participants? Although we do not have systematic data to bring to bear on this question for all the years of ET's operation, some suggestive findings exist. For example, in the first year of the program, the demographic and education and employment-related characteristics of ET job finders closely matched the characteristics of ET participants (see Mass. DPW 1987). As the composition of the ET participant pool changed, however, the characteristics of job finders changed in the same direction (see Table 17-3). ET participants of different sex and race appear to be able to obtain jobs roughly in the proportion in which they participate in the program (see Table 17-3). This relationship between participation rates and placements seems to have been maintained over the history of the program.

How Good Are ET Jobs?

As discussed in the introduction to this chapter, the ultimate goal of any work and welfare program is economic independence. For the single-headed (usually female-headed) families on welfare, this means doing at least as well in income and benefits on the job as they do on welfare. A job that does not leave a person as well off as he or she would be on welfare is not likely to allow a welfare recipient to achieve stable economic independence. "Job quality" can be defined as the degree to which the job replaces and surpasses the income/

benefits package under welfare. The breakeven point for each welfare recipient may be different, however, given differing expenses associated with work and the fringe benefits available through the job. For example, an ET graduate that gets a job that offers and subsidizes family health insurance will need less income to replace welfare benefits. Alternatively, an individual whose child care expenses increase because of the job will likely need more income to replace welfare benefits. Nevertheless, a convenient rough guide for the breakeven point is the income and benefits package on welfare for a family of one parent and two children (the "typical" AFDC family in Massachusetts). The family of three receives a maximum annual AFDC grant of $6,900 and an additional $1,700 in food stamps. If one values Medicaid insurance at an estimated premium value of about $3,400 annually, the breakeven point for this family would be $12,000, or about $5.75 an hour for a full-time job. How does the income available through ET placements measure up against this benchmark?

For the state fiscal year 1987 (1 July 1986–30 June 1987), the average hourly wage for "ET priority jobs" was $6.42, or about $13,400 in annual income. Eighty percent of those jobs had some employer-subsidized health insurance associated with the job. This is the gross income, and even a family earning this amount will likely pay some taxes. Nevertheless, the amount is above the breakeven point for a typical welfare family. Just as the other measures of program performance have changed, so too have the wages for ET jobs: the average hourly wage for a full-time ET job has increased from $5.01 in fiscal 1984 to $6.42 in fiscal 1987 (Mass. DPW 1986b).

Even as the average wage for an ET job placement has increased since the beginning of the program, the increase for black and Hispanic ET graduates has been greater. For example, while the overall average ET hourly wage for full-time jobs has increased 28 percent since the first year of the program, it has increased 33 percent for blacks and 42 percent for Hispanics in the program (Mass. DPW 1987).

Another issue concerning job quality is the occupational distribution of ET placements. Perhaps not surprisingly, the occupational breakdown of ET jobs reflects the fact that a vast majority of ET participants are women and most of the jobs are entry level positions. For example, 36 percent are clerical jobs and another 22 percent are service jobs; these represent the largest occupational categories. On the other hand, however, only 3 percent of the jobs are in relatively low-paying retail sales positions and ET graduates are placed in jobs in the construction trades at the same rate at which they appear in the total Massachusetts economy (4 percent) (Mass. DPW 1988 [for ET job distribution]; Massachusetts Division of Employment Security [for the distribution of jobs in Massachusetts]).

To What Degree Do Those Finding Jobs Leave Welfare?

Another important outcome of the program that is an indicator of its success is the degree to which those getting jobs through ET leave welfare and achieve economic independence. When reviewing the record of the program in promoting financial independence, two factors should be remembered. First, many people leave welfare every month for many different reasons; ET is not the only route out of welfare. Second, some of the individuals who did leave the welfare rolls after getting a job through ET may have left welfare in the absence of the program; as suggested above, absent a rigorous evaluation, this number cannot be estimated.

With the reservations listed above, the best available indicator of the success of the ET Choices Program in encouraging economic independence is the proportion of ET placements that subsequently leave the welfare rolls. We consider this measure at three different times. First, for all ET placements between 1 October 1983 and 30 April 1985 as of 1 July 1985, 52 percent were closed cases, 16 percent were cases with reduced AFDC grants, and 27 percent were at or above their original AFDC grant (5 percent are unaccounted for) (Mass. DPW 1986a). Second, for all ET placements as of June, 1986, 57 percent were closed cases, 20 percent had reduced grants, and 23 percent had grants at or above the level at time of program enrollment (Mass. DPW 1986b). Finally, by June 1987, 66 percent of all ET placements (and 77 percent of ET "priority" placements) had closed cases.

Summary and Conclusion: ET and Welfare Reform

On 22 June 1988, Governor Michael Dukakis, soon to be chosen by the Democratic National Convention as the party's nominee for the 1988 Presidential election, held a news conference in Boston announcing the 50,000th ET job placement. This event by itself was not surprising; what was perhaps surprising was the fact that a man running for President in 1988 would tout a work and welfare program, a "social program," as an example of his leadership abilities. Perhaps equally surprising was the fact that the national news media was already quite familiar with the ET Choices Program and its stature as a "model" welfare reform proposal.

Indeed, ET has been getting national attention for several years. Although as we have indicated there has as yet been no rigorous evaluation of the program's impact, the program is thought by many to be highly successful, and by some to be the answer to welfare reform.[18] Unfortunately, because there is no estimate of the impact of the program, we do not have at our disposal one of the most powerful decision-making tools in policy analysis— a benefit/cost ratio for the program—to help decide if the principles of the

ET Program—voluntary participation, a broad menu of relatively expensive services, customized service delivery—ought to be the foundation of national work and welfare policy. Nevertheless, there are some observations we can make about the national influence of ET and about the way the ET Program has transformed the Massachusetts Department of Public Welfare.

ET and National Work and Welfare Policy
The attention given to the ET Choices Program has dovetailed with the national debate about employment and training policy in particular and welfare reform in general. At the state and local levels, many welfare commissioners have been under pressure from their governors and from the public to develop programs like ET in either design or result. Over the past several years, many states on their own initiatives and with state funding have attempted to develop new employment and training programs for welfare clients. Some of the ideas embodied in ET have surfaced in these programs either by direct influence or independently. In addition, in the spring of 1988, both houses of Congress passed more comprehensive welfare packages that contain provisions for employment and training programs with some similarities to ET. We review these developments below.

Three recent examples of state-initiated employment and training programs that share some central features with the ET Choices Program are the California Greater Avenues for Independence (GAIN) Program, the Investment in Job Opportunities (IJO) Program in Maryland, and the Comprehensive Employment Opportunity Support Centers (CEOSC) Program in New York. While it cannot be said that these other programs are copies or clones of ET, they share some basic policies with ET.

The California GAIN Program is an initiative of the California legislature that shares some central features with the ET Choices Program. For example, the GAIN Program makes available to welfare recipients a wide variety of education, employment, and training services, including adult basic education, English as a second language, career assessment, vocational training, supported work, and others. In addition, although some GAIN participants must engage in a specific sequence of activities at the beginning of program participation, there is some attempt made to customize services according to individual needs and career aspirations. The GAIN Program does differ significantly from ET, however, in its provision that a certain group of AFDC recipients (usually those with school-age children) must actively and continuously engage in some program activity for as long as they receive welfare. In this sense, the GAIN Program is more like workfare than ET.

In contrast to the California GAIN Program, the IJO Program in Maryland and the CEOSC Program in New York are more closely related to the ET Choices Program. The IJO Program is largely voluntary, although some county welfare departments have included provisions for mandatory participation. IJO offers a wide range of services, from remedial education to skills training; in addition, IJO individualizes the service plan according to the needs of each participant. Finally, the IJO Program is relatively expensive and makes the same long-term gamble that ET does. That is, the IJO Program is taking the risk that the larger per capita investment in services will allow the program to serve more needy individuals and to help them secure more stable, higher-quality jobs.

The CEOSC Program in New York State also shares some important program features with the ET Program. Like ET, it is a voluntary program with a broad range of service and provisions for an individualized approach to training. Unlike ET, however, the CEOSC is targeted on adult AFDC recipients with preschool children. For this reason, the investment in CEOSC for support services is greater than in ET. In many of the CEOSC sites (CEOSC was a pilot program implemented in 1987 in nine sites) on-site child care is available. In addition, each CEOSC participant has a case manager responsible for her progress and success in the program. The cost per participant in CEOSC is even greater than for ET, but the target population is a group that is more likely than average to become long-term welfare recipients. In this respect, CEOSC is an attempt to develop a "poverty prevention" program along the lines of ET.

In addition to wholly state-initiated programs, the ideas embodied in the ET Program have exerted some influence on national welfare reform legislation, the Family Support Act of 1988. The major assumption underlying this act is that public assistance should provide support for a relatively brief interval until the recipient is securely established in employment. Furthermore, it assumes that public assistance programs should facilitate and motivate this result. The legislation reflects these principles in some of its changes to the AFDC Program, including:

- strengthening the role of employment and training programs, both by making participation mandatory for more recipients and by requiring states to provide a broader range of services;
- guaranteeing child care availability during employment and training and increasing child care deductions in AFDC benefit calculations; and
- increasing transitional support, including both Medicaid and child care, for AFDC families whose earnings take them over the eligibility limit for normal AFDC benefits.

ET and Welfare Reform in Massachusetts: A Model for the Nation?
Besides exerting an important influence on the national work and welfare policy debate, the ET Choices Program has helped transform the Massa-

chusetts Department of Public Welfare. In the 1970s, under the influence of national policy guidelines, most state welfare departments had separated the administration of income maintenance programs like AFDC from more traditional "social services" programs like child-abuse prevention or foster care. In theory, this approach was supposed to help remove the stigma attached to welfare by making it basically a clerical operation as opposed to an "examination" by a social worker, and the separation of income maintenance and services was supposed to improve the administration of both through more specialization.

By the beginning of this decade, most welfare departments in the nation had managed to achieve the separation of income maintenance programs from social service both in fact and in spirit. Income maintenance departments became "paper-processing plants" concerned chiefly with establishing program eligibility and calculating and delivering benefits accurately. With the increasing pressure to move welfare clients into jobs, however, income maintenance departments have once again gotten into the business of both referring clients to, and delivering, services. This issue was even more pressing for ET, since the program is voluntary and succeeds only by attracting recipients to participate. Welfare offices and workers now discovered that in order to fulfill their quotas for participation and placements, they would have to "relearn" how to deliver social services to their clients. In this respect, the movement to decrease the rolls of welfare programs has led to the reintroduction of more traditional social work to income maintenance agencies.

In Massachusetts, the Welfare Department has reclassified its income maintenance workers as "case managers" and has tried to redefine the caseworker's role from essentially clerical to antipoverty. That is, each case manager has as part of his or her tasks the development of a plan by which each welfare client can achieve economic independence and the ultimate realization of that goal through ET or other means. It is in this sense of redefining the work of a state's welfare agency from the precise calculation of benefits to the realization of economic independence for its clients that the ET Program will likely find its greatest resonance in national welfare policy.

Although the ET Program is an excellent work and welfare program and has helped change the institutional culture of the Massachusetts Department of Public Welfare from that of an income maintenance agency to an antipoverty agency, it does not represent the full answer to the problem of welfare reform. There are at least two important additional ways in which social policy must change if poverty among single-parent families with children is to be substantially decreased. First, policies must be developed to decrease the burden on the single-parent family (overwhelmingly the mother) by stimulating two-parent family formation, depressing out-of-wedlock births, and increasing child support from the absent parent. A welfare department can directly help increase child support. Indeed, in some states, welfare departments and other public agencies have aggressively pursued absent parents (when they can be identified) in order to establish court-ordered payment schedules and to collect monies through wage attachment and other means.

A second important element of welfare reform concerns the provision of transitional aid to a client beyond the first year or two after he or she leaves the welfare caseload for a job. While a program like ET can successfully train and place welfare recipients in jobs (especially in an expansionary economy like that enjoyed by Massachusetts in the 1980s), it cannot fully compensate for the many difficulties faced in the labor market by poor families with young children, even when both parents are present in the household. The practical and financial pressures experienced by families with low incomes and few work-related benefits often become too great to sustain economic independence. Many poor families that experience a spell on welfare will return to the rolls for want of financial or in-kind help with child care, medical insurance and expenses, the cost of housing, and so on. Some form of broader assistance to the working poor is needed to sustain the financial independence that a program such as ET can help welfare recipients to realize: This assistance includes, for example, universal child allowances, national health insurance, and a meaningful and large-scale low-income housing program. The ET Choices Program is an effective program for preparing some welfare recipients for jobs. However, it was not designed to be a full-scale social program for the poor, and it would be a mistake to think that ET is the complete answer to welfare reform in the United States.

Notes

1. Originally, the ADC Program contained no provision for aid to the adult guardians of dependent children, although states could offer such aid on their own. In 1950, however, the Social Security Act was amended to provide for federal matching funds for aid to one adult guardian.

2. The growing tendency of single mothers to enter the labor force is reflected by the fact that the proportion of all female heads of family receiving AFDC declined from a historic high of 69 percent in 1973 to 46 percent in 1985. See Robert A. Moffitt, "Work and the U.S. Welfare System: A Review," written with support from the U.S. Department of Health and Human Services, February 1987.

3. The other current "big gun" in the armament of welfare reform is tougher child support enforcement policy. While just 10 years ago the idea of "forcing" poor men to pay for their abandoned children may have been considered being too tough on the poor in some political circles, it is now an idea whose time appears to have arrived.

4. For a review of the results of evaluations of some of these programs that have been developed as WIN Demonstration programs, see, for example, the many Manpower Demonstration Research Corporation evaluation reports listed below in References, and in Chapters 15 and 16.

5. The Baltimore City Department of Social Services operated a WIN Demonstration called OPTIONS prior to the implementation of the ET Choices Program. Some observers claim that the OPTIONS Program anticipated the ET Choices Program design; in fact, however, the OPTIONS Program served WIN mandatory recipients, as well as volunteers.

6. The Urban Institute is now under contract with the Massachusetts Department of Public Welfare to evaluate the ET Choices Program, although the focus of the evaluation is not on program impacts. The evaluation had not been completed as of the writing of this chapter.

7. No rigorous evaluation of WTP was conducted, although there are two independent summary studies of the first year of the program. One study was prepared by Meredith and Associates, Inc. (1983), a Boston-based welfare advocacy organization, and the other was prepared by the Office of Family Assistance, U.S. Department of Health and Human Services (1985).

8. The issue of mandatory versus voluntary participation in employment and training programs for welfare recipients is part of a longstanding policy debate. The issue is intimately wrapped up with a range of ideological responses; most notably, those favoring mandatory participation want to appear tougher on welfare recipients than those who favor voluntary participation. In practice, there is usually no simple distinction between "voluntary" and "mandatory" programs. For example, some "mandatory" programs have been notoriously lax in their procedures to sanction non-compliant welfare recipients, whereas most "mandatory" programs have not been funded at high enough levels to serve every mandatory client; those that do get served often are those who step forward to be served and who behave a lot like "volunteers" for the program.

To my knowledge, although the MDRC work and welfare evaluations have tested the feasibility of implementing a mandatory participation requirement, there has been no "head-to-head" rigorous test of the effectiveness of a mandatory program as opposed to a voluntary program. Since there is no conclusive objective argument for either approach, therefore, the debate usually is based on a combination of political, ideological, and ethical principles, rather than on efficiency.

9. The wage guide illustrates the evolving nature of the ET Program. The guide was not used in the early years of the program but was developed later in response to concerns about the ability of the program to place individuals into jobs sufficient to maintain economic independence.

10. Until 1987, the JTPA program and the Division of Employment Security were two different state agencies. In that year, however, the two state agencies were consolidated into a single jobs and training agency. The Welfare Department now contracts with this consolidated agency for the delivery of many ET services.

11. This is not entirely correct. The JTPA system has federally mandated performance standards for participation and placements for welfare clients. These standards are different than those used by the ET Program and the sanctions that back up the federal standards are different from those used by the ET Program. It is felt by the Welfare Department that the ET standards for JTPA are more demanding and more finely tuned than the federal JTPA standards.

12. For a summary of the findings of the National Supported Work Demonstration, see Masters and Maynard (1981), and Kemper, Long, and Thornton (1981).

13. It should be noted that even though the ET Program has committed relatively large resources for child care and other support services, there remain serious problems for single women with young children both in the ET Program and in the labor force. The ET Program can only compensate so much for the tremendous practical, financial, and logistical problems faced by single mothers on the job or in training with one or more children of various ages. In part these difficulties are the result of an inadequate supply of convenient, inexpensive day care (particularly at or near the job or training site) in our society. It is likely that one of the reasons why so few ET participants take advantage of the day care voucher system is that they cannot conveniently "package" all the institutional or family day care they need and rely on neighbors, older siblings, and relatives coming into the home to babysit.

14. In 1988, the Massachusetts State legislature passed a bill authorizing a system of universal health coverage for all citizens of the state. When this system becomes fully operational by 1992, it is likely that the form that transitional health insurance for ET graduates takes will change.

15. The question of the appropriate evaluation design needed to evaluate an employment and training program is the subject of intense debate in the evaluation and policy analysis community. There are essentially two schools of thought on the subject. One school believes that the only unambiguous way to evaluate program impacts is through a classic experimental design in which clients are randomly assigned either to a treatment group that gets program services or a control group that is denied program services. The impact of the program on any given measure is then the difference between the average value for that measure among the two groups. The other school of thought argues that the program impact can also be estimated (or, as the more strident anti-experimentalists insist, can only be accurately estimated) through the use of statistical techniques that "simulate" an experiment with greater purity than is possible in practice. For the latest salvos in this debate, see, for example, Burtless and Orr (1986); Heckman and Hotz (1987); LaLonde and Maynard (1987).

16. For more on the welfare dynamics of the "hard-to-serve," see, for example, Bane and Ellwood (1983); Ellwood (1986).

17. This is not to imply that women or minorities are *intrinsically* "less employable" than white men, but only that, *on average,* white men fair better in the labor market. This is doubtless due to a number of factors (perhaps discrimination is one of them).

18. Some critics have argued that one of the secrets of ET's success has been the fact that it has not yet been evaluated. Although there is no reason to believe that the program will prove to be a failure in its effectiveness, it is true that evaluating any social program presents certain risks. First, if the total benefits to society of the program do not exceed the program's costs, the program may be seen as yet another transfer of resources from taxpayers to welfare clients. Second, even if the program does prove to have a positive impact, that impact is bound to be lower than the raw outcomes that have been announced publicly for many years. That is, for example, the number of jobs that the ET Program helps welfare recipients obtain *above and beyond the number of jobs they would have gotten on their own* will almost certainly be less than the total number of jobs obtained by individuals in the program.

References

Bane, Mary Jo, and David T. Ellwood. 1983. "The Dynamics of Dependence: The Routes to Self-Sufficiency." Cambridge, Mass.: Urban Systems Research and Engineering.

Burtless, Gary, and Larry L. Orr. 1986. "Are Classical Experiments Needed for Manpower Policy?" *Journal of Human Resources* 21 (Fall): 606–39.

Ellwood, David T. 1986. "Targeting 'Would-Be' Long-Term Recipients of AFDC." Princeton, N.J.: Mathematica Policy Research.

Fraker, Thomas, and Rebecca Maynard. 1987. "Evaluating Comparison Group Designs with Employment-Related Programs." *Journal of Human Resources* 22 (Spring): 194–227.

Gueron, Judith M. 1988. "State Welfare Employment Initiatives: Lessons from the 1980s." *Focus* 2, no. 1 (Spring).

Heckman, J., and V. J. Hotz. 1987. "On the Use of Nonexperimental Methods for Estimating the Impact of Manpower Training Programs: Re-Evaluating the Evaluations." Typescript.

Kemper, Peter; David Long; and Craig Thornton. 1981. *The Supported Work Evaluation: Final Benefit-Cost Analysis.* Final Report 5. New York: Manpower Demonstration Research Corporation.

LaLonde, R., and R. Maynard. 1987. "How Precise are Evaluations of Employment and Training Programs: Evidence from a Field Experiment." Typescript.

Massachusetts Department of Public Welfare. 1986a. "An Analysis of the First 25,000 ET Placements." Boston, August.

———. 1986b. "Follow-Up Survey of the First 25,000 ET Placements." Boston. August.

———. 1987. *An Evaluation of the Massachusetts Employment and Training Choices Program: Interim Findings on Participation and Outcomes.* Boston: January.

———. 1988. "ET Chartbook." Boston, February.

Massachusetts Division of Employment Security. 1988. "Employment Review." Boston, January.

Masters, Stanley H., and Rebecca Maynard. 1981. *The Impact of Supported Work on Long-Term Recipients of AFDC Benefits.* Final Report 3. New York: Manpower Demonstration Research Corporation.

Mead, Lawrence. 1986. *Beyond Entitlement: The Social Obligations of Citizenship.* New York: The Free Press.

Meredith and Associates, Inc. 1983. "Massachusetts Department of Public Welfare Employment and Training Program." Boston, August.

Rodgers, Charles S. 1981. "Work Tests for Welfare Recipients: The Gap Between the Goal and the Reality." *Journal of Policy Analysis and Management* 1, no. 1: 5–17.

U.S. Department of Health and Human Services. Social Security Administration. Office of Family Assistance. 1985. "First Year Evaluation of the Work Incentive Demonstration." Washington, D.C., February.

———. Social Security Administration. 1988. *Social Security Bulletin* 51, no. 1 (January).

U.S. General Accounting Office. 1982. *An Overview of the WIN Program: Its Objectives, Accomplishments, and Problems.* Washington, D.C.

————. 1987. *Work and Welfare: Current AFDC Work Programs and Implications for Federal Policy.* Washington, D.C.

————. 1988. *Work and Welfare: Analysis of AFDC Employment Programs in Four States.* Washington, D.C.

Wallace, John, and David Long. 1987. *GAIN: Planning and Early Implementation.* New York: Manpower Demonstration Research Corporation, April.

Werner, Alan; Christopher Kane; Gary Silverstein; and Jean Layzer. 1988. *Review of the Implementation of the Maryland Investment in Job Opportunities Program: Synthesis of Findings.* Prepared for Maryland Department of Human Resources, Office of Welfare Employment Policy. Cambridge, Mass.: Abt Associates.

Werner, Alan, and Bonnie Nutt-Powell. 1988. *Evaluation of the Implementation of the New York State Comprehensive Employment Opportunity Support Centers.* Volume 1, *Synthesis of Findings.* Prepared for New York Department of Social Services, Office of Program Planning. Cambridge, Mass.: Abt Associates.

18/Denying Independence: Barriers to the Education of Women on AFDC

Marilyn Gittell and Janice Moore

Lower-income and minority women are more likely than other women to suffer from low-quality education in inferior schools, lack of support for completing school, and sharply limited opportunities to pursue a postsecondary education. They experience especially harshly the dilemma of desiring work while being denied the quality of education necessary to circumvent sex stereotyping and acquire employment that leads to economic independence and security. Also, lacking the ability to relocate, they must usually take the lowest-paying jobs without medical and other fringe benefits. Ironically, their dependence on the welfare system is significantly related to those short-sighted public policies that deny low-income women quality education and work experiences.

As Becker (1964) suggests, any activity that raises the future productivity of individuals is part of a society's investment in human capital, even though it may entail opportunity costs in foregone short-term earnings. Yet in general, American economic, education, and employment policies seek immediate returns on expenditures. The cumulative effect of those policies is disinvestment in human capital. While it is understandable that lower-income and minority women are often forced to make short-term decisions about investment in their own human capital, social policies that eschew long-term investment in women's development are counterproductive. These policies contribute directly to the discriminatory pattern that places lower-income and minority women into the secondary labor market, depriving them of an adequate education and creating and reinforcing the need for welfare dependency. For example, women receiving Aid to Families with Dependent Children (AFDC) are rarely offered the opportunity to pursue postsecondary education in state employment and training programs. The denial of this opportunity stems in part from a lack of awareness by policy makers about the needs of many AFDC women and the failure of society to recognize the benefits of education for this segment of the population.

445

A recent U.S. Department of Labor study on female workers shows that the average single mother in poverty supports a family of 3.4 persons and is a high school graduate aged 33.4 years. Yet, employment opportunities now open to these heads of household are unlikely to change their economic status. The highest rates of poverty for working women were reported for women in traditional occupations: service-sector jobs, private household work, operative work, and sales. Black single mothers who worked in private households had a poverty rate of 63.7 percent; service workers had a rate of 47.3 percent. The lowest poverty rates for working women who maintained families were for professional, technical, managerial, and administrative employees. But to reach these more lucrative and stable jobs, single female heads of household must have an education beyond the high school level (U.S. Department of Labor [USDOL] 1983).

The type of employment a woman has and her resulting income are clearly linked to the amount and type of education she has obtained. For example, a study of occupations and incomes of college graduates in 1982 found that 84 percent of graduates were employed in the higher-paying professional, technical, and managerial areas, and that women college graduates surpassed the average earnings of their cohorts who finished their education with high school within two years of graduation (Henderson and Ottinger 1985). To earn a salary sufficient for supporting a family, many women will require a postsecondary education. For some women that will mean vocational training in well-paying fields. For others it will mean obtaining two-year or four-year degrees from community colleges, universities, or other degree-granting institutions. In addition to higher earnings and the promise of a greater lifetime earning potential, AFDC women also see their education as example-setting for their children. The possibility that their educational pursuits would encourage their children to set their own goals high may even be its greatest benefit.

Benefits of a college education for some college-ready AFDC mothers accrue to society. Henry Levin, professor of economics at Hartford University, has recently expressed concern about the hesitancy of U.S. policy makers to invest in the education of citizens living below the poverty level. The consequences of such hesitancy could be a deterioration of the labor force and a continuing decline in the competitiveness of U.S. labor (Levin 1985). Support for the view that investment in college education can be seen as an investment in human capital is not easily found in cost-benefit analyses. Recent economic developments, however, validate the need for investing in a highly skilled labor supply to respond to a changing deindustrialized economy (Beck 1985).

Blaug (1985) has argued that investment in postsecondary education for the greater productivity of a highly skilled labor force is a secondary gain for society. The most lasting value of the college experience is its socializing function. His argument is particularly relevant to the status of lower-income women in the "hour-glass" shape of the 1980s economy, where the greatest job growth is at the bottom and the top of the skill and wage scales. While school-leavers will leave educational institutions with the learned traits of compliance, punctuality, persistence, docility, and concentration, college graduates will be those prepared for the upper-level jobs, having learned not only skills but also the necessary traits of self-esteem, self-reliance, versatility, and leadership. In short, the college experience screens out those workers privileged to enter the primary labor market, while the others must face the increasingly dead-end employment of the secondary labor market. If society is to avoid a "screen" that filters out exclusively the economically disadvantaged, ethnic minorities, and women, then the opportunity to gain through a college experience the social qualities sought by primary labor market employers must be broadened. This is vitally important as trends continue toward the "feminization of poverty" and opportunities for lower-income women decline.

Finally, society's failure to deal with the welfare population and the problem of poverty as integral parts of larger social and economic goals is reflected in the lack of integration among economic development, education, and welfare policies in states and cities. State and local economic development plans explicitly exclude poor people from their blueprints. Higher education institutions are reluctant both to work with private-sector employers and to direct their programs to the needs of this population. Welfare bureaucracies are notable for their failure to communicate with other agencies to serve the needs of their clientele, at times precluding the possibility of allowing their clients to obtain the education that would make them economically self-sufficient.

The study reported in this chapter was conducted with a grant from the Ford Foundation to explore state and city policies and programs in education, employment, or economic development and how they influence the status of lower-income women, particularly AFDC recipients. We were particularly interested in linkages among the programs within the states and each city.

A second dimension of the study concentrated on interviews with 85 AFDC women enrolled in education or training programs. Questions were designed to elicit responses from women about their life goals, what barriers have kept them from meeting those goals in the past, and what barriers still exist. AFDC women's educational goals were a major theme of our interviews, which sought to examine the diversity of their needs ranging from postsecondary training programs to community college and university options.

A two-dimensional case-study approach was employed in three major cities in 1985: Philadelphia, Boston, and Baltimore. Each city was approached as one case study. Boston was chosen as a city in exceptionally good economic health, as a model site of the Massachusetts Employment and Training Choices Program (ET), which achieved a national reputation for its high rate of placing welfare recipients into jobs, and as a city with several innovative education programs for low-income women. Both Baltimore and Philadelphia are less economically healthy than Boston and have diverse programs, private or public, that serve the perceived needs of urban women in poverty. Baltimore has a history of exceptional city manpower programs, and its OPTIONS program serves as a welfare work model. Philadelphia has various strong educational programs and recently embarked on a saturation demonstration for placing AFDC recipients in jobs.

Two three-day site visits to each city were made, during which interviews were conducted with AFDC women, heads of city or state welfare or human service departments, heads of city or state manpower programs and departments of education, private developers and representatives of economic-development corporations, the directors of local Private Industry Councils (PICs), elected officials actively concerned with this population, the presidents of each city community college, and the heads of all education and training programs that could be identified as serving lower-income populations. Also, in each city a focus-group meeting was held which brought together relevant city and state officials. The following discussion presents our research findings on the postsecondary training and education needs of AFDC recipients and the barriers to meeting those needs.

Economic Independence Through Education: A Means to an End

Almost all of the AFDC women we interviewed placed full-time employment as their strongest personal goal. One of the reasons women most strongly articulated for wanting full-time employment outside the home was to be financially independent and to have control over their lives. AFDC as a means of support was seen as imposing, demeaning, and unreliable. Women commented frequently about the loss of privacy suffered under AFDC; others cited the "indignities of welfare," such as being questioned about the cost of clothes they are wearing, about the sources and values of gifts, about their friends, boyfriends, and sex lives. Many spoke of being driven to tears in the welfare offices. Others talked about the low self-esteem they developed "waiting for checks." "You get into the postman mentality," one woman told us. Neighbors are made aware of their welfare status because of the distinctive "brown envelope" arriving in the mail. One woman said she hid her "brown envelope" from her son for years so he would not know they received AFDC: "But their friends find out and say, 'Here comes your momma's welfare check.' " Many women had been "dumped," or randomly taken off AFDC without warning. Even though they were later put back on AFDC with reimbursement for the loss, it did not erase the hardship they and their family had endured when left suddenly without an income.

for enrolling in educational and employment programs was to acquire a good job—with an adequate income, benefits for their family, stability and security, and a job that is interesting to them, a job they really want.

Public policies do not match the perceptions or reality of the needs of this population. In the highly publicized ET work program for AFDC recipients in Massachusetts, up to 1 January 1985, 12,000 were placed in jobs at an average yearly income of $9,700 (Stein 1985). Most jobs were in the clerical and service occupation categories, the jobs that account for the greatest growth in Massachusetts. From 1 July to 1 December 1985, these categories combined accounted for 46 percent of all ET placements (Massachusetts Department of Public Welfare [Mass. DPW] 1986). These are the sectors where women workers have been traditionally concentrated and salaries remain at a constant low level with little chance for advancement.

For many of the women we interviewed, concern about their low level of educational attainment circumvented any ambitions to change their welfare status. Most of those who had dropped out of high school were occupied with plans to first complete their education, then plan careers. For these women, their life goal was to have an education—not just as a means of finding good employment but to fulfill a dream. To interviewees holding a high school degree, a college education would fulfill their dream. Women without high school degrees sought to finish high school or earn an equivalency degree; many hoped to earn a GED first and continue on to college programs. This was especially true for young mothers who had left high school when they became pregnant. Two women at ABCD (Action for Boston Community Development) were working on their GEDs. Both were older teenagers who had had babies while they were in high school and had dropped out. One told us it was hard for her to leave her 1-year-old in a day care center, but she wanted to do something with her life and that meant finishing high school. Her plans after finishing are to enroll in a local two-year college so that she can continue her education.

An older WEAVE student in Boston said in an interview that she grew up on a farm in the South and could not attend school. "I only went to school on rainy days." She helped with sharecropping until she turned 20, when her sister brought her to Boston. But by then she had a 1-year-old child and again stayed away from school. Now she has four children ages 20, 14, 12, and 4. With her youngest almost school age, she now wants to fulfill a dream of getting an education.

A woman with a 7-year-old daughter told us her child missed having more exclusive attention since she began attending Sojourner-Douglass College. But she explained it as a positive experience for her daughter to see her studying every night: "My career sets an example for her." When the daughter attended the college's day care center, she took part in mini-classes for children and received a certificate for completing the course. The mother explained, "She ran home with that piece of paper saying, 'See, Mom, I got my diploma before you!'" Women made similar comments when they spoke of how children viewed mothers leaving the house to work or go to school. They explained that children are more anxious to go to school "like Mom." "They don't see you sitting home," said another. A mother attending Roxbury Community College (RCC) told us her daughter and she are competing for grades: "It influences her and she thinks, 'Mommy is doing it, so I can do it.'" Another in that interview explained that if her children bring home a low grade she can say, "I got an 'A', you can, too!"

Mothers explained their determination to learn basic skills in another way: "I don't want my son to ask me, 'What's this, Mommy?' and I can't read it." Being able to help children with their homework was a high priority for many of those interviewed. Most of the women enrolled in educational programs mentioned that they do their homework with their children in the evenings and it is important to them that they can read and help their children with math problems.

Barriers to Work and Education: An AFDC Perspective

One explanation for the variety of responses from interviewees on employment and life goals is found by examining the demographics of the larger AFDC population. The diversity of these women is seldom recognized because policies aimed at them conveniently address a stereotyped population with programs narrow in scope. Our research indicates that AFDC women vary substantially by age, level of education, amount of prior work experience, number and ages of children. While the largest proportion of AFDC women are 21–29 (44.9 percent), 31 percent are 30–39 and 14 percent are 40 and older. Sixty percent of the AFDC families have children under 6, and over 42 percent have children 7–13 (Stein 1985). These figures point to a wide variance in program needs, such as day care and health care, and indicate differences in early work experience and levels of employment skills.

But the least recognized diversity is in level of educational attainment. National data show that 37.2 percent of adults on AFDC in 1975 had completed at least 12th grade (Hollister and Maynard 1984). A profile of the education level of women below the poverty level who are heads of household in the three cities we studied also reveals high percentages of high school graduates: 48.4 percent of AFDC women in Boston, 41.5 percent in Philadelphia, 34.1 percent in Baltimore—with the largest percentage of women who graduated from high school in the youngest age group, 15–24 (see Table 18-1). About 10 percent had some college education. Only in Boston did the 25–64 years

Table 18-1/Level of Education of Head of Family with Female Householder Below Poverty Level, by Age and City, 1979

	FEMALE HOUSEHOLDER, NO HUSBAND PRESENT			
EDUCATION	*15–24 years old*	*25–64 years old*	*65 years and older*	*TOTAL*
	BALTIMORE			
TOTAL	4,088	19,018	1,363	24,469
Completed 4 years of high school	1,412	4,645	162	6,219
Completed some college	372	1,703	40	2,115
Percent high school graduates	43.6	33.4	14.8	34.1
	BOSTON			
TOTAL	2,533	9,986	466	12,958
Completed 4 years of high school	828	3,806	66	4,700
Completed some college	259	1,274	47	1,580
Percent High School Graduates	42.9	50.9	24.2	48.4
	PHILADELPHIA			
TOTAL	6,641	34,134	2,626	43,401
Completed 4 years of high school	2,378	12,012	330	14,720
Completed some college	615	2,625	65	3,305
Percent high school graduates	45.1	42.9	15.0	41.5

Source: U.S. Bureau of the Census 1980, from Table 247.

age group have a larger percentage of high school graduates (50.9 percent). In the latest year for which data is available (1979) women in the 15–24 years age group made up some 20 percent of the total population of women below the poverty level who are heads of household in each of the cities, and that number is increasing (U.S. Bureau of the Census 1980). As evidenced in our interviews, many of those who did not finish high school left school because they became pregnant and had children or they were not learning anything in the schools they attended.

These data suggest that higher education is an important option for many of these women. Our interview data suggest as well that they want to go to college, that they have the potential to develop more advanced skills, and that they can be prepared for more stable, long-term employment. Other AFDC recipients need basic skills training, a GED, or job-readiness training before they are ready to undertake postsecondary education. By asking the AFDC women we interviewed what barriers to their employment goals they encountered, we attempted to understand the diversity of program needs among the more general AFDC population.

In our interviews we asked women who set employment as their goal what barriers prevented them from achieving this goal. Responses were similar in all three cities. The following is a summary list of the major obstacles women spoke of most often:

1. Education:
    —lack of basic skills
    —lack of job skills
    —lack of credentials
2. Day care:
    —problems with availability
    —expense
    —location
    —quality
3. Welfare
4. Clothing, lunch expenses
5. Type of job needed:
    —need for a good income
    —need for medical and job benefits
    —need for hours appropriate for single parents
6. Availability of good jobs
7. Transportation problems
8. Husband/boyfriend interference
9. Confidence/self-esteem

Barriers to Work

Reflecting the data indicating that the majority of AFDC recipients do not have a high school degree, the most frequently mentioned impediment to success was the lack of an education. Primarily, women spoke of lacking basic skills, job skills, and credentials. We questioned them about their early schooling to understand why they did not succeed in school as children and teenagers, and from their responses, we conclude that most of those interviewed are now suffering because they received poor training in the public schools or because their needs went unaddressed and they dropped out. Even for those with a high school degree, many cited the poor quality of their high school experience as a reason for needing further education. We interviewed a woman who was graduated 15 years ago from a West Philadelphia high school and is now enrolled in a basic skills pre-employment program. To enroll in this program she had to send for her high school transcript, and when she received it she understood why her skills were so bad: "I had all C's and D's. I shouldn't have graduated at all and was completely unprepared in math skills. I wanted to go into nursing, but now it's trouble: chemistry is hard—you have to have that math training."

Women asserted that teachers, school counselors, and staff did not encourage them or help them identify their goals. A woman enrolled in Philadelphia's YWCA Education Program echoed, "No one then talked about goals. Your family didn't emphasize that and no one else was saying, 'What do you want to be?'" Some had career counseling in their last two years of high school, but, as several exclaimed, "That's too late!"

For many, their school experiences were negative and discouraging. We heard one woman describe her last school experience: "I had a teacher that divided the classroom. Smart kids sat on one side, dumb kids and black kids sat on the other. I just wasn't interested in that." "I was bored and dropped out in the 11th grade," said one woman. "I was bored" was a comment repeated many times as women described high school instructors and courses that did not relate to their own lives.

The main reason women gave for dropping out of high school or junior high school was that they became pregnant. Several mentioned remaining in high school through their pregnancy and finishing school, but the majority was either made to feel uncomfortable ("I was the only pregnant girl there") or were asked to leave. Ironically, it is because of their children and their increased responsibility as single parents that they are now anxious to get their GED or high school diploma, or to learn job skills. In Baltimore, an early high school dropout at the Harbor City Learning Center told us, "Earlier I was acting younger. I wanted to dance and take driver's education. I didn't want to finish and get a job." At Lutheran Settlement House, a GED student described the transition she had to make: "I like school this time. Before I went dancing three nights a week. Life has changed. My responsibility is bigger now with three children."

If an education is the primary barrier to those wanting decent employment, it is not to say that all need the same type of education. We found that desiring an education that will make work a real possibility meant different things to different respondents. For those who never finished high school, the first barrier to overcome was having no high school diploma or equivalency. "Doors are closed to you without a GED," we heard in one interview. "You can't hope for something better without the GED," said a GED program graduate who is now enrolled in business management courses at the Community College of Philadelphia. In addition to the many replies such as these, the need for a GED to advance toward career goals was evidenced by the numerous survey participants enrolled in community colleges, community-based colleges, and job training and education programs who first took a GED course and passed the equivalency exam. In fact, Jenny Ramos, who heads

Intake and Assessment at the Boston ABCD Center for Jobs, Education, and Career Training, told us that more than half of the women coming to the Center need their GED before starting job training. This fact is virtually ignored in workfare policies. For those who seek a college education, the GED is essential.

A woman who had been out of school for some time stressed that she especially needed a basic math review before going to work: "If you've been out of school you need that." Women at the Baltimore OPTIONS program cited basic skills as their first barrier to overcome, "You need the basics first!" In Boston, a Roxbury Community College student told us she wants to get a R.N. degree and be a nurse, but to enroll in the degree program she wants to attend at the University of Massachusetts, her English and math needed strengthening: "I needed to strengthen my academic skills first. Otherwise, I don't think I'd make it through one term at U. Mass." Similar comments were made by a Boston WEAVE student: "After high school I had a hard time getting a job. You come out of school not knowing anything, having no basic skills." For many AFDC women, a basic skills education alleviates their most immediate barrier to employment.

But for other survey respondents, the education they feel they most need is in job skills. They are anxious to work but do not have the specific training they need, or they desire additional training to get a better job than they now have. One bright young woman, just finishing a job training course at the ABCD program, described to us how she was setting and accomplishing her goals. She dropped out of high school when she had her child but decided, "I want to do something with my life." First she got her GED and then started thinking about what vocations she was qualified for; realizing her job skills were minimal, she began to search for training with the goals of getting an education, finding a good job with benefits, and "getting off welfare." She considered training as a dental assistant since it is a stable, high-paying occupation. "But the training was just too expensive." Her sister told her that ABCD has free business training, so she enrolled and took accounting, typing, business math and English, and office skills. When we spoke with her she was scheduled for a job interview the following day for a clerical/filing position. Even if she did not take the job, she said, her job skills had improved and she would continue to go for interviews. Ultimately, she wants more accounting instruction because accounting is a higher-paying area, usually with good benefits. This woman's experience is generally descriptive of the situation most respondents found themselves facing. Once they finish high school or a GED program, they are still not ready for a job, they need other credentials. "Just high school won't get you far these days," a WEAVE student confirmed.

For some AFDC women a GED, basic skills, or job training removes a barrier to employment; for many others, a two- or four-year college degree or college program certificate is needed. At the Community College of Baltimore, we found women who had finished high school and had years of work experience as nursing assistants, but after staying home with their young children for some years they found that to be a nursing assistant, the state of Maryland now requires certification and a college degree. Before returning to work, they had to pay $100 and lab and book expenses, and they had to complete the Community College certificate program.

Other women in this job area told us that the income it pays is inadequate for supporting a family. Most chose to apply their nursing experience toward a nursing degree and were looking at R.N. programs. Tuition, fees, and living expenses while they pursued this, however, made the college degree a difficult barrier to overcome. In business, the women we interviewed encountered similar difficulties: women who held clerical or secretarial positions found the income they earned was too little for supporting a family. Although many desired an A.A. or B.A. in business management, administration, computer programming, accounting, or other areas, the expenses of college discouraged them from looking closely at the college option.

Child care is essential to these women for education and employment. Since quality day care is extremely expensive, women rely on assistance from welfare to cover day care costs for job training, educational programs, or work. Through Boston's Employment and Training (ET) Department, women are able to get a child care voucher that reduces their costs to $5.00 a week. The women we interviewed relied absolutely on this voucher; without it there was little question that most of them would have no choice but to remain at home.

There are other problems, however. Often we were told that centers wanted "something extra" to take children with vouchers. One woman was able to get her son into a center with her voucher but was required to pay three weeks in advance, "Getting that $15.00, that was hard." We spoke to one AFDC mother enrolled in a college-training program whose six children were all school age, but she said when her youngest son needed day care she found that, "It was just too much to go through for that voucher. I paid for his day care." It was $65.00 a week, and she worked summer jobs to cover the extra expense, but when her welfare caseworker discovered her "extra" income, she was required to go for a hearing and is now paying the money back.

But the problem most peculiar to Boston is a catch-22 situation created unknowingly by the various training and educational programs and Boston's ET Department. Most programs reported that women are unlikely to finish training and classes unless they have arranged in advance for day care. Ilene Strier, placement director at SCALE (Somerville Center for Adult Learning Experiences), told us, "It's really frustrating trying to keep them in the program. They used to sign up and then have trouble finding day care and drop out. Now women must say they already have day care and we encourage them to have a backup." Women at SCALE must sign a contract stating that they are ready to go into the training program and have made day care arrangements. ABCD also requires women to sign a similar contract. Boston's ET Department, however, requires women to produce a letter of acceptance to an education or training program before a day care voucher is approved. "What are we supposed to do?" women asked in focus groups. "We can't get in without day care, and we can't get day care without that letter from school!"

Jay Ostrower, director of Employment and Training at ABCD, acknowledged this catch-22 in an interview and said that ABCD tries to be flexible by preparing a form letter for the women so they can get the day care voucher from ET, and then formally admits them to the program once the women have arranged for day care with their vouchers. For women in other programs, however, unless they lie to the educational programs about their arrangements through ET, they will not be accepted into the program and will not be granted day care vouchers.

In the Boston interviews, day care was a special concern. The Massachusetts State law governing the use of Employment and Training day care vouchers requires that they be used only with fully licensed day care centers. Shortly before the Boston site visit, a number of child abuse cases in some of the licensed centers used by AFDC women became the focus of local news stories. Although the incidents were isolated, the mothers we spoke with were extremely concerned. Many expressed anger that they were restricted from using vouchers for baby-sitters in their own homes. Several told us they knew of reliable neighbors they felt comfortable leaving their children with and who charged less than day care centers; but vouchers will not cover such care and the women cannot afford to pay sitters without them.

In Baltimore and Philadelphia, complaints about day care were less severe, but still women in both cities mentioned having their names on long waiting lists to get their children into centers; they spoke of the expense of day care when they were turned down for subsidies and worried about the quality and safety of child care centers. Some of the Philadelphia and Baltimore AFDC mothers we interviewed mentioned knowing other women who stay at home primarily because they have no affordable day care options; some women referred to themselves as the "lucky ones" because they have parents or relatives willing to look after their children without charge. In all three cities, however, women clearly could not attend the job preparation, job search, and training and education programs they needed in order to get employment without having help with child care. Some women received help from their families, but most women, without financial support for day care costs from city and state agencies or from the training and education programs, would have to remain at home.

While education and day care are the major barriers to employment identified by the AFDC mothers we interviewed, several other problems were frequently mentioned as well. From women in all three cities we heard comments like, "AFDC has you in a bind"; "Welfare does not help you get off welfare"; and "You try to get off AFDC despite them." Mostly women were referring to a lack of information about services and options ("They don't tell you anything") and to a lack of cooperation when women had to keep appointments at the welfare office that disrupted their training class schedules or interview commitments. One student at Women's Technical Institute (WTI) in Boston told us, "They don't care!" She explained that her appointment with her caseworker took two hours even though there was little business conducted and she was mostly kept waiting. When she explained that she was late to classes at WTI where she was studying drafting, the caseworker told her she should not be in school. Another student told a similar story and concluded: "They treat you like dirt. It's upsetting, but you survive despite them."

Another obstacle, in addition to the discouraging attitudes of caseworkers, is the cutoff point of AFDC and benefits. While Boston's ET continues day care support for 12 months and Medicaid for four after closing an AFDC case, most agencies such as Baltimore's OPTIONS, provide no assistance once women are placed into jobs. Usually employers need some time to process an employee for payroll, and women reported going for up to four weeks without an income. The prospect of such an income lapse can make employment a frightening option. Losing medical benefits was the most often mentioned concern when women spoke of going off AFDC. They were worried that employers might not cover medical expenses and said that employment is more attractive for them when it includes health insurance. "I hate to give up that medical" was often heard. One group suggested that "transitional support"—medical coverage, food stamps, day care and transportation —would make employment more possible. Philadelphia women suggested, "They should have a better way to funnel you off welfare." They explained that most employers' health insurance begins after six months of employment and that if they were taken off assistance gradually, they could hope to have an increase in salary or an addition of benefits.

Employment and training staffs who place women into jobs described immediate withdrawal of public assistance support services as a significant barrier for AFDC women. Ilene Streier of SCALE says, "Students cannot work for under $5.10 to $5.25 per hour and break even. This means hard placements—they are still a low-skill group and have been out of work for some time." The staff of ABCD concurred. They do counseling sessions with students to determine what income they must have in order to work. With the help of a "resources worksheet" developed by Sondra Stein, formerly of WEAVE, students are encouraged to calculate the dollar value of their AFDC income and benefits and what will be their new expenses to determine what their "new income" must be. Day care and medical costs are the two expenses most difficult to cover, and Jay Ostrower, of ABCD's ET program, concluded, "Benefits are crucial." But there is also clothing for work and transportation and lunch money to take care of in addition to adequate income to support one's family. Steve Savner of Boston's Legal Services has also assisted women in determining if they can afford to take ET jobs and uses a similar worksheet. If women can at least break even and have job benefits, he found that they are usually willing to choose work over AFDC.

The cost of transportation to work was generally a problem in all three cities. In Boston, ET covers women's lunch and transportation costs while they attend a training or education program, but as with other benefits, whether women receive the full benefit depends on their caseworker. Boston's ET, for example, can pay up to $10 a day in transportation assistance, but women are seldom made aware of this available aid. One woman told us she thought assistance could be up to $3 a day, "But ET is mean . . . I always get $2." Some women told us it was too much bother to try to get the extra assistance— having to produce a time sheet, a letter from their school or training program —and it was not worth the time. Philadelphia women described a similar situation.

In Baltimore, several women mentioned distance as a barrier to employment. Although buses are good, and the women can get a bus pass, some jobs require cars, which is unaffordable transportation for them. Distance becomes more of a barrier in all three cities when women have to go farther for day care. This often creates a daily ritual of getting children ready for the day care center, going with them by bus and sometimes transferring to a second bus, dropping them off at the day care center and waiting for another bus or two to go to work or to their classes. At the end of the day, they repeat the journey. Several women at Women's Technical Institute in Boston described this long process and said at the end of their classes they will look for a job close to their children's day care or take a job that has on-site day care. This narrows job options.

Even if women are anxious to work, have the training or education needed, and are able to overcome day care barriers, the availability of jobs at the necessary "new income" level, with security and workable hours for a single parent, is limited. Women in Boston seemed relatively confident that they would find adequate employment, but women in Philadelphia, and especially in Baltimore, listed availability of jobs as something they worried about. Women in training for construction jobs at Baltimore's Mt. Winans site said they are willing to take a job with income potential, but they had some doubts about whether such jobs are available. At the Community College of Baltimore, women in the nursing assistance course had similar reservations: "These days nurses are expected to do more of the work that aides used to do. They're training too many people here for the jobs that will be open."

In order to leave AFDC for employment some women must overcome the interference of a boyfriend or husband. One woman told us she had a good record with several employers, but, "My children's father is my biggest problem. He always shows up on the job. He's in jail for this—for three years, and then for a 12-year term." For other women, the interference is sometimes less severe but also persistent. They speak more often of jealousy from their boyfriends when they start education, training programs, and jobs. "He just ripped my books up one day," a young woman told us. Some are beaten or verbally abused. Others are discouraged by the jealousy or resentment. Comments such as "He doesn't want me to work"; "He resents my going to work"; or "He hassles me" were common.

Of the major barriers to employment women described in interviews, many cited a lack of confidence and self-esteem resulting from racial and sexual discrimination, from discrimination as a welfare recipient, or from other demeaning life experiences. In Baltimore, a black woman described her experience: "Black women are indoctrinated into thinking you're only capable of doing certain things, unless you have a lot of self-esteem. I got knocked down so many times I finally said, I have to stop." A young black woman told us, "What kept me from my personal goals started with my background: the way I was raised I didn't recognize that I should have any goals." An older white woman explained that a barrier for her was her low self-esteem as an AFDC mother who had been out of school for 16 years and that she felt insecure in the "work-world." Some women were abused spouses who left their husbands but feel insecure as they return to school, begin job training, and start to support themselves and their children.

Barriers to Postsecondary Education

A Boston woman's experience illustrates the complex combination of problems AFDC and low-income women encounter when they try a college option.

I came out of high school with no academic background, but somehow got a five-year scholarship at Northeastern University. It covered tuition and books but no living expenses. So I lived with my sister and her kid. That made it hard to study—your family just doesn't understand having to study.

She also said most of the other students were whites and she felt "out of place." When she had trouble academically, a minority organization counseled her and provided tutors to try to keep her in school, but "I was just surviving, not knowing what I wanted to do." Finally she dropped out and enrolled in Training, Inc., a training program for lower-income women. She wanted to quit the program and stated, "I'm surviving for the three months, but when you come out you have skills." She still has the opportunity to continue at Northeastern on her scholarship but explained that housing was her biggest problem. By getting training and a job she hoped eventually to find an apartment of her own. Until then, attending the university and studying were unlikely. The combination of an unsupportive family, of having inadequate housing as a student, and being one of few minority students on a mostly white campus created too many barriers.

Other black women pointed to racism as a barrier that discouraged their attempts to consider different college programs. Still others spoke of colleges as being intimidating for different reasons: "I want to go to college," a Community Women's Education Project student told us, "but they're too fast and too big. I'd be chewed up and spit out in college." Most women who have been out of school for some time prefer a program designed for their special needs. Usually this includes basic skills education first. These women expressed a need for counseling, day care, someone to help them put together financial aid, and help with the necessary forms and applications, especially with complicated administrative arrangements. Women at RCC complained that no one helped them with their arrangements between ET and the college. It is complicated, they explained, and if no one helps to expedite ET or financial aid checks, they sometimes suffer from lapses in payments. Women especially stressed the importance of a supportive atmosphere, such as that encountered by women at Sojourner-Douglass College, who said, "They make you feel good about yourself. That's important." Another requirement many women had is similar to women's requests for work hours suitable for a single parent: if colleges make day classes available to women, they can go to courses while their children are in school or day care and be home for dinner and to help children with their homework.

When we asked women who set education as their goal what prevented them from achieving this, the major barrier AFDC women said they face is an uncooperative and often difficult welfare agency. We were told in the Boston interviews, for example, that "ET makes going to school hard," although program administrators insist they support education as an option. Women complained that ET gave them no information about the option they have under ET to choose an educational program. "They don't tell you you can go to school," women told us at Women's Technical Institute. Women at the University of Massachusetts ARMS (Advocacy for Resources for Modern Survival) program also said that when women are not informed of their education option and choose a work option, or training, they later have trouble switching into an educational program once they find it is also an option.

Other women, enrolled in RCC, described difficulties with ET when they attended college. One told us, "Welfare clients who try to do something for themselves get a hard time. When you get a Pell grant, they deduct it from your food stamps. You can keep work study money and it isn't taxed, but you might lose your AFDC." Another RCC student agreed: "You start to get up and they knock you back down. I went to the welfare office because I needed day care for my 5-year-old and they told me no day care for my 5-year-old son if I'm 'just going to school.' " A third said she still received notices of job interviews from ET even though she informed her caseworker that she is a full-time student. If she does not notify them to cancel the interviews, they can delay her AFDC and food stamp checks. When speaking of the extra transportation, day care, and lunch money, these students said the trouble they go through to get the assistance is more trouble than it is worth, "When I don't have to be troubled with them, I don't." ET students were also supposed to get vouchers for books, but the Roxbury focus group explained that ET never paid for the books they purchased so the bookstore will no longer accept the vouchers.

Women at the Community College of Philadelphia were more concerned that they could lose their AFDC support if their caseworkers knew they were enrolled in college programs. One described frustration that she could not get information from her caseworker about what benefits might help her through school. "People would go to them for information if they could. I used to sit on the phone trying to get information, but confidence is necessary to do this and welfare workers make you feel so low." Another said that if AFDC workers find out about any school aid or college work study, they subtract if from their benefits. Consequently, these women were afraid to let their caseworkers know they go to school, and so they cannot apply for transportation, day care, or tuition assistance through the welfare office. Some of the women in this focus group said they do have contact with caseworkers who "look the other way"; but all agreed they receive no help or information, that they fear losing food stamp and medical benefits, and that in general the welfare office is their major barrier to a postsecondary education.

Covering tuition expenses is another major obstacle. Women in Baltimore described having no aid to subsidize their tuition. Although some discussed loan options for covering tuition, one woman explained, "Several girls I know are afraid to go to school out of fear they'll lose AFDC money plus have to pay a loan back right away." Again, some women feared that applying for a loan or grant might lead to their school enrollment's being "discovered" and losing all of their benefits: "Get help with tuition? No, they'll discover that income!" For some women their lack of information about how students cover tuition and school expenses keeps them from considering education as an option. A Philadelphia woman told of her frustration with welfare: "I said, 'I'm going to quit this crap and get into a career.' I thought about an A.A. degree, but how will I live for two years?"

Education as an Option in State Welfare Policies

Work Incentive (WIN) programs starting in 1967 and reinforced by the 1981 changes in the Omnibus Budget and Reconciliation Act (OBRA) established that, except for women with children under 6, the primary policy goal is to employ AFDC recipients. The OBRA stresses immediate job placement, overlooking the evaluations of employment and training programs that demonstrated the value of combining education and work experience in preparing lower-income populations for employment (Auletta 1983; Berlin 1985).

In 1987 new federal regulations completed the shift in emphasis from service and income relief in the welfare program to employment, job creation, and maintenance. States are working furiously to develop their own workfare programs, but there is often a lack of concern for the development of policies that will provide the most effective preparation of this population for productive work experiences.

From its inception in the 1930s, the AFDC program was maintained as a state program, allowing the states to determine eligibility and income standards even as federal funding grew and federal regulations increased. Some states have been more liberal than others in setting standards for eligibility, in encouraging recipients to work, and in preparing them for work. States have also interpreted the OBRA requirements differently, some seeing work registration requirements as binding with no option, and others feeling less compelled to immediately place AFDC recipients in jobs.

A major purpose of this research was to compare linkages between welfare and education programs in the three cities and states (Massachusetts, Maryland, and Pennsylvania) to determine whether or not city or state practices and policies offered possible alternatives for expanding options for preparing AFDC women for employment. In examining state AFDC plans submitted to the federal government and the state welfare codes, we found that state codes are ambiguous, broadly stated, and no more restrictive than the federal regulations. Major discretion is left to state and often local administrators to interpret federal and state regulations on work registration requirements.

Administrators in Massachusetts and Maryland pride themselves on their "liberal" interpretations of federal legislation and their ability to find "loopholes" that allow them to support AFDC women who choose college. A Maryland administrator explained that the OPTIONS program put full-time students on "long-term hold" from WIN requirements. This was not a formal procedure but "administratively operational." Massachusetts considers college attendance part of "manpower service, training, employment and other employment related activities" and therefore in conformity with federal regulations. We also discovered that Wisconsin and California have adopted procedural agreements to facilitate AFDC women's enrollment in college without loss of benefits. In Wisconsin, administrative discretion has allowed AFDC women to attend college as a prerequisite to job training. Other states have created flexibility by requiring job searches in longer intervals and allowing part-time school attendance while the searches are carried on.

State discretionary power under the ambiguous federal and state rulings benefits AFDC recipients who want to pursue an education in liberal states, but there are many more conservative states that narrowly interpret the regulations and prohibit college attendance as an option. For example, Pennsylvania administrators, who do not consider college education a viable option for AFDC women, interpret federal regulations to exclude college attendance as a response to work requirements.

An important way in which state policies affect the educational opportunities of women on AFDC is through their implementation of college financial aid programs. Federal Public Welfare Title 45 draws specific restrictions around what monies an AFDC recipient may keep without having them included as income and deducted from benefits. Section 233.20 of Title 45 excepts from what it defines as income: "loans and grants, such as scholarships, obtained and used under conditions that preclude their use for current living costs." There is also an exclusion for income from JTPA participation, and "Any grant or loan to any undergraduate student for education purposes made or insured under any programs administered by the Commission of Education." This includes Pell grants and federal loans, but whether it includes college work study is an issue interpreted differently by state courts. The most recent case concluded college work study dollars cannot be counted as income, but there is some skepticism that this would be applied to future state court cases (Rosen 1983). Again, differences in state practices prevail.

Maryland interprets the federal regulation loosely and their state plan excludes as income educational loans or grants used not for living expenses but for educational expenses: "tuition, books, transportation, etc." "Etc." is loosely interpreted to mean when "the cash doesn't touch the recipient's hands" but is a direct payment to colleges. These payments are considered "vendor payments" and not available for living costs.

Paul Franklin, an education researcher, concluded that how grants are treated by AFDC offices is the most difficult obstacle to college attendance. The primary issue is "which money is counted first" by student financial aid administrators. If agreements are articulated between state student financial aid offices and state departments of public welfare, then it is more likely that grants will not be counted as living expenses. Also, agreement on the issue between state offices and local welfare offices will further clarify the need to avoid having grant money or private scholarships counted as income and deducted from benefits. Food stamp benefits are more fragile in this way (Franklin 1985).

In general, for states to formalize these procedures with the federal government they must specify the amount of money to be excluded as income and the length of time the "disregard" will continue (Title 45, Sec. 233.20). Such action, however, risks rejection of state plans and could bring state practices under closer scrutiny.

Federal law makes it illegal for state welfare departments to count certain federal school grants as income or to deduct the amount of such aid to reduce AFDC payments. Clearly in this action Congress intended to support and perhaps encourage AFDC women who choose to go to college. Yet, there is a widely held view that AFDC women would be given exceptional support and advantage over working poor if a college education were to be officially considered an option to work. In addition, other issues might be raised, including how many years of college education could be supported and in what fields.

The lack of coordination between state education policy on student aid and welfare policy on student income and cost-of-living calculations results in conflicting policies on financial aid that are insensitive to the needs of recipients. Ambiguous state regulations in many states about the relation between student financial aid and welfare leave considerable discretion to caseworkers in calculating costs and income. Local welfare agencies and caseworkers tend to be more restrictive in the interpretation of the regulations if there is no specific commitment or policy directive from higher-level officials to allow or encourage education as an option under work regulations. Our interviews indicated that AFDC recipients in college perceive that caseworkers are generally not supportive of their college attendance and are inclined to interpret regulations narrowly.

States can, even under current federal law, be supportive of students or provide disincentives by the process they use to calculate aid. There is a tendency in some states to discourage a college option since states would have to bear the additional costs. In most states now, the cost-of-living standard is calculated at a lower level by welfare offices than by student financial aid formulae. This has created an area of conflict between state departments of welfare and education. Wisconsin is the only state that has officially adopted a policy accepting the higher standards of student financial aid cost-of-living requirements for AFDC recipients.

The order in which different sources of student aid are applied to student financial packages is of extreme importance: for example, if a college determines a student with three children requires $10,000 to attend college for one year and AFDC covers the family's living expenses of $4,000, student financial aid offices will try to create an aid "package" of $6,000. If state and federal aid are combined to total $6,000, then an additional grant or scholarship provided by private sources will likely be deducted from the AFDC payment. It is necessary for private grants to be added into aid packages first to avoid this problem. Similarly, state aid should be added second and before federal aid since some federal assistance programs, such as "College Work Study," are still being deducted from AFDC payments. Even though this practice has been challenged in state supreme courts, the issue is not yet resolved.

A recent report for the College Board recommends that welfare agencies and colleges, especially financial aid officers, establish a continuous and close relationship so the most up-to-date information is available and disseminated to students, and conflicts in policies will be resolved in favor of AFDC recipients (College Entrance Examination Board 1984). Some states are working in this direction. California established the Cooperative Agencies Resources for Education (CARE), sponsored by the Social Services and Employment Department and the Chancellor's Office of the Community College System, which provides for local AFDC offices and local community colleges to work together. The Massachusetts Board of Regents also established a fund to support limited community college tuition waivers for AFDC recipients. Recently proposed New Jersey legislation clearly establishes higher education as an option for AFDC women under its workfare program.

Availability of Education Opportunities

For a single AFDC mother, the idea of taking time and scarce family resources to pursue an education seems far too costly for consideration unless clear encouragement is presented. State and local welfare departments, however, do not advertise college options and prefer fast-track training programs over education options for dramatic short-term reduction of welfare rolls. The paucity of educational opportunities and wider availability of training programs in the three cities studied bears testimony to the lack of priorities among these welfare policy-makers and administrators.

Postsecondary Education

Our review of postsecondary programs for AFDC women in these three cities found a lack of concern for this population and a dearth of programs and support services in traditional colleges and community colleges.

One exception to this observation about traditional colleges was the University of Massachusetts–Boston. Although we heard several criticisms from black interviewees about the University of Massachusetts–Boston, the college does provide a course specifically aimed at AFDC mothers. Take-A-Long-Look, or TALL, is an employment assessment option of the Massachusetts ET Program. Women take a six-week course in how to take time to consider their life options and goals. After the six weeks, many go into the regular university program. A university student organization of women on welfare started four years ago also encourages women at the University of Massachusetts. Advocacy for Resources for Modern Survival (ARMS) was formed to provide information, referral, advocacy, self-help, and organizing around public assistance issues, particularly the issue of lack of information available to AFDC women about their education option as part of ET. ARMS is now the Boston chapter of the statewide welfare rights organization, the Coalition for Basic Human Needs.

In all three cities, we also looked at the programs in traditional community colleges that include a population of AFDC women. They offer relatively low-cost vocational training for women, basic skills, and GED programs. For AFDC women who are college-ready, community colleges can lead to careers in accounting, bookkeeping, business administration, and technical jobs providing an adequate income for family heads. AFDC women must overcome several problems, however, in attending these traditional community colleges. First, lower-income women are not generally addressed as a population with specific needs. In interviews with the presidents and provosts of the three community colleges, we found that they prefer to treat this population as part of the mainstream, because they feel that these women's needs are no different than those of the rest of their students.

Although community colleges must have large numbers of AFDC students, they do not differentiate services and programs to respond to their needs. Some do have satellite campuses or community service sites in lower-income neighborhoods that offer literacy and basic skills programs, as well as college-level courses for credit. The YWCA of Germantown is a Community College of Philadelphia (CCP) community service location providing courses for college credit; Community Women's Education Project is another CCP community service location. In general, however, college officials rationalize their "mainstreaming" approach on ethical and educational grounds, denying the special needs of AFDC women.

Traditional educational institutions were often found to keep no records on how many of the students are AFDC or low income or how many are single parents, and none did any follow-up on what happens to students when they leave the program. Such follow-up, especially of first-time college students who are low-income women with children, would be valuable in determining what keeps students in school, what barriers arise that make school impossible, and what opportunities are available to them upon completion of programs.

At the CCP, no record is kept of how many AFDC students attend the college and no day care or special support services are provided for them. President Judith Eaton told us, "We're an educational institution first. Support services are not a priority; educational service is." CCP does receive JTPA funding for literacy and occupational programs, which may attract AFDC women.

None of the three community colleges made special arrangements to address the particular problems of AFDC women. In the summer 1984 term, for example, Roxbury Community College had 20–30 women under ET, but when ET was slow in paying the college, a decision was made to withhold the students' grades. This "mainstreaming" philosophy is also reflected in the comments of AFDC interviewees, who find the "bigness" of community colleges difficult. Some need help in filling out forms and applications and in following through with office personnel to receive checks and enroll in classes. Financial aid, which is essential to their college enrollment, is difficult to calculate and apply for; testing requirements present another barrier; remedial courses, which many lower-income women need to pass placement tests and to prepare for college classes, are not covered by financial aid; some women need assistance acquiring child care or help with welfare department caseworkers to get transportation, day care, or tuition expenses covered. These special needs indicate that even college-ready AFDC women require additional support services from counseling and financial aid offices within community colleges.

A major difficulty evident in community colleges is their reinforcement of sex-stereotyped education. Evidence of sex-stereotyping in curriculum programs was found in the community colleges in each of the cities. At Baltimore Community College (BCC), 98 percent of the fall 1984 secretarial majors, 90 percent of the nursing majors, and 89 percent of the gerontology majors were women, while women made up only 10 percent of electronics majors, 20 percent of engineering majors, and 25 percent of drafting majors. At CCP, the higher-paying fields were dominated by men; in the fall 1983 term, 81 percent of engineering majors were men and 89 percent of electronics majors were men. While community colleges have not given special encouragement to women to major in drafting, electronics, or engineering, it is those non-traditional job areas that provide the opportunity for self-sufficiency for single parents who are women.

When those AFDC women not yet prepared for college seek job training, however, the structure of the community college curriculum is a problem. Marion Pines, commissioner of Neighborhood Preservation and Manpower Programs in Baltimore, found problems using BCC for vocational training for AFDC recipients and made attempts to encourage the development of special programs for them. Job training courses were finally made available in office occupations, respiratory therapist, and dental assistant. Problems arose as the courses were developed. The provost of BCC, Rodney Fields, described lower-income students as in need of literacy instruction first: "You cannot design training courses like a college course." He said community colleges assume students have already attained a minimum skill level, which means they usually leave out the "drill and study" needed by these students. Muriel Berkeley, chair of the department of Vocational Education at BCC, suggested that a "pre-curriculum" program is needed to first provide basic skills instruction. Of the 30 students enrolled in BCC by the Baltimore Manpower Department in 1985, only four could pass the placement tests, while others needed remediation. She estimated if they add basic skills, the program must be lengthened to over one year. Linda Harris, head of the Baltimore Manpower Department, explained the basic problem with community colleges: "There is a big gap in philosophy. They are an educational institution thinking in 'terms' and 'credits' and 'requirements.' " She suggested that most welfare clients need a basic skills background, but in a shorter time, something a community college curriculum is not designed to do.

Those programs that tailored their courses and support services to women and either targeted AFDC women or offered them extensive services, were overwhelmingly found to be community-based and nontraditional education programs. Community-based colleges in each of the cities gave evidence of successfully providing college opportunities for lower-income women.

In Baltimore, Sojourner-Douglass College provides a complete college program for AFDC women. Created in 1972 as a four-year black university associated with Antioch University, Sojourner-Douglass College began operating as a fully accredited independent four-year university on 1 February 1980. The student body is primarily comprised of low-income black women with an average age of 30 years. The college concentrates on raising the self-esteem of its more than 300 students by offering courses in black culture and history, by stressing pride and self-awareness in classes and counseling, and by creating a supportive atmosphere. On-site day care is provided at a fee of $2.00 a week.

Another successful community-based college, Community Women's Education Project (CWEP) in Philadelphia is a comprehensive center for women using the combination of a traditional college program, basic skills instruction, and job training. Concentrating on adult female students, CWEP's program offers accredited college courses as a community service location of the Community College of Philadelphia in general studies and data processing, and provides basic skills classes in math, English, and computer literacy. A majority of the more than 1,600 students who have attended CWEP since 1977 are lower-income adult women. One program, Women at Work, was specifically designed for lower-income women returning to the job market and AFDC women desiring to move into employment. The participants are almost all AFDC recipients and minorities. CWEP is now negotiating with the Community College of Philadelphia to expand Women at Work and to create a mentoring program for women in nontraditional fields.

In addition, CWEP regularly holds computer literacy courses and workshops on community issues. Basing course work on community concerns and shaping the program for adult women who have been away from school or work for an extended period, CWEP is able to serve women who might otherwise find postsecondary programs overwhelming. Of the 47 people who attended workshops in fall 1984, 29 entered the college program. Preparatory courses, extensive counseling, workshops, and free on-site day care are the support services provided that especially suit a population of low-income women.

Our review of educational institutions pointed to their failure to translate research findings into educational practice. Although several comprehensive studies have identified cooperative education, part-time work, and part-time study as the most successful approach to the AFDC population (Zwerling 1986), we found no cooperative education program in these cities. In fact, we know of only one urban community college, LaGuardia College in New York City, that has an extensive cooperative education program. It is astonishing that other colleges have not pursued similar programs, especially for this special population, which could greatly benefit from work experience tied to education.

Nontraditional Education
We found only one program in the three cities devoted entirely to nontraditional training for women. The Women's Technical Institute (WTI) in Boston, a private postsecondary institution, is a national model for training and placing women into high-paying jobs in electronics and drafting. Beginning as Women's Enterprises in 1976, the organization was primarily funded through government contracts as a nonprofit trade school for women. Now as Women's Technical Institute, the technical training school serves mostly adult, low-income women. WTI receives funding from over 150 local and national foundations and corporations. Students are about 20 to 54 years old, mostly with high school degrees. Approximately 66 percent of the student population is white and 34 percent minority. Of the 230 students enrolled in 1984–85, about 48, or 21 percent, were AFDC recipients. Full-time students attend training courses in either drafting or electronics for six months and are then placed into jobs. The school places 85 percent of its graduates in jobs at an average salary of $15,000. Although there is no provision for day care at the WTI, counseling is available and the peer support created at the all-women school contributes to the high completion rate of the students.

Nontraditional training was also found at one site in Baltimore's city-funded Manpower Programs, OPTIONS. The Mt. Winans site is a low-income housing project that is now being rebuilt by AFDC women residents who are in construction training to rebuild their own homes. The Mt. Winans project was not created specifically to give women nontraditional job training but rather to train women within their communities to do community improvement work. The project was linked with community-based organizations already in the neighborhood. When women have completed training, it is hoped that they will become involved with other improvement projects in their neighborhoods.

In Baltimore, New Directions for Women began in 1973 to do nontraditional training for lower-income women and ran successfully for several years. When the program lost federal CETA funding, however, the problems of being a nontraditional training program for women grew. Mandy Goetze, founder and former director of the program, described her main problems as racism and sexism. Most of her clients were low-income black women whom she had trouble placing with white male employers. The trade jobs required union memberships for the women, which the primarily white male organizations resisted. More recently, the program has shifted to more traditional employment for women, more suburban students, and "paying" students.

In fact, the majority of city training programs in Baltimore, Boston, and Philadelphia were fast-training sessions in traditional job areas, such as clerical and secretarial skills, word processing, and typing. They are aimed at training AFDC women quickly and placing them in jobs. Some were more business-management centered, such as Training, Inc., in Boston, which combines basic skills training with office and business management course work. Training, Inc., began as a Boston YMCA careers training program in December 1983. A year later it was funded by Bay State Skills Corporation to train 45 women in clerical and word processing and it continues to rely on this funding source. The participants are mostly single, minority female heads of household who have previously worked in only unskilled or low-skill jobs.

The Lack of Coordination in Public Policies

In our exploration of policies and practices in several policy areas—education, employment, and economic development—we were constantly confronted with the extent of separation and even conflict in these areas of policy at the state and local levels and the lack of long-range goals for education and employment. Separate departments and agencies administer programs in each area and make plans without consideration for or knowledge of related activities in the other agencies. Often in our interviews with policy makers we were the source of information about programs within the state or city that had not been disseminated to interested administrators in other policy areas. More compelling is the fact that agencies are more dedicated to controlling their own funds than to developing cooperative programs with related agencies.

In our interviews in Maryland, we found that coordination is achieved at the local level and minimally at the state level. Marion Pines, the Baltimore commissioner of Neighborhood Preservation and Manpower, has had long and thoughtful experience with the problems of employment and poverty and views solutions as inextricably tied to economic development. Unfortunately, the economic development managers in Baltimore are not so thoughtful and have to be cajoled and pressured by the commissioner to concede some concern for the unemployed in their plans. They have agreed at least to request new businesses to interview trainees for new jobs.

Although the governor of Massachusetts created an employment task force that includes economic, education, and welfare officials to seek ways to coordinate policies, the policy process still ignores that fact. Strong economic growth in the state and the low level of unemployment (3.8 percent) tends to overshadow the problem of lack of linkages. New legislation in Boston, however, requires hiring JTPA trainees in businesses that have received tax concessions under the economic development program.

In Pennsylvania, there is no evidence of state recognition of the interrelatedness of these policy areas. Maryann Steinberg, the administrator in charge of the welfare demonstration program in Philadelphia, after several months of investigation and deliberation about how to organize the new program, concluded that the employment picture for Philadelphia was an overwhelming limitation on any effort the welfare department could make in work placements for AFDC recipients. To the extent that jobs were available for these women, they would be at the lowest possible level, with no opportunity for advancement and without adequate health or child care benefits. No provision was being made by the state to coordinate job training or education with job placement. Efforts to engage the state education department in the allocation of education or vocational education funds for the AFDC clients to better prepare them for jobs met with no success. The best that the saturation program could hope to do was to provide more intensive counseling to 1,500 AFDC recipients in the next year and place them in minimal-level jobs. Candidates would be given assessment tests and some small percentage would be placed in job training programs with JTPA funding. Even the JTPA arrangements took extra efforts by the new saturation unit staff to include AFDC women in ongoing programs. The state welfare department would be cooperative, but this demonstration effort was clearly to be limited to short-term training to secure job placement. More long-term education will not be an option.

We found no JTPA programs in any of the cities specifically targeted to the AFDC population and its needs. We also found that Private Industry Councils (PICs) lack female members who might provide insights into these special concerns. JTPA staffs, unless they were forced to respond to outside pressures, preferred to ignore this population. A recent report on JTPA explains the failure of the program. "The reasons range from problems in the structure of JTPA itself, to deficiencies in local implementation that demonstrate both a lack of understanding of the special needs of women, and in some cases outright discrimination (Dalby 1985)." Dalby also suggests there is a lack of adequate study of the particular job training needs of women and the unique problems they face.

Recognizing that training AFDC women is more costly because of the need for support services, many PICs are fulfilling their obligation to serve welfare recipients by accepting male general assistance recipients. In some jurisdictions, AFDC women have been excluded from JTPA because they would be "unavailable" for mandatory work programs. JTPA legislative goals include coordination of welfare and job training programs; however, we found no evidence that this was happening. In our interviews we found strained efforts in each site to access JTPA funds to serve AFDC women, and only in Massachusetts did we observe real results.

State education departments do not consider women on welfare their clientele. Higher education departments and institutions have also removed themselves from the issue. Community colleges, many originally created to serve lower-income and less well prepared students, fear the possible loss of status if they specifically address the needs of women on welfare. When some of these women find their way, against all odds, into institutions of higher education, they face not only lack of recognition of their special needs but also insensitivity to their circumstances. Community colleges in each of the cities enrolled AFDC students, but none knew exactly how many were registered nor did they make any effort to provide special orientation, training, or preparation for them. In addition, as one community college president told us, "The community colleges are the worst offenders" when it comes to gender-based programs. Vocational career programs, to which lower-income women are invariably directed, are now screening applicants more carefully and demanding more skills and experience.

Throughout our interviews with training and education program administrators, we pressed to find out why greater effort was not made by government agencies to use colleges and particularly community colleges to conduct programs for AFDC women. Invariably we were told that colleges do not know how to train people for jobs, that their curriculums are not suited to these purposes, and that they are unable to convince college administrators and faculty that the traditional time alloted to complete programs is too long to suit their needs. Private proprietary schools and community-based organizations, they claimed, are more flexible in developing and scheduling programs.

Joint efforts by training and education experts probably can offer the most thoughtful response to the problem. The example of Harbor City Learning Center in Baltimore suggests this is so. That program combines the knowledge and experience of training and education personnel in a cooperative education program that offers work experience and traditional learning skills and job placement. LaGuardia College in New York City has long and successful experience with cooperative education with a largely lower-income population, and their success could be used as a model for education programs for AFDC women. A different emphasis but an important one is the North Carolina community college system, which stresses the role of the colleges in economic and community development and uses vocational education funds to educate students for specific jobs connected to their development activities.

Many of the community-based colleges have organized their programs especially to serve lower-income women. Easy access to facilities in the neighborhood and availability of day care in these colleges are important attractions. In addition, these colleges make major allocations for remedial courses, counseling, and student aid advisement, which they know are special needs of their students. Our research indicated that government officials had limited knowledge of these institutions and their long experience with lower-income populations. The colleges have not been particularly successful in developing relationships with training and welfare agencies to conduct funded programs.

Vocational education programs are an underused resource in the training and education of lower-income women. Federal and state funds historically allocated to local school systems and more recently to community colleges have not adequately served women. In recognition of this fact the 1985 Vocational Education Act (the Carl D. Perkins Act) specifically addresses this shortcoming. The legislation strengthens the programs and funding for vocational training for women and girls, and in nontraditional areas. Title II of the act allocates funds to educational institutions and community-based organizations specifically targeted to programs for displaced homemakers and single parents. However, states will surely be tempted to continue to allocate their vocational education funds in the same ways as they have in the past unless pressures are brought to bear on them or incentives are offered for them to do otherwise.

Conclusions and Recommendations

There is general agreement among policy makers, the public at large and AFDC women that economic independence is preferable to welfare. There is not agreement about whether *any* employment constitutes independence or whether training and education is a reasonable alternative to immediate employment because it offers greater opportunity for economic independence in the future. Policy makers and the public seem to accept that any job is better than welfare; AFDC women know that is not true.

The issue of whether or not AFDC women should have the option, the opportunity, or in fact, an incentive to pursue an education has been subverted, ignored, or rejected out of hand by social policy. As a society we have tended to blame poor people for their condition, ignoring the failure of macro-economic policies to address their needs. In addition, we refuse to recognize the importance of government policies as determinants of dependency. While the mythology of American democracy stresses the value we place on education, we eschew its importance to this population.

Our interviews indicate that there is a significant interest in education and career training on the part of AFDC women, particularly as a means to more gainful employment. A multiplicity of personal, social, economic, and political barriers, both real and perceived, impede their pursuit of these objectives. Our research also found that public policies are a deterrent to these goals and that there is a lack of appropriate training and education opportunities available for these women.

Many women on AFDC, while eager to be free of the welfare system, recognize that they lack the skills, the experience, and the self-confidence to secure employment that is more stable and offers opportunity for advancement. There are AFDC women in career training programs and attending college, some at great sacrifice to themselves and their children and often without the knowledge or support of welfare agencies. An even larger number would choose to attend college or any advanced training program if they could acquire basic education, if there were reasonable incentives to do so, and if the many existing barriers were reduced.

Increased communication between training and employment departments, JTPA programs, and welfare departments directed at allocation of public funds and improvement of training and college education for AFDC women should be promoted at the state and local levels. Task forces comprised of representatives of these various agencies can informally integrate their activities to better serve AFDC women.

The experience of training programs developed over the last several decades could be brought to bear in the effort to address the needs of AFDC women in preparing them for work. There should also be continued effort to take advantage of the enormous resources and experience of institutions of higher education to develop opportunities for this population.

Discretion for changing policies that will provide encouragement and support for AFDC students resides in the states, and commitment to a longer-term investment in their education and training will add to their immediate costs. As in all policy areas, states will differ significantly in their response to the issue. Even without federal action, some states can be encouraged to pursue these goals in formal or informal ways. Other states will continue more restrictive policies. Historically, the more liberal states have been the source of new ideas and programs that are later adopted in other states and as national policy. For this reason every effort should be made to encourage states to experiment with changes in the options for education for AFDC women; one way of accomplishing this could be to encourage state-sponsored scholarships for AFDC women.

The individual and institutional barriers to education for AFDC women must also be addressed. Our finding of a lack of appropriate education programs and a shortage of possible choices among those programs available calls for external incentives to create new opportunities and enhance effective ones. Many of the individual needs cited by the women in our interviews can be provided for in institutional programs if they are thoughtfully developed and tailored to the target population. If one attempts to respond to those needs in the programs, they will have certain identifiable characteristics. The institutional and program requirements of a model program are listed below. The more of these available in a program, the more likely it will be to serve AFDC students.

- General Institutional Characteristics
  Small size
  Neighborhood location
  Demonstrated ability to develop programs for discrete populations
  Sympathetic to the needs of lower income populations
- Curriculum Characteristics
  GED available
  Basic skills and developmental courses
  Nontraditional education for women
  Cooperative education
  Degree programs
  Certificate programs
  Liberal arts
  Technical career training
  Career education
  Special programs for discrete populations
  Independent study and internship credit
  Student orientation
  Test preparation
  Problem oriented inquiry method
- Services
  Child care
  Career counseling
  Job development and placement
  Peer group support system
  Referral services and personal counseling
  Flexible class scheduling

Acceptance of the principle that education or career training is a desirable option for AFDC women requires that several issues be addressed: (1) policy barriers to the achievement of the goal must be eliminated or alleviated, (2) incentives need to be provided to encourage the election of an education or training option, and (3) education and career training programs that best respond to the special needs of this population must be developed and encouraged.

In the area of public policy, ideally federal and state legislation can be amended to define college and career training as forms of job preparation and options to immediate job placement. Such action could then clear the way for establishing administrative regulations defining AFDC students as a special category of AFDC recipients, recognizing the cost-of-living standards for student financial aid and integrating student financial aid with welfare payments. This would reward rather than punish AFDC women for electing a longer-term investment in their futures.

A second-best strategy to legislative action would be to adopt administrative regulations that encourage cooperative agreements between welfare, education, and employment programs to recognize the special needs of this population, to pool their resources, and eliminate conflicting regulations affecting potential college students. Wisconsin provides a model for this kind of action. Some reorganization and reorientation of welfare departments and caseworkers is essential to the acceptance of more sympathetic approaches to training and education as an option to work. Segregation of AFDC students offers the possibility of developing more sensitive policies and staff to support their needs. Welfare departments and caseworkers need to know more about what the demands are on women in college, and they should be familiar with all sources of available support for students and have some knowledge of education institutions. Welfare departments can potentially act as facilitators in encouraging education institutions to adopt appropriate programs and remove unnecessary barriers to AFDC women.

References

Auletta, Ken. 1983. *The Underclass*. New York: Vintage Books.

Beck, Norman. 1985. "Financial Aid Today: An Economic Perspective." *The College Board Review*, no. 137 (Fall).

Becker, Gary S. 1964. *Human Capital*. NBER, General Series, no. 80. New York: Columbia University Press.

Blaug, Mark. 1985. "Where Are We Now in the Economics of Education?" *Economics of Education Review* 4, no. 1.

Boeckman, Margaret. 1984. *Study of Barriers to Employment for WIN Mandatory Welfare Recipients*. Baltimore: Maryland Department of Human Resources, Office of Welfare Employment Policy, November.

Center for National Policy Review. 1985. *Jobs Watch Alert*, 9 January. Whole issue.

College Entrance Examination Board. 1984. *College Opportunity and Public Assistance Programs*. Washington, D.C.

————. 1982. *Income Maintenance Programs and College Opportunity*. Washington, D.C.

Dalby, Nancy. 1985. "Women Facing Problems Under JTPA." *Jobs Watch Alert* (9 January): 6–10.

Franklin, Paul L. 1985. *Helping Disadvantaged Youth and Adults Enter College*. Washington, D.C.: College Entrance Examination Board.

Grant, Sally, and Donna Moore. 1985. "Legislative Alert." Typescript. National Association of Commissions on Women, West Orange, N.J., 11 February.

Henderson, Cathy, and Cecilia Ottinger. 1985. "College Degrees . . . Still a Ladder to Success?" *Journal of College Placement*, Spring.

Hollister, Robinson G., and Rebecca A. Maynard. 1984. "The Impacts of Supported Work on AFDC Recipients." In Robinson Hollister, Peter Kemper, Rebecca Maynard, eds., *The National Supported Work Demonstration*. Madison: University of Wisconsin Press.

Levin, Henry M. 1985. "The Educationally Disadvantaged: A National Crisis." Report prepared for the Stewart Mott Foundation, Flint, Mich.

Marano, Cynthia. 1985. *The Carl D. Perkins Vocational Education Act: A Sex Equity Analysis*. Washington, D.C.: Wider Opportunities for Women, January.

Maryland Department of Employment and Training. 1985. *State Plan and Annual Report*. Baltimore: Department of Employment and Training.

Massachusetts Department of Public Welfare. 1986. *Massachusetts Employment and Training Choices Program: Program Plan and Budget Request, FY87*. Boston: Executive Office of Human Services, January.

Massachusetts Work and Welfare Advisory Task Force. 1983. "Recommendations of the Work and Welfare Advisory Task Force." Photocopy. Boston.

Mellor, Earl F. 1984. "Investigating the Differences in Weekly Earnings of Women and Men." *Monthly Labor Review*, June.

Rosen, David Paul. 1983. "Resolving the Contradictions of Federal Public Assistance and College Opportunity Policies: Legislative Recommendations." Unpublished document presented to National Commission on Student Financial Assistance. (March): 9.

Stein, Sondra Gayle. 1985. "Women, Poverty and Welfare: Breaking the Cycle." Report prepared for "Women, Welfare, and Higher Education: A Policy Conference" at Smith College, 1–2 April.

U.S. Bureau of the Census. 1980. "Poverty Status in 1979 of Families and Unrelated Individuals by Years of School Completed." Washington, D.C.: Government Printing Office.

U.S. Code of Federal Regulations. 1984. Public Welfare Title 45. Ps. 200–499. Revised October 1.

U.S. Department of Labor. Bureau of Labor Statistics. 1984. "Employment in Perspective: Working Women." Report 716. Fourth Quarter.

————. Bureau of Labor Statistics. 1977. *The Work Incentive (WIN) Program and Related Experiences: A Review of Research with Policy Implications*. Employment and Training Administration. R&D Monograph no. 49. Washington, D.C.: Government Printing Office.

————. Women's Bureau. 1983. *Time of Change: 1983 Handbook on Women Workers*. Bulletin no. 298. Washington, D.C.: Government Printing Office.

U.S. Public Law 88-210. "Carl D. Perkins Vocational Education Act." 18 December 1983. 98th Congress of U.S. 2d Session.

Zwerling, L. S. 1986. *The Community College and Its Critics*. New Directions for Community Colleges, no. 54. San Francisco: Jossey-Bass, June.

V

Public Training
for the Private
Sector

Introduction to Part V/*Sharon L. Harlan*

The critical determinant of the training system's effectiveness is how well
it interfaces with the labor market. Public training programs are frequently
criticized for operating without due consideration for how the market functions or employers' needs for certain skills or types of employees. A popular consensus about the "failure" of public training was responsible for a
major 1980s policy shift that gave the private sector a larger role in directing
training programs for the economically disadvantaged. Yet, as we have seen
throughout this book, immediate business needs are often at odds with those
of female training participants.

The two chapters in Part V step back from considerations of the specific
content of occupational training programs and focus on the relation between
public employment and training policy and the private labor market. Both
Goldstein and Osterman agree that the current interconnection is unproduc-
tive, one finding fault with industry's behavior and the other critical of a disorganized employment and training system. Using the microelectronics and
semiconductor industries as her examples, Goldstein shows how multinational corporations have diverted public resources to further their own profit-
maximizing self-interest at the expense of women's opportunities. Moreover,
operating in an atmosphere of economic crisis, firms have refused to retrain
and upgrade female workers and have assigned affirmative action a low pri-

ority. Osterman sees the employment and training establishment as confused about its mission, uncertain of whether it should be an instrument of labor market policy or part of the income transfer system for the economically disadvantaged. He proposes a restructuring of the public training function that would allow it to be used as an instrument to help firms provide greater employment security for their workers.

The emerging training environment is being shaped by economic turbulence that Goldstein documents at the industry level and Osterman observes in the entire U.S. economy. Because of the restructuring occurring in American industry, more and more firms are vacillating in their commitment to guarantee jobs to employees and this is causing a number of dilemmas. Technological change plays an important role in forcing layoffs, creating high unemployment rates among dislocated workers, and throwing employer/employee relationships into turmoil. Whereas both authors can point to positive examples of firms that have adopted policies for smooth transitions, they agree that this has not happened on an industry-wide or national scale.

Both Goldstein and Osterman are primarily concerned with *retraining* workers who are already employed, mostly by large corporations. They are similar in their desire to see public employment and training policy used as a way to provide employment security and cultivate loyal, stable work forces with low turnover. Osterman's particular vision is a public policy that would improve the efficiency of individual mobility within and between firms and minimize the penalties for job loss by offering extended unemployment insurance, health insurance, and training programs.

Goldstein's central dilemma is why the electronics industry has laid off women production workers during downturns in the business cycle rather than retrain them for a growing number of technicians' jobs. She analyzes several reasons why the firms preferred to hire new technicians from the external labor market. Interestingly, Osterman also discusses the "paradox" of firms laying off one category of workers while hiring in another area. He believes that under the right conditions, such as offers of subsidies for retraining, firms would undertake that responsibility. Goldstein, however, claims that private firms have already managed to subsidize themselves by convincing public training institutions to assume the costs of general and specific training for technicians.

A second concern of these authors is how the employment and training system can function more effectively in getting unemployed workers, particularly the poor, minorities, and women, to penetrate the private labor market. Osterman maintains that the current system, which segregates the poor into separate programs, stigmatizes them and makes private employers reluctant to hire them. By mainstreaming disadvantaged groups into a unified system (while still permitting remedial education programs) and enforcing equal employment policies, he argues that the traditional targets of federal employment and training policy will be better served. He would eliminate the means testing for program eligibility, make the labor exchange system cover all noncollege occupations, and strengthen the Private Industry Councils of JTPA to organize local labor markets around security, placement, and training. With the exception of strengthening PICs, these changes, combined with aggressive affirmative action, should have positive impacts on women.

Goldstein also favors integrating women into the educational pipeline which feeds high tech industries. However, her analysis raises some tough issues about the economic disincentives for educators and managers to train female employees and the unacceptability of poor and working-class women to managers in jobs other than production. The gender and class segregation of jobs makes managers far more comfortable in hiring middle-class youths as technicians. They are assumed to be more "career oriented" and superior at the communication and interpersonal skills that are needed to get along in the industry. These examples are reason to wonder whether a single employment policy would really eliminate a two-tier employment system.

Goldstein and Osterman appear to agree on several important courses of policy action. First, they are critical of public institutions carrying out federal policy and they single out community colleges as having substantial potential, but numerous flaws, as training institutions. Osterman wants better treatment for training staff and greater consistency in quality across states, while Goldstein suggests more public funding for programs and becoming more responsive to women's financial and family needs. Second, both authors argue for the necessity of a strong, broad-based training system that is integrated with a larger industrial policy and monitors private industry's affirmative action record. Third, each expects industry to bear a larger share of the responsibility for financing general and specific training. Osterman wants a tax levied on firms that is proportionate to the value of their payroll. He argues that this will result in a stable revenue source, enhance their identification and involvement with the policy, and encourage them to engage in general training for incumbent workers.

The relationship between public training institutions and private employers remains one of the most difficult and important issues to be resolved. The tension between meeting women's long-term economic needs and serving the immediate interests of employers will not be eased without breaking out of the narrow frameworks that currently dominate the strategies of both private industry and government. It is clearly not reasonable to expect individual firms operating in competitive labor markets to jeopardize themselves by acting altruistically in hiring the disadvantaged. However, we think public policy makers have been too complacent—overly willing to take the goals of the private sector as a given while exclusively altering training to suit it.

Industry cannot expect to accept government training subsidies without government regulation to insure decent wages, benefits, and equal opportunity for women workers. If these standards were applied consistently across all employers, they would remove the competitive advantage of those who are willing to exploit their female work forces.

19/Management Training Strategies in High Tech Electronics

Nance Goldstein

The high tech electronics industry is one that depends critically on its employees to develop new and better ideas for products and for the operations of the complex production technologies. It is an industry that highly values training: new and upgraded skills are continually needed to produce the newest models of computers and semiconductors. It also is an industry that employs a large number of women in the U.S. and overseas. Most of these women, however, work as semiskilled assemblers and operators, a job that is rarely thought of in connection with training, and is increasingly being automated. This threat to women's jobs has been hidden by the many years of unprecedented industry growth. While the high tech slump of 1985 and 1986 hit production workers, many regions had a sufficiently diverse electronics industry to reemploy many and to cloud the impact of adopting new technologies on job opportunities. Yet, industry managers and experienced production workers now acknowledge the threat.

Have women workers chosen to retrain for other more promising industry jobs, such as for electronics technician, one of the nation's fastest growing occupations? Have workers sought upgrading opportunities to find better and more secure jobs? Have young women wanting to work in the industry trained to qualify for these jobs? Have managers upgraded their workers to fill these technicians' jobs, providing these workers with a more promising employment future?

This chapter will attempt to answer these questions by looking at many of the factors that frame these training/retraining decisions, including the company and industry-specific conditions, the regional labor market situation, and the emerging relation between the education sector and the industry. This analysis relies heavily on research on the high tech electronics industry in Scotland. It is based on a 1984 survey of managers, technology educators, industry

485

experts, and female workers in mainly U.S. multinational corporations. The survey examined technology and employment strategies in an industry that depends on very expensive, rapidly changing production technologies. Scotland was chosen because it has the largest global concentration of integrated circuit producers outside of California, including a large group of leading computer multinationals.

This data has been supplemented by more recent interviews with technology educators in Massachusetts and secondary source material on California. These two states each account for a large share of the industry's plants and jobs: Silicon Valley and the region circled by Routes 128 and 495 outside of Boston house about 46 percent of the plants in the U.S. semiconductor and computer industries (Markusen 1986). While the analysis looks only at selected industry sites, the findings point to important developments applicable to the industry as a whole.

After looking at the employee composition of the industry and the extent of gender segregation, the chapter will assess the link between college-based programs in electronics technology and the maintenance of segregation. It will then examine whether women in the industry have chosen to retrain as technicians as well as what the industry's involvement is in retraining. A final section argues for direct intervention to alter the gender segregation of the industry's employment and training.

Occupations in the High Tech Electronics Industry

Three occupations dominate the development, design, production, testing, and servicing of semiconductors and computers—engineer, technician, and "semiskilled" production worker. Engineers usually hold bachelor's degrees in electronic, industrial, or chemical engineering. Employers look for people with higher degrees only for a few highly specialized tasks, particularly product design.

Technicians conventionally have some formal training at the postsecondary level, often involving a technology certificate or an associate's degree.[1] In practice, however, their responsibilities vary widely and those of experienced technicians frequently overlap those of engineers. Once on the job, technicians test, adjust and repair equipment, following the instruction and supervision of engineers and scientists. They determine the correct functioning of circuits, locate any faults, prototype and test new products, and assist professionals in the design, selection, installation, calibration, and testing of production equipment and products. Most technicians specialize in just one type of equipment, but some apply their skills over a range of different types that can extend from radio, radar, sonar, and television to industrial and medi-

Table 19-1/Employment in the U.S. Computer and Semiconductor Industries

	1970		1980	
	Number Employed	*Percent Women*	*Number Employed*	*Percent Women*
Electrical/electronics engineers	47,004	2	67,320	4
Electronics technicians	31,454	11	60,299	15
Operatives, fabricators, transporters, and laborers	519,221	58	591,091	58
Assemblers	158,191	74	208,284	72
Electronics assemblers	NA		55,879	77

Sources: Strober and Arnold 1985, Table 1. Also taken from U.S. Census, Population Characteristics Special Report, *Occupation by Industry*; for 1970, Table 8; for 1980, Table 4.

cal measuring and control devices, navigational equipment, and computers. Often they maintain and service equipment, either on the shop floor or at the customer's location. Technician is a particularly important occupation in high tech production, because the work of technicians is critical to maintaining production.

Semiskilled production workers are those who operate or mind the production machines. These workers may also assemble products, either wiring or soldering together individual or groups of components or putting together and packaging the final product.

The Gender Segregation of Jobs

Since the industry's beginnings, men have held the overwhelming majority of engineer and technician jobs, while women have been concentrated in the operator and assembler jobs (Green 1983; Keller 1981; Siegel 1980). In the U.S. in 1980, 96 percent of the electronics engineers and 85 percent of technicians were men, dominating these jobs as they did in 1970 (See Table 19-1). By contrast, 77 percent of electronics assemblers were women. In Scotland, the absence of women technicians was even more acute. In the 21 semiconductor and computer and related firms surveyed, 97 percent of all electronics engineers and 93 percent of technicians were men; 76 percent of the industries' semiskilled production workers were women.

Throughout the 1970s and early 1980s, the phenomenal growth in the U.S. computer and computer-related industries was accompanied by a slight increase in the number of women getting jobs as technicians. Yet, women remained only a small minority of the industry's technicians, increasing over the decade to 15 percent from 11 percent (which represents a numerical growth of 161 percent; Strober and Arnold 1985, Table 1). In Massachusetts, women claimed a smaller share of electronics technician jobs, but that representation did increase over the decade—from 8.7 percent to 12.7 percent (employment data from the U.S. Bureau of the Census, 1970 and 1980).

Moreover, there was a wide gap in earnings between semiskilled workers and technicians. A 1986 Massachusetts manufacturing wage survey, for example, indicated that typical assemblers earned an hourly wage of $6.00–$6.99, compared with technicians' average wage of $9.62 to $10.82.[2] And, despite the 1985–86 industry slowdown, Massachusetts training experts claimed that labor market competition, particularly for experienced technicians, continued to push technicians' wages up.

Trends in Occupational Composition

The industry's reliance on technical personnel increased steadily throughout the 1970s and early 1980s. These were years of employment growth, with expansion in physical capacity, the number of establishments, and overall employment. Yet, the share of production jobs fell: in the U.S. semiconductor industry employment, it dropped precipitously from over 72 percent to less than 54 percent in 1977. In the computer industry production, production workers as a percentage of the total work force decreased from 51 percent to 44 percent (1968–1978; Markusen 1986). The share of production workers continued to decline during the early 1980s: by 1985 production workers comprised only 40 percent and 34 percent of the U.S. semiconductor and electronic computing equipment work forces, respectively.[3] The 1985 convulsion in the computer and semiconductor industries further led to more than 7,000 layoffs among Massachusetts firms in these industries and the loss of more than 10,000 jobs (High Tech Research Group [HTRG] 1986). The job loss was heaviest among semiskilled production workers (Massachusetts Division of Employment Security [Mass. DES] 1986).

Several strategic changes help explain the occupational shift—the drive to automate production, to improve product quality, and to adjust quickly to rapidly changing markets. By 1983–84, management in leading firms in both industries had decided to invest heavily in more automated production equipment and computer-intergrated manufacturing systems as the way to reduce unit costs. Computerization, by increasing the precision of manufacturing, would also reduce the number of defects in output, minimizing the high costs of waste and time delays. Also, with computerization, the same equipment can be quickly adapted to reflect the firm's production experience or customer specifications to manufacture the right product for the market. Combining computerized control with greater automation of tasks eliminated a lot of female-dominated manual work: the same semiskilled work force could thus oversee more machines and perform additional tasks. Also, competition from the Far East has mounted unabated since the late 1970s: particularly in the computer industry, many producers have shipped assembly activities overseas to reduce unit production costs (HTRG 1986; O'Connor 1985; Russell 1984).

Competitive pressures also compelled managers to seek capital-saving measures: managers focused on hiring technical people to maximize the productivity of their investment in these technologies. Company performance and profits depended on well-trained personnel who could fully exploit the expensive information-intensive equipment: the faster and more creatively technical labor could use information to improve the product or to design a new one, the more sales could be generated using the same production equipment before it became obsolete. With the growing importance of special order markets and technical support for customers, the faster personnel recognized a problem or a product idea and turned it into a product delivered to the customer, the more sales the firm could make.

Both the increasing reliance on technical labor to meet market product demands and the automation or exporting of production activity seem likely to continue over the next years (Goldstein 1988). These factors are bound to impede the further growth of semiskilled production jobs in the U.S. Similarly, managers in Scotland claimed that through growth, layoffs, and natural wastage their semiskilled work force would decline over the next five years (in some cases dramatically) while the number of technical staff would continue to increase. A few even predicted the ratio of technically trained to lesser-skilled workers would soon be one or even two to one.

By contrast, while the 1985 layoffs in individual firms included technical personnel, the industry has maintained continued demand for technicians, as well as for engineers. Furthermore, even if the fortunes of the computer and semiconductor industries falter, increasing numbers of companies and industries, such as hospitals, investing in a wide variety of sophisticated electronics technologies need electronics technicians to maintain and repair their equipment. In fact, electronics technician has been identified as one of the top fastest-growing occupations in the U.S. (to 1995; U.S. Bureau of Labor Statistics [USBLS] 1986).

The declining importance of production jobs endangers the job security of the microelectronics industry's female workers and makes the industry an uncertain source of jobs for working-class women in the future. Women with qualifications for electronics technician jobs would face a better employment future. These jobs offer better pay as well as a more interesting and secure work life. What are the prospects, then, for retraining production workers to become electronics technicians? Or even for expanding the proportion of women in general in electronics technicians jobs? Not very good, as the next sections will show.

The Gender Barriers in Technology Education and Training

The education sectors in both the U.S. and Scotland have responded vigorously to the demands of the growing microelectronics industry to expand industry-specific training and higher education (Stern 1985; Zemsky and Meyerson 1985) to produce a larger technical labor force. The expansion of industry-specific technical training in higher education resulted in part from active lobbying by high tech industry leaders and employers' associations (as, for example, Massachusetts High Tech Council). Managers eagerly wooed the public sector. Training was high on the agenda of formal national and state commissions like the California Commission on Industrial Innovation (Saxenian 1981).

In addition, corporate managers contacted individual college and university faculty to persuade them to design new courses and to subsidize industry-relevant training. They pressed educators to reshape these courses to meet specific industry skill requirements by sitting on curriculum development committees and by donating equipment and company personnel. Proximity to the schools allowed managers continuing opportunities to communicate with and influence educators.[4]

The education sector also benefited from closer links with industry. These links were important because of the projected decline in the college-age population from the early 1980s through 1995 and the restrictive fiscal situation of many regional education systems in both the U.K. and the U.S. Setting up programs that promised close collaboration with the high tech industry and access to the industry's jobs was a competitive advantage for any college. Also, participating in collaborative projects with firms and winning private sector research contracts brought in outside funding to support faculty research threatened by public-sector cutbacks.

Courses to train electronics technicians proliferated in U.S. public and private junior and community colleges, technical institutes, and engineering universities. Students wanting a technician's job could choose from one- and two-year certificate courses, two-year associate's degree programs, bachelor's degree courses, as well as shorter programs often supported by federal funding. The trend in recent years, however, has been for the education sector to offer longer programs leading to an electronics technician qualification, "paraprofessionalizing" (Hacker and Starnes 1986; Noyelle 1985) the job of technician.[5] Education and training experts in Massachusetts explained that companies preferred to hire graduates of an associate's degree program over those from shorter vocational training certificate programs, because graduates would have both the knowledge of the technology and the communications and interpersonal skills associated with academic credentials. In turn, colleges hungry for improved student numbers shifted their resources to longer, more academic programs. The opportunities for gaining a qualification in a program shorter than a two-year associate's degree dwindled.

Data from Massachusetts community colleges confirmed this trend. The share of community college students completing a technology qualification with a two-year associate's degree grew from 42 percent in 1980–81 to 99 percent by 1984–86 (data from Commonwealth of Massachusetts 1987). Similarly at one well-respected Boston technology college, the majority of its recent graduates shifted to the associate's and bachelor's degree programs. The proportion of their electronics technology students completing a full-time degree program had risen to approximately 75 percent in 1986 from about 50 percent only six years earlier. Gaining an associate's degree had become the best ticket to a technician's job in the Massachusetts and California high tech industries (see also Stern 1985).

At the same time that they were updating and expanding their technology degree programs, universities and colleges were competing with one another to offer short courses about fast-changing technologies for industry employees. In these courses, faculty offered brief, highly specialized classes to retrain and upgrade employees in the use of a particular technology (U.S. Office of Technology Assessment [USOTA] 1984). The courses were tailored to a specific industry and often to individual company needs. The courses were oriented to engineers and sometimes to technicians, because these employees were most able to turn information into returns to the company rapidly. Thus, to win industry support and financing, educational institutions eagerly assumed responsibility for and a lot of the costs of highly specific industry training.

Few Women Graduates

In 1980, women constituted 42 percent of all community college graduates in electronics technology courses in Massachusetts. By the end of the 1985 academic year, however, women's share of graduates had dropped off sharply to 14 percent. The picture of women's involvement in electronics technician programs, if Massachusetts can be used as an example, is clear. Unless programs were targeted to women, few participated—either as new workers first entering the labor force or as adults retraining for better jobs. This was true in both the community college system and, as we shall see below, in private-sector colleges and schools specializing in electronics.[6] This section examines the barriers women have faced.

Community colleges are an important supplier of a region's technical labor: they are financially and geographically accessible to working-class students and adults. Courses are inexpensive, are usually convenient to home or work, and have schedules suitable for people with jobs. Add to this state intervention to increase enrollments and the result was a sharp rise in women's participation in community college electronics technology courses.

Because of the growing high tech industry demand for technicians in the late 1970s, colleges developed programs using federal funding—the Comprehensive Employment and Training Act (CETA) and the Vocational Education Act—to train disadvantaged populations for these jobs. CETA and Vocational Education thus funded training for women on welfare and "displaced homemakers" (among others) that qualified them for available jobs. High Tech Prep and Women in Technology are examples of the courses colleges developed in 1979 and 1980 and 1981 to serve both the target populations and industry demand. They were short courses, usually six to eight months. While they did not lead to a formal credential, the graduates were accepted as technicians by the young, expanding high tech industry.

Women's participation plunged for two interrelated reasons: the nature and application of government training money changed and few women enrolled in the academic degree programs. Reviewing the history of this rapid turnaround will demonstrate some of the problems in getting women to enter nontraditional fields.

Shifting of Training Resources

The 1980s were turbulent years for the high tech industry and technology training. With the advent of the Reagan administration, there were changes in federal funding. CETA funding began falling in 1980. When the Job Training Partnership Act (JTPA) replaced CETA in 1983, the new program further reduced funding for disadvantaged worker training. At about the same time, funding for vocational education was made more restrictive (the Carl D. Perkins Act of 1984). Targeting programs to displaced homemakers became practically the only way to gain vocational education funds. The allocation of vocational education money to Massachusetts had meanwhile been shrinking in real terms since the late 1970s.

These developments in effect reduced the number of women enrolling in technician programs. First, technology education faculty had to compete for shrinking federal funds with educators from many other disciplines designing new programs targeted to displaced homemakers. Second, even this source of funding to help women in the labor market could not replace lost funding from CETA: targeted to women reentering the labor market, these programs could not help working women who wanted retraining or upgrading.

Furthermore, college educators recognized that these graduates were having trouble getting hired into the industry by the late 1970s, so they began questioning the promise of these specially funded short courses. High tech developed very quickly during this period into a much more advanced and sophisticated industry: as a result, firms wanted technicians with a more thorough education. The short technician course was no longer considered adequate for dealing with the problems of new production technologies. Then, with the major slump in 1981–82, interest in electronics technician courses in general faded.

College educators responded to these developments in several ways. First, as mentioned above, they diverted technology education resources into new, longer academic programs leading to an associate's degree to provide the more theoretical training high tech employers wanted. In addition, the colleges raised the entry requirements in math and English for these associate's degree programs, in many cases requiring a minimum grade or placement tests. While community colleges have open enrollments in general, students without satisfactory academic entry requirements must pass remedial classes at the college before being allowed to enroll in these programs. Such requirements add at least one semester if not more to a two-year full-time program.

Second, community colleges diversified their programs for target groups, offering more specialized technology programs geared to other industries. Adult women were counseled to take short courses in personal computer repair and robotics, for example. They also were guided into entirely new areas, such as radiology technician. Educators explained that this shift was due not only to changing labor market demand but also to the failure of past programs. For instance, the technician courses had been targeted to unemployed women with little if any math or science background. They often had a significant fear of math, slowing if not blocking their progress. The short-course format did not allow enough time to train them well enough to assume the good technician jobs in the industry.

Third, the constituencies of community colleges were changing. Educators had succeeded in improving women's college enrollment throughout the 1970s. By the early 1980s, colleges were looking at the large numbers of Asian and Hispanic immigrants needing education to improve their employment opportunities. Resources were channeled to meet the educational needs of these minority groups rather than to women.

Other Training and Employment Barriers

Thus, it was women's high participation in these special, short-term programs in electronics technology in Massachusetts that was unique. Women's high participation in these courses contrasts sharply with electronics and other technology education and training programs at other institutions.

Women's participation in associates degree programs in electronics has been low and that did not change as male participation in these courses grew. Women were only 9.5 percent (on average) of Massachusetts community college degree graduates (1980–86). The same was true in private technical colleges, consistent with the history of low women's participation in most of technology and science education. The Boston area technology college cited earlier graduated on average only 5 women with associate's degrees annually from 1980 through 1986 in classes averaging 170.

Women's low participation in private technology schools is especially troubling because, according to many of industry analysts, employers preferred hiring graduates from these schools, often run in association with high tech corporations, over those with academic degrees. GTE Sylvania Tech and Control Data Institute in Massachusetts, for example, have provided well-respected "short-term high impact" training programs. These are courses that focus on skill areas industry has identified as having urgent and essential needs and that emphasize "hands on" experience in modern, sophisticated electronics laboratories. The availability of these facilities, too expensive for most colleges to provide, is a major attraction for students and employers. Experience using advanced equipment enables trainees, once hired, to be productive more quickly than those with more academic backgrounds.

These schools have trained few women: student populations at both schools have run 90 percent male or higher since 1980, even during 1981–83— years of significant enrollment growth. One of the schools had scheduled a part-time morning course primarily to attract displaced homemakers. Instead, night-shift workers—predominantly men, working as office or data processing clerks and wanting to retrain—filled the class. In many cases they were sponsored by their employers.

The structure of technology education associated with high tech contains formidable barriers for women's entry into this nontraditional field, either as pre-employment vocational students or as workers seeking retraining. The academic atmosphere has been extremely competitive. With a growing number of largely male students, managers were able to compete for "the best and the brightest." In fact, they preferred to delay hiring if they failed to attract "the cream." Surviving this extremely competitive and male environment without encouragement or support is a formidable and uncomfortable project for any woman.[7]

Faculty, burdened with fast-growing teaching loads and busy seeking external funding, had no time for or interest in actively recruiting women for technology courses (in many cases already fully subscribed). There was no acknowledgment among the technology faculty of the need for counseling, remedial assistance, or other institutional support mechanisms to attract and retain women students. Except for the services available to the college population as a whole, no facilities existed.

Gender frames the students' employment opportunities as well. Faculty with good contacts in industry found research projects and jobs in the industry and recommended their students for these opportunities. While there is no doubt that exceptional female students were put forward, it can be very difficult for a good female student to get attention in an almost entirely male environment. The small minority of female students in these programs had no affirmative action or monitoring mechanisms to ensure that they received their share of the benefits that the new "old boy" network of academic-industry links created.

For women workers in the early 1980s, retraining from a production employee to a technician meant earning an associate's degree. This choice represented a greater academic and financial commitment than was formerly necessary to obtain middle-level jobs in manufacturing. A woman considering retraining would now have to leave the labor market and commit herself to two years of full-time academic study, or many more years of part-time study if she decided to keep her job. Add to this even more time if she had to take additional courses to meet the higher math and English entry requirements.[8] If she works and has children, or comes to this program with a fear of math, her difficulties are further compounded. Not surprisingly, given these obstacles, female workers indicated that they were discouraged by the highly academic nature of available programs and the time commitment involved in arranging logistics and studying for a long course.

According to educators, the cost of tuition deters women's completion of programs. In the industry schools and the private college, tuition runs approximately $5,200 for seven months of intensive training (1986) and $5,750 for a full-time academic year (1987), respectively—a sum prohibitive for most working women. Tuition for community college programs is much less expensive: two Massachusetts colleges offered full-time two-year programs at approximately $900 an academic year.[9] Even here, one has to add to this the costs of transportation and study materials. However, working women with children conventionally devote their earnings to household and family expenses, not to self-improvement (McCulloch, Wolkowitz, and Young 1984).[10]

Increased academic requirements, increased competition for vacancies, and reduced government funding to attract women have combined to discourage women from training/retraining for technicians' jobs. By contrast, the Women's Technical Institute in Boston offers some additional evidence that affirmative action objectives backed by resources are critical to enabling women to *choose* to become electronics technicians. It has succeeded in graduating a growing number of adult women from its six-month electronics technician training program since it opened in 1983. That success derives from features that, as described above, cannot be found in the rest of the technician education and training sector. The course curriculum, recruitment practices, class scheduling, counseling, and financial and job placement assistance are all tailored to helping adult women retrain in nontraditional fields. The average age of students was 30–34. The rate of job placement upon course completion was approximately 90 percent.

Management Training Strategies: Production Workers vs. Technicians/Engineers

Despite a tight technician labor supply in parts of Scotland, and perhaps in Massachusetts as well, firms did not retrain female production workers to fill technical jobs. Among U.S. multinationals in Scotland surveyed, only two firms reported that they had upgraded women to technicians, representing only eight workers out of the more than 3,600 semiskilled production workers in the 11 of 12 companies dominating the industries' 1984 regional employment.[11]

Instead, companies pursued profoundly different approaches in financing training for production workers and technical/engineering staff. Management's training allocations reflected decisions about the structure of work and the value of different employees for competing successfully in trying and unpredictable markets. It reflected as well very different expectations of the respective contributions of production workers and technicians to the work and development of the firm.

While management lavished upgrading opportunities on engineer and technician employees, female workers were offered training programs limited to preparing them for their assigned task in production. Where the boundaries between the work of engineers and technicians were often fluid, barriers sharply divided production and technical work and the opportunities that flowed from each.

Technicians were given in-depth specialization; they were taught everything necessary for total responsibility for their equipment in off-site training programs and on-the-job supervision. Managers also encouraged technical workers to pursue training opportunities that would enhance their jobs. They were sometimes sent on short courses that would help them learn new technical capabilities, and, if they showed interest, they were sponsored in part-time courses offered at a growing number of colleges to upgrade their technical skills and qualify for better jobs.[12]

Training for production workers was quite different: because the new technologies had reduced the number and complexity of production tasks, operator training was short and focused on increasing their speed in extremely restricted oversight and mechanical work. The operator was taught to recognize good and poor quality output, to adjust machine dials minimally, and to call a technician or engineer when a problem developed. Production workers seldom knew how their work fit into the finished product.

and with *no* technical qualifications. In Massachusetts, managers evidently also frequently hire people who have completed only part of a technician education course or direct from a technical high school. In both cases, the firm trains these new recruits on the job or sponsors them in obtaining their degree, often on day-release. In all cases in the Scotland survey, the unskilled recruits were young men. Employers thus supported extensive training for unknown recruits from the external labor market while refusing to invest in their female employees. How can this inconsistency be explained?

Company recruitment practices are fundamentally shaped by managers' desire to find "the right people" for technical work: most of all, they wanted to ensure that new employees would fit into the high tech work culture. The quality of "fit" is variously characterized as "someone with drive" and eagerness, a well-rounded "people person," a good team member, someone with good social skills.

Managers wanted technicians who could articulate technical analysis, work well in teams, and cope with pressure, work long hours, and face unexpected problems with composure and good humor. Solving technical problems rapidly involved collaboration. Communication skills facilitated the structure of work between engineers and technicians, especially around tasks associated with complex new technologies. Personnel managers and community college educators report that candidates with good communications and interpersonal skills frequently were hired over those with superior technical qualifications but without social skills.

Unfortunately for women, the maleness of this technical culture seems bound to define who fits in and who does not. After all, most managers are male engineers, and the experience of an almost exclusively male partnership around technical work will surely influence who these managers perceive as a good fit. Male managers and technical staff will generally be more comfortable with other men much like them. The code of "homosocial reproduction," as Rosabeth Kanter (1977) labels it, anticipates that the men making hiring decisions will expect men, not women, to fit in easily and quickly. And, such gender homogeneity is even received as productive: the shared knowledge and collaboration across occupations that Hirschhorn (1984) argues makes microelectronics-controlled manufacturing technologies more productive and adaptable depend on minimizing social awkwardness and tensions.

Not only has the work structure influenced the gender of the jobs, but gender (along with class) may also have shaped the organization of work. The more fluid organization of engineer's and technicians' work in Scotland may be due to comfortableness and operational successes of the male work environment in the plants. This is reinforced by the increased likelihood that candidates for technician jobs will be middle-class youth who remind male managers of themselves when they started out.

Because few women have held technical positions, most managers have had little experience to challenge their expectations. Managers have experienced women primarily as subordinate production workers, who are not viewed as good candidates to join the more collaborative world of technical work.[19] Where managers have had female technical workers, they have often raved about them. Not surprising, most managers did not acknowledge this dynamic of gender exclusion, nor did they consider it their responsibility to alter the situation. Aware of it or not, when managers invested in "growing their own" skilled labor inside the firm, they were more likely to risk investing in men than in women.

Progressive Company Programs

There have been some exceptional firms that have undertaken affirmative action initiatives, ostensibly because employers seem to have judged that retraining existing production workers provided cost savings or other compelling returns to the firm.[20]

Some employers considered that they had a responsibility to improve the employment situation of their workers through sponsored training. For example, as part of its policy to support the advancement of female employees, Motorola, a semiconductor firm with a major plant in Austin, Texas, set up a facility to train semiskilled production workers as technicians. (Fraser 1987).

In several other firms, escalating salaries in the competitive labor market for electronics technicians seem to have been the incentive behind upgrading programs. Texas Instruments, a semiconductor producer, developed a pilot project to train digital wire board designers (USOTA, 1984). Students were selected for an intensive one-year course both from a pool of recent high school graduates and from the firm's own production workers. Women employees proved to be only a minority of the people trained through the program. Wang Labs in Lowell, Massachusetts, set up a Twilight Tech program in 1980, providing their assemblers, inspectors, testers, and materials handlers with an opportunity for promotion. The nine-month program has averaged about 20 graduates a year; usually about half are women. The number of students selected for each class is tied to the expected in-company demand for technicians, which means that a very high percentage of those completing the course are placed in technician jobs. The program is organized during the working day so that half of the four daily hours of classes are on company time.[21] Honeywell, Gould Modicom, and Varian Exitron, other Massachusetts electronics firms, have brought community college faculty in-house to run retraining/upgrading programs for employees. When the initiative was targeted to assemblers, as was the case with one program at Gould Modicom, the interest and participation among women was high.

Perhaps the most thorough and expensive program has been developed by Western Electric in Massachusetts. Negotiated by a union that represents a large share of the work force, it enrolls approximately 380 workers in a program lasting anywhere from six to 18 months. The Communications Workers of America bargained for this upgrading program in exchange for streamlining the grading structure. Here management was willing to bear the costs of upgrading only because this very large and competitively besieged firm won greater flexibility in the organization of work.

The course begins with a preparatory math course, followed by an intensive electronics program. This first program was designed for high-grade testers with some technical training. Because this occupation tends to filled by men, the group included few women. However, the firm plans to extend upgrading opportunities to more grades of workers over the next five years. The program will be for lower-level testers, and eventually a course will be targeted to production workers, where the firm's female employees are concentrated. This program also will award college credits that can be applied toward an associate's degree.

Given the absence of unions from most of high tech industry, it is important to consider whether there is any economic rationale for retraining women production workers in the industry. The recruitment and training practices of the one Japanese multinational corporation in the Scotland survey suggest that firms can reap medium-term economies by turning to their production workers to maintain and repair new production technologies. Management had structured work so that all jobs from the bottom up were enhanced (relative to many competitors). Operators were trained extensively in-house in the use of their machine and its role in production. Managers then selected experienced operators—about half of whom were women—to train to become operator trainers and "setters." The tasks in these jobs, which involved routine machine maintenance and repair, were conventionally done by technicians. Advanced technicians were sometimes recruited from the external labor market, yet management was also willing to support advanced training for setters.

This commitment to richer, more responsible jobs throughout the work structure and continuing training/retraining throughout the worker's "lifetime employment" was made possible by two additional policies. The firm recruited youth with high academic achievement in math, science, and English: success in scholarship satisfied management that the recruits would be quick learners on the job. Also, the corporation invested in only the most advanced production equipment. Thus, workers were freed from many routine tasks that became automated. Furthermore, the computer controls in the new machines stored and processed more of the relevant technical information. All these practices combined to minimize the firm's reliance on highly qualified engineers and technicians who commanded escalating salaries in the competitive labor market. It also reduced labor turnover and employers claimed that low turnover resulted in higher productivity. The commitment to upgrading production workers, then, was a cost-minimizing strategy.

Although academics have promoted the importance of upgrading training and enhanced jobs to make complex new microelectronics technologies work smoothly and efficiently (Hirschhorn 1984; Appelbaum et al. 1986), U.S. managers have not recognized the cost-minimizing advantages of retraining production workers. Retraining female workers could save firms hiring and adjustment costs. Experienced operators and assemblers have familiarity with company production processes and protocol as well as contextual information that can speed up adjustment to new product requirements or the assessment and correction of unanticipated production problems. Commitment to retraining female production workers would also serve to minimize technician turnover, given women's reduced mobility because of family responsibilities and (inevitably) the reduced transferability of in-house training. Moreover, training facilities, which were part of the original location decision by firms in California (Saxenian 1981) and Scotland (Goldstein 1988), would allow managers to upgrade workers quickly and inexpensively as vacancies develop.

Policy Implications

It is very difficult for an outsider to identify and evaluate all the factors involved in management training and employment practices. These are decisions that depend heavily on individual executives, their relationships with their managers, and the economic and strategic expedients that change rapidly in this industry. The outcomes reported here are consistent with broadly defined short-run business interests attempting to minimize risks and uncertainties in a highly volatile market. Management strategies and their implementation were shaped by gender-defined perceptions that female workers were "wonderful operators" and men were good technicians and engineers. In that context, few managers recognized or rated highly the potential long-run financial savings of upgrading female workers in programs such as the one developed by the Japanese corporation in Scotland. Cash-flow crises and the development of new products overwhelmed management's consideration of the social and economic benefits of affirmative action. Although managers claimed that new technologies threatened the long-term employment of semiskilled female workers, they expressed no commitment to these largely loyal workers and their continuing employment.

Moreover, the difficulties of moving women into this historically male field of technology have been exacerbated by colleges struggling for resources and by their genuine excitement about getting involved in this high-profile industry. Faculty were too busy to recognize that the maleness of the electronics technology field is itself a major barrier to women's involvement.

Examples cited above demonstrate that the labor market and other pressures can alter management's willingness to invest in semiskilled female employees. However, U.S. managers did not feel compelled to consider this option. To see the economic return of retraining, firms must have the capability to calculate the benefits and costs to inform their training and investment decisions. Furthermore, weighing the medium-term, as well as the short-term, returns and being required to bear more of the costs of lay-offs and training would change the way firms make these decisions, as the practices of the Japanese firm demonstrate. Government intervention is critical to make more attractive the benefits of company investment in its women workers.

The industry must bear more of the responsibility—even if only the financing—for training and retraining its female employees. That this should be the case for specific training is uncontroversial, but even here, the industry has increasingly shifted training to the education sector. However, firms rarely pay the full cost of provision of short courses, thereby draining public monies for individual firm gains. The colleges frequently assume, for example, the planning costs, costs of canceled programs, and perhaps even capital costs in purchasing technologies that change yearly. This constrains the use of public resources for other facets of technology education.

Furthermore, it can be argued that industry should contribute more to what is considered general technology education. Many of the fiscal problems colleges face in planning and implementing technology training and education are a direct result of high tech industry competition over new technologies that results in an extremely rapid pace of change in electronics products and production technologies. Educators, responsive to management pressure to update and provide more specialized technology programs, may find it difficult to decide which developments deserve institutional support, thus spending scarce resources on incorporating the newest technology at the expense of improving the quality of the education and making it truly accessible to everyone.

These factors have precluded a debate on exactly where industry responsibility for its own training begins and where higher education responsibility for educational goals ends. While the dilemma of how to divide the responsibility of training between the public sector and industry has no simple or single solution, it does call for a visible debate and a clearly articulated policy.

A policy advocating greater company responsibility for training and greater resources for the employment and training of women could be built on public-sector technical assistance to industry and on financial incentives. Public-sector agencies could provide program development and evaluation assistance. Incentives could be created to compensate for the company's perceived short-term costs. Just as technological assistance grants have helped industry to reap the benefits of new technologies, affirmative action grants would induce managers to accept and plan internal training/retraining programs. While such programs would require substantial funding in an era of balanced budgets, governments have long provided financial incentives to shape management decisions. Concerned by the erosion of manufacturing employment in traditional industries (USOTA 1986; Governor's Commission 1984), state and local governments have used tax and other incentives to promote their regions as the lowest cost option and lure investment by high tech firms. The federal government has also supported and subsidized the industry in many ways (for example, R&D funds).

However, the situation demands even more than investment. It requires an independent body to stand outside the competitive constraints of the individual firm to promote better access to training. As an industry-wide priority. The industry cannot on its own be expected to develop a thoughtful, comprehensive training system—one that would set training objectives for transferable skills, insure nondiscriminatory access to training and jobs, as well as monitor and modify programs. A tripartite mechanism with representatives of industry, the government, and workers might be an appropriate governing structure. Because of the high tech industry's low level of unionization, it is particularly important to ensure that all workers—men and women, minority and white—are represented and share in the benefits.

Whatever the route of policy implementation, it is important to make the high tech electronics industry accountable for the quality of and access to training and employment opportunities. There are many ways to allocate training resources and to organize work, even within competitive constraints: accordingly, there needs to be greater exploration of ways to achieve work force flexibility and stability and to enhance women workers' skills, pay, and contribution to the firm. Failure to redirect the internal dynamics of this industry, in essence, supports the continued exclusion of most women from the industry's technical jobs and the continued consignment of women production workers to a ghetto of increasingly routine, repetitive, and insecure jobs.

Notes

1. There are however almost as many routes to becoming a technician as there are interpretations of what a technician does. To complicate matters, there is no single data source for employment or training levels for the occupation; in fact little data exists.

2. The wage data refer to the occupation and so concern electronics assemblers and technicians working throughout the economy, not just in high tech electronics. Technicians' earnings can be, and in many cases are, much higher than what is recorded here, depending on the firm, specialization, and regional market conditions.

The *Boston Globe* in 1986 spotlighted a man who had worked at Wang Labs in Lowell, Massachusetts, as a $3-an-hour assembler. He took the in-house training for technician skills and worked his way up to a $37,000 salary as a senior technician in charge of transferring product designs to manufacturing.

3. The data compared should be interpreted only as showing a general trend of decline in production employment: Markusen's data are from the Census and the more recent data from the U.S. Bureau of Labor Statistics (USBLS).

4. The reliance of the industry on the education sector is an important and distinguishing feature of this industry's development in the U.S., Scotland, and a few select Far Eastern locations (e.g., Singapore). The industry has in effect externalized many formerly internal recruitment and training costs. Proximity allows companies to add specific skills to their existing work force rapidly and cheaply when they need it through special short courses. That is less expensive than hiring someone new or waiting for someone with a formal qualification to finish his or her degree. Also, employers arranged for students at nearby colleges and universities to work on special projects in the plant or over the summer. This gave managers the chance to see if they are suitable employees, reducing the costs of making a hiring mistake. Further, firms had called on faculty and research students at the universities to solve unanticipated and medium-term technical problems: the university in effect relieves the firm of hiring additional employees. This easy access to a supply of technical labor and technology resources had become by the early 1980s a major determinant in corporate decisions about where to locate advanced manufacturing plants (Goldstein 1988).

5. The U.S. high tech industry has been instrumental in shifting the responsibility for the supply of technical labor on to the education system. Eliminating the traditional industrial apprenticeship reduces business costs and silences unions through which workers had a significant voice in the conditions of training. The definition of qualifications, monitoring of both the on-the-job and classroom components of the training, and the number and wages of trainees were determined by management in negotiation with labor. The numbers of trainees and length of training were determined in part by unions exercising their power in controlling the labor supply and maintaining high wages for their members already working in the occupation. In addition, the apprenticeship system, where workers trained other workers, fostered a trade consciousness (Cockburn 1983; Ryan 1984) and camaraderie that nurtured unionism. By contrast, the education sector supplies technical people with a career orientation. Recruits from an educational institution would have learned the intellectual basics of their occupation and the value of "high performance" by competing in an academic environment, a kind of training particularly important to the individualism of the high tech "culture." This "paraprofessionalization" of the occupation suited the aim of industry management to avoid if not prevent the development of unions and the associated wage pressures and work practice agreements.

6. A complete picture of training/retraining in Massachusetts would have to include secondary school enrollment and participation in further education programs in vocational high schools, all private technical schools, and all colleges and universities offering relevant training programs (e.g., through extension courses). However, the lack of or confused state of data limits this discussion to training centers where data existed. This sample included the leading high tech firms most consistently relied on, the state's

best-known private technology schools, a well-respected academic technology college, and the community college system.

7. This interpretation of the male-dominated technical education environment, a problem that has been cited in many evaluations of women in nontraditional vocational education, was corroborated by the author's experience teaching classes of electronics engineering students that had at most one or two women. Cockburn (1984) contends that women are essentially "on strike," simply refusing to take on the difficulties training in male-dominated technologies require.

8. The function of additional entry requirements is unclear. Educators emphasized that greater sophistication in the technology demanded more and more math usage. However, the higher entry requirements may more importantly serve to screen applicants rather than prepare them for the course. (See, for example, Hacker 1983.) As there are many levels of technicians and technical training, female workers in Scotland wondered the same thing. If true, this in effect discourages women who have little math interest or prior training.

9. Financial aid for tuition was available at all the schools but frequently requires students at the private suppliers to take on debt.

10. In Scotland there was an additional and particularly salient factor influencing female workers' reluctance to retrain. In the large multinational corporations that were the primary subject of the research, management had established higher than average wages and benefits packages. Women employees knew they were earning more than most women working not only in electronics but in any other "women's jobs" in the region. In addition, firms regularly had a lot of overtime work: workers were frequently working extra hours at time and a half and double time. Working overtime was an easier and more flexible way to improve one's income than retraining for a technical job. Also, the unpredictableness of overtime—and the expectation that workers would do it—made it difficult for workers to consider committing themselves to evening classes over a long period of time. It is not known how important these factors were in a woman's decision about retraining in the U.S.

11. In one of the firms four operatives were upgraded in the one year for which data was provided: in the other, only four technicians in the firm's work force had been upgraded within employment. One of the major employers in the region did not submit data on internal retraining.

12. While many of these opportunities required employees to devote their own time to training, managers expressed their willingness to give them company time for exams or special workday sessions.

13. While no manager indicated he would refuse to sponsor semiskilled workers in part-time upgrading programs, it seemed to be considered an extraordinary event—neither in the usual progression of things in management's view nor a common request by female workers.

14. Management made an exception to short-term personnel planning for engineers. They all recruited a certain number of engineer graduates annually. While the actual level of annual recruitment varied with company forecasts, managers considered engineers a significantly important ingredient in their future technical capability and profitability to hire new talent yearly.

15. This impression was corroborated by other surveys that found that managers expected production workers, particularly older workers, to be unable or resistant to

learning new procedures and unlearning old habits for new jobs (Rothwell and Davidson 1984).

16. The survey in Scotland's high tech industry revealed management preference for younger people in all occupations. Management implied and at times expressed this concern when hiring young women for semiskilled jobs. In some cases women applicants were asked if they were married, pregnant, or planning to start a family, as those questions are legal in the U.K. Also, in most cases, women had medical exams before being hired; the exams often included urine tests. The expectation that family responsibilities interfere in women's commitment to the job had become a major factor in hiring women as production workers because of management's concern to hire stable workers. It can only be expected that these same concerns were influential in managers' implicit and explicit decisions not to upgrade women workers to technicians.

17. The head of a well-respected electrical engineering department in a Scottish college said that his staff would discourage anyone over 25 from taking the course for a technician qualification. He claimed older students would have great difficulties getting a job.

18. In addition, in areas with a well-developed high tech industry like Silicon Valley, Route 128 outside Boston, and Silicon Glen in Scotland, employers can also recruit experienced technical employees from competitor firms and research institutes. Poaching, as it is called, has significant benefits and it was widely practiced in Scotland —in hiring engineers especially—despite managers' denials. Experienced technical staff join a firm with a proven track record in a specialization; that reduces the time necessary for in-company training. They also bring to the new employer important competitive information about their former employer. This, however, is an expensive recruitment strategy. It fuels the salary inflation that plagued the industry in the late 1970s and early 1980s. The growth and development of the industry in Scotland was at least in part the result of management strategy to mediate the rapidly escalating labour costs and turnover resulting from the growth of the industry labour market in Silicon Valley (Goldstein 1988).

19. The point here is that management wanted female production workers to remain production workers. Production yield (the proportion of output that is free of defects, so immediately salable) in semiconductors and computers critically affects cost-minimizing and profits. As indicated earlier, a stable production work force is a major contributor to high and improving yield. So managers placed great emphasis on keeping their female production workers content in their job and with the company. Managers in every survey firm in Scotland had attempted to improve the image of production workers and to enhance these jobs by offering their female production workers good pay (relative to other "women's jobs" in the region), merit-based pay increases, excellent benefit packages, and inclusion in company communications networks, and so on, to convince them of the importance of their jobs and performance. Providing a regular route out of these jobs into technician jobs would be expected to disrupt production and would contradict these efforts to keep female workers at their benches.

20. This discussion draws on what little published data on firm training policies exist and on what interviews with Massachusetts educators revealed. The difficulty in finding out private-sector training practices clearly impedes any attempt to discuss all "best practice" cases and to identify the incentives that supported their development.

21. Trainees on the course earn credits that can be applied, if they choose, toward

a degree program at a community college. The worker would only have to fulfill the nontechnical requirements to earn an associate's degree in electronics technology.

References

Appelbaum, Eileen; Peter Albin; and Ross Koppel. 1986. "International Competition in the Service Industries: Impacts of Technological Change and International Trade on U.S. Employment." A Report prepared for the Office of Technology Assessment, Washington, D.C.

Cockburn, Cynthia. 1983. *Brothers: Male Dominance and Technological Change*. London: Pluto Press.

———. 1984. "Women and Technology: 'Opportunity' Is Not Enough." Paper presented at the British Sociological Association Conference.

Commonwealth of Massachusetts. Division of Employment Security. 1987. "The High Technology Industry in Massachusetts." A report prepared for the Commonwealth of Massachusetts, Division of Employment Security, Boston.

Fraser, Bryna Shore. 1987. "New Office and Business Technologies: The Structure of Education and (Re)Training Opportunities." In Heidi I. Hartmann, ed. *Computer Chips and Paper Clips: Technology and Women's Employment*, vol. 2. Washington, D.C.: National Academy Press.

Goldstein, Nance. 1988. "Women's Employment in Silicon Glen." In Diane Elson and Ruth Pearson, eds., *Women's Employment and Multinationals in Europe*. London: Macmillan.

Governor's Commission on the Future of Mature Industries. 1984. *Final Report*. Boston: Commonwealth of Massachusetts.

Green, Susan. 1983. "Silicon Valley's Women Workers: A Theoretical Analysis of Sex Segregation in the Electronics Industry Labor Market." In June Nash and Maria P. Fernandez-Kelly, eds., *Women, Men and the International Division of Labor*. New York: SUNY Press.

Hacker, Sally. 1983. "Mathematization of Engineering: Limits on Women and the Field." In Joan Rothschild, ed., *Machine* ex Dea: *Feminist Perspectives on Technology*. New York: Pergamon Press.

Hacker, Sally, and Charles Starnes. 1986. "Computers in the Workplace: Stratification and Labor Process Among Engineers and Technicians." Typescript.

High Tech Research Group. 1986. *Whatever Happened to Job Security? Layoffs in the 1985 Massachusetts High Tech Industry*. Boston: HTRG.

Hirschhorn, Larry. 1984. *Beyond Mechanization: Work and Technology in a Post-Industrial Age*. Cambridge, Mass.: MIT Press.

Kanter, Rosabeth. 1977. *Men and Women of the Corporation*. New York: Basic Books.

Keller, John. 1981. "The Production Workers in Electronics-Industrialization and Labor Development in California's Santa Clara Valley." Ph.D. Diss., University of Michigan.

McCulloch, Rosalyn; Carol Wolkowitz; and Kate Young, eds. 1984. *Of Marriage and the Market*. London: OSE Books.

Markusen, Ann. 1986. *Oligopoly and Regional Development*. Cambridge, Mass.: MIT Press.

Noyelle, Thierry. 1985. "The New Technology and the New Economy: Some Implications for Equal Employment Opportunity." Report prepared for the National Research Council Panel on Technology and Women's Employment, Washington, D.C.

O'Connor, David. 1985. "Global Trends in Electronics: Implications for Developing Countries." Report prepared for the World Bank, Washington, D.C., September.

Rothwell, Sheila, and David Davidson. 1984. "Technological Change, Company and Personnel Policies and Skill Development." Manpower Services Commission, London, June.

Russell, J. 1984. "If You Don't Buy in Asia, Wait a Minute." *Purchasing Magazine*, November.

Ryan, Paul. 1984. "Job Training, Employment Practices and the Large Enterprise: The Case of Costly Transferable Skills." In Paul Osterman, ed., *Internal Labor Markets*. Cambridge, Mass.: MIT Press.

Saxenian, Annalee. 1981. "Outgrowing the Valley." Working Papers 8, no. 5, September.

————. 1985. "In Search of Power: The Organization of Business Interests in Silicon Valley and Route 128." Typescript, May.

Siegel, Lenny. 1980. "Delicate Bonds: The Global Semiconductor Industry." *Pacific Research* 11, no. 1.

Stern, David. 1985. "Education for Employment in California—1985 to 2010." Typescript. University of California at Berkeley, School of Education, January.

Strober, Myra, and Carolyn Arnold. 1984. "Integrated Circuits/Segregated Labor: Women in Three Computer-related Occupations." Stanford, Calif.: Institute for Research on Educational Finance and Governance, Stanford University, November.

U.S. Bureau of Labor Statistics. 1986. Occupational Projections and Training Data. Bulletin no. 2251, April.

U.S. Office of Technology Assessment. 1984. *Computerized Manufacturing Automation: Employment. Education and the Workplace*. Washington, D.C.: Office of Technology Assessment.

————. 1986. *Plant Closing: Advance Notice and Rapid Response—Special Report*. Washington, D.C.: Office of Technology Assessment.

Wickham, Ann. 1983. "The State and Training Programmes for Women." In Liz Whitelegg, ed., *The Changing Experience of Women: An Open University Reader*. London: Martin Robertson.

Zemsky, Robert, and Martin Meyerson. 1985. "Training Practices: Education and Training Within the American Firm." Report by the Higher Education Finance Research Institute, University of Pennsylvania, Philadelphia.

20/New Directions for Employment Policy

Paul Osterman

Interest in employment and training policy has been uneven. Although very much at the forefront of the War on Poverty, these efforts were discredited (many would argue unfairly) by the disrepute of the Public Service Employment component of the Comprehensive Employment and Training Act (CETA) and have been substantially reduced by the budget cuts of recent years. However, for at least three reasons the topic is pushing its way back onto the national agenda.

Macroeconomic turbulence, the trade deficit, and technological change have combined to generate growing numbers of so-called dislocated workers. These are typically skilled workers who are laid-off and unable to find comparable or nearly comparable employment. The numbers of such individuals are substantial (more will be said on this below) and they are better connected politically than the typical poverty-level client of the training system.

Training is also increasingly seen as an element of industrial policy. A labor force with broad skills is thought to be better adapted to taking advantage of the potential of new flexible computer-based technologies. This is true on the factory floor and in the office. Given that the American labor force will never be competitive in wage terms, the emphasis on skill and technology seems persuasive.

Finally, the perennial issue of welfare reform is increasingly focused on job training for eligible recipients. The wide acclaim given to the Massachusetts Employment and Training Program (ET) has partially defused the traditional coercive "workfare" connotation of such efforts and a number of other states are engaged in or considering similar efforts, and recent Federal legislation mandates these programs.

Despite all these signs pointing toward new importance and resources for an employment and training system, there is good reason to fear that little of substance will be accomplished. The evaluative evidence lends slight basis

510

for optimism about the effectiveness of training programs. Many would argue that this is because the system itself is confused and fragmented, torn between serving the broader labor market and serving the most disadvantaged at the bottom. Our contention is that the problem is deeper: we lack a good way of thinking about how employment and training policy fits into the labor market, and hence programs tend to be marginalized and irrelevant.

The plan of this chapter is as follows: we will first examine the evidence concerning the need for an employment policy. This evidence will be drawn from survey data on the economic well-being of individuals. We will then briefly review the evidence on the poor performance of employment and training programs in the past. We will then turn to an analysis of the difficulties facing firms as they seek to organize work in internal labor markets. From this material we will develop a case for the potential role of employment and training in the economy. With that case in hand we will then sketch out the nature of possible program interventions and discuss the realism of such suggestions.

The Case for an Employment Policy

Why should we be concerned about employment policy? To answer this we examine information on two concerns: low income and worker dislocation.

In thinking about low earnings it is important to distinguish between transitory difficulties and persistent inadequate earnings. Most people whose earnings dip below a cutoff are experiencing transitory problems, and to the extent that public policy should intervene, the appropriate vehicle is the transfer system not training. However, people who year after year fall into the lowest earnings categories clearly require more substantial intervention. In order to make these distinctions and to estimate the prevalence of persistent low earnings in the labor market we employ a longitudinal data set that tracks the same individuals over 11 years. We are interested in the number of years in which an individual's annual earnings fell below 50 percent of the median annual earnings of full-time workers. The age range of the sample precludes retirement as an issue and we also eliminate those who report serious medical disabilities. The data are presented in Table 20-1.

The first column shows the number of years in which men in the survey fell below the cutoff. If we classify those with three or more years below the cutoff as troubled, then 13.6 percent of the sample are of concern; if the criteria is five years of problems, then the group falls to 8.3 percent. Even 8.3 percent represents a very substantial number of people: if we apply this percentage to 1980 labor force data we are talking about 3.9 million men who are labor market participants between the ages of 25 and 63 and who have had five or more years of persistent low earnings.

Estimating the number of women who fall below a similar standard is

Table 20-1/Number of Years Individuals Fell Below the Earnings Cutoff, 1971–1981

FREQUENCY BELOW CUTOFF (YEARS)	MEN (%)	WOMEN			
		Heads		*Wives*	
		MALE STANDARD (%)	FEMALE STANDARD (%)	MALE STANDARD (%)	FEMALE STANDARD (%)
0	70.3	25.4	41.4	21.9	30.9
1	9.0	13.7	12.6	9.6	13.6
2	7.2	4.4	8.4	7.1	10.2
3	1.6	4.2	3.7	5.6	9.4
4	3.7	5.3	6.9	7.8	7.3
5	2.0	4.4	7.0	6.6	5.9
6	1.1	6.6	6.0	7.5	4.9
7	1.1	2.8	5.2	5.6	4.4
8	0.9	6.6	3.8	5.5	4.5
9	1.5	7.0	2.8	5.9	3.5
10	0.7	7.0	1.1	7.3	3.3
11	0	0	9.4	0	2.1
N	1,582	162	162	1,061	1,061

Source: Osterman 1988. Table is drawn from data on computer tapes from the Institute for Social Research, University of Michigan, Panel Survey on Income Dynamics.

Note: The sample is limited to individuals between the ages of 25 and 53 in 1971 who had no long-term disabilities and who had never retired. An individual falls below the cutoff only if he/she had positive earnings in the given year. The median earnings data for the period 1971–81 are taken from annual reports in the *Monthly Labor Review* for the period up until 1978 and from *Employment and Earnings* for 1979–1981. The data in fact refer to median weekly earnings of full-time workers, and we have calculated the annual figure by multiplying by 52. The data from which we calculate the distribution of people who fall below the cutoff is the Michigan Panel Survey on Income Dynamics. The earnings figure with which we work includes all labor income, not simply wages and salaries.

more difficult. Defining the cutoff itself is problematic because of the intermittent participation rates of women in the labor force. With respect to the cutoff the question is whether to use the male earnings standard or a comparable figure for full-time women. The argument in favor of the male standard is that to do otherwise is to legitimate the male/female earnings gap. Set against this is the special topic of interest to us here; we are less concerned with the general question of sex discrimination—a problem faced by all women—than with identifying the size of the group who face particular problems. This calculation would be confused by conflating the problem of sex discrimination with the special needs of a particular group.

Even using the female standard does not resolve all ambiguities. Many women choose not to work full time, yet the earnings standard we are employ-

Table 20-2/Employment Status in January 1984 of Job Losers by When Lost Job and Age

	Lost Job 1983–1984			Lost Job 1979–1982		
	Age 20–25	*Age 26–55*	*Age 56+*	*Age 20–25*	*Age 26–55*	*Age 56+*
MEN						
Working[a]	49.3%	50.2%	23.5%	75.9%	75.2%	43.1%
Unemployed	43.8	44.3	58.5	18.4	18.9	23.4
Out of Labor Force	6.7	5.4	17.9	5.6	5.7	33.3
WOMEN						
Working[a]	46.4	44.0	24.8	60.8	63.5	38.3
Unemployed	37.4	38.6	50.5	13.9	14.5	11.5
Out of Labor Force	16.1	17.3	24.5	25.1	21.9	50.0

Source: Osterman 1988. Table is drawn from data on computer tapes from the U.S. Dept. of Commerce, Bureau of the Census, Current Population Survey, January 1984.

[a] Working refers to those who lost a job between 1979 and January 1984 and were working as of the January 1984 date of the CPS Survey.

ing is based on full-time work. We deal partially with this by only counting toward the total figure those years in which people actually have positive earnings.

If we use the more conservative standard of requiring five or more years of low income to classify a person as troubled, then 26.9 percent of female household heads and 28.6 percent of wives fall beneath our standard (see Table 20-1). These estimates are still inflated because within each group are some individuals who choose not to work full time, and hence their incomes fall below the cutoff as a result of choice. Nonetheless, taken together with the results for males, we have clear evidence that persistent low earnings is a problem for a substantial number of people.

The Impact of Unemployment

The second issue of interest in considering the case for employment policy is unemployment. The level of unemployment in the economy is a macroeconomic issue, but we want to ask about the consequences of unemployment for those who experience it. How well does the labor market reabsorb job losers?

The best source for addressing these questions is a 1984 Census survey in which data were collected from a sample of individuals who reported that they had lost their job because of plant closings or layoffs sometime in the five years preceeding the survey. In Table 20-2 we examine the employment status of job losers after controlling for the most important of the conditioning variables.

Table 20-3/Relation Between Current Earnings and Earnings on Lost Job, by Percentage

	MEN, BY AGE			WOMEN, BY AGE		
	20–25	*26–55*	*56+*	*20–25*	*26–55*	*56+*
Lost more than 25%	29.4	33.4	34.4	26.9	30.8	54.3
Lost 10–24%	10.0	13.5	17.5	18.5	14.5	13.6
Remained 10% plus or minus	24.4	24.3	29.3	20.5	20.6	12.9
Gained more than 10%	36.0	28.7	18.6	34.0	34.0	18.9

Source: Osterman 1988. Table is drawn from data on computer tapes from U.S. Dept. of Commerce, Bureau of the Census, Current Population Survey, January 1984.
Note: Sample is limited to individuals who experienced layoffs at some point between 1979 and 1984 and who were re-employed at the time of the January 1984 interview. Earnings for current and lost jobs are in constant dollars and are weekly earnings.

This table tells a striking story. A remarkably large percentage of people who lose their job fail to find new ones. For those who lost their job over a year ago the unemployment rate for prime age (26–55) women was 20.0 percent (the rate is calculated by dividing the number unemployed by the sum of the unemployed and employed), and the rate for comparable men was 19.9 percent. As a comparison for people in the same survey who had not been laid off, the unemployment rate for women was 4.7 percent and for men 3.3 percent. In addition, the unemployment rate understates the problem, since many of those out of the labor force are people who became discouraged and stopped looking. Finally, a more recent survey whose preliminary results were just released shows a similar pattern.[1]

The Situation of Job-Finders
It is apparent that large numbers of people are simply unable to become reemployed over a reasonable period. Now, what about those who did find work? How do their new jobs compare with those which they left?

In Table 20-3 we examine the situation of those who *found* jobs, and we classify this sample into four groups: those whose wages (after adjusting for inflation) in the current job are 25 percent or more less than in the job they had lost; those whose wages in the current job are between 10 percent and 25 percent less than the earlier job; those whose current wages are plus or minus 10 percent of the earlier wages; and those wages are 10 percent or more above the old job.

It is apparent that the impact of layoffs varies considerably. The losers (the two loss categories taken together) outweigh the winners: for the sample as a whole, 45 percent of the men and 47 percent of the women are losers, compared with 30 and 33 percent, respectively, as winners. At the same time, for both sexes we cannot overlook the 30 percent of the sample whose earnings in the new job were higher than in the old one. The conclusion, then, has to be that on balance a layoff is costly even for those who do find work but that a nontrivial minority gain.

There are at least two grounds on which the foregoing may be criticized. First, it is possible that even had the individuals remained in their jobs they would have experienced earnings losses. This might be true if there is a tendency for those who are about to be laid off to be working in declining industries or weak firms. Second, the earnings losses may be due to unobservable characteristics of the individuals involved. They may, for example, be poor workers and their next employer learned this and reduced their wage. More sophisticated statistical procedures that control for these concerns leave the findings unchanged.[2]

Finally, there is the more difficult challenge, which is that it is not unexpected that in a dynamic economy some wage loss accompany structural change. If individuals' wages never adjusted downward, our labor market would be rigid and inefficient. The problem here is that there is no simple standard against which one can judge how much wage loss is appropriate or inappropriate (unless one assumes that whatever the market generates is by definition appropriate). The best reply is that one would hope that most of the burden of adjusting to shifting demand patterns would be born by new entrants, not by experienced workers who have already made substantial investments in skills and communities. Further, to the extent that these experienced workers are required to accept reduced earnings, the fall should not be so great as to disrupt established life-styles. If the drop is great the pain to the individual and his or her family may be substantial. This distributional cost alone justifies policy, but as we will see, there are social efficiency costs if the consequence of job loss is too high. These arise as fellow workers, observing the consequences of change, more fiercely dig their heels in to protect their jobs and in doing so limit the possibilities of innovation on the shop floor and in the office.

If one asks about the future, then a strong case can be made that problems of adjustment will become more, not less, serious. The labor force is becoming older as the large baby-boom cohort moves into middle age. Middle-aged workers are substantially less mobile than younger people,[3] and hence even a constant degree of turbulence in the macro environment may elicit heightened adjustment problems. These problems will not only impinge upon the affected individuals but will also play themselves out politically and in the workplace as job security becomes an increasingly salient issue.

The evidence of adjustment problems, the prospect of future difficulties, and the earlier material on low earnings, all direct our attention to the capabilities of the employment and training systems for dealing with these problems.

The Past Performance of Employment Policy

It is possible to identify three categories of American employment policy. These are remedial or ameliorative programs, the labor market exchange, and skills training for the masses. We will describe each of these in turn and provide a summary of what the social science evaluation literature has to say about their effectiveness.

The Remedial System

A significant, and in the minds of many observers major, element of American employment policy are those programs aimed at helping people at the bottom of the labor queue. These programs are typically income targeted and the "clients," must be "economically disadvantaged," that is, have family income below some specified level.[4] The programs offer a range of services such as remedial education, classroom-based skills training, assistance in job search skills, and so on. In addition, programs may have tools for providing incentives (subsidies) to private firms to hire program participants. The modern history of these programs began with the Manpower Development Training Act in 1961. They expanded during the War on Poverty and CETA and contracted during the Job Training Partnership Act (JTPA). Throughout this period there have been various improvements (for example, considerable effort went into upgrading the quality of summer placements for youth) and changes (such as JTPA prohibits stipends for trainees), but in the main the programs and many of the service deliverers have remained surprisingly constant. Perhaps the biggest change has been in the direction of increasingly sophisticated evaluation.

How well have these programs worked? After nearly three decades what can we say about their effectiveness? In answering this question we should be very clear about what the goals of the programs are: they are aimed at raising the earned income of the participants. Although other objectives—such as reduced crime—are often proclaimed, increased earnings has always been the single most important objective against which success is measured.

Before reporting results, it is worth noting that a troublesome issue is whether the programs included in the evaluation are representative of the best programs in the field. In fact they almost certainly are not. At one extreme, many of the demonstrations suffered from start-up problems and implementation difficulties. At the other extreme, evaluations based on national samples included many mediocre efforts along with good programs and hence are not generalizable to what the best might accomplish. These caveats are necessary and support the claim of many hardworking field staff that their programs accomplish more than might be suggested by the evaluation research. Nonetheless, the policy question is what might be expected from a national effort,

an effort that must include good as well as bad programs and poorly implemented efforts as well as effective execution. Policy must be based on average
effects and for this purpose the evaluation literature is useful.

Although the results of all evaluations are not identical, when they are
taken as a whole, a clear message does come through. Employment and training programs raise annual earned income by somewhere between $500 and
$1,500 a year.[5] This gain (given typical program costs) is large enough to
justify the programs on a cost-benefit basis and, for someone whose annual
income might be at the poverty line, the extra funds are important. However, I
would argue, these results suggest strongly that the programs are not a success
and, in fact, fail to achieve their central goal. A person entering a program
most likely has experienced a sporadic work history and employment in a low-
wage and dead-end job. Program participation (on average)[6] does not change
these facts. The modest earnings gains are generally due to longer hours, not
higher wages, and in any case do not suggest that in any fundamental way the
person's life circumstances have changed. The participants in these programs
remain at the bottom of the income distribution and there is no evidence that
they have been placed upon a new trajectory with respect to lifetime earnings.
There is also evidence that in the past these programs have tracked women,
for example, by placing them disproportionately into classroom training versus
direct job placements (Harlan, Chapter 2).

The discussion has focused on training programs, but a similar conclusion
emerges concerning the various subsidies that have been offered firms to
induce them to hire the disadvantaged. Evaluations of the Targeted Job Tax
Credit provide no evidence that the hiring of groups intended to benefit was
increased by the subsidy, and similar conclusions flow from evaluations of
other, smaller scale, subsidy efforts.

Seen in this light, employment and training programs, we must conclude,
are marginal to the operation of the labor market. Whatever process generates the low earnings of the system's clients is only glancingly affected by the
existence of the programs. The system is also marginal in other ways. The
changing federal legislation has so frequently shifted the respective roles of
federal, state, and city governments that consistent governance has been difficult. However, it is at the point of program delivery that the true nature of the
programs are apparent. Regardless of the particular federal legislation in place
and regardless of the overall administrative structure, the actual service deliverers have always been a collection of community action groups and social
service agencies, national community-based organizations, and city agencies.
The chief characteristic of many of these "program operators" has been their
instability and lack of a consistent internal structure. In sharp contrast to the
most analogous institution—the school system—these agencies come into and
go out of existence, there are no accepted certification or training requirements

for staff, curriculum varies over space and time and changes without warning, and career lines for staff are virtually nonexistent (Osterman 1981, 434–46). The system is a haphazard collection of agencies of widely differing quality —some good but others very poor—but the deeper point is that there is no expectation (except by hardworking staff) that it be different. In effect the unevenness is designed into the structure.

Equally indicative of its marginal character, and more damning of the possibility of success, is the tenuous relation of the employment and training system to the private economy. American business takes training seriously and expends considerable resources to accomplish it. Given this one might expect that firms would eagerly turn to a public system that was prepared to under-write some of the costs. Yet this has not proved to be true. Employment and training programs have found it very difficult to involve companies and have not found firms to be an eager customer for the trainees. As an example, in a recent survey of firms concerning training programs, the Bureau of National Affairs found that only 9 percent had any involvement at all with JTPA (Bureau of National Affairs 1986, 22). When companies do make contact with these programs there is usually the aura of public service and charity. These are perfectly legitimate motives but do not suggest that the business community expects the employment and training system to be of significant assistance in meeting human resource needs.

The Labor Exchange

It would seem logical, and indeed Beveridge suggested almost a century ago, that the employment exchange be at the center of a well-designed employment and training system. At once in touch with both firms and workers, with information available for advice, and with the power of referral to jobs or training, the employment exchange could manage the flow of people through the labor market.

Despite this promise, the United States Employment Service (ES) has long been regarded as unable to fill any but menial jobs. With impressive consistency employers complain that the Service fails to screen workers and, whenever they list a vacancy, sends them large numbers of unqualified applicants. For their part, job applicants claim that good jobs are rarely listed with the Service and when listed are not filled with Service referrals.[7] A recent study which examined the benefits of ES referral found that for men there was no statistically significant difference between treatment and controls in earnings in the six-month follow-up period for the two groups, while for women the results were much like those discussed earlier for training programs: the payoff was statistically significant but only on the order of $300 for six months (or $600 difference in annual earnings) (Johnson, Dickinson, and West 1985, 117–35).

Much as was true for training programs, there is no reason in principle why the public employment exchange should fail. Just as firms conduct their own training so they also employ private employment exchanges to recruit, screen, and refer applicants. Companies pay a fee for this service, and on first glance, a public subsidy should be welcome. Some observers of the United States Employment Service explain its failure by pointing to the burden placed on the system by other administrative tasks that have been delegated to it, but, as the data provided by Lester (see n. 7) suggest, the ES has been ineffective for many decades. Instead, we must conclude that the ES suffers from the same fundamental ills that plague the training system: the system was not conceived and designed to provide genuine service to the private economy. Instead it has been largely tied to the transfer system. For many years it was a mechanism to enforce the job search requirement for the receipt of unemployment insurance benefits: recipients had to satisfy officers of the ES that they were looking for work and in practice that meant ritualistically calling ES referrals. This gave the system its basic character from which it has not recovered and in recent years it has also been used to enforce work requirements for receipt of welfare payments.

Skill Training for the Masses
Most adults who receive subsidized vocational training and placement do so through different systems than those described above. They use vocational education programs at the high school level and community colleges at the postsecondary level. To give a sense of magnitudes, at the high point of the CETA system 3.6 million adults a year were served compared to 5.5 million youth who received occupational training in high school and 4 million youth and adults who attended two-year colleges (National Commission on Employment Policy 1981). With the decline of the CETA/JTPA system the balance has shifted even more in favor of vocational education and community colleges.

Vocational education has certainly proven itself a large, stable, and durable system with a clear administrative structure and reliable funding. Along these dimensions it stands in sharp contrast to the federal training system described above, yet surprising as this may be, the results are no different. Although the situation is perhaps better than in 1964 when 85 percent of students in vocational education courses studied agriculture or home economics (Ruttenberg 1970, 17), recent evaluations leave little room for optimism (National Research Council 1984). The clear message from this literature is that youth who attend vocational programs earn no more—after controlling for differences between these students and others—than those who do not, and even more surprising, there is no relation between the occupations students prepare for and what they eventually do. That is, a student who studies machining has a no higher probability of working as a machinist after graduation than does another student in a general education track in the same high school.

The case of community colleges is a bit more complicated.[8] These institutions, which offer two-year degree programs after high school, have experienced explosive growth in the past two decades and their character has changed considerably. Between 1960 and 1980 enrollment grew from 650,000 to 4 million. To put matters even more sharply, whereas in 1960 they accounted for 16 percent of all higher education enrollments, by 1983 that figure had risen to 38 percent, and more startlingly, they claimed 54 percent of all freshmen first time higher education enrollments. (Pincus 1985, 2). Along with this growth came a substantial change in the mission of the community colleges: they shifted from institutions intended to help students transfer to four-year colleges to essentially vocational training centers. While in 1965, 13 percent of all community college enrollment was in vocational programs in 1984 the figure was 66 percent (Pincus 1985, 2).

Given the growing importance of these institutions and the reasonable expections of success, the amount and nature of the evaluation evidence is frustrating. There have been few evaluations and those that do exist tend to be focused upon the wrong question for our purposes (that is, rather than asking whether attendence in community colleges pays off relative to entering the job market, they instead ask how the benefits of a community college degree compare to that of a college degree). In addition it seems reasonable to think of community colleges as containing two broad tracks: highly specific vocational programs and more general degree programs. Evaluations should, but do not, distinguish between these.

The best evaluation we know of, by Wellford Wilms and Stephen Hansell (1982, 43–60), followed a sample of entering students in six occupational fields in four cities. They found that for the three fields that they termed "high level" (accounting, computer programming, and electronic technician) there was no relation between years of attendance or graduation, and the field of subsequent job or after-graduation earnings. For low-level occupations (secretary, dental assistant, and cosmetologist) a substantial fraction of the students did find work in their field of training and the earnings of graduates exceeded those of dropouts. Hence, the results of this study are ambiguous and there is no explanation of why the results differed across occupations. In addition the study suffers from failing to compare enrollees to a control group of nonenrollees. The reasonable conclusion from this study is that the impact is highly variable and uncertain but this is a conclusion which we can only tentatively hold. Therefore, our bottom line on community colleges has to be agnostic and it is not even clear what our prior beliefs suggest. On the one hand, the large and growing enrollments suggest that there should be some payoff. On the other hand, the consistent failure of other vocational training programs is cause for skepticism.

Some Cross-Cutting Themes

With these results in hand, what are some conclusions we might draw about the nature of the American employment and training system? One observation that immediately comes to mind is that the term "system" is hardly descriptive if by that we mean a set of elements that fit together in a rational way. To begin with, none of the three major components we have identified—training for the disadvantaged, training for the masses, or the employment exchange—has a consistent or regular relation with any other. Their reporting responsibilities at the federal level are different, and at the state and local level there is in general little effective coordination. This confusion has been noted by observers for 30 years and seems impervious to reform.

The fact that poor people constitute the overwhelming majority of participants in federal training programs and are a small percentage of participants in vocational education and community college programs points to another characteristic of the federal system: its uncertain identity as between being an element of labor market policy or a part of the larger transfer (welfare) system. On its face, the system is a labor market program aimed at providing skills and finding jobs for its clients. Yet we have seen that the private economy hardly takes it seriously. Set against this is the fact that the system has consistently been used as an adjunct of the welfare system. In part this occurred when stipends for training were sufficiently attractive that people enrolled in training simply to receive the cash. Under these circumstances the training programs were literally welfare and transfer programs. (This is not to say that the majority of enrollees signed up for this reason but that the problem was sufficiently widespread so that the character of the programs were affected. In fact, the inability to pay stipends is unfortunate since it limits the length of training programs and tends to eliminate those most in need.) Although this is no longer possible for adults, it continues, in effect, in the summer youth jobs program, which is largely a transfer and hot weather "fire insurance" effort.

The connection of employment and training to the welfare system extends beyond direct transfer. With growing public concern about the legitimacy of welfare, participation in training is often made a requirement for the receipt of transfer payments. This trend began with the WIN (Work Incentive) Program and continues under that rubric today and in various workfare programs and training programs for welfare recipients passed or under consideration at the state level and in the new federal legislation. Commendable as this may be from the perspective of the welfare system, and even in terms of the mission of many job training programs (which after all are intended to help people escape poverty), this effort, and the many others like it across the country, reinforce the view that job training and welfare are parts of the same overall system for dealing with a particular segment of the population. Under these circumstances it is hard to argue with the view that training is really an element of the welfare system, and as such, we should not be suprised that the employer community views the system with suspicion. Just how serious that suspicion is was demonstrated by a recent experiment in which two randomly selected groups were sent to look for work. The first group identified themselves as clients of the employment and training system and offered employers a voucher good for partial subsidy of their wage. The second group made no such representation and carried with them no subsidy. The groups were alike in all other respects, and remarkably, the hiring rate of the second group was substantially above the first. The connection with the employment and training system was so negative that it outweighed a wage subsidy (Burtless 1985, 105–14).

We are forced to conclude that the employment and training system taken as a whole is disorganized, stratified, and confused about its mission. Nonetheless, it is difficult to blame the poor results on these characteristics. The pattern of failure is so consistent across the different elements of the system, each element having a different structure and a different history, that it is hard to believe that purely administrative considerations can explain the problem. If the federal training system has a constantly shifting delivery system and uncertain funding base, the same cannot be said of vocational education. If a system aimed at serving only poor people might be expected to fail, why should the failure extend to vocational schools? Why cannot the employment service provide the "simple" service of matching job searchers with vacancies? The answers to these questions must take us beyond organization charts and raise the question of the relation between these programs and the private economy. In the end, it is the hiring and promotion practices of firms that determine labor market outcomes. To understand how employment policy might work we need to learn what are the issues facing companies as they plan their human resource strategies.

Employment Policy from the Perspective of Firms

If employment policy has been ineffective in the past, one important reason is that it has been divorced from the human resource considerations of firms. We have seen that few firms rely on the public training or placement system as a source of recruits and that the system in fact tends to stigmatize its clients and render them less rather than more desirable. All of this raises the question of how a public employment policy might become better integrated into the interests of the private sector. Our argument is that by understanding some of the emerging tensions in the evolution of firms' human resource policies it may be possible to identify an opening for public employment policy. To accomplish this we need to see how internal labor markets are evolving within companies.

The discussion that follows emphasizes issues facing primary labor market firms. The reason is that we hope to find ways to link employment policy to the perceived human resource issues in these firms and hence to develop new ways of opening up employment in those firms to groups that in the past have been confined to secondary labor market employment.

Firms and Internal Labor Markets

The internal labor market strategies of firms—their so-called "human resource management"—are in flux. This can be seen from the frequent reports of "soft" experiments, such as team production, shop floor participative decision-making, and quality of work life efforts, and "hard" experiments such as aggressive concession bargaining to change work rules. To understand these tensions and how management perceives the problems it faces we conducted a large number of interviews with firms in a wide range of industries.[9] It is apparent from these interviews that firms perceive several alternative ways of organizing work, that is, several different internal labor market models. Each of these has its own strengths and weaknesses according to the objectives and constraints of firms. Although it is not clear which pattern will prevail, there are good reasons to believe that one model (which we term the "salaried" model) is perhaps the most desirable along several dimensions and that a substantial element of the employer community recognizes this. However, it is difficult to get "from here to there" because of a set of actual and perceived costs and uncertainties. High on this list are issues of employment security. It is here that the possibility of public employment policy emerges. Such a policy might be "useful" to firms by facilitating the transition between internal labor market models while at the same time accomplishing other public purposes.

The two broad alternative ways of organizing work in internal labor markets we term the *industrial* and the *salaried* models. Each of these comprise a set of rules (concerning wages, promotion, training, internal deployment, and job security) that fit together in a logical way and form a coherent system.[10]

The industrial model of organizing blue-collar work, which had its origins in the ideas of scientific management and industrial engineering, became the norm because of the unionization drives of the Great Depression and was solidified in the era of postwar prosperity. Work is organized into a series of tightly defined jobs with clear work rules and responsibilities attached to each classification. Wages are attached to jobs and hence an individual's wage is determined by his or her classification. Management's freedom to move individuals from one job to another can vary from situation to situation, but the typical case is that both promotions and lateral shifts are limited by seniority provisions and by requirements that workers agree to the shift. Finally, there is no formal job security and it is understood that management is free to vary the size of the labor force as it wishes. However, when layoffs do occur they are generally organized according to reverse seniority. Although this model became the dominant institutional form as unions grew, it should not be construed as limited to unionized situations. Because of fear of unions, government pressures for uniformity, and employer imitation, the model spread throughout the economy.

The salaried model combines a more flexible and personalistic set of administrative procedures with greater commitment to employment security. Although individuals have job descriptions, much as industrial employees have work rules, these descriptions are not intended to have legal or customary force. They are subject to revision by superiors, and the employees are prepared to take on new activities as demanded. By the same token, the clearly defined job ladders and promotion sequences that characterize industrial settings are absent here. There is a considerably greater scope for merit considerations in pay setting, and the wages of two individuals in the same job can vary considerably.

The salaried model clearly characterizes much white-collar work. The career patterns of most managers and many professionals who work in bureaucracies are accurately captured by the model. However, the salaried model is not simply another way of describing white-collar work. There have also always been a few American firms that have stood outside the mainstream industrial model for their blue-collar workers. These firms are viewed as pointing to alternative directions for blue-collar employment.

In the industrial model, rigid job classifications and reliance on non-personalistic procedures "buy" worker acquiescence by limiting employers' freedom to determine who can be laid off and by placing some numerical constraints through limitations on combining or redesigning jobs. In the salaried model, employment security is the central element of the system. Once individuals pass a probationary period they can expect either lifetime employment with the firm or that the firm will make extensive efforts to avoid layoffs. This role that employment security plays in the two models is very important to our argument. Workers are aware of the difficulties, described above, of finding comparable new employment after layoffs. Hence they will not readily forego the protections of the industrial model and provide the flexibility and commitment of the salaried model without some level of assurances. At the same time, providing assurances is costly and risky and this makes it difficult for firms to easily move to a salaried model.

The salaried and industrial models each entail distinctive costs and benefits. The industrial model often implies considerable rigidity in wage structure and managers' freedom to assign labor as they wish. However, it provides firms with flexibility in adjusting employment levels through layoffs. On the other hand, the salaried model with its attention to employment security restricts the flexibility of the firm concerning employment numbers. However, in return the firm gains a measure of internal flexibility and commitment that may be lacking in the rival system.

Much of uncertainty of the current period reflects changes in the relative costs and benefits, as perceived by firms, of the industrial and salaried models. Indeed much of the recent widespread innovations in human resource practices can be interpreted as efforts to move from one model to another.

The industrial model is under extreme pressure from several sources. The greatest source of tension flows from the nature of new technologies. First, computer-based technology leads to pressures for altering traditional job classifications to encompass new, and frequently broader, ranges of tasks. This implies a one-time change in what has frequently become an unwieldy system of organizing work. However, the pressures are deeper than this. Increasingly, firms are adopting computer-based technologies that both upgrade skills (blurring the difference between blue- and white-collar labor as both increasingly work with computers) and permit firms to shift between products and designs. These technologies imply that job duties will continue to shift as the flexibility inherent in the technologies interacts with volatility in product markets. This implies that job classifications should *remain* loose and subject to change, and it is this thrust that is most inconsistent with the premises of the industrial model. Additional pressures flow from the perception that the industrial model cannot deliver the level of worker commitment and product quality that the salaried model can provide.

Employers face tension from a different source for white-collar work. These jobs are already organized along the lines of the salaried model. However, the model is somewhat endangered as competitive pressures and the nature of new technologies lead to white-collar employment reductions and hence call the job security aspect of that model into doubt. In recent years many firms have announced large reductions in management layers and more seem to be in store.[11] If these reductions are too severe, employers may lose the commitment of their white-collar employees and other consequences, such as union organization, may follow.

Employers therefore feel in a bind. For blue-collar work many want to shift to a salaried model. However, macroeconomic uncertainty and unwillingness to permit labor to become too great a fixed cost leads them to fear that employment security is too high a price to pay. For white-collar employment they want to maintain the salaried model but at lower employment levels. However, it is not clear how to reduce employment without undermining the premises of the model. The central question, then, is: What are the alternative resolutions of these dilemmas? It is uncertain how events will play out, and this uncertainty explains the co-existence of very different tendencies in human resources, ranging from employer aggression and concession bargaining, on the one hand, to participatory systems on the other hand.

For firms that do want to move in the direction of the salaried model for blue- and white-collar workers, one possible solution is to offer employment security (or a commitment to make every effort to avoid layoffs) to a core of more or less permanent employees and surround that core with a "periphery" of temporary, contract, and part-time workers who enjoy less protection. The workers in the "core" will be willing to work under the salaried model and to provide both flexibility and commitment to the firm. The peripheral labor force provides the firm with a buffer against either macroeconomic—cyclical —downturns or labor force reductions necessitated by technical change. In a sense this "core-periphery" model is a strategy for having it both ways. It enables firms to achieve substantial internal flexibility with a highly trained and committed labor force while at the same time maintaining the ability to adjust employment levels at will.

Given these advantages one would expect the "core-periphery model" to expand and it has. There has been a very substantial growth in temporary help firms, in subcontracting arrangements, and in two-tier arrangements in which part of a firm's labor force is granted employment security while the remainder is not.[12] Nonetheless, there are also good reasons to believe that there are limitations to this arrangement that restrict its ability to resolve the dilemma we have posed. Youth and women have been the traditional source of peripheral workers, but because of the declining size of the youth cohort and the increasing interest of women in full time, labor force commitment, the size of the labor force available for peripheral work will not increase substantially in the coming years. Furthermore, there are limitations to the fraction of work that firms are willing to trust to a noncommitted work force. For these reasons the core-periphery model, while attractive to firms and destined to grow, has significant limitations. In addition, from a social perspective, serious consideration must be given to the implications of a greatly expanded "have-not" labor force.

An alternative resolution, pursued by some firms, is simply to force through "reforms" of internal labor market rules without any compensating concessions to employment security. With unionized blue-collar work this takes the form of "concession bargaining," while large-scale white-collar lay-offs are the relevant analogy in that sector.

The current era is one of substantial employer strength relative to the work force, and it is far from clear that this strategy will not succeed. It may seem particularly promising in the short run. There are, however, also good reasons to believe that the long-term stability of this solution is problematic. Several research efforts suggest that product quality and productivity is influenced by the quality of shop-floor labor relations.[13] Hence, there may be substantial cost to this strategy. Furthermore, the forces that posed the problem in the first place—product market uncertainty and technical change requiring a flexible labor force—are on-going and imply continuous adjustment. While the concession strategy might work once, it is difficult to envision repeated successful applications in the same firm.

Perhaps the deepest source of uncertainty about the long-term viability of this strategy is that the current balance of power between management and labor is unlikely to persist. As working conditions worsen, it is likely that new opportunities for union drives will emerge. Firms must fear that either the expansion of a peripheral labor force or continued aggressive employer militancy will lead to renewed union activity. Indeed, our interviews suggest that the human resource staffs in white-collar settings, as well as in the more blue-collar firms that are now structured along salaried lines, are acutely aware of this possibility and constitute an internal lobby against employer militance strategies.

The foregoing arguments are not intended to predict the direction in which we can expect internal labor markets to evolve. We are in a period of considerable uncertainty and confusion in which competing forms coexist. Instead, the point is to describe analytically what some of the choices are and where they came from. In addition, we are interested in highlighting an opening for public employment policy. The salaried model has a great many attractions, both normative and practical. It would seem desirable that as large a fraction of the economy as possible evolve in that direction. However, there also appears to be significant obstacles, notably issues of employment security and the consequences to workers of labor market adjustment. As the earlier material on labor market adjustment demonstrated, employees have good reason to be highly risk averse in the face of any changes in the arrangements that provide a degree of job security. Hence, absent credible assurances, those working under the industrial model will resist giving up its limited protections, while firms must fear that those employed in salaried settings will react strongly to cutbacks. By the same token, firms now organized along the lines of the industrial model will be reluctant to provide the degree of security implied by a shift to a salaried model. This results both from the perceived costs and loss of flexibility in employment levels as well as from an ideological reluctance to forego the higher degree of managerial discretion inherent in the industrial model. Either the employer militancy strategy or marginal adjustments will seem the safer alternative. Hence, from both sides of the equation, workers and firms, the salaried model may seem too uncertain and too costly. The question then is whether it is possible to envision how public policy can assist in the transition to the salaried model and help firms already organized along those lines to maintain it.

Toward an American Employment Policy

The foregoing arguments point to four goals for employment policy. The first three are:

- *Enhance prospects of intra-firm mobility for the incumbent work force.* This is an important objective because as the labor force becomes more mobile and flexible, it is better able to adapt to changing conditions without layoffs.
- *Improve the efficiency with which inter-firm mobility occurs.* It is not reasonable to expect that firms will never need to adjust the size of their labor force. We have seen that the American labor market does a poor job of moving experienced workers from one firm to another, yet without sufficiently hopeful mobility prospects, workers will remain attached to traditional forms of job protection.
- *Assist individuals in persistent labor market difficulty.* For our purposes this assistance should take the form of employment and training efforts, although it is clear that other interventions, such as basic skills education, are also often necessary.

These three goals are reasonable objectives for an expanded employment and training system. However they are limited, at least at a first approximation, to enhancing the mobility and employment prospects of individuals. Yet a major thrust of our argument has been that a pressing objective of public policy is to encourage the shift from industrial to salaried internal labor markets (in much of blue-collar work) and to preserve the salaried internal labor markets in white-collar settings. This, then, is a fourth objective. It is clear that there are other aspects of public policy, particularly regulatory efforts, that are as important as employment and training policy in this regard and we are making no claim here that an effective employment policy is sufficient to accomplish the goal. Nonetheless, for the reasons we have developed at length, employment policy is important.

Employment policy can help achieve this fourth objective in several ways. First, as we have repeatedly argued, if a reasonable level of employment security can be maintained, then the transformation will be eased. There are two forms employment security can take. Internal security can be provided by firms that are willing and able to stabilize employment. This is possible to an extent but is, as we have seen, quite difficult. External security can be provided if the penalities for job loss are not great. This can be accomplished by a combination of safety net efforts (unemployment insurance, extended health insurance, and so on) and by employment programs that can overcome the barriers to mobility between employers. The extreme European efforts can be interpreted as attempts to deploy public policy (laws prohibiting layoffs) to achieve internal security. By contrast, our suggestions are aimed at using public policy to provide a higher degree of external security, both because such external security has merit on its own terms and because it can provide the basis for reform of internal practices.

In addition to the direct provision of security, employment policy can be important if it creates indirect incentives to transform internal labor markets. If, for example, public support expands general training within firms, this in turn will create pressure to utilize the new skills. The boundaries surrounding jobs may weaken and intra-firm mobility may ease. The pressures, and opportunities, that derive from a highly skilled labor force may subtly move the internal labor market in the direction of salaried patterns.

The Employment and Training System

In thinking through the shape of policy two major issues emerge: the institutional structure in which that policy is embedded ("who does what to whom") and the programmatic content of the policy. It is our strong view that it is more important to focus upon the creation of a credible system than upon specific programmatic interventions. There are two reasons for this. The first is that the needs of individuals are too varied to admit a single category of intervention, and there is also considerable variation in the tactics that are appropriate to different kinds of firms. The issue then is whether a system can be put into place that is flexible enough to shape programs to particular circumstances.

The second reason why it is important to emphasize the development of a strong system is more subtle but probably more important. We have argued that a central function of employment and training programs is to provide the labor force with sufficient security that on-the-job flexibility is forthcoming. Specific programs are too ephemeral; they lack "presence" and hence are unlikely to accomplish this objective. Instead, what is needed is the visible, concrete bureaucratic existence of an agency that has the appropriate responsibilities and that can be held accountable for meeting its objectives. This agency needs to have an active and vigorous presence at the local level and to have at its disposal a variety of programmatic tools to meet different needs. As this system proves itself and gains credibility, it can meet the broad goals we have established.

Our discussion of the shape of an effective system will focus on four topics: eligibility, the structure of the system, financing the system, and staffing the system. After discussing these institutional issues we will then describe specific programmatic interventions that the system might deliver.

Program Eligibility
We have already described the consequences of an employment and training system that is means tested. It becomes perceived as part of the welfare system

gives the PICs a potentially distinctive mission (in contrast to the Employment Service, which also has local offices) is that the PICs are tripartite and representatives from government, business, and labor sit on them. Hence they are best positioned to achieve the sort of corporatist control and commitment that characterizes European models. A PIC that reaches its potential could organize a labor market around a set of objectives for employment security, placement, and training. The rub is again practical. The great majority of PICs contain third-level business representation, limited union participation, and far too many government officials. It is a rare PIC that has begun to conceive of its role, much less act upon it, in any but the most pro forma terms.

The true administrative power at the local agency is the so-called service delivery agency that houses the staff that administers the JTPA grant. Typically this agency is under mayoral control and is the successor to the former CETA administrative agency. The staff of this agency generally constitutes the most experienced group of employment and training professionals in an area. Most PICs depend upon this staff, and while there are exceptions, it would be naive to expect most PICs to develop substantial independent expertise.

In the end then the best option appears to be to strengthen PICs and to rely on the combination of a strong PIC and service delivery agency. This agency would (as is done now) develop financial agreements with training agencies, particularly community colleges, to provide services.

As noted above, the placement function of the Employment Service should be central, yet as constituted, the ES is unable to deliver quality services and none of the (internal to the ES system) administrative reforms of the past two decades has changed this. This implies that one major organizational change is warranted: placing local Employment Service offices directly under the control of the employment and training agency we have described. JTPA in fact recognizes that the two institutions should work together and attempts to accomplish this by requiring that the PIC approve the annual plans of local offices. However, as a practical matter, this is pro forma, since local offices report to a central state ES agency and that central agency has discretion over the distribution of resources and over personnel decisions. The only way to improve the Employment Service and to integrate it into the Employment and Training System is to alter radically the power and reporting relationships.

Financing the System

It is clear that we envision a substantially expanded employment and training effort and that this in turn will require increased funding. Normally one would expect resources to be derived from general revenue, and doubtlessly a substantial portion will be. However, there is a strong case to be made for consideration of a training payroll tax.

Such a scheme would levy a percentage tax upon firms, based on the value of their payroll. It would be undesirable to increase the tax burden on labor, since that would create a disincentive to expand employment. Such a tax need not, however, have this effect. Several states have already reduced the unemployment insurance tax by a given amount (in California by half a percentage point) and replaced it with a training tax. Federal legislation could mandate such a system nationally.

The advantage of a training tax (with or without a reduction in unemployment insurance taxes) are several. Given that there is substantive importance to establishing a stable and credible training system, then the identification of dedicated and relatively stable revenue becomes programmatically important. In the past the roller coaster budgets of training programs have destroyed, not enhanced, the sense of a institutionalized system that can reliably deliver services. Given the importance of achieving organizational credibility, the payroll tax takes on substantive importance.

The second advantage of the payroll tax is that it enhances firms' identification with the training system. In many states the politics of unemployment insurance is such that the employer community takes a proprietary attitude toward funds and are active players in policy making concerning any disbursements into non-unemployment benefit purposes. Given that an important goal is to tie the training system and the employer community more closely together, then giving employers a financial stake in the system makes good sense.

The final advantage of payroll tax funding is that it can set the stage for some interesting program designs. In particular, a fraction of the funds can be returned to firms in return for enhanced training and mobility prospects for incumbent workers. The goal here is to encourage firms to provide more general training (as compared to very specific job-related training) and in doing so to make the labor force more mobile both internally and externally. Typically, firms are reluctant to provide such training for fear of losing the investment as workers leave. The arrangement proposed here avoids this disincentive, however, since the firms would pay the tax regardless and, from the firm's perspective, there would be no reason not to reclaim a portion of the tax for internal training.

Staffing the System

We have already noted that one characteristic of the remedial employment and training system is the tremendous institutional instability of service providers. Organizations come in and out of existence and there are no clear career lines for staff. Since one of our major objectives is to create a visable and stable presence, it will be important to alter these past patterns. In part this can be accomplished by greater reliance on more stable institutions, notably community colleges. In part it will be necessary to raise salaries, establish career devel-

above would be responsible for administering this program and monitoring the training. Clearly this definition is not watertight, and there would remain considerable slippage; nonetheless, widespread underprovision of general training suggests that this modest redirecting of the already existing unemployment insurance tax is worth undertaking.

It is clearly not possible to administer a training tax/subsidy program like the one outlined above in all firms because the cost of administration and monitoring would be prohibitive. A firm size cutoff is therefore necessary. This, however, raises a difficult problem, because a strong case can be made that it is in small firms that the greatest underprovision of general training occurs. Several studies have shown that training is underprovided in small firms for two reasons.[16] First, these firms are often simply unable to devote management time to human resource issues. They are often early in their product life cycle or operate in more competitive environments and hence have more pressing product development and product market concerns. Second, small firms lack an extensive internal labor market and hence will be even more concerned than large firms that any resources devoted to training will be lost as workers leave.

Given these considerations it makes a great deal of sense for a consortium of small firms along with the public authority to jointly sponsor training at an external institution. The role of the training agency is crucial here as a catalyst to bring the firms together, to develop an accurate assessment of common training needs, and to help finance and organize the program. If most of the relevant firms in the area participate, then it is not unreasonable to expect some financial participation by the firms, since they will be protected from "free riders." A logical extension of such an approach, although one with more radical implications, is to create a common labor pool so that workers who are temporarily redundant in one firm will be loaned to another. Arrangements of this kind seem common in Japan and there are a few examples in the United States. A model of this sort would require a set of firms that share relatively similar skills but tend to be at different points on the product cycle or the business cycle. It clearly would not work if all firms needed to divest themselves of employees at the same time. However, whether or not this particular extension is viable, the general model of industry-centered joint training agreements with a strong placement component has considerable promise.

Turning to other efforts at adult training and placement, in recent years an important thrust has been efforts to assist the victims of plant closings and large-scale layoffs. These are the dislocated workers whose situation we discussed earlier. The typical program today centers on a worker assistance center that provides counseling, placement, and training services for laid-off workers who are searching for employment elsewhere. Although these efforts often ameliorate the situation of the displaced, they suffer from being reactive.

They are typically triggered by a plant closing or large-scale layoff. The crisis nature of the intervention and the short time usually available (even if advance warning is practiced), and the institutionally ad hoc nature of the response all limit the effectiveness of such efforts. This is not to imply that such efforts are not important; when a layoff or closing occurs, a response is necessary, and our training agency should take an active role. However, our point is that the most effective response will have been the prior training and placement efforts that will have created a more flexible and mobile labor force and hence make the last minute responses less desperate.

These points notwithstanding, in addition to the worker assistance center approach there are several other creative policy responses to layoffs that have been sporadically tried but that deserve diffusion. The first two of these seek to reduce (although not avoid) layoffs. Several states have experimented with part-time unemployment insurance (UI), under which firms can reduce a full-time employee to parttime and the worker can collect UI for the lost hours. This would reduce the number of workers permanently separated, since the firm can attain the appropriate reduction in hours without laying people off. As already noted, such a scheme is less attractive in U.S. settings than it is in Europe, because many American layoffs end in recalls anyway. Furthermore, the seniority system may create a disincentive for more senior employees to accept reduced hours, given that their full-time jobs are relatively secure and the brunt of adjustment falls upon younger employees. This suggests that the program may be easier to implement in nonunion settings. Furthermore, in many cases the firm's technology may make part-time work cumbersome and the fixed costs (benefits, for example) associated with each body employed may make two part-time employees more expensive than one full-time worker. Nonetheless, this plan has been intensively used by a number of employers (Motorola is often cited as making the greatest use in Arizona and California), and its slow diffusion may be attributable to the limited number of states (12 as of 1986) that permit it and the fact that most employers even in those states are not fully familiar with the possibilities.

It is worth considering the implications of the paradox that firms that are laying off one category of employees are often at the same time hiring another. For example, a company may be reducing its ranks of middle managers and blue-collar production workers but expanding employment of technicians and sales people. There are several reasons for this paradox. First, and most obvious, the firm may believe it impossible, too expensive, or too time-consuming to train a blue-collar worker to be, for example, an effective salesperson. Second, except at the most senior levels (and senior executives are generally unconcerned with the details of personnel actions), different managers who do not connect with each other are responsible for the two actions.

A worthwhile experiment would be for the training agency described above (which has as part of its function keeping in touch with the actions of

7. These complaints are longstanding. Richard Lester, after arguing that the Employment Service should be at the center of an employment and training system, went on to note that (in the early 1960s) only 30 percent of all placements made by the Service were nonfarm jobs of over three days' duration. See Lester 1966, 71.

8. I am grateful to Norton Grubb and Jerry Karabel for sharing with me drafts of their very insightful work in this area. My analysis has been influenced by their views.

9. The industries included banking, insurance, high technology manufacturing, and other durable and nondurable manufacturing. The interviews were typically conducted with senior personnel staff as well as with line managers.

10. There is a third model for organizing work, which might be termed "secondary." This model entails high turnover and few advancement opportunities, that is, occupations that are not attached to job ladders. Many clerical occupations can be understood in these terms. For an extended discussion of this model see Osterman 1987, 46–67.

11. For example, *Business Week* reports that 89 out of the 100 largest firms have begun programs to substantially reduce their white-collar employment. See *Business Week*, 16 September 1985, p. 34.

12. For evidence on the growth of these arrangements see the Bureau of National Affairs 1986.

13. See, for example, Katz, Kochan, and Gobeille 1983, 3–17. Also see Weiskopf, Bowles, and Gordon 1983, 381–450.

14. For evidence on the effectiveness of affirmative action see Leonard 1985, 3–20.

15. Useful discussion of these and other agreements is provided by Savoie 1985, 535–47, and Straw and Hilton 1985.

16. These studies are reviewed in Pannell 1981.

References

Barnow, Burt. 1987. "The Impact of CETA Programs on Earnings: A Review of the Literature." *Journal of Human Resources* 22 (Spring): 157–93.

Bassi, Laurie, and Orlie Ashenfelter. 1986. "The Effect of Direct Job Creation and Training Programs on Low-Skilled Workers." In Sheldon Danziger and Daniel Weinberg, eds., *Fighting Poverty*. Cambridge, Mass.: Harvard University Press.

Betsey, Charles, et al. 1985. *Youth Employment and Training Programs: The YEPDE Years*. Washington, D.C.: National Research Council.

Bloom, Howard. 1984. "Estimating the Effect of Job Training Programs Using Longitudinal Data: Ashenfelter's Findings Reconsidered." *Journal of Human Resources* 19 (Fall): 545–55.

Bureau of National Affairs. 1986. *The Changing Workplace: New Directions in Staffing and Rescheduling*. Washington, D.C.: General Accounting Office.

———. *Personnel Policies Forum Survey* no. 140. Washington, D.C.: General Accounting Office.

Burtless, Gary. 1985. "Are Targeted Wage Subsidies Harmful? Evidence From A

Wage Voucher Experiment." *Industrial and Labor Relations Review* 39 (October): 105–14.

Johnson, Terri; Katherine P. Dickinson; and Richard West. 1985. "An Evaluation of the Impact of E.S. Referrals in Applicant Earnings." *Journal of Human Resources* 20 (Winter): 117–38.

Katz, Harry C.; Thomas Kochan; and Kenneth Gobeille. 1983. "Industrial Relations Performance, Economic Performance, and QWL Programs." *Industrial and Labor Relations Review* (October): 3–17.

Leonard, Jonathan. 1985. "What Are Promises Worth? The Impact of Affirmative Action Goals." *Journal of Human Resources* 20 (Winter): 139–52.

Lester, Leonard. 1966. *Manpower Planning in a Free Society*. Princeton: Princeton University Press.

National Commission on Employment Policy. 1981. *Seventh Annual Report: The Federal Interest in Employment and Training*. Washington, D.C.: Government Printing Office.

National Research Council. 1984. *High Schools and the Changing Workplace*. Washington, D.C.

Osterman, Paul. 1987. "Choice of Employment Systems in International Labor Markets." *Industrial Relations* 26, no. 1 (Winter).

———. 1988. *Employment Futures; Reorganization, Labor Markets, Dislocation, and Public Policy*. New York: Oxford University Press.

———. 1981. "The Politics and Economics of CETA Programs." *Journal of the American Institute of Planners*, October.

Pannell, Patricia Flynn. 1981. "Employer Response to Skill Shortages: Implications for Small Business." Proceedings of the Small Business Research Conference 2. Waltham, Mass: Bentley College.

Pincus, Fred L. 1985. "Customized Contract Training in Community Colleges: Who Really Benefits?" Paper presented to the 1985 American Sociological Association, Washington, D.C.

Ruttenberg, Stanley, and Joyce Gutchess. 1970. *The Federal-State Employment Service*. Baltimore: Johns Hopkins University Press.

Savoie, Ernest J. 1985. "Current Developments and Future Agenda in Union Management Cooperation in Training and Retraining Workers." *Labor Law Journal*, August.

Straw, Ronnie J., and Margaret L. Hilton. 1985. "Training for Employment Security and Personal Growth: The CWA Approach." Paper presented to the Twentieth Atlantic Economic Conference, Washington, D.C., 31 August.

U.S. Department of Commerce, Bureau of the Census, 1981. *Current Population Reports*, ser. P-20. Washington, D.C.: Government Printing Office, December.

Weiskopf, Thomas; Samuel Bowles; and David Gordon. 1983. "Hearts and Minds: A Social Model of U.S. Productivity Growth." *Brookings Papers on Economic Activity*, pp. 381–450.

Wilms, Wellford W., and Stephen Hansell. 1982. "The Dubious Promise of Postsecondary Vocational Education: Its Payoffs to Graduates and Dropouts in the U.S.A." *International Journal of Educational Development* 2.

About the
Contributors
and Index

Joan M. Greenbaum is associate professor of computer information systems at La-Guardia Community College of the City University of New York. For the last 20 years, she has worked with and taught about computers and their impact on working life. She spent the last two years as a visiting professor in Denmark, studying the social aspects of computer system use.

Judith M. Gueron is president of the Manpower Demonstration Research Corporation (MDRC). Since 1974, Dr. Gueron has directed numerous major studies, including the National Supported Work Demonstration, the Youth Incentive Entitlement Pilot Projects, Project Redirection, the Demonstration of State Work/Welfare Initiatives, and the JOBSTART Demonstration.

Lois Haignere is director of research, United University Professionals. In this position and in her previous employment as senior research associate at the Center for Women in Government, State University of New York at Albany, she has designed and directed many research projects on employment equity for applied settings, encompassing issues of pay equity, affirmative action, and job training. Dr. Haignere received her Ph.D. in medical sociology from the University of Connecticut.

Leslie Lilly is in the Community Development Office of the North Carolina Rural Economic Development Center. Before holding this position, she was the founder and executive director of the Southeast Women's Employment Coalition. She is chair of the Winthrop Rockefeller Foundation and a board member of Women and Foundations/Corporate Philanthropy. A southerner by birth, she has worked in the rural South for 15 years on issues of social and economic justice.

Jing Lyman is the president and founder of HUB Co-ventures for Women's Enterprises, Inc. She has been chair and co-founder of Women and Foundations/Corporate Philanthropy, is a commissioner of the National Commission on Working Women/Wider Opportunities for Women, and is on the Board of Directors of Catalyst. She has been a member and leader of two dozen diverse advocacy organizations.

Jill Miller is executive director of the Displaced Homemakers Network. She has been an independent consultant on women's employment and training issues and a senior associate at the Institute for Women's Concerns. She is chair of the National Coalition for Women and Girls in Education and Chair of POWER: Promoting Older Women's Employment Rights.

Janice L. Moore is a Ph.D. candidate in political science at the Graduate School and University Center of the City University of New York (CUNY). She teaches American politics and urban politics at Brooklyn College, CUNY. Her current research focuses on resident participation in urban development policy making in West Berlin and New York City.

Roger J. O'Brien is a principal of O'Brien and Marmo Associates and adjunct faculty in the Graduate School of Business Economics at Southern Connecticut State University. As a private consultant, he conducts strategic planning and program evaluation studies for education and job training organizations. He is former director of employment and training programs for the South Connecticut Regional Council of Elected Officials. He holds a Ph.D. from New York University.

Paul Osterman is associate professor of human resources and management, Sloan School, Massachusetts Institute of Technology. He is the author of *Employment*

Futures: Reorganization, Dislocation and Public Policy (Oxford). Dr. Osterman has served as acting director of planning, policy and research in the Office of Training and Employment Policy in Massachusetts.

Sarah C. Phillips is a private consultant and formerly was director of the New York City Office of the Center for Women in Government, State University of New York at Albany. In this capacity, she implemented several pioneer projects to increase the number of women in nontraditional municipal uniformed jobs. She also provided training on sexual harassment prevention and on integrating women into previously all-male work forces.

Denise F. Polit is president of Humanalysis, Inc. She recently completed a five-year follow-up project of the women in the Project Redirection sample and, for the past two years, has been involved in New Chance, a demonstration designed by the Manpower Demonstration Research Corporation. Dr. Polit is the co-principal investigator of the evaluation of the Office of Family Assistance's Teen Parent Demonstration. Both demonstrations involve efforts to enhance the self-sufficiency of adolescent parents.

Deborah Stern is the associate director of development for the 92d Street Y, where she is responsible for government fundraising in the performing arts, education, and social service programs. She has consulted on projects related to women's economic development, including the HUB Co-ventures for Women's Enterprises, Inc., and the MS. Foundation for Women. She holds an M.B.A. from the University of California, Berkeley.

Louise Vetter is a senior research specialist emeritus at the National Center for Research in Vocational Education, the Ohio State University, and the owner of LBC Ventures. She has over 23 years of experience in research on women's career development and equity issues in vocational education. She is an honorary life member of the Vocational Education Equity Council, American Vocational Association. She received her Ph.D. in counseling psychology from the Ohio State University.

Sandra Watson coordinates the Office Automation Training Program at LaGuardia Community College of the City University of New York.

Alan Werner is a senior policy analyst at Abt Associates Inc. Before joining Abt, he was director of research for the Massachusetts Department of Welfare (during the early years of the Employment and Training Choices Program, an innovative voluntary program) and senior research associate at the Center for Employment and Income Studies, Heller School, Brandeis University. Dr. Werner is currently project director for the evaluation of welfare reform efforts in Maryland and New York State.

Index